BOOKS BY ANDRÉ CASTELOT

Josephine
The Turbulent City: Paris
King of Rome
Queen of France

JOSEPHINE

"Empress Josephine"

André Castelot

JOSEPHINE

Translated by Denise Folliot

Harper & Row, Publishers

New York and Evanston

To my friend Marcel Jullian

The portrait of Josephine used on the frontispiece is by Baron François Pascal Gérard. Detail from "The Coronation of Napoleon and Josephine" on the endpapers is by Jacques Louis David. Both photographs of these paintings are used courtesy of Brown Brothers, Photographers.

This book was originally published in France in 1965
by Librairie Académique Perrin.
© Librairie Académique Perrin, 1964.

Contents

II. EMPRESS, QUEEN, AND DUCHESS

I. VICOMTESSE, CITIZENESS, AND GENERALE

"She was all woman . . ."—NAPOLEON

1. When Josephine Was Called Rose

In the village of Trois-Ilets in Martinique, one morning during the reign of Louis XVI, the Carib fortuneteller, Eliama, saw two Creole girls enter her taboui, a cabin covered with flowering bougainvillea and jasmine at the mouth of the Croc-Souris River. She was well acquainted with one of the visitors, the daughter of M. Tascher de La Pagerie, whose plantation was quite near. The girls's name was Rose.

The other, her distant cousin and school friend, was called Aimée du Buc de Riverny. Laughing to cover their embarrassment, the two girls explained the reason for their visit—to know their future. The Carib took Aimée's hand, looked at it, then declared: "One day you will be a queen."

Some time later, indeed, the ship in which Aimée du Buc had embarked was captured by Turkish pirates. Sold as a slave at Algiers, the girl was offered by the old Dey of that city to Sultan Selim III of Constantinople, and the Commander of the Faithful made her his favorite. And so the "French Sultana"—the Sultana Validé, otherwise called "the first lady of the palace"—was to become the mother of Mahmud II.

Eliama gazed for a long time at the trembling hand which Mlle. de La Pagerie held out to her, then raising her head looked at the girl in amazement.

"You will soon be married," she murmured. "The union will not be happy. You will become a widow, and then . . ."

There was a pause, while Rose felt her heart beating, and finally the fortuneteller concluded: "And then you will be more than queen." (This tale might seem the fabrication of a writer of the "True Romance" fiction, but for the fact that both Napoleon and Josephine separately recounted it.)

She was right. After a first unhappy marriage, Rose Tascher de La Pagerie was to become the Josephine of fabulous destiny, Queen of Italy and Empress of a French Empire extending from Brest to Warsaw and from Hamburg to Rome. Her husband, the first Emperor of the French, was to reign also over the Confederation of the Rhine, Switzerland, the Kingdom of Naples, Spain and Portugal. Her daughter would become the Queen of Holland, her son Viceroy of Italy. One of her grandchildren was to become Napoleon III and six others were to marry the Queen of Portugal, the Crown Prince of Sweden and Norway, the Emperor of Brazil, Prince Hohenzollern, the Grand Duchess Maria Nicolaievna of Russia and the Count of Württemberg. Today the blood of Josephine flows in the veins of nearly all the royal and princely families of Europe.

The most extraordinary destiny in history had begun not far from Trois-Ilets, in a melancholy valley brightened scenically by an amazing symphony of greens studded with yellow, pink or purple flowers: the Pagerie plantation.

Today the ruins of the sugar factory have been cleared of overgrowth, the walls of the kitchen and of Mme. de La Pagerie's boudoir rebuilt, and a little museum set up. Here one's eye is first drawn to a locust-wood bed said to have belonged to Josephine, that little Creole from the Windward Islands, whose husband—called Napoleon—was to write to her:

"I have never passed a day without loving you. I have never passed a night without holding you in my arms. I never drink a cup of tea without cursing the fame and ambition that keep me apart from the soul of my life."

Like her, he was born on an island, Corsica, which at the time of his conception was still Genoese. Similarly, it was not until June 14, 1763, nine days before Josephine's birth, that Martinique was restored to France as a result of the Treaty of Paris, after having been taken away from Louis XV by the British in the previous year.

The little wooden-steepled church of Trois-Ilets, restored and enlarged after a damaging cyclone in 1891, still stands, and it was under this same vaulted roof—the upturned keel of a ship adorned with crystal chandeliers—that one July morning in 1763 a Capuchin, Brother Emmanuel, baptized the child of a neighboring landowner, a daughter born at la Pagerie on June 23.

One woman who did not sign the register was yet perhaps the most moved of all those present, the slave Marion, the buxom black wet nurse, or "da," who for five weeks had been nursing the daughter of her masters. On this day, in her flowered dress, the blouse adorned with short open-work sleeves, and wearing gold cuocs, in her ears, she proudly carried the newly baptized child.

It was in this same church that the future Josephine's mother, Rose Claire des Vergers de Sanois, had been baptized and had married on November 9, 1761, Joseph Gaspard de Tascher, owner of la Pagerie, who had been born on July 5, 1735, at Carbet, the very place, it appears, where Christopher Columbus had landed, believing himself in the Indies. The Vergers de Sanois were an old family, originally from Brie but settled in the island since 1644. The Tascher family (pronounced taché), who had come from the Blois district in 1726, were of less ancient lineage but were descended on the female side from the famous Pierre de Belain, Seigneur d'Esnambuc, who had obtained the Antilles for France at the beginning of the seventeenth century.

M. Tascher de la Pagerie devoted little attention to the running of the plantation, a considerable property which employed 150 slaves. In the archives preserved at la Pagerie one can still read the names of some of them: Faisan, Manon, Théodule, Appolino, Dorothée. In 1807, when Mme. Tascher, now the Empress's mother, died, the estate of la Pagerie, consisting of 165 slaves, 28 mules, 5 horses, 20 cows and 46 sheep, and approximately the same amount of land as in 1763, was valued at nearly 600,000 francs, a figure to be multiplied by five today.

M. de La Pagerie preferred spending his time at Fort-Royal—

later Fort-de-France and at one time Fort Napoleon—where, his wife observed sadly, "he finds more pleasure than he does with me and his daughter." A little later, when she was expecting another child, she hoped it would be a boy.

"Perhaps," she sighed, "that would make his father have more affection for me."

The child was another girl, Catherine Désirée. The advent of a third daughter, Manette, does not seem to have brought about any change in M. de La Pagerie. It seems a fact that he sometimes preferred the company of the dark beauties of Fort-Royal or even the conversation of his sister and brother who lived in the town, to the melancholy surroundings of Trois-Ilets and the society of his wife.

Rose—they called her Yéyette—was just over three when on August 13, 1766, a Carib chief, an ouboutou named Pakiri, announced that he had lit a log of green wood on one of the mornes, the remains of ancient volcanoes that surrounded the property, and that the smoke had gone up quite straight and had inclined suddenly to the north when very high in the sky. Moreover, on the evening before the sun had sunk "in blood." Undoubtedly a hurricane—the Carib chief called it a ioüallou—was about to sweep over the island.

The church bell at Trois-Ilets began to sound the alarm. A few moments later mosquitoes rose in swarms and birds fluttered down to take refuge near the houses, the ocean heaved and began to foam, and fish from the sea suddenly swam up the rivers. The cloud-covered sky was streaked by éclairs titiris, dazzling flashes of lightning that take their name from the myriad tiny silver fish in the river at la Pagerie. It was the beginning of a terrible hurricane.

This time it was not a "banana storm," which only blew down the fruit trees, but a real hurricane. The Tascher family and their slaves took refuge in the stone building of the sugar mill, which was solid enough to resist the unleashed elements. On their knees they recited litanies to the Virgin. Outside, a tidal wave, accompanied by flooding rains and a wind that flattened the palms like grass, ravaged the island. Roofs were torn off, cabins blown away, and the ships in the harbor driven ashore.

When calm returned the great wooden house and the veranda surrounding it no longer existed and the Taschers set up housekeeping on the second floor of the sugar mill.

This was the earliest childhood recollection of the future Josephine.

In the valley through which the Pagerie River flows—it was also known as the Croc-Souris, from the name of the bluff where it rises—the little girl lived a happy and carefree life surrounded by a small court of the slaves' children until she was ten.

Then one morning after taking the winding road through the sugar cane to the little bay called Trou Morin, Rose, still called Yéyette, and her mother boarded a gommier, to make the trip across the bay to the island's capital. The long bark was to take the child to the Dames de la Providence, a convent at Fort-Royal. Going by boat across the bay was the shortest route to the capital, only a quarter the length of the road which went through Rivière-Salée and Lamentin. Seated quietly in the boat, Rose passed the three tiny islets that gave her native village its name—Charles, Sixtain, and Tebloux—then the long Vache Island, a real one this time, nick-named Mandoline Island because of its arched contour rising high out of the water. A good hour later—an hour of sailing through one of the most beautiful landscapes in the world—Mme. de La Pagerie and her daughter reached La Savane. On this great esplanade along the harbor of Fort-Royal, a statue of Josephine would be erected one day, all white in the sun and surrounded by palms. Today some of the little peasant girls coming from upcountry to work in Fort-de-France make the sign of the cross before it.

Rose walked through narrow streets past wooden houses built in tiers up the steep sides of Mount Carbet. When they arrived at the convent her mother kissed her and the doors closed behind her.

For four years Rose followed the precepts laid down by Father Charles François de Coutances, Apostolic Vice-Prefect to the Wind-ward Islands of America, according to which it was necessary "to instil early in young girls that decency and modesty of feeling which are the finest ornament of their sex, that gentleness and goodness of character which make them the embellishment of society."

"Take pains," he added to the nuns, "to give your pupils simple, plain manners; affected ways spoil the best natural qualities. Since dancing helps give them an attractive manner and bearing you need not scruple to provide a master for them, though with discretion in your choice."

Mistakes in class were punished by tying a black ribbon to the hair, while the successful pupils wore a white one. The only

diversion for the new boarder was a visit to her grandmother de
Sanois or to her father's brother and young sister, Robert Tascher, a
naval lieutenant, and Françoise Rose, Aunt Rosette, who endeav-
ored to amuse the shy little girl.

When she left the Dames de la Providence, the future Empress
possessed "an attractive manner and bearing," could sing, play the
guitar, thanks to her teacher, M. Francis, and knew "the language of
the heart." Back with her family at Trois-Ilets, she resumed her idle
existence, her close companions being the mulatto Euphémie, her
nurse Marion, and her confidant, the slave Brigitte.

Often, without even leaving her hammock, Rose would eat habi-
tants, enormous, tasty Martinique prawns, tourlourous, red land
crabs served with rice, and coffres, fish so wonderful that the
fishermen usually prefer to keep them for themselves. Her favorite
dessert was pineapple described as "France," that is, delicious. For
even now, in this too neglected province, when they wish to indicate
that something is fine and good they call it "France." "Here the
earth turns into gold," they say. It is an extraordinary country. One
breadfruit tree will provide for several persons and in some villages
one can see centuries-old trees apportioned to as many as ten
families, each of which has its branch. When one makes a hedge of
fresh-cut stakes along a path, it will take root, produce leaves and
branches a few weeks later—and sometimes even fruit.

Each day Rose took the shady path bordered with coconut palms,
ginger and breadfruit trees, the path following the Croc-Souris
River, which can be glimpsed through the creepers, hibiscus and
orchids. After ten minutes' walk she would reach the spot where the
little stream, now deeper, spread out in a graceful bowl. There,
among the fallen rocks, beneath a tall coconut palm and a plum
tree, she would take off her clothes and bathe, then lie in the sun on
the great slab of rock at the "queen's lake," as the bathing place of
the future empress is still called.

She would often make excursions through the island, from Mont
Pelée in the north to the Devil's Table, opposite Ste. Lucie's Canal,
in the south. Or she would go as far as the town of Le Diamant and
gaze at that extraordinary rock rising abruptly out to sea which
gives its name to the village. A few years later, Diamond Rock was
to become a name in history through the exploit of 120 British
sailors who clung to the steep sides of the gigantic rock for

seventeen months, resisting the attacks of the French forces. The British commissioned the rock a sloop of war, H.M.S. *Diamond Rock*. Thereafter Her Majesty's ships always saluted the heroic pinnacle as they sailed by.

Rose was now nearing fifteen. A witness describes her as "formed with every grace," although "more attractive than pretty." She had a dazzling complexion, silky hair of a light chestnut—it became darker with age and assumed attractive red lights—and eyes which must be called changing. Some observers called them dark blue, and painters usually showed them as brown, like black coffee, but her two passports, issued in 1795, describe them as "dark yellow" and "black." The discrepancies no doubt result from the fact that she nearly always kept her eyes "half closed by long, slightly arched lids fringed with the most beautiful lashes in the world." She displayed then, and still more later, the charm of her gentle glance, her supple carriage, the languor of her movements, her smile and her voice. From the passports one can also note the height she was to reach—five feet. One of the descriptions calls her mouth and nose "small," the other "well made"—which fits—whereas her chin was seen as "round" by one and "slightly prominent" by the other.

For the moment Rose was in love with her hammock, where she spent hours dreaming, in love with guava jelly, in love with the sweet aniseed prepared by Marion, in love with Versailles, of which she heard from her father, who had been page to the charming Dauphine Marie Josèphe de Saxe, daughter-in-law of Louis XV.

Was she also in love with love? How could she not be, in that country where everything spoke of it, a country where modesty was unknown, a country in which Negroes and mulattoes wore head kerchiefs which were in fact love signals. In those days—many of whose customs have persisted until now—a kerchief with one end knotted meant: an untouched heart, with two knots: a heart to be won, with three: a heart occupied. Some would even knot them in such a way that four ends stood up proudly and shamelessly announced, by way of invitation: a passionate heart.

If one believes a certain Tercier, a Vendean general (and I am not sure one should), Rose had an affair with him. He was a captain in the Martinique regiment and was received by the best society in the island. "It was among these people," he wrote, "that I made the acquaintance of Mlle. Tascher de La Pagerie, the famous Empress Josephine. I was very intimate with her family. I often spent several days at her mother's house. She was young then, and so was I . . ."

The dots are those of the General, who wrote his Memoirs much later, after being a determined enemy of Napoleon. I prefer to believe the tradition which asserts that Marion advised Rose: "Pas d'amou po toué" (No loving for you).

During the carnival of 1779 Comte d'Estaing's squadron was anchored for six weeks at Fort-de-France. There were 150 officers for whom dances were given and it is possible that Rose innocently allowed herself to be courted by a nineteen-year-old lieutenant serving in the *Marseillais*, called Scipion du Roure. She met him again much later and he became her lover. But at this time Rose was engaged, and the whole of la Pagerie was in a flutter at the event.

It was a situation which had developed in several episodes. The Marquis de Beauharnais, who lived in France, was the lover of Rose's aunt, Marie Eugénie Tascher—the wife of a M. de Renaudin —and had asked for the hand of Rose's sister, Catherine Désirée, for his son Alexandre.

Of course everyone knew Alexandre, since he too had been born in Martinique, in 1760, three years before Josephine, when his father was Lieutenant General and Governor of the French Antilles, which then comprised not only Martinique, Guadeloupe, La Désirade and Marie-Galante, but also Dominica, St. Lucia, Grenada, the Grenadines, Tobago, St. Vincent and Cayenne. Indeed, young Alexandre had remained at Fort-Royal after the departure of his parents and Mme. de Renaudin, who had entrusted him to Mme. Tascher de La Pagerie, Rose's grandmother.

It was Mme. de Renaudin, of course, who had arranged this unhoped-for alliance for a Tascher girl with no dowry. Unfortunately, by the time the offer of marriage arrived at Trois-Ilets Catherine Désirée had died of tuberculosis. Her father then suggested his third daughter, Manette, "whose health and gaiety of character" were joined to "a face which will become interesting." But Manette was only eleven and Mme. de La Pagerie did not want to be parted from her. So on June 24, 1778, Gaspard Tascher de La Pagerie offered Rose. She was fifteen the day before and, her father pointed out proudly, was "well-formed for her age and in the last five or six months grown so much as to appear eighteen." She was endowed with a very sweet character. Moreover, she played the guitar a little and had "a pretty voice, a fine complexion, beautiful eyes and beautiful arms."

The Marquis replied: "I will not say which of your two girls I should like to accompany you. The one you consider best suited to my son is the one we should wish. Start from that and indicate which one you are bringing."

M. de la Pagerie chose his elder daughter and thus Rose found herself engaged to Alexandre de Beauharnais. The banns were published in the church at Trois-Ilets on April 11, 18, and 25, 1779. Immediately there began a correspondence between M. de la Pagerie and his sister. Mme. de Renaudin took pleasure in describing the bridegroom. According to her, the young man had everything to make him pleasing: "an agreeable face, a charming figure, intelligence, ability, and all good qualities of soul and heart are united in him, a factor of inestimable worth. He is loved by all around him." Moreover, he had a pretty fortune: an income of 40,000 francs and expectations amounting to a further 25,000 francs a year.

According to a less partial witness, his future regimental comrade Louis Amour de Bouillé, Alexandre's physical appearance was nothing out of the ordinary but, being gifted by nature "with many outward attractions, gentle, amiable manners and graceful ways," he was already pleasing to women. He had had many adventures and "this kind of success flatters his self-esteem and completely preoccupies him." Discretion was not his strong point and he would recount his good luck to his comrades. "He even showed me the documentary proofs," said Louis Amour, "which he preserved and arranged as another man might have done with his titles to fame."

"If only I could take wing and come to get you!" Mme. de Renaudin wrote to her brother. "Come, come, it is your beloved sister who begs you."

But France was at war with England and M. de La Pagerie had been appointed Captain of Dragoons in the Militia. It was not the moment to leave Martinique, just when the English had seized the neighboring island of St. Lucia. And then was it wise to undertake the long crossing with a very young girl when the English ships were patrolling the ocean? Mme. de Renaudin shrugged her shoulders. Supposing "the young man's ardor" should cool by waiting?

In spite of the expense entailed by the journey, a decision had to be reached. So at the end of August, 1779, M. de La Pagerie, his sister Rosette, the mulatto Euphémie and the most important person in the expedition—Rose—finally left Fort-Royal.

During the long crossing in the naval supply ship *Isle-de-France*, Rose may have dreamed of her nineteen-year-old fiancé, a king's officer in a smart white uniform with whom she might have played when he was living with her grandmother Tascher.

. Fourteen years earlier, Beauharnais, a very pretty child, had made the same crossing to rejoin his parents. His mother died nineteen months after his return. The little boy had been brought up by Mme. de Renaudin, his godmother, who was separated from her husband and living conjugally with the former Governor. The couple entrusted Alexandre to a pretentious tutor named Patricol, who accompanied the boy and his brother François first to the school at Plessis and then to the University of Heidelberg. From letters in the tutor's inflated style we learn of Alexandre's progress in learning. An admirer of Voltaire, Patricol writes: "It is singular how he has taken the bait of his catechism. I feared lest a mind like his, for so long brought up to strict rules, might find much to discount in all these arguments and might make objections to which I would find it difficult to reply, but fortunately he himself cut the knot of all difficulties by discovering the principle that one must not go deeply into the holy mysteries that Holy Church orders us to believe, that we must sacrifice our reason to her since she cannot deceive us. A completely false principle, but one which I respect and which I am very fond of on account of the service it renders me on this occasion."

At the age of fifteen the Chevalier Alexandre, who had been an honorary musketeer for the past year, was already a lover whose vigor and prowess were emphasized with satisfaction by his tutor.

On December 8, 1776—at the age of sixteen and a half—Alexandre became a second lieutenant in the Sarre Infantry and efficiently carried out his duties. It goes without saying that he was in love. First, with a certain Mme. de Caumon, who nicknamed him her "cabri." "She always calls me that," Alexandre explained to his beloved godmother Renaudin, "because of the stray hairs I have on the end of my chin, so that in the regiment too they call me cabri, or little goat."

The Cabri was sent to the garrison at Le Conquet, three leagues from Brest. "Pity me," he wrote to his aunt, "for I am in the most miserable spot you could ever see. It is at the end of the world. One could go no farther and we are almost surrounded by the sea. Imagine a hamlet inhabited by poor people who speak a language we cannot understand and who can give us as lodging only holes in the wall for which we pay dearly."

But soon Le Conquet was no longer at the end of the world, for the Chevalier made the acquaintance of Marie Françoise Laure de Girardin de Montgérald, who was very pretty and eleven years older than her young lover. It is in these terms that he describes his happiness to his father's mistress: "Who would ever have said that I was to be so happy at Le Conquet? Yes, I will not conceal it from you: your Chevalier has tasted of love in this district. He is loved by a charming woman. . . . Her husband, who went away three days ago, told me he had orders to stay away for three weeks. I hope with all my heart that nothing obliges him to come back earlier."

Marie Françoise was married to M. Le Vasseur de La Touche de Longpré, a very distant relative of the La Pageries. He was a naval officer and occupied a post at Brest. He was away from home so often that soon Mme. de Longpré was expecting a child by her lover. "I had never before experienced true love," Alexandre wrote to Mme. de Renaudin. "The person who has made me feel it for the first time is so virtuous and so sensitive that I am in the greatest despair at seeing the moment approach when I must leave her for a long time."

He had indeed to leave his mistress to follow his colonel, the Duc de La Rochefoucauld. When he returned, as a captain, Mme. de Longpré had given him a son, christened Alexandre like the lover, but also like the husband.

However, young Beauharnais now had to return to "the bosom of his family" to marry Rose. Before he left Le Conquet Mme. de Renaudin prevailed on him—between two embraces with Mme. de Longpré—to tell his father what he thought about marrying "the elder Mlle. de La Pagerie." "The attachment and desire which this person shows to become acquainted with her aunt decide me in her favor," he replied, "and I am very flattered already to have that feeling of tenderness in common with her."

In his eyes the marriage was to be simply an affair of convenience. To marry the niece of the woman who had been a mother to him for nearly twelve years would simply make the event more "in the family." His wife would thus be somewhat less of a stranger to him, a kind of cousin. At that time many young gentlemen had hardly seen their wives before marriage. Out of affection for his aunt, and above all because a captain of nineteen ought to marry, Alexandre agreed to wed the "person" chosen by Mme. de Renaudin, and left Brittany for Paris without any feelings of foreboding.

In the family house in the Rue Thévenot, on October 20, 1779, the Chevalier learned that his fiancée and her father had landed at Brest, not far from his beloved Le Conquet, on the 12th. So, in the company of Mme. de Renaudin, Beauharnais hurried into a post chaise. M. Tascher de La Pagerie was so ill of a liver ailment that he was feared to be dying, and at Morlaix Alexandre transferred to a horse, not in order to be more quickly with a fiancée who might be in mourning, but so as "to prepare Mme. de Renaudin for the eventuality." Happily, in the fortnight since his arrival, Rose's father had somewhat recovered.

For a fortnight Rose, her eyes still full of the sun of Martinique, had been discovering France by living in a dark, cold inn at Brest and hardly ever leaving her father's bedside. Brest has the heaviest rainfall of any town in France and in late October is frequently drowned in drizzle. To entertain her, Rose had nothing but the sighs and complaints of Aunt Rosette and the conversation of Euphémie, who acted as lady's maid and must herself have been feeling very homesick. When she saw Alexandre on Wednesday, October 27, handsome, distinguished, with elegant "Versailles" manners, her fiancé must undoubtedly have fulfilled her sixteen-year-old dreams.

As for him, his heart certainly beat no faster, not even with curiosity, on seeing for the first time the girl who was to bear his name. We have proof of that by a letter he wrote to his father the day after his first meeting with his fiancée. "I have been dashing about ever since I got up. The number of things our new arrivals need and the meager resources of this gloomy town we hope to leave soon have given me a lot of trouble. The essentials are now completed. I have bought a cabriolet in good condition for which I was asked forty louis [800 francs]. Our departure appears fixed for Tuesday morning. We cannot fix the time at which we shall start off. The only thing I can assure you of is the lively impatience of us all to be with you."

He finally decided to come to the main point: "Mlle. de La Pagerie will perhaps strike you as less pretty than you expected, but I think I can tell you that the honesty and gentleness of her character will surpass anything you can have been told."

This is not particularly exciting.

On November 2, 1779, All Souls' Day, they set out. It was cold and Rose shivered in the clothes she had worn on the island of perpetual summer. It took them four days to get from Brest to Rennes, four days during which, somewhat tightly packed in the cabriolet, the engaged couple got to know each other. Alexandre was not in love, of course—in that frivolous and cynical epoch it would have been very bad taste—but the Creole's charm seems to have worked a little. From Rennes he wrote to his father: "The pleasure of being with Mlle. de La Pagerie, with the one to whom your son's name seemed so sweet, was the only cause of my silence." The journey was so slow that the expenses of the little caravan amounted to nearly 3,800 francs.

In mid-November Rose entered Paris for the first time, the Paris over which she was one day to reign. How far away the dark, narrow cold Rue Thévenot (near the Cour des Miracles) must have seemed from the luminous, vivid landscapes of her youth. But the home of the Marquis de Beauharnais was elegantly furnished and its comfort—relative if one had just come from Trois-Ilets— must have consoled the young fiancée. And then the sixteen-year-old girl would soon be married to her handsome, amiable Chevalier, who in expectation of his marriage was already using the title of Vicomte. The little La Pagerie girl would be a vicomtesse. It was all the more impressive since Alexandre had no right to use the title.

The day after her arrival Mme. de Renaudin took her niece to the shops to collect her trousseau. The girl does not seem to have brought much from Martinique since her aunt spent 20,872 francs— no doubt of the Marquis's money. The banns were hastily published in Paris, at Saint-Sulpice, the parish church of the Rue Thévenot, and at Noisy-le-Grand, where Mme. de Renaudin lived and where the marriage was to be celebrated.

The Archbishop of Paris granted a dispensation of the last two banns, so eager were they to end the camping out at Rue Thévenot. Rose's father had a relapse and kept to his bed. And on December 10 the notary, Maître Trutat, arrived "in the apartment which M. de La Pagerie occupies in Mme. de Renaudin's house." According to custom, the guests who were to honor the newlyweds by signing the contract were present at the reading of the banns. It was not a particularly brilliant gathering. There was Alexandre's elder brother, who had assumed the title of Marquis, also without any right; an uncle, Comte des Roches-Baritaud, squadron commodore, whose son Claude, following his cousins' example, became, on his own authority, Comte de Beauharnais; and finally naval supply officer Michel Bégon, a distant relative of the bridegroom. That was all of the Beauharnais side. None of those resounding titles redolent of old France which one finds at the foot of so many marriage contracts at that time. On Rose's side there were no distinguished names. There are simply the signatures of a certain Tascher, prior of Sainte-Gauburge, almoner to the Duc de Penthièvre, and of two Mlles. Ceccouy, doubtless friends of Mme. de Renaudin.

Alexandre brought an income of 40,000 francs from a still undistributed inheritance from his mother. It was the revenue of important property at Santo Domingo valued at 800,000 francs.

The future Empress brought nothing but her trousseau "lent" by Mme. de Renaudin and a promised income of 5,000 francs which M. de La Pagerie undertook to pay his daughter—when he could. Her aunt, Mme. de Renaudin, showed more generosity in giving her niece—still out of the Marquis's money—her furnished house at Noisy which she had bought, she said, "out of her diamonds," a euphemism modestly concealing her lover's presents. Naturally she kept a life interest in the house. In short, all Rose received was "expectations."

On December 13 M. de La Pagerie, who was still ill, stayed in bed and was unable to attend the nuptial blessing given in the church at Noisy-le-Grand. The prior of Sainte-Gauburge took his place. In the parish register are the names of those invited to sign the contract, plus that of the tutor Patricol and those of a few friends and distant cousins. A certain Nouël de Villamblin signed his name and this signature was to bring him the title of comte and a prefecture under the Empire.

The house at Noisy was not equipped for winter living—Frédéric Masson calls it a weekend cottage—and the "high and puissante Dame Marie Josèphe Rose de Tascher de La Pagerie," in company with her husband, the "high and puissant Seigneur Messire Alexandre François Marie, Vicomte de Beauharnais, Captain in the Sarre Regiment," moved into the Marquis's house, in gloomy Rue Thévenot.

Rose had been dazzled by her attractive husband, by his fine form, his elegant bearing, and even by the fashionable cynicism so much admired in the reign of Marie Antoinette. Besides, he had introduced her to love and presented her with her first jewels: a watch, a pair of bracelets and earrings. When she was not wearing them she kept them in her pocket and stroked them with pleasure. She was in love, but he had not been won over in the least. And how should this dandy have been conquered by a sixteen-year-old girl from a rural village on the shores of the Caribbean? The new Mme. de Beauharnais had hardly any breeding and even less conversation and was far from the feminine ideal of the age: the eighteenth-century woman steeped in grace, charm and, above all, wit, expected to possess an acute sense of the ridiculous and to be able to make use of mockery and impertinence. What would later attract so much male desire—Josephine's incomparable grace, her caressing look, her island languor—were still undeveloped. Even her body, which was to give pleasure to many men, would not flower until later.

Rose hoped her husband would introduce her into society and take her to Versailles. She already saw herself in the celebrated court dress, the heavy ceremonial trappings, performing her three curtsies before the Queen. She was deluding herself.

M. de Beauharnais, a self-styled vicomte, could not be allowed to ride in the carriages of the King, had no right to follow His Majesty at the hunt, and was not invited to receptions at court. Like many people at that time, the Beauharnais had usurped their nobility and could not claim to have been "presented." But Alexandre danced so well that he was one day invited, without his wife, to one of Marie Antoinette's famous balls. Only once. And the bitterness he felt on account of this single occasion was one day to hurl Citizen Beauharnais enthusiastically into the Revolution.

So Alexandre did not go to Court, but he also took care not to share his other social life with his wife. According to him, she had not been educated.

"I have made a plan to begin her education over again and zealously to make amends for the neglect of the first fifteen years of her life."

She must set to work to satisfy her pedantic husband. And above all she must not always show him her love and must never reveal jealousy. That would be utterly vulgar. Did Rose dare suspect her libertine husband of unfaithfulness? This feeling was considered unfashionable and appropriate only for the lower classes, particularly in a marriage of convenience. Worse than that—she dared write to him about it. What bad taste!

"Count on my propriety," he recommended, "and do not poison the pleasure I feel in reading what you write to me by reproaches which my heart will never deserve."

Poor Rose knew her husband thought her ignorant—he was always saying so. Alexandre had had a good education and the little Vicomtesse was an ignoramus, a Creole who had just grown in the sun. She promised him, sweetly and sincerely, to do everything to learn what she did not know and thus do honor to the man whose name she bore.

"I am delighted," Alexandre replied, "at your expressing the wish to improve your mind. This taste, which one is always in a position to satisfy, procures pleasures which are always pure and has the valuable advantage of leaving no regrets at having yielded to it. It is by persisting in the resolution you have formed that the knowledge you acquire will raise you above others and, joining learning with modesty, will make you an accomplished woman."

The little Creole must have shed her first tears on reading these lines from a pedant of twenty who had been influenced by the insupportable Patricol. With unadulterated joy and amazing self-satisfaction the vain Vicomte wrote hollow, inflated sentences for the young wife whom he did not love. His conceit is enough to make one shudder. "In truth—I admire my self-esteem; I speak as a man sure of being loved, of being desired." Poor Rose!

"The letter of yours I have just been handed is very tender, very pretty and the heart that dictated it must be very sensitive, very worthy of being loved. And so it is . . ."

These unexpected lines were written by Alexandre (who had gone to Brest to rejoin his regiment) and addressed to his wife. He also wrote to her: "My trust must deserve yours and if I do not yet possess it I do not despair of ever obtaining it. Farewell, my love. If I kissed you as much as I love you, your plump little cheeks would still feel it. Farewell a thousand times. Your faithful friend and tender husband."

Rose's tears had dried and she seems to have succeeded, if not in captivating her husband at least in disarming him by not troubling him too much with her burdensome love. "Yes, my love," he continued, "it is true that I love you, that I very much want to see you again and that that moment, however near it may be, seems very distant to me."

Needless to say—it would be too much to expect otherwise—the pedagogue reappears at the end of this same letter: "I was delighted with the news you gave me of your household. I desire nothing so much as peace in the home and domestic tranquillity. Remember, my dear, that one can never do too much to obtain it, that hardships are nothing when their aim is to recall and fix happiness in the bosom of the family. It is there that one can experience true joys and withdraw from the trials of life."

He seemed to realize that this was not the tone to take when addressing a seventeen-year-old bird of the islands, and he inquired: "Don't you find me very moralizing, very boring today?"

He was so every day and retained his preaching spirit even when inspired by a more tender feeling: "You do not speak to me of your talents. Do you always cultivate them, my dear? I should like you always to send me the drafts of your letters. Perhaps I should find some faults in the expressions, but my heart would easily unravel the feelings of yours."

Yet these letters were a joy to the little exile, whose only amusements were Euphémie's songs. She knew no one in Paris except the tradesmen and drapers to whom she went with her aunt. All that could rouse her from her inexpressible boredom were the care of M. de La Pagerie's very uncertain health and the arrival and departure of the mail.

However, Alexandre wondered whether the letters Rose wrote him were not inspired by her aunt. A new letter from his wife opened his eyes. "I well recognize your charming style," he wrote to Mme. de Renaudin. She asked him if she should continue to prompt

her niece's letters. Certainly not, Alexandre replied. "By being sure
that she alone has held the pen, I shall have more pleasure in
hearing the flattering things she says to me and I shall be convinced
that she has drawn them from her heart. As for the turns of phrase,
what matters their correctness? Besides, to judge from her last
letter, she has made considerable progress and need not be
ashamed of writing to anyone."

Alexandre's regiment left Brittany for the garrison at Verdun and
Rose was happy to see her smart husband arrive in the gloomy
house in the Rue Thévenot, particularly as Alexandre left tangible
traces of his visit. A few weeks later she became aware that she was
pregnant.

But after this bright interval the clouds continued to gather in the
sky. Alexandre made no attempt to return to their home. He preferred to spend his leave with his conquests or in parading his
vanity from château to drawing room. According to his wife, "his
unfortunate spouse" must complain of his "extreme dissipation" and
"antipathy for his home." And she did complain. "Unfortunately,"
she was to explain, "her husband's heart was closed to the impressions she hoped she had made on it."

Mme. de Renaudin was sorry for her niece. She instructed the
ineffable Patricol to address reproaches to his former pupil. He did
so, and Alexandre replied that he had thought at first that he could
live happily with his wife and "begin her education," but the little
inclination Rose showed to learn had convinced him he was "wast-
ing his time."

"So," he explained, "I decided to renounce my plan and leave it to
anyone who wished to undertake my wife's education. Instead of
spending a great part of my time at home, with a person who has
nothing to say to me, I go out much more than I had intended and
have partly resumed my old bachelor life. I imagined that if my
wife had any real affection for me she would make an effort to
attract me and to acquire the qualities I like, qualities capable of
holding me." But the contrary had happened. The person with
nothing to say to him refused to "take the path of learning and
talent. She has become jealous and has acquired all the characteristics of that fatal passion. That is our situation today," Alexandre
concluded. "She wishes me, in society, to pay attention only to her.
She wants to know what I am saying, what I am doing, what I am

writing, etc., and never thinks of acquiring the real means of attaining this end."

When forwarding Alexandre's explanations, Patricol advised Mme. de Renaudin "to acquaint her niece with our literature by making her read our best poets and reading them with her." She would do well, he added, "to furnish her memory with the most striking passages from our theatrical works." Since M. de La Pagerie was still in France, perhaps he could help too, and teach his daughter spelling and geography. Patricol promised on his return to Paris to find someone to "direct Mme. la Vicomtesse in her studies during the whole winter." Alexandre certainly had "a tender heart," but he could not be expected to become attached to a woman incapable of filling, by her attainments, "the long intervals between the pleasures of love."

In short, let Rose learn grammar and a few elements of geography and her husband would stop deceiving her and be at her feet! Patricol took the opportunity for moralizing: according to him, a wife should try rather to inspire friendship than love.

However, Alexandre took Rose to see Mme. de Montesson, the morganatic wife of the Duc d'Orléans, at whose house the young woman became acquainted with Mme. de Genlis and the Comtesse de Rohann-Chabot, née Montmorency. Quite frequently the couple also saw Alexandre's young aunt, Fanny de Beauharnais, who was married to his cousin, Comte Charles, though she was already separated from him. She received in her salon writers and also some politicians. Rose, still very much a schoolgirl, said little, but listened. Sometimes she would play the harp, and then the Vicomte showed a bit more pride in his little savage.

On September 3, 1781, Alexandre was at his wife's bedside when she gave birth, in the Rue Thévenot, to a boy who was one day to be Prince Eugene and Viceroy of Italy. There was a truce in the house. For two months the Vicomte kept his wife company, but "the taste for liberty" and an uncurbed willfulness led him to go to Italy, in spite of Rose's pleas, and not to return until July 25, 1782.

His father-in-law and Aunt Rosette had returned to Martinique and the Vicomte found his wife living with the Marquis de Beauharnais and Mme. de Renaudin in a house in the Rue Neuve-Saint-Charles, now Rue de la Boétie.

During this long absence Rose had devoted herself entirely to little Eugene. Once the fine days came she went to breathe the pure air of Noisy. She saw only the few friends of the family and never went out into society. After staying long enough to start another child on the way, Alexandre left his home once more. In the two years and nine months of his marriage, the Vicomte de Beauharnais had lived with his wife for only twelve months.

This time he did not dare inform Rose of his flight. On awakening, Mme. de Beauharnais received a letter from her husband, written from Paris at three in the morning, asking her to forgive him for having left without saying good-by—"without having told you for the last time that I am yours." He had left, he asserted, because his heart was divided between two feelings, "the love of my wife and the love of fame." And he was going to seek this fame in Martinique, since the island, dear to their hearts, was once more threatened by the English. Alexandre explained rather lamely that if he was leaving Europe, "it was in order one day to have more claims on your tenderness." He was sure that, although his wife might resent his departure now, a day would come when she would admire him. Until then she must have faith in him. She must assume, he wrote, that he had "enough sense to know how to behave and enough soul not to forget my duties as a father and a husband." But for the moment those duties were subordinate to his duties as a soldier. And this irritating man concluded with these words: "Your injustice does not prevent my relying on your hopes for my success, and I shall live up to them punctiliously and give you all news of me."

To do the young woman credit, she took this harsh desertion very nicely, which gained her a letter from her husband, who was waiting to embark at Brest. "I read your expressions of sadness and your loving promises with rapture. I turn back to thank you for them, to embrace you as much as I love you, my adorable friend, my dear wife, to beg you to think of me, to write to me by nearly every courier until I leave. I have only your dear letters and news of you to moderate my ardor and to recompense me for the pain of being far from everything I love most in the world. Farewell a hundred times."

Undoubtedly Alexandre loved his young wife as much as that egotistic, demanding, impulsive and egocentric person could love.

Unfortunately Rose missed one post and Alexandre seemed genuinely grieved as he wrote these lines very characteristic of the age: "Ah! beware of forgetting me! Above all, beware of trying to put me out of your mind in order to distract yourself! I should soon be far from your heart and I do not wish ever to leave it. It is in your soul that I wish henceforth to find my sweetest pleasures."

Unfortunately—was it carelessness, or the laziness in letter writing of which her second husband was to complain, or was Beauharnais beginning to bore her a little?—Rose once more let the courier start off for Brittany without sending a letter, and Alexandre, apparently delighted at being able to complain, sent his wife another lecture. He was indeed right to leave! Around him all those who, like him, were waiting to embark, had received letters from their wives, "who wept for their husbands' absence and gave proof of it." Alexandre thought he merited even more than his companions "the tenderness of his better half." And yet he was completely deserted.

Finally a letter did arrive at Brest, but having made this effort Rose fell into apathy once more, which brought her a new reprimand: "This inconceivable negligence puts me into a mood which I cannot shake off. Ah! how light are your feelings! Your love never existed in your heart. I shall do my best to imitate you. If, as I am beginning to fear, our marriage turns out badly, you will only have yourself to reproach."

Alexandre was all the more unjust in that at Brest he had again met his former mistress, Mme. de La Touche de Longpré, now a widow, who was also going to Martinique to take over the estate of her father, M. de Girardin, whom Rose had called her uncle, although he was not, and who had just died at Fort-Royal. As might be expected, M. de Beauharnais became once more Mme. de Longpré's lover and he quite calmly asked his wife to look after his mistress's two children, one of whom, Alexandre, was his own child.

The frigate which was to transport Alexandre still did not sail, as English cruisers had been blocking the roadstead for a month. This allowed him at last to receive several letters from his wife. Once more properly affectionate, he took up his pen: "The tears came to my eyes on reading the words your hand had traced and your tears had watered in the bitterest sorrow. This letter is a thousand times tenderer than any other and why, my good and beloved one, do you not always miss me? Why is your heart not always as full of love for me? Indeed I have often thought that now I shall be in love with you without your returning it. Filled with sorrow at no longer seeing you, I have again congratulated myself of making a long journey which may make me indifferent to you, but God preserve me from such a wish! Love is what I want to enjoy and it is from you that I wish to have my happiness. Farewell, my dear wife, farewell. Kiss Eugene and may my tenderest embraces convince you that I have left my heart with you, never to take it back. Farewell a hundred times."

The English ships still cruised before Le Goulet, which allowed Alexandre to counsel his wife: "Ah! my kindest friend, remember the little life you carry. Take care of it and particularly of your own health. Caress and look after Eugene. And above all think of your husband. He loves you and will love you all his life." Of course he was as always lavish with advice, but this time it concerned Eugene. "You well know that one of your holiest duties is to undertake his education. You must begin now to convince yourself that there are other means of proving your love for him than caressing him."

At last, on November 18, Alexandre and Mme. de La Touche de Longpré boarded the frigate *La Vénus*, which instead of heading for the Antilles made a long halt in the Basque roadstead, not far from the island of Aix. This time it was contrary winds that prevented the ship's leaving. Rose wrote only once to La Rochelle, no doubt thinking that her letters would not arrive until her husband had left. This silence gave Alexandre a long-awaited opportunity. He was furious. His wife was writing to him only "to be obliging." "It would have been too much trouble for you to repeat the pleasure!" One can feel that he was profoundly wounded, not in his love but in his pride. "Forgive my letter, but I am in a rage." He certainly was. He, who thought himself admired by every woman, was disdained by his own.

Finally, on December 21, *La Vénus* set sail westward, bearing Alexandre and his fortunes.

Admittedly, since his marriage Beauharnais had been disarmed by Rose's pretty ways. He seems even to have resigned himself to his child-wife's ignorance and somewhat annoying jealousy, even to her schoolgirl foolishness, her childishness, her awkwardness, and her Creole frivolity. The marriage of convenience might have become a successful marriage if Rose, having been first intimidated by her husband and then falling in love with him, had not begun to be irritated by his pedantry and conceit. Or so it would seem.

Undoubtedly this versatile man, this pontificating intellectual, this person swollen with pride, who imagined he knew everything, must have been absolutely unbearable to live with. The drama which was to begin in Martinique was to prove still more that these two people were not made for each other.

During his long crossing Alexandre was a prey to remorse. His letter from La Rochelle had been much too severe. Then he reconsidered and put it in a different way: "I tried to give myself the illusion that you loved me a little."

On January 21 *La Vénus* anchored at the entry of the splendid bay of Fort-Royal and when he disembarked Beauharnais learned that peace preliminaries had been signed the day before and that therefore the fame he had come to seek in the Caribbean risked being very slight. At first he was astonished by the "extraordinary country," taken aback by the "indecent" dress—slaves of both sexes generally went about bare to the waist—and disturbed by "the appearance of licentiousness" prevalent in the island.

Alexandre went to Trois-Ilets, where he found M. de La Pagerie "at work making sugar." It is probable that Alexandre was somewhat disappointed by the simplicity of his wife's natal estate. He had been five or six years old when he left the island and his memories of it must have been rather vague. The main house had not been rebuilt since the hurricane of 1766 and the Taschers were still living on the second floor of the sugar mill, now a ruin, and in a few adjoining buildings, of which two still remain. Alexandre made the acquaintance of his mother-in-law—"loving and missing you always," he wrote to Rose—and of M. Tascher's other daughter Manette, soon to die. She struck him as pretty and "very sweet," but, he observed, "spoiled by skin blemishes which are all the more unpleasant in that they reveal a corruption of the blood." [Manette was suffering from scurvy. Ed.] Because of this Alexandre gave up the scheme he had formed of marrying his sister-in-law to one of his friends, probably the Comte de Barrin. Finally he paid his respects to Rose's grandmother, who had only two and a half years left to live. "Your grandmother Sanois is still lively for her age, very strong, in good health and depriving all her little dogs of her caresses in favor of me."

Beauharnais admitted that he spent only a day and a half at La Pagerie, having "duties to perform." No doubt the young captain went to pay a call on the director of the port, Baron Tascher, who was his wife's uncle, and to General de Bouillé, then governor, who agreed to take M. Beauharnais on as aide-de-camp. But, although not getting the fame he had come to Martinique to find, Alexandre was extremely interested in "the young people" and paid court to several women, not omitting Mme. de Longpré. In his excuse it must be said that Rose's silence persisted. So her husband considered himself entitled to write to her on April 12, 1783: "I remember, my dear, your prediction that if ever you were unfaithful to me I would notice it either from your letters or from your behavior to me. Doubtless this moment has now arrived since, during the three months I have been here, ships have arrived from every port and not one has brought me a single word from you . . . Embrace our dear son from me. Take good care of the coming one."

Two days before he wrote Rose had given birth to the "coming one," who was a girl who was to become Queen Hortense of Holland. Christened the next day in the Madeleine Church of the Ville l'Evêque district, she had for godfather, by proxy, Rose's father and for godmother Alexandre's cousin, Comtesse Claude de Beauharnais.

Rose's silence toward Alexandre persisted, which did not prevent her writing to her parents and even to Aunt Rosette. To the latter she declared that she had learned to correct in herself the lively feelings her husband had known how to arouse in her. "Your tone in speaking of your husband," wrote Alexandre, to whom Rosette, not without pleasure, had showed the letter, "is more than indifferent. What I read, combined with your obstinate silence since I left France, shows me how you have changed."

And whose was the fault if not Alexandre's? He had never ceased being unfaithful, had had numerous affairs, and had spent only one day in three with his wife, all the while employing an unbearably moralizing and didactic tone to her. Moreover, one may well suppose that Rose knew her husband had gone off to seek fame in Martinique in the company of his former mistress, Mme. de Longpré.

Still, Alexandre was profoundly mortified. He had written to his wife letters as burning as such a boring and egotistical person

could conceive. He, Vicomte de Beauharnais, wrote letter after
letter to his little Creole wife—a provincial from overseas—who
replied with a silence strongly resembling contempt.

At this point, the beginning of June, 1783, Perraud, M. de La
Pagerie's former valet from Paris, arrived in Martinique. He was
questioned by Alexandre. No, he brought no letter from the Vicomtesse. Before he left he had asked Mlle. Philippe, Mme. de Beauharnais's maid, to give him any letters from Mme. de Beauharnais
and Mme. de Renaudin, but Mlle. Philippe replied—and Perraud
showed the Vicomte the maid's letter—that the time was too short
"seeing that the ladies had many engagements, balls and suppers."

Alexandre was very bitter. There he was, miles away in the
Caribbean, among savages, striving to add to his laurels, and
meanwhile his wife was dancing and supping. Not for one moment
did his own betrayals come into his mind, though he was "involved
with several women." Apart from Mme. de Longpré, he was also
later the lover of Mme. de Turon, in whose house he had taken
lodgings in Fort-Royal. This did not prevent his acting the part of
the victim. "I ask you now what I must think of all this," he wrote to
his wife. "A dreadful truth . . . Well, time, the great destroyer of
our woes and our pleasures, will throw light on my misfortune by
giving me the strength to bear it or by undeceiving me."

Rose still did not write and on July 8, 1783, the storm broke.

2. "This Union Will Not Be at All Happy . . ."

"If I had written to you in the first moment of my rage, my pen would have scorched the paper."

It was in these violent terms that Alexandre began a letter to his wife on July 8, 1783.

Toward the middle of June he had learned, though not from Rose, of the birth in Paris of little Hortense. In the drawing room of Mlles. Hurault in Fort-Royal the happy and proud father was being congratulated. Then that plague of a woman, Mme. de Longpré, intervened more or less in these words: "Mme. de Beauharnais's daughter cannot be yours, my friend, considering that it was born about twelve days short of the nine months. You know women are more likely to be late than early."

The future Queen of Holland had been conceived on M. de Beauharnais's return from Italy, on July 25, 1782, and since his wife's pregnancy, and without ever doubting his paternity, the Vicomte had in many letters frequently alluded to the coming birth of his second child, an event with which he was delighted. With a son in mind he had even chosen the name Scipion. Admittedly there

28

are only eight months and sixteen days between July 25, 1782, and April 10, 1783, and being aware of her flightiness in this sphere one might be permitted to wonder whether, while awaiting her husband's return, Rose had not yielded to some consoling arm. Yet it seems that Hortense really was the daughter of the Vicomte de Beauharnais.

In any event, Alexandre began by shrugging off the suggestion. He was no simpleton! Then Mme. de Longpré—if not jealous, at least irritated by her lover's affection for his young wife—told him she had made inquiries in the island. She had questioned one of the slaves at la Pagerie, the Negro Maximin, who had told her that Rose had had many affairs before leaving for France. The slave had even given names, that of a certain officer called "M. de B.," whom we have not been able to identify, and of "M. d'H."—M. d'Heureux.

Maximin talked because Mme. de Longpré "showered" money on him. M. de Beauharnais's mistress then turned to Brigitte, who had served Rose at la Pagerie—but without success. Brigitte would say nothing. Alexandre then decided to question Brigitte himself. We know of the scene through Mme. de La Pagerie. The young slave denied everything that Maximin had told Mme. de Longpré. Undoubtedly Mlle. de La Pagerie, "very sweet and amiable," had attracted to her father's house officers of either her father's or her uncle's acquaintance, but she had never gone alone anywhere; her mother, father or uncle had always accompanied her.

"Now then, Brigitte," Alexandre interrupted, "stop pretending. Your mistress confessed to me that she several times wrote to M. d'Heureux, that it was you who hid these letters in your box, for fear her mother should come across them, that you must still have some which she told me to ask you for. As I am now her husband it would be unpleasant for me if anyone saw these letters. Give them to me and I shall take care of you. I shall give you ten moedes for each letter. Give me just one and I shall make you a present of twenty gold moedes."

Without losing her head, Brigitte replied that her mistress could not have made such an admission to the Vicomte.

"I have never known her to flirt," she explained. "I have never seen her write to anyone."

"Don't be afraid," Alexandre resumed. "You have nothing to fear, since it is your mistress who told me to ask for them."

"I fear nothing, sir," replied the slave. "I have no letters. I know of no one to whom my mistress wrote. She never gave me any letters. She cannot have told you I have any. I have so little fear that you may hand me over to justice and even torture without my saying anything else."

"So you won't tell me anything. Take care not to talk of what I have told you, for if you do you will have me to deal with. Your life depends on it. So remember not to breathe a word to anyone."

Hoping to have more success with Maximin, M. de Beauharnais then questioned him, but in spite of the 15 moedes he had received the slave refused to repeat the slanders that, according to Alexandre, he had told Mme. de Longpré. But Alexandre still believed his mistress's calumnies, which were also repeated by his landlady and the other mistress Mme. de Turon, who, incidentally, was being kept by her husband indoors since he had learned of his misfortune. M. de Beauharnais questioned Aunt Rosette, whose answers were full of insinuations. Crabbed, cantankerous, embittered by her enforced celibacy, her allusions to the conduct of "young girls today" only made matters worse. She had such an unpleasant character that it was perhaps she who gave birth to an expression still used in Trois-Ilets on hot, thundery days: *"Au joué mam' Tasché!"*—It's a day like Mme. Tascher.

On July 8, 1783, the husband wrote his wife an extravagant letter:

In spite of my soul's despair, in spite of the rage that chokes me, I shall be able to control myself, I shall be able to tell you coolly that in my eyes you are the vilest of creatures, that my stay in this country has taught me your abominable behavior here, that I know in every detail your intrigue with M. de Be . . . an officer in the Martinique regiment, and that with M. d'Heureux, who embarked in the *César*, that I am unaware neither of the means you took to satisfy yourself nor of the people you employed to make things easy for you; that Brigitte has her freedom only in order to keep her silent, that Louis, who has since died, was also in the plot. . . . It is therefore no time for pretending and as I am aware of every detail there is only one thing you can do, be frank. As for repentance, I do not ask it of you, you are incapable of it: anyone who, during preparations for her departure, receives a lover in her arms when she knows she is destined for another, has no soul; she is lower than any slut on earth. . . . By yourself you have deceived a whole family and brought opprobrium and ignominy to another family of whom you were unworthy. After so many crimes and atrocities what is to be thought of the disputes that arose in our household? What can be thought of this last child arriving eight months and a few days after my return from

Italy? I am forced to accept it, but I swear by the sky above me, it is another's, a stranger's blood flows in its veins! It will never know my shame and I take another oath that it will never know, either by the care given to its education or its upbringing, that it owes life to an adulterer, but you will see that I must avoid a similar misfortune in future. Make your arrangements, therefore. I shall never, never put myself in a position to be deceived again and as you are the kind of woman who would impose on the public if we lived under the same roof, be good enough to retire to a convent when you receive my letter. This is my last word and nothing in nature can make me go back on it. . . . You persist in denials because from your earliest youth you have made a habit of untruthfulness, but at heart you cannot but be convinced that you are getting only what you deserve. . . . See the shame with which you and I and our children will be covered as a punishment from heaven which you have deserved and which should earn me your pity and that of all honest souls.

Farewell, madame, I shall write to you in duplicate and these will be the last letters you will receive from your despairing and unfortunate husband.

P.S. I leave today for Santo Domingo and I expect to be in Paris in September or October, if my health does not succumb to the fatigue of such a journey added to such terrible circumstances. I think that after this letter I shall not find you in my house and I must warn you that you will find me a tyrant if you do not punctually carry out all I have said.

This indictment was entrusted to Mme. de Longpré, who was going back to France. She made the journey in company with Comte Arthur Dillon, who had replaced Alexandre in her heart and was waiting to become her husband. So M. de Beauharnais found himself thrown over by both his mistress and his wife, whose incomprehensible silence continued.

The following month Mme. de La Pagerie provided a few explanations to the Marquis de Beauharnais, who was as astonished as his daughter-in-law: "I would never have thought that our son-in-law would have been so influenced by Mme. de Longpré, his traveling companion, that she would have turned his head to the point of forgetting himself and his duty as he has done. This woman who has apparently never felt anything for her own family has inflamed his imagination and filled him with suspicion and jealousy toward his wife and, no doubt in order to attach him to herself forever, decided to separate him from his wife. To do this she has had the baseness to incite him to suborn one of my slaves whom each of them made say whatever they wanted by giving him much

money and making many promises. The Vicomte gave him fifteen
moedes in two installments! Now where is the slave who would not
be corrupted by such a sum and where is the one who would not
sell his masters for half? I have him in chains. I wish it were possible to send him to you for questioning. You would judge for
yourself, sir, all the lies he has been made to say by all the mistakes
into which he has been led. Can such base conduct, such vile means
be put to use by a wellborn, intelligent man? . . . It is not possible
for my daughter to remain with him unless he gives her really
sincere proofs of a true change of heart and a complete exoneration."

Separation, indeed, appeared inevitable.

"All your acquaintances, all your friends," wrote Mme. de La
Pagerie to her daughter, "pity you and are filled with indignation to
know you so abominably insulted."

Alexandre did not go to Santo Domingo as he had told his wife.
His excessive grief, so he affirmed, forced him to keep his bed. In
fact he had fallen ill of an inflammatory, or "putrid," fever (typhus)
at Mme. de Turon's. Beauharnais did not leave Martinique for
France, in the frigate *Atalante,* until August 18. Before embarking
he had had the audacity to go to say good-by to his father-in-law at
Trois-Ilets.

"And so these," M. de La Pagerie said to him, "are the fruits of
your journey, and the wonderful campaign you were to wage
against the enemies of the state. It has been confined to making war
on your wife's reputation and on the tranquillity of her family."

On September 15 Alexandre disembarked at Rochefort very ill,
still from his "excessive grief," he claimed, and went first to Châtellerault to recover. He lodged with relatives of Mme. de Longpré.
Perhaps he wanted to try for a reconciliation with his former
mistress, in spite of his "completely disturbed health." At Châtellerault, learning that his wife was still living with her children at the
home of the Marquis de Beauharnais, he wrote to ask "without
bitterness" and "without temper" whether she still considered co-
habitation possible after "what he had learned." To live under the
same roof would be folly. "You would be as unhappy as I from the
perpetual image of your wrongdoing. . . . I advise you to take the
easiest way, that of acceding to my wishes. I can see no obstacle, if
you should wish to return to America, to allowing you to do that

and you may choose between a return to your family and the convent in Paris."

Knowing his wife to be at Noisy, he asked her to send a carriage and horses to Paris for October 26. "If Euphémie wants to take this opportunity to bring Eugene I shall be very grateful and shall be indebted to her for the pleasure." Alexandre ended his note by stating that no attempt, no effort, no steps aimed at moving him should be undertaken either by Rose, Mme. de Renaudin, or the Marquis. His resolution was unshakable. "Submit, therefore, as I do, to a painful line of conduct, a distressing separation, for your children particularly, and remain assured, madame, that of the two of us you are not the most to be pitied."

However, on October 26 Rose returned to Paris in the hope of making peace. She would undoubtedly have preferred a separation for herself, but she tried nonetheless to avoid the irreparable. Beauharnais, learning of his wife's presence in the Rue Neuve-Saint-Charles, went first to a hotel in the Rue de Gramont and then asked for hospitality from the Duc de La Rochefoucauld. Parents and friends all intervened to prevent a definitive rupture, but in vain, and on November 27, 1783, Rose, having entrusted Eugene to Euphémie and boarded out Hortense at Noisy, retired, accompanied by Mme. de Renaudin, to the Bernardine nuns of the Abbey of Penthémont in the Rue de Grenelle. To this pious refuge came women who were separated from their husbands or abandoned by them or who were in need of a temporary shelter. The accommodations of this guest house were agreeable, the society select, the manners and conversation befitting the times, that period just on the eve of the Revolution in which a whole world would disappear.

On Monday, December 8, 1783, at eleven in the morning, Louis Joron, King's Counsel and commissioner at Chastelet, and his secretary, Jean d'Esdouhard, presented themselves at the Abbey of Penthémont and were at once shown into parlor number three on the third floor where "Madame Marie Rose Tascher de La Pagerie, aged twenty, Creole of Martinique" came to receive them. It was at her request that these gentlemen had come, so that they might take down her complaint against "the Sieur Beauharnais, her husband."

In those days it was not exactly easy to break a marriage. Of course what the Church had united remained indissoluble. Divorce did not exist, but a judicial separation could be obtained from the Parliament. Still, incompatibility of temperament, and even blows, were not enough to obtain the desired freedom. The story is told of the little Comtesse de Forcalquier who, having been slapped by her husband, hoped to obtain a separation. Not succeeding, she walked into her husband's study and declared, joining action to the words: "Here is your blow, sir, I can't do anything with it!"

Rose had not the smallest slap to include in her report. She could produce only one document, the insulting letter sent from Martinique on July 8 of that same year.

But she had a "very pretty tone of voice." We know that from the father of Jean d'Esdouhard, who later also came to visit the recluse. In this melodious voice she recounted her woes to the two men of law. For the first time we have evidence written at a time when the little Creole seemed in no way fated to become a figure in history. Rose seemed to her visitors "very interesting, of excellent breeding, perfect manners" and "very gracious." "One really cannot understand," added Félix d'Esdouhard, "when one sees and hears her, her husband's wicked behavior and the wrongs he has done her."

Mme. de Beauharnais in fact described all her conjugal life to Louis Joron and his secretary. Having recalled Alexandre's eagerness and his satisfaction at the time of the wedding, Rose spoke of his frequent absences and his "great dissipation." Had she reproached him with this indifference? Of course, but unhappily her husband's heart had remained closed.

"He was stronger than I and gave me no proof of his sensibility."

Of course the birth of Eugene had strengthened their ties. "The Vicomte gave the complainant his companionship until her recovery from lying-in, at which time his taste for liberty and for following absolutely his own inclinations made him decide to travel."

"On his return he seemed delighted to be with me again, but this happiness did not last long."

Once more the Vicomte abandoned "the said Dame de Beauharnais." And yet his letters "breathed only tender and affectionate sentiments." For example, M. de Beauharnais had congratulated himself on learning that his wife was expecting another child.

"Alas," sighed Rose, "how was I to expect that the news of my delivery would give my husband a pretext for overwhelming me with unjust reproaches?"

And Mme. La Bicomtesse showed the lawyer the two letters written by Alexandre from Fort-Royal and then from Châtellerault, "which contained the most atrocious imputations, and not content with accusing the complainant of adultery also described her as infamous and added that he despised her too much to live with her henceforth." Then Rose, with tears in her voice, continued the story of her misfortunes.

"He threatened to behave as a 'tyrant' if I refused to shut myself up in a convent. If these horrors had been only the effect of the first impulse of jealousy, my husband's youth might make me excuse them, but they are so considered and thought out for the purpose of shaking off a yoke that weighs on him that it is impossible for me to suffer such affronts patiently. It would be failing in what I owe myself and what I owe my children."

She also pointed out that the Vicomte had not wished to refer for information to her parents in Martinique, to the Marquis de Beauharnais, or to "any of the respectable people who have always borne witness to her honesty."

On December 11 the request for "a separation of person and dwelling" was introduced by Mme. de Beauharnais. Two months later the Provost of Paris finally authorized Rose to remain in the Abbey of Penthémont and ordered Alexandre, who was considered guilty, to pay the costs of his children's board and upbringing.

But legal proceedings were not enough for Alexandre. On Friday, February 4, 1785, he had little Eugene carried off "by open force." Rose, in tears, begged for help from the Provost of Paris and complained of the "cruel procedure" adopted by her husband, which had caused her "the most painful disturbance" and "the most terrible suffering." M. de Beauharnais must return "this dearest pledge" to his mother as soon as possible, even "through a seizure of his goods and income." Fortunately that was not necessary.

One month to the day after the kidnaping, on March 4, 1785, Alexandre, no doubt thanks to Mme. de Renaudin, laid down his arms. Rose obtained total reparation. With humility the Vicomte admitted "that he was wrong to write on July 8 and October 20 to the said lady the letters of which she complains and which were dictated by the impetuosity and excitability of youth, and which he regrets all the more having indulged in, as, on his return to France, the testimony of the public and of his father has always been in her favor." In short, Alexandre honestly withdrew all his complaints. He no longer accused his wife of having led a wild youth and recognized Hortense as his daughter. Moreover, he had gone to see her at Noisy and brought her "trinkets from the fair." M. de Beauharnais also declared himself ready to accord to "the lady his wife" all that she might have obtained by law.

So Rose found herself free before the age of twenty-two. For herself and her daughter she received 6,000 francs a year—30,000 present-day francs—and Eugene was to be handed over to his father on reaching the age of five. Henceforth the young woman could reside wherever she liked. But she was so comfortable at Penthémont and the society there was so pleasant that she stayed there until the fall. In those parlor-drawing rooms, in those gardens, those elegantly furnished bedrooms the "little American," as some still called her, became a refined Parisienne, a Parisienne of the eighteenth century, acquiring the inimitable and never equaled grace of that dying epoch.

The chrysalis was about to become a butterfly.

She learned how to develop what her Creole birth had given her: that delightful languor, that innate seductiveness, that caressing walk natural to girls born in the Caribbean islands, that supple body, all dimples, and by this time well formed for love. For now her beauty was to appear. She knew now—and always would know—how to make the best of it. Her teeth were to decay early, so then she laughed with her lips barely parted, letting the laugh bubble in her throat which, she well knew, made her even more attractive. She had learned how to embellish a conversation with charming remarks, rather trifling, no doubt, but prettily turned, and delightfully phrased. The possession of this knowledge, this turn of the tongue, one might call it, makes any woman seem intelligent. By daily contact with women like Mme. de Béthisy, Mme. de Mézières, the abbess of Penthémont, or the Comtesse de Polastron, lady in waiting to Marie Antoinette, by being received into this society which was moving, with laughter and wit, toward the guillotine, prison or exile, Rose had acquired "bon ton"—two words untranslatable in our twentieth-century vocabulary. Nowadays one would say of her, "she has wit." Vicomtesse de Beauharnais was appreciated by the members of the guest house. Her misfortunes had made her "interesting." She was pitied. She was touching, and her company was sought after.

Nevertheless, in September, 1785, Rose decided to leave the abbey and its social gatherings to stay with the Marquis de Beauharnais and Mme. de Renaudin, who had gone to live in the Rue de Montmorin at Fontainebleau, since Alexandre from pressing motives of economy had removed the furniture from the house in the Rue Neuve-Saint-Charles. But Rose still paid 300 francs rent to retain a room at Penthémont.

In that same month of September, when Rose was leaving Paris for Fontainebleau, a little King's scholar at the Military School of Paris placed 42nd out of 137 candidates in the annual examinations and was commissioned a second lieutenant. He was just sixteen and his name was Napoleon Bonaparte. (The name originally was Napoleone Buonaparte, since his birthplace, Corsica, was a part of Italy.)

On his way to Lyons by coach on Monday, October 31, to join the unit to which he had been posted—the La Fère regiment stationed at Valence, he stopped to dine at Fontainebleau, where Mme. de Beauharnais had been living for eleven days. Their two destinies had crossed for the first time.

The next day as the coach was going slowly up hill the future Emperor jumped out and began to run and gambol about the road like a madman, shouting: "I'm free! I'm free!"

At Fontainebleau Rose, too, might have shouted out her joy at finding herself finally free and her own mistress. The life of each was just beginning.

In the fall the Court was in the habit of spending a few days at Fontainebleau. They did so in 1785 and again in 1786. In 1787 the watchword was economy—the monarchy had gone bankrupt and had filed its petition by summoning an Assembly of Notables. That year only the King and a group of hunters galloped after the deer and boar.

Although Rose used the title Vicomtesse, which everyone gave her, she could not, as we have seen, claim to be presented at Court and she made no such request. But Alexandre, now aide-de-camp to the Duc de La Rochefoucauld, was scheming to be presented to the King. Captain de Beauharnais had on his side the Duc de Coigny, equerry to the King, wearer of the blue ribbon and a friend of Marie Antoinette. In spite of this powerful backing, Sieur Berthier, genealogist of His Majesty's Orders of Nobility, wrote a letter on March 15, 1786, which succeeded in alienating Rose's husband from a royalty which denied him its honors.

Monsieur le Duc,

Monsieur de Beauharnais is not entitled to the Court Honors which he solicits. His is a good middle-class family of Orléans which an old genealogy filed in the office of the Order of the Holy Ghost describes as having been originally known under the name of Beauvi, which it later abandoned to take that of Beauharnais. Some of its members were merchants, magistrates and minor judges in the tribunals of the same town, and others were counselors to the Parliament of Paris. One of its branches, known as Lords of La Bretesche, was condemned by a judgment of M. de Machault, Intendant of Orléans, on 4 April, 1667, as usurping a title of nobility, to pay 2,000 francs fine, which was reduced to 1,000.

I am, with the profoundest respect, Monsieur le Duc, your most humble and obedient servant.

Berthier

One can understand the rage of the future President of the Legislative Assembly. Had not the Châtellerie of La Ferté-Aulain, which belonged to his father, been raised to a marquisate in 1764? This was doubtless true. But nobiliary titles, particularly when they were only twenty years old, were not "inherent to the nobility," and it was impossible for the Beauharnais family to assemble the necessary quarterings for taking its place in the privileged class. Moreover, it must not be forgotten—and Alexandre knew it well—that, although after November, 1750, all officers who were not noble might have acquired nobility provided they were Knights of St. Louis, this did not give them ancestors and, further, nobility was not transmissible except in certain conditions which M. Beauharnais could not claim to fulfill.

The Taschers seem to have belonged to the old nobility. Unfortunately they had sold their la Pagerie estate in the Blois district at

Vievy-le-Ragé, but they had kept the name. The Beauharnais, by assuming titles to which they had no right, comte, vicomte or chevalier, by having someone in the family who had occupied an important position—that of governor and lieutenant general—and by having received the titles of marquis and baron, might appear of better family than the country squires of Martinique, but the latter could lay claim to a Nicolas de Tascher, who had fought in Palestine with St. Louis. Because of these facts Rose's father, although not titled, could no doubt have managed to be received at Court by giving proof of his knightly nobility. But the "Vicomtesse" de Beauharnais, separated but still married, could obtain nothing official. Still this may account for Rose's receiving permission to follow the Court hunts during the three years when she spent much time at Fontainebleau. She took part energetically in all weathers. "The Vicomtese is galloping over the fields," her father-in-law wrote. "She was at the boar hunt and saw one. She was soaked to the skin: she put a good face on it, after changing everything and eating a little." Alexandre, who had come to visit his father, was not invited. "He was very annoyed," reported the Marquis, "and in his disappointment has left for Blois."

But it is more likely that the Vicomtesse owed these favors to the sentiments of three gentlemen at Court, the Marquis de Montmorin, the Comte de Crenay and the Duc de Lorge. According to André Gavoty, whose knowledge of Josephine's amorous life is unrivaled, it was at Fontainebleau, riding through the forest, that Rose, generous with her body, had known her first lovers. At her father-in-law's house she had met his neighbor, the Marquis de Montmorin, Governor of the château, whose wife was lady in waiting to the Comtesse d'Artois. Rose was invited to Montmorin and became acquainted with the Comte de Crenay, Mme. de Montmorin's brother-in-law, Master of the Wardrobe to the Comte de Provence, and married to another lady in waiting of the King's sister-in-law. We do not know whether it was in 1786, '87 or '88 that he obtained Rose's favors. Also at the Montmorins' Rose got to know the Duc de Lorge, whose wife was lady of honor to the Duchesse d'Artois. The Duc de Lorge, né de Durfort-Civrac, Peer of France and colonel of cavalry, paid assiduous court to Rose which the young woman did not in the least resist. We know this from Napoleon himself. De Lorge was forty, attractive and, if the Emperor at St. Helena is to

be believed, had already been one of the "causes of dispute"
between Rose and Alexandre.

Although this is only supposition, Rose's third conquest may have
been the brother of the Duc de Coigny. His title was Chevalier de
Coigny, but he was called "Mimi." He was a handsome, fashionable
boy, harebrained, a wag and conceited, according to his contemporaries. As such he would have pleased Rose. He would certainly
have made her laugh. Be that as it may, the indulgence granted to
Mimi under the Consulate, the clemency toward him indeed while
he was conspiring vigorously against Bonaparte under the name of
"gros-Voisin," and the pension he obtained from the new regime,
paid to him even when he was expelled from France, later gave rise
to gossip. Without doubt Mme. Bonaparte did not forget the
weaknesses of the Vicomtesse de Beauharnais.

In November, 1787, the royal hunting horns rang through the
forest for the last time before the Revolution.

In Paris, during the same month, Lieutenant Bonaparte took pity
on a "person of the fair sex" who in spite of the cold was "walking
up and down the passages" of the Palais Royal.

"Let us go to your room," she said.

"What shall we do?"

"We shall warm ourselves and you can have your fill of pleasure."

That evening he knew love for the first time. He was eighteen.
And if, as is customary, she asked him what he was called, the name
her client uttered and his pronunciation of it, "Napoleone," may
well have sounded unfamiliar to her ears. In a few years the name
would seem less strange.

Although Mme. de Beauharnais had some charming comforters,
she also had very serious money trouble. Her pension from the
Vicomte was often late in being paid. M. de Beauharnais had heavy
personal expenses. He had just given a child to a girl who was
"young, pretty and of very good family." He coolly started a suit
against Rose regarding some undivided property in Martinique.
Rose also had great difficulty in getting money from Trois-Ilets. To
soften her father she told him of little Hortense, who often thought
of her grandparents and of "Aunt Manette." "She asks me, 'Mama,
will I see them soon?'" wrote Rose.

Baron Tascher came to France and gave his niece a bill of
exchange for 2,789 francs, which was all M. de La Pagerie had been
able to scrape together. Rose lamented that it was not more. She

could not put her creditors off with such a paltry sum. She then tried to obtain a reimbursement of the money due her from the royal treasury. The results were even worse. So the future Empress became a petitioner for the first time, a role which hard times would often force her to play before she found, as she expressed it, "a position."

In June, 1788, she decided to go to Martinique with Hortense. Why this long voyage, this difficult and dangerous crossing, particularly with a little girl of five, when Mme. de Renaudin had just been ill and little Eugene had recently arrived at Fontainebleau for the holidays? According to some historians, it was an escapade connected with a love affair. Perhaps she wanted to run away from one love or join another. Could the man have been Scipion du Roure, who had flirted with her before her marriage and who was, in fact, at Fort-Royal? Perhaps there is a simpler explanation: Rose's grandmother was dead, her father was ill and her sister dying and, as her daughter Hortense was to relate in her Memoirs, "my mother's position, brilliant though it was, could not make her forget her country and her family. She had left an aged mother there, whom she wished to see once more." The Vicomtesse's position was not brilliant, as we know from the debts she left behind on her departure, which Mme. de Renaudin settled while she was away. She had to sell certain objects, including her harp, to pay for passage for herself and Hortense. There were also 2,000 francs to be found for the annual payment of Eugene's board at the Institution de la Jeune Noblesse in the Rue de Berry.

The *Sultan,* in which Rose, Hortense and Euphémie had embarked at Le Havre on July 2, 1788, was almost wrecked at the mouth of the Seine shortly after weighing anchor. The crossing was a long one and it was not until August 11 that the ship arrived at Fort-Royal. After embracing her uncle and aunt Tascher, Rose went to Trois-Ilets, where she found her family and her childhood memories. Hortense was in seventh heaven. She later related:

I was five years old, I had never shed a tear, I was spoiled by everyone. No harsh word, no disapproval even, had ever arisen to force me to repress any desire or feeling. We were living in my grandmother's house. One day I was playing near a table on which my grandmother was counting out money. I watched her and when a coin fell from her hand I hastened to pick it up and give it back to her. I saw her make a dozen small piles of coins, which she then left on a chair, going out of the room with the rest of the money. I don't know how the idea came to me that she was giving me the money to dispose of, but I so thoroughly convinced myself of this that I put all the piles in my skirt, which I held up to form a pocket, and went off with this treasure without the least remorse, being positive that it rightly belonged to me. I went to find one of the mulatto servants in the house and said to him:

"Jean, here is a lot of money my grandmother has given me for the poor Negroes. Show me their cabins, so that I can take it to them."

It was scorchingly hot, for the sun was at its strongest, but I was so pleased that I did not want to delay one moment.

Jean and I discussed how we could help the largest number of the poorest people. I went into all the Negro cabins, still with the money in my skirt, which I held firmly, loosening it only to take out what Jean had decided I should give. My mother's nurse received a double share.

When my treasure was exhausted and I saw myself surrounded by all these Negroes, who were kissing my hands and feet, I went home in triumph, proud and happy with so many blessings. On entering the house I found a great commotion. My grandmother was looking for her money. She did not know whom to accuse for its disappearance and the poor servants trembled for fear of being suspected. The truth came to me like a flash and in despair I confessed at once to my grandmother, but at what cost! I had lied, I had stolen and I was rebuked for it. . . . My imagination had done it all, it is true. I had seen piles set apart—there was no doubt they were for the poor. Leaving them on a chair within my reach was telling me to distribute them. That was what I had imagined and I had made a reality out of that fiction.

Rose preferred Fort-Royal, the seat of the island's government, where Uncle Robert Tascher was still port commander, to the melancholy valley of la Pagerie, somewhat overshadowed by the surrounding hills. The King's ships often anchored in the harbor, their officers were entertained by the port administration or at Government House and Rose wrote to Mme. de Renaudin to send her "a low-cut, lawn ball dress" and a dozen fans. One day the brig *Levrette* arrived at Fort-Royal and the second lieutenant hastened to visit all his "old acquaintances." He saw Mme. de Beauharnais. "Without being precisely pretty," he was to write later, "this woman attracted because of her figure, her gaiety and her kindness of heart. Being engrossed in pursuing the pleasures to which her age and her attractions gave her some right, she publicly scoffed at people's opinion of her, whether flattering or not. But as her fortune was extremely limited and she liked spending, she was often forced to dip into the purses of her admirers." This document was published by Jacques Janssens and we must agree with him that when one knows "Josephine's personality and the way in which she was later to make use of it to obtain resources for herself without being hampered by any scruples, there is really nothing surprising in her actions here."

A frequent arrival at Fort-Royal was the vessel *Illustre*, flying the flag of M. de Pontèves-Gien, Commander of the Leeward Islands. One of the officers was Scipion du Roure, who was undoubtedly the pretty Vicomtesse's lover. So that was why Rose preferred Fort-Royal! And yet her parents' plantation would have been a more peaceful refuge for her, for, like Saint-Pierre, the other town on the island, Fort-Royal was at that time in full revolt—a repercussion of the taking of the Bastille and the abolition of privileges in France. The troubles began with the refusal of old M. de Vioménil, the Provisional Governor, to wear the tricolor cockade.

"I would rather die a thousand times," he replied, weeping, "than to besmirch forty-two years of honorable service by tolerating this symbol of independence."

He had to give way and reluctantly recommended the wearing of "this pledge of peace, union and concord." A Te Deum was sung and life resumed its normal course.

But Rose had learned that her husband, elected deputy of the nobility of the Blois district, had been one of the first representatives of his rank to join the Third Estate, or the common people (the other two Estates were the clergy and the nobility). It is certain that she was not at this time seduced by the new ideas. First, because her parents remained profoundly royalist—Mme. de La Pagerie was to remain so even under the Empire, when she had become Napoleon's mother-in-law—and then because, in the Antilles, the revolution was soon complicated by the problem of slavery or antislavery. Since the French in France were acclaiming liberty, since the planters, the great ones who resided in France, had embraced the new ideas, the mulattoes who had been emancipated found it quite natural to claim the same liberty. In their joy they indulged in excesses, in "outbursts," according to a report, such as striking a grenadier, and forced the whites to take up arms. The result was chaos. The agitation was complicated by the fact that the Revolution in France moved more quickly than the news of it crossing the Atlantic.

Meanwhile a Colonial Assembly was set up and in imitation of

Paris the two towns, and even some villages, formed committees, assemblies, deputations, nominated delegates and commissioners, and brandished large words like "motions," "deliberations" and "public tranquillity."

In February, 1790, troubles between the troops and the "citizens" flared up again. The barracks of the Martinique Regiment were sacked and the people "occupied the batteries and dragged the cannons along the avenues." The slaves stood on the sidelines, but soon were drawn into the fray, armed by one camp or the other. Saint-Pierre was in revolt. The return of the regular Governor, the sick and elderly M. de Damas, did not help matters. "I know of no more embarrassing situation than mine," he wrote to the Minister. "If Saint-Pierre is not brought to its senses I do not know what stand to take. If I had troops, I should not be in such an alarming position."

M. de Damas received no reinforcements and was evidently not able to restore order. Soon, on June 16, whites and mulattoes came to blows, the Negroes revolted, occupied the royal fortress, and turned the cannon on the town. Meanwhile the mutinous troops, who sympathized with the Negroes, occupied Fort Bourbon. M. de Damas took refuge at Gros Morne, a village on the road to Trinité, while Rose's uncle, who had become mayor of the town and was sent as a delegate to the insurgents, was held by them as a hostage. "The revolutionary wave," wrote Sainte-Croix de la Roncière, the historian of Martinique, "was to flow over the whole island and civil war reigned in our finest possession in the Antilles until the day when the English, taking advantage of the situation, would come to take possession of it."

Uncle Tascher was freed and Rose came to ask him to get her away from the island. She embraced her parents and her sister, feeling sure that she would not see them again. (M. de La Pagerie was to die two months later on November 7, 1790. Manette, Marie Françoise, died on November 4, 1791, and by an error of the vicar was buried under Rose's name of Demoiselle Marie Josèphe Rose.) She took refuge at Fort-Royal. La Pagerie would have been safer, but Scipion du Roure was at Fort-Royal.

On September 3 it was announced that on the following day the forts, still occupied by the rebels, were going to fire on the town. That same evening, on her uncle's advice, Mme. de Beauharnais sought shelter in the frigate *Sensible,* which had Scipion du Roure on board. "Yielding to circumstances," the ship was preparing to leave the harbor for France. But the insurgents did not wait until the next day to open fire. As Rose, her daughter and Euphémie were crossing La Savane a shot fell near them. They managed to embark without any other incident and the *Sensible* immediately left port.

The following day the mutinous soldiers, mulattoes and Negroes were masters of the town and ordered the vessels to re-enter the port. Durand d'Ubraye, who was also in command of the naval station, replied by hoisting sail. The forts opened fire. For three quarters of an hour grapeshot was fired at the ships, but they were soon out of range. The *Sensible* remained at the entry of Fort-Royal harbor for three days under sail but, receiving no message, the frigate, followed by *Illustre, Levrette* and the corvette *Epervier,* steered for the Bermudas, where the little squadron hoped to find favorable winds for return to France.

Hortense and Rose had embarked in such haste that they had no baggage with them.

"Hortense, who was charming and gay, who danced the Negro dances well and sang their songs with great accuracy, greatly amused the sailors who, since they constantly paid attention to her, were her favorite company," Rose was later to tell Georgette Ducrest. "Whenever I dozed off she would go on deck and, as the object of general admiration, would repeat all her little accomplishments to everyone's satisfaction. One old boatswain was particularly fond of her and when he had any time off from his duties he would devote it to his 'little friend,' who loved him madly. With all this running, dancing and jumping my daughter's little shoes wore out completely. Knowing she had no others and fearing I would forbid her to go on deck if I noticed the state of her footwear, she hid this circumstance from me. One day I saw her come back with her feet covered in blood. Frightened, I asked her if she had hurt herself.

" 'No, mamma.'

" 'But look at the blood on your feet.'

" 'I assure you it's nothing.'

"I wanted to see what was wrong and discovered that her shoes were quite in rags and that she had been horribly cut by a nail. We were only halfway across, it would be a long time before I could get another pair of shoes and I was already upset at the grief I would have to cause poor Hortense by making her stay in my horrible little cabin and at the harm this lack of exercise might do to her health. I wept bitterly. . . . At this moment our friend the boatswain arrived and inquired frankly the cause of our 'sniveling.' Sobbing, Hortense told him that she could no longer go on deck because she had torn her shoes and I had no others to give her.

" 'Bah! is that all? I've an old pair in my chest, I'll go and get them. You'll cut them, madame, and I'll sew them up as well as I can. In a ship you've got to be able to do anything. We're not toffs or fops. As long as we have the makings, that's all that counts.'

"Without giving us time to reply he went off to find his old shoes, which he brought with an air of triumph. . . . We went to work with great zeal and at the end of the day my daughter again had the pleasure of amusing the crew."

The crossing was long—fifty-two days. As the result of an error in navigation, after passing through the Strait of Gibraltar the *Sensible,* which was making for Toulon, nearly ran aground on the coast of Africa. An anchor was thrown out and everyone, including Rose, had to stand to the ropes to pull the frigate out of this fix.

On landing at Toulon on October 29, 1790, Rose learned that she had become a somebody without knowing it. Alexandre de Beauharnais was in fact an influential member not only of the Assembly but also of the Jacobins, of whom he was soon to become the president, having been twice president of the Constituent Assembly. He was listened to, in spite of his inflated style, and, as shown by the *Moniteur,* spoke from the tribune on the subjects of the Jews and the floods, as well as on monks and roads and bridges. He imagined he knew everything.

Scipion du Roure had landed first and had rented for his mistress—and for himself too, no doubt—a modest apartment at 7 Rue Saint-Roch. When she left Toulon for Fontainebleau Rose borrowed 2,000 francs from her lover and another 1,600 francs from a naval officer, Auguste de Meyronnet Saint-Marc, which were to be repaid only by Mme. Bonaparte.

3. "Sans-culotte Montagnarde . . ."

Rose, Hortense and Eugene were all at Fontainebleau with her father-in-law, the Marquis de Beauharnais, on the evening of Tuesday, June 21, when they learned that that very morning the royal family, prisoners of the Revolution, had escaped from the Tuileries to join Bouillé's army.

This event brought Alexandre into history, since he was to "reign" for a week. Undoubtedly, if Louis XVI had not fled from Paris, M. de Beauharnais would never have been known except as the first husband of the Empress Josephine, but it was he who that morning, in his capacity as President of the Assembly, had to go to the Tuileries with La Fayette to verify the royal family's departure. He then took his place at the tribune of the Assembly and declared:

"Gentlemen, I have some distressing news to announce to you: the King and part of his family were abducted last night by enemies of the public weal."

The King's abduction was the euphemism he had decided on a few moments earlier with La Fayette and Bailly to explain Louis XVI's departure. All through that tragic week, which was to give birth to the Republican party in France, Alexandre with undeniable skill directed the Assembly. The deputies were in permanent session and it was he who guided their voting on a variety of questions. And later on Wednesday, June 22, at ten in the evening he was to announce to his colleagues that Louis XVI had been arrested at Varennes the night before. He then had passed "the most urgent and active measures for protecting the King's person"—another euphemism to describe the return of the fugitive, henceforth a prisoner.

On the 25th, from the terrace of the Feuillants convent, he watched the passing of the frightful procession of captive monarchy walking alongside and surrounding the overloaded royal coach, in which the patriots were riding. Seeing Louis XVI, white with dust, cast a dazed look around at the crowd, M. le Vicomte de Beauharnais must have remembered the letter, by which the genealogist of the Orders of Nobility six years before had informed Rose's husband that he was not entitled to the honors of the Court. And on this day, June 25, 1791, he had respectfully been brought the key of the royal coach, he who had never been given the right to enter the King's carriages.

Meanwhile, at Fontainebleau, the crowd gathered in front of the house at 8 Rue de France, where the President of the Assembly's family were living, and when Eugene and Hortense were seen to appear at a window a voice cried: "They are our Dauphin and Dauphine now!"

On June 27 Alexandre sent to his father at Fontainebleau a letter in that astonishingly pretentious style he had learned from Patricol. "I would reproach myself were my present situation, which circumstances have rendered more perilous, painful and honorable than any other presidency, to prevent my offering you an expression of what I feel. I am worn out with fatigue, but I draw strength from my courage and from the hope that, meriting by my zeal at least part of the praise that has been heaped on me, I may be of use to the common weal and to the maintenance of the kingdom's tranquillity."

Alexandre's celebrity reflected on Rose, and there was now a relaxation in their relations. The children, their studies and their welfare, were undoubtedly the cause of this *modus vivendi*. Their relations were decorous, courteous even, as they were supposed to be in the eighteenth century, between spouses who had nothing in common apart from their surname.

During the two and a half years that followed her eventful return from Martinique, Rose lived first in the Paris house of the Asturias, Rue d'Anjou, then in the Rue Neuve-des-Mathurins, finally renting an apartment in the Rue Saint-Dominique.

Did she have any adventures? The name of the witty Joseph Robbé de Lagrange who, like Rose, was fond of the good life, has been put forward without proof. However that may be, she behaved with a discretion that is the despair of present-day historians. She had money troubles, not because Alexandre had to be forced to pay the agreed allowance, but because Mme. de Beauharnais—as later Mme. Bonaparte or Her Majesty the Empress and Queen— spent far more than her means, principally on clothes. She got into debt, borrowed from various sources, even from her children's governess, the devoted Mlle. de Lanoy. She had to be elegant. She had friends more fortunate than herself before whom she had to "make a show." She visited the Marquise d'Espinchal, the inevitable ✓ Mme. de Genlis, and the Marquise des Moulins, who had a literary salon. A subscriber to several theatres, the Marquise offered Mme. de Beauharnais her box. Rose was also seen at the houses of the Prince de Salm and of his sister, Princess Amalia de Hohenzollern- ✓ Siegmaringen, who had taken a fancy to her.

In September the Constituent Assembly died and the deputies scattered, after declaring heroically but rather stupidly that they were ineligible for the Legislative Assembly, just as they were beginning to know something about their work.

War was starting, a war of twenty-three years. Begun by Rose's first husband, it would end in the defeat of her second. Alexandre was obliged to resume service in the army. He was appointed adjutant general and at Valenciennes, on April 27, 1792, before going on campaign, he made his will. Rose was not mentioned; Patricol was made his executor. His children were evidently his heirs, although he did not mention them. A natural child, Marie Adélaïde de La Ferté, who was born in June, 1785, near Cherbourg and baptized at Clamart in 1789, was bequeathed 600 francs a year. This half sister of the future Queen Hortense was the daughter of the girl, "young, pretty and of very good family" mentioned earlier. Alexandre had introduced the girl to a friend, Mme. Le Breton des Chapelles, who took care of mother and child, under the name of Mlle. de La Ferté, a pseudonym no doubt inspired by the village of Ferté-Aurain, which later became La Ferté-Beauharnais.

Alexandre rose in rank—lieutenant colonel, adjutant general—

and was soon brigadier general. His activities consisted in fighting as little as possible and sending the Legislative Assembly as many reports as possible. He was present at the first setbacks and ended his account in these terms: "My fate like yours is, as you know, indissolubly united with the success of the Revolution. I fear lest fresh disasters should prevent my still serving with a leader's responsibility, but I shall always be a soldier. I shall stay in the ranks, I shall get myself killed, and I shall not survive my country's loss of liberty."

The monarchy fell and the former Vicomte proclaimed his republicanism and called for the tyrant's head. He was rewarded on March 8, 1793, by the rank of general and on May 11 by the command of the Upper Rhine Division. On May 23, though he still had never really fought, the Convention appointed him to the head of the Rhine Army. But he did refuse the post of Minister of War, although this would have kept him far from the battlefield. Mainz was besieged, but Citizen General Beauharnais, who had 60,000 men under his orders, did not fly to its aid.

He rushed through proclamations, still wrote reports covering himself with glory, and hesitated so long that Mainz capitulated. Alexandre immediately retreated and ten days after the fall of the town offered his resignation. "Belonging to a proscribed caste," he wrote, "it is my duty to relieve my fellow citizens of all grounds for anxiety which might arise concerning me in these moments of crisis."

Alexandre, who had already left his post on his own authority, was at last able to retire to Blois, whence he wrote to assure his father that his "head is not idle, it exhausts itself in plans for the safety of the Republic, just as my heart spends itself in efforts and wishes for the happiness of my fellow citizens."

In spite of the turmoil, Rose continued to divide her life between Paris, Fontainebleau and Croissy, where she lived in Mme. Hosten-Lamothe's country house. It was in the house of this Creole from St. Lucia, who was said to hold advanced opinions, that she got to know Tallien, the son of a butler, who was directing a little revolutionary newspaper.

"Humor him," Mme. Hosten-Lamothe had told her. "We might need him."

We have no idea whether Rose humored him to the point of

giving herself to this "brutal lover," whose face, however, was far from unattractive. We are equally in doubt about Pierre François Réal, the son of a gamekeeper, who as prosecuting attorney was brought close to fame by the Revolution and later, under the Consulate, became Councilor of State and assistant to the Minister of Police. She had met Réal in the house of Jean Chanorier, former lord of the manor at Croissy and now mayor. It was there that Rose also met Mme. de Vergennes, one of whose daughters became Mme. de Rémusat, a lady in waiting to the Empress. Mme. de Beauharnais was to make use of her "red" friends to see that the Vergennes were not disturbed—for the moment at least, but the day was to come when this friendship would compromise her. Rose was arrested on the same day as M. de Vergennes.

But that was not yet. In 1793 she was still able to help her friends of Penthémont, Fontainebleau or Croissy. She managed to save Mme. de Montmorin from the scaffold. She "put her life in peril," the latter was to say, "to shield me from the furious factions." Rose had been less fortunate with Armand de Montmorin, the former Governor of Fontainebleau. He was arrested after August 10 and massacred in September. But, as Mme. de Montmorin was later to bear witness, "there was nothing her tender heart would not risk to save my unfortunate husband."

To obtain graces, favors and enough to live on, Rose undoubtedly yielded her person from time to time. The young woman was free, she loved love and when she was told that she was pretty and pleasing felt no shame in according what was asked of her. "Mme. de Beauharnais's accommodating ways," wrote a contemporary Albert de Lezai-Marnésia, "her leanings toward intrigue and her natural kindness attracted people to her house and even provided her, by her many relations with several influential men of the day, with the means of rendering numerous services."

Although she was friendly with the powerful men of the day, when the Princess of Hohenzollern left Paris for the country, and then for England, and proposed taking Hortense and Eugene with her, Rose agreed to her children's removal from the turmoil. But Beauharnais, then at Strasbourg, had been informed. He objected to the emigration of his son and daughter and a courier caught up with the fugitives at Saint-Pol, in Artois.

There is no doubt that the questions of the day were beyond her. Rose was always to attach more importance to the color of a ribbon

or the skill of her lovers than to politics. But influenced by Rous-
seaumania, which was then in fashion, she brought up her children
"in the Spartan way." Hortense learned dressmaking with her
governess, "citizeness Lanoy," and poor Eugene was a carpenter's
apprentice under old Cochard, the policeman for the commune of
Croissy. He was even given a sword and rifle.

"I hope they will be worthy of the Republic," she said.

For the moment at least Rose proclaimed her Republican opinions. On asking Vadier, President of the Committee of General
Security, to free her sister-in-law, Marie Françoise de Beauharnais,
the future Empress wrote to him "frankly" and, she stated, "as a
sans-culotte extremist." (Her words were *"sans-culotte monta-
gnarde,"* *montagnards* being the name given to the Jacobins and
other extremists from the fact that they sat in an area of raised seats
in the National Assembly called "The Mountain.")

So Mme. la Vicomtesse de Beauharnais had become a sans-
culotte extremist. One must not blame her for the phrase. To live
one had to howl with the wolves, and Rose wanted intensely to live.
But the man who appeared Republican on January 21, 1793, seemed
tepid and reactionary a year later, and Beauharnais was beginning
to be suspect. His wife wrote to Vadier: "Alexandre has never
deviated from his principles. He has always toed the line. If he were
not a Republican he would have neither my esteem nor my affection. I am American and if I were allowed to see you, all your
doubts would be swept away. My household is a Republican
household. Before the Revolution my children were not to be
distinguished from sans-culottes. . . . Farewell, worthy citizen, you
have my entire confidence."

Not in the least moved by the letter from the American sans-
culotte extremist, Vadier was the first to sign the warrant of
summons for Citizen Beauharnais. In vain did Alexandre "exhaust"
his head and "spend" his heart; in vain did he increase his patriotic
activities in Blois; in vain did he assert his civic devotion, get
himself appointed president of the Jacobins of Chaumont and
elected mayor of Ferté-Aurain, where he set up a people's association and a committee of revolutionary surveillance—the former
Vicomte was accused of not having flown to the help of Mainz.
At Strasbourg, instead of "attending to the common weal," he had
"spent his days in wooing the civilians and his nights in arranging

balls for them." Although he was defended by three of Rose's friends, Réal, Barère, and Tallien, who objected to "vague charges" being brought against the General, Alexandre was arrested and imprisoned first in the Luxembourg and then, on March 14, 1794, in the Carmelite Prison.

Rose's turn was not long in coming. An anonymous denunciation recommended that the Committee of Public Safety "beware of the former Vicomtesse Alexandre de Beauharnais." So on April 20 the Committee sent two of its members, Citizens Lacombe and George, to 953 Rue Dominique "in the La Fontaine-Grenelle section" to search and examine any papers they might find in the suspect's house. They turned the apartment upside down and found "in a drawer of a desk in a little study belonging to the said apartment" and "in two wardrobes in an attic" the correspondence and "effects" Beauharnais had entrusted to his wife. The members of the Committee read the confiscated documents and came to the conclusion that "after the most scrupulous researches" they had "found nothing against the interests of the Republic, on the contrary a multitude of patriotic letters that can only redound to the credit of this citizeness."

Nervously Rose signed the report, making a big blot on the *i* of Beauharnais. The footsteps of the national guards died away down the street and the young woman began to take hope again. But very early the next morning Citizen George, accompanied this time by another member of the Committee, Citizen Elie Lafoste, came to arrest "the said Beauharnais, wife of the former general." To this end they were "authorized to take all necessary civil and military action." Rose did not want Eugene and Hortense to be waked and kissed them while they were still sound asleep. She entrusted them to Mlle. de Lanoy and to the faithful Euphémie and then, surrounded by guards, she went to the Rue de Vaugirard, where the Carmelite Prison was. At the prison Elie Lafoste gave the warder the warrant for arrest telling him to "receive Citizeness Beauharnais, wife of the general, a suspect under the law of September 17 last, and to detain her until otherwise ordered in the interests of public safety. 2 Floréal, Year II of the Republic one and indivisible."

The name of the Carmelites is strangely evocative. In this former convent in happier times the Barefoot Carmelites used to manufacture their extract of balm and the famous "Carmelite white" a pure-

white paint as brilliant as marble. It was here that perhaps the most
atrocious scenes of the September Massacres took place.

The appearance of 70 Rue de Vaugirard remains unchanged
today. One can still climb the short flight of steps, as Rose did on
entering the prison, where twenty months earlier seventy-six priests
and other prisoners had been massacred, with the killers even
pursuing their victims out into the garden. She must have closed her
eyes in horror on seeing the bloody marks left by the swords which
the murderers had leaned against the wall once their "work" was
finished. Those "signatures" are still there. Beginning the day after
the slaughter, the convent of the Carmelites was used for nine
months as a public dance hall, The Lindens, before becoming once
more a place of detention.

The new prisoner quickly dropped her attitude of "sans-culotte
extremist." Except for the setting, she could have imagined herself
back in the days of Penthémont. She again met, or became acquainted with, the Duchesse d'Aiguillon, born a Noailles, Mmes. de
Lameth, de Bragelonne, de Jarnac, de Paris-Montbrun, the Duc de
Béthune-Charost, Comte de Soyécourt, Chevalier de Champcenetz,
Prince de Salm-Kyrbourg, Admiral Duc de Montbazon-Rohan and
the Marquis de Gouy d'Arsy.

There was laughter in this anteroom of the guillotine. But, as a
contemporary remarked, "one had to have known that kind of
gaiety to understand its value." Rose was in a dormitory of eighteen
beds. Her closest neighbors were Mme. de Custine and Mrs. Eliott,
who had been the mistress of Philippe-Egalité (Duc d'Orléans, a
revolutionist). Rose quite won her heart. "She is one of the most
accomplished and amiable women I have ever met," Mrs. Eliott was
to say. "All the little arguments we ever had were about politics. She
was what was called 'a constitutional' at the beginning of the
Revolution, but she was never in the least a Jacobin, for no one
suffered more than she did from the Reign of Terror and from
Robespierre."

The female prisoners all made their own beds, but only Mme. de
Beauharnais and her two companions, now friends, cleaned their
room. "The other prisoners did not bother," Mrs. Eliott recalled.
There was, incidentally, a slovenliness in the Carmelites which did
not exist in other prisons. "The male prisoners do not take any care

of their person," an eyewitness relates. "They are unbuttoned, for the most part without cravat, in dirty shirts and breeches, their legs bare, a kerchief round the head, unkempt and with long beards. The women, our sad companions in misfortune, gloomy and pre-occupied, wear a little dress or pierrot, now of one color now of another."

When the turnkey rang his bell all the women came out of their cells and went to the refectory, where they were served with a meal of what the men had left—for the latter ate first. According to some, the food was adequate, according to others the meat was dubious and the eggs might have been laid under the ancien regime. When the meal was over and the table cleared the refectory became a drawing room. The men returned and strutted about trying to be amusing. "We talked, we gossiped . . ." Others strode along the filthy corridors. The first person in the Carmelites to kiss Mme. de Beauharnais's hand was Alexandre. He was then madly in love with Delphine de Custine of the astonishingly fair hair and aquamarine eyes, who occupied the bed next to Rose. Her husband, poor Armand de Custine, had just died on the scaffold. He had loved his wife—the "queen of roses," as Chevalier de Bouffiers had named her—but she had had for him only "the tenderest friendship." Before going to his death he had written to her: "It is the end, my poor Delphine, I embrace you for the last time. I cannot see you and even if I could I would not want to. Parting would be too difficult and this is no moment for weakness." Delphine had put on black, which suited her so well that she inspired a consuming passion in Alexandre, who soon became for her "a person after her own heart who gave her a taste of happiness in the very shadow of the scaffold."

For in the Carmelites, as in other French prisons, a kind of amorous frenzy reigned. "Everywhere the sound of kisses and lovers' sighs penetrated the very depths of the dark corridors," an eyewitness relates. "Husbands became lovers again, lovers increased in tenderness. The sweetest kisses were taken and returned, without either resistance or scruple; favored by a bit of darkness, love found its tenderest desires fulfilled. It is true that these pleasures were sometimes disturbed by the sight of the unfortunate ones who passed through the room on their way to appear before the Revolutionary Tribunal. Then there would be a long moment of silence, an interchange of anxious looks, then we embraced tenderly and gradually the ordinary course of things was resumed."

Thanks to the complicity of the jailers, it was possible with the aid of substantial tips to be locked up with the lady of one's heart.

"France is probably the only country in the world, and French-women the only women, capable of offering such singular intimacy and displaying themselves at their most attractive and voluptuous in the midst of the most repugnant and horrible circumstances the universe can provide," wrote Beugnot, who was a lodger in the prisons of the Terror. "The proximity of women furnished us pleasant distractions. We talked agreeably about everything without dwelling on anything. Unhappiness was treated like a naughty child at whom one only laughs and in fact we laughed openly at the divinity of Marat, the priesthood of Robespierre, the magistracy of Fouquier, and seemed to be saying to that bloodstained rabble, 'You may kill us when you please, but you will not prevent us from being pleasing!' "

In the evening, when men and women separated to go back to their horrible dungeons, Delphine would show Rose the burning messages Alexandre sent her. "Do you wish for my blood? I will shed it with pleasure if, as it flows for you, it may inflame yours and imprint my image more strongly in your memory. . . . Then, being in your heart as a lover, a friend, a brother, I shall mingle with everything that is dear to you and live on love, even in the sighs that prevent other bonds."

Decidedly Alexandre had never written like that to his wife.

It would show little knowledge of Rose to imagine that she would be content just to be Delphine's confidante. Her love affair with the famous General Hoche, introduced to her by Alexandre, began in the Carmelite Prison. He was in a neighboring prison and had to pass through Rose's dormitory to climb the fifteen steps to his cell.

And how did one start a love affair in the month of Floréal, Year II? In the morning, when the men were still locked up, Rose would send a flash of sun into the depths of the General's dark cell with the aid of a mirror: so many flashes of light meant so many heads fallen into the basket the day before. Thus began one of Josephine's two great loves, the other being for Captain Hippolyte Charles. Her heart beat quite differently for her two husbands.

Rose was thirty-one and Lazare Hoche five years younger. He was tall and sinewy, his frank countenance was scarred—an attractive attribute to some women—and he talked grandly. His father had been groom in Louis XVI's stables and before becoming a volunteer in the French Guards he himself had curried the King's horses. Hoche, however, had been educated by his foster brother, General Le Veneur. This strapping fellow gave an impression of strength for which Rose undoubtedly felt a great need. Looking at him one would not have imagined that he would die of consumption in three years.

The month before, on March 11, Hoche had married a girl of sixteen. Sent first from Thionville to Nice and then arrested, he had been separated from the "angel of his life," his dear Adélaïde, after only eight days' honeymoon. Once he had met Rose he began to bear prison life with good humor and to suffer much less from having had to leave his "cherished, tender spouse."

"My health is good," he wrote gaily to a friend who had evidently sent him food. "There is nothing so agreeable as a good dinner when one is hungry. . . . Long live the Republic!" Once after ordering a choice meal he added, "Send me my wife's portrait with my dinner," but he seems not to have waited for his freedom before forgetting Adélaïde in Rose's arms. At this time their love affair would last only twenty-six days, since Hoche was sent to the Conciergerie. Not until later were matters between Mme. de Beauharnais and the handsome General Hoche to take a more passionate turn. As for Rose, she found a "consoler"—that is her own word for him—in the person of "General" Santerre, the boastful brewer, who had taken Louis XVI to the scaffold and claimed to have ordered the roll of drums which cut short the unhappy King's speech. He had been less brilliant with the Army of the West, where he had commanded ragged, disorderly volunteers who, at the first attack of the Chouans, the royalist insurgents, had retired "at furious speed" with their general leading.

One should not misjudge the term "consoler" as used by Rose. Her two cellmates, the Duchesse d'Aiguillon and Mme. de Custine, called him the same thing.

He was not yet "the infamous Santerre," and the Faubourg Saint-Antoine had nicknamed him "Gros-Père." He was in fact fat, chubby, expansive and smiling and his character was as frank as his appearance. He was kind, charitable and of a happy disposition, qualities much appreciated in prison, where each evening the roll call of prisoners to be sent to the Conciergerie, that anteroom of the guillotine, echoed dismally.

Whenever he could Alexandre visited his blonde mistress . . . and his wife. Alexandre often spoke to his wife of their children, to whom they sent joint letters. "My dear little Hortense," wrote Rose, "it pains me to be separated from you and my dear Eugene. I am always thinking of my two dear little children whom I love and embrace with all my heart." Then Alexandre took up the pen and, so as not to lose the habit, wrote in moralizing sentences: "Think of me, my child, think of your mother. Give cause of satisfaction to those who are taking care of you and do your work well. It is by this means, by the assurance that you are employing your time well, that we shall have even more confidence that you miss us and remember us. Good morning, my little girl! Your mother and I are unhappy at not seeing you. The hope of soon embracing you sustains us and the pleasure of talking about it consoles us."

Possibly from the same cell, and certainly in the same style, he wrote to Delphine's brother Elzéar: "Brother of a goddess, grant your beneficent aid to a weak mortal, the tenderest that ever was, the most passionate, the most adoring of your Delphine."

Every day Hortense and Eugene went to the Carmelites and at the beginning managed to see their parents. But, as Hortense was to relate: "Entry to their prison was forbidden us and soon correspondence was prohibited. We tried to make up for this by writing at the bottom of a list of clothes, 'Your children are well,' but the porter was barbarous enough to erase this. As a last resort we would copy out the list ourselves in turn so that, seeing our writing, our parents would at least know we were alive." For a time Rose's little pug dog Fortuné, bad tempered but obliging, acted as postman. He could enter the prison and carry notes in his collar. Alexandre's friend Calmelet, a lawyer devoted to Rose, tried to get the Beauharnais freed. He had the children sign a petition to be sent to the Convention. "Innocent children beg of you the liberty of their affectionate mother, their mother who can be blamed only for the misfortune of belonging to a class to which she has proved herself a stranger, since she surrounded herself only with the best patriots, the most excellent montagnards. Having asked for a permit in conformity with the law of 28 Germinal, she was arrested without being able to discover the cause. Citizen representatives, you will not let innocence, patriotism and virtue be oppressed. Restore life to unhappy children, citizen representatives. They are not old enough for grief." But Calmelet was imprudent enough to have the children also send a petition to the Committee of Public Safety asking for their mother to be tried. "When one has no fear of judgment, one burns to have it given." This was exceedingly unwise. At that time of madness it was better to be forgotten.

One day a strange woman arrived in the Rue Saint-Dominique, giving Rose's name, and mysteriously took Hortense and Eugene to the Rue de Sèvres. They went through the garden and the lady took the children to the second floor of a gardener's house, where she led them to a gable window. Opposite was a gray, dirty building, the Carmelite Prison, in which a window opened. "My father and mother appeared at it," Hortense related. "Full of surprise and emotion, I cried out, I stretched my arms toward my parents. They signaled to me to be silent, but a sentry at the foot of the wall had heard us and called out. The unknown woman quickly took us away. Later we learned that the prison window had been pitilessly walled up. That was the last time I saw my father."

Beauharnais, who felt (correctly) that he might never see his children again, increased his petitions. He asserted that his wife, "also a very good Patriot," had never left the territory of the Republic since the beginning of the Revolution. As for himself, it was a crime to leave him in the Carmelites, he must be freed. "If the freedom I have constantly served is restored to me," he promised, "I wish to use it only to increase hatred for kings in my children's hearts"—those children who were each one day to wear a crown.

General Beauharnais was not to perish for having let Mainz be lost. At that time heads were falling like roof tiles in a high wind. At the beginning of Thermidor—the end of July, 1794—the Terror was at its height. Fouquier's machinery had developed a new procedure, for emptying the overcrowded detention centers, prison conspiracy. A bar in a window at the Saint-Lazare had been sawn through in order to give the impression that the prisoners were trying to escape. Elsewhere prisoners found themselves being accused of seeking the company of the aristocrats they were locked in with. And so on July 22 an officer from the tribunal came to interrogate forty-nine inhabitants of the Carmelites before transferring them to the Conciergerie. Alexandre was one of them. He rushed to Delphine and gave her the Arab ring from his finger, but he dreaded Rose's tears and merely wrote to her. "From the interrogation to which quite a number of the prisoners were subjected today," he wrote, "it would very much appear that I am the victim of the wicked calumnies of several self-styled patriotic aristocrats in this place. The assumption that this infernal plot will follow me to the Revolutionary Tribunal leaves me no hope of seeing you again, my dear, or of embracing my dear children. I shall not speak of my regrets; my tender affection for them, the fraternal attachment which binds me to you, can leave you in no doubt as to my feelings on this subject as I depart this life."

The interrogations went on, and Alexandre took advantage of this to write these lines intended for his wife and for posterity: "I regret equally being separated from a country I love, for which I would have given my life a thousand times. . . . I shall die with that serenity which still allows one to be moved by one's dearest attachments, but with the courage that characterizes a free man, a pure conscience and an honest mind whose most fervent wishes are for the prosperity of the Republic. Farewell, my dear. Console yourself with our children, console them by instructing them and above all by teaching them that it is by virtue and civic duty that they must efface the memory of my agony and recall my services and my offices to the gratitude of the nation. Farewell. You know those I love. Be their consolation and, by your care, prolong my life in their hearts. Farewell, for the last time in my life I press you and my dear children to my heart."

On the next day, 5 Thermidor or July 23, Alexandre bravely mounted the scaffold.

Only five more days and he would have escaped death—and Josephine would doubtless never have become an empress.

Prostrate on her bed, Rose did not dare move. The prison continued to empty, a situation which was not calculated to calm her. Would she have to follow her husband? She might well think so, and the little Creole had little courage in the face of death. She spent her days reading the cards in secret and weeping before everyone, "to the great scandal of her companions," says a prisoner, for it was bad form to tremble at the thought of the tumbril.

Fortunately there was Charles de La Bussière. A playwright and actor in the little theatres of the Boulevard du Temple, he was a clerk to the Committee of Public Safety, in charge of the filing system. Unable, at the risk of being caught, to take bundles of papers home with him, this heroic man tore them into small pieces and swallowed them. An admirer of the Comédie-Française, he began his salvage operations with the actors there. He managed, it appears, to eat 1,200 documents. We have no idea whether he knew Rose or whether one of her friends had asked him to save her, but as he was later to tell—he ate the papers that would have enabled Fouquier-Tinville to send the wife of the former President of the Constituent Assembly on the same road as her husband. (La Bussière sank into poverty, and under the Consulate he was given a benefit performance at the Porte Saint-Martin. Josephine went to it with Bonaparte and paid 100 pistoles—approximately $400—for her box.)

Two days after Alexandre's execution, a woman of ravishing and seductive beauty sent this famous note from prison to her lover, Tallien: "The director of police has just left; he came to tell me that tomorrow I am to go to the Tribunal, which means to the scaffold. This is very different from the dream I had last night. Robespierre was no longer living and the prisons were open. But thanks to your notorious cowardice there will soon be no one in France capable of bringing about my dream."

She was Thérésia Cabarrus and, like Rose, was separated from her husband. To save this goddess from death Tallien was to find the supreme courage to attack Robespierre. One morning, five days after Alexandre's death, a prisoner, looking into the street from her cell window, saw a woman going through what seemed at first incomprehensible motions. "She kept holding up her dress without our understanding what she meant. As she persisted, I called out, 'Robe?' She nodded. Then she picked up a stone, put it in her skirt, which she again showed me, lifting the stone in her other hand. 'Pierre?' I called out again. She was delighted that we understood. Finally, putting dress and stone together, she rapidly went through the motion several times of cutting her throat and then began to dance and applaud. This extraordinary pantomime filled us with indescribable emotion since we dared to think that it was telling us of Robespierre's death."

The news ran through the prison. Rose learned that the Terror was over, thanks to Tallien, her friend Tallien. Hope was born again. Undoubtedly Tallien and Hoche, who had been freed on August 4, would do everything to open the doors of the Carmelites. The future Mme. Tallien, whom Paris now called "Notre Dame de Thermidor," had gone to reassure Hortense and Eugene as to their mother's fate the moment she was free.

On the evening of August 6 a name was called out by a turnkey in the Carmelites: "The widow Beauharnais!"

She was free. The prisoners applauded on hearing that the pretty widow who trembled and wept with so much charm was to rejoin her children—and her lover. As for Rose, she fainted from joy.

On this same 19 Thermidor Salicetti, deputy for the army, denounced the general commanding the artillery of the Italian Army, the Corsican Bonaparte, friend of Augustin Robespierre. . . . Salicetti, who had discovered the "intelligent captain" Bonaparte, had placed him at the head of the artillery at Toulon and made him battalion commander and then general.

Three days later, on August 9, Bonaparte was committed for trial. "He thought he was lost," wrote M. Laurenti, a rich businessman of Nice with whom the young General lodged, and who had just refused his daughter's hand to the penniless officer. On seeing the officer suddenly suspected, placed under strict arrest, and guarded by an armed sentry, he must undoubtedly have congratulated himself on his wise decision.

4. The Gay Widow

"Your beloved image is constantly in my heart . . . My love only increases with each day."

It was not to Rose that Lazare Hoche addressed these ardent words but to his wife, who was still in Lorraine. On leaving the Conciergerie, he immediately informed her that he was leaving for Thionville "on foot, as becomes a republican." But two days later he had not yet started out. Rose had now been freed and the "beloved image" was forgotten.

While he was ardently celebrating his new-found freedom with his mistress, the General had only one fear: that Mme. Hoche would appear. He therefore counseled her not to leave. So as not to arouse his young wife's jealousy, he assured her that he lived in concealment and did not "frequent any public place and never the theaters." Yet he was seen with Rose at Mme. Hosten's, where his liberation was celebrated.

Rose was really in love. With Hoche she was happy and, as Barras would later reveal, found love in his arms. Ah! if the gallant General could only divorce his wife for her—Josephine admitted much later that she has thought seriously of this possibility. Hoche, though, was attached to his mistress only by sensual bonds. But, as we know from his letters, he continued to love her with passion for a year and a half more.

It is possible that, as Barras affirmed, only Hoche's "tender esteem" for his "young and virtuous wife" prevented his getting a divorce. Adélaïde fought and won her first victory as a result of her freshness and charm. Hoche had been appointed to direct the army at Cherbourg—he was later to command the whole of the West—and before leaving Paris he asked Adélaïde to bring him his sword, pistols and horse. Once he saw his child wife he melted and for twenty-four hours forgot Rose's expert caresses, which were later to "inflame the blood" of Bonaparte, and tenderly loved the gentle "Adélayde," as he wrote her name.

"Ah, my friend, how happy I am," he wrote to his father-in-law before setting out. "Twenty-four hours spent with my wife have made me forget all my troubles."

During the next year Hoche was to live hardly more with Adélaïde than with his mistress. When he next saw his little wife in March, 1795, he wrote: "She is charming. I love her, my good friend, more than I have ever done."

But on returning to Lorraine Adélaïde's heart was heavy. She had guessed the presence of a rival. Hoche defended himself as well as he could. "I shall not stoop to justifying myself . . . exert yourself, my dear, to rebuild a union which should never have been broken. . . . If you still love me try to redress all my wrongs, I am sometimes a little mad."

Adélaïde was right to be uneasy. Her husband loved Rose, in a different way but quite as much, in spite of the money she was costing him. He had taken Eugene with him as a young volunteer and "apprentice aide-de-camp." But his mistress showed very little gratitude. Her letters were too infrequent and Lazare complained: "I am in despair at receiving no answer from the woman I love, the widow whose son I have become accustomed to thinking of as mine."

He suffered from being separated from the "widow," but even more from knowing her courted and flattered. The vanity which, according to him, now filled Rose's heart, together with her coquetry, gave him infinite pain.

"There is no more happiness for me on earth. I cannot go to Paris to see the woman who is the cause of all my grief."

Perhaps if Rose had now asked him to divorce his wife he would have agreed, but there was shortly to be no question of that for the loyal General. Adélaïde would be expecting a child—a living reminder of her visit to Rennes in March, 1795.

At the end of September, 1794, Rose had rented an appartment at 371 Rue de l'Université "near the Rues de Poitiers and Belle-Chasse," from Mme. de Krény, who was to become her confidante and "woman of all work." She lived there first at the expense of Hoche, from whom she borrowed shamelessly—in spite of his sighs. She also asked Mlle. de Lanoy's brother-in-law for 15,000 francs and had from Citizen Desrez, a lawyer, another 500 "which he has lent me today and which I shall return to him at his first request."

The pretty widow's chief problem was how to live. Thanks to Tallien, who had supported her petition as an "act of justice," she had been able to recover her "linen, clothes, furniture, jewels and other effects" placed under seal at the Rue Saint-Dominique and belong to "the citizeness widow Beauharnais and her children." But the gold louis was to go up to 4,000 francs—five times that amount today—and on some days it rose by 100 francs an hour. A cord of wood went up by 2,000 francs in two days. A pair of shoes or a turkey cost 250 francs, a leg of mutton 1,248 francs, and one paid a crown (three francs) to have a shirt washed. Rose paid 700 francs a pair for her stockings—"gray silk with colored clocks"—500 for a short length of muslin and 1,200 for a shawl. So in order to dress the young woman got an advance from her friend Emery, the banker, on the very uncertain income expected from Martinique. Emery, who was a very liberal man, a former deputy to the Legislative Assembly and a former mayor of Dunkirk, did business with the Antilles and granted Mme. de Beauharnais this overdraft. On November 20, 1794, Rose was able to inform her mother: "A person leaving for New England has undertaken to deliver this letter to you, my dear mother. . . . No doubt you have heard of my misfortune. I have been a widow for four months. My children are my only remaining consolation and you, my dear mother, my only support."

This discreet appeal to her only support had no result. A little later, therefore, she explained the situation frankly to her mother. "Without the attentions of my good friend Emery and of his partner I do not know what would have become of me. I know your affection too well to have the slightest doubt of the eagerness with which you will supply me with the means to live and to acknowledge my debt to M. Emery by paying him."

Mme. de La Pagerie sent what she could, but it was not much. So, without embarrassment, Rose drew a bill of exchange on her mother for £1,000 sterling. Since the beginning of the Revolution she had been living mainly on loans from the obliging banker. "You may judge from this," she wrote to her mother, "that I owe him considerable sums." Later the wife of the First Consul was to advance Emery and his partner 200,000 francs—without interest.

The widow Beauharnais was the official guardian of her children, together with the faithful Calmelet, and as such appealed to Mme. de Renaudin, who came to her rescue by lending her 50,000 francs in promissory notes—2,644 real francs—which allowed Rose to pay her contribution to the forced loan floated by the hard-up government.

Rose did have a small staff. Besides Citizeness Lanoy, who left her when Hortense was boarded out, she was served by a lady's maid, Agathe, and a manservant, Citizen Gontier. Mme. de Beauharnais paid them only occasionally, usually borrowing money from them instead.

Her difficult situation in this year of 1795, a famine year, was well known and when she dined with certain of her friends, such as Mme. de Moulins, she was allowed to dispense with bringing her own bread, as was the custom then.

Paris had become a huge junk shop and Rose, too, was obliged to sell anything she could spare, disposing of stockings and items of clothing among the women of her acquaintance. On leaving prison she had been obliged to indulge in trading like everyone else.

Rose's greatest friend at that time was the dazzling Thérésia, soon to be the wife of Tallien.

"Mme. Tallien is infinitely good and beautiful," Rose wrote to her aunt Renaudin. "She makes use of her vast influence only to get favors granted to those unhappy people who apply to her, and she gives everything with such an expression of satisfaction that you would think it was she who owed you thanks. Her friendship for me is spontaneous and affectionate. I assure you that mine for her is like what I feel for you, which should enable you to imagine my feelings for Mme. Tallien."

"She is the Venus of the Capitol," exclaimed the future Duchesse d'Abrantès, "but even more beautiful than the work of Phidias!"

Thérésia's fame reflected on her friend Rose. Everyone knew of the part she had played at Bordeaux, where she had saved many aristocrats from the guillotine. They knew that, thanks to her famous letter, Tallien had overthrown the "tyrant" and ended the Terror, and a wave of homage and gratitude mounted toward her, toward the man whom she could not choose but marry, and also toward Rose, the couple's best friend and godmother of the little girl to whom Mme. Tallien had given birth as she left the Théâtre-Feydeau—Thermidor Rose Thérésia, who symbolized the wonderful new beginning.

Mme. de Beauharnais often visited the Cottage, which the pair had just bought in the Allée des Veuves, now the Avenue Montaigne. In those days it was almost in the country and the house had a thatched roof and creepers climbing over the carved wooden balconies. Indoors there was a surprising contrast—a luxurious classical décor with a Pompeian hall, tall lamps on tripods and pillars of multicolored marble. Before the bed draped in jaune fifi effarouché, a greenish canary yellow, was a statue of Diana in the bath, made in the likeness of Thérésia. At the Cottage the Talliens received the new masters of France, those who, during that night of supreme fear, had found the courage to overthrow Robespierre, and chief among them was Barras.

Thérésia Tallien and Rose, remembering that they had been the Marquise de Fontenay and the Vicomtesse de Beauharnais, also brought to the Cottage women of the former society, such as the attractive little bacchante Aimée de Coigny—the Jeune Captive of André Chénier's poem—Mme. de Staël, quite unembarrassed at finding herself in such mixed company, and Mme. Permon, whose daughter was one day to be Duchesse d'Abrantès and who claimed to be descended from the Comnenus line of Byzantine emperors. It was Rose who brought the young and virginal Mme. Récamier to the Allée des Veuves.

Everyone liked Rose, even the women. A contemporary wrote: "Her even temper, her easygoing disposition, the kindness that filled her eyes and was expressed not only in her speech but also in the very tone of her voice; a certain indolence natural to Creoles . . . all this gave her a charm which counterbalanced the dazzling beauty of her two rivals—Mme. Tallien and Mme. Récamier. Besides, although she had less brilliance and freshness than they, she was also beautiful, thanks to the regularity of her features, the elegant suppleness of her figure and the gentle expression of her face."

Undoubtedly Rose no longer had the same bloom as when she was twenty, but she was so clever in making up and in dressing her long, silky hair that she drew men's glances even more now. She knew how to walk, to sit, to recline so as to enhance her languorous Creole grace, and how to cast on those she wished to attract her "irresistible" glance, letting it glimmer through the curling lashes of her dark-blue slanting doe eyes.

"As beautiful in joy as in sorrow," as a contemporary tells us, she knew so well how to adorn her small but perfectly modeled body, to let her voice sing prettily, like all Creoles barely sounding the letter *r*—a mannerism which also happened to be very fashionable at that time in France—and she had a skin so "dazzling in its fineness" that she could compete with the prettiest women of the day. The times were far from unhelpful. In an inevitable reaction from the deliberate simplicity of the Revolution women freely indulged in the delights of self-adornment.

One day, for example, Rose appeared to the guests at the Cottage as a "beautiful violet."

"She wore a long dress of pink and white watered silk, the bottom of the train trimmed with black fringe; the bodice six fingers deep and with no fichu; the black gauze sleeves short; long gloves reaching above the elbow, in nut brown, a color which suits this beautiful violet; shoes of yellow morocco; white stockings with green clocks."

Although the "gay widow" adopted the fashion of tunics slit up the side, she did not go so far as Mme. Tallien who, an amazed eyewitness recounted, exhibited herself one evening with "her bust encircled by a diamond necklace; on an undulating chain, the diamonds curved round her breasts in a line of sparks; they fell and rose with each heartbeat, throwing a thousand fiery stars on the smooth skin. This was the cartouche, the name given to this more elevated girdle of Venus, and Mme. Tallien rivaled Minerva and Juno." Neither did Rose imitate her friend Mme. Hamelin—"the most licentious woman in France"—who made, and won, a wager to walk from the Luxembourg to the Champs-Elysées one summer day with her bosom entirely exposed to the sun.

"For two thousand years now," a journalist wrote, "women have been wearing shifts, it is an age-old and deadly habit!" And the shifts, like all other restraints, were thrown off.

However, Rose did adopt the method which "tends to enhance the brilliant lily of a beautiful breast and emphasize the rosebud which is its natural ornament." Black velvet was placed "crosswise over the heart" and fastened above the left breast. As the dress was transparent one could very distinctly see the velvet "which drew attention to the bloom of the rosebud through the tunic." Mme. de Beauharnais was certainly able to permit herself this extravagance, in spite of what Barras was to remark about her "premature decay." I prefer to believe Bonaparte when he wrote, two years later, of "the little, white breast so resilient and very firm."

Rose had not wanted the hangman's scissors to chop off her hair bluntly, but, imitating her prison companions, she had cut it off herself, and now like all the elegant women she dressed it à la Titus. She resembled a Greek shepherd and it suited her admirably. When Thérésia launched the fashion of brown, gold or red wigs, Rose hastened to order these accessories, which cost 25 louis each. They were not yet paid for when it became necessary to change to blue, green or purple ones to avoid disgrace. When wearing a hat she did her hair à la Minerve or à la Liberté. Suddenly from one day to the next everything had to be in peasant style and Rose ordered a "gleaner's hood."

Dancing went on everywhere. The capital had 640 dance halls and Rose went where society dictated, from the Calypso in Faubourg Montmartre to the famous balls of the Hôtel Richelieu, described by Mercier in "Tableau de Paris" as "the abode of transparent gowns, lace-drenched hats, of gold, of diamonds, of gauze and of muffled chins. For entry a certain affluence is necessary. In this enchanted place a hundred perfumed goddesses crowned with roses drift about in Athenian dresses and try in turn to catch the eyes of our Incroyables [unbelievably dressed men of the Directory period] with their tousled hair and Turkish slippers."

A dance hall was opened even in the grim prison of the Carmelites, where Rose and so many others had been incarcerated.

"Every class has its dancing society," wrote Mercier, "and from
the smallest to the largest, that is from rich to poor, everyone
dances; it is a mania, a universal fashion." For Rose the preparations
for a ball were a real vigil at arms, as witness a note she sent
Thérésia.

"There is some talk, my dear friend, of a magnificent evening at
the Thélusson dance hall; no need to ask if you will be there. I write
to beg you to meet me there with that peach-flower underskirt you
like so much and which I do not dislike myself. I propose wearing its mate. As it seems important to me that we should be
dressed in exactly the same way, I give you notice that I shall have
on my hair a red kerchief knotted Creole fashion with three curls on
each temple. What may be rather daring for me will be perfectly
normal for you as you are younger, perhaps no prettier, but
infinitely fresher. You see I am fair to everyone. But it is all part of a
plan. The idea is to throw the Trois Bichons and the Bretelles
Anglaises into despair. You will understand the importance of this
conspiracy, the need for secrecy, and the enormous effect that will
result. Till tomorrow, I count on you."

The three Bichons and the Bretelles Anglaises were probably
some fashionable young men who attracted the two friends. It was
at the Thélusson that the Bals des Victimes were given. One's
partner was greeted à la victime, by imitating the movement of a
head being inserted in the lunette, that invention of the good Dr.
Guillotin.

Like her friend Thérésia, like all those who had learned to live in
the shadow of the guillotine, Rose wanted to drown her thoughts.
The sound of the violins was to prevent their hearing, in memory,
the sinister voice calling out at evening the names of those summoned for their appointment with death. One would have had to be
a saint to resist this mass hysteria, this morbid gaiety, and Rose was
not. Besides, her tastes coincided so well with those of the age, with
these times in which only love and beauty counted; and the joy of
dressing oneself differently every day, or spending without thought
for the morrow, of dancing, of drinking were to drive away the
nightmare—and also to avoid seeing the misery around one.

The winter following Thermidor was a terrible one. There was nothing to be found in the food shops, no meat, candles or wood. Even that black sticky mixture called bread, made of a conglomeration of sawdust, beans and chestnuts, became rare. The homely cabbage had risen from 8 sous to 8 francs, when it could be found. To top everything off the Seine began to freeze, and in spite of woodcutting in the Bois de Boulogne and at Vincennes many Parisians died of the cold. Some died of hunger too. All the more reason not to forgo any opportunity for a feast, if only to efface the memory of the stinking soup from the kitchens of the Carmelite and La Force prisons.

It was also fashionable to consult cartomancers, fortunetellers and other soothsayers whom Rose, superstitious like all Creoles, never failed to visit—it reminded her of Martinique. Accompanied by Thérésia, Mme. Hamelin or Julie Talma she went to 5 Rue de Tournon, which still exists, to see the famous Mlle. Lenormand, who had thirteen ways of answering her clients' questions: "the examination of corpses, the evocation of shades, the apparition of specters, water reflected in a mirror, ashes thrown to the north wind, candles, laurel, verbena, white of egg, fingernails, fire, birds, a cock nourished on special grain and placed among the letters of the alphabet."

We do not know whether Mlle. Lenormand also predicted that Rose would end up "more than queen," but the fortuneteller may have given her the formula for settling with her tradesmen: to let herself be kept.

With no husband and with two children to rear, she cannot really be blamed for having sought influential, rich protectors. Rose found herself unarmed in the face of life. That was her weakness: aside from love nothing counted. Nature had "formed her of lace and gauze," as Bonaparte was to say.

It was for the Marquis de Caulaincourt, father of Napoleon's Master of the Horse, that the irresistible Creole proved most expensive. A former lieutenant general under Louis XVI, he had never emigrated. Before the Revolution Rose had met this attractive man, now in his fifties, at the Marquis de Montmorin's in Fontainebleau. She first did him a service by providing a recommendation for his son Armand, whom the difficult times had turned into a sergeant major, although he had formerly been a lieutenant and aide-de-camp. His second son, Auguste, had no employment. Rose did what she could, but without appreciable results. Fortunately, thanks to other influences, Caulaincourt was successful in his attempts and, most important, received three years' pay due him as a retired general, of which Rose hastened to appropriate a large share. This enabled her to go on being an elegant woman—which was what counted most for her. The Marquis paid willingly, for he had fallen really in love with Rose. The general's fifty-four years did not perturb the lady of thirty-two, although her tastes ran rather to men younger than herself—a predilection that was to remain right up to her last lover.

It would even seem that Caulaincourt, "a slave to the devil of middle-aged passion," that notorious demon de midi that walks in the high noon of a man's life, had considered divorcing in order to marry the fascinating widow. For Rose, the idea of becoming the Marquise de Caulaincourt might have been tempting. Her suitor had money and owned the fine estate of Caulaincourt, which had not been seized. However, at that time Rose still thought that Hoche might have the courage to part from the simple Adélaïde.

And then, other love beckoned to her. Shortly after settling in the Rue de l'Université, Mme. de Beauharnais decided to have Barras visit her. With Tallien he was certainly the most powerful member of the Convention, the "grand profiteer" of the blow struck in Thermidor. He was President of the Convention, member of the Commission of Five, member of the Committee of Public Safety, and general in command of the Army of the Interior, and would one day be a director, one of the five "kings" of France during the Directory.

At the beginning of 1795 she wrote to him: "It is a very long time since I have had the pleasure of seeing you. It is very bad of you to abandon an old acquaintance like this. I hope you will be moved by this reproach. I am now living at 371 Rue de l'Université."

Barras came to see her, of course, but not often enough to please Rose, who sent him another message in February: "Tell Barras that I have been ill in bed for three days with a cold and that it is unkind of him not to have come to see me, and that one has to be a very good friend of his to forgive him."

She was to be his friend and to forgive him. Did Rose love him? Could one love the regicide Vicomte Paul de Barras, who may have been intelligent, handsome, elegant, of attractive bearing, brave, refined and witty, but was for all that most appallingly corrupt? This does not seem to have stopped Rose. As for him, he loved only money—money and luxury. To get them he would have done anything. He also loved women, the "goddesses of his 'Cult of Reason,' " but was completely incapable of loving one alone.

"Democracy is love," he would say. And on occasion he did not disdain young boys. This vain, cynical gambler, this vicious politician, enjoyed not only power but what power could obtain for him. It was said that "he loved the throne for its velvet." He enjoyed the passing moment, said someone who knew him well, "living from day to day with his wit, his purse, his mistresses and his conscience." But not much with the last-named, as he had none. Yet he was obliging. "He was pleased to do a service," said Mme. de Chastenay, "and showed no discrimination or conceit in doing it or timidity in attempting it." Rose was to make the utmost use of him. The "General's" support obtained for her the gift of a cow for Croissy—a valuable animal in the Year III—and two horses and a carriage to compensate for the equipage which Alexandre had left to the Army of the Rhine, and which had been taken over by the Representatives.

Historians do not agree on the date when Rose became part of Barras's harem, a harem composed of new, future and former mistresses. Some think she became one of his friends in October, 1794, others in the course of the winter or spring of 1795. According to André Gavoty, who knows most about the subject, their liaison did not begin until after Vendémiaire. But if the question had later been put to the two people in question they might not have been able to reply. For to Paul de Barras and Rose de Beauharnais their physical relations, taking place among other adventures, were not so important as to be marked by remembering the date. As Barras was to say later, "Mme. de Beauharnais was one of the series of ladies who made up Tallien's and my company."

And being "one of the series" for the Roi des Pourris (king of profiteers) was to enable her to extend her "business affairs." There was no question now of sugar loaves or pairs of stockings. She had larger ideas. Robert Linet was to note that one day Gabriel Ouvrard came to offer him 100,000 francs for a contract to supply the army. The member of the Committee of Public Safety, later to be Minister of Finance under the Directory, exclaimed, "Leave, sir, or you will leave by the window."

"I can't offer you more," the banker replied placidly. "I am giving the same amount to Barras and Mme. de Beauharnais."

Emboldened perhaps by her "business dealings," on August 17, 1795, Rose indulged in an expenditure undoubtedly well above her means. On that day she rented from Julie Carreau, formerly Louise Julie Talma, a small house not far from the Chaussée d'Antin and the Faubourg Montmartre, at 6 Rue Chantereine. It was a pretty place, the charming "folly" of a kept woman—as Mlle. Carreau was, by the Vicomte de Ségur. Rose moved in on October 2, two days before 13 Vendémiaire. An entrance gate gave access to the little flowering courtyard by a narrow path bordered by lime trees. At the entrance were two tiny lodges: the stables where two black horses were kept and the coach house for the carriage given her by the Republic. Set in a cluster of fine trees which gave the impression of a park, it was a dream come true: a little building with four windows in the main façade and at the side a bay window through whose glass doors one could reach the garden. In the basement were the kitchens and storage cellars, on the top floor rooms for the cook, Gallyot, the maid, Louise Compoint, who had succeeded Agathe, and Citizen Gontier, the man of all work.

The house was furnished in the course of the following months. The elevated ground floor, reached by a flight of steps, comprised an entrance hall furnished with an oak buffet, an armoire and a wall fountain; a small room used as a dining room with four mahogany chairs with black seats and an extension table. Against the wall were two console tables with marble ornamentation. The rounded bay was furnished as a boudoir. It contained a piano but was used chiefly as a dressing room. It had a profusion of mirrors, some on stands, a pier glass, and a dressing-table mirror, which enabled Rose to see herself from every angle. The fourth and last room, the bedroom, was completely done over. Mme. de Beauharnais bought chairs with curved backs, which she recovered in blue nankeen, and a little bed of bronzed wood. From the Rue de l'Université she had brought her harp, her lime-wood desk from Guadeloupe, a marble-topped table of the same wood, and a bust of Socrates, somewhat out of place, perhaps, in a setting so far removed from wisdom.

There was no provision for rooms for Hortense and Eugene. The children were boarded out, Hortense with Mme. Campan and Eugene, back from the army, with Citizen Patrick MacDermott, Director of the Irish College, who was also at Saint-Germain. So Rose could live as she pleased, and one knows what that meant.

There were some luxuries in the house, but the necessities were lacking. It was the same with the country house at Croissy for which Barras, then or later, paid the rent. "Mme. de Beauharnais suggested that I should take over the remainder of the lease of a country house she had rented at Croissy," he was to relate. "I agreed. Once installed she confessed that she could not pay the current rent, let alone the arrears. I assumed responsibility for everything." After he had become a director, when he came to lunch with Rose, he was preceded by gendarmes and baskets of provisions. "Poultry, game and rare fruits were piled high in the kitchen," recounted a neighbor, the future Chancellor Pasquier. "It was a time of shortages and they had no saucepans, glasses or plates, and they would borrow these from our scantily supplied household."

Sometimes, too, Rose would be the hostess at Barras's little house in the Rue de Chaillot, at the spot where the Galliéra Museum now stands.

One day in Prairial or Messidor in the Year III Mme. Tallien invited to the Cottage an odd, sorry-looking officer she had met no one knew where. Perhaps at the house of Mme. Permon, who knew the man's family well, but more probably with Barras, who had been his patron since 1793. His ill-powdered hair hung "like spaniel's ears" on either side of his thin, yellow face. He had no gloves and was dressed in an old, worn overcoat and his boots had certainly not seen polishing for several months. Surprising as it might seem, this man was a general, but he had been temporarily detached and his half pay allowed him only one meal a day. At midday he made do with a cup of black coffee, which he would take at the Café Cuisinier. He lived quite a long way from the Allée des Veuves, near the Pont Saint-Michel, and to visit his patroness he went on foot, for he could not afford even a hack. His name was Napoleon Bonaparte.

If he came to see Thérésia it was first of all because he was courting her. "At that time Mme. Tallien was pretty enough to eat," he was to say on St. Helena. "One was glad to kiss her arms and anything else one could." He also came because he wanted to get a pair of uniform breeches, which was almost impossible, as he had no commission and cloth was issued only to officers on active duty. Moreover, under pretext of illness, he, an artilleryman, had just refused to take command of an infantry brigade and be posted to the Army of the West, commanded by Hoche. He had often heard Barras exclaim, "Women are good for something in this world; they are more obliging than men."

And so he took courage and explained his clothing problems to Mme. Tallien. Thérésia found it amusing to busy herself with the affair and a few days later she greeted the unfortunate man by calling out to him across the drawing room, "Well, my friend, you've got your breeches!"

We do not know if Rose had noticed him or if she remembered that one evening Barras had introduced this little Corsican officer to her. In any case he had made no impression on her. Yet this poor devil had fine features and the lines of his mouth were "full of charm." "It seems to me today," wrote someone who saw him at this time, "that from the curves of his fine, delicate and firm mouth one could deduce that he despised danger and that danger did not make him angry."

No doubt Barras had the same feeling when, during the night of 12–13 Vendémiaire Turreau, the former commissioner, proposed Bonaparte's name. The Convention was to disband, giving place to the Directory. The Deputies had just passed decrees which the sections of the right considered "injurious to the nation." The sovereignty of the people had been violated and future candidates deprived of two thirds of the seats in the new Assembly, since the Convention—less naïve than the Constitutent Assembly of 1791— had reserved them for itself. In short, Paris was showing signs of rebellion.

The mild General Menou, confused by this revolt of the right, gave way. The members of the Convention realized, in their own words, "that the revolutionary lightning had become extinguished in their hands." Frightened, the Convention nominated as general in command of the Army of the Interior Barras, who on 9 Thermidor had marched on the Hôtel de Ville against Robespierre. The former sublieutenant of colonial troops under Louis XVI knew he was only a makeshift general and wanted another—a real one—preferably an artilleryman.

"Bonaparte," said Turreau.

Fréron, who was in love with Paulette Bonaparte, agreed. Barras, who had seen Bonaparte at work during the siege of Toulon, accepted.

"Go and get him," he told Fréron.

Barras's Memoirs—written in part by Rousselin de Saint-Albin—are a tissue of intentional errors. Neither Fréron nor Turreau comes into Barras's story:

"Nothing could be easier than to replace Menou. I have the man you need, a little Corsican officer. He won't make so much fuss."

If Barras is to be believed, Bonaparte was not to be found; he had gone to sound out the royalists, who would have nothing to do with him.

According to other witnesses, he was at the Feydeau Theatre when he heard the rumor that the royalist sections of Paris were marching against the Convention. He then went to wait around in the Assembly corridors, where he was found and taken to the Carrousel, Barras's headquarters.

It is amusing to read the account of that famous night in Barras's Memoirs: "The only army at my disposal was but 5,000 men of all kinds. Forty pieces of cannon were at Les Sablons, guarded by fifteen men. It was midnight and several reports told me we should be attacked at four in the morning. I said to Bonaparte:

"'You see there is not a moment to lose and I had good reason to chide you for not coming sooner. Go at once to find that artillery and bring it with all speed to the Tuileries.'

"Bonaparte at once dispatched my order. Murat left with 300 horse."

As though Bonaparte merely "dispatched" Barras's order! And by this simple act earned the nickname of General Vendémiaire, the rank of general of division on October 16 and on the 26th the post of commander in chief of the Army of the Interior!

Whatever the case may be, he astonished those who did not know him, in other words, everyone. He was a strange general, this whippersnapper wearing a little hat decorated with "a makeshift plume" and with a sword knocking against his thin calves, "that sword which, indeed, did not appear to be the weapon likely to make his fortune."

On the evening of 13 Vendémiaire Rose may have been dining with Barras—Napoleon implied as much in a somewhat ambiguous remark on St. Helena. Mme. de Beauharnais certainly rejoiced at the government's victory. "Far from being in the least in league with the sections," Barras was to write, "Mme. Beauharnais was entirely of our party, in so far as one may say that she was ever anything." She learned that evening from Barras's own lips how the royalists had been fusilladed on the steps on Saint-Roch in the Rue Saint-Honoré and how they had been crushed by that same little Bonaparte whom she had met at the Cottage. Thérésia Tallien's friends were the only people able to reply when it was asked where the unknown man had sprung from, this man whose Christian name had not yet been heard, and whose family name was so difficult to spell that its owner pronounced it: buona-parté. And that was how *Le Moniteur* of 22 Vendémiaire spelled it.

That same issue of *Le Moniteur* tells us that five days earlier, on the 17th, Barras had announced to the Convention that the "committees of the government had issued a decree to the effect that the Lepelletier and Théâtre-Français sections were to be disarmed." And he added: "I have ordered all the inhabitants of these two sections to deposit their weapons at the town hall in each section within three hours. This order has been carried out."

On learning of this decision, Eugene, moved by honorable feelings of filial devotion, although he was not living in one of the sections in question, feared that he might be obliged to part with the "sword my father had worn and which he had rendered illustrious by honorable and outstanding service." Hoping to keep the sword, the fourteen-year-old future Viceroy of Italy, on his mother's advice, asked for an audience with Bonaparte. That day the new military commander of Paris was lunching at Barras's house with La Montansier, a theatre director, in earlier years a prostitute who was now more than sixty. Andoche Junot came in search of his general. Bonaparte received Eugene and was touched at the sight of his tears. He knew the boy was the son of a friend of Thérésia and Barras and gave him back the sword.

The next day Rose paid a visit to Bonaparte to thank him and, probably on the following day, the General went in his turn to the

Rue Chantereine, where Mme. de Beauharnais had just settled in. Or at least that is how Napoleon, Josephine and Eugene—not to mention Hortense—were to tell the story of "my father's sword" which Barras, who had nothing to do with it, persisted in treating as a legend.

Bonaparte came again to see Rose, but his visits were infrequent, although he knew that if he wished to succeed he must not be afraid of feminine society.

"Women are everywhere," he had written to his brother, "in the theatres, out walking, in the libraries. You see pretty women in the scholar's study. This is the only place in the world where they deserve to be at the helm; and the men are all mad about them."

Yet he seemed to shun this pretty woman who was almost pursuing him. Was it because he knew Rose was Barras's mistress? Right up to February she was issuing "At Home" invitations for 8 Rue Basse-Pierre at Chaillot. It may have been that he was completely absorbed in his military duties. In any case, although he found her very pretty and was charmed by her "old world" manner of receiving him, he was not yet in love. But perhaps a certain shyness checked him when faced with this elegant vicomtesse.

On the eve of Vendémiaire, when he was still barely able to keep the wolf from the door in his modest lodging at the Cadran Bleu, he was still in love with Désirée Clary. On arriving in Paris at the end of May of that same year, he had received this letter from his little fiancée from Marseilles: "Every moment pierces my heart as it separates me from the dearest of friends. . . . Oh! my friend, may your vows be as sincere as mine and may you love me as much as I love you. . . . It is an hour since you left and it seems a century!"

He had replied: "I received your two charming letters, they refreshed my soul and gave it a moment of happiness, which was a sad illusion dispelled by your remoteness and the uncertainty of the future. Yet I do feel that with the love of my good friend I cannot be unhappy. . . . I beg you not to let a day pass without writing to me, without assuring me that you still love me." (It is thanks to M. Girod de l'Ain, the great-grandnephew of Désirée, that we know these details of the idyl between Bonaparte and his fiancée.)

Then his inactivity in his cheap little room (he paid three francs a week), his vaguely defined and humble work in the topographical bureau led him into apathy. He often told Désirée that if she loved another she should not hesitate to abandon the poor brigadier general with no brigade—and no money, so little money that he even thought of killing himself. But there was another way of extricating himself. He had confided in Barras, if the latter is to be believed: "If I were the only person concerned I could wait patiently. A man's needs are not great. But I have a family in the greatest distress. I know we are nearing the end of our misfortunes. In a revolution, bread must be found for everyone and the aristocrats have had the good things of the world for long enough. Our turn must come. But while we wait we are suffering."

Barras is then supposed to have suggested the means for escaping from this situation: "A marriage. . . . I've seen many people do that. All our ruined nobles, or those who couldn't be ruined because they were born without money, settled their affairs in this way. They kept an eye out for the daughters of merchants, bankers, financiers. They never missed one. If I have the time to nose around a bit I could find you something."

And the Vicomte, laughing up his sleeve, suggested that Bonaparte should marry La Montansier, who was born in 1730.

The former actress possessed 1,200,000 francs and, just before 13 Vendémiaire, she agreed to meet her "suitor."

"We got up from the table," Barras relates. "The fiancés drew near to each other and began to talk intimately. . . . As I was about to join in the conversation of the two turtledoves, someone came to warn me that there was trouble in Paris and that I was summoned by my colleagues to the Committee of Public Safety.

" 'I leave you in charge of the house,' I said to Bonaparte and Mlle. Montansier.

"And I left them together."

This affair between a woman of sixty-five and a man of twenty-six would seem purely a figment of the imagination were it not that after Vendémiaire Bonaparte had thought of marrying a friend of his mother, Mme. Permon-Comnène, a widow who was still charming but who could have been his mother. Little Laure, her daughter, later the Duchesse d'Abrantès, was in a neighboring room when Bonaparte made his strange offer. She heard her mother burst out laughing after a moment of surprise and reply to her suitor: " 'My dear Napoleon, let us talk seriously. You think you know my age?

Well, you don't know it. . . . I shall only tell you that I could be not only your mother but Joseph's also. Let us drop this joke, it distresses me for you.'

"Bonaparte told her several times that he did not care about the age of the woman he would marry if, like her, she appeared only thirty, that he had given mature consideration to what he had told her and he added these very remarkable words:

" 'I want to marry. They want to offer me a woman who is charming, good, pleasant and associated with the Faubourg Saint-Germain. My Paris friends wish this marriage, my old friends dissuade me. I myself want to marry and what I propose to you suits me in many ways. Think of it.'

"My mother stopped the conversation by saying, laughingly, that she had made up her mind."

The "charming, good, pleasant" woman could only be Rose and the "Paris friends" Tallien and his wife, for, on his own admission, Barras did not intervene until much later when he gave up Rose for Mme. Tallien. In which case it must have been at the instigation of Thérésia that the woman "associated with the Faubourg Saint-Germain" finally sent this well-known note intended to stir up the man who seemed to have forgotten her:

You no longer come to visit a friend who is fond of you; you have completely abandoned her. You are wrong, for she is tenderly attached to you.

Come to lunch tomorrow, Septidi. I want to see you and talk with you about your affairs.

Good night, my friend, I embrace you.

Widow Beauharnais

If it was not a plot conceived by the two women, Rose and Thérésia, by what feelings was Rose impelled? Perhaps she was thinking of what her friend Ségur had said to her one day: "That little general could become a great man."

Of course she already had Barras, one of the five kings of the Republic since October 30, and at that time he passed for a great man. But she could not be unaware that this protector was only a temporary one. She needed more, someone who could cope with the endless drain of her expenses. And then she found Bonaparte "odd."

She called him "drôle" in her musical Creole voice. Granted this was
not exactly exciting. To make a long story short General Bonaparte,
who had broken with Mme. Permon and who thought the widow
Beauharnais had money, came on that famous Septidi, and Rose
cleverly gave him to understand that between Barras and herself
there was only a great friendship. What was said about them was
mere calumny. The naïve little General was prepared to believe
everything.

Then he talked of his affairs to the pretty widow who seemed
willing to listen. No doubt he spoke of his hopes of being given
command of the Army in Italy, and no doubt also of his family.
"You know," he had written to his brother Joseph, "I live only for
the pleasure I can give my family." Being now out of difficulties he
had sent money to the clan. "I have sent the family fifty or sixty
thousand francs in money, bills of exchange and clothes. . . . They
lack nothing. . . . They are well supplied with everything."

He had asked for a position as consul for Joseph. Lucien, already
on a mission as Fréron's assistant, had been appointed commissioner for war on October 28. Two days earlier Bonaparte had had
Louis made an artillery lieutenant and on November 12 made him
his own aide-de-camp. At the end of the year he was to take charge
of little Jerome and send him to school.

"I cannot do more than I am doing for them all."

The clan should have been satisfied, but always felt that he never
did enough.

Bonaparte returned several times to the Rue Chantereine, in
spite of the presence of the pug, Fortuné, which was jealous, barked
and tried to bite the intruder's legs. The luxury—the appearance of
luxury of a woman living on the largess of admirers—dazzled him.
He admired everything, including the charming way Rose had of
receiving him, of saying exactly the right thing to everyone, the tact
with which she conducted a conversation or her way of preparing
the coffee she served him herself. "Coffee from Martinique which
her mother sends her from their own plantations." He had no idea
that there were any debts, that the servants were rarely paid and
the tradesmen even more rarely, and that Rose possessed far more
robes and shawls than shifts and petticoats. In the presence of this
"lady" he felt provincial and of very modest birth. He was unaware
then that the title vicomtesse was a usurped one. He was under the

spell of "the incomparable Josephine." For it was thus that he already called her, not wishing to use the name of Rose, which had been uttered by too many men's lips. He loved her now as he had never loved before.

"I really loved her," he was to confess on St. Helena, "but I did not respect her. She was too untruthful."

But for the moment he noticed nothing. He did not hear her lies, he did not perceive her schemes or the superficial side of the Creole any more than he suspected her generosity, her obligingness, her inability to hate, her simplicity. He hardly understood the beatings of his own heart. He knew only that "she had an indescribable way of pleasing."

She knew this, of course, and made use of all the arts of seduction in which she was so highly skilled. She was amused by the burning passion she had aroused and the day after she had given herself to him—an act which cost her very little—she was somewhat surprised on deciphering, not without difficulty, his first letter:

7 in the morning.
I awake full of you. Your image and the memory of yesterday's intoxicating evening leave my senses no rest. Sweet and incomparable Josephine, what a strange effect you have on my heart! Are you angry? Do I see you sad? Are you uneasy? Then my heart is broken with grief and there is no rest for your friend. . . . But can there be any more rest for me, when, surrendering to the deep feelings that master me, I draw from your lips and from your heart a flame that burns me. Ah! last night I really perceived that your portrait is not you! You leave at noon, I shall see you in three hours. Meanwhile, *mio dolce amor,* receive a thousand kisses, but do not give me any, for they sear my blood.

He was bewitched. He had been fascinated by holding in his arms that sensuous, languorous and dimpled body, as supple as a palm tree, a body breathing love. He, who was without experience, was amazed by the skill of his partner, who was so clever as to make him believe that she was discovering and acquiring this delightful knowledge with him.

The marvelous adventure which was to make the light-minded, and still more light-virtued, Creole into the sovereign of a vast empire and of a kingdom had begun.

5. *"Incomparable Josephine"*

On the evening of March 9, 1796—19 Ventose, Year IV—five people met in the fine gilded drawing room on the second floor of 3 Rue d'Antin. This room with its Regency décor is now the manager's office of the Banque de Paris et des Pays-Bas. In 1796 it was the room used for marriages in the town hall of the second arrondissement, and on that evening a bride, three witnesses and Commissioner Collin-Lacombe, a Bourbonnais with a wooden leg, who was an unauthorized replacement for the Registrar Leclerq, doubtless gone to bed, had been waiting for more than an hour for the groom and the fourth witness, in other words, Bonaparte and his aide-de-camp Lemarois.

From time to time Rose, now Josephine, looked at Barras, for with Tallien and the devoted Calmelet, he was one of the witnesses of this astonishing marriage. He had been quite surprised at seeing this simpleton of a little general request the hand of a woman who could be had by merely asking politely. He smiled on remembering that he had reproached Bonaparte for his excessive generosity.

"You seem to think of the Beauharnais woman as one of the soldiers of 13 Vendémiaire who ought to be included in the list of awards. You would have done better to send the money to your family, who need it and to whom I have again been sending help."

Bonaparte had reddened and then defended himself: "I have made no gifts to my mistress. I did not wish a virgin to seduce. I am one of those who prefer to find love already in existence rather than love that has to be created . . . Well, no matter what Mme. Beauharnais may be, if I entered seriously into relations with her, if those presents you reproach me for making were wedding presents, what would you have to say to that, Citizen Director?"

"Are you serious in what you have just proposed?"

"For one thing, Mme. Beauharnais is rich," Bonaparte replied, "impetuously."

Finally, Barras had replied: "Well, since you are consulting me seriously I shall reply in your own words: why not? You are on your own, you have no ties. Your brother Joseph has shown you the way. He has extricated himself from his difficulties with the Clary dowry. Get married. A married man has a place in society, he presents a broader surface and more resistance to his enemies."

According to Napoleon, who recounted it on St. Helena, Barras added: "She is connected with the old regime and the new. She will give you standing. Her house is the best in Paris."

This was a bit exaggerated.

In the white and gold room of the Rue d'Antin all eyes were on the clock, except those of Citizen Collin, who had fallen asleep in his armchair. Josephine looked anxiously at the hands and then, seeking comfort, she glanced at Calmelet, who had advised her to marry Bonaparte. As she had been unable to get a birth certificate, it was he who had certified to a notary that he knew the widow Beauharnais "perfectly" and that she had been born on June 23, 1767. She thus lost four years which, in her situation, she could well do without.

Bonaparte was now more than an hour late. Supposing he didn't come! But that was not possible. He had adored her since that day not long ago when she had given herself to him. But was this marriage foolish, perhaps? He was jealous, thrifty, methodical. She was frivolous, extravagant, disorderly. There was also a six-year age difference between them. When she spoke of this he would sing, out of tune:

Believe me, if one can but please
One is never more than twenty!

Of course he was now better dressed and far from lacking in
charm. His look and smile were attractive. But she did not love
"Bonaparte," as she called him—and was always to call him, finding
his first name too unusual. She had hesitated a long time before
marrying him. For her Bonaparte was only a "street general,"
sprung from the pavements of Vendémiaire. At first she had been
flattered by the burning passion she had aroused in this "puss in
boots" with the somber countenance. For her, to please was a joy, a
joy for herself. Advantage, reason came later. Then Bonaparte's
somewhat overwhelming love had disturbed her.

She had explained it to a friend: "Do you love him? you will ask.
No. . . . Then you feel aversion for him? No, but I find myself in a
state of indifference which displeases me. . . . I admire the General's courage, the extent of his knowledge, the liveliness of his
mind, but I am frightened, I confess, by the influence he seems to
wish to exert on everything around him. . . . If when we are
united he should cease to love me, would he not reproach me with
everything he had done for me? What should I do then? I should
weep."

Her feelings for Barras had made her hesitate. She adored the
Vicomte's elegance and refinement. If she closed her eyes, she could
see him, Victorine de Chastenay, "seated in one of the large, gold-
trimmed, red velvet chairs with which his apartment was furnished.
He would listen in turn, to right and to left, somewhat like a
confessor, to the problems people wanted to discuss with him and
accept the petitions handed to him."

Barras played very well at being a king. Ah, if only he had
wanted her. But this was unimaginable. From the very beginning of
their liaison he had cast greedy eyes on Mme. Mailly de Châteaure-
nault. And soon Josephine had been obliged to share her lover with
her rival, then with Thérésia. It was a trio that could not go on and,
as Rose later said, "I gave up my place to those ladies, being a
resigned and obliging friend."

But marrying Bonaparte perhaps need not keep her from still
seeing her dear director. Three weeks earlier she had been presiding
over a dinner at Chaillot. She had said to him, "It is you I shall

always love, you can count on it. Rose will always be yours, at your disposition whenever you make the sign."

She took her strong physical attraction toward him for love, and had left in tears. "Pressing me in her arms," Barras related, "she accused me of no longer loving her, repeating that I was what she had loved most in the world and that she could not part from me, at the very moment when she was about to become the wife of the little General. . . . I left my study with Mme. de Beauharnais, not without some embarrassment on my side."

To explain the traces of tears to her fiancée, who was impatiently waiting at her house, the wily woman had accused Barras of misusing her. Bonaparte was immediately on his high horse.

"I shall ask him for an explanation!"

Josephine had calmed him down. "He has rather brusque ways, but he is very good, very obliging. He is a friend, that's all." And of course he had believed her.

Then a little later, according to Napoleon on St. Helena, Rose had confessed that she had indeed been Barras's mistress and "that she was pregnant by him."

"It is very unpleasant," she sighed, "and I don't know what to do."

He had at once proposed: "Well, let's get married. I don't see any difficulty."

Was it this extraordinary "obligingness" of her suitor that had made her decide to become Citizeness Bonaparte? There was another reason as well. She simply had to "settle down." Thirty-two is no great age, but youth is nevertheless behind one. Of course, as Bonaparte's intoxication proved—the spectacle she presented when undressing in her mirrored boudoir was as ravishing as ever: her high bosom, her breathtakingly beautiful legs, her Creole walk, were enchanting, but she had studied herself very, very closely. The little wrinkles were there, ready to deepen, the complexion losing its freshness under its layer of makeup and powder. Yes, she had to settle down. She was now alone. Hoche and Caulaincourt no longer appeared willing to leave their respective wives to marry her. So Josephine had decided to marry her lover, considering it no more difficult to offer her hand than her body. There was no reason for thinking otherwise. The new society attached hardly any importance now to legal union, since one could divorce as easily. If Hoche and Caulaincourt had wished, they could certainly have "legally" left their wives for Josephine with no difficulty.

Marriage had become "a lease that could be canceled any week or any night." It is said that "on returning to barracks for the winter soldiers would marry, having agreed in advance to divorce when they left." Marriage was an amusement, no more. But catching a husband had become difficult.

It was unusual to find a candidate as eager as Bonaparte, so for Josephine he was an opportunity to be seized.

The groom was now two hours late. During the long wait it was Barras who was most anxious. If Bonaparte had changed his mind, Barras might have Josephine on his hands again. He remembered the visit his mistress had paid him to announce her marriage.

"For my part," she had said, "I did not think it necessary to confide the secret of my extremely straitened circumstances. He thinks that I have a certain fortune at present and that I have great expectations from Martinique. Don't let him learn what you know, dear friend, you would spoil everything. Since I don't love him, you will understand that I can manage this affair. . . . But I know well that you no longer love me," she had added, in a burst of those tears she could always shed to order. "That is the greatest of my griefs. When one has loved a man like you, is it possible ever to have another attachment?"

"What about Hoche?" he had replied, almost laughing. "You loved him also above all . . ." And he gave the names of some of her lovers. "And *tutti quanti!* Get along with you, you're a great humbug!"

Indeed she was, and she had given much pain to poor Hoche, who had insisted that she hand back his love letters. "As she has 'obtained the favours of the heroes of her age,' I despise her!" He could not understand how she could prefer to him a little police general who had refused to fight under him in the Vendée and who, on top of everything, was insolent. Hoche remembered that day at Mme. Tallien's when Bonaparte had assumed the voice and manners of a fortuneteller and had dared to say to Hoche "in a solemn tone," after looking at the hand held out to him: "General, you will die in your bed."

Bonaparte had still not arrived. A candle stuck in a pewter sconce threw a glimmering light on the cupids playing in the gilded frieze. The bride mused by the dying fire.

She had also had to overcome the resistance of her children. On the preceding January 21, at a dinner given to celebrate the third anniversary of the death of Louis XVI, Hortense had found herself seated between her mother and "a general" who, she was to relate, "whenever he spoke to her leant forward with so much eagerness and perseverance that he tired me and forced me to push my chair back. Thus, in spite of myself, I watched his face, which was handsome, very expressive, but remarkably pale. He talked with ardor and seemed exclusively occupied with my mother. It was General Bonaparte."

On seeing Bonaparte's attentions, Hortense guessed that her mother was about to marry again.

"She will no longer love us as much," she observed to her brother.

"When the General visited us he noticed our coolness toward him. He took some trouble to dispel it, but in a way which did not succeed with me. He liked to tease me, speaking ill of women, and the more warmly I defended them the more eagerly he attacked them."

One day, as Josephine remembered, Hortense had thrown herself weeping into her mother's arms, begging her not to marry again. Josephine had not the courage to announce her marriage to her daughter. Mme. Campan undertook to do so and the girl had been "deeply distressed" by it.

They had been waiting in the town hall for more than two hours. No one thought of cutting the wick of the candle, which had formed a "long nose." Collin dozed. Josephine still mused. She had told him she had a large fortune. But she was aware that Bonaparte had gone to Emery for information about her property. The banker had explained the situation: the Pagerie plantation produced only 50,000 francs a year. Each year Josephine could present to Emery a bill of exchange for 20,000 or 25,000 francs. It was in fact no gold mine and it was certainly not what he had thought.

Josephine no longer dared look at the clock. To calm herself she thought of her "dowry": the Army of Italy. Barras had implied that it was he who had named Bonaparte to command the Army of Italy, an appointment reserved for the husband of his mistress. In fact the

idea had come from Carnot, but Barras had seconded it in the
Council. Had the Corsican asked for her hand in order to have his
dream realized? A few days earlier Josephine had reproached her
betrothed with having "sought her out through personal interest."
Back at home, he had written to her:

Nine in the morning.
I left you with very painful feelings. I went to bed very angry. It
seemed to me that the respect due to my character should have prevented
that last thought which disturbed you yesterday evening. If it were to
prevail in your mind, madame, you would be very unjust and I very unhappy!
So you thought I did not love you for yourself!!! For whom then?
Ah! madame, I would have had to change a great deal! Could such a
base feeling be conceived in so pure a soul? I am still astonished by this,
but less than by the feeling which, when I woke, brought me back to
your feet without rancor and without will of my own. Indeed it is impossible to be weaker and more degraded. What, then, is your strange
power, incomparable Josephine? One of your thoughts poisons my life,
tears my heart with contradictory wishes, but a stronger sentiment . . .
brings me back still guilty. I feel truly that if we have quarrels you must
impugn my heart, my conscience; you have captivated them, they are
still yours.
But you, *mio dolce amor*, did you sleep well? Did you think of me, if
only twice? I give you three kisses: one on your heart, one on your
mouth, one on your eyes.

The end of the letter showed that she was perhaps wrong to be
alarmed.

But then there was his family, those Corsicans who frightened
Josephine before she even knew them. Fearing their reactions
Bonaparte had concealed his marriage from them. He had informed
neither the head of the family, his brother Joseph, nor his mother,
Mme. Letizia—*la madre*. Josephine could imagine their shock. A
widow, older than her husband and encumbered with two children,
who would have to be supported although they did not belong to
the clan. An elegant, extravagant, frivolous Parisienne; a woman
who would overwhelm them with her luxury; a former vicomtesse,
widow of a general and former President of the Constituent
Assembly. How would she regard her sister-in-law? And this fine
lady had prevented dear Napoleon from marrying the little Clary
girl, who wept on being "no longer allowed to love him and think of

him." Poor Désirée had just written to her former fiancé: "You, married! I cannot get used to the idea, it kills me. I cannot bear it. I shall show you that I am more faithful to my promises and, although you have broken the ties that united us, I shall never become engaged to another, I shall never marry."

She did marry. She even became Queen of Sweden and Norway, but for the moment one thing was certain—Julie, Désirée's sister and Joseph's wife, was to be Josephine's enemy.

Suddenly the sound of a sword banging against the stone stairs was heard. The door opened. It was Bonaparte, followed by Lemarois. Without bothering to apologize he made straight for the Commissioner and shook him awake.

"Come on, sir, marry us quickly!"

Still half asleep, Collin droned out that extraordinary act of marriage in which the groom ("Napoleone Bonaparte, son of Charles Bonaparte, of private means, and Letizia Ramolino") gained eighteen months in age, in which the bride ("Marie Josèphe Rose Tascher born on the Island of Martinique, Windward Islands") became younger by four years, in which Lemarois was not of age, although the document declared he was, and had no right to be a witness, in which, finally, the mayor's substitute was not qualified legally to unite the two citizens and had the act signed by Leclercq on the following day.

Five minutes later everyone was saying good night on the pavement of the Rue d'Antin. Barras and Tallien climbed into a carriage —the former lived at Luxembourg, the latter at Chaillot—Calmelet and Lemarois set off on foot, while Josephine, returning on her husband's arm to the house in the Rue Chantereine, was in her turn making her entrance into history. But who could have foreseen the dazzling future?

On their arrival in the bedroom, Fortuné refused to be dislodged. He bit Bonaparte in the calf and the bridegroom had to be resigned to putting up with the pug.

The next day, March 10, the newlyweds visited Hortense at Mme. Campan's in Saint-Germain. The thirteen-year-old girl regarded her stepfather with neither admiration nor affection.

Pretending not to notice the little girl's sulky looks, Bonaparte pinched her ear and said to Mme. Campan: "I must send my little sister Caroline to you, but I warn you she knows absolutely nothing. Try and make her as learned as dear Hortense."

√   Caroline, in fact, could neither read nor write, and she was fifteen.

There was one more night of love, with the pug Fortuné as the third person present. On Friday, March 11, Bonaparte hardly left the little sitting room. Bending over a map of the Alps spread out on the round table, he was studying his next campaign. For he was leaving that night to join the army at Nice. The honeymoon had lasted less than forty-eight hours. From time to time Josephine entered the room. He kissed her, but, to her great surprise, sent her away.

"Be patient, my dear!" he cried. "We shall have time to make love after the victory."

√   "How odd he is," Josephine would say.

That evening the post chaise in which his aide-de-camp, Junot, and Chauvet, paymaster of the Army of Italy, were waiting drew up at the end of the little path. He tore himself from his wife's arms, making her promise to join him soon. She promised, but, naturally, to leave Paris for camp life struck her as a mad scheme. One last kiss and the carriage left the Rue Chantereine.

What would happen now? Had the Directory not wanted to get rid of Bonaparte? Was this Italian campaign only a rash venture? Moreau and Jourdan, generals who had proved themselves, were marking time at the head of the Army of the Rhine. And her husband, that backstairs, bedroom general, that "little freak with disheveled locks," that protégé of Barras and women, was off to fight the Austrian Empire and Piedmont with 37,000 unpaid scarecrows whose stomachs were empty and whose feet were shod in woven straw.

From Châtillon-sur-Seine Bonaparte sent her a power of attorney so that she could draw "various sums owing to him"—70 louis and 15,000 francs in promissory notes. The following evening, a Monday, on arriving at Chanceaux, a village twelve leagues from Châtillon, he wrote to her to tell her of his sadness. He addressed his note to "Citizeness Beauharnais." Perhaps he feared the postman would not find the house of "Citizeness Bonaparte." Each turn of the wheels that bore him from his voluptuous Josephine, each moment that separated them further, left him weak. His thoughts never left her. He imagined she was sad and his heart was torn; he

imagined she was gay, "frolicking with her friends," and he reproached her with forgetting their separation.

"Ah! do not be gay but a little melancholy. And above all, may
your mind be free from grief as your lovely body from illness."

There was no doubt that she was not suffering. The day after he
left she started to write to him. It took her four days to finish the
letter—and she addressed him formally as "vous." When he received
it he exploded:

> You call me *vous! Vous* yourself! Ah, wicked one, how could you write
> that letter? How cold it is! And then, from 23 to 26 is four days. What
> were you doing, since you were not writing to your husband? Ah! my
> friend, that *vous* and those four days make me sorry not to possess my
> old indifference. Woe to whosoever may be the cause of it. *Vous! Vous!*
> Ah, what will it be in a fortnight! My soul is sad, my heart is enslaved,
> and my imagination terrifies me. . . . You love me less. You will be
> consoled. One day you will love me no longer. Tell me so. At least I
> shall earn my misfortune. . . . Farewell, woman, torment, happiness,
> hope and soul of my life, whom I love, whom I fear, who inspires in me
> tender feelings which summon me toward nature and eager impulses as
> volcanic as thunder. I ask neither eternal love nor fidelity but only . . .
> *truth*, unlimited frankness. The day when you will say to me 'I love you
> less' will be the last day of my love or the last of my life. . . .
> P.S. A kiss to your children, whom you do not mention! At least that
> would make your letters half as long again. Those visitors at ten in the
> morning would not have the pleasure of seeing you. Woman!!!

The three exclamation marks score the paper. And did she want
to know the warmth of his heart, the force of that burning love?
There came the wonderful declaration:

> I have never spent a day without loving you. I have never spent a night
> without holding you in my arms. I have never drunk a cup of tea without
> cursing the fame and ambition which keep me apart from the soul of my
> life. In the midst of affairs, at the head of the troops, on going through
> the camps, my adorable Josephine alone is in my heart, occupies my
> mind, absorbs my thoughts. If I leave you with the speed of the tor-
> rential waters of the Rhone's, it is in order to see you again more quickly.
> If I rise to work in the middle of the night, it is to advance the arrival
> of my sweet love by a few days.

She had no intention of arriving, but since he complained of the
coldness of her letter she wrote him a few burning lines, and it
would seem from his response, erotic. (All the letters Josephine

wrote to Bonaparte during the Italian campaign have been lost. An archivist of Villach town hall, near Klagenfurth, Austria, was said to have kept "passionate letters from the Empress Josephine" which had been left behind in Carinthia by Bonaparte. This seems unlikely, however, as the town archives were apparently destroyed during World War II.)

Bonaparte was overwhelmed. "What are you thinking of, my adorable one, to write to me in such terms? Don't you think my state is hard enough without increasing my regrets and troubling my soul? What a style! What feelings you describe! They are all fire, they burn my poor heart!" She had become the one thought in his life. "If I am tired of the turmoil of activity, if I fear the outcome, if men disgust me, if I am ready to curse life, I put my hand on my heart. Your image is beating there." He gazed at the charming features and took courage. But not for long. "The idea that my Josephine might be uneasy, the idea that she might be ill and, above all, cruel one, the dreadful idea that she might love me less, withers my soul, makes me sad, dejected, and does not even give me the courage of fury and despair." As she thought more of her body and her face than of him, he wrote: "Love me as you love your eyes. But that is not enough. As yourself. More than yourself, then your mind, your life, your all. . . . Sweet one, forgive me, I rave.

"P.S. Farewell, farewell, farewell. I go to bed without you. I shall sleep without you. I beg you, let me sleep. I have been holding you in my arms for several days."

On arriving at Marseilles on March 20, he went to see Mme. Letizia, handed her a letter from Josephine and wrung from her a promise to reply to this daughter-in-law who had been imposed on her. *La madre* took nine days to write a letter, affected, trite, but elegant. She spoke French badly, and wrote it even worse, and it is likely that someone wrote the letter for her, perhaps Joseph, who was in Genoa at that time.

On March 30, four days after his arrival at Nice, Bonaparte wrote to his wife, "the pleasure and torment of my life"—"My soldiers show inexpressible faith in me."

His short stature and pale, undistinguished countenance had made a bad impression at first. "The portrait of his wife, which he held in his hand and showed to everyone," Massena, one of the divisional commanders, related, "did not help matters. It took the close questioning to which he subjected his commanding officers, the heroic language in which he spoke to his men, those gemlike, immortal phrases he flung to them, to make them all understand that soon they would be able to say with pride: 'I was in the Army of Italy.' "

The epic had begun. He was going to "crack the enemy's center"; the eyes of everyone would be fixed on the peninsula. Everyone except Josephine, who, for one letter written in hot blood—was it really hers?—would send him ten other short, cold letters to which he replied angrily:

"You cannot manage to spend another moment to write to one 300 leagues away from you, who lives, is aware, exists only to remember you, who reads your letters with hunger. . . . I am not satisfied. Your last letter is as cold as friendship. I found no trace of that fire which lights your eyes and which I sometimes thought to see there."

He himself asked why he complained of his wife's coldness since a certain oversensual letter had "attacked his rest." But this one was worse. It was "the iciness of death." From afar he sent her "a kiss lower down, lower than the breast." And he underlined the last words three times.

He wrote to Barras that on April 23, after having engaged in battles, he had made 12,000 prisoners, killed 6,000 Piedmontese, taken 21 flags and 40 cannons. And in the same letter, as though asking a reward, he added: "I should very much like my wife to join me."

When this letter reached Paris, Josephine was throwing back her head to laugh at the puns of a handsome young lieutenant of hussars who bent over her. The officer's lips almost brushed her beautiful hair with its chestnut lights.

She found him irresistible. Josephine had fallen in love with Lieutenant Hippolyte Charles, adjutant to General Leclerc, who was nine years younger than herself. The thought of her husband did not trouble her in the least. She felt no remorse at the prospect of giving herself to the dazzling hussar. The first flourish and bow of the seductive lieutenant had conquered her. "You will be mad about him," she told Talleyrand. "Mmes. Récamier, Tallien and Hamelin have all lost their heads over him, his is so beautiful." Josephine was also to lose her head over this officer in his attractive sky-blue uniform with scarlet belt. He knew better than anyone how to throw out his chest and make the most of his uniform, his jacket with eighteen rows of braid, Hungarian breeches embroidered in silver, and a cloak trimmed with fox fur. She could not take her eyes from his round chin with its dimple, his beautiful black, tousled hair, not to mention his blue eyes and his charmingly upturned nose. Finally: "He dresses with such taste. I believe that no one before him ever knew how to arrange a cravat."

There is no doubt she had met the man who was to be her great love. Charles was a southerner, somewhat below middle height, but a very attractive young man with his bronzed complexion, long whiskers and black mustache. Some historians have presented him as a good-looking fop, a cross between a Marseilles hairdresser and a Toulouse commercial traveler, in an attempt to show that the delicate Josephine could have had no more than a passing physical attraction toward this figure of fun, and as proof of their theory have compared Charles with the hero of Italy, forgetting that, in this matter, a pretty, sensual woman will always have a different opinion from a stern member of the Academy of Moral Science. Admittedly, according to the Duchesse d'Abrantès, Charles expressed himself solely in puns and "played the fool," but, she added, "he was what is called a comical fellow, he made you laugh. It would be impossible to find a more amusing man."

The pun was a very fashionable method of jesting during the Directory; one had to make puns to be up to date. In order to make Josephine laugh, Charles surpassed himself. How could she resist the handsome man who talked of the little general "qui est sur le Pô, ce qui est bien sans Gênes" (who is on the River Po which is well outside Genoa, or who is very unceremoniously on the chamber pot).

In the delightful setting of the Rue Chantereine, Josephine and Charles sighed, adored, possessed each other, declared they had never thought it possible to love so much. What did they care for the names of those Italian villages her husband was in the process of carving on the pediment of history. They loved each other breathlessly and beyond reason. Nothing else existed.

The name of General Bonaparte was on everyone's lips except those of his wife. Only Hippolyte mattered to her. Their embraces were interrupted only by the too frequent arrivals of couriers bearing to Citizeness Bonaparte, 6 Rue Chantereine, burning letters which she may even have gone so far as to read aloud to her lover.

"I have received a letter which you broke off in order, you said, to go to the country. And after that you affect to be jealous of me, who am overwhelmed with work and fatigue. Ah! my dear one. . . . It is true, I am in the wrong. The country is beautiful in spring. And no doubt the nineteen-year-old lover was there?"

But someone came as a killjoy—Colonel Murat, her husband's chief aide-de-camp. He came to announce the recent victories and—most important for Bonaparte—to bring a letter for Josephine earnestly begging her to start on her journey. He suggested that she should travel with Murat. Her lodgings were ready at Mondovi and Tortona.

"How happy Murat is . . . little hand. . . . Ah! if you don't come!!! Bring your maid, your cook, your coachman. I have carriage horses here you can use and a fine coach. Bring only what you need personally. I have silver and china plate here that you can use."

With difficulty, for he wrote very badly, she deciphered the burning words: "No woman was ever loved with more devotion, fire and tenderness."

Of course reproaches followed:

My life, how can I not be sad? No letters from you. I get one only every four days. Whereas, if you loved me, you would write twice a day. But you have to chat with your gentlemen callers at ten in the morning and then listen to the idle talk and silly nonsense of a hundred coxcombs until an hour past midnight. In countries with any morals everyone is at home by ten in the evening. But in those countries people write to their husbands, think of them, live for them.

Good by, Josephine, to me you are an inexplicable monster. . . . I love you more each day. Absence cures small passions but increases great ones.

A kiss on your mouth or on your heart. There is no one but me there, is there? And then one on your breast.

Did she murmur her usual "How odd he is?" One thing is certain: she gazed admiringly at the tall, handsome, strapping Murat. It is said, without proof, that she bestowed her favors on him.

It seems, however, that Charles alone reigned over Josephine's heart. But by a disturbing coincidence, on the very day of Murat's arrival in Paris, Bonaparte broke the glass on Josephine's miniature. He paled "in a terrifying way," relates his aide-de-camp, and exclaimed, "Marmont, my wife is ill or unfaithful!"

And he wrote to Josephine: "Think of me or tell me with disdain that you no longer love me."

He threatened her with "Othello's dagger" if she had the misfortune to deceive him. She read the letter to her friend Arnault, who related: "I can still hear her reading a passage in which, seeming to repress the anxiety obviously tormenting him, her husband said to her: 'But if it were true! Fear Othello's dagger!' I can hear her say, smiling, in her Creole accent: 'Qu'il est drôle, Bonaparte.'"

She lisped in her soft island accent and threw the note carelessly into a drawer. But the courier had to take her answer with him and was allowed only four hours' repose. Instead of taking her ease with Hippolyte, Josephine had to take her pen and hastily write a letter which Bonaparte, with reason, was again to consider "as cold as friendship."

Two days after Murat's arrival came Joseph Bonaparte and Junot. The former brought the Piedmontese request for an armistice and the latter flags taken from the enemy. Naturally both were also the bearers of letters for the "générale."

"I warn you," said the note handed to her by Joseph, "that if you delay you will find me ill. Fatigue and your absence, that is too much at one time."

Now it was Junot's turn to deliver his letter. Again Josephine deciphered: "You must come back with him, do you hear? If this does not happen at once, let him not return. Unhappiness without remedy, grief without consolation, endless pain if I have the unhappiness of seeing him return alone. My adorable one, he will see you and breathe in your abode! Perhaps you will even accord him the unique and priceless favor of kissing your cheek? And I shall be alone and far, far away! But you will come back, won't you? You will be here at my side, on my heart, in my arms, on my mouth.

"Take wings, come come. . . . A kiss on your heart and then a little lower, much lower!"

She laughed. It was not to be taken seriously. Fifteen days' journey including crossing the Alps! She could not leave Paris and its pleasures, Paris which paid her homage in celebration of her husband's victories. It was in company with Junot, Mme. Tallien and Mme. Récamier that she had gone to the festivities given by the Directory. Josephine had borne very well comparison with Thérésia and Juliette. "I can still see the three of them," the poet Arnault recounted, "in the dresses best calculated to enhance their different advantages, their heads crowned with the finest flowers, on a lovely May day, entering the room where the Directory was to receive the flags. One might have thought it was the three months of spring come to celebrate the victory."

"As they left," Laure d'Abrantès related, "Junot offered his arm to Mme. Bonaparte who, being the wife of his general, had a right to the first place, particularly on this solemn day. He gave his left arm to Mme. Tallien and so descended the staircase of the Luxembourg with them. The crowd was immense. People pushed and shoved to see better.

" 'There, that's his wife.'

" 'And how pretty she is!'

" 'Long live General Bonaparte!' the people cried.

" 'Long live Citizeness Bonaparte! She is good to the poor people.'

" 'Yes, yes,' said a fat woman from the market, 'she's certainly Notre-Dame des Victoires!' "

And meanwhile, at Lodi, Bonaparte was weaving the fabric of his fame. "After Lodi," he was to write, "I no longer considered myself as just a general, but as a man called on to influence the destiny of a people. The idea came to me that I might well become a decisive actor on our political stage. Then was born the first spark of high ambition."

At Lodi the whole of Italy was conquered for the Republic. But as he ordered the march on Milan Bonaparte was thinking only of his wife.

Joseph was in no hurry to leave the capital. He was scheming to obtain a post as consul and wanted to buy a country house. But Murat could not stay there forever. As for Josephine, it was out of the question for her to leave Paris and dear Hippolyte. So she invented a pretext for not setting out: "I am pregnant."

Murat may have been deceived or it is possible that Josephine took him into her confidence. Josephine's maid, Louise Compoint, was in the plot and, by making use of her charms, undertook to disarm Junot.

On May 13 the news reached Lodi. "And is it then true that you're pregnant? Murat wrote to tell me. But he says it has made you ill and that he does not think it wise for you to undertake a long journey.

"I shall therefore continue to be deprived of the happiness of enfolding you in my arms! I shall still be several months distant from all I love! Is it possible that I shall not have the happiness of seeing you with your little belly? It must make you very interesting! You write that you have greatly changed. Your letter is short, sad, and in a shaky hand. What is the matter, my adorable one? What can disquiet you?"

There was nothing the matter with her—except love. She preferred the sparkling lieutenant to the solemn general, the lieutenant his friends nicknamed "l'éveillé" (the wide awake).

Bonaparte was anxious and deeply distressed by his wife's cold, lifeless letters. And so, in order to gain time, she wrote that she was ill. And he replied: ". . . my heart is in indescribable anxiety. You are ill, far from me. Be gay and take great care of yourself, you whom, in my heart, I prize more than the universe. Alas! the thought that you are ill makes me very sad."

Her husband advised her to divert herself: "Ah! do not stay in the country. Go to town. Try to amuse yourself. And believe that my soul feels no acuter suffering than to know that you are ill and sad. I thought I was jealous, but I assure you I am not. Rather than know you were melancholy, I think I would give you a lover myself."

Perhaps it was with her lover that she read those lines!

"So be gay and contented and know that my happiness is linked with yours. If Josephine is not happy, if she yields to sadness and discouragement, she does not love me."

Once again he softened at the thought that she was bearing his child: "Soon you will give birth to another being who will love you as much as I do . . . No, it is not possible. Your children and I will be constantly about you to convince you of our care and our love. You won't be bad-tempered, will you? No 'hum!!!' except as a joke. Then three or four scowls. Nothing is prettier. Then a little kiss and all is made up."

Forty-eight hours after sending this letter, on Whitsunday, the victorious General mounted his white horse, Bijou, and made a triumphal entry into Milan. At the city gate were waiting Masséna, Count Trivulzio, and Archbishop Visconti, with whom he was to stay. The last two were stupefied at the sight of their conqueror, wearing a hat with a tricolor plume, his powdered hair falling in locks to his shoulders, that thin little man advancing alone followed by his tatterdemalion army. In the streets there was wild enthusiasm. He was acclaimed because he was going to wrest Milan from the grasp of Austria. There were cries of *Viva la Libertà!* There was joy among the Milanese that evening, at the archbishopric, when he declared at the end of a splendid banquet:

"You shall be free. You shall be free and more certain of being so than the French. Milan will be your capital . . . you will have 500 cannons, the eternal friendship of France. . . . You will touch both seas, you will have a fleet. A truce to regrets and quarrels. . . . There will always be rich and poor. . . . If Austria should return to the attack, I shall not abandon you."

"Well," he said to Marmont on going to bed, "what do you think they are saying about us in Paris? Are they satisfied?"

"Their admiration must be at its height."

"They have seen nothing yet and the future holds much greater successes for us than we have so far accomplished. Fortune smiled on me today and I shall not disregard her favors. She is a woman and the more she does for me the more I shall ask of her. In our time no great idea has ever been conceived. It is for me to set the example."

Napoleon was beginning to take shape beneath Bonaparte, but only Josephine continued to be unaware of this.

She was leading an intensely active life. No evening without a ball or a theatre. No day without a new dress. No day without being paid court to. Life in Paris continued its giddy pace and Mme. Bonaparte was now queen of the capital. As Marmont said, "she was more concerned with reveling in her husband's triumphs in Paris than with going to join him." Marmont was fighting at her husband's side but the poet Arnault was observing her way of living. "The love Josephine inspired in a man as extraordinary as Bonaparte obviously flattered her, although she took it less seriously than he. She was proud to observe that he loved her almost as much as glory; she enjoyed that glory, which increased every day, but she liked to enjoy it in Paris amid the acclamations that rang out along her path with each piece of news from the Army of Italy."

As she received courier after courier, galloping night and day to bring her husband's burning love letters more quickly, she laughed again. In the intervals of embracing Charles she had other pre-occupations. She had given up her black wig and had a wonderful blonde one made. The newspaper *Ami des lois* asserted with the same earnestness that it brought to serious problems: "A woman with black hair would be scorned in good society and dark-haired men are fashionable." This was perfect, since Hippolyte's hair was a handsome brown.

On May 18 Bonaparte awoke happy. Surely it was an omen. Josephine was better, the first difficulties of pregnancy were over, she had left. And he embraced this fancy.

This thought fills me with joy. Of course, you will go by Piedmont, the road is much better and shorter. You will come to Milan, where you will be very pleased, as this country is beautiful. As for me, I shall be mad with happiness. I long to know how you carry children. It must give you a majestic, respectable look which I think should be very amusing. Now, don't get ill! No, my dear, you will come here, you will be very well, you will produce a little baby as pretty as its mother and who will love you like its father. And when you are old, really old, when you are a hundred, it will be your consolation and happiness. But until then mind you don't love it more than me! I am already beginning to be jealous.

Adio, mio dolce amor, adio, beloved. Come quickly to hear beautiful music and see beautiful Italy. Only the sight of you is lacking. You will embellish it. In my eyes, at any rate. You know, when Josephine is any-where I see only her.

On May 23, before leaving Milan to return to headquarters at Lodi, he tried to make her jealous.

"They gave a great festival for me here. Five or six hundred pretty faces tried to please me. But none was like you. None had that gentle, harmonious countenance so deeply engraved in my heart. I saw only you, I thought only of you. That made everything unbearable and half an hour after entering I went sadly to bed, thinking, 'See that empty hollow, my adorable little wife's place.' Are you coming? How is your pregnancy?"

He became more affectionate still: "Ah! my lovely one, take good care of yourself, be gay, take plenty of exercise, don't be upset by anything, don't be anxious about your journey. Go by short stages. . . . I constantly imagine seeing you with your little belly. It must be charming."

He barely put down his pen before galloping to fresh glory. He advanced on the Austrians, who were camped out in the country. But on the 25th he was obliged to return to Milan. Violent revolts had broken out and he ordered repressive measures. When order had been re-established, he left again, not without scolding his absent wife. Soon the Austrians were expelled from Italy. On June 5 at Brescia he signed an armistice with Naples, which retired from the coalition. But he had only one thought: to return to Milan where he was sure Josephine was waiting for him. But when he arrived at the Serbelloni Palace on June 6 he found neither his wife nor any letters from her. One thing alone was certain, that on 12 Prairial, May 31, she had still been in Paris. This time he would have burst into tears if he could.

"My soul was open to joy," he wrote to her. "It is filled with sorrow. All the couriers arrive without bringing me letters from you. . . . When you do write, your few words and your style never show deep feeling. You loved me as the result of a passing whim. You already feel it would be ridiculous to let it detain your heart."

One wonders if he suspected the presence of the handsome hussar at her side.

"It appears that you have made your choice and know who is willing to replace me. I wish you happiness, if it can be gained by inconstancy. I do not say perfidy. . . . You never loved me."

For him there remained only glory, but would it be enough to make him happy? "It is the seed of death and of immortality."

With some anxiety Josephine read the letter in which her husband considered separation. "As for you, may the memory of me not be hateful to you. My misfortune is not to have known you well enough. Yours is to have considered me to be like the other men surrounding you."

He drew up the account of their love: "My heart has never felt anything in half measure. . . . It had shielded itself against love. You inspired a limitless passion, an intoxication that degrades it. The thought of you had a place in my mind above all else in nature.

Your whim was a sacred law to me. To be able to see you was my supreme happiness. You are beautiful, gracious. Your gentle, heavenly soul is depicted in your countenance. I adored everything about you. Had you been less experienced, younger, I should have loved you less. Everything pleased me, even the recollection of your errors and of the distressing scene that took place a fortnight before our marriage."

It was true that she had confessed part of her highly charged past—by no means all—and he had still asked for her hand. He had been very angry, and very grieved, when she had declared, doubt-less from coquetry, that he did not love her for herself but for her fortune, which she did not possess, for her title of vicomtesse, which she did not possess either, or for her influence over Barras, whose intention was to end his brief affair with her.

Now, in the second half of June, 1796, Josephine's uneasiness became anxiety on receiving this terrible letter. Supposing she had to begin again the search for a husband or protector. She had, of course, continued to pile up debts, but she knew he would pay them someday. Would the love she felt for her amusing puppet, Hippolyte Charles, outweigh the glory of being Mme. Bonaparte? As she read on, he continued to speak of their union in the past tense.

"For me virtue was what you did. Honor was what pleased you. Glory attracted my heart only in so far as it was pleasing to you and flattered your self-esteem. Your portrait was always on my heart. Not a thought without looking at it and covering it with kisses. You left my portrait for six months without taking it out. Nothing escaped me."

Bonaparte no longer seemed willing to be the only one to love.

"If I were to continue, it would be I alone who loved. And of all roles that is the only one I cannot adopt. Josephine, you would have ensured the happiness of a less singular man. You have been my unhappiness, I warn you. I felt it when my heart was becoming ensnared, when every day yours won a limitless empire over me and enslaved all my senses. Cruel one!!! Why give me hope of a sentiment you did not feel!!!! But the reproach is not worthy of me. I never believed in happiness."

Yet the idea of living without her appeared insupportable:

"Every day death hovers round me. . . . Is life worth making such a fuss about!!! Farewell, Josephine, remain in Paris, write to me no more, and at least respect my refuge. A thousand knives pierce my heart. Do not drive them in farther. Farewell, my happiness, my life, everything that existed for me on earth."

This time she did not say, "How odd Bonaparte is!" Perhaps all was over. But three days later she received another letter. He was suffering, but no longer spoke of his union with her as of something dead.

"Josephine, where will they hand you this letter? If it is in Paris, my unhappiness is certain, you no longer love me! There is nothing left but to die . . .

"Oh! you! . . .

"My tears flow. No rest or hope. I respect the will of the immutable law of fate. It covers me with glory in order to make me feel my unhappiness more bitterly. I shall become accustomed to this new state of things, but I cannot become accustomed to no longer esteeming you."

He could not envisage life without her:

"It is not possible! My Josephine is on the way, she loves me at least a little. So much promised love cannot have vanished in two months. . . . I detest Paris, women and love. . . . I am in a dreadful state . . . and your conduct . . . But should I accuse you? No. Your conduct is that of your destiny. So lovable, so beautiful, so gentle, were you to be the instrument of my despair? In spite of fate and honor I shall love you all my life. This evening I reread all your letters, even the one written in your heart's blood. What feelings they aroused in me!"

Perhaps nothing was lost, since he had read the letter written "in her blood" and in which she reminded him, no doubt vividly, of the hours spent in his arms.

The same courier who left Milan on June 11 reached Paris on the 18th or 19th, and brought these discouraged lines to Barras: "I am in despair. My wife is not coming. She has some lover who keeps her in Paris!"

Had he guessed the truth?

6. *"Ah! Josephine! . . . Josephine! . . ."*

Barras and all the government were anxious.

The war was not over. There was still much to do to conquer and pacify Italy. Yet the whole situation threatened to collapse because Josephine still refused obstinately to join her victorious husband. A letter from Bonaparte to his brother Joseph shows the depressed state of mind of the commander in chief: "My friend, I am in despair. My wife, all I love in the world, is ill. I cannot concentrate. . . . Reassure me, tell me truly, you know my heart. You know how ardent it is. You know that I never loved before, that Josephine is the first woman I adored. . . . I love her madly and I cannot remain far from her. If she no longer loved me there would be nothing for me to do on earth."

He had to be brought out of this slough of despond. The fate of Italy was at stake, and there were the negotiations with the Pope, the still-unsigned peace with Rome, and the massing of the Austrians for a return. But in her last letter to Milan Josephine was still talking of illness. Barras, who was not deceived, confirmed the news to Bonaparte in order to gain time. He asserted that the Directory was opposed to her departure. Citizeness Bonaparte could not travel since she was ill.

Napoleon was cast down at having dared to order his poor wife
to travel. The unfortunate man begged her pardon. "I have done
you so much injustice that I do not know how to atone for it. I
rebuked you for staying in Paris, and you were ill! Forgive me, my
dear, the love you have inspired in me has taken away my reason, I
shall never recover it. One does not recover from that illness. I have
such dire forebodings that I shall confine myself to seeing you,
pressing you to my bosom for two hours and then dying together.
Who is taking care of you? I suppose you have sent for Hortense."

With feverish impatience he waited for the courier, who had been
ordered to stay only a few hours in Paris, to give Josephine time to
write "ten pages." She must explain her illness to him. "If it is
dangerous, I warn you that I shall leave for Paris at once."

He applied for leave. Since she could not come, he would hasten
to her. This time Paris was seriously disturbed. The conquest of
Italy depended on Josephine's little bed. She would have to go,
even accompanied by her lover. Carnot, doubtless at Barras's request, signed this letter to her husband:

"The Directory, which had opposed Citizeness Bonaparte's departure, fearing that the attentions her husband might give to her
should distract him from those to which glory and the salvation of
the motherland call him, had agreed that she should not leave until
Milan was taken. You have taken it and we make no more objections. We hope that the myrtle with which she will be crowned will
not displace the laurels with which victory has already crowned
you."

At this time Milan had been occupied by French troops for six
weeks.

Josephine finally gave in. She would leave. And while she was
preparing her luggage letters arrived every day. Bonaparte, whom
Carnot had soothed, no longer spoke of separation; he seemed more
in love than ever.

"All my thoughts are concentrated in your bedroom, in your bed,
on your heart. Your illness is what preoccupies me, day and night. I
have no appetite, no sleep, no interest in friendship, glory, the
motherland, you, you, and the rest of the world exists no more for
me than if it had been annihilated. I care for honor since you care
for it . . . for victory since it pleases you. If it were not for that I
should have left everything to place myself at your feet . . .

"You are in bed, ill, more beautiful, more interesting, more adorable. You are pale and your eyes are languid, but when will you be cured?"

The unfortunate man imagined that his wife might be jealous. It meant nothing to her and she must have smiled on reading this recommendation:

"In your letter, my dear, take care to tell me that you are convinced I love you beyond anything that can be imagined, that you are persuaded that every moment of my life is dedicated to you, that never an hour goes by without my thinking of you, that it has never occurred to me to think of another woman, that in my eyes they are all devoid of grace, of beauty and of wit, that you, you as I see you, as you are, can alone please me and absorb all the faculties of my soul."

And yet on St. Helena he would dare to say that "love does not really exist."

But he did not manage to dispel the thought that she had a lover who kept her in Paris. "You know well that I could never bear your having a lover, still less give you one. Tearing out his heart and seeing him would be the same thing for me!"

Josephine had not yet dared tell him, in any of the three-line notes she had been sending him for a month, that her pregnancy was no more than a memory, and the coming of the child still touched her husband, the child he envied since it would be near her. "A child as adorable as its mamma will see the light of day and will be held by you for several years in your arms. Unfortunate that I am! I should be content with one day. A thousand kisses on your eyes, your lips, your tongue, everywhere.

"Adorable woman, what is your power?"

Josephine could not back out now. Barras kept on telling her she must leave Paris. But to do so, money was necessary. As may be imagined, she had nothing but debts. Then she received a visit from a friend she had met before her marriage, Hamelin, son of a head clerk in the Finance Ministry, now ruined by the new regime. He was married to Fortunée, one of Josephine's companions in pleasure, a young, pretty, flighty Creole of twenty, the one whom we have already seen walking with bare breasts along the Champs-Elysées. Hamelin asked if Josephine could do anything for them.

"Why don't you come to Italy?" she suggested. "I am sure that on my recommendation Bonaparte would do something for you."

In fact her husband had just written to her: "If you have anyone you want to find a job for, send him to me here and I will find a place for him."

A few weeks earlier Josephine had been paid 10,000 francs for a contract for 20,000 blankets for the army. The business had given her so little trouble that she hoped to be able to repeat it. "A single idea common to everyone," a contemporary tells us, "united many different people: the desire to make money, and any means of getting it was all right. The most elegantly dressed woman was not above dealing in supplies and would undertake to show samples of the merchandise in which she or her protégé was speculating, and in those days protection could be obtained only by sharing profits."

Hamelin immediately told his friend Monglas about the conversation he had had with the wife of the General commanding the Army of Italy.

"I shall go with you," Monglas decided.

Josephine had asked Hamelin if her "two partners" could lend her 2,000 francs and they quickly obliged her. On receiving the money she begged Hamelin to get her some English veiling from a draper for 300 francs. Then she arranged to meet them at Mme. de Renaudin's in Fontainebleau. From there they were to set off for Italy, where she would recommend her "partners" to her husband.

Josephine had promised to perform the same service for a former admirer, the elegant Joseph Robbé de Lagrange, a friend of Alexandre de Beauharnais from Blois and now aged about fifty. Lagrange had done more than Hamelin and Monglas. By making the most of his former relations with Mme. de Beauharnais to a group of financiers, he had founded a company to finance the expedition. He went to the Rue Chantereine and asked Josephine why she did not set out. She was careful not to mention the 2,000 francs paid by Hamelin and Monglas.

"I have not the means to go," she sighed.

"Never mind that. I am prepared to advance you 10,000 francs."

She accepted and once the money was received made the same rendezvous at Fontainebleau with her former admirer and with her two other accomplices.

On June 24, "plunged into deepest grief, dissolved in tears," according to an eyewitness, "sobbing as though she were going to the scaffold," Josephine entered her coach after a dinner given by the Directory. She was to stay two days at Fontainebleau with her former father-in-law Beauharnais and her aunt Renaudin, who had finally been able to regularize their union. Mme. de Renaudin was now a marquise.

Meanwhile Bonaparte was writing several letters a day to Josephine which he dared not send. "Because they are too stupid . . . Yes, that is the word."

The very day of her departure, not knowing that she was setting out, he addressed to her these lines, which she was not to read until much later: "At last, my incomparable little mother, I shall tell you my secret: make fun of me, stay in Paris, have lovers and let everyone know, never write, yet I shall love you ten times more."

"Have lovers." Why should she feel any scruples? And in fact in the coach where Joseph and Colonel Junot had taken their seats, opposite her, their knees touching, was Hippolyte. She was taking her lover with her.

On the evening of Thursday, June 30, Bonaparte arrived in Florence. A courier was waiting for him, having brought a letter from Joseph which announced Josephine's imminent arrival.

"Berthier," he cried, mad with joy, "Berthier, she is coming, you hear, she is coming! I knew she would make up her mind to in the end!"

He ordered Marmont to go to meet his wife. It was important that, when she entered the Kingdom of Sardinia, as the territories of the house of Savoy were called at that time, the King Victor Amadeus III should receive her with the honors due to a sovereign.

At last he was to see his wife again and live with her. It was not only desire for that body, the memory of which had haunted his nights for four months and made him write letters throbbing with passion. He loved her with his whole heart. It was certainly not the Bonaparte of 1796 whom Mme. de Rémusat described when she wrote: "He has always attached too much importance to himself to be detained by feelings of affection of whatever kind. He knows almost nothing of the ties of blood, the claims of nature."

That was to be true of Napoleon, but it was not yet true of Bonaparte.

Citizeness Bonaparte's coach pursued its way toward Italy. With her and Hippolyte were Joseph Bonaparte and Colonel Junot, not forgetting Fortuné, the pug, which fawned on the lover, but had been so fond of the husband's calves that Bonaparte still had a scar on his leg. Colonel Junot showed off, described the life of his general in Italy, told barrack-room jokes and made Hippolyte jealous, as he considered himself the only one who could make Josephine laugh. When Junot realized the situation, he returned to his ardent courtship of Louise Compoint, the lady's maid, who was following in another carriage with two servants. Prince Serbelloni, President of the Directory of the Cisalpine Republic, traveled with Nicolas Clary, Désirée's brother, while Hamelin and Monglas followed in a post chaise. In this way everyone benefited from the escort provided for the General's wife. The roads were by no means safe. The courier from Lyons had been murdered on this very route, and the boxes of promissory notes intended for Bonaparte stolen.

The procession was preceded by the courier Moustache, a cavalryman from the Army of Italy, who had the horses brought out at the posts and ordered the rooms at night. Those of Hippolyte and Josephine were always adjacent, as were the quarters of Junot and the pretty Louise, who had not proved obdurate and had resumed her temporarily interrupted affair with the handsome aide-de-camp. She now ate with her mistress and was very good company. Joseph was more taciturn. He was languishing from a love affair, tending to his health and writing a novel called *Moïna*.

At Lyons, on July 7 and 8, Josephine was treated as a sovereign for the first time: troops in full dress, more flowers than she knew what to do with, speeches listened to as yet without boredom, a cantata which had to be rewarded with a smile and a not very amusing performance of *Iphigenia in Aulis*. Robbé de Lagrange was partly responsible for this welcome. He had preceded Josephine and scattered gold in order to flatter Bonaparte's self-esteem. The General would know—he would see that he did—that it was thanks to Lagrange that Josephine had been welcomed in this way.

While his wife was rolling along the roads toward him, Bonaparte was continuing to build his fame, creating sister republics, exacting millions for the Directory's empty coffers and dispatching to Paris convoys of works of art, his *spolia opima*, the spoils of war.

On July 1 he went with Berthier and Murat to Florence to dine

with Grand Duke Ferdinand. This brother of the Austrian Emperor
Francis could not have guessed that on that day he was entertain-
ing, in Florence—which would become the capital of the French
department of the Arno—the man (Murat) who was to become
King of Naples (after Joseph Bonaparte) and so dethrone his aunt
Marie Caroline, Queen of Naples, consort of Ferdinand IV, later
Ferdinand I of the Two Sicilies. Nor could he have imagined that in
the person of Berthier he had invited to dine the man who, bearing
the title of Prince of Neufchâtel, would later marry his niece Marie
Louise of Austria as proxy on behalf of Bonaparte, the third guest,
who would become emperor of a realm extending over half of
Europe.

They passed through Chambéry, Lanslebourg, Mont-Cenis,
Novalesa . . . And then Turin, where the wife of the Commander
in Chief of the Army of the Republic was very well received by the
King of Sardinia. Marmont was waiting for her with his cavalry.
Finally, after eighteen days on the road, she met Bonaparte at the
gates of Milan on July 13.

He could not take his eyes from his treasure. The "incomparable
Josephine" was there. And in a few hours she would be his,
although she had not been slow in telling him of her fatigue and the
pain in her side. Josephine and her husband made their entry into
the city in a six-horse carriage and halted in front of the monumental façade of the magnificent Serbelloni palace, furnished with
taste and adorned with flowers on Bonaparte's orders.

During the two days they spent together Josephine succeeded in
having Charles and her protégés, Lagrange, Monglas and Hamelin,
invited. "After lunch," wrote the last-named, "Mme. Bonaparte
would often take me to her apartments in order to have someone to
whom she could chat at ease. The General appeared to approve and
there I saw him in a most intimate setting: he loved his wife
passionately. . . . As for her, she had never been enamored of him
for the simple reason that she had always been enamored of
someone else. I knew the situation with regard to M. Charles and I
felt uncomfortable at seeing that the young General, already
covered with a glory that reflected on his wife, was the unlucky rival
of a whippersnapper whose only attributes were a pretty face and
the elegance of a hairdresser's assistant."

As yet Bonaparte suspected nothing and Josephine had not dared talk business to him. She still pretended to be ill, which enabled her to put a certain check on the meetings in the *camera matrimoniale.*

On July 15 Bonaparte left for the siege of Mantua and two days later wrote to his wife: "Since leaving you I have been perpetually sad. My happiness is to be near you. Endlessly I go over in my memory your kisses, your tears, your agreeable jealousy, and the incomparable Josephine's charms constantly kindle a bright, burning flame in my heart and in my senses. . . . I thought I loved you a few days ago, but since I have seen you I feel that I love you a thousand times more. I have adored you more every day since I have known you, which proves that La Bruyère's maxim that 'love comes all at once' is false. Everything in nature has a course and different degrees of growth. Ah! I beg you to let me see some of your faults. Be less beautiful, less gracious, less tender, above all less good."

Josephine was not happy since Charles had also had to return to headquarters.

But she was reigning. she adopted the Milanese custom of driving to the Corso, in the cool of the day, in a *bastardella,* a carriage low enough to allow conversation with passers-by. After one turn the carriage stopped and the chatter started. Then the carriage moved on and halted again in front of the popular ice-cream shop, the Corsia de Servi, where one could be served without leaving one's *bastardella.* This was fashionable, as was also the pony-tail style of hairdressing. "A scandal!" exclaimed a conservative eyewitness. "Everything is sown with flowers, feathers, gold more or less false, and topped with a little military helmet from which a tuft of untidy hair escapes, a kind of imitation tail imitating the dragoons' headgear."

At night, in the Serbelloni palace, Josephine, assisted by Joseph, would receive in the rooms with French windows opening on the park. The wives of the highly placed French officials came, representatives from the Doge of Venice, from the Grand Duke of Tuscany, the King of Sardinia, not to mention the pretty Milanese, as undressed as ever.

Josephine had so much to do that she did not write to Bonaparte. Naturally he sent her letter after letter.

I had a post from Paris. There were two letters for you; I read them. Yet, although this seems to me a very simple thing and you gave me permission the other day, I am afraid it will make you angry and that grieves me much. I would have liked to seal them again, but no! that would have been revolting. If I am guilty I ask your pardon. I swear it was not from jealousy. Indeed I have too high an opinion of my adorable one for that. I wish you would give me permission to read all your letters. In that way there would be no remorse or fear. Achille has come with the courier from Milan; no letters from my adorable one! Farewell, my only blessing. When can you come to join me? I shall come and fetch you myself from Milan. A thousand kisses as burning as my heart, as pure as you.

I summoned the courier. He said he went to your house and you told him you had no orders for him. Fie! naughty, ugly, cruel, tyrannical, little, pretty monster! You laugh at my threats and my nonsense. Ah! if I could, you know I would shut you up in my heart, imprison you there.

Tell me that you are gay, well and very affectionate.

She was better, but neither gay nor affectionate.

Milan gave feasts for her. Under the acacias in the public gardens platforms had been erected on which puppets and jugglers acted and orchestras played. When night came one danced to exhaustion in the garden lit with lanterns.

But Josephine was not enjoying herself. "I am bored to death here," she wrote to Mme. Tallien. "Amid all the superb feasts they give me I constantly miss my friends of Chaillot [the Talliens] and of the Luxembourg [Barras]. Joseph keeps me company faithfully . . . My husband does not love me, he adores me. I think he'll go mad."

Hippolyte had not come back to Milan, and this was the source of the trouble.

Bonaparte did everything he could to distract his wife. Between two battles he did shopping for her. "I send you something to make a fine Florence taffeta skirt, it will do for Sundays and days you dress up. You see how generous I am, it cost me more than 30 francs. But that is not all. I want to send you a fine crepe dress. Write and tell me the quality, color and quantity. I shall send to Bologna for it."

Josephine had sent to him Hamelin and Monglas, who had tactlessly asked for the advances made to Mme. Bonaparte. "Your protégés are a bit impatient. I suppose they realize I am bound to do anything for them which pleases you."

Lagrange, being cleverer, had stayed in Milan near Josephine, who recommended him to her husband "for a contract." Who had spoken to Bonaparte of Mme. de Beauharnais's former lover? He wrote to her, underlining these words: "Perhaps you have found the lover you came to look for. But you will have found him without my proposing him to you. . . . By the way, I am told that you have known the gentleman you recommended to me for a contract for a long time and *very well.* If this is true, you are a monster."

"Very well" is underlined three times. But he soon brushed aside this thought and continued his letter, written at Castiglione on July 21 at eight in the morning. "What are you doing now? You are asleep, aren't you? And I am not there to inhale your breath, to contemplate your charms and overwhelm you with my caresses. Far from you, the nights are long, dull and sad. Near you, one regrets that it is not always night. *Farewell, beautiful and good, all incomparable, all divine.* A thousand loving kisses, everywhere, everywhere."

The next day he told her that "the requirements of the army" called for his presence near Castiglione. Why should Josephine not join him at Brescia, "where the tenderest of husbands awaits you"? he wrote.

She had rebuked him, with reason, for opening her mail. She had cleverly made him think she was jealous. "I am in despair," he wrote, "that you should think, my dear one, that my heart could be open to others than yourself. It belongs to you by right of conquest and that conquest will be firm and eternal. I do not know why you speak to me of Mme. Te . . . for whom I care nothing, any more than for the women of Brescia. As for your letters, if you are annoyed at my opening them that will be the end of it."

He was still tormented by jealousy. "Your letters are cold, the warmth of your heart is not for me. After all, I'm the husband. Someone else must be the lover. One must be like everyone else."

"On 7 [Thermidor]—July 25—at Brescia, all right?" he had written to her. She had to leave Milan for Brescia, breaking the journey in Bassano. But she did not go alone. Robbé de Lagrange and Hamelin accompanied her. On arriving at Brescia, Josephine pleaded Lagrange's cause. Bonaparte, who had come out to meet his wife, was too happy enfolding her in his arms to refuse her anything. On July 27, the "carpetbagger" received a valuable letter of recommendation to the Directory from the general. Without waiting further, he galloped to Paris, but he arrived too late. He was not to get the contract for the Army of Italy.

"But in compensation," said the Minister for War, Petiet, "I can offer you the fodder contract for the Armies of the Pyrenees and Italy. Take that anyway."

Lagrange was very disappointed.

"What can I do with that?"

"Take it, believe me," answered Petiet, showing him out.

After reflection, Lagrange followed the Minister's advice. He provided the fodder, and this was followed by other contracts for Italy. He recived a substantial fixed sum, plus three sols interest on the profits of the operation. Of course Josephine was to have her share, which she drew without her husband's knowledge. So she became involved in those notorious speculations in porous cardboard boot soles or moldy fodder. And Bonaparte complained of the vile traffickers, not knowing his wife was mixed up with them.

On July 29 Bonaparte was drinking coffee with Josephine and Hamelin on the balcony of the house Louis XVIII had once occupied in Verona. He kissed his wife ardently, his hands exploring. As usual, he was without shame, prodigal with those "conjugal liberties which constantly embarrass you," as Miot de Mélitot was to relate. Josephine seemed happy. Headquarters were being installed in Verona, and Charles might soon be near her.

Between two sips of coffee they suddenly saw in stupefaction long columns of white-coated soldiers streaming down the mountain. Messéna, who had been entrusted with guarding the gorges commanding the provinces of Venitia and Lombardy had unfortunately been driven aside by the Germans and Wurmser's Hungarians, who were out to rescue Mantua. Before leaping onto his horse, Bonaparte ordered Hamelin to escort Josephine and Louise Compoint, with a few dragoons, to Peschiera, six hours from Verona at the southeast extremity of Lake Garda, where there was a fortress as impenetrable as it was uncomfortable. Josephine spent the night there fully dressed.

The next morning, July 30, Junot arrived with an escort. They were to retire to Castelnuovo. But on the road along the lake shore, just before the Sermione Peninsula, an Austrian gunboat began to fire on the coach. A dragoon was hit and fell from his horse.

Josephine seemed to be living again through those moments at Fort-de-France when she was crossing the quay with Hortense to board the *Sensible*. A good tactician, Junot made the General's wife, his dear Louise and Hamelin get out of the coach. While it continued at full gallop, serving as a target, the travelers, crouching like Indians on the warpath, crept through the ditch alongside the road. Josephine showed great courage during this adventure, but was glad to find the coach again when the road turned away from the lake. The narrow streets of Desenzano were filled with dead and wounded. Masséna was fighting Wurmser's troops not far away. Josephine was in tears when she rejoined Bonaparte, who had come via Castiglione and Montichiari.

Bonaparte vowed that Wurmser would pay dearly for Josephine's tears. However, the General realized that his wife's place was not in the middle of the fighting. The road to Milan was cut, since Brescia had been retaken by the enemy; an action in which Lannes and Murat had been taken prisoner. There was only one solution—to go south to Florence. Once more Josephine was entrusted to Hamelin. They were also given a colonel, Colonel Milhaud, the courier Moustache, and an escort of dragoons.

Bonaparte now found himself forced to conquer, or to lose everything—as would be the situation right up to Waterloo. As he set out with 42,000 men to fight 80,000, Josephine went south, avoided Mantua, where an artillery duel was raging, crossed the Po not far from Cremona and halted at Parma, where she met Fesch, her husband's uncle. Mme. Letizia's brother, who was to be Cardinal Fesch under the Empire, could think of nothing but paintings. He was requisitioning them for the French museums and occasionally appropriated some for his own collection. Josephine did not linger there, as Parma was too near the fighting zone. In hot, sunny weather she crossed the Apennines and arrived in Florence, where the representative of France, Miot de Mélitot, gave her shelter. The Grand Duke of Tuscany received General Bonaparte's wife with courtesy, and invited her to dinner, in spite of the fact that at this very time her husband's soldiers were fighting at Lonato against the Uhlans of his brother the Emperor, and hurling them back along the Mincio River and Lake Garda. On Wednesday, August 3, Bonaparte took 2,000 prisoners, and two days later, on Friday, swept Wurmser from the town of Castiglione.

But no one in Florence knew that luck had deserted Bonaparte for only two or three days. There was already a rumor that the Neapolitans and the Pope intended to break the armistice and march north. A story was circulated that the French had been crushed and that Josephine had brought her husband's body in her luggage to have it buried in the Legation gardens. Mme. Bonaparte had no regrets on leaving the banks of the Arno for the little republic of Lucca in Tuscany, where the Senate treated her as a princess, complimented her, presented her with the "oils of honor" and gave feasts and receptions for her. The fact that at this moment Bonaparte could tell the Directory "another campaign has been completed in five days" no doubt had a good deal to do with the welcome she received from the people of Lucca. But they were unaware that Josephine, as she wrote to her aunt Renaudin, was terribly bored and cared nothing for "the honors of this country."

She had hoped to find Hippolyte somewhere between the Adige and the Arno. Unfortunately Lieutenant Charles was at war and, unlike her husband, could not ask his mistress to join him between two battles.

One fine morning Moustache arrived with a letter from his chief. Bonaparte wanted his wife. She was to return to Brescia where, as on July 25, "the tenderest of lovers" awaited her. As it happened, however, the lover she found there turned out to be not Bonaparte but Charles. On arriving at Brescia on Wednesday, August 17, after a long circuitous trip, Josephine and Hamelin learned that Bonaparte was waiting for them at Cremona. Josephine refused to go back fourteen leagues farther to the south, although Hamelin advised it. It would have meant a long night journey. He insisted, but in vain. Hamelin tells the reason for Josephine's refusal: "She took her husband's apartment and I that of an aide-de-camp.

" 'Go up to your room,' she said to me, 'I am going to lie down. They can put the table by my bed and you and I will take supper together.'

"When I came down again I saw three places laid and I asked who was the third guest.

" 'It's poor Charles,' she replied. 'He's on his way back from a mission and has stopped at Brescia on hearing I was here.'

"He came in at once and we supped together. The meal was soon

over and we were retiring, but as we went out the door a languid
voice was heard recalling Charles. I went my way. Before going to
bed I noticed that I had left my hat and pistols in the parlor
adjacent to the bedroom. I wanted to go and fetch them, but the
grenadier on duty at the door said that no one could go in.

" 'Who gave you your orders?'

" 'The lady's maid.'

"I realized that the heroine of Peschiera had once more become
the light woman of Paris."

The following day Bonaparte returned to take his proper place
and Charles vanished. This time, since Hamelin had "undergone the
baptism of fire with Mme. Bonaparte," as André Gavoty puts it, the
General could do no less than appoint him collector of contributions
for the army. Now Hamelin was launched. As a military agent he
could also indulge in trading for himself. It was a gold mine.
Naturally he did not ask Josephine for the money she had borrowed
in Paris. Even better, he soon handed her 12,000 francs as her share
in a particularly fruitful affair—60,000 present-day francs. She
would now be able to settle her debts and pay for her children's
keep, not to mention helping a Tascher great-aunt who was living in
poverty at Blois, and also sending subsidies to Aunt Renaudin, who
was always short of money.

When opening his wife's mail Bonaparte was surprised to notice
that she was signing large letters of exchange, for from 3,000 to
4,000 écus. "She was robbing me," he explained later. It was the
army she was robbing, her husband's army, from which she made a
living. After a week at Brescia—the longest time Bonaparte and
Josephine had lived together since they were married—they had to
part once more. On Thursday, August 25, Bonaparte and his wife
went back to Milan, which he left the next day for Verona to "push
victory to its ultimate end," drive Davidovich's troops back toward
the Tyrol and give the final blow to Wurmser, whose army had been
re-formed in a hope which was soon crushed. During these battles
Charles, "assistant to the adjutants general," fought with gallantry
and was mentioned by Bonaparte in his report to the Directory.

Josephine had resumed her life as sovereign of Italy. She kept
open house, presided at popular celebrations, followed the im-
provised processions, received delegations, honored balls with her

presence, and during a brief visit by Bonaparte watched the planting of a tree of liberty from a balcony of an inn, the Coperto da
Frigini. Banners embroidered with the words "Lombardy raised up
by genius" floated in the air, the artillery thundered and salvos were
fired. Speeches hailed "Bonaparte, messenger of the happy day
bringing to Lombardy the era of Liberty and Equality."

When he was away from her their correspondence was resumed:
love and burning messages from the husband, indifference from the
wife, constant reproaches.

"You, to whom nature has given sweetness, charm and everything
that pleases," he wrote, "how can you forget him who loves you so
warmly? Three days without letters from you, although I have
written to you several times. Absence is horrible, the nights are long,
tedious and insipid, the day is monotonous. Today, alone with my
thoughts, work, writing, men and their high-flown schemes, I have
not even a note from you that I can press to my heart."

And again: "No letters from you, I am really anxious. Yet I am
assured that you are well and even that you have been for an
excursion to Lake Como. Every day I wait impatiently for the mail
by which you will send me news. You know how much it means to
me. I am not living far from you, the happiness of my life is with my
sweet Josephine. Think of me! Write to me often, very often, it is
the only remedy for absence, which is cruel but, I hope, only
temporary."

He wrote to her from Ala before throwing a bridge over the
Adige. Two days later, on September 5, he entered Trent. On
September 8 came the victory at Bassano. He was so happy that for
the first time, apart from two affectionate lines, he wrote only
military news to her. "Eighteen thousand prisoners and the rest
killed or wounded." Wurmser could do nothing but take refuge
behind the strong walls of Mantua. "We have never had such great
and constant success. Italy, Friuli and the Tyrol are secure for the
Republic."

On September 12 he announced that Wurmser was surrounded
with his 9,000 men. On the 17th he resumed his amorous style to
complain of the silence into which the careless Josephine had once
more sunk. "You are wicked and ugly, as ugly as you are frivolous.
It is treacherous to deceive a poor husband, a tender lover! Must he

lose his rights because he is far away, laden with work, fatigue and trouble?"

Two days later he was in her arms, in Milan. Bonaparte "still loves me with adoration," wrote Josephine to Barras. He stayed until October 12 in this town which was to become the capital of the Lombard, or Transpadane, Republic. (Ferrara, Bologna, Reggio and Modena would become the Cisalpine Republic on October 16.) On October 15 Bonaparte was at Modena. He went to bed with a violent headache and the next day he stayed in bed with a fever. The absence of news did not improve it. For, naturally, Josephine was as lazy as ever. Finally, on Monday the 17th, he received letters from Josephine. Before leaving he pressed them to his heart and lips unread. "At that moment I saw you near me, not willful and angry but gentle, tender with that soothing kindness which is my Josephine's exclusive property."

He opened the letters. "It was a dream!" The reality was there, before his eyes. "Your letters are as cold as fifty years, they are like fifteen years of marriage. In them one sees the friendship and feelings of that winter of life. Fie, Josephine! . . . It is very naughty, very bad, very treacherous of you. What is there left for you to do to make me really to be pitied? Love me no longer? Well, that's already done. Hate me? I wish it were so. Everything degrades except hate. But indifference with marble pulse, fixed eye and monotonous step! . . ."

In one letter to her husband at this time Josephine spoke of her "little belly." Perhaps she was pregnant this time. She may have been afraid it was the result of the night of August 17 spent with Charles and considered it to her interest to have as ally on the spot Berthier, the chief of staff, on whom Charles, incidentally, was dependent. Josephine treated him with care. Even more, she favored his love affair with the ravishing Mme. Visconti and took him as her confidant. She wrote him such a charming letter that Berthier could not help reading it to Bonaparte.

Afterwards he related the scene to Josephine. "On rereading the letter you sent me, your husband said: 'You must admit that I have a charming wife. Yes, I love her very much and I confess there is no one like her in the world. Come, Berthier, we must go to Milan someday. How glad I shall be to embrace my little wife!' I think that, like you, when he said embrace he was thinking of something more."

It can be seen that Josephine had once more been playing a part by making Berthier believe that she missed being with her husband. A good actress, she was also able to convince him, a little later, of her jealousy. She was indeed to be jealous, very jealous, one day, but for the moment she adopted this pose solely to divert possible suspicion on the part of her husband.

Berthier calmed her: "I am so attached to you that I swear I would tell you if Bonaparte had done you the slightest wrong. No, he has not. He loves you, he adores you. He is unhappy at these imaginings of yours. I have not left General Bonaparte all through the campaign. So, be happy! I swear by all that is most sacred that he has always devoted himself to you. No, there is no woman more loved, more esteemed than you. How many times has he said to me: Admit, my dear Berthier, that I am very unfortunate! I am mad about my wife, I think only of her, and judge how unfair she is to me!"

On the fighting front things were going badly. On November 14 Bonaparte was unable to overcome the resistance of the Austrian General Josef Alvinczi. He feared the worst and did not hide it from the Directory. "Perhaps we are on the eve of losing Italy! None of the expected help has arrived. . . . The Army of Italy, reduced to a handful of men, is exhausted. The heroes of Lodi, Millesimo, Castiglione and Bassano have died for their country or are in the hospital. All that remains to the forces is their reputation or their pride."

Mme. Bonaparte was living in anguish. She knew merely that her husband had left Verona on Sunday night to march on Ronco, on the banks of the Adige. She had learned that on the evening of Monday, the 15th, he had managed to enter the town after a fierce battle. Since then there had been silence. From Ronco three roads crossed the marshes. The middle one passed in front of a town entered by a bridge straddling the Alpone—a bridge and a town called Arcole.

At last Josephine received a letter announcing victory. It was written from Verona, which Bonaparte had entered to a triumphal welcome that same day, Friday, November 19. "At last, my adorable

Josephine," he wrote, "I am born again. Death is no longer before my eyes and glory and honor are still in my heart. The enemy has been beaten at Arcole. Tomorrow we shall remedy Vaubois's mistake of abandoning Rivoli. In eight days Mantua will be ours."

On the morning of the 15th he had been no more than the head of a retreating horde. If the bridge of Arcole became part of history on Monday, November 15, 1796, he himself became a legend, the legend which, over the years, was to show him seizing a flag under a hail of shot and shell, and advancing to the bridge sweeping along the men with whom he was to conquer the world. Naturally the legend overlooked the second episode, that of the soldiers dragging their general from the bridge, bearing him along in their flight and dropping him in the marsh, from which Marmont and Louis Bonaparte with difficulty snatched him out of the mud, to perch him on his horse again. Legend returns to show the hero of Italy charging the enemy and forcing him to evacuate the village. But the victory—the victory of Arcole—did not take place until two days later, on Wednesday, November 17. The French were then able to extricate themselves from the marsh and to overthrow the enemy on the plain.

While the Austrians were fleeing in disorder to Vienna, he returned to Verona and wrote: "Think of me often. If you ceased to love me . . . or if your heart grew cold . . . you would be horrible, unjust, but I am sure that you will always be my tender lover as I shall always be your tender friend. Death alone can break the union formed by sympathy, love and feeling. Give me news of the little belly. A thousand, thousand tender, loving kisses."

For two days he rested at Verona and on the evening of Sunday, November 21, before seeking his camp bed, he wrote for her these burning lines which by their tone recall those sent at the beginning of the year.

"I am going to bed, my little Josephine, with my heart full of your adorable image. . . . You never write to me; you never think of your good friend, cruel woman! Do you not know that without you, without your heart, without your love, there is no happiness or life for your husband. Good God! How happy I should be if I could be present at your delightful toilet, little shoulder, a little white breast, resilient and very firm; above all a little face with a kerchief tied around it, Creole fashion, good enough to eat. You know I don't forget the little visits; you know, the little black forest . . . I give it a thousand kisses and wait impatiently to be there. Everything is for you; life, happiness and pleasure are only what you make them. To live in a Josephine is to live in Elysium. A kiss for the mouth, the eyes, the shoulder, the breast, everywhere, everywhere!"

Two days later, the 23rd, still without news, he wrote: "I no longer love you at all. On the contrary, I detest you. You are wicked, very awkward, very stupid, a Cinderella. You never write to me, you don't love your husband. You know the pleasure your letters give him and you don't write him six careless lines! What are you doing all day, madame? What important business leaves you no time to write to your very good lover? What attachment stifles and pushes aside the tender, constant love you promised him? Who can be this wonderful, this new lover who absorbs all your moments, tyrannizes over your days and prevents you from paying attention to your husband? Josephine, take care, one fine night the doors will be broken down and there I shall be!"

The next day, the 24th, he announced his imminent arrival in a letter of four lines: "I love you furiously. I am writing to Paris by this post. Everything goes well. Wurmser was beaten yesterday at Mantua. All your husband needs to make him happy is the love of Josephine." (Some of these letters, published by Queen Hortense, have been toned down. M. Fleury, head of the secretariat of H.I.H. Prince Napoleon, to whom these passionate letters of Bonaparte to his wife now belong, has confirmed that the suppressions are very slight and principally concerned with the "little black forest.")

On Saturday, November 27, he dashed madly up to the Serbelloni palace. His carriage stopped before the monumental façade with its Ionic columns, its stone glittering in the pale, autumn sun. He ran four steps at a time up the stairs to the gallery on the second floor where Josephine's boudoir and their *camera matrimoniale* were. He opened the door, but the apartments were empty.

Josephine had gone to Genoa. With tears in his eyes, Bonaparte went to his desk and wrote: "I have arrived in Milan, I hurried to your apartments, I left everything to see you, to press you in my arms . . . you were not there. You are gallivanting about after festivals; you leave me just as I arrive. You no longer care for your dear Napoleon. A whim made you love him, inconstancy makes you indifferent.

"Being accustomed to danger, I know the remedy for the tedium and evils of life. The unhappiness I feel is incalculable; I had a right not to expect it. I shall be here until nine o'clock. Don't put yourself out; seek your pleasures; happiness is made for you. The whole world is only too happy if it can please you, and your husband alone is very, very unhappy."

The next day Berthier, more fortunate, showed his general a letter Josephine had just sent him from Genoa. In a rage Bonaparte wrote to his wife:

"My intention is that you should not alter any of your plans or the parties offered you. I'm not worth the trouble, and the happiness or unhappiness of a man you do not love has no claim on your interest. . . . Be happy, reproach me for nothing, don't bother about the joy of a man who lives only in your life, enjoys only your pleasures and your happiness. When I demand from you a love like mine I am wrong; why should one wish lace to weigh as much as gold? . . . But what I deserve from Josephine is her consideration, her esteem, for I love her to madness and her alone. Farewell, adorable woman, farewell, my Josephine. May fate heap on my heart all the griefs and sorrows, but may it give my Josephine prosperous and happy days. Who deserves them more than she? When it is proved that she can no longer love, I shall lock up my profound grief and content myself with being able to be useful and helpful to her.

Fearing to have wounded her, he reopened his letter "to give her a kiss." And he added: "Ah! Josephine! Josephine!"

The next day Clarke arrived from Paris. He found Bonaparte "haggard, thin, the skin clinging to his bones, his eyes bright with constant fever." His thoughts were always with the absent one, who did not return from her escapade until December 1. Then she threw ✓ herself into his arms. But the hurt left a mark on her husband's heart. He was also to remember the letters of exchange "for three or four thousand écus to pay her debts." The wound was a slight one as yet. But after that Saturday when he had not been able to repress his tears, after those four dreadful days when he realized that she had been lacking in "consideration" for him, as he wrote, he was to write to her tenderly, perhaps, but never again such ardent letters, letters which had made Josephine say in a note to her aunt, two months earlier, that she had "the most amiable husband one could ever meet," a husband who never gave her "time to wish for anything." "My wishes are his," she had added. "He spends all day in admiration before me, as though I were a divinity." Now this was over and she would never be a "divinity" for him again. He was to love her simply as a woman.

7. Mme. Bonaparte

Gros, a pupil of David, came to Milan to paint Bonaparte's portrait. He wanted to show him bareheaded, a flag in his hand, advancing on the bridge at Arcole. But the General could not keep still. Josephine intervened. Every day after lunch she took her husband in hand, forced him into the pose—and the painter could begin making his sketches. It was at Genoa that Mme. Faytpoul, wife of the French Minister, had introduced Gros, an artist whom the hard times had forced to lay aside the brush for the rifle. He had charmed Josephine and, since he wished to paint the General's portrait, she had brought him back with her.

Josephine was playing the part of a happy woman, but in reality she was bored to death. Even though Charles was at headquarters, he could not come to see her as much as they both desired. Josephine was already reigning. She wrote to the pretty Mme. Hamelin: "Come quickly and you will see an extraordinary sight. Everyone is madly gay here." Everyone, but not Josephine. The licentious Fortunée Hamelin came hurrying, and she was not alone. Many of the other arrivals in Milan were ladies of easy virtue, and the tone they imparted to Mme. Bonaparte's "court" was by no means a dignified one. Josephine's days were concerned with love and a succession of amusements, idle talk and confidences, with trying on new dresses, with place seekers, the usual circle of acquaintances and, above all, with visitors. We know that the charming Creole excelled in the art of conversation. Her ease of manner was astonishing. Among so many upstarts she was a great lady. Women from the Italian aristocracy "collaborated" with the occupation and accepted Josephine's invitations. Among them were the Marchesa Paola Castiglione, who spoke Latin and Greek, and her sister, Maria, of the beautiful black hair, with whom Murat was in love, the graceful Contessa Aresa, who declared she was in love with Bonaparte, and finally Mme. Visconti, who also claimed to love the conqueror. "I think I never saw a more charming head than hers," wrote the Duchesse d'Abrantès. "She had delicate but regular features, and in particular the prettiest nose possible." She threw herself at Bonaparte, but he gave her to understand, bluntly, that his heart was already taken and, as though it had been a staff matter, passed this little marvel on to Berthier. The inexperienced chief of staff, who was deformed and almost stuttered, fell hopelessly in love with this goddess from Olympus, and had her husband—for there was a husband—named ambassador to Paris from the new Cisalpine Republic. Thus began a rather odd triangle which provided conversation for Josephine's entourage until her death.

On December 10, 1796, Josephine gave a grand ball in honor of General Clarke, a booted diplomat who had been charged with negotiating with Austria should occasion arise, though Bonaparte was not to give him time to do so. While he was waiting, Clarke observed the General and, as he wrote to the Directory, considered him the most important man of the Republic. For the first time the judgment which posterity was to confirm was bestowed on Bonaparte. One wonders what the heedless Creole may have felt on hearing Clarke say: "His coolness in the midst of the most fast-moving actions is as remarkable as his extreme promptness in changing his plans when unforeseen circumstances dictate this. He belongs neither to the royalists, who calumniate him, nor to the anarchists, whom he dislikes. The Constitution is his guide. If he rallies to it and to the Directory which supports it, I think he will always be useful and never dangerous to his country."

He concluded: "Bonaparte will be placed by posterity in the
ranks of the greatest men."

Josephine's husband was absent when, escorted by Fesch, a little
marvel arrived in Milan: Paulette, Napoleon's sister, affectionately
called by him Paganetta, little pagan. The future Princess Borghese ✓
was then sixteen. "There was something unreal, fine, dainty about
her which it is impossible to describe," Maxime de Villemarest said
of her. The poet Arnault, who made her acquaintance shortly after
her arrival in Milan, commented: "She is the prettiest little person
one could find and the least sensible one can imagine. No more
poise than a schoolgirl, talking disconnectedly, laughing at nothing
and at everything." With this lack of seriousness and her perpetual
laughter and later a knowledge of coquetry rarely equaled, Paulette
was irresistible, and it must be added, no one did resist her. She
herself offered little resistance to the desires of her partners, since
yielding herself to love seemed to her the most agreeable way of
life.

The first man to be inflamed by the mere sight of Paulette—she
was no longer Pauletta and not yet Pauline—had been Lieutenant
Junot, already aide-de-camp to the young General Bonaparte. In the
spring of 1794 he had accompanied his chief to the Château Sallé at
Antibes, where the Bonaparte family was living, and had fallen
madly in love with Paganetta, then aged fourteen. He plucked up
courage, during a walk, to ask Bonaparte for his sister's hand. He
considered himself not a bad match since he would inherit 1,200
francs a year on his father's death.

"Let us sum things up," replied Bonaparte. "Your father is in
good health, you will have a long wait for your income. For the
moment, apart from your lieutenant's insignia, you have nothing.
Paulette has nothing and what is the total? Nothing. You cannot
marry at the moment. Let us wait for better times."

For Paulette those "better times" would wear the seductive face
of the elegant Fréron, the Directory's commissioner at Marseilles at
the end of October, 1795. The proconsul of the Year II, the former
Don Juan of the Terror, now aged forty, was trying to efface the
memory of his past as a terrorist in that same Marseilles where, two
years before, he had cheerfully waded through blood. In courting

Paulette he was also trying to forget that in Paris he had left his mistress, Mlle. Masson of the Théâtre des Italiens, with the two children she had already given him and a third she was expecting. Finally, he was trying to hide as best he could his need for "spirits and his effeminate tastes."

Would Bonaparte and Mme. Letizia consent to this marriage? Paulette, who had fallen in love with Fréron, had no doubt of it. At first Bonaparte had not said no. It was Mme. Letizia, rather, who had shown little enthusiasm for having this drinker of blood come into the clan. We know this from a letter written by Fréron to Bonaparte: "I beg you to write at once to your mother to remove all difficulties. Why postpone these ties which have been formed by the most delicate love? My dear Bonaparte, help me to overcome this fresh obstacle, I count on you."

But Josephine was aware of Maximin Isnard's reproach: "Fréron, at every step I take in the South I find the trace of your depredations and of the blood you caused to flow. . . . Wherever I meet a crime I find Fréron!" So Josephine had worked to separate the two lovers.

"My friend," Paulette had written to Fréron, "everyone works together to cross us. I see from your letter that your friends are ungrateful, even Napoleon's wife, who you thought was on your side. She writes to her husband that I should be dishonored if I married you. In this way she hopes to prevent it. What have we done to her?"

Napoleon had asked Josephine to write to Barras to work against Fréron. The match had been broken off and one can imagine with what looks the little bacchante eyed her sister-in-law when she met her in Milan. Bonaparte had summoned Paulette to Milan with the idea of changing her ideas and marrying her to Marmont. However, the future Duke of Ragusa guessed that his general's sister would not make an exemplary wife. Meanwhile, Paganetta proved capricious, unprincipled, made fun of everyone, stuck out her tongue at Josephine—who in spite of everything prepared charming apartments for her—and did not hesitate to nudge her companion under the table with her knee—it was Arnault on one occasion—if he did not pay enough attention to her tricks. Bonaparte glared fiercely, but in vain, at Paganetta. "The authority of the commanding

General of the Army of Italy was shattered by a little girl's flightiness."

Having tried her best to conciliate Paulette, unsuccessfully, Josephine ended by taking a dislike to the insupportable madcap, who before long was calling her "the old woman." For the moment Josephine merely displayed a little jealousy and made a face when she heard her husband's soldiers sing about Paulette.

After remaining in Milan for more than a month—for most of the period from November 27 to January 7—it took a great deal of courage for Bonaparte to remount his horse and take the road to Mantua, where the siege was nearing an end. Josephine was anxious. Her husband looked ill, "with pale and hollow cheeks," and he thought he had been poisoned.

"He's as yellow as one could wish," his enemies said.

Burning with fever he launched this new campaign, writing whenever he could to Josephine, who trembled less for him perhaps than for the fate of the army in which her lover was fighting. Yet she was not unaware that a defeat would be the end of her life as a near-sovereign in Milan as well as in Paris. Now she watched for the courier. She learned that three horses had died of exhaustion under Bonaparte, that ill horseman who, at dawn on Saturday, January 14, had planned one of his finest battles, Rivoli. At ten o'clock he shouted, "They are ours!" then successively beat the left, the center and the right of the enemy. As evening fell, 24,000 prisoners and 60 guns were captured and the fame of Napoleon increased.

The next day Bonaparte finished off the last of the enemy troops, those of Alvinczi, then went to bed and wrote to his wife, confessing that he was "dead tired." This did not prevent his winning the battle of La Favorita next day. He wanted her to join him as soon as possible. This time she obeyed without reluctance and, accompanied by Paulette and Mme. Visconti, joined her husband at Bologna. On the same day, February 1, Bonaparte declared war on the Pope. Wurmser surrendered the next day and the French finally entered Mantua. The house of Austria had lost the contest and Bonaparte bore down on Ancona.

But Josephine had hardly settled in Bologna when her husband left her "to have done with Rome." He did not see his wife again until February 24. "I am still at Ancona," he wrote to her a few days later. "I shall not have you come here because everything is not yet over. Besides this is a very gloomy country and everyone is fearful. . . . I have never been so weary of anything as this dreadful war. Farewell, my sweet one, think of me."

While in Bologna, where she had nothing much to do, the indolent Creole answered her husband no more than when in Milan or Paris. So on February 16 he wrote: "You are sad, you are ill, you no longer write to me, you want to go to Paris. Do you no longer love your friend? This thought makes me unhappy. My sweet one, life is unbearable for me since I learned of your sadness. . . . Perhaps I shall make peace with the Pope and soon be with you. It is the most ardent wish of my soul. . . . I give you a hundred kisses. Believe me, nothing equals my love except my anxiety. Write to me yourself every day. Farewell, dearest friend."

Of course he still loved her, but a hundred kisses had replaced the thousand thousand of former times and there was no more talk of the "little black forest."

Three days later, on February 19, having sent her a bulletin of victory from Tolentino, "peace with Rome has just been signed," he added, "If your health allows it come to Rimini or Ravenna, but I implore you to take care of yourself."

He need not have worried, she was taking great care of herself, not even exerting herself to write to him, and he again grew angry. "Not a word from you. Good God! what have I done then? Thinking only of you, loving only Josephine, living only for my wife, taking pleasure only in my love's happiness, should that earn me such harsh treatment from her? My dear, I beg you to think often of me and write to me every day. You are ill or you do not love me! Do you think my heart is of marble? . . . You, to whom nature has given wit, gentleness and beauty, you alone who can reign in my heart, you who are doubtless too aware of the absolute empire you have over me!"

On February 24 he came to take her to Mantua, then left her immediately to begin his decisive campaign: the attack on Vienna. Thanks to reinforcements brought by Bernadotte, the commander in chief of the Army of Italy now had 74,000 men at his disposal. Without anxiety Josephine saw him leave Mantua on March 8 to transfer his headquarters to Bassano. Undoubtedly she did not yet realize she had married a genius—she was not to be convinced of this until the morning of the coronation—but she believed in his extraordinary luck and Bonaparte's entry into Vienna was not to surprise her unduly. Besides, she was absorbed by other, infinitely more trifling problems, not to mention the all too hasty meetings with Hippolyte, whom Bonaparte had sent to Rome with Marmont to take a letter to the Pope. Josephine had entrusted her lover with some shopping for her in the eternal city, but on his return Charles had to rejoin the army in Gorizia, while his mistress had been obliged to return to Milan.

So the General's wife resumed her life in the Serbelloni palace, "an existence steeped in boredom," she declared. The only palliative, always the same one, was the arrival of couriers with fresh news from her husband and her lover. This time Bonaparte was facing an adversary of equal stature, the Archduke Charles, but this did not prevent him, supported by Masséna, from advancing into the heart of the Austrian Territories and throwing fear into the man who would one day be his father-in-law. But Bonaparte, weakened by the absence of the garrisons he had had to leave behind him, was wise enough to stop at Leoben, twenty leagues from Vienna. This enabled him to write a letter to his adversary with these words worthy of the legend he was so cleverly creating: "I should be prouder of a civic crown which I deserved than of the sad glory which comes from military successes."

It was the peace preliminaries at Leoben which enabled Bonaparte to toss before the Directory this menacing hint of his candidature for power: "I ask for rest . . . having achieved more fame than is necessary for happiness. . . . My civil career, like my military career, will be single and simple."

For the moment General Bonaparte's rest consisted in joining Josephine at the castle of Mombello, or Montebello, a magnificent residence mostly baroque in style, which he had rented at Crivelli, not far from Milan. Here they both behaved like sovereigns. There was no question now of admitting aides-de-camp and officers to their table. Bonaparte would often dine alone in public, in the tent he had had pitched in front of the castle, while the inhabitants of the country filed by. As a diplomat of the time who had seen these manifestations of glory said, "he was no longer the general of a victorious republic, he was a conqueror in his own person."

No headquarters had ever more closely resembled a Court. Arnault has described it: "Surrounding the General, but keeping their distance, were the high-ranking officers, the administrative heads of the army, the magistrates of the town and also a few ministers of the governments of Italy, all standing, like himself. To me nothing was more remarkable than the attitude of that little man among the giants whom he dominated by his character. . . . Berthier, Kilmaine, Clarke, even Augereau (later a marshal of France) waited in silence until he spoke to them, a favor which not everyone received that evening." "That man," I said to Regnault as we returned home, "that man is a man apart. Everything yields to the superiority of his genius . . . he is born to dominate as others are born to serve. If he is not fortunate enough to be carried off by a bullet, in four years' time, he will either be in exile or on a throne."

Like her husband, Josephine had adapted herself wonderfully to these excessive honors and comported herself with as much ease as if she had been born to the throne.

On June 1 Bonaparte's mother, Mme. Letizia, arrived at Montebello with Jerome and her two other daughters. Bonaparte, who had gone to Milan to meet his mother, was still young Napoleone to her and he hastened to give her his arm as she stepped from her carriage. There followed Annunziata, soon to be called Caroline, and Marianna, who had become Elisa. Then came a great, clumsy fellow, Felix Bacciochi, a relative of the Pozzo di Borgo family, who had just married Elisa. Bonaparte had been opposed to his sister's marriage with this thirty-five-year-old captain with no future, but for Letizia the fact that Bacciochi was a Corsican was paramount, and she overrode her son. Bonaparte frowned, but Josephine, wishing to win over her mother-in-law, whom she was meeting for the first time, persuaded him that it was useless to dwell on the subject. They would make up for it by marrying Pauline to Adjutant General Leclerc, the son of a miller from Pontoise, who seemed destined for a brilliant future. In any case he was of higher rank than Junot. He had met Paulette during the siege of Toulon, when she was just a little girl, and since then, it was said, had never stopped thinking of her. He loved her first because she was bewitching and also because she was the sister of his general, whom he idolized.

For Pauline only one thing counted, she was being married. The ceremony took place on June 14, 1797. On the same day the marriage of Elisa was regularized, for she had not been united to her silly Bacciochi before God. The groom was appointed battalion commander and sent to take charge of the troops defending Ajaccio. Like Paulette, Elisa received 40,000 francs dowry from her brother.

The whole clan was thus reunited, for Lucien and Joseph, now ambassador to Rome, had come to the court of Montebello to gaze on their brother and receive a few crumbs from the feast.

Josephine's children were still at Saint-Germain and were to spend the summer with the Marquis and Marquise de Beauharnais. Eugene went in for sports and even won a prize for running, a feat which could hardly be expected to bring a smile to the aunt's face, she was so angry with her niece. Not only did Josephine not write, but all those honors seemed to have turned the head of the little Rose of former days. Why did she never show any interest in the elder Beauharnais's problems? The Office for the Liquidation of Emigrés' Debts refused to pay him the arrears of an annuity. One word from Josephine would settle everything. But the General's wife, too preoccupied with herself, had not taken the trouble. Mme. de Beauharnais wrote to Calmelet on April 18: "I share her glory with all my heart. But I confess that her thoughtlessness toward us wounds me cruelly, particularly aware as I am that, under the circumstances, she is our sole resource. I have just written to her about what she owes us. But will she have the time to read my letter and will she pay any attention to it?" (This letter and thirteen others written by the Marquise de Beauharnais to Calmelet belong to M. André Gavoty. See "Sources," page 485.)

It is certain that in the years when Josephine was separated from Alexandre and later as a gay widow, she had often begged her aunt and father-in-law for help and had received assistance and subsidies from them. It is true, she was rather out of touch with them, but she could not help knowing, from Calmelet, that the Marquise was living on a grand scale.

However, it may have been in order to reduce her aunt's expenses somewhat that Josephine asked her husband to have her son Eugene sent for. On his arrival at Montebello, on June 28, he was immediately appointed aide-de-camp. Two days later he was promoted to second lieutenant, and he was not yet sixteen. We catch sight of him at Montebello, "playing pranks" with the Bonaparte girls. With "every mark of the gentleman," a good dancer, unself-conscious, a pleasant singer even, always smiling, he knew how to please "without inspiring jealousy."

Josephine was no longer so young, but she knew how to dress, to wrap herself in Indian muslin and thin silks. "White suited her," a contemporary tells us, "she knew it and hardly wore any other color. On her wonderful hair, not yet adorned with the crown of dia-monds, she usually placed a garland of ivy, or she tucked a few flowers from her garden into the gauze turban which was to become the fashion."

Bonaparte and Josephine accompanied Paulette on her honey-moon trip to Lake Como. There was no privacy possible for the young couple. Dragoons served as guards and brought up a proces-sion which consisted of more than thirty people. At the Villa Passabacqua there was a reception of notables, and illuminations on the lake. Josephine finally took pity on Paulette and gave the signal for retreat.

Josephine tried in vain to soften her stern, cantankerous mother-in-law. Mme. Letizia continued to look on her daughter-in-law not only as the woman who had taken away from her the heart of her favorite son, but also as an ex-vicomtesse, a too promiscuous widow, an overly fashionable woman who, as an added grievance, had not yet managed to give her husband a child. Moreover, *la madre* spoke a French heavily larded with Italian which made the Parisiennes in Josephine's train smile.

Montebello was the scene of a little drama. The cook's powerful mastiff one morning killed Fortuné, who had left his mistress's bed rather earlier than usual. Josephine wept and Charles got her a new pug. It is reported that the cook apologized to his master, promising to keep his dog firmly tied up in the future, but that Bonaparte advised the cook to let his beast prowl since the new pug was as ill-tempered as the unfortunate Fortuné.

Bonaparte had promoted Charles to the rank of captain in the 1st Hussars on June 24, 1797, and Josephine was able to watch him ride in the procession during the extraordinary July 14 celebration in Milan.

Josephine had accompanied Bonaparte to Passeriano in Friuli, but she saw little of him there. He often worked until dawn, and conferences with the Austrian delegates began in the evening and ended in the middle of the night.

At that time a contemporary remarked that Josephine would weep several times a day "for the slightest of reasons." Certainly Passeriano, a former country house of the Doges near Udine, was a gloomy place, and Montebello or Milan seemed like a haven of delight in comparison. Her only distraction was talking to Barras's secretary, Botot. But if her eyes were full of tears, the principal reason was the absence of Charles, who in mid-October had returned to Milan after his leave. The rumor ran, too, that the fickle Hippolyte was paying assiduous court to Pauline, then two months pregnant, and that he had been the lover of Mme. Lamberti, a ravishing Lombard who had bestowed her favors on the Hapsburg Emperor Joseph II and then on General Despinoy. But when Josephine returned to Milan at the beginning of November, Charles seems to have been forgiven, since a fortnight later, while Bonaparte was scorching the road on his way to Rastadt to bring the war to a provisional halt, Josephine went off on a trip to Venice, with Charles, before returning to France.

The Republic of Venice received its conqueror's wife royally, with a succession of illuminations, gondola outings, feasts and balls in an enchanted setting. The Venetians chose to forget that the famous bronze horses of St. Mark and the celebrated Lion had found their way to Paris.

Whether the two lovers were careless or not, it is certain that Bonaparte had his suspicions. Perhaps, as has been said, that adorable little plague of a Pauline, having guessed the truth and having been thrown over by Charles, had wanted to make her brother suspicious. In any case, while at Rastadt, Bonaparte told his chief of staff to send this urgent order to Milan: "Citizen Charles, aide-de-camp, is ordered to leave Milan on receipt of this and go with all diligence to Paris, where he will receive further orders. Signed: Alex. Berthier."

The order doubtless reached its recipient belatedly. In any event, Berthier arrived in Milan on December 22—his master having left Rastadt for Paris—he signed a new order, made at the request of Josephine, which puts a somewhat different face on the staff officer's disgrace and considerably weakens the first order: "Alexandre Berthier, Commanding General, acting on the request of Citizen Hippolyte Charles, attached to the General Staff, for permission to go to Paris to take care of family matters necessitating his presence there, authorizes Citizen Hippolyte Charles to proceed to the Minister of War in Paris in order, with the present authorization which he will present to the Minister, to obtain three months' leave."

Charles immediately leaped on his horse, not in order to deal more quickly with his family matters, but to follow Josephine, who was, in fact, on her way to Paris.

In Lyons, on December 19, she was received like a queen. In spite of the cold the town was illuminated, there was dancing, and Josephine went to the Grand Theatre to be acclaimed with shouts of "Long live the Republic! Long live Bonaparte and his wife!"

The people of Moulins did even better. The town had been awaiting Mme. Bonaparte's arrival for three days. Her carriage had suffered damage at Tarare, and then at Roanne, and it was not until Christmas Eve that Josephine made her entry into the capital of Allier to shouts of "Long live the Republic! Long live Bonaparte! Long live his virtuous wife!"—they did not yet know her very well.

The inn where "the wife of the conqueror of Italy" was staying was lit up by luminous transparencies.

But let us hear the speech of the mayor, Citizen Radot:

"To see within our walls the virtuous wife of the greatest of heroes is a joy more keenly felt than it can be expressed. You, the wife of him who had neither model nor rival, you who, by your literary attainments and your virtues, share in his glory, come share in the national gratitude."

The "president of the municipal administration" was the first to speak thus of Josephine's virtues. He was to have imitators all through the First Empire and even in the Second, when Napoleon III himself alluded one day, in an official speech, to his grandmother's virtues. By dint of so much repetition people came to believe in them. Josephine responded gracefully:

"I lack words to show my gratitude for the warm welcome you have given me, I am extremely sensible of it. If my husband has had such brilliant successes, it is because he was fortunate enough to command an army in which each soldier is a hero. Bonaparte loves the Republicans and he is still ready to shed the last drop of his blood for them."

The next day the reports were: "dawn brings the painful thought that Citizeness Bonaparte is to leave Moulins. It was hoped to retain her for just one day, but she burns with the desire of seeing her husband again. . . . Let us not impede the wife's journey."

Josephine burned principally with the desire to see Hippolyte again. And he did not delay. A few hours later, outside Nevers, the beloved puppet jumped into the carriage of the "virtuous wife." This was such a wonderful Christmas present that Josephine dawdled with her lover before returning to Paris, where Bonaparte was waiting for her.

The Creole had not only been billing and cooing with her lover, they had talked business. Josephine had seen Botot, Barras's secretary, at Passeriano and the Bodins at Lyons the week before. Since Charles had obtained three months' leave, they might perhaps, while the new captain was waiting to get his complete freedom, form a company—the Bodin company. Hippolyte would work at it while the General's wife would provide support from her connections—particularly those she still entertained with Barras, the master of the Directory.

And so was created that organization of doubtful honesty which, thanks to the support of the General's wife, was to deliver as mounts to the Quartermaster General horses originally destined for the boneyard.

The future looked good. There was no doubt that, thanks to their common business interests, Josephine and Hippolyte could love each other at leisure.

Citizen Muller, gardener and florist, was in despair. It was the third time that M. de Talleyrand, Minister for External Relations, had made him bring out and then take back the 930 shrubs intended to adorn the gardens of the Hôtel Galliffet on the occasion of the great feast the Minister wished to give "in honor of Mme. Bonaparte." To Bonaparte's fury, Josephine did not come and Talleyrand spent his time giving counterorders to his gardener and putting off his guests, whose invitation cards bore the words: "You will judge it proper, I am sure, to refrain from wearing anything coming from English factories."

While he waited for his wife, Bonaparte continued to live like a king. To verify this it is sufficient to read the Memoirs of Hortense, who was taken to the Rue de la Victoire one morning by her grandfather Beauharnais. "What a change in our little house, formerly so quiet! Now it was filled with generals, and officers. The sentries had difficulty in pushing back the common people and those from society who were impatient and eager to see the conqueror of Italy. Finally, in spite of the crowd, we got in to see the General, who was having lunch surrounded by a numerous staff. He welcomed me with all the tenderness of a father."

Finally, on January 2—13 Nivôse—after a week of love, Josephine, temporarily deserted by Hippolyte at Essonnes, returned to the Rue Chantereine which, the day before, had become Rue de la Victoire, in honor of her husband.

Bonaparte did not give her a good reception. His wife's attempts to offer a plausible excuse for her delay did not succeed in calming him. He felt there was some danger. He had been very much displeased on arriving in the Rue Chantereine. While still in Italy, Josephine had written to Calmelet: "I wish my house to be furnished with the utmost elegance." She had been obeyed. The Jacob brothers had let themselves go and the expenses had exceeded 300,000 francs. Napoleon was later to say: "Everything was of the latest model, made to order." The bedroom on the second floor had become a tent of striped material with drum-shaped chairs. The classical style beds could be pulled closer or farther apart by an ingenious spring. Josephine had decided to place the gifts received in Italy in the ground-floor rooms, one of which became "the General's study." Her husband must now have a setting that befitted his fame.

The arguments about this costly installation had been all the more difficult to bear as Hippolyte was not there, and it was with ill humor that at ten in the evening of January 3 Josephine went to the entertainment given by Talleyrand. For the fourth time Citizen Muller had brought out his shrubs, the five hundred guests had received their invitations and the rooms were perfumed with amber. Applause broke out when Barras, in full dress, went to meet Bonaparte, Hortense and Josephine. The General was wearing the green uniform of the Institute, to which he had just been elected, and Josephine, the heroine of the evening, was dressed in a yellow tunic embroidered with black and a gilded cap very much in the "Doge of Venice" style. The ladies—people were already leaving off the word "citizeness"—lined up as though in the presence of royalty. Josephine spoke to everyone with kindness which was commented on by all those who met her. Bonaparte took the arm of the Turkish Ambassador and, looking at his old and pretty friend Mme. Permon in her dress of white crepe, murmured something. The representative of the Ottoman Porte looked at her wide-eyed with interest.

"I told him you were of Greek origin," the General explained to Mme. Permon, shaking her hand.

After this exchange of commonplaces the future Duchesse d'Abrantès and her mother were the cynosure of all eyes. It was almost like being back at Versailles.

Mme. de Staël, who hoped for "a situation," presented the conqueror with a laurel branch.

"You should leave laurels to the Muses," Bonaparte replied coldly.

There was no doubt that this bluestocking irritated him. She persisted: "General, what woman do you love most?"

"My wife."

"That's simple, but whom would you most respect?"

"The one who knows best how to run her household."

"I can understand that too. But who, for you, would be the greatest of women?"

"The one who had the most children, madame."

Mme. de Staël, left stranded by the General, who had turned on his heel, was dumfounded.

"Your great man is a very peculiar one," she said to Arnault.

She was soon to swell the ranks of his enemies. And, indeed, they were already numerous. "This sulphur-faced Scaramouche," Mallet du Pan wrote the next day, "has had a success due merely to curiosity. He is done for, absolutely done for!"

He was only fifteen years off.

At eleven o'clock the ball stopped and the ladies sat down at table and were served by the men. Behind Josephine stood Talleyrand, who raised his glass of champagne.

"To the citizeness who bears the name most dear to glory."

Josephine went every day to 100 Faubourg Saint-Honoré, where Louis Bodin lived. It was there—for the Bodins could do no less for her—that she would meet her dear Hippolyte.

8. "My Hippolyte!"

"They have all my hatred, you alone have my tenderness and my love."—JOSEPHINE

When in the arms of her "puppet" Josephine did not talk solely of love. The frivolous Creole was in debt and urgently needed money. Bonaparte would certainly not understand how his wife could need thousands of francs for her clothes. So she borrowed 400,000 francs from Botot and tried to obtain from him, for the Bodin company, the contract to supply the Army of Italy. She was soon all the more free to love Hippolyte and run her business affairs as Bonaparte had to leave Paris on a tour of inspection in the North with a view to a possible invasion of England.

He was already becoming bored. The incense burned before him by the Parisians had not intoxicated him. The applause that greeted his arrival at a theatre embarrassed him. Soon disillusioned, he had said to Bourrienne: "In Paris no one remembers anything. If I remain doing nothing for long I am lost. One reputation quickly replaces another in this great Babylon. By the time they have seen me three times in the theatre they will no longer look at me, so I shall go only occasionally."

Josephine and his old friend from Brienne had tried to argue with him. "Was it not pleasant to see his fellow citizens come in crowds to meet him?"

"Bah! the people would come just as eagerly if I were going to the scaffold!"

On January 29 he had confided to Bourrienne, now his secretary: "Bourrienne, I do not want to stay here, there is nothing to do. They won't agree to anything. I can see that if I remain I shall soon decline. Everything wears away here, I have already no more fame, Europe is too small to provide enough. I shall have to go to the East, that is where the greatest glory comes from. But before that I want to make a tour of the coasts to see for myself what could be undertaken. I shall take you, Lannes and Sulkowsky. If the success of an attack on England seems doubtful to me, as I fear, the Army of England will become the Army of the East and I shall go to Egypt."

That was the first mention of the word "Egypt." But before convincing the Directory that London was on the banks of the Nile he had to make a show of inspecting the Army of England.

While, for ten days, in the bad weather of the month of Pluviôse her husband was to be seen from Boulogne to Antwerp, Josephine went with Charles to boxes at the theatre, walked with him in spite of the cold, spent intoxicating moments in the Rue Saint-Honoré, never for a moment forgetting to keep after Botot about the Bodin company. She begged, demanded and importuned Barras, to whom she wrote on February 21: "Good day, my excellent friend, I embrace you and love you tenderly." The former lover was asked to give a helping hand to the new.

On February 15 she was able to send her dear Hippolyte this announcement of victory: "27 (Pluviôse), 11 in the evening.—Botot, whom I saw this evening, has been charged by Barras to tell me that Citizen Bodin's business is developing well, that the Minister for War has told Barras of my interest in it and that Barras has taken the opportunity to urge him to bring it to a conclusion. Barras has had me notified to go and see him tomorrow morning."

She was continuing with her endeavors, but her husband arrived and Josephine was obliged to send a word to Botot: "Bonaparte arrived last night. Please, my dear Botot, express my regrets to Barras at not being able to dine with him. Tell him not to forget me. You know my position better than anyone, my dear Botot. Good-by, my best wishes."

Her position was difficult, indeed. What if Bonaparte learned of what she was doing? He had already scolded her on discovering that she had accepted "presents" from the speculators.

He had returned from Belgium in a good humor. On February 20, accompanied by Josephine, he was seen to laugh "heartily on several occasions" during the performance of the comedy entitled *The Bewigged Head.* Being for all practical purposes generalissimo of the French troops, he met the Directors every day in order to organize the expedition to Egypt. For the insane invasion of England was substituted the no less insane "war in the East." But the five "kings" who were governing France saw in these farfetched schemes only one thing: the removal of Bonaparte. France might be invaded by Europe from one day to the next, but that mattered little to the Directory as long as they saw the specter of military dictatorship receding.

Bonaparte himself thought only of his dream. "It seemed as though the earth burned his feet," said one of the Directors, bewildered. He had a fever—as did his wife, who had caught a chill—and kept to his bed, but asked Barras to come to see him "for one minute one evening." The Director had obeyed, and had promised to help him get away as many men as possible.

And while Bonaparte finally obtained a free hand to organize what coolheaded people called his suicide—dragging 45,000 men to the ends of the earth to harm England—Josephine too was able to announce a victory. Louis Bodin had got the longed-for contract. She was to share in the profits, 1,500,000 francs being divided between her, Barras and Schirer, the Minister for War—7,500,000 present-day francs. Charles would be able to resign as a captain and devote himself to business. For the moment he was the indispensable financial intermediary between his mistress and the Bodins. There was much for him to do, from the bribes to be paid to the Minister for War to the letters of recommendation to be got from Barras. And Josephine's love letters to Hippolyte assumed a half-loving, half-business style.

"I have just written to the Minister for War to tell him that I could not see him today as I am going into the country, but I shall go tomorrow to hand him a *packet* which has been given to me for him. I also wrote to Barras and begged him to hand the *letters he promised me* to the bearer of my note. I am awaiting his reply. I am going into the country, my dear Hippolyte. I shall be back at five and at half past five or six I shall go to Bodins' to meet you."

But now a drama was to begin.

Act One: Louise Compoint enters. Napoleon was to relate this on St. Helena when he had preserved no illusions about the faithfulness of "incomparable Josephine":

"On my return from Italy a lady's maid Josephine had dismissed, who had disapproved of her sleeping with Junot, wanted revenge. She told me that a young adjutant from the General Staff, Charles— a little whores' delight you probably saw in Italy—followed Josephine about, slept in the same inns and traveled in her coach. I could have done without this information."

When Louise left the stage, Bonaparte questioned Josephine about her information.

"Tell the truth. There's no great harm in it and after all one can sleep in the same inn and travel together without . . ."

"No, it's not true."

She wept, which disarmed her husband and enabled Josephine to complain to her lover.

"Yes, my Hippolyte, my existence is a perpetual torment! Only you can restore my happiness. Tell me that you love me and me alone. I shall be the happiest of women."

But business could not wait. "Send me 50,000 through Blondin" (one of the servants of the Bonaparte household). "Farewell, I send you a thousand tender kisses. Always thine."

On March 16 Charles left the army and was now able to remain at home.

Act Two: March 21: Bonaparte burst into his wife's boudoir. He had finally learned everything, or nearly everything, from his brother Joseph.

"Do you know Citizen Bodin with whom Captain Charles lodges?"

Bonaparte was well informed. He knew that it was his wife who

had procured for Bodin the contract for supplying the Army of
Italy. He mentioned that Charles lodged at 100 Faubourg Saint-
Honoré. Josephine denied everything, of course.

"But you go there every day. You have no need to make use of
such means."

At once her tears gushed out. "I am the most unfortunate of
women and the unhappiest. I know nothing about what you are
telling me. . . . If you want to divorce me you have only to say
so."

The amorous Josephine cared nothing for the fame of the victor
of Arcole, the conqueror of Italy. And in describing the scene to her
lover (in a letter discovered only a few years ago by Louis Hastier)
Josephine added, speaking of her husband and his brother, "the
Bonapartes":

> Yes, my Hippolyte, *they* have all my hatred, you alone have my tender-
> ness, my love. They must know how I loathe them from the terrible state
> I have been in for several days. They see my regrets and despair at being
> deprived of seeing you as often as I wish. Hippolyte, I shall kill myself.
> Yes, I want to put an end [to a life] which will henceforth be a burden
> if it cannot be devoted to you. Alas! what have I ever done to those
> monsters? But whatever they do I shall never be the victim of their
> atrocities. Please tell Bodin to say that he does not know me, that it was
> not through me that he got the contract for the Army of Italy. He must
> tell the porter at No. 100 that if anyone asks him if Bodin lives there he
> is to say that he does not know him. Bodin is not to make use of the let-
> ters I gave him for Italy until some time after his arrival in that country
> and when he needs them. Ah! although they torment me they will never
> detach me from my Hippolyte. My last sigh will be for him.
> I shall do everything possible to see you during the day. If I cannot,
> I shall go to Bodin's this evening and tomorrow morning I shall send
> Blondin to you to make an appointment to meet you in the Mousseaus'
> garden. Farewell, my Hippolyte, a thousand burning kisses, as burning
> and loving as my heart.
> Alas! what have I ever done to those monsters?

What had she done? Poor, unthinking Josephine! She was a
woman—delightfully and irritatingly so—and, with the help of
tears, she would manage, once again, to make Bonaparte believe
that everything Louise and Joseph had recounted was sheer calumny—at least where her marriage was concerned. But, for all that,
tragedy had entered the Rue Chantereine. "My sister-in-law nearly

died of grief," Pauline was to say. "For myself I consoled my
brother, who was very unhappy."

Hippolyte was afraid of being arrested. His resignation was not
due to be officially accepted until March 30. For those ten days he
was still under the jurisdiction of the army, and hence of the
husband. Yet Bonaparte considered it unworthy of himself to take
such a revenge. Charles was not disturbed and the contract with the
Bodin company remained valid.

It would seem that on thinking the situation over Josephine
had been frightened. There were drawbacks in becoming Mme.
Charles after being Mme. Bonaparte. Once divorced she would
undoubtedly lose her influence and Hippolyte's affairs would be
much less successful. She would not even be able to keep the house
she was so fond of. And in fact on March 26, Bonaparte, doubtless
influenced by the word "divorce" uttered by his unfaithful wife,
bought the house in the Rue Chantereine from Julie Talma. Josephine was no longer in her own home.

She pulled herself together and in order to make up with Bonaparte offered to go with him to Egypt. Or rather—for she was clever
enough to do it—she made her husband suggest taking her. No
doubt Josephine hoped that at the last moment a way would be
found for her not to be separated for so long from Hippolyte and
their kisses "as burning and loving" as her heart.

Before leaving, M. and Mme. Bonaparte, like a good married
couple, discussed the purchase of a country house near Paris. They
visited that charming Malmaison, belonging to M. Lecoulteux, who
had been looking for a buyer for two years. Like many who have
experienced a "shock," Bonaparte was seeking the indispensable
haven, but he had no time to deal with the matter. They would see
about it later. Perhaps Josephine would return before her husband
did. Or perhaps the Egyptian campaign would be shorter than was
thought. As the new head of the army said to Bourrienne, they
would either both be back in a few months or he would not return
for six years.

On April 29 Josephine and her husband, together with the aide-de-
camp Lavallette, went to Mme. Campan's in Saint-Germain to see
Hortense and Caroline. At first the two girls had not got on well
together.

"I hoped very much to become friendly with Caroline Bonaparte, who was almost my age and whose character I was sure would suit mine," Hortense related. "If there was no intimacy between us it was the General's fault. He too frequently proposed me to his sister as a model and made too much of my weak talents to her. But what most distressed her was the scheme to send her to Mme. Campan's with me. I tried in vain to persuade her that nothing could be more agreeable than life at Saint-Germain, that our pleasures there were just as good as those of Paris. I had difficulty in convincing her. Caroline already knew the world and enjoyed it. In the end, despite her tears, she had to obey the General. I took a great deal of trouble to make her first arrival bearable. I explained her backwardness in study by ascribing it to her long voyages. I made the most of what she did know. I touched up her drawings so that she would receive a prize. But for all that I never won her heart. Her estrangement from me even led her to unjust complaints. She accused me to the General of constantly shining at her expense and of being the cause of little humiliations to which our companions subjected her. Hurt by conduct I knew I had not deserved, I wanted to have it out with her. Her frankness disarmed me; she acknowledged she was wrong and disclosed to me that she loved Colonel Murat and had been trying every means to get back to Paris. I was touched by her confidence and from that moment we were once more united."

One may imagine the excitement at the school that morning. Laughter and shouts on every floor, while all the girls crowded to the windows to see the arrival of the conqueror of Italy. Only Emilie, daughter of François de Beauharnais and Hortense's cousin, was sulky. The man who had become her uncle by marriage, so to speak, had decided to marry her to one of his aides-de-camp, Antoine Lavallette. And her heart beat for Louis Bonaparte, the General's brother. But there could be no question of disputing the great man's decisions. On seeing her betrothed Emilie was astounded—a pink baby face, tiny eyes and a nose the size of a pea. He seemed already to have developed a potbelly, which was supported by two little legs. But he touched her by saying, once they were left alone together, "Mademoiselle, I have only my sword and the General's favor and in two weeks I shall be leaving you for Egypt. Open your heart to me. I feel inclined to love you with all my heart, but this is not enough. If this union is not to your liking, confide in me. I shall get myself sent away, you shall not be harassed and I shall keep your secret."

Josephine's niece lowered her eyes and for sole reply handed her fiancé the bouquet she was holding. They were married quietly, as Emilie's father was an émigré and her mother, who had divorced him, had married a dark-skinned mulatto. The few days she spent with her husband after the ceremony did not win Emilie over, far from it.

"Just imagine, Flavie," she wrote to a friend, "your poor friend with her heart irretrievably engaged in spite of itself to a master whom she did not know, of whose very name she was unaware a week ago, and whom she has not been able to judge, in spite of the appearances of a noble character, except from the impressions made by an exterior which a heart and eyes already occupied cannot find bearable. That is my position and I have to state that I think I should be less unhappy with anyone else whatever."

Later she was to be moved by Lavallette's qualities, his uprightness, his honesty and his nobility of sentiment. She was touched and forgot the short legs, and tiny nose and eyes. She was to see only the heart and mind of her husband and began to love him with all her heart and soul. As for him, he had loved Emilie from the moment that Hortense had brought her blushing companion to him in the garden at Saint-Germain, the prettiest of all Mme. Campan's boarders.

At four o'clock on the morning of May 4 Bonaparte entered his carriage with Josephine and Bourrienne. The day before he had explained to Arnault: "The Parisians shout but they would not act. If I mounted my horse no one would follow me. We shall leave tomorrow."

On May 6 they met Eugene, who was also taking part in the campaign, at the Auberge de Provence, Place Bellecour in Lyons. The next day they embarked on the Rhone, thus arriving in Aix before nightfall. Then after a long night journey—Bonaparte jumped on his horse, rode ahead of the carriage and shouted to the guards posted at the entrance to Toulon: "Je suis Général en Chef Bonaparte!"

A quarter of an hour later Mme. la Générale and her son halted in front of army headquarters. There were the army, the fleet, the savants, the whole of the future Empire, from Louis, one day to be Josephine's son-in-law and King of Holland, Murat, her brother-in-law and one day King of Naples, Eugene, one day to be Viceroy of

Italy, to Generals Berthier, Davout, Lannes, Marmont and Duroc, Kléber and Desaix.

Josephine announced that she was tired. A short stay at the waters would do her good. On the eve of the expedition she "reported sick." Moreover, it was announced that an English squadron was prowling about somewhere between Malta and Corsica. Josephine became very doleful. Must she come under enemy fire for the third time in her life? Bonaparte decided to leave his wife in France. She could take the waters and then come to join him. She wrote to her daughter:

"I have been in Toulon for five days. I was not tired by the journey but very upset at leaving you so quickly without being able to say good-by either to you or to my dear Caroline. But, my dear daughter, I am somewhat consoled by the hope of soon embracing you. Bonaparte does not want me to sail with him. He wants me to take the waters before undertaking the journey to Egypt. He will send for me in two months' time. So, my Hortense, I shall once more have the pleasure of pressing you to my heart and assuring you that you are well loved."

Josephine paid a visit to the *Orient* on which her husband, son and brother-in-law embarked on May 19 at six o'clock. And from the headquarters building which overlooked the harbor she watched the departure of the squadron and waved her handkerchief while the guns roared and the bands played.

"He has gone at last," Barras noted. "The sword moved farther off."

As for Josephine, she was in tears. She could, to be sure, now meet Hippolyte again and she had avoided a long exile from Paris. But these thoughts comforted her less than usual. Was she beginning to love her husband? In any case she seemed now to realize what she would lose in being separated from him. She was now undoubtedly more "attached" to him. And henceforth she would find herself a target for the hatred of Lucien and, more particularly, of Joseph, charged by his brother to give her 40,000 francs a year—200,000 present-day francs. That was a respectable amount for the wife of a commanding general, but hardly enough when one had debts and so many needs. Josephine winced at the thought of having to depend on her brothers-in-law. Therefore, as he had promised, Bonaparte wrote to his brother on May 29: "If my wife is in your vicinity, please treat her with consideration."

Josephine stayed in Toulon for another week in order to have news from the dispatch vessel *Chasseur,* which had joined the *Orient* off the Cape of Corsica on May 23 and returned to Toulon the same day. After a few days in M. Filhe's house at Hyères Josephine set out again for Plombières. She did not forget her business dealings with the Bodin company and from Lyons wrote to her dear Barras on June 10 asking his attention to certain problems.

Josephine then arrived at Plombières, with Citizeness Cambis and Mme. de Krény, now spoken of as "dear little one." She lodged just opposite the Hôtel des Dames, in the Pension Martinet, "a very respectable house," in which "the husband and wife are just like [Ovid's] Philemon and Baucis." We have no idea whether Charles had been with her since Lyons or would join her later. In any case, Josephine now spoke differently of her husband, as witness this letter to Barras: "I wrote to you the day before yesterday, my dear Barras. I am afraid my letter did not reach you, as I was not aware of the regulation that it should be franked. I asked you, my dear Barras, to tell me news of you often and to pass on immediately any news of Bonaparte. I need it. I am so distressed at being parted from him that I am overwhelmingly sad. Moreover, his brother, with whom he keeps up a correspondence, is so horrible to me that I am always uneasy when away from Bonaparte. I know he said to one of his friends, who repeated it to me, that he would never be easy until he had made a breach between me and my husband. He is a vile, abominable creature whom you will get to know someday."

Hoping Barras would come to join her, she went on: "I do wish, my dear Barras, that the waters of Plombières would be prescribed for you and that you would decide to take them. It would really be kind of you to be ill just to please me."

Remembering her husband's anger during the Italian campaign at her laziness in writing, she strongly enjoined Barras to forward the letters the government might receive from Bonaparte in Egypt and to send hers to her husband. "You know him and you know how annoyed with me he would be if he had no news of me. The last letter he sent me was very affectionate and very tender. He tells me to join him quickly, as he cannot live far from me. So I am hurrying up with the cure prescribed for me so that I may quickly join Bonaparte, whom I love in spite of his little faults."

Josephine had a way of reducing her husband and his epic to engaging proportions.

She followed her cure conscientiously. Each day she went to the Capuchin spring, from which emerges the effervescent water which for centuries has had the reputation of making sterile women fruitful.

When not drinking the waters Josephine made excursions to the Jacquot farm, to Moulin-Joli, to La Feuillée, the leafy gallery overlooking the beautiful Val d'Ajol. She received, paid visits, was invited by the Director Reubell, a colleague of Barras who was also taking the waters, though in a military fashion, his safety being watched over by two battalions of infantry and sixty dragoons.

On June 20—Bonaparte had just left Malta—Josephine was hemming kerchiefs, which were so useful for protecting her hair from the steam when she entered the Capuchin baths. She was chatting with General Colle and Citizen Latour when Adrienne de Cambis, who was looking into the street from the balcony, called to Mme. Bonaparte that a very pretty dog was passing in the street. Josephine, who adored dogs, hurried to the balcony. The General and Latour followed—and the accident happened. The balcony broke under their weight and the four of them fell fifteen feet. The men landed on their feet, the two women in a sitting position. Josephine, badly bruised, uttered terrible cries. She hurt all over. The spa doctor, Martinet, immediately bled "the wife of the young hero." After this fashionable remedy he made her drink a "tealike infusion of arnica" and then plunged the still sobbing Josephine into a hot bath.

"I had administered an enema before the bath," he reported, "and she passed it satisfactorily and urinated. I then applied leeches to the parts which had hit the pavement and were the most bruised. . . ." Aided by all the doctors in Plombières, he put compresses on his client's charming seat and "on top, hot, soothing remedies," not omitting "boiled potatoes." To end his bulletin he added proudly that "the stomach was kept free by enemas." This therapy was later to earn him a scholarship for his son and a pension for his daughter.

In any case, Josephine seems to have suffered dreadfully, even more, perhaps, than Citizeness Cambis, who had a broken thigh. Twelve days after the accident Mme. Bonaparte wrote to Barras: "I take advantage, my dear Barras, of the first return of calm I have experienced since my fall to thank you, my friend, for the interest you have shown and the charming letter I had from you. It soothed my wounds by bringing me fresh proof of your friendship. I am taking a long time to recover from my fall, my dear Barras, I cannot walk yet. I have dreadful pains in my back and abdomen. I am made to take baths every day. They are waiting until I am a little stronger to make me take douches, the only thing, according to the doctors, that will cure me. Meanwhile I suffer terribly."

Yet, if Dr. Martinet's letter to Barras four days earlier is to be believed, Josephine was getting better. "Citizen Director, today (June 28) there is good news of our interesting and good patient. There is still some pain in the lumbar region, but that does not prevent the patient's sleeping and having an appetite. I hope that tomorrow she will go out for a walk."

Happily the "interesting and good patient" was somewhat diverted by the presence of a valet-hairdresser found in the town, whom she was to take with her when she was able to leave Plombières. His name was Carrat and he was such a gifted talker that he made Josephine smile and young Hortense, whom Euphémie had fetched from Saint-Germain, laugh until she cried.

Battalion Commander Lahorie had installed himself at Josephine's bedside, having asked leave "to care for" the woman who had been the wife of his friend Beauharnais. Josephine at once wrote to Barras: "It would be very pleasant for me, my dear Barras, to repay so much attention by getting the rank of adjutant general for him." It was unfortunate for Josephine that Barras did not think it right to grant this rank to one who had made it his duty, as he wrote, "to take an interest" in Josephine's injuries. This "ingratitude" was to throw Lahorie into the arms of the opposition, and was the reason that in 1812 he followed General Malet, who asked his help in overthrowing the French Empire. This adventure then led to his being shot at Grenelle.

Josephine was inherently kind. She begged favors as easily as she breathed. From Plombières she wrote to Barras recommending a fellow patient, General Beurnonville, who was "going to Paris to ask you to take an interest in him and prevent an injustice which is being planned against him." She warmly backed up Rémusat's request to "obtain the post of deputy in charge of the first division at the War Office," as he "deserves promotion from every point of view, having worked in the administration for a long time." Even the chief of police of Plombières was supported by her when he had recourse to Citizeness Bonaparte's benevolence.

In every letter she complained of her health. "I have received a charming letter from Bonaparte," she told Barras. "He tells me he cannot live without me and that I am to go and embark at Naples. I wish my health allowed me to leave at once, but I can set no date for my recovery. I can neither stand nor sit for ten minutes at a time without feeling terrible pains in my back and abdomen. I do nothing but weep, the doctors assure me that I shall be better in a month. If I find no relief in a fortnight I shall return to Paris. My dear Barras, you have no idea how much I suffer!"

Finally she was better and set out for home. At the theatre in Nancy she was offered a crown of laurels, which she refused. But at the end of the play, *Le Pari*, she accepted the olive branch held out to her while on the stage verses praising Bonaparte were sung.

Back in Paris, and almost cured, she "received" Mme. de Vaisme, Mme. Visconti, Mme. de Chauvelin, Mme. de Lameth, Mme. de Castellane, Mme. de Luçay and, of course, Mme. de Kreny and Mme. Hamelin. Among the men were writers and poets, such as Andrieux, Lebrun—Pindar—who went around with his pockets stuffed with verses which he read out to everyone. Chevalier Auguste de Déis, the author of patriotic songs, also found his way to the Rue Chantereine, as did Deschamps, author of an opera, *The Bards*, who later became the Empress's secretary.

She received Desprès, a former friend of André Chénier and author of a Latin ode on "Snowballs." The gayest and most talented of the visitors was undoubtedly Désaugiers, "song personified," the author of delightful little comedies. There was also the witty, prolific Hoffmann, who in spite of a slight stammer was able to argue with astonishing skill. Sometimes Chénier's brother was to be seen—whose plays *Charles IX* and *Caius Gracchus* were very successful.

The serious, rather pompous Volney, who had written a book on Egypt and Syria which Bonaparte had taken with him, had accepted an invitation from Citizeness Bonaparte. He spoke Arabic, had lived in the Middle East, and his conversation was listened to respectfully in the Rue Chantereine. Another visitor was Lemercier, the author of tragedies; another who came was Arnault, formerly secretary to Louis XVI's brother, the Count of Provence (who would become Louis XVIII). He never ceased to admire his hostess's "equable temper," her "easygoing character" and "the kindness that shone in her eyes."

Bouilly, another frequent visitor to the Rue Chantereine, was also under the spell of Josephine's "natural grace." "There no longer existed," he wrote, "that tone of elegance and polite charm which I used to find in the society of 1788, but in gatherings at Josephine's one could still find some precious reminders of those perfect models of grace and breeding."

Meanwhile Bonaparte had made a successful landing at Alexandria and, having beaten the Mamelukes for the first time, had advanced on Cairo. On July 19 he was at Wardan—or Ouardan. Bourrienne, who was standing some way away, saw him talking to Berthier, his aide-de-camp Julien and, in particular, to Junot. Bonaparte looked even paler than usual. There was even, Bourrienne observed, "something convulsive in his face and wild in his look." He struck his head several times. His secretary had never seen him "so displeased, so preoccupied." Bonaparte came towards him "with a disturbed countenance" and said "in a broken voice" and a "sharp, stern tone": "You are not devoted to me. If you were you would have told me everything I have just learned from Junot, who is a true friend. Josephine! . . . and I am 600 leagues away . . . you should have told me! Josephine! . . . to have deceived me thus! . . . she! . . . woe to them! . . . I shall wipe out that race of fair-haired whippersnappers. As for her, divorce, yes, divorce, a glaring public divorce! I must write! I know all! . . . It is your fault, you should have told me!"

He knew everything and he suffered horribly. Gradually he calmed down, kept his head and, two days later, won the battle of the Pyramids. But no smile lit his features. He was sad, terribly sad, even when making his entry in Cairo on July 24.

That evening Eugene wrote to his mother from his tent at Gizeh: "My dear mamma, I have so much to tell you that I do not know how to begin. For the last five days Bonaparte has appeared very sad and it is the result of a conversation he had with Julien, Junot and even Berthier. He has been even more greatly affected than I thought by this talk. From everything I can hear [it seems that] Charles was in your carriage until three stages from Paris, that you saw him in Paris, that you went to the Théâtre des Italiens with him in the fourth-tier boxes, that he gave you your little dog, and that even at this moment he is with you—these scraps are all I was able to hear. You may well understand, mamma, that I do not believe it, but what is certain is that the General is very upset. Yet his friendship for me increases. By his actions he seems to be saying that children are not responsible for their mothers' faults, but your son likes to think that all this gossip has been invented by your enemies. I hope that when you come all will be forgotten."

The next day Bonaparte wrote to Joseph from Elfi-Bey's house in Cairo to tell him that he had "much domestic grief, for the veil has been horribly torn asunder." And he sighed: "It is very sad to have for the same person in the same heart all kinds of feelings."

Hoping that he might soon return to France—but in the following month the disaster to the fleet at Aboukir was to keep him a prisoner in the land he had conquered—Bonaparte spoke of his misogyny to his brother: "Arrange for me to have a country house when I get back, either near Paris or in Burgundy. I intend to shut myself up there for the winter. I am tired of human nature. I need solitude and isolation. I am weary of greatness. My feelings are dried up. Glory is insipid. At twenty-nine I have exhausted everything and all that remains is to become completely self-centered. I intend to stay in my house. I shall never give it to anyone."

The two letters, from Eugene and Bonaparte, together with all the mail from the Army of the East, were intercepted by Nelson. Having been sent to London, they were, somewhat tastelessly, published in English and French by the English government, in the *Morning Chronicle* on November 24.

The next month some of the captured letters were reproduced in Paris, but at Barras's request Bonaparte's letter to his brother and Eugene's to his mother were suppressed. Josephine may not have seen the issue of the *Morning Chronicle* but had evidently been made acquainted with the facts by Barras. One can imagine her anxiety. The loss of the fleet prevented all communication with Egypt and the "faithless wife" could not correspond with her husband. Perhaps she hoped to win him over again once she was face to face with him, and to get him to admit, as on the last occasion, that everything was a base calumny. Perhaps she thought that matters would be cleared up when Louis returned from Egypt on March 11, 1799. She had confirmation from him of her misfortune, and yet her brother-in-law brought a letter for Joseph, a letter several months old, in which Bonaparte enjoined him: "Be attentive to my wife. Go and see her sometimes, I am asking Louis to give her some good advice." But the clan refused to see Josephine and did not accept her invitations. "Advice" as regards Charles would have been opportune, for the lovers had quarreled, although only temporarily at this time. Josephine seems, from some fancy for the past, to have resumed her affair with Barras. On her return from Plombières she had written to him: "I came home during the night, my dear Barras. My first care was to send to your house for news of you. . . . Permit me to come and see you this evening at nine. Give orders for no one to be allowed in. Farewell. Your friend."

As often as she saw Barras she pestered him. First of all, there was a scheme to marry Hortense to Jean Jacques Reubell, battalion commander and son of the Director, who had seen the girl at Plombières. Barras was entrusted with arranging interviews but the scheme came to nothing, as the Director did not consider the match good enough for his son. This refusal made it possible for Hortense one day to become Queen of Holland.

And then, and above all, there was business. Josephine interceded with her former lover on behalf of the Lagrange company and, in particular, the Bodin company, which had acquired a very bad reputation. There was a matter of cattle requisitioned but not paid for which was somewhat troublesome. Bodin was arrested and then freed, thanks to Barras's secretary Botot, but the company was hard hit and among the Director's papers can be found letters like the following, signed by Josephine: "It is impossible for it to go on unless someone comes out in defense of it. It is not looking for a new contract but the fulfillment of the existing one. . . . I count on your good offices which the company has never more urgently needed."

Slanders about Josephine were repeated to the Director and she defended herself like an insulted mistress: "Put me face to face with that woman and you will learn the truth. You will see, my dear Barras, that I have never stopped loving you and respecting you and that I should die of grief if I had compromised you for a moment. I want to talk to you for an instant tomorrow. Let me know if I can come at five or half past. I cannot live with the thought that you could for one moment doubt my attachment to you, it will last as long as I do."

And Charles? Had he got wind of something? Was he jealous of Barras? He too played the wounded lover and sent Josephine a cutting letter calling her every name a deceived lover could think of. Josephine sent the letter to her friend and confidante Mme. de Krény, and added: "My dear little girl, please read the letter I have just received and have the person come to your house so that you can find out what can have been the motives for such a letter. I find it so uncalled for and so little deserved that I am not taking the trouble to answer it and, as I have no reason to reproach myself, I clearly see that a rupture is being aimed at. The person has wanted one for a long time but should employ more straightforward, less hypocritical methods."

To Charles, after a few lines on business, she wrote: "Please grant me a few moments to speak to you of an object in which I am interested. You can be assured, after this interview, which will be the last, of being no longer tormented either by my letters or by my presence. An honest woman who has been deceived retires without a word."

The "honest woman" knew as well how to forgive as how to implore forgiveness and a reconciliation with Hippolyte took place soon after Louis's return.

On April 21 Josephine bought Malmaison for 325,000 francs—her home, the house whose name cannot be uttered without evoking her and where we shall so often follow her steps. Four hundred acres of land, vines producing a sourish but attractive wine, a château flanked by two slate-roofed pavilions. The deed of sale mentions a sum of only 225,000, thus reducing the transfer charges by nearly 10,000 francs. The importance of this was only relative, since Joseph had taken advantage of Bonaparte's letter to stop paying Josephine's allowance. So she did not even have the 15,000 francs needed to enable her to take possession of her estate. They were lent by the steward, Jean L'Huillier, on condition that he keep his post.

Hippolyte, now reconciled, was soon at home there. He appeared so much as one of the family that a neighbor made a mistake: "She can be seen from the road and, on moonlit evenings, when in her white dress and veil she leans on the arm of her son [sic], who is in black or blue, the effect is almost eerie: they look like two ghosts."

Gohier, the President of the Directory (who had married his cook), lectured her, but Josephine refused to break a tie "which nevertheless seemed to be approaching its end."

"Well, then, get a divorce," Gohier advised. "You tell me you and

M. Charles are merely friends, but if this friendship is so exclusive that it makes you fly in the face of conventions, I shall say the same as if you were in love: Divorce, because friendship so destructive of all other feelings will take precedence over everything with you. Take my word, all this will bring you trouble."

She often received Gohier at Malmaison and flirted with him, which exhilarated him. Things were not going well with Barras, but even worse with Charles. She was sure Hippolyte was deceiving her. The rupture of which Josephine had spoken to Mme. de Krény soon appeared definitive, and their reconciliation had lasted only for the spring. Josephine was very depressed. "Since I have been living in the country," she wrote to Barras, "I have become such a savage that the great world scares me. Besides I am so unhappy that I do not care to be an object of pity to others. You, my dear Barras, who love your friends even when they are unhappy, even you I shall visit only for yourself and when you can see me alone. Be kind enough to tell me on what day you can give me lunch. I shall come from Malmaison expressly for that and I shall be with you at nine in the morning. I want to talk to you, ask your advice. You owe it to the wife of Bonaparte and to her friendship for you."

In asking for advice, Josephine may have learned that her husband was being seen about with beautiful Pauline Bellisle (Mme. Fourès) whom his soldiers called "Bonaparte's Cleopatra" and his officers "Bellilotte." Or she may have known that he had fallen really in love with the young dressmaker of Carcassonne who for love of her husband had dressed as a soldier and followed him to Egypt with the army.

Bonaparte, in fact, knew of the publication by the English of the letter to Joseph and Eugene's letter to his mother. All Europe knew he was a deceived and ridiculed husband. All Europe had learned of his intention to divorce. There could be no question of forgiving his wife, so he carried on a blatant liaison and made sure that everyone knew he was not an inconsolable husband. He played his part so well that the English knew all about it. When they intercepted Fourès, his mistress's husband, who had been sent to the Directory with dispatches so that the General could have free rein, they hastened to disembark him on the shores of Egypt and smilingly wish him good luck.

Bonaparte succeeded in getting the Fourès pair to divorce and even offered to marry his mistress if she gave him a child. For Bonaparte complained: "The little fool can't have one!"

"My goodness, it's not my fault!" she replied, laughing.

Bellilotte was treated as "queen of the East" and many people thought she was about to succeed Josephine. But Bonaparte did not go so far as to take his sultana with him when—on learning of the loss of Italy and the threat to France's borders—he decided to leave the army and return to France in the little frigate *Muiron*.

"I might be taken by the English," he said to Cleopatra, "and you must have a care for my fame. What would they not say if they found a woman on board?"

But he had nonetheless decided not even to see the unfaithful Josephine again. Josephine herself did not really grasp the seriousness of the situation and in her heedlessness wrote this postscript to a letter from Hortense to her brother: "I am waiting for the moment that will reunite me with all I love. I shall have nothing left to wish for, particularly if I find Bonaparte as he was when he left me and as he ought always to have been for me. Then, my dear Eugene, [will be forgotten] all I have suffered from your absence and from his."

This letter is dated October 4. Two days earlier Bonaparte had been at Ajaccio; two days later he was to set sail for France.

Josephine was dining in the Luxembourg Palace with Gohier when a telegraphic dispatch dated October 9 was brought: Bonaparte had landed at Fréjus.

Josephine rose: "President," she said, "do not fear that Bonaparte is coming with designs fatal to liberty. But you must work together to prevent any wretches capturing it. I shall go to meet him. It is important for me not to be forestalled by his brothers, who have always detested me."

With Hortense she hurried to a carriage and went to meet her husband by the Burgundy road. Her heart beat fast as she scanned each turning in the way, wondering if her treachery would be forgiven, if her charm could still work. But she was now thirty-seven. On returning from Plombières Hortense had come close to getting married and Josephine could almost be a grandmother. She could not think what she would do if Bonaparte insisted on a divorce. She owed a million francs to tradesmen, and Malmaison was not paid for. The house in the Rue de la Victoire was not hers. Things were going badly with Charles, whom she saw only occasionally when business required it. Moreover, Barras might no longer receive her once she was nobody.

She passed Sens, then Joigny, Auxerre, Chalon and Mâcon. "In each town," Hortense related, "in each village, triumphal arches had been raised. When we stopped to change horses the people crowded round our carriage and asked us if it was really true that their *savir* was coming, for all France was then giving him that name."

As Josephine drew nearer Lyons she reassured herself. If she could speak to him first she was saved. At Lyons, on October 12, she learned the disaster: Bonaparte had passed through Lyons the day before and had taken the Bourbonnais road through Cosne, Nevers and Moulins. Everything seemed to crumble around her. Josephine closed her eyes. As in a nightmare she could see Joseph already speaking to his brother. She could hear the two men arranging the forthcoming divorce.

Bonaparte arrived in Paris on October 16 at six in the morning and found the house empty. Of course he could swear she had gone off with Charles.

"The warriors of Egypt," he exclaimed, "are like those of the Siege of Troy. Their wives have been equally faithful."

His anger was "terrible and deep." Before leaving Egypt he had written to Joseph: "My friend, I intend to return to France soon. I received your letter through Tunis. Start proceedings so that my divorce will be prepared on my arrival. I am sending you my proxy. My resolve is irrevocable. I know you will approve. . . . I am sometimes very unhappy. But I am twenty-nine. Forgetfulness will come."

Joseph had not received this letter and had not begun proceedings. But matters could be hastened. Undoubtedly Eugene had tried to calm his stepfather, pointing out that the General could make no decision before seeing his wife. The old Marquis de Beauharnais himself—he was over eighty-five—came from his new house in Saint-Germain and begged Bonaparte not to "bring despair down on his white hairs." "Whatever her wrongs, forget them."

But the whole clan, with Mme. Letizia at their head, was on the watch. Joseph never stopped blackening Josephine. He collected all the gossip and constantly talked to his brother of Charles, the lover who had made fun of him—of him, the man revered by all the French. He mentioned the debts, "Rose's" past, the shady affairs into which she had dragged his name. Bonaparte's mind was made up. He swore to divorce her, but his eyes filled with tears.

The supplier to the Army of Italy, a "thickset man with the face of a white Negro" called Collot, who had frequently done the General a service, entered his office. He saw the General angrily poking at the fire.

"So you want to leave your wife, do you?" exclaimed the financier.

In fact all Paris was talking of nothing but the divorce. Still holding the tongs, Bonaparte said, "Doesn't she deserve it?"

"I don't know, but is this the moment to bother about it? Think of France. Her eyes are fixed on you. She expects to see your every moment devoted to her salvation. If she sees that you are occupied with domestic quarrels your grandeur disappears and in her eyes you are nothing but a husband out of Molière. Leave your wife's wrongs and start by raising up the state—"

"No!" Bonaparte interrupted violently. "She shall never set foot in my house again. I don't care what they say! They'll gossip for a day or two and on the third no one will speak of it again. Among all the press of events what importance has the breaking of a marriage? Mine will not be noticed. . . . My wife will go to Malmaison. I shall stay here. The public knows enough not to be mistaken about the reasons for her going away."

Collot still tried to oppose him.

"So much violence convinces me you are still in love with her. She will appear, exculpate herself, you will pardon her and you will be calmer."

His hands clenched on his chest, Bonaparte cried: "Me? Forgive her? Never, do you hear? Never!"

9. Brumaire, or the Entry into History

Josephine's carriage had halted in front of the gateway adorned "with military emblems" which led through a covered passage to the little house in the Rue de la Victoire. It was eleven in the evening. She knocked.

The porter came down from his room above the gateway. He stammered out that the General had forbidden him to open the door to Madame. Her possessions had been stored in the lodge. Josephine felt the tears come to her eyes, but she shrugged her shoulders and forced her way in. In the little hall hung with ticking and adorned with sculptured and painted trophies she found Agathe, the lady's maid who had replaced Louise Compoint and who was utterly devoted to Josephine. She informed her that the General had shut himself up in his bedroom. Leaving Hortense downstairs, Josephine mounted the spiral staircase leading into the drawing room. She stopped in front of the door and knocked timidly.

"It is I!"

There was silence. Then she began to speak. She recalled their memories, their love. For that evening she was sincere and, seeing the gulf opening before her feet, believed she loved him. It was impossible, she said, that he could refuse to see her, that he was unwilling to hear her explanations, that he should be so inexorable when she wished to exonerate herself from the slander that once again had been directed at her. She would tell him everything, explain everything.

Bonaparte, perhaps with his head under the pillow in order not to hear her, would not reply. He knew that if he were to open the door to her his resolutions would vanish. He could not bear her tears. For now she was weeping behind that hopelessly shut door. He could feel she was on her knees. Suddenly he heard her, still sobbing, retire and slowly go down the stairs. Perhaps she had understood.

Of course he still loved her, but in a very different fashion from his feelings during the Italian epic. Now he knew the joys of power, the intoxication of glory. There was no question of isolating himself in the country, as he had written to Joseph. He knew that tomorrow he would sweep away the immoral government of profiteers and take the destiny of France, this dying France, into his own hands. All the way from Fréjus he had been acclaimed and applauded by everyone, except the highway robbers, who had pillaged his luggage as though he had been any other traveler.

No one believed in anything any more. The workers in the faubourgs were turning away from politics. The Parisians resignedly allowed the successive royalist or Jacobin conspiracies to fight over a bloodless France. Nothing, they thought, could be worse than the present situation. The streets of Paris reflected both the poverty of the inhabitants and the luxury of the merchants, tradesmen and their mistresses who were living off the body of the dying Republic. A passer-by, on his way from the Odéon to the Louvre, had met only eight cabs and one private carriage. At the city gates could be seen decaying coaches drawn by old hacks harnessed with ropes. On the other hand, in front of the pleasure garden Tivoli or Idalie there was a press of phaetons, *wiskeys, dulcinés* and *bobgheis* all shining with gold and precious stones.

When Bonaparte had reappeared, even in his curious half-civilian, half-Oriental dress—tall hat, green overcoat and Turkish scimitar—there had been a sigh of relief. A coup d'état seemed inevitable, and one led by him. There could be no question of taking power legally, or asking for a revision of the Constitution.

The procedure envisaged in the law would have required nine years. Action must be speedy. France must awake and find her soul.

When, two days earlier, he had entered the Luxembourg escorted by a delirious crowd, the old soldiers of the Guard had wept with joy.

But wasn't there the risk, if he appeared as a flouted husband, that the legend already beginning to envelop him would be tarnished? Might not divorce bring about a worse scandal and an official separation do him even more harm? Cuckoldry did not fit the people's image of the hero of Italy. In a word, if he were to be publicly separated from Josephine, would he become that sword Sieyès was seeking? Might not Josephine even be able to help him in his schemes and to create in Paris, by her charm, the kind of Court she had managed to form in Italy at Montebello or the Serbelloni palace? But there was also the memory of Hippolyte Charles, that whippersnapper. Repulsion, indignation and exasperation filled his mind.

There were sounds in the house. Eugene had come down from his attic room to find his mother sobbing in Hortense's arms at the foot of the stairs. Everything was over for her. What would become of her, particularly as her love for Hippolyte, that love "as burning as her heart" was dead? And the realization of her age was constantly present.

Suddenly Josephine mounted the stairs again with her two children. A few moments later Eugene and Hortense called, wept and begged together before the bedroom door. Josephine implored Bonaparte to pardon her. The two children joined in with their prayers and sobs.

We do not know how long the scene lasted. Finally Napoleon opened the door. He seemed very distressed and he, too, was weeping. It is probable that when they saw Bonaparte, deeply moved, take their mother in his arms Hortense and Eugene retired, leaving them to have it out together.

One thing is certain. When Lucien came to see his brother next morning Bonaparte summoned him into the bedroom. There he found the husband and wife in the twin beds which had been brought close by the spring. Josephine was smiling in modest triumph and pouting in her subtle Creole way. She had promised not to see Charles again which, as so many of her interests were at stake, did not prevent her later doing business with him and perhaps even occasionally tasting the forbidden fruit in his company.

For the moment her heart still beat at the thought of what she might have lost. Gradually a twofold feeling for her husband was to develop and stand in place of love. First, under the influence of those about her, she began to feel a certain admiration for Bonaparte, without perhaps realizing that she was the wife of the greatest genius in history. Also, and above all, she would be grateful to him when she saw what he was to make of her: a little Creole of easy virtue, a spurious vicomtesse, burdened with debts, who had passed through many hands, transformed by him into a "consuless," then into an empress and a queen.

Besides, it was not until these last days of Vendémiaire and the beginning of Brumaire, not until those nineteen days, that she was to wake up to the situation and begin to think that Bonaparte might rise to a higher position than her first husband (the President of the Assembly) or her former lover Barras (President of the Directory). She was to back him up and help him with all her might to capture France, which was asking nothing better than to be seized.

To start with, there was Gohier.

"I do not know if he is a partisan of mine," Napoleon was to say later, "but he used to pay court to my wife."

This plump quinquagenarian grew lively at the very sight of a pretty woman. He kept the list of his successes as carefully up to date as the list of victims he used to draw up when he was Minister of Justice during the Terror.

Preening himself, he greeted Josephine and Bonaparte, who went to dine at the Luxembourg on October 22, two days after their reconciliation. While observing the other guests Josephine noticed the unfrocked priest, the ex-Abbé Sieyès, then a Director.

"What have you done?" she murmured to her suitor. "Sieyès is the man Bonaparte most detests. He is his bête noire."

Gohier may have had Bonaparte's bust on his chimneypiece, possibly from love of Josephine, but though he was at this time President of the Directory he understood nothing. The "national mess," as people called it, did not bother him. The situation did not strike him as intolerable and the noxious smells arising from the entrails of the regime did not trouble him. Even if it had been otherwise he would have replied that, without Sieyès, nothing could be done. It was, in fact, indispensable to organize the coup d'état from within and consequently to have on the spot—that is, among those governing—one or two accomplices, or rather one or two leaders. The not very shrewd Gohier could follow, but not take command. It was the same with Roger-Ducos. Barras, the greatest profiteer, the greediest, the most shameful, had served too long, particularly himself, and was no longer usable though believing himself indispensable. The Jacobin General Moulin never spoke a word to anyone, and everyone knew that he owed his rank solely to politics.

So Sieyès was the man of the moment. He had, moreover, appointed himself and had for months been searching for the sword that would save the Revolution by instilling order and authority at home and preventing the imminent invasion from abroad. He had first considered General Moreau, who was also dining that evening, but the conqueror of Hohenlinden had himself indicated Bonaparte.

"There's your man. He will carry out your coup d'état better than I would."

The ex-abbé had already seen Bonaparte when he paid his official visit to the Directory on October 18. But the General had been annoyed because the drummers on guard at the Luxembourg did not beat a salute when he stepped out of his carriage. Both wings of the doors of the Council Room were not opened for him. He had frowned. He might almost have thought himself a prince of the blood royal.

Bonaparte undoubtedly had an aversion for Sieyès. "His natural disinclination for having anything to do with women" was certainly one of the reasons for this feeling. The ex-priest moved in a slow, languid way and his manner of greeting was icy. Moreover, he was unspeakably proud. Once in the old days when he was saying Mass for the Duc d'Orléans, he noticed that Orléans had gone out in the middle of the service. He immediately stopped short and left the chapel, exclaiming: "I do not say Mass for the riffraff."

Bonaparte confided frankly in Gohier. "I was almost as surprised to meet Sieyès in your drawing room as I was to find he was one of the Directory, when I came back to France. In refusing to be a member when it was organized he did himself justice. If you do not watch out, President, this spurious priest will betray you to the foreigners."

Then he began the assault and, in the words of the late Albert Ollivier, dangled "a bait with a view to proposing himself."

"When I arrived in Paris a host of good citizens assured me that when Reubell had retired there was regret that I was not then in France. But if that was a misfortune it would be easy to remedy it."

Gohier did not take the bait, not even in view of the fact that if Josephine was the wife of a Director she would be living near him. He answered cautiously:

"It is certain that you would have had all the votes if an unambiguous article in the Constitution had not stood in the way of your election. There is no doubt that, having defended the Republic, you are fated one day to be at the head of the government whose stability your victories have always assured. But our articles of association have rigorously laid down the age of forty for becoming a member of the Directory."

"And would you yourself abide strictly by that rule which might deprive the Republic of men as capable of governing as of defending it?"

"In my eyes, General, nothing could excuse any infringement of it."

"President, you are observing the letter of the law that is fatal."

It seemed better, therefore, to fall in with Sieyès and organize a "consulate," particularly as, a few days later, Gohier was clumsy in defending Bonaparte when the General was summoned by the five Directors to be rebuked for having abandoned his army a thousand leagues from France. That day Bonaparte showed his teeth.

"It has been put forward here that I did so well for myself in Italy as to have no need to return there. That is an unworthy statement, for which there is no foundation in my military conduct."

Then, looking at Barras, he said, "Moreover, if it were true that I did well for myself in Italy it would not have been at the Republic's expense that I made my fortune."

Gohier then spoke. "I do not know who reported to you the

remark that offended you. No one here blames your conduct in Italy, but I must point out that if you had really made a fortune in Italy, it could only have been at the expense of the Republic."

In fact—without counting Josephine's arrangements—Bonaparte had brought back from Italy two million in gold. But Barras's presence should have kept Gohier quiet, for one doesn't speak of rope in the house of the hanged. However, Bonaparte asserted confidently, "My so-called fortune is a fable which even those who invented it cannot believe."

"The Directory is convinced, General, that the laurels with which you have covered yourself are the most precious treasures you have brought back from Italy and it was in order to offer you fresh opportunities for glory that we wished to speak to you. A general like yourself cannot remain inactive when the armies of the Republic are fighting and triumphing on all sides. The Directory leaves to you the choice of the army whose command it is resolved to give you."

Sieyès was still annoyed at being overlooked by the budding dictator. Even before the meeting he had made himself clear.

"Instead of complaining of his inactivity, let us congratulate ourselves on it. Far from placing weapons in the hands of a man whose intentions are suspect, far from wanting to set him in a new scene of glory, we should stop devoting our attention to him and try, if possible, to make everyone forget about him."

Bonaparte understood that he must take the step and, in spite of his repugnance, become friendly with Sieyès. Neither could—or dared—make the first move. Fortunately Comte Pierre Roederer was excited by what he called a "patriotic conspiracy." He had been with Louis XVI during his last night as king and wanted to be with Bonaparte during his first as dictator. With the help of Talleyrand he began to meet Sieyès in secret.

"Twice Talleyrand took me at night to the Luxembourg, where, as a Director, Sieyès lived," he was to relate. "He left me in his carriage and went in to see Sieyès. When he was sure that Sieyès had no other person with him and was expecting no one from outside (for in order not to offend his four colleagues who, also, lived in the Luxembourg, he never shut his door) a message was sent to me in the carriage where I had stayed and the meeting between Sieyès, Talleyrand and myself would take place. In the last days I went openly to Sieyès and even dined there."

So, for the moment at least, a meeting between the two principal actors in the coup d'état was avoided.

Bonaparte would have liked to have General Bernadotte on his side. Josephine, Désirée (Bernadotte's wife and Bonaparte's one-time fiancée), and Paulette tried to bring the two men together. Mme. Bonaparte invited Bernadotte to the Rue de la Victoire.

"A change of government is necessary," declared Bonaparte, a little too precipitately.

"It is impossible to change it," Bernadotte replied.

When Désirée's husband had left, Bonaparte burst into the office where Bourrienne was working. Hardly able to contain himself, he exclaimed: "What do you think of Bernadotte? You have just crossed France with me, you saw the enthusiasm my return caused, you said yourself that in it you could see the wish of all Frenchmen to escape from the disastrous position in which our defeats have placed them. Well, here's Bernadotte boasting, with ridiculous exaggeration, of France's brilliant, victorious position! He spoke of the Russians beaten, Genoa occupied, countless armies rising up everywhere, and I don't know what else. He spoke of external enemies, internal enemies; at the last words he looked at me. . . . But patience, the moment will soon be ripe. . . . You know Josephine, her grace, her skill. She was in the drawing room. Bernadotte's probing glance did not escape her, and she turned the conversation to another subject. Bernadotte saw in my face that I'd had enough and he left. All right, I'll let you work. I am going back to Josephine."

A few days later, however, Désirée's husband returned to the Rue de la Victoire. Bonaparte received him in the presence of his wife, his stepdaughter and his secretary. Once more the conversation went very badly.

"Yes, General," Bonaparte almost shouted, "yes, I would rather live in the woods than in a society that affords no security."

"But, good heavens," Bernadotte replied, "what security is lacking?"

Once more Josephine intervened and changed the conversation.

With the money from Italy Joseph had bought the estate of

Mortefontaine. Bonaparte and Josephine were to spend two days there, October 29 and 30. The evening before they had been to the Théâtre-Français and on coming away met Bernadotte.

"At first, not knowing what to say, I asked him if he was coming on our excursion today," Bonaparte told Bourrienne. "He said he was, then as we were passing his house in the Rue Cisalpine I boldly asked him for a cup of coffee and told him I should be delighted to spend a little time with him. He seemed to me to be quite pleased."

At Mortefontaine the next day, while Josephine and Désirée were gossiping with Julie—they conspired as a family—Bonaparte made fresh advances. Once again he spoke to Bernadotte about the evils from which the Republic was suffering, but Bernadotte replied curtly, looking the General straight in the eye: "I do not despair of the Republic and I am convinced that it will resist its enemies both internal and external."

Josephine was right to fear Bernadotte's reactions. She confided to Bourrienne, speaking of her husband: "You know that our friend is not always very discreet. I am afraid that he may have said too much to Bernadotte about the need to bring about changes in the government."

In fact the former Sergeant Bellejambe, thinking the Directory in peril, had gone to warn Barras. Josephine therefore urged her husband to visit her former lover with the hope of making him a party to the schemes. Barras, no doubt at Josephine's request, invited the General to dinner with a small party. After the meal he took Bonaparte aside and declared: "The Republic is dying; nothing works well any more; the government has no strength; we must have a change. Hédouville must be appointed President of the Republic."

Hédouville was Hoche's former chief of staff and an ex-governor of Santo Domingo. Admittedly, as commander in chief of the Army of the West, he had managed to pacify the Vendée, but he was not a person of sufficient stature to save France. Besides, the name Bonaparte hoped to hear from Barras's sensuous lips was his own and not that of an Hédouville whom later Napoleon was to make a diplomat and a chamberlain.

Barras still considered Bonaparte as his protégé and under an obligation for having been given a start. To him Josephine's husband was still the little, unemployed general in run-down boots whom he had seen coming out of the Rue de la Huchette one Vendémiaire evening; the man, moreover, to whom he had given his mistress, the unkempt General who, in Barras's opinion, owed all his Italian successes to him. Without noticing Bonaparte's cold glance, Barras continued:

"As for you, General, your intention is to return to the army, and I, ill, no longer popular, worn out, I can do nothing but return to private life."

"Oh, the fool! The fool!" Réal is said to have exclaimed of Barras, when Bonaparte described this scene to Josephine, Talleyrand, Fouché and Roederer.

Urged by Josephine, Fouché and Réal then went to the Luxembourg and made clear to Barras his mistake. The next day Barras arrived at the Rue de la Victoire at eight in the morning. Bonaparte was in bed with Josephine. The Director forced his way into the house and the General quickly received him. All Barras's excuses— he had been misunderstood . . . of course if his friend had any plan he could count on him—went for nothing. Bonaparte did not trust him and made a great pretense of friendship, and of weariness—all he wanted was rest. And Barras left the Rue de la Victoire convinced of Bonaparte's good intentions.

The future Consul's mind was thoroughly made up. The previous evening he had seen Sieyès and without loss of time had offered his cooperation.

"Citizen," he had said, "we have no constitution, or at least not the proper one. It is for your intelligence to give us one. Since my arrival you have known my feelings. The time to act has come. Are all your arrangements made?"

Sieyès began to present the fruit of his vigils. Bonaparte interrupted him.

"I know all that from what my brother tells me, but presumably you have no intention of presenting France with a new, ready-made constitution which has not been discussed soberly, article by article. This is not the affair of a moment and we have no time to lose. Your task is to establish a provisional government. I agree that this government should be reduced to three people and, since it is judged necessary, I consent to be one of those three with you and your colleague Roger Ducos."

Sieyès's idea had been that Bonaparte's role would be confined to commanding the troops and now he was demanding the chief post. The abbé frowned, but when Bonaparte had left he confided to Joseph: "The General seems to be as much in his element here as on the battlefield. We must follow his advice. If he withdrew all would be lost, and his acceptance of the provisional consulateship assures our success."

While awaiting this success, Josephine "received" almost every day. All those to be won over to the cause, those who were asked to shut their eyes, or those who were to be the principal actors in the coup d'état, came in procession to the Rue de la Victoire, indulged in witty conversation, drank a cup of tea, listened to Talleyrand wearily toss off an epigram or watched Réal's tiger face break into a laugh. One evening it was learned that Sieyès was taking riding lessons in anticipation of the great day and there was a shower of jokes.

Leaning against the chimneypiece, Bonaparte declared, "The idea of attacking the government is a sacrilegious one."

Uniformed hussars with embroidered capes fluttered around the women or conversed seriously apart. A few scholars also were invited so that, as Taine said, the intelligent Republic would come face to face with the intrepid Republic. And all the time Josephine, smiling, perceptive, interrupted conversations that might become dangerous, and brought to bear her incomparable charm, knowingly avoiding clashes and keeping open house.

By dint of secret meetings and private conversations—all carried on between two smiles and two cups of tea offered by the mistress of the house—the plan was settled. Two of the Directors, Sieyès and Roger Ducos, were to take part in the new government. But this was to be a transitional regime. In any case, Bonaparte preferred matters to be left vague. As for Barras, he could be bought—cheaply. A handful of gold would make him retire from history. General Moulin would return to the oblivion from which politics had drawn him. In the case of Gohier, Josephine would undoubtedly be able to keep the fire burning. With the Directory suppressed, the two Assemblies would remain. It would be best to carry out the operation in two parts. The Five Hundred and the Ancients, the two elected chambers, would be made to believe that there was going to be a "day." Phrasing it in this particular way was meant to suggest that the Parisians were about to invade the sessions chambers. In the language of the time, it would be shouted that "the skeleton of the Republic" was about to be thrown "to the hands of the vultures who would fight over its fleshless limbs." The Convention had in the past been subjected to such harassment. So the Ancients, won over in advance, and the Five Hundred, presided over by Lucien Bonaparte, would vote for the transfer of the legislative body to some location outside Paris—to Saint-Cloud for example—while Bonaparte, appointed commander of the armed forces, would be charged with maintaining order, in other words, with creating a new order.

Of course, the talk everywhere was of changes in the government, but the scope of the upheaval planned by the conspirators was not known. Some people thought there would merely be "revisions." In the end Bonaparte was afraid of some indiscretion. On returning from Talleyrand's one evening, he told Josephine how frightened he had been. Several carriages surrounded by horsemen had been drawn up in front of Talleyrand's house, 24 Rue Taitbout. He thought they had come to arrest him. They had both blown out the candles and what they saw from the window of a lodge calmed their fear. It was merely that a wheel had broken on one of the cabs which, under heavy guard, were transporting the receipts of the gaming houses of the Palais-Royal.

Josephine probably trembled at this tale. She now looked at Bonaparte with different eyes. We know this from a letter preserved at Malmaison and addressed to Citizen Vanhée, a cousin of J. M. Emery. She had found Bonaparte, she wrote, "more loving than ever" and so she was "extremely happy."

The day after writing this, on November 6—15 Brumaire—Josephine watched her husband leave. He was going, with considerable anxiety, to a banquet for seven hundred people being given in honor of himself and of Moreau in the church of Saint-Sulpice, now the Temple of Victory. Bonaparte was afraid of being poisoned and ate only hard-boiled eggs. Under the high-vaulted roof of the church the air was icy, as icy as the conversation. Everyone watched everyone else or whispered his fears, or his hopes, to his neighbors.

"I'm bored, let's go," said Bonaparte.

On returning to the Rue de la Victoire he found Fouché, Arnault and the inevitable Gohier. When the Director and the Minister had left, Arnault, convinced that the coup was to take place next day, 16 Brumaire, asked, "What time tomorrow?"

"Nothing tomorrow. Nothing! The game has been put off."

"At the stage matters have now reached?"

"The day after tomorrow everything will be over."

"But think what might happen tomorrow? Don't you see, General, the secret is leaking out."

"The Ancients are all timid. They want twenty-four more hours to think things over."

"And you granted it to them?"

"Where's the harm? I'm giving them time to realize that I can do without them what I can do with them. Till the 18th, then!"

On 16 Brumaire Gohier, who, as André Gavoty said, "still believed as strongly in the purity of his seductive friend's intentions as he did in the excellence of the regime over which he presided," visited Josephine. Every afternoon at four he went to see the woman he loved. She would receive him sitting on her sofa, bringing to bear on him her smiles, her Creole lisp and her soft eyes, always hoping to bring him into the conspiracy. But enraptured, as blind as only a quinquagenarian can be, he was unaware of her dissembling and when Fouché arrived Gohier asked him:

"What's new, Citizen Minister?"

"Nothing new, really, nothing."

"Is that all?"

"Still the same gossip."

"What?"

"Still the old conspiracy."

"Conspiracy!" exclaimed Josephine cleverly, assuming a frightened look.

"Yes, conspiracy, but I know where I stand. I can see clearly, Citizen Director, trust me. It is not I who am attacked. If there really had been a conspiracy, during all the time it's been talked about, we should have had proof of it in the Place de la Revolution or at Grenelle."

Always a good actress—she was "completely feminine," her husband was to say—Josephine appeared thoroughly scared. Gohier smiled and thought to calm her by saying:

"The Minister speaks as one who knows. If he says such things in front of us it proves there is no reason to do them. Be like the government, don't worry about such rumors. Sleep in peace."

In the evening Josephine gave a dinner to which Bernadotte, Roederer and, in particular, Moreau, were invited. After dinner, while his wife kept the conversation going with small talk, Bonaparte took his rival Moreau by the arm and drew him aside.

"Well, General, what is your opinion on the state of the Republic?"

"I think, General, that if the men who govern so badly are not removed and if a better order of things is not set up, we shall have to despair of the safety of our country."

"I am pleased to discover that these are your feelings. I was afraid you might be one of those who are wedded to our unsatisfactory constitution."

"No, general, I am convinced that modifications are needed in our institutions, but these must not attack the essential principles of representative government or the great principles of liberty and equality."

"Of course," Bonaparte replied, "everything must be done in the interests of the people, but a stronger government is needed."

Moreau offered the support of his Jacobin friends who, according to him, were all ready to rally to his cause. Bonaparte shrugged.

"I cannot do anything with you and your friends, since you are not in the majority. You frightened the Council by your motion to declare the country in danger and you vote for the men who dishonor your ranks."

He already spoke as though he were the master.

On 17 Brumaire, the eve of the great day, the hours were taken up by practical details. Between two riding lessons Sieyès drafted the decrees. The two Presidents, who were in the plot, prepared the summons which were to be taken to the Deputies in the middle of the night. Regnault de Saint-Jean-d'Angély wrote out the texts for the posters and the "Addresses to the Parisians" which Roederer's son was to set in type. As for Bonaparte, he was looking for a horse.

He had only a cabriolet—and one cannot take France in a cabriolet—so Admiral Bruix lent him a black horse with a fiery eye, not a very docile steed. Bonaparte wanted to make an imposing

effect and be surrounded by a large staff when he went before the
Council of Ancients, who were to appoint him to his post and before
whom he would take the oath. So he summoned all the available
officers and the forty adjutants of the National Guard for eight in
the morning of 18 Brumaire. He let the three cavalry regiments of
Paris know that he would review them at first light in the Avenue
des Champs-Elysées. Sébastiani, who was in the plot, agreed to post
several infantry units in the Place de la Concorde.

That evening, after dining with Cambacérès, Bonaparte asked his
wife to send Eugene to the Luxembourg with this note for her
bashful lover, Gohier: "Come, my dear Gohier, with your wife and
breakfast with me at eight in the morning. Don't fail, as I have some
very interesting things to talk to you about. Farewell, my dear
Gohier, you can always count on my sincere friendship. Lapagerie-
Bonaparte."

"Everything is permitted during a conspiracy," Bonaparte remarked. His aim was simple: to have Gohier at hand.

"I should then have made him ride with me willy-nilly."

Josephine and Bonaparte had spread their nets for Gohier, but
without taking into account Mme. Gohier, who was already disturbed by her husband's daily four-o'clock visit to the too-attractive
Mme. Bonaparte. The early hour—does one pay visits at eight in the
morning?—seemed odd in spite of her own presence, not to say
suspicious. So she went alone to the Rue de la Victoire. She was
astonished. The road, the little drive and the garden were full of
officers who, seeing how many of them had been summoned,
realized that "today was the day." Mme. Gohier was greeted by
Bonaparte, who was banking equally on Gohier's passion for Josephine and on Mme. Gohier's docility and blindness.

"Isn't the President coming?"

"No, General, it's not possible."

"It is absolutely essential that he come. Write to him, madame,
and I shall have your letter taken to him."

Mme. Gohier thought herself clever in writing to her husband:
"You did well not to come, my friend, everything going on here
convinces me the invitation was a trap. I shall not delay in returning
to you."

Now there was no reason for Josephine to hide the truth. In a few moments, as soon as the Ancients summoned him, Bonaparte would mount his horse.

"Everything you see, madame," she said in low tones to the obstinate woman, "must give you a presentiment of what must come about without fail. I am very sorry Gohier did not come at my invitation, which was arranged with Bonaparte, who wants the President of the Directory to be one of the members of the government he intends to set up. By sending my letter through Eugene I emphasized how much importance I attached to it."

"I am going to join my husband," said Mme. Gohier wildly.

"I am not stopping you, but tell him to think well, and both of you consider the wish I was authorized to pass on to you. It is not his interests only that are at stake. The influence Sieyès and his friends will have on the events in preparation depends on the stand the President takes. Use all your influence to persuade him to come."

Meanwhile Bonaparte bore off Bernadotte who, summoned like so many others, had come in civilian dress, alleging loudly that as he was not on duty there was no reason for him to be in uniform.

"You will be in a moment."

"Nobody told me, I should have had my orders earlier."

He refused to understand. A general without a uniform! He might as well be in slippers, thought Bonaparte, who raised his voice: "Your Directory is hated, its constitution worn out. We must make a clean sweep and give the government another head. Go and put on your uniform. I can't wait for you any longer. You will find me at the Tuileries among all our comrades."

The future King of Sweden remained unmoved.

"Bernadotte," the apprentice dictator resumed, "do not count on Moreau, or on Beurnonville, or on the generals of your party. When you know men better you will see that they promise much and perform little. Don't trust them!"

"I do not want to take part in a rebellion."

"A rebellion!" Bonaparte exclaimed in describing this scene to his secretary. "A rebellion, Bourrienne, can you imagine it? A lot of fools, men who quibble in their hovels from morning to night! It was all in vain, I could not overcome Bernadotte, he's like an iron bar. I asked for his word that he would do nothing against me. Do you know what he answered?"

"Something unpleasant, no doubt."

"Unpleasant? That's a good one! Worse than that. He said, 'As a citizen I shall stay calm, but if the Directory gives me orders to act I shall march against all the disturbers of the peace.' But, after all, I don't care. I have made all my arrangements and he shall not have a command."

Meanwhile they waited. The decree from the Council of the Ancients had not yet arrived, but everyone knew that they had been in session for an hour. Lefebvre's powerful voice could already be heard shouting: "Let's throw all those damned lawyers in the river!"

At last the commissioners of the Council of the Ancients were seen arriving in a grand procession. Everything had gone as had been foreseen. The Deputies, summoned at seven, had believed—or appeared to believe—that the Republic was placed in danger "by the anarchists and the foreign party." One of the conspirators had cried: "Measures must be taken for the public safety. We are sure of the support of General Bonaparte. In the shadow of his protecting arm the Councils can discuss the changes necessary in the public interest."

Bonaparte received the delegates, who were accompanied by a messenger wearing plumes and a high-collared cloak. They had come in this style to read the decree to him:

Article I. The Legislative body is transferred to Saint-Cloud; the two Councils will sit in the two wings of the palace.

Article II. They will proceed there tomorrow, 19 Brumaire, at noon; all performance of functions and discussion is forbidden elsewhere and before that time.

Article III. General Bonaparte is charged with the execution of the present decree. He will take all necessary measures for the safety of the national representation.

General Bonaparte is summoned to the Council to receive a copy of the present decree and to take the oath.

The reading of the decree was over. Bonaparte was with Josephine in the little round dining room that was also used as an antechamber. He turned to his aides-de-camp and the officers present. "Follow me!"

Before opening the door to the garden he once more asked Bernadotte to accompany him, but Bernadotte refused. Then, as Bonaparte was hurrying out he called to Bourrienne, "Gohier didn't come, too bad!" He was already on his way up.

"Come with me!"

The officers acclaimed him. A group of them remained "outside
the movement," but the majority imitated Bonaparte, who jumped
on to his admiral's horse.

Josephine remained with Bernadotte and Bourrienne. They listened to the diminishing sound of the uproarious procession, which
had taken the boulevard road and was to meet, at the corner of the
Rue du Mont-Blanc, the 1,500 horsemen Murat was to command.
Bernadotte left immediately and Josephine could give way to her
anguish. Bourrienne tried to calm her.

"Do you know Gohier very well?" she asked him.

"We have not exchanged one word on the situation."

"I'm sorry for that, I would have asked you to write to him to
urge him not to make a fuss and to imitate Sieyès and Roger, who
are going to hand in their resignations voluntarily, and not to side
with Barras, who is probably being forced to hand in his at this
moment."

This was true. Barras was preparing to take a bath and could not
receive Gohier and Moulin, who were astonished to find him in
blissful ignorance while the tramp of boots and hoofs could be
heard beating through the town. After a final lesson Sieyès had left,
on horseback, for the Tuileries, where he made a conspicuous
entrance. Under pretense of "seeing what the news was," Roger
Ducos had also left the Luxembourg. When Barras left his bath,
after an hour's soaking, he carefully shaved and then declared he
was ill and refused to see his two colleagues, who were wandering
about aimlessly. He had in fact just learned of the transfer of the
two Assemblies to Saint-Cloud and hoped to receive a visit, if not
from Bonaparte, at least from one of his emissaries, summoning him
to the Tuileries. No one came, except his secretary, Botot, whom
Bonaparte himself had taken to task on leaving the Tuileries. Before
reviewing his troops, the General, always a good actor, had pounced
on him and cried:

"What have you done with the radiant France I left you? I left
defeats! I left you the millions from Italy and I find everywhere
laws of dispossession and poverty! What have you done with the
hundred thousand Frenchmen I commanded, my companions in
glory? They are dead! This state of things cannot last. In three years

it would lead us to despotism. But we want the Republic to be based on equality, morality, civil liberty and political tolerance."

On hearing this, Barras felt that a wind was beginning to rise which might well shake him. A visit from Mme. Tallien, full of "charming vivacity," did not restore his self-possession. A little later he smiled scornfully on hearing Merlin de Thionville talk of "making Bonaparte's head roll at the feet of Liberty." Finally, at noon, Talleyrand and Admiral Bruix came with a letter of resignation carefully drafted by Roederer and needing only Barras's signature. After an inflated sentence on his passion for liberty, a sentence of twelve lines, Josephine's former lover was made to say:

"The glory accompanying the return of the illustrious warrior for whom I was fortunate enough to open the way to glory, the striking marks of confidence given him by the legislative body and the decree of the national representation have convinced me that, to whatever post the public interest may summon him, the perils to Liberty have been surmounted and the interests of the armies guaranteed. I return with joy to the rank of simple citizen, happy, after so many storms, to hand over undiminished and as unsullied as ever the destinies of the Republic in whose founding I shared."

He had all the more joy in returning to the rank of simple citizen as Talleyrand and Bruix also brought with them a very large sum of money provided by the banker Ouvrard, who was betting on Bonaparte, having seen the glorious procession pass his windows that same morning.

A few minutes later Bonaparte's dragoons provided a so-called escort of honor to accompany the ex-Director to his house at Grosbois. So Barras quits the pages of history, inelegantly, leaving Gohier and Moulin sole arbiters of the situation.

All day Josephine waited. As Bourrienne, who never left her, said, they "wished they could hasten the passing of time."

The city seemed quiet. It was pouring rain, which made the Parisians disinclined to go out and see what was happening. It was night when Bonaparte finally came back and could reassure his wife. Everything had gone well. But "18 Brumaire" was really to take place the next day, the 19th, at Saint-Cloud, where he would have to bury the Directory, force acceptance of a new constitution, and create the Consulate. This last had a slightly Roman air which did not displease some people. But would it be enough? Although the Ancients, once convened, had so far acted as one man, there were some who had been intentionally forgotten and who must have been furious. There were also the Five Hundred. All this made up "the great unknown." These gentlemen had been deliberating in little groups all day long. A short while before, when the conspirators were in council at the Tuileries, Sieyès had even suggested arresting forty opponents, but Bonaparte, as he told Josephine, had exclaimed:

"I swore this morning to protect the representatives; I do not wish to violate my oath this evening; I have no fear of such weak enemies."

He was wrong, as he was later to admit.

Then there were Gohier and Moulin, who refused to resign. For the time being Moreau's soldiers were on guard at the Luxembourg— a sentry had even been stationed at the door of Gohier's apartments, where a bust of Bonaparte still stood on the chimneypiece. Of course, if the following day passed off without any clashes the Directory, now composed of two Directors out of five, was bound to collapse.

The next morning Josephine, still in bed, heard her husband putting heart into his officers and saying to Lannes: "You are wounded and we shall be a long time on horseback. Stay here."

Then he turned to Berthier, who was trembling.

"What's the matter with you, Berthier? Are you in pain?"

"I have a carbuncle developing and I'm covered with poultices."

"Well, stay here."

"No, indeed," Berthier replied. "If I have to drag myself along in agony, I shall not leave you."

At that moment Josephine asked Bonaparte to come up to their bedroom. She wished to embrace him.

"Good, I'll come, but this is not a day for women."

We do not know what she said, but we can guess. This time she was not the woman who had treated her husband so carelessly. He was not the man she had found "odd." It was not physical love but something that could take its place and was certainly much deeper.

As Bonaparte was getting into his carriage Bourrienne and Lavallette, on their way to Saint-Cloud, were passing through the Place de la Concorde past the spot where the scaffold had stood for so many months.

"My friend," Bonaparte's secretary sighed, "either we shall sleep at the Luxembourg tomorrow or we shall end here."

And tomorrow Josephine would be the wife either of a man condemned to death—even possibly summarily shot—or of the master of France.

She remained without any news until half past five. Then a courier sent by Bourrienne at Bonaparte's request restored her calm. It was a deliberately optimistic message—Bonaparte knew how anxious his wife must be and had ordered Bourrienne to hasten to her shortly after leaving the Council of the Ancients.

But things had not gone as they had hoped. The General had made a sudden, and illegal, entry into the Ancients' chamber.

"Yesterday I was untroubled," he declared, "when you summoned me to inform me of the decree removing the Assembly and to instruct me to execute it. I at once assembled my fellow soldiers and we flew to help you. Now, today, I am already being covered with slander. People talk of Caesar, of Cromwell, of military government. If I had wanted a military government would I have hastened to give my support to the national representatives?"

Then, at the first interruption, when Linglet shouted, "And what about the constitution?" he began to get confused. Faced with those men in their red togas he lost his assurance and cried:

"The men of Prairial, who want to bring back to the land of liberty the scaffolds and the horrible rule of terror, are surrounded by their accomplices and preparing to carry out their dreadful schemes. The Council of the Ancients is already being blamed for the measures it has taken and for having put its trust in me. I myself am not shaken. Shall I tremble before the factious, I whom the coalition could not destroy? If I am a traitor, be you all Brutuses."

He had then threatened, turning toward Berthier and Bourrienne: "And you, my comrades who accompany me, you, brave grenadiers whom I see outside this building, let those bayonets with which we have conquered together be turned at once on my heart. But if any orator, in the pay of foreigners, dares pronounce against your general the word 'outlaw,' may the thunder of war crush him instantly."

The Ancients protested. Then he stupidly hurled a phrase that had quelled the Arabs at the council chamber in Cairo: "Remember that I march accompanied by the God of War and the God of Fortune."

The Assembly had now become openly stormy and Bonaparte had definitely lost ground. "One cannot possibly imagine what it was like without having been there," Bourrienne related. "There was not the slightest consistency in what he stammered out with, it must be admitted, the most incredible incoherence. Bonaparte was not an orator. One must suppose that he was more accustomed to the sound of battles than to that of parliamentary discussions. His place was at the head of a battery rather than facing the chair of the President of an Assembly."

Bourrienne tugged at Bonaparte's sleeve, muttering: "You must leave, General, you don't know what you're saying."

So Bonaparte left, with the almost ridiculous cry of "Let him who loves me follow me!"

Bourrienne obviously concealed the pitiful side of this scene from Josephine, whose fears were somewhat lessened, but only somewhat, as the Five Hundred still remained to be dealt with. Had she but known, nothing had in fact been accomplished. What had that morning seemed bound to pass off without a hitch had been a total failure.

The hours went by heavily, slowly, oppressively. The little garden began to fill with visitors coming for news when suddenly Mme. Letizia and Paulette appeared in great agitation. They had come from the Théâtre-Feydeau. At half past nine the actor Elleviou, stepping out of his role, had advanced to the front of the stage. Making a bow, he declared: "Citizens, General Bonaparte was nearly assassinated at Saint-Cloud by traitors to the country."

A great cry was heard. It was Paulette, who had nearly fainted. "Let us go to the Rue Chantereine, to my daughter-in-law," Mme. Letizia had decided. "We shall get news there."

Josephine, indeed, soon learned that everything was going well. The army had had to intervene and expel the Five Hundred. At that very moment they were trying to catch the Deputies who, feeling bayonets tickling their spines, had fled across the park, dropping their Roman costumes in the bushes and on the grass in order to run faster. But enough of them had to be collected to give the appearance of legality to the coup d'état and to set up a consular commission.

The visitors left and Josephine went to bed. Shortly after four in the morning she finally heard the carriage containing Bonaparte and Bourrienne stop before the house. A few moments later the two men were with her. She questioned them feverishly. This time it was over and successful, but it had been very difficult. The Five Hundred had threatened Bonaparte with unparalleled violence. Without his grenadiers he would have been a dead man. However, assisted by Sieyès and Ducos, he was from now on Consul of the Republic. The Directory was no more than a bad dream, thanks to the bayonets—those bayonets whose power Mirabeau had evoked ten years before. The Revolution was over.

"What about Gohier?" Josephine asked.

"What do you expect, my dear?" Bonaparte answered. "It's not my fault. Why did he refuse? He's an honest man, a fool. He doesn't understand! Perhaps I ought to have him deported. He wrote against me to the Council of the Ancients, but I have his letter and the Council never knew anything about it. Poor man! Yesterday he was expecting me to dinner—and he thinks he's a statesman! Forget him!"

"What about Bernadotte?" Josephine asked.

"Have you seen him, Bourrienne?" Bonaparte said.

"No, General."

"Neither have I. I've heard nothing about him. Can you imagine it? I heard today of a lot of plots being hatched around him. If you can believe it, he was asking for nothing less than to be appointed as my colleague in the command. He talked of mounting his horse, of coming with the troops he would be given to command. He said he wanted to uphold the Constitution. What is more, I am assured that he had the audacity to add that if it were necessary to proclaim me an outlaw, it would be done and that there would be soldiers capable of carrying out the decree."

"All this must make you realize the strictness of his principles, General."

"Yes, I understand. He is perfectly sincere, for if it were not for his obstinacy my brothers should have been able to win him over. They are allies. His wife, who is Joseph's sister-in-law, has great influence over him. But I ask you, didn't I make enough advances to him? You saw it yourself. Moreau, whose military reputation is quite different, came at once. Anyway I am sorry that I coaxed Bernadotte, so I shall think of a way of separating him from all his cliques but in a manner which will not give rise to talk. I cannot take any other revenge. Joseph likes him and I should have everyone against me. Ah! family considerations are a stupid business! Good night, Bourrienne."

His secretary bowed, but as he was going to the door Bonaparte called him back.

"By the way, we shall be sleeping at the Luxembourg tomorrow."

It was the first step toward the throne.

10. "Consuless" Josephine

On November 15–24 Brumaire—Josephine, "wife of the provisional Consul," gave a sad sigh. That day she was leaving forever her charming little house in the Rue de la Victoire to live in the severe, heavy Luxembourg Palace.

Sieyès and Roger Ducos had taken their former apartments. Bonaparte had installed himself in the rooms formerly occupied by Moulin on the ground floor "to the right of the Rue de Vaugirard entrance." Josephine, now the wife of one of the three kings of the Republic, henceforth had her own apartments on the second floor, those formerly belonging to Gohier, where she had so often visited her elderly lover. A small, concealed staircase enabled her to reach her husband.

Already the mirrors of the Rue de la Victoire, which had reflected her dark-blue eyes shaded "by the most beautiful lashes in the world," seemed far away. She was now the first lady in France and soon to be treated as its sovereign. And, as Désirée Clary, a queen in spite of herself, was one day to sigh: "Courts are no fun if you haven't been brought up in them."

Josephine was so bored that one can believe Barras when he states that she came secretly to see him one evening at Grosbois, wearing a black dress. "My friend," she sighed, "throwing herself in tears" at his feet, "why didn't we marry? Today I should be the mistress of Grosbois and happier than I am now."

For the present Bonaparte and his wife were living only "temporarily" in the Luxembourg. Nothing was settled. Bonaparte was "Consul of the day" only on one day out of three. In the evening, three times a week, while Josephine went to the Opera or received visitors, Bonaparte would attend the legislative committee meetings on the second floor, one headed by Lucien, the other by Lebrun. Their task was to replace the provisional arrangements by a definitive government. Sieyès, who always had a draft of a constitution hanging out of his pocket, proposed that the Senate should nominate "a grand elector for life," sitting at Versailles, whose only function would be to choose two Consuls, one for war and one for peace. Bonaparte exploded.

"How could you imagine, Citizen Sieyès, that a man of honor, a man of talent and of some capacity for affairs, could ever consent to be a mere calf being fattened by several millions at the royal château of Versailles?"

Sieyès would have liked to be that "fatted calf," and at the sight of his disappointed face laughter broke out. They came back to the formula of three Consuls, but there was no more laughter, Fouché recounts, "when the suggested decision was to have a First Consul, invested with supreme power, having the right of appointment and dismissal for all posts, and with the other two Consuls having only a consultative voice."

"If General Bonaparte assumes the function of supreme magistrate without preliminary election, he will display the ambition of a usurper and justify the opinion of those who claim that he carried out the coup of 18 Brumaire for his own benefit only."

Bonaparte was offered "the position of generalissimo with the power to make war or peace and to treat with foreign powers."

"I wish to stay in Paris," Bonaparte exclaimed angrily, biting his nails. "I wish to stay in Paris, I am Consul."

Marie Joseph de Chénier, breaking the silence, "spoke of liberty, of the Republic . . . of the need of putting a brake on power."

"That shall not be!" cried Bonaparte in a rage, stamping his foot. "Sooner than that, blood will flow knee-deep!"

"At these words, which changed a hitherto calm discussion into a scene," Fouché related, "everyone was taken aback, and a secured majority gave the power, not to three Consuls with the second and third having only a consultative opinion, but to one alone, appointed for ten years, re-eligible, empowered to promulgate laws, appoint and dismiss at will all the agents of executive power, make peace or war and finally to nominate himself."

On December 12 there took place what Lucien Garros has justly called the "armchair coup d'état." The three Consuls had to be elected. "A ten-litre measure placed on the table served as a voting urn. During the balloting Bonaparte leaned against the chimney-piece, warming himself. As the counting was about to start he went over to the table, picked up the slips of paper and prevented their being unfolded. Turning to Sieyès, he said very gravely: 'Instead of counting, let us give a further proof of our gratitude to Citizen Sieyès by assigning to him the right to appoint the three chief magistrates of the Republic and let us agree that those he appoints shall be considered to be those in whose nomination we have been engaged.'"

The ballots were quickly burned. The constitution of the Year VIII was settled. Sieyès eliminated himself, Roger Ducos, realizing that he did not carry enough weight, retired, and Bonaparte, "appointed" by Sieyès, himself chose his two satellite assessors. He first named Cambacérès, who after Thermidor had been President of the Committee of Public Safety and of whom it was said that he was the best fitted to bring an air of gravity to contemptible actions. Bonaparte then chose Charles François Lebrun, René Maupeou's former secretary, who in a way represented what was good in the past, that is to say "enlightened despotism" with a dash of Voltairism.

Bonaparte thus became First Consul and Josephine his "consuless," although not bearing this title. "It is a function, which has no feminine form," Bonaparte was to say.

However, Josephine was henceforth wife of the Head of State and could no longer, as before, go to the "little theatres" or to public balls. Bonaparte would not have allowed it. He also forbade his wife to see her old frivolous—and shiftless—friends of Directory days, such as Mme. Tallien, who was reigning at Grosbois before leaving Barras for Ouvrard. At St. Helena Napoleon was to assert that Josephine herself no longer cared to receive her former friend.

"Who can read a woman's heart! She would say that Mme. Tallien recalled memories of a liaison she wanted to forget. The fact was that Mme. Tallien was too pretty."

There had, perhaps, been some jealousy in Josephine's attitude, but this did not prevent her saying to the former Notre-Dame de Thermidor, who had come to complain of being ostracized by Bonaparte: "I assure you I have done everything friendship could suggest, but in vain. You are the only woman whose name he has erased from the list of my intimate friends."

Mme. Tallien wept and through her tears recalled the heroic days when she used to receive Bonaparte at her house.

"Just because he governs France does he hope to tyrannize over our private lives? Must we sacrifice our friendships to him?"

Her former protégé told her himself in explanation of his attitude: "I don't deny that you are charming, but think what you are asking, consider it and judge for yourself. You have had two or three husbands and children by everybody. One would doubtless think oneself happy to have shared in the first lapse; one would be annoyed by the second, perhaps one would forgive it, but after that, and again and again! Now consider, what would you do in my place? I who have undertaken to restore some decorum!"

Perhaps, too, the future Emperor remembered the too-famous remark: "Well, my friend, now you have your breeches!"

Later he even became violent and, once more forbidding Josephine to receive her former friend "under any pretext whatever," he added, "A wretch married her when she had eight bastards. I despise her more than ever. She was a pleasant girl; she has become a horrible and infamous woman." This is a far cry from the "little kiss on the mouth" which he asked Barras to give Mme. Tallien from him during the Italian campaign.

Decorum even led the new master to require his women guests to give up transparent materials or dresses cut too low. One day, in his wife's drawing room, he repeatedly gave orders for wood to be put on the fire until the servant exclaimed, "There is no room for any more, Citizen Consul."

"That will do," Bonaparte replied, in a rather loud voice. "I wanted to be sure there was a large fire as it is extremely cold and these ladies are almost naked."

The first meal of the day was served at ten in the morning and dinner at five. There were always at least twenty guests. Bonaparte liked having people to lunch. There was no display. They were still camping out. The servants of "Citizen and Citizeness Bonaparte" wore neither braid nor livery. There was only one butler—which for the times was surprising. Only his Egyptian servant Rustum, dressed as in Cairo, brought a touch of color and acquired the habit—which he always kept—of standing behind his master's chair. The guests were often booted. A few Ministers would come, or some of the higher civil servants, and frequently Joseph and Lucien.

After lunch Bonaparte would quickly get hold of Bourrienne. "Come and work."

In the evening, after dinner, there would be conversation. A few ladies, "Mme. Bonaparte's little committee," would sit round Josephine and listen to the mistress of the house with great pleasure. Witnesses are unanimous: she was undoubtedly the most unassuming and affable woman in Paris. But she was always careful not to open her mouth when she laughed. "If she had had any teeth," said Laure d'Abrantès, "I don't say pretty or ugly teeth, but any at all, she would certainly have outshone many ladies at the Consular court who could not equal her."

The men—Cambacérès, Lebrun, Sieyès, Roger Ducos, soldiers, officials and Deputies—remained on their feet. When the conversation was not general, Bonaparte would often go from one to another, disconcerting those who did not know him by a rain of questions. He struck them as "severe and cold," but managed to put them at their ease with an "affectionate, beautiful" smile.

Josephine frequently threw anxious glances at the man she was always to call "Bonaparte." If he frowned or if his voice hardened, she trembled. She was afraid now of losing a husband—and a generous husband. What would she do without him and what would become of her at thirty-six, an age which, it cannot be overemphasized, was not considered young in those days. On 24 Brumaire he had been able to line up nearly two million in national property in the Dyle Department (of which Brussels was the capital) which were intended for the dowry of Marie Adélaïde, Alexandre de Beauharnais's natural daughter, who was to marry Captain Lecomte. Josephine was as grateful to him for his generosity as for the pardon he had bestowed on her. As Frédéric

Masson has said, "no woman was ever better rewarded for having
deceived her husband." Her tears and her charm had won her a
"position." She was undoubtedly bored, but "constantly" repeated,
and repeated until her death, "In my position."

There were also the debts that had accumulated during the
Egyptian campaign. She had not the courage to be the first to
mention them and it was Talleyrand who one evening dared face
his new master and explain that Josephine's unpaid bills were
having a deplorable effect on the public. The First Consul immediately summoned his secretary.

"Bourrienne, Talleyrand has just been talking to me about my
wife's debts. Ask her for the exact total. She must confess everything. I want to have done with them and not have to go through it
again, but don't pay them without showing me all the bills from
those rogues, who are a set of thieves."

The next day Bourrienne told Josephine what was happening. At
first delighted, she soon grew gloomy when Bourrienne asked for
the exact total of what she owed.

"Don't insist on it, Bourrienne," she begged.

"Madame," he replied, "I cannot conceal the First Consul's
feelings from you. He believes that you owe a considerable sum and
he intends to pay it. You are in for some sharp reproaches and
probably a violent scene, but it will be the same scene for the
amount you admit to as for a larger sum. If you conceal a great part
of your debts, the complaints will begin again after a time, it will
reach the First Consul's ears, and he will be in an even worse
temper. Take my advice and admit everything. The result will be
the same, you will have to listen to the unpleasant remarks he will
make to you only once; holding back anything now will mean a
constant repetition of them."

"I can never tell him everything," the Creole sighed, pouting. "It's
quite impossible. Please don't repeat what I am going to confess. I
think I owe roughly 1,200,000 francs, but I want to admit only to
600,000. I shall not run into debt again and I shall pay the rest
gradually out of my savings."

"I have to repeat my first remarks, madame," Bourrienne replied.
"As I do not think he estimates your debts as high as 600,000 francs
I can guarantee that you would not have any more unpleasantness
for 1,200,000 than for 600,000 and if you mention the higher sum
you will be rid of it forever."

"I shall never do it, Bourrienne. I know him and I could never bear his violence."

Bourrienne therefore regretfully stuck to the sum of 600,000 francs—three million present-day francs—and Bonaparte, after a moment of speechlessness at the enormity of the sum, agreed to pay. But the secretary asked for the bills and was petrified. Josephine was being robbed. They had dared charge her 1,800 francs for a hat with heron's plumes. And during the same month the extravagant woman had ordered 38 hats. Bourrienne offered to pay most of the tradesmen only half their bill. They accepted, smiling. "One of them," Bourrienne added, "received 35,000 francs instead of 80,000 and had the impudence to tell me he was still making a profit." So the 600,000 francs allocated by Bonaparte were enough to settle everything.

Having paid his wife's debts, Bonaparte considered that he need not scruple to take one of Josephine's diamond necklaces, the finest, to give to his sister Caroline (she still signed her name as Maria Annonciatta), who was to marry Murat on January 20.

Wishing to gain the good will of her sister-in-law, who was madly in love with the dashing Murat—at least she would then have one ally in the terrible clan—Josephine had supported the cause of the future King of Naples, recommending him to her husband, who had not at first wanted to hear of the marriage. Off the battlefield he did not care at all for the impetuous cavalier, whose affectation in dress already irritated him.

"Murat is the son of an innkeeper," he told his wife. "In view of the right rank to which fortune and fame have raised me, I cannot have my blood mingled with his! Besides, there is no hurry, I'll see about it later."

Josephine persisted, and recalled the soldier's courage.

"Yes," admitted Bonaparte. "Murat was superb at Aboukir."

Finally he gave way, consoling himself with this thought: No one will say that I am proud, or trying to make great alliances. If I had given my sister to a nobleman, all the Jacobins would have talked of counterrevolution.

The contract was signed in the Luxembourg on January 18, in the presence of Bonaparte and his wife. M. and Mme. Murat then went through a religious ceremony in "the decadal temple of Plailly" near Mortefontaine.

Josephine was pleased with her triumph. But a shadow remained:

the loss of her necklace. She must have another. The jeweler Foncier had a magnificent collection of pearls said to have belonged to Marie Antoinette. Josephine decided to buy them and have a necklace made. In order to find the necessary 250,000 francs she applied to Berthier, the new Minister for War. "Berthier, biting his nails as usual," wrote Bourrienne, "arranged a prompt liquidation of debts owed for the Italian hospitals, and as purveyors in those days were very grateful to their protectors the pearls passed from Foncier's shop into Mme. Bonaparte's jewel box."

The operation went all the more smoothly as Josephine, realizing that the First Consul's wife could no longer have direct contact with the speculators, had asked Lagrange to collect for her "the hidden receipts due to her from the suppliers." We owe this information to the publication by André Gavoty of a letter written by Josephine to Lagrange on December 13:

"Please settle my share in the military supplies and clothing company according to the directions of the Minister for War and manage this affair with all the discretion and delicacy of which you are capable."

Perhaps it was Lagrange who, indirectly, paid for the necklace. In any case, the most difficult point, which Josephine had not at first considered, remained: how to explain to Bonaparte the presence of this magnificent necklace around his wife's neck. So for two weeks the pearls never left their case. Finally Josephine grew bolder.

"There is a great reception tomorrow, Bourrienne," she said to her husband's secretary, "and I simply must wear my pearls. But you know Bonaparte, he will scold me if he notices anything. Please, Bourrienne, stay close to me. If he asks me where the pearls come from I shall immediately reply that I have had them for a long time."

Of course Bonaparte noticed the necklace.

"Well, what have you there?" he asked his wife. "I don't think I know those."

"Good heavens!" Josephine replied, smiling, "you've seen them a dozen times. It's the necklace the Cisalpine Republic gave me that I used to wear in my hair."

"But I think . . ." Bonaparte went on.

"Well, ask Bourrienne, he'll tell you."

"What do you say, then, Bourrienne? Do you remember?"

"Yes, General, I well remember having seen them before."

"Seeing Mme. Bonaparte's self-assurance," Bourrienne wrote, "I involuntarily recalled Susanna's remark about the ease with which honest women lie" (in *Le Mariage de Figaro* by Beaumarchais).

Josephine, it must be admitted, had often behaved like a not very honest woman. She was also to have a way of secretly procuring money which strikes us as very odd, to say the least. In order to know what went on in Bonaparte's house, Fouché was soon to pay Josephine 1,000 francs *a day*—5,000 present-day francs—on the pretext of giving more adequate protection to the First Consul and of being kept informed of his sayings and doings. Fouché also claimed to have engaged Bourrienne for 25,000 francs a month. This is not impossible to believe when one knows that Bonaparte was one day to get rid of his old comrade for "underhanded financial dealings." Thus the Minister of Police had as his chief informers the wife and the confidential secretary of the Head of State. It sounds like a dream.

Josephine had certainly decided to give up trading on her influence and not to make anything out of army supplies, but she was to succumb to temptation. On December 27, 1799, Rouget de l'Isle, who had been one of Josephine's friends before her marriage, sent her husband this offer of service:

"The neglect, which you have caused me to suffer or which you have acquiesced in, the coldness with which you received me some time ago, all proclaim that someone has done me an ill turn with you. Whether this conjecture is true or false, it forces me to remain at a distance. If the Republic and you should have need of yet another brave man, count on me. With respectful greetings."

The First Consul did not reply. Josephine intervened, insisted and, for the sake of peace, Bonaparte commissioned a "Battle Song," which was played at the Opera on January 3, without the slightest success. The wing of genius brushed the composer of the *Marseillaise* only during that famous night in Strasbourg.

Since her husband refused to make use of the composer, Josephine, returning to her old ways, asked him to lend his name for a deal in army supplies. The firm of Goisson had sent a certain Citizen Maunier to offer her a comfortable sum if she would obtain an important contract for them. The incorrigible Josephine agreed and asked her old friend if, in return for a large percentage, he would draw her profits from the business. Rouget, having at first refused, consented to play the part of intermediary. Thanks to Josephine, the contract was obtained, but at the end of the following year, when the story came out, Rouget was brought up for questioning. "Had I not been extremely cautious," he wrote to Josephine, "I could have mentioned you ten times in the first interview and compromised you directly or indirectly."

This might appear slanderous had we not seen the letters from the author of our national anthem. At this point the firm of Goisson went bankrupt, the affair became serious and Rouget, considering himself freed from his promise, as his protectress had not been able to save him, wrote to the "Citizen Consul" to reveal "numerous details" which were "of a kind to have as their expounder and interpreter" only Josephine's husband and himself.

Bonaparte being thus informed, the affair was hushed up. But Josephine received such a lecture that she was henceforth to be content with her monthly stipend from Fouché and to eschew, apparently, any bribes offered her.

Josephine always gave a kind reception to petitioners, particularly royalists "of a rank formerly higher than hers." They were beginning to return to France and would ask the former Vicomtesse de Beauharnais if their names could be erased from the list of émigrés, so that their confiscated property might be returned and they might have some hope of getting employment. To be received by Citizeness Bonaparte they had only to present a small oval card, a permit signed by Bourrienne. Nearly all the files of émigrés in the National Archives contain a letter or note from Josephine, who had become the "guardian angel of the royalists and the émigrés." From London the Comte d'Artois sent the Duchesse de Guiche to the wife of the First Consul to open negotiations aimed at the return of the monarchy. But, faithful to her commitments, Josephine informed Fouché, who had the messenger deported.

The Comte de Provence thought he would be more successful than his brother by writing directly to Bonaparte to "reveal the hopes" he was building on the man who now united "power and talent." But the First Consul refused, in noble phrases, to be "the savior of France" as the Pretender to the throne called it. His intention was to save France for himself.

Bonaparte did well to refuse. The day after Marengo, and two days after sending Bonaparte a second letter saying that "glory awaited him" if he would bring back the monarchy, the Comte de Provence wrote to Cadoudal, a lifelong supporter of the royalists who had headed the Chouan troops, describing "the conqueror of Lodi, Castiglione and Arcole" as a tyrant.

For her part, Josephine was sorry that the efforts to restore the monarchy had failed. She had even insisted, as had Hortense, that the Consul should accept "Louis XVIII's" proposals.

"The sword of the connétable [the first official of the French King's household, and earlier, until 1627, commander in chief of the French armies] would suit you better," Hortense had dared to say one day when fastening his Turkish scimitar.

Bonaparte had shrugged.

"These wretched women are crazy. The Faubourg Saint-Germain has turned their heads. They have made themselves the guardian angels of the royalists, but no matter, I'm not angry with them for that."

Josephine's attitude can be explained by fear of the future. If Bonaparte were to become sole master of the fate of France, if he were to make himself "king," her position might become delicate. Since the establishment of the Consulate, she had been thinking of that divorce to which she had nearly fallen a victim on his return from Egypt and which she guessed would be inevitable if her husband wanted to found a dynasty requiring an heir—the heir she could not give him.

So when Bonaparte appeared for the first time in his uniform of First Consul—red with gold embroidery—and asked her, "How do you think this costume suits me?" she answered sincerely, "Less well than that of connétable."

It had been suggested that he wear a red cap, but he had replied—and it was also a profession of faith: "Ni bonnet rouge ni talons rouges" (Neither the red cap of the revolutionary nor the red heels of the nobleman). He was the future and nothing from the past would do for him.

On February 19 Bonaparte, taking another step toward the throne, declared to his secretary, who had come to wake him: "Well, Bourrienne, today we are at last going to sleep in the Tuileries. You're lucky, you are not obliged to make a spectacle of yourself, you can go there quietly. I shall have to go with a procession. I find it tedious, but one must appeal to the eye, it does the people good. The Directory was too simple, so it never gained any respect. In the army simplicity is a good thing. In a great city, in a palace, the head of the government must use every means to draw all eyes to him, but we must proceed gently. My wife will go and watch the review from Lebrun's apartments. If you like you can go with her."

From one of the windows of the Pavillon de Flore, where Lebrun lived, Josephine, "radiantly beautiful" in the words of Mme. d'Abrantès, was able to watch the spectacle together with Hortense, Caroline and "a kind of Court." And it was indeed a spectacle. Three thousand soldiers, accompanied by their bands and commanded by Lannes, Murat and Bessières, were lined up in the courtyards of the Tuileries and the Carrousel. The procession entered the Place du Carrousel, a relatively narrow, lopsided square between the Louvre and the Tuileries in which the streets of the district converged. After a cluster of heavy cavalry came the State Councilors packed into hackney-cabs, which were described as coaches by the newspapers, their registration numbers being hidden with strips of paper. Then came a military band composed of fifty musicians bedizened with gold. They preceded the general staff, on horseback and fluttering with tricolor plumes. After the Ministers—also in hired cabs—came Bonaparte's Guides, horsemen in busbies and green cloaks with red epaulets. Rustum, on his prancing Arab horse, preceded the Consul. Their coach, surrounded by Guides, all trumpets sounding, was drawn by the six white horses presented by the Emperor Francis after the battle of Campo Formio. A great shout of "Long live Bonaparte!" rang out.

On arriving in front of the Pavillon de l'Horloge the hero of the occasion descended from his carriage, threw a glance at Josephine, and mounted his horse. While those two figureheads, his colleagues, went to their apartments, the First Consul reviewed the troops. He lingered before the new Consuls' Guard. Drawn up in two lines stretching from the gate of the Carrousel to the door of the Tuileries, the Consular Guards wore bearskins and a tricolor uniform of dark-blue jacket, white gaiters and facings, and red epaulets and frogging.

Then the troops marched past their commander. When the flags of the 96th, the 43rd, and the 30th half brigade passed, flags of which there remained only the blackened staff and a few rags riddled by bullets, Bonaparte took off his hat and bowed over his horse's mane.

Then with a brisk step he entered his new dwelling—the dwelling he found "as depressing as grandeur."

There, too, the traces of the Revolution were to be removed. "Take all that away, I don't want such rubbish," he had ordered, pointing to the red caps to be seen almost everywhere.

On the very day he entered the Tuileries he gave orders that the numerous Trees of Liberty planted in the courtyard should be pulled up, as they deprived the rooms of light—orders of symbolic significance. He also ordered the removal of an inscription which up to then could be read on one of the sentry boxes flanking the iron gate of the Carrousel: "August 10, 1792, royalty is abolished and will never rise again."

"Being in the Tuileries is not everything," he told Bourrienne, as they walked in the Galerie de Diane; "it is necessary to stay there. Who hasn't lived in this palace? Brigands, members of the National Convention . . . Look, there's your brother's house. From there I saw the Tuileries besieged and that good Louis XVI taken away. But don't worry, just let them try coming!"

He installed himself in Louis XVI's former apartments on the second floor. Josephine preferred the ground floor giving on to the garden, but unfortunately one could not see the lawns and flower beds when seated inside, as the windows were placed high and were curtained. Josephine could not help thinking of the Queen. This was where Marie Antoinette had lived during the slow death of the monarchy. Here she had sat during the evening of October 6, 1789. Here, on returning from the terrible Varennes journey, she had looked into the mirrors of her bedroom and had seen that her hair had gone quite white.

"I shall never be happy here," Josephine murmured as she and Hortense made a tour of the rooms which had been decorated "à la moderne," a style which did not match the ceilings and paneling of the period of the Roi Soleil.

After the anteroom, which opened on a flight of steps leading to the Carrousel, at the corner of the Pavillon de Flore, came the first drawing room done in a violet-blue fabric embroidered with a honeysuckle design in light brown. The second was hung with yellow and brown satin. This was Josephine's famous "yellow drawing room," whose mahogany chairs were covered with striped satin. To brighten the room looking glasses had been added which were draped instead of framed, and there was a chimneypiece against which Bonaparte would often lean, with his back to the hearth, talking, explaining, interrupting, or turning around between two sentences to poke the fire. Josephine smiled as she listened and worked at her tapestry, for which the canvases were prepared by Mlle. Dubuquoy.

What used to be the Queen's bedroom was now hers. It was a symphony in blue and white. The bed was of solid mahogany, ornamented with bronze.

"It seems to me," Josephine was to say, "that the Queen's ghost comes to ask me what I am doing in her bed. In this palace there is an odor of kingship which one cannot breathe with impunity."

The apartment also contained a bathroom—formerly Marie de Médicis's oratory—a little library, its walls hung with green, and finally a boudoir-dressing room with a low ceiling. Its curtains were of embroidered muslin. Josephine spent long hours here, attentive to her makeup and her wrinkles. Bonaparte would sometimes come and fetch her for meals. "Not ready yet?"

He took pleasure in teasing her, criticizing her coiffure.

He would remove the flowers from her hair, Hortense, whose little bedroom communicated with her mother's dressing room, tells us: put them back, affirm that they looked much better than where the hair-dresser had put them, call on me to support his good taste and all with a serious air that made one laugh. On days when he was preoccupied with business he would come in looking grave, sit in a large armchair near the chimneypiece or walk up and down not paying attention to anyone. And he would always say, "Not ready yet?"

We would finally sit down to table. Dinner lasted ten minutes. Some-times he even got up before dessert was served. My mother would point this out to him. He would smile, sit down again for a moment and then leave at once, without having spoken a word to us. When he was in this frame of mind everyone trembled before him. No one would have dared interrupt him for fear of distracting him from some serious thought or of receiving a harsh reply. Then we said to each other: "He's in a very bad temper today. Is there anything new?" And after questioning each other we were no wiser.

For Josephine to be any wiser she had to wait until evening when her husband joined her. There was a little staircase from his study to his wife's bedroom by which he used to go down to her.

On the night of February 19–30 Pluviôse, Year VIII—as they were going to bed, he had said to her, laughing, "Come, little Creole, come and sleep in the bed of your masters."

The bed of her masters was no consolation for Josephine's boredom, particularly as her daughter had preferred to leave the palace and return to Mme. Campan's at Saint-Germain. Bonaparte talked incessantly to Hortense of marriage and this sort of "inquisition" annoyed her.

When her daughter had been away for six days Josephine could not bear the grandeur any longer. She soon had Hortense come back, but when the girl spoke of leaving a second time Josephine, who had always wept easily, began to cry like a child.

"You like being away from me," she reproached her.

Hortense tried to explain why she preferred Saint-Germain to the Tuileries, but nothing would calm her mother. In the midst of this grief Bonaparte entered.

"Do you imagine you had children just for your own sake?" he asked, laughing. "Consider that when they are grown up they no longer need their parents. When Hortense marries she will belong to her husband and you will be nothing to her."

Hortense did not agree and Bonaparte continued his teasing:

"Children always love their parents less than they are loved by them. It's natural. Look at the little birds. When they can fly they go away and never come back."

Josephine's tears increased and the First Consul took her on his knees and said, smiling, "Poor little woman! How unhappy she is! She has a husband who loves her and that is not enough! It is I who should be angry. You love your children much more than me."

"No," Josephine replied, "you cannot doubt my attachment, but if I don't have my children near me my happiness cannot be complete."

"What is there lacking in this happiness? You have a husband as good as the next man, two children who give you nothing but satisfaction. Go on, you were born under a lucky star."

"It's true," she admitted, smiling through her tears.

"And gaiety succeeded weeping," writes Hortense in her account of the scene.

But the tears soon returned. Once again Josephine was frightened. Together with Eugene, who had been promoted to the rank of captain on December 22, Bonaparte left Paris on May 6, 1800, to fight against Austria. His intention was to invade Italy—as had Francis I—by crossing the Alps. Their last evening had been spent at the Opera, where the First Consul had been greeted with acclamation, and the bulletin on Moreau's victory at Stockach read. At two in the morning, having kissed Josephine, Bonaparte left in a post chaise. He thought he need not worry about leaving, since Paris had resumed its joyous, elegant existence.

Although run down, Paris was enjoying itself. Women were preoccupied with their long sheathlike train dresses of gauze and their new straw hats, which fashion decreed must be "worn far back with a high turn-up in the front, shaped like an oval shell." Carriage drives were resumed and the "dance mania" of the Consulate conceded nothing to that of the Directory. In the Champs-Elysées there was a crowd under every tree. "Here a piano, there a harp, next to it a guitar, farther on a whole concert." The great city was full of bastringues (public dance halls). The sound of violins and clarinets could be heard everywhere. "See what richness," wrote a reporter, "what splendor, what freshness, how many pretty women all different, and young men all alike . . . luxury, simplicity, day, night, ladies, prostitutes, vice, decency, all are mingled."

Yet gradually as the days went by fear settled on Paris. Josephine was faced with the realization that Bonaparte's absence was giving rise to a certain anxiety. He had left to go "with all speed to the help of the Army of Italy." But would he arrive in time to give a helping hand to Masséna, besieged in Genoa? If he did not, if he was beaten, what chaos would result! The royalists took heart, rejoiced and began to conspire seriously. Schemes were already being plotted. Discontented "Thermidorians" and "Brumairians," such as Sieyès, were preparing a "government in reserve" in case "he" returned beaten. Intrigue increased. Even Joseph, who was Minister of the Interior, refused to visit Josephine in the Tuileries. He set himself up as "heir presumptive" and would not "work with the Consuls." Unquestionably Cambacérès and Lebrun were not up to the job.

On May 15 Bonaparte wrote to Josephine: "I have been in Lausanne since yesterday. I leave tomorrow. My health is fairly good. This country is very beautiful. I see no objection, in ten or twelve days, to your joining me, but you must come incognito and not say where you are going, because I don't want anyone to know what I am doing."

She did not in the least want to join him. Although she was anxious about him, Josephine, always lazy, rarely wrote to him, and before he left Lausanne her husband rebuked her, just as in the old days. "I am leaving at once to spend the night in Saint-Moritz. I have had no letters from you, that is not right. I have written to you by every post. . . . A thousand tender messages to you, my good little Josephine."

Another letter from Ivrea, on May 29: "I am in bed. I leave in an hour for Vercelli. Murat should be at Novara this evening. The enemy is completely baffled and does not yet know what we are doing. I hope in ten days to be in the arms of my Josephine, who is always very good when she is not playing the *civetta* (the coquette). A thousand tendernesses. I received Hortense's letter and I shall send her a pound of very good cherries by the next post."

His next letter, written in Milan, where he had arrived soaked through and suffering from a bad cold, brought Mme. Bonaparte, who had retired to Malmaison, the news of the crossing of the St. Bernard Pass. On learning that the Consul had repeated Hannibal's exploit—not on a prancing horse, as David shows him, but more modestly on a mule—Paris took hope. "This news has electrified all the good citizens," said a police report, "and at the same time has disturbed the seditious of all parties. It spread at once throughout the whole city and produced a very good effect, particularly in the faubourgs."

But on June 14 there was renewed dismay at the news that Masséna had had to surrender. Genoa was lost.

"Paris today is not in the least like the Paris of a week ago," one of the Prince de Condé's agents reported to his master. "The surrender of Genoa, which frustrates so many promises and so many plans, has made a strong impression on everyone's mind. The revolutionaries, who are much more on the lookout for news than the royalists, announce it openly in the streets. In former times they would have guillotined as alarmists anyone daring to do so. They do not fail to add that it is not Masséna's fault, but Bonaparte's."

On the same day, in the plain between Alexandria and Tortona,

Bonaparte, with fifteen guns against a hundred, was giving battle
not far from an obscure village called Marengo, which that evening
swiftly took its place in history. Eugene attacked at the head of his
men, which earned him promotion to the rank of major—at nineteen. But, suffering heavy losses, the French Army was obliged to
give way before the Imperial troops. From the church tower of San
Giuliano Bonaparte watched the disaster, affecting a calm he did
not feel. Desaix, with 6,000 fresh men, was to recoup the situation
and turn the retreat into a victory, but the bad news was already
hastening toward Paris and reached the Tuileries on June 20.
Josephine's anguish was the greater since an unofficial dispatch
mentioned the death of "a great chief." These vague rumors soon
gained credit and Paris was heavy with anxiety. On June 22
Josephine awoke with the thought on her mind that on this day she
had to appear at the reception of the diplomatic corps, at which the
Ministers were to be present. Many of them—such as Fouché, who
"was banking on a defeat"—would be making a show of compassion. The reception was being prepared when, around eleven in the
morning, there was a noise in the courtyard. A courier had just
brought the news of the victory of Marengo. He was followed by a
second and a third messenger, giddy with exhaustion and white
with dust. One of them handed Josephine a gold laurel branch
which Berthier had detached from the crown surmounting one of
the fifty Austrian flags captured from the enemy. The diplomats,
Ministers and members of the little Court congratulated the Consuless with an eagerness and a joy proportionate to their defeatism
of the day before. To them all the First Consul's wife passed on the
few details Cambacérès and Lebrun had received. Desaix's soldiers,
after being exhorted by Bonaparte, had attacked the enemy, who
were under the impression they had already won. But while turning
defeat into victory General Desaix had fallen at the head of his
division.

"Why am I not permitted to weep?" the First Consul is supposed
to have sighed.

From the direction of the Invalides the cannon began to thunder.

"I hope the French people will be pleased with their army,"
Bonaparte had written.

For the first time, as Cambacérès noted, public rejoicing was
"spontaneous." The delight was general, as it was never to be again,

and Bonaparte's name was in every mouth. And Hyde de Neuville, that determined royalist conspirator, having reckoned "the incalculable consequences of the event," sighed: "It is the baptism of Napoleon's personal power; the power he holds in his hands has become a part of himself."

Josephine was asleep when Bonaparte returned to the Tuileries on July 2, 1800, at two in the morning. Having embraced her, he fell asleep, tired by the journey, but when he woke Josephine found him worried, although a crowd had come to the Tuileries to applaud him. Mme. Bonaparte learned the reason for her husband's ill humor when she heard him say to Fouché: "So, they thought I was lost and they wanted to try a Committee of Public Safety again! I know everything, and they were men I had saved, had spared! Do they think I'm another Louis XVI? Let them try and they'll see! Let no one make any mistake. For me a battle lost is a battle gained. I fear nothing; I shall cast all those ingrates and traitors into the dust. I shall be able to save France in spite of malcontents and muddlers."

Two days later, on July 4, he seemed calmer when taking part in the traditional Quintidi review. Charles Nodier related:

A young Mameluke he had brought back from Egypt headed the column. He was dressed with Oriental magnificence, a long Damascus blade at his side. He carried a bow and his appearance had something extraordinary and romantic about it. Then came four aides-de-camp, covered in gold embroidery. Behind them modestly rode a man in gray, his head bowed, advancing without display or pretention; it was Bonaparte. None of his portraits is like him. It is impossible to catch the distinguishing marks of his countenance, but his expression is overwhelming. . . . His face is very long, his complexion dark, his eyes very deep-set, very large, steady and as bright as crystal. He looked sad and downcast and occasionally sighed. He rode a white horse, one of those the King of Spain sent him. The horse was covered with trappings of red velvet embroidered with gold. The bit, bosses and stirrups were all of gold and on this richly harnessed horse was the greatest man in the universe dressed in clothes that Garat (the singer) would not have liked to see his groom wearing.

Was he proud of himself? Not yet. During that same week, on June 30, as he was crossing Burgundy with Bourrienne, he had said to his secretary, "Well, now, with a few more great events like this campaign I shall be able to go down to posterity."

"It seems to me," Bourrienne replied, "that you have already done enough to make people speak of you everywhere for a long time."

"Oh, yes, done enough! That's nice of you! It's true that in less than two years I've conquered Cairo, Paris and Milan. Well, my dear fellow, if I died tomorrow I should not, after ten centuries, have as much as half a page in a history of the world."

The Court was taking shape. There were still no chamberlains and the aides-de-camp took turns in acting as attendants in the antechambers.

"It was not precisely a court," a foreign lady was to say, "but it was no longer a camp either."

When she did not take her meal alone with Bonaparte, which frequently happened, Josephine gave luncheons at the Tuileries for women invited without their husbands.

"In my opinion," the Duchesse d'Abrantès tells us, "it was a charming custom to invite women still too shy to shine in a salon among men so superior as to intimidate them very much. By talking with Mme. Bonaparte during luncheon, which was always an informal meal, of fashions, theatres and society gossip, these young women grew bolder and were less likely to be mere silent ornaments in the First Consul's drawing room when he came for a little relaxation. Mme. Bonaparte presided with charming grace over these luncheons. There were usually five or six of us, all of the same age, with the exception of the hostess."

Josephine soon had "ladies in waiting," who were on duty in rotation. The Duchesse d'Abrantès has very neatly sketched Mme. de Lameth as "spherical and bearded, neither attribute very pleasing in women, but good and witty, qualities which always became them well." John Law's charming little niece, Mme. de Lauriston, "always of an equable temper"; Mme. d'Harville, "rude by design and polite by chance"; a friend of Plombières, Mme. de Talhouët, "who was too mindful of the fact that she had been pretty, and not enough of the fact that she was no longer so"; Mme. de Luçay, "so exquisitely considerate." Mme. de Rémusat, née Claire de Vergennes, was not appointed until 1802. A plump brunette, with bright eyes and a dimpled smile, she often played the part of confidant to the Consular, and later the Imperial, household. "To a lively imagination and a judgment rare for her age," says Charles de Kunstler, "she added good breeding and wit, also much common sense, which came to the aid of her independent and somewhat inflexible temperament." She was to leave her Memoirs, a collection of much-discussed—and sometimes debatable—gossip, which nevertheless enables us to cast an indiscreet eye on the inside story of M. and Mme. Bonaparte.

In the afternoons Mme. Bonaparte would sometimes grant audiences. The ladies' chairs formed a circle and the men stood in the background while the First Consul and his wife would walk past, as though at a review, having the visitors they did not know presented to them and exchanging a few commonplaces about fashions or the theatre. "Mme. Bonaparte managed the gathering with charm and grace," Mme. de Rémusat wrote. "She was elegantly dressed in a style similar to the classical. That was the fashion of those times, when artists had quite an influence over the customs of society."

Bonaparte's small dinners were given in his wife's apartments, but the "great crushes"—as they were always known—took place on the second floor in the Gallery of Diana. On some evenings there were twelve or fifteen times as many men as women. Little by little Bonaparte fell into the habit of leading the way to the table, Josephine following with the chief guest. Needless to say the meal was served at a gallop. It rarely lasted more than twenty minutes or half an hour.

"To eat quickly one should dine with me," Bonaparte would say. "To eat well, with the Second Consul, and to eat badly, with the Third."

After the official dinner those invited to come in the evening invaded the drawing rooms and tedium fell on the Tuileries. Another review, more presentations, more commonplaces. Bonaparte, as Bourrienne was to relate, was not particularly amiable. "Politeness to women was not one of Bonaparte's usual characteristics. He rarely had anything pleasant to say to them and indeed often paid them backhanded compliments or said very odd things. Sometimes it was, 'My goodness, how red your arms are!' or 'Oh, what an ugly hair style! Who bundled up your hair like that?' Sometimes again, 'Your dress is very soiled. Don't you ever change your dress? I've seen you in that one twenty times.' In this respect he was merciless and generally liked to see money spent. He often concerned himself with his wife's clothes and as her taste was so exquisite it may have made him rather exacting about the dress of other ladies."

There is a story of the reply made to him one day by a witty woman whom he had asked bluntly:

"Do you still like men?"

"Yes, when they are polite."

Fortunately Josephine's charm was often able to smooth things over.

When there were no great crushes the evenings were spent more simply. "After the Consul's dinner," wrote Mme. de Rémusat, "we were informed that we could go upstairs. How long we conversed depended on whether we found him in a good or a bad humor. Bonaparte would then vanish and generally was not to be seen again. He would return to his work, give a private audience, receive a Minister, and go to bed very early. Mme. Bonaparte would play cards to fill out the evening. Between ten and eleven someone would come to say, 'Madame, the First Consul has gone to bed,' and then she would dismiss us."

On the evening of December 24, 1800—3 Nivôse—Bonaparte and his wife had made plans to attend the first performance of Haydn's *Creation.* After dinner Bonaparte was sitting by the fire and did not appear very eager to go out. The night was foggy and cold, and it did not seem worth while venturing out in it when it was so comfortable poking the fire. But Josephine and Hortense were waiting, hoping they had not got dressed for nothing.

"Come along, Bonaparte," said Josephine, "it will be a diversion for you, you're working too much."

The Consul closed his eyes and after a pause declared, "You can go, I shall stay here."

His wife replied that in that case she would keep him company. "There was a contest between them," Hortense related, "which ended by the horses being put to the carriages."

A few minutes later it was announced that the carriages were waiting. Bonaparte went toward his. Was it he, as Hortense says, or Rapp, as Laure d'Abrantès affirms, who noticed that Josephine's shawl did not match her dress or was badly draped? Whoever it was, Josephine allowed her husband to leave while she quickly returned up the steps of the Pavillon de Flore to change her shawl or let Rapp arrange it "in the Egyptian style."

Less than three minutes after Bonaparte and his escort left, Josephine's carriage, which contained also Hortense and Caroline—the latter nearly nine months pregnant—crossed the Carrousel in its turn toward the Rue Saint-Nicaise. This street ran parallel to the château, for a dozen yards formed one of the sides of the Place du Carrousel, and ended at the Rue Saint-Honoré. Almost immediately after it came the Rue de la Loi, which led to the Opera.

At the very moment when Josephine's carriage was about to enter the Rue Saint-Nicaise a frightening explosion shook it and broke the windows.

"It's meant for Bonaparte!" cried Josephine before she fainted.

The terrible infernal machine constructed by the Chouans Limoelan, Saint-Régent and Carbon had just gone off. On coming out of her swoon Josephine repeated: "It's meant for Bonaparte! It's meant for Bonaparte!"

Finally a guard from the escort came to reassure her. The attempt had failed. The First Consul's carriage had already reached the Rue Saint-Honoré when the powder barrel exploded, mowing down the rear of the escort and killing ten or twelve people.

Had it not been for the shawl Josephine also would have perished. The First Consul's wife bravely gave orders for the carriage to proceed, by a different route, to the Opera.

"It was nothing," murmured Bonaparte as he greeted his wife.

A few minutes later the news of the attempt was known by the public and spread rapidly. All the spectators rose and—"like an electric spark"—a wave of applause rose toward the Consular box. Bonaparte remained unmoved. Josephine was not so self-controlled. Her face was anguished. "Her very bearing, always so graceful, was no longer her own," recalled Laure d'Abrantès. "She seemed to shudder and try to shelter behind her shawl." Josephine let the tears run down her pale cheeks. And "when she looked at the First Consul, she shuddered once more."

Back at the Tuileries and seated in the great drawing room, which gradually filled with visitors, she continued dabbing at her eyes. Bonaparte, "with his rare but expressive gestures," marched up and down, shouting violently:

"It is the work of the Jacobins; it is the Jacobins who wished to assassinate me! Neither priests, nor nobles, nor Chouans are mixed up in it! I know what to believe and I am not to be imposed on. It is the *septembriseurs,* mud-spattered wretches who are permanently conspiring, a solid phalanx against successive governments. Well, this is the same clique, the blood drinkers of September, the assassins of Versailles, the brigands of May 31 the conspirators of Prairial, the authors of every crime committed against all the governments. If they cannot be chained up they must be crushed. . . . There must be no pity for such wretches!"

That evening Josephine heard Fouché accuse the royalists. Like Bonaparte, at first she regarded him with scorn. Of course the regicide, the assassin of Lyons, wanted to save his former friends. But in the end she was impressed by the conviction shown by her paymaster and, with Lannes, Réal and Regnault, agreed with Fouché, who kept on saying: "This is the work of the royalists, the Chouans, and I ask only a week to bring proof of it."

The Minister needed not a week but twenty-five days to arrest one of the three conspirators, who turned in the other two. It was indeed royalists who had planned the attempt.

Josephine was convinced that the assassins would try again. The Chouans were steeped in hatred.

To kill the Consul Louis XVIII's partisans soon were drawing up another plan involving attacks on coaches, in which they were experts. When he went to Malmaison with Josephine Bonaparte was escorted by only fifty mounted grenadiers. In those days Neuilly, Puteaux, Nanterre and Rueil were only little villages separated by waste land of dubious report, pitted with quarries in which a whole troop could hide, while waiting to attack the escort. Georges Cadoudal, chouannerie personified, came to Paris and approved the idea of "taking the road to Malmaison," but he deemed it necessary to return to London in order to come to an understanding with the English rulers and government about it. He was, however, to put in an appearance later.

Meanwhile the assassins reviewed possible methods: a pistol shot, a barrel of powder to be placed in the cellars of the Tuileries. Others thought the most thoroughgoing method would be to effect an entrance through the ground floor of the château into the room of the usurper and his wife, and kill them both as they slept.

Josephine had persuaded her husband that as she slept very lightly she would wake up if anyone dared enter their bedroom, so they continued to sleep together.

This sometimes gave rise to very homely scenes, as for example on the night when Bourrienne came into the First Consul's bedroom to defend himself against accusations that seemed to him unjust. Bonaparte, who had believed them, had ordered his former fellow student to stop opening his mail as he had hitherto done. "I let Bonaparte go downstairs to bed," Bourrienne was to relate. "Half an hour later I went to his apartments. I was always allowed in at any time. I was carrying a candle, I picked up a chair, went straight to his bed and placed the candle on a bedside table. He and Josephine woke up.

" 'What has happened now?' he asked in surprise.

" 'General, I have come to announce that I cannot remain with you. If I am not trusted, my position is unbearable. You know how devoted I am to you, if you wish to reproach me at least let me know the cause, but my situation for the past three days has been much too painful.' "

Josephine then inquired hastily, "What has he done to you, Bonaparte?"

"It's none of your business."

Then, turning to Bourrienne, he explained: "Yes, I certainly have a complaint against you! I know you have spoken about important matters in a way that does not please me."

His secretary tried to defend himself. Suddenly, Bourrienne relates, "I still seem to see and hear that good Josephine, half-sitting up, say to him with the most winning gentleness, 'Now then, Bonaparte, how could you suspect Bourrienne, who is so attached to you, and is your only friend? . . . My God, how I detest all your police!' "

Bonaparte began to laugh and said to her "jestingly": "Now, now, go to sleep. You look after your dresses, women don't understand anything about government affairs."

One can imagine the scene. Josephine was undoubtedly still the companion of her husband's bed. Bonaparte was still attached to her physically, but he now saw her with different eyes. Her treachery and the discovery of her love affair with Charles had a lot to do with this.

If his eyes had not been opened just before entering Cairo he would undoubtedly have remained faithful to her. Bellilote, that ravishing blonde with clear eyes, had made him temporarily forget Josephine's kisses, those kisses that used to "burn his blood." But when "Cleopatra" arrived in Paris from Egypt Bonaparte had no wish to take that fresh, attractive body in his arms again. He even refused to see her, merely sending her money quite often. And Josephine sighed with relief, particularly as the First Consul, to make matters quite clear, married off his former mistress to a certain Henry de Ranchoup.

Yet the specter of divorce was to be present to Josephine for ten years. Every time there was another woman in her husband's life, it was the fear of being abandoned and losing her position that aroused her jealousy—not love. This jealousy annoyed her husband extremely.

"She worried more than she need," he would say. "She is always afraid I will fall seriously in love. Doesn't she know that love is not for me? What is love? A passion that puts the whole universe on one side and on the other sets up and sees only the beloved object. It is certainly not my nature to be so exclusive. So what do these diversions matter to her when my affections are not involved?"

She was to tremble again, nonetheless, after Marengo, when Bonaparte, who had been seduced at Milan by Grassini's golden voice, spent some agreeable moments with the dark-haired, warm, twenty-seven-year-old prima donna of La Scala. He brought her back to Paris and made her sing duets with the tenor Bianchi to celebrate the Fourteenth of July and the victory of Marengo. Grassini was by no means faithful to the First Consul, deceiving him with the violinist Rode. This ended her liaison with Bonaparte, but not his protection. And there were occasional revivals of their relationship whenever La Grassini was staying in the capital. At the beginning of 1803 Josephine had some reasons for showing jealousy as Bonaparte had just resumed his affair with the Italian and was being very unpleasant to his wife, obviously irritated by Josephine's suspicions, complaints, spying and readily wakened jealousy. Mme. de Rémusat was to say: "He was hard, violent and pitiless toward his wife the moment he had a mistress. He lost no time in informing her of it and in displaying an almost savage surprise when she did not approve of his indulgence in diversions which, as he would demonstrate so to speak mathematically, were both permitted and necessary to him."

"I am not like other men," Bonaparte would say, "and the laws of propriety and morals cannot be made for me."

"Declarations such as these aroused Mme. Bonaparte's displeasure and tears. Her husband sometimes responded with a violence whose excesses I would not dare to relate."

Josephine would then unburden herself to her kind friend Mme. de Krény, her former lodger from the Rue de l'Université.

"I am very unhappy, my dear, every day Bonaparte makes scenes although I have done nothing. It's no way to live. I tried to find out what could be causing them. I have learned that La Grassini has been in Paris for a week. It must be she who is the cause of all my misery. I assure you, my dear, that if I were in any way in the wrong I should tell you frankly. Would you please send Julie [Mme. de Krény's maid] to see if anyone visits her. Also, try to find out where that woman lives."

Bonaparte was hiding the singer in a little house in the Rue Chantereine, a step from his old house.

Another brief infatuation disturbed the household: the actress Duchesnois. In this case Josephine was wrong to be anxious. One evening the famous actress was summoned to the Tuileries. She came. Constant, Bonaparte's valet, announced her arrival to his master, who was at work.

"Tell her to wait," he said.

Two hours later the Consul was still working and Constant reminded him of the lady's presence.

"Tell her to get undressed."

Mlle. Duchesnois obeyed. It was cold, so cold that Constant came once more to his master's door to inform him of the fact.

"Tell her to go to bed," growled Bonaparte.

The night was half over when the valet, at the request of the actress, went once more to the First Consul. Without raising his head, he remarked, "Tell her to get dressed and go home."

It was different when an affair was more serious. Josephine was made perfectly well aware of the end of a liaison by her husband's renewed tenderness for her. Mme. de Rémusat, who lived at close quarters with the couple, has described this. "He would then be moved by her grief and instead of insults give her caresses as unbridled as his violence and, since she was gentle and pliant, she would recover her feeling of security."

She was soon to lose it. Mlle. George had entered the First Consul's life, and this was to be a serious affair. If Josephine had been able to witness the intimate scenes between the two lovers, her anxiety would have been even greater. It is said that the first time Bonaparte received the actress in private he had remarked, "You have kept on your stockings, you must have ugly feet."

But ignoring her "vulgar extremities," to use his own phrase, he offered his mistress actions and attentions like those he had once kept for Josephine. "He would gradually demolish all my toilette," Mlle. George recounted. "He acted the lady's maid with such gaiety, grace and modesty that one had to give way, whatever one might think. And how could one not be fascinated and drawn toward that man? To please me he became like a little child. He was no longer the Consul, he was a man in love, certainly, but a man whose love was neither violent nor hasty. He embraced you gently, his words were tender and respectful, it was impossible, when with him, not to feel what he himself felt.

"For the first fortnight he gratified my scrupulous delicacy and, if I may say so, my modesty by repairing the night's disorder while appearing to remake the bed. He would help me dress, put on my shoes and even, since I had garters with buckles that made him impatient, had round garters made for me to be put on over the foot."

Meanwhile Josephine would wait in vain in her bedroom for her companion. She soon learned the name of her rival and her jealousy turned to real fury.

She constantly brooded over her fears. "It's a great misfortune for me not to have given Bonaparte a son. That will always be one means by which hatred can trouble my peace."

One evening after midnight she guessed that Mlle. George was with Bonaparte.

"I can't bear it any longer," she said to Mme. de Rémusat. "I'm sure Mlle. George is up there, I want to surprise them together."

Her lady in waiting tried in vain to dissuade Mme. Bonaparte from this foolish action.

"Follow me," Josephine ordered. "We shall go up together."

Nothing Mme. de Rémusat could say was any use and the two women—Josephine "overexcited" and her companion holding the

candle and "very ashamed" of the part she was forced to play—
went up the private staircase leading to the First Consul's room.
Suddenly they heard a slight sound. Mme. Bonaparte turned round.

"Perhaps it's Rustum, Bonaparte's Mameluke, guarding the door.
The wretch is capable of cutting both our throats."

"At these words," Mme. de Rémusat relates, "I was seized with a
terror which, ridiculous though it may have been, did not permit me
to listen further, and without thinking that I was leaving Mme.
Bonaparte in total darkness, I went downstairs still holding the
candle and returned to the drawing room as quickly as I could. She
followed me shortly afterwards, astonished at my sudden flight.
When she saw my terrified face, she began to laugh, and so did I,
and we gave up our scheme."

However, Bonaparte got to know of the scene on the staircase
and used it to draw Mme. de Rémusat into his family disputes.
Which one was in the wrong? She got out of it as best she could.
Certainly she was very sorry for Mme. Bonaparte, but conceded
that the Consul's wife was lacking in dignity "when she tried
through the spying of her servants to obtain proof of the unfaithfulness she suspected." Hence came "endless words and little scenes"
between husband and wife, in the course of which Bonaparte was
"by turns imperious, hard, overdefiant, then suddenly touched,
softened, almost gentle, and with a good deal of grace made
amends for the wrongs he admitted to but nevertheless did not
renounce."

Josephine gained nothing. Alleging his wife's jealousy of Mlle.
George or of other infatuations as reasonable, Bonaparte began to
keep more often to his own room. When he did come to her by the
famous staircase Josephine took care that the whole Court should
know it.

"That's why I got up so late today," she was to explain with an
exhausted, happy look.

Yet the liaison with Mlle. George was to go on all during the time
of the Consulate.

"He left me to make himself emperor," the actress was to say
proudly to Alexandre Dumas one day.

As for Josephine, she was seeing Charles again and looking after
his interests. By her own account, an hour after receiving a request
from her dear Hippolyte concerning one of his friends she wrote to

Cambacérès and to the Minister of Justice to recommend Charles's protégé. She failed and wrote to the man who had been her lover: "I am all the more vexed at not having succeeded since I should have been delighted to prove to you that my feelings are still the same, that nothing will make me change, that I love you with the tenderest and most lasting friendship."

If all that remained between her and Hippolyte were memories, was Josephine faithful to her husband? Most probably not. In a letter written about this time to Mme. de Krény, Josephine speaks of an alleged, unknown "gardener," who may well have played a part in the life of the amorous Creole.

"Bonaparte decided at seven in the evening to spend the night at Malmaison, an idea which was carried out at once. So here I am, my dear, confined to the country for I don't know how long. This year Malmaison, which used to hold so many attractions for me, is no more than a tedious desert. I left so hurriedly yesterday that I did not have time to send a message to the gardener who had promised me some flowers. As I particularly want to write to him, let me know what I must order from him. I don't know what you have agreed on with him, but I want to tell him my disappointment, particularly, my dear, as it is very real.

"I have not forgotten your fifty louis, you shall have them the day after tomorrow."

Is it likely she would have had a "very real disappointment" because her hurried departure from the Tuileries had prevented her taking a bouquet picked for her? Especially as she was going to Malmaison, which was full of flowers. Moreover, it was to her intimate friend Mme. de Krény that she was telling the whole business. It is not impossible, of course, that the "gardener" was Charles.

Only one thing would have quieted Josephine once and for all— maternity.

"A child would have kept Josephine calm," Bonaparte was to say with truth, "and would have put an end to a jealousy that gave her husband no peace."

Undoubtedly he found her tears and scenes—for which she had a genius—insupportable, but he still loved her and was to love her for many more years. When he was at Pont-de-Briques, near Boulogne, at the end of 1803, preparing for the invasion of England, he wrote her lines of such affection (although Mlle. George was still a part of his life), that Josephine wrote him this very tender letter, one of the few we possess:

"All my grief disappeared as I read the kind, touching letter which contains such loving expression of your feelings for me. How grateful I am to you for devoting so much time to me, your Josephine. If you knew, you would congratulate yourself on being able to give so much joy to the woman you love. A letter is the portrait of a soul and I press this one to my heart. It does me so much good! I want to keep it always. It will console me during your absence, guide me when I am near you, for I want always to be in your eyes the kind, tender Josephine, preoccupied solely with your happiness. If your mind has an impulse of joy, if sadness troubles you for a moment, you must pour your happiness and your grief into the bosom of your friend. You shall have no feeling I do not share. That is my desire, these are my wishes, only to please you and make you happy. . . . Good-by, Bonaparte, I shall not forget the last sentence of your letter. I have taken it to heart. How deeply it is engraved there, with what transports my own responded to it! Yes, my wish too is to please you, to love, or rather to adore you."

A few weeks later he sent "a thousand remembrances to the little cousin," probably a synonym for the "little black forest," or "Josephine's three islands," a sensual memory he was to recall on St. Helena.

11. The Mistress of Malmaison

Malmaison—three leagues (eight miles) from the Tuileries, on the Cherbourg road, in the parish of Rueil. Malmaison—three syllables woven into Josephine's life and where, even today, one can still sense her presence at the turn of a path or on opening a door. Malmaison, whose slate roofs she could glimpse when, as the young Vicomtesse de Beauharnais, she was living at Croissy.

This "Trianon of the Consulate" was Josephine's real home. From Octidi to Primidi what one might call the weekends of the Revolutionary calendar—the Consular household would go there with its suite. From the spring of 1801, and until the stays at Saint-Cloud began at the end of 1802, Bonaparte was to reside much more frequently with the mistress of Malmaison—for Josephine was really at home here—than in the Tuileries.

The inventory we possess gives us a detailed description of the furniture Josephine and Bonaparte bought with the buildings of Malmaison. The general effect is not luxurious. Among the most prized objects are the two "great stoves heated from below with marble tops and adorned with two figures," which were placed in "the great antechamber giving on to both courtyard and garden." The cost of the furnishings of the Great Drawing Room—couches, easy chairs, armchairs of mahogany covered in green taffeta, console table, fire irons, curtains of green silk, and mirrors—reached the sum of 2,072 francs. The master bedroom held a "Polish-style bed with its curves," and two couches, two easy chairs and two low chairs. The curtains were of striped muslin. This was undoubtedly the Consular family's main bedroom.

After the purchase of Malmaison from the Lecoulteux de Moley, on April 20, 1799, the house had been gradually refurnished and the estate considerably enlarged by the purchase of 153 hectares of woodland and the acquisition of the Pavillon de la Jonchère and the Toutain and Butard parks. The house itself had been much improved. For 600,000 francs Josephine had Percier and Fontaine, government architects, build two Doric lodges either side of the entrance gate, then two wings projecting from the main courtyard, and finally a peristyle whose tent-shaped ceiling was supported by lances. On its walls were bundles of lances and the window curtains revealed bars which were a "trellis of zinc lances."

"It looks like a show-cage for animals at a fair," Bonaparte exclaimed.

It was a cage, perhaps, but a very attractive one. The great hall led to the park by a little bridge between two obelisks. A gallery was added for the works of art. Finally, the private apartments on the second floor and the small apartments on the third for officers and guests were fitted out.

The Council Room, too, had the air of a tent. There were more fasces, armor, cardboard helmets and, of course, lances. Beyond the circular study one entered the wonderful library divided into three parts—as the building's lack of structural strength made the addition of supporting Doric columns necessary. Here Bonaparte's presence can still be felt. One can imagine that the First Consul has just left his study by going over the little bridge where he liked to work in summer under a canvas awning.

"When I am in the open air," he used to say, "I can feel my ideas spreading higher and wider. I cannot understand how some men can work successfully near a stove and deprived of all communication with the sky."

In all the rooms were bouquets from the hothouses or gardens of Malmaison. From her years in Martinique Josephine had preserved a passion for flowers. One has to have strolled across the *mornes* of the Antilles to realize the extraordinary range of colors in the vegetation of the Ile des Revenants. Using greenhouses of varying temperatures, Josephine, instructed by the botanists Ventenat and Soulange-Boudin, introduced many new species into France. Thanks to her, to Brisseau de Mirbel, "director of her botanical establishments," and later to her own botanist Bonpland, 184 kinds of plants hitherto quite unknown are now to be found in many gardens there.

The peace preliminaries between France and England had only just been signed when, on October 11, 1801, Josephine wrote the French Minister Plenipotentiary Otto in London: "Do you not think that the King of England might consent to give me a few of the plants from his beautiful garden at Kew?"

Once the Peace of Amiens was signed, in March, 1802, the English streamed over to France and Josephine received a friend of Fox at Malmaison.

"Mme. Bonaparte," he recounted, "did the honors with that attractive affability which readily justified the First Consul's attachment to her. The park is designed in the same taste as ours—none of those straight lines imposed on grass and flowers. . . . She took us through her magnificent hothouses, giving the names of those rare plants which the art and patience of man (and woman) cause to vegetate . . . in our climate."

"It is here," she told them, "that I have felt happier, in studying the crimson of the cactus, than in contemplating all the pomp that surrounds me. It is here that I should like to reign among these vegetable tribes. Here is the Hortensia, which has recently been given my daughter's name, the Alpine Soldanella, the Parma violet, the Nile lily, the Damiette rose, these spoils from Italy and Egypt never made Bonaparte any enemies! But here is my own acquisition," she added proudly, showing her fine Martinique jasmine. "The plant sown and cultivated by me reminds me of my country, my childhood, and what I wore for ornament as a girl."

"Indeed, as she said this, her Creole's voice sounded like music full of expression and tenderness," added the Englishman.

France owes to Josephine many other species, such as the purple-flowered magnolia, the eucalyptus, the hibiscus, the phlox, the catalpa, the camellia, the Louisiana cypress, the lacquer tree, the

Virginia tulip tree and varieties of myrtle, rhododendron, mimosa, dahlia, tulip, geranium and double hyacinth.

She hesitated at nothing, and it is said that one day she paid 4,000 francs for a tulip bulb, the flower she most loved after the rose.

It was to Josephine that the extraordinary progress of the rose in France was due. She had plants sent from Australia and managed to collect in Malmaison 250 varieties, nearly all the roses then known, which her painter, Pierre Joseph Redouté, Marie Antoinette's former drawing master, was to immortalize in those plates which are a joy to the eye. Josephine also caused the creation of the Malmaison rose—shading from white to pink—and the Josephine rose with its blue tones. There were also the *Souvenir de la Malmaison*, the *Belle sans Flatterie* and the *Aimable Rouge*.

She herself wrote to Thibaudeau on March 19, 1804: "It makes me happy to see plants from abroad flourish in my gardens. I hope that Malmaison soon will be a model of plant cultivation and become a rich source for all the departments. It is for this reason that I am having innumerable trees and shrubs from the Southern Hemisphere and Northern America reared there. I should like every department, in ten years' time, to possess a collection of valuable plants from my nurseries."

She applied everywhere to enrich her collection. "Please collect a large quantity of seeds and plants," she wrote to M. Soult, the French consul at Charleston. "It would be a kindness for which I should be most grateful, for you are aware that I delight in the cultivation of foreign plants."

She supervised her plantings herself. Brisseau de Mirbel was made her Minister for Flowers.

But it was not only flowers that aroused her enthusiasm. She did not wait for the signing of peace with England to ask Otto to send her carriage horses "dapple-gray or light bay, with a spot on the head." She also wanted "two gentle saddle horses, suitable for carrying a lady." She was fond of all animals and wanted to fill Malmaison with them. Apart from the 500 merino sheep from Spain and a herd of "wonderful cows" imported later from Switzerland and looked after by Bernese in costume, ponies from Ushant were to be seen galloping freely over the lawns, and white or black swans, Carolina and Mandarin duck swimming on the lakes. Gazelles, kangaroos, chamois, a gnu and a graceful African antelope disported themselves in paddocks. There was even a seal. In the aviaries were parrots, parakeets, cockatoos, West Indian birds, white blackbirds, squirrels, pigeons from the Moluccas. She was sent rare birds from Guadeloupe—at her expense—and had storks dispatched from Strasbourg, for a price.

Bonaparte had scant respect for his wife's "zoological park." One day, during the Empire, he asked Rustum for his gun in order to shoot at the swans from his bedroom window. Hearing the shots Josephine rushed in "in her chemise and wrapped in a large shawl."

"Bonaparte, please don't fire at my swans!"

"Leave me alone, Josephine, it amuses me."

She managed to get the weapon away from him while Napoleon "laughed like anything."

All the visitors—whether from over the Rhine or over the Channel —praised the First Consul's wife. To them Josephine was "the ideal mistress of the house. They praise her taste and her wit, of which in fact she has a very small allowance. They admire her botanical and zoological hobbies, which make her appear skilled in every science and give her the reputation of being a lover of nature."

A swarm of young women clustered round her: Mme. Savary, née de Faudoas, whose teeth were as bad as those of the mistress of the house, Mlle. de Ghéenenc, soon to be Mme. Lannes and described as "a Raphael virgin," the fresh Mme. Bessières, Mlle. Auguié, niece to Mme. Campan and later wife of General Ney, her sister, Mme. de Broc, and finally Caroline, still laughing and gay at that time.

Josephine's society also included Mmes. de Chauvelin, d'Aiguillon, de Vergennes, de Nicolaï, MM. de Girardin, de Ségur, de Montesquiou, de Noailles, de Praslin, de Mouchy. For there were many members of the nobility who no longer held apart.

At Malmaison Bonaparte and his wife could relax. Simplicity was so much the rule that a visitor from Germany remarked scornfully that "the general appearance was of a rich banker's house" and that there was not even "the etiquette that prevails in the court of the smallest German prince."

However, there is no better guide to life with Josephine than Laure d'Abrantès.

"Life at Malmaison, at the time of my marriage, was like life in any country house where there are a great many visitors. Our apartments consisted of a bedroom, a dressing room and a room for our maid, just as in the country houses of rich people. The furniture was very simple and the rooms of the daughter of the house, which were next to mine, differed only by having a double door. . . . The rooms were not parqueted, which surprised me, knowing how fastidious Mme. Lecoulteux herself was. They all gave on to a long corridor, reached by a step; off to the right were Mme. Bonaparte's rooms and the little room where we lunched."

Lunch, which took place without Bonaparte, was at eleven and, except for members of the family, no men were present. After lunch Josephine would talk, read the newspapers, work on her embroidery or receive petitioners.

One day there arrived at Malmaison a certain M. de Céré, who had been dismissed as the First Consul's aide-de-camp for taking two weeks too long in carrying out a mission. At Savary's request Josephine gave him an audience. Just as he was leaving his house he had met his tailor, who handed him a bill. He arrived at Malmaison, was struck by Mme. Bonaparte's "charming and gracious" welcome, presented his petition, eagerly swallowed her promise to intercede with her husband for him, returned home intoxicated by hope—and discovered his petition in his pocket. By mistake he had handed Josephine his tailor's bill. The unhappy man could not sleep all night and the next day called on the First Consul's wife.

The moment Josephine noticed M. de Céré in the pillared hall, she hurried forward and gave him her hand.

"How glad I am! I handed your petition to the First Consul. We read it together. It was wonderful. It made a great impression on him. He told me he would report to Berthier and that everything would be settled in two weeks. I can assure you that this success, for I regard the affair as settled, made me the happiest woman in the world yesterday."

M. de Céré did not dare say anything, but, Mme. d'Abrantès concluded, "one may deduce that Mme. Bonaparte, although very good and kind-hearted . . . was not always a person on whom one could rely entirely. . . . She was benevolent, and really wished to be obliging, but this wish gave way before the slightest fear of upsetting the First Consul."

She herself was to say to Carnot one day, "Pay no attention to my recommendations. They are forced from me by importunity and I give them to anyone at all."

At six o'clock Bonaparte, who had spent the day working and

receiving Ministers, generals or councilors, joined his wife for
dinner. There were present Josephine's ladies, the aides-de-camp,
their young wives and a few friends. Every Wednesday what was
almost a banquet took place. Afterwards they moved to the drawing
room. Josephine went to her harp. Sometimes she played it, but
always the same tune. She undoubtedly preferred her tapestry. She
would work while listening to Arnault, who had come from Paris
with one of his colleagues. Ducis needed no urging to recite scenes
from his plays, others would declaim verses or read. The little Court
also played chess or reversi (a card game) or went to the little
private theatre where Louis, Eugene, Hortense (a charming
actress), and others, including Bourrienne (the cleverest of them)
would act a comedy. Eugene was the principal leader of the little
group. Now twenty-one, he had just been appointed colonel of the
Chasseurs de la Garde, with 30,000 francs a year pay, which was to
be increased to 150,000 at the end of 1803. His stepfather had given
him the magnificent Neufville-Villeroy house in the Rue de Lille. He
was very eligible. Eugene was charming, cheerful, always gay, and
the girls at Malmaison always had designs on him, and he collected
hearts one after another. Laure d'Abrantès relates:

When it was fine the First Consul would order dinner to be served
in the park. A table would be placed to the left of the lawn in front of
the house. . . . We spent little time at table and the First Consul
thought dinner was long if we spent half an hour over it.
When he was in a good humor, if the weather was fine and he could
snatch a few moments from the constant work which was then overwhelming him, he would play at prisoners' base with us. He cheated,
just as he did at reversi. He would trip us up or come up behind us without having shouted Barre! But this cheating always gave rise to happy
laughter. On those occasions Napoleon took off his coat and ran like a
hare, or rather like the gazelle, to whom he gave all the tobacco in his
pouch, telling it to run after us; and the wretched animal tore our
dresses and quite often our legs too.
One day, after dinner, it was fine. The First Consul said, "Let's play
prisoners' base."
At once his coat was on the ground and a conqueror of the world
was running like a little schoolboy.
At that time there was an open ditch running along part of the road, that
is, by the field which was later bought for the great plantation of plane
and tulip trees. By entering this field the curious could easily observe
from a distance what was happening in the park. On the house side

there was an iron railing on which one could lean. Mme. Bonaparte, who was not playing prisoners' base, was by this railing with Mme. de Lavallette when, going forward a few steps, she was frightened by the sight of two men whose air and countenance were calculated to inspire fear, particularly at a time when France was still trembling from the Nivôse attack. The two men were ill dressed and spoke in low tones as they watched the First Consul. I was not playing any more and came up to Mme. Bonaparte just then. She took my arm and asked Mme. de Lavallette to find her husband or Eugene, but to take care that the First Consul did not see her, since he hated inquiries and precautions of that kind.

"Do you want anything, citizens?" she asked them in a trembling voice.

"Indeed no, citizeness. We are watching. Aren't we allowed in this field?"

"Of course, of course," Mme. Bonaparte hastened to reply, "but . . ."

"Oh, it's because we're watching the First Consul? That's because it's astonishing, as I was saying to my brother, to see the head of the government enjoying himself just like the poorest Frenchman in the Republic. There now!" said the man, grabbing his friend's arm and pointing at the First Consul, who was holding my husband by the ear, "there now, see how he's got hold of Junot! . . ."

As the man stopped speaking he was spun round and found himself facing Rapp, whom Mme. de Lavallette had met and who . . . had needed no urging to go where there might be even the shadow of danger for his general.

"What are you doing here?" he asked in a voice of thunder. "What do you want? Alms? Get moving. Why are you looking into the garden and frightening these ladies with your ruffianly looks? I'll have you arrested, I will, if you don't answer."

"Things are going badly, it seems to me, Colonel," replied the man who had not yet spoken. "Since when can't we watch our general? Has he given orders that he is to be hidden from his old soldiers? I'm quite sure he hasn't."

"Ah, I'm sure he hasn't!" repeated the other man.

"Are you soldiers?" Rapp asked, softening a little as he saw the men were professionals.

"Are we soldiers? What a question! Now here's a man who won't send us packing."

It was Eugene, who had got away from the game as soon as he could and had come running up to see what Rapp was about with the men. . . .

"So it's you," he said to one of the men, who lacked an arm (which we had not noticed before, as he wore a big coat round him).

"Yes, Major, and here's a colonel who wants to put us in prison, but you'll stop him, won't you?"

"Arrest you, my lad! But what are you doing here anyway?"

"I came to speak to you, Major. I came to tell you that the Austrian bullet that took off my arm has not given me another one to serve my country, so I'm discharged, but not asking alms, as that citizen said. However, no hard feelings. . . . I have a nice little pension, but that's all the more reason for being grateful. So I brought my brother here, a fine chap of thirty-one, strong, well and brave. As far as that goes he wants nothing from anyone. I ask a horse and gun for him, Major, and you'll see what he can do if needed."

The First Consul, who had eyes that saw without looking and ears that heard without listening, had grasped the gist of the story from the first word, for he had recognized the sergeant of his Guides. At Montebello or Marengo the man had had his arm shot off while defending his badly wounded superior officer . . . whom the Uhlans were trying to finish off. The First Consul had himself seen that the man was carried from the field on the crossed rifles of soldiers. And the sergeant had later been presented to him once on parade so the man's face had stayed in his mind.

"Well, well, here come the invalids. Good morning, my lad. So you came to see me? Well, have a look round. Obey your general's orders once more. Take him along, Eugene."

The old Guide presented his brother to the First Consul and pointed out that he did not come under the law of conscription.

"He's joined voluntarily, General, and you are his recruiting officer."

The good fellow was so happy. He moved about with his eyes full of tears and the stump of his arm waving in his sleeve as though he wanted to rub his hands together.

"If I'm the recruiting officer," said the First Consul, "the conscript must drink my health and that of the Republic. Eugene, my son, take your soldier with you and entertain him for me."

The old Guide watched the First Consul move away. As long as he thought he might turn round he kept a good countenance, but once he could no longer see him his defenses gave way and he burst into tears. . . .

That evening the house slept. From time to time a mounted Guide rode round the park. Laure recounted:

Suddenly there was a shot. It came from the moat. At once, with no more delay than was required to draw a breath suspended by fear, everyone was up. The women, dressed only in an underskirt, the men with only trousers. The First Consul was already in the corridor in his dressing gown, with a candle in his hand, crying out in his loud, resonant voice: "Don't be frightened! It's nothing!"

He was as calm as though his sleep had not been disturbed and I am certain of this because at that moment, curiously enough, I was occupied only with him and particularly with examining his countenance at such a time. It was calm and unmoved, without being indifferent, but one could see that he felt far above the common danger. His destiny was not yet fulfilled and he could feel this. Rapp and M. Lacuée, or perhaps it was Lemarrois . . . came up from the park . . . and announced that the Guide's horse had fallen after stepping on a molehill while crossing the lawn in front of the house. As he fell the rifle had gone off and roused the whole house. When the First Consul heard his aide's report he began to laugh and standing on the little stool at the end of the main landing shouted: "Josephine, don't cry any more. It was a mole that did everything. That's quite understandable, for it's an ugly animal. As for the Guide, two days' arrest to teach him not to cross my lawn on his horse. As I assume he got quite a fright himself, his punishment won't be any longer. Good night, ladies, go back to bed and sleep well."

As he was returning to his rooms, he said, "Good heavens, Mme. Junot, how pale you are! Were you frightened?"

"Yes, indeed, General, very much so."

"Really? Fancy that! I thought you were so brave. Anyway, this is no concern of women, but they must not cry." . . .

All her life Josephine was to remember the painful scene of Le Butard. That day she had a bad headache and wanted to remain at Malmaison. Bonaparte was very anxious to visit Le Butard, Louis XVI's former hunting lodge, which he had just added to Malmaison.

"Come along with us," he said to her. "The air will do you good. It's a sovereign remedy for all indispositions."

Josephine dared not refuse, and entered the carriage with Emilie Lavallette and Laure Junot, who was expecting a child.

"Napoleon was ahead of us with Bourrienne," the latter related. "The aide-de-camp on duty had not been summoned for this trip, with which the First Consul was as delighted as a schoolboy on holiday. He was on horseback and galloped in front of us, returning to take his wife's hand, as a child running in front of his mother, goes, comes back, leaves, returns again to kiss her and runs off once more."

Suddenly the carriage stopped before a stream with fairly high banks. Questioned by Josephine, the groom replied that fording the river might be dangerous.

"I don't want to go to Le Butard by this road!" exclaimed Mme. Bonaparte. "Go and tell the First Consul that I am returning to the château, unless he knows another way."

The carriage turned round, but Bonaparte came galloping back. He looked furious.

"What's this new whim? Go back to where you were," he ordered the driver, touching his shoulder with his whip.

The carriage turned round and stopped before the stream.

"Now, then," said Napoleon to the young postilion who was driving. "A good bound, then ease the reins and you'll be over."

Josephine uttered a piercing cry which, in Laure's words, "sounded through the forest." She began, naturally, to cry and clasped her hands.

"You can't make me stay in the carriage. Let me get out! Bonaparte, I beg you, please let me get out, let me get out!"

Bonaparte shrugged.

"That's childish. You'll get over, and in the carriage. Now, then, did you hear me?" he called to the postilion.

Laure Junot then intervened.

"General," she said, signing to the groom to open the door, "I am responsible for the life of another. I cannot stay here. There will be a violent bump, which might not only do me harm but kill me," she said, laughing, "and you don't want that, do you, General?"

"I!" exclaimed Bonaparte. "My God! I do you any harm! Get out, you're quite right, a shock might do you harm."

Mme. Junot prepared to leave the carriage with Bonaparte's help. She lingered in order to back up Josephine.

"But," she went on, "a shock might harm Mme. Bonaparte too, General. After all, supposing she were like me . . ."

At these words, she said, "the First Consul looked at me with such a comic air of amazement that, instead of jumping to the ground, I stayed on the step laughing like the girl I was. And suddenly he responded with a single outburst of laughter, so loud and clear that we started. At last I jumped down and Napoleon, who was serious again, remarked that I had been foolish to jump like that. Then, as though he feared he had not shown his displeasure with his wife strongly enough, he said, in a voice that admitted no answer, 'Put up the step and let the carriage cross.'"

Poor Josephine was so pale that Laure could not help saying, "General, you seem unkind, and yet you are not so. Mme. Bonaparte is ill, she has a fever. Please let her get out."

This time he grew angry. "Mme. Junot, I never liked being remonstrated with, even as a child. Ask Mme. Letizia, ask Mme. Permon. Do you think I have become more pliable since?"

Then, as Josephine sobbingly asked the postilion "to wait another moment," "You rascal!" Bonaparte exclaimed, striking the postilion over the shoulders with his whip, "are you going to carry out my orders?"

The carriage then passed over the obstacle. The shock was so great that the body of the coach was damaged beyond repair.

Mme. Bonaparte sobbed all the way to Le Butard.

And when Josephine, getting out, showed her husband a tear-stained face, he displayed not merely ill temper but rage. He even pulled her somewhat roughly out of the carriage and taking her a little way off into the forest continued to scold her, as we could hear, with all the more violence as he had been prepared for a cheerful outing when he left that morning. He was wrong in forcing his wife to cross the stream, but in what followed he was in the right. Josephine apparently reproached him with other things than crossing the stream, for I heard Napoleon reply:

"You are crazy, and if you repeat such a thing I shall say you were wicked as well, because you don't believe what you're saying. Besides, you know I loathe all this senseless jealousy. . . . You'll end by pushing me into it. Come on, kiss me and be quiet, you're ugly when you cry, I've told you that before."

As can be seen, she took every opportunity to complain of her husband's "betrayals."

Yet Josephine would have been right to be jealous of Bonaparte's feelings for Laure. . . . Josephine was taking the waters at Plombières when one morning at Malmaison Laure was wakened by a loud knock at her door.

I immediately saw the First Consul near my bed. I thought I was dreaming and rubbed my eyes. He began to laugh.

"It is I indeed," he said. "Why so surprised?"

A minute had been enough to wake me. In reply I smilingly stretched my hand toward the window, which I had left open because of the heat. The sky was still that bright blue that follows the dawn. One could see from the dark green of the trees that the sun had hardly risen. I took my watch, it was not five.

"Really," he said, when I showed it to him, "is it so early? Good, then we'll talk."

Taking a chair, he placed it at the foot of my bed, sat down, crossed his legs and settled there, just as he used to, five years before, by my mother's chair at La Tranquillité.

After chatting for half an hour, Bonaparte pinched Laure's foot through the covers and went away happily, "humming a few notes off key."

But the next day, when Bonaparte came to wake the woman who had undoubtedly attracted him, he found a locked door. On the following day, trying once again, he found Junot sleeping at his wife's side.

After that Laure would never spend the night at Malmaison, not even when Josephine was in the house. One evening, a year later, Mme. Junot had been invited to dinner. She recounted:

As I was about to leave a terrible storm broke out in which the trees in the park were felled by the violence of the wind. Mme. Bonaparte said she did not want me to leave in such a tempest and she would have "my room" prepared. I thanked her and said I was expected at home right away.

"I won't let you leave in such a storm, Mme. Junot," said Mme. Bonaparte, going to the door to give her orders.

I stopped her, giving as my reason that I had no clothes and no maid with me.

"They'll give you one of my nightcaps and one of my gowns, you'll have everything you need. One of my women will be at your orders. Do stay. That's settled, isn't it? Besides, how could you go through the woods, alone, at this hour? It would be risky. Do you know the woods of Bougival are not safe?"

"I'm not afraid, madame, I have four men with me and I assure you that there are no wild beasts in the woods of Le Celle and Bougival. Allow me to take my leave of you and go."

The First Consul was by the fire, poking the embers with the irons and taking no part in the conversation. But from where I was I could see him clearly and I saw him smile, but not unkindly. It was plain to me that he was remembering something I had said. Finally, as Mme. Bonaparte was insisting more strongly that I should stay, he said from his place, without putting down his fire irons or turning his head, "Don't tease her any more, Josephine. I know her, she won't stay."

The Consul had undoubtedly had a weakness for Laure, but this time Josephine had not noticed it.

Bonaparte, who wanted to show the Parisians that a king might be "nothing much," invited the Infante Louis of Parma and his wife Marie Louise, both Bourbons descended from Louis XIV, to visit him in June, 1801. The Treaty of Lunéville had placed them on the throne of Tuscany, which under the First Consul had become the Kingdom of Etruria.

The amazed Parisians watched the entry of the King, the Queen and their son, three puppets, parading in a coach dating back to

Philip V and drawn by mules whose harness was covered with bells. Gesticulating, grotesque and noisy, the King was endowed with an uncommon imbecility. The Queen was repellently ugly, monstrous, inhuman. As for their child—the Contino, aged five—"he merely gave you his hand to kiss," Laure related. The success of the spectacle exceeded Bonaparte's intentions.

That was not all, as was seen when Josephine had the Parmas to dinner at Malmaison. "The King was taken ill on leaving his carriage," Mme. Junot recounted, "and in the strangest way. I was crossing the pillared hall to go to the drawing room when I found myself in the middle of the tumult caused by this event. The Queen appeared very upset and tried to hide her husband, but there is no way of concealing from so many attentive people the sight of a king, however insignificant, when he falls from an attack of grand mal epilepsy, and it appeared that the unfortunate prince was a sufferer from this terrible illness. When I saw him that day he was as pale as death and his features were contorted. But I must say that this fainting spell, whatever the cause, was not as long as an attack is supposed to be, but it was frightening. When he entered the drawing room Mme. Bonaparte asked him kindly what was the matter.

"'Oh, it's nothing, nothing, is it, Louisa? It's nothing, an upset stomach. I'm hungry, I shall have a good dinner. I'm hungry. I was saying to Pepita, wasn't I, Pepita?'

"And that laugh on his still white and contracted lips had something terrifying about it."

At the Opera, where the astonishing couple went with Bonaparte and Josephine, Voltaire's *Oedipus* was presented for them. At the line "I have made kings, but would not reign myself" the whole audience turned toward the Consul's box and applauded. The King began to laugh stupidly, jumping "with both feet" on his chair.

"The new generation growing up now did not know what a king looked like," said Bonaparte, looking at the pitiful puppet. "Well, we've shown them one!"

On July 7, 1801, "the citizeness wife of the First Consul," per- petually hoping to have a child, left Malmaison for her cure at Plombières, in company with Mme. Letizia, Hortense, Mme. de Lavallette and Rapp.

It was an unpleasant journey. They ate badly: "spinach cooked in lamp oil" or "red asparagus stewed in curdled milk," if one is to believe Hortense, who added: "We are growing visibly thinner." The mother-in-law still treated her daughter-in-law with disdain, particularly as it was on Josephine's account and not on hers that the authorities came to meet the travelers and that Plombières and Luxeuil gave balls and receptions. In the intervals between baths Josephine met Astolphe de Custine and his mother Delphine, whom Alexandre de Beauharnais had loved; and after seven years filled with stirring events memories of the Carmelites came back to "Rose."

Meanwhile Bonaparte stayed in Paris. "Malmaison without you is too sad," he wrote to her.

While gossiping with Mme. Hamelin and Mme. de Chauvelin, Josephine watched with affection the languorous, eighteen-year-old Hortense dancing with Astolphe. Although not very beautiful, the future Queen of Holland, like her mother, had immense charm, was "as fresh as a flower" and, it was said, joined Creole nonchalance to French vivacity. Her hair was described by another woman as "the most beautiful blonde hair in the world." Her eyes were blue and "infinitely gentle." To all this was added a "gentle" gaiety and a "sparkling" malice. Moreover, she painted and sang very prettily, played the piano cleverly and was a delightful actress. Undoubtedly the little marvel would have to be married. Hortense was in love— or thought she was—with Duroc, her stepfather's favorite aide-de-camp.

"I could never get used to calling you Mme. Duroc," her mother said to her one day. They would think about it on their return.

On the road to Paris Josephine was received like the wife of a king. On August 4 the civil and military authorities came to meet her at the boundary of the Meurthe Department. In the evening she dined in the government palace at Nancy and then went to the theatre with Madame Mère. The next day she visited the town and lingered in the botanical garden in the Rue Sainte-Catherine. After lunch she set off again for Paris with Mme. Bonaparte. La madre was visibly more and more ill-humored. The honors paid to her daughter-in-law irritated her. So, immediately on their return, anxious to improve her relations with the "clan" and wishing to disarm them, Josephine set about giving her young daughter to her brother-in-law Louis. If Hortense and Louis had a son, moreover, why should he not be adopted by Bonaparte? In this way Josephine would consolidate her position and the specter of divorce, always present to her mind, would retreat. To succeed—and to sacrifice her daughter to her own interests—she had to fight. Bonaparte favored Duroc and wanted to settle matters at top speed. He summoned Bourrienne.

"Where is Duroc?"

"He has gone out, to the Opera, I think."

"When he comes back tell him that I have promised him Hortense, he shall marry her. But I want it to be in two days at the most. I shall give her 500,000 francs and appoint him to command the 8th Division. He will leave for Toulon with his wife the day after his wedding and we shall live apart. I don't want any son-in-law in my house. As I want it settled, tell me this evening if that suits him."

"I don't think it will."

"All right, she'll marry Louis."

"Will she want to?"

"She'll have to."

"The First Consul made this proposal in a short tone," related Bourrienne," which led me to believe that there had been some lively domestic argument and that he was proposing this ultimatum for the sake of peace and so as not to hear any more about it."

Duroc returned at half past ten. Bourrienne gave him a verbatim report of the First Consul's proposal.

"If that's the way it is, my dear chap," exclaimed the aide-de-camp, "he can keep his daughter. I'll stick to whores." And with "indifference" he took up his hat and left.

"Before going to bed the First Consul was informed of Duroc's reply and Josephine received assurance of her daughter's marriage to Louis."

"Perhaps we shall not have any children," Bonaparte told her. "I have brought Louis up and look on him as my son. Your daughter is what you hold dearest in the world. Their children shall be ours. We shall adopt them and this adoption will console us for not having any. But the young people must be content with our plan."

Bourrienne was sent to Hortense.

"I am instructed to propose to you something your mother and the Consul keenly desire. They wish to unite you to Colonel Louis

Bonaparte. He is good, sensitive and he has simple tastes. He will fully appreciate your worth and he is the only husband suitable for you. Look around you; whom would you wish to marry? The time has come to think seriously of this. Until now no one has attracted you and if your heart made a choice which was not approved by your parents would you consent to disobey them? You love France. Would you like to leave it? Your mother could not bear the thought of seeing you joined to a foreign prince who would separate you from her forever. As you know, her misfortune is no longer to have hopes of children. It is for you to make up for this so as perhaps to prevent a greater misfortune. You must know that there are constant intrigues around the Consul to persuade him to divorce. Your marriage alone is capable of tightening and making firm the ties on which your mother's happiness depends. Can you hesitate to do this?"

"I had let Bourrienne speak without interruption," Hortense related. "I learned for the first time that it was in my power to contribute to my mother's peace. How could I refuse? But I needed to become accustomed gradually to the idea of joining my lot with that of a man I did not deeply love. Such a match required mature reflection."

Particularly as a kind of instinct informed the girl how unhappy she would be with Louis Bonaparte.

"Little fool," Josephine is supposed to have said to her, "does the heart count in marriage? You are not asked to love beforehand, but to marry him. Love will come later."

Hortense, with a chill at heart, had accepted and on January 4, 1802, the marriage was celebrated in the Tuileries. That evening she wept as she observed how little enthusiasm her gloomy husband displayed.

The day after the wedding, when Hortense and Louis came to dine in the Tuileries, Josephine wept in her turn. Perhaps she realized that she had brought about her daughter's unhappiness. Bonaparte tried to dry her tears by speaking of their coming journey to Lyons.

"What do the public say?"

"That you are going to have yourself elected King of Italy."

The First Consul began to laugh and in reply quoted the line from Voltaire's *Oedipus* which had so pleased the unfortunate King of Etruria: "I have made kings, but would not reign myself."

Before setting out with Josephine, Bonaparte discovered that Louis had sent out wedding cards in his own name and Mme. Bonaparte's. The Consul flew into a violent rage. He looked on himself as the head of the family, even though Joseph was the eldest. The scene, which took place in the presence of Hortense and Josephine, was a violent one.

"What business is it of yours? If I had wanted to follow the conventions I would have sent cards in my name. Am I not as your father? Is it not my stepdaughter you have married? By what right do you use my wife's name without my permission? You ought to know that my position as First Consul would require that the French authorities and foreign ambassadors should be informed and be present at the wedding. It took place in privacy only in order to avoid the bother of ceremony. They will not know the motive for this oversight and will not suppose that it came from you. Your stupidity will fall on me. You shall not be independent, I will not allow it."

The newlyweds spent their honeymoon at Malmaison. When, one day, his young wife allowed herself to laugh, for some reason her husband did not know, Louis exclaimed: "What do you take me for? Do you think I will let myself be your plaything? I warn you that only light women can allow themselves to laugh at their husbands and treat them as nothing and I shall leave you rather than let myself be so humiliated."

"I cannot describe my despair," Hortense related. "In one moment I saw all thought of happiness, even of peace, vanish. I could not understand the character revealed to me. It made me afraid for the future." And what a future!

She was to weep later as she saw him in their bedroom putting on a shirt already worn by someone with skin disease—intended, according to the therapy of the day, to draw out "peccant humors." As the result of badly treated venereal disease, Louis was a perpetual invalid, going from doctor to doctor. He was soon to drag from spa to spa his cerebral pains, his paralyzed arms, his locomotor troubles and his dizziness. To strangers he appeared serious and tender and seemed to have "reserved, gentle" manners, but in private Louis was a sad specimen, full of perpetual suspicions about everything and nothing.

There is no doubt that Josephine sacrificed her daughter to her own interests. She induced her to marry a valetudinarian who was also appallingly eccentric.

Josephine left for Lyons with her husband, on her first official journey, at midnight on the night of January 8–9, 1802. Snow, cold and wind followed them. After a night spent at the posthouse of Lucy-le-Bois, they reached Chalon on the next evening and Lyons on January 11 at eight in the evening. Josephine presided over balls and concerts. At a silk factory she watched them weave a velvet screen with her initials. On January 20 a fete was held, more for her than for her husband. "A deputation of Lyons ladies presented her with a basket of flowers," an eyewitness wrote, "which she received with as much grace as feeling. . . . The general gaiety was generated by agreeable music, dazzling illumination, a prodigious crowd, and above all by the presence of the First Consul and his wife."

Dressed in silk—made in Lyons, of course—and without Bonaparte, who that day, in Lyons itself, became President of the Italian Republic, she presided over a fete given at Sainte-Marie de Belle-cour and took her place on a platform over which were the words: "The Graces joined with valor." Then with her husband she watched a review of troops returned from Egypt. As was his custom, Bonaparte talked to and questioned his former companions. What a long way he had gone since, as General Bonattrape, he had abandoned them and left Alexandria secretly!

Two days later, on January 27, they returned through Roanne and Nevers. Josephine had managed so well, had given such a good impression of not being bored, had shown such a gift for listening to and answering compliments, had, in fact, been able to make each person believe that she knew him and had come solely for his sake, that now Mme. Bonaparte herself was associated with the position of head of the state which her husband had held since Brumaire.

The next month Josephine was at Notre-Dame, in the gallery separating the choir from the nave, for the Te Deum to celebrate the signing of the Concordat. Somewhat dazzled, she watched the ceremony of the bishops taking the oath with their hands between her husband's. France was once more the Church's eldest daughter, although Bonaparte was wearing his Egyptian scimitar and the six horses that preceded his coach were held by Mamelukes. Their green and gold liveries were new and, as in the days of kings, the domestic staff surrounded the ceremonial coaches which were escorted by shining troops.

The Prussian Minister wrote to his court: "Everything around the First Consul and his wife is taking on the air and etiquette of Versailles. Ceremonial luxury, coaches, liveries, numerous servants reappear on every side. Foreigners are carefully selected for admission and the foreign ladies presented to the First Consul in his wife's circle are named by one of the palace officials. He is developing a taste for hunting and the forests in which the Kings of France and Princes of the Blood used to hunt are now to be reserved for him and the officers of his suite."

Before going to live at Saint-Cloud Josephine went back to Plombières in June, 1802, still in the hope of overcoming her sterility. In saying good-by, Lucien had remarked ironically, "Now, my sister, give us a little Césarion!"

She traveled like a queen, escorted by detachments of gendarmes or carabineers. At Nancy there was a great dinner in the Prefecture. This time she would have preferred more simplicity. "I feel I was not born for so much grandeur," she wrote to her daughter on arriving at Plombières, "and that I should be happier in retirement, surrounded by the objects of my affection."

She had hardly begun her cure when she received a letter from her husband, then at Malmaison, where Hortense, already pregnant, took her mother's place. "I have not had any news of you. I believe you have already started taking the waters. We are rather sad here, although the charming daughter does the honors of the house wonderfully well. . . .

"I love you as on the first day, because you are above all good and lovable. . . . A thousand kind thoughts and a loving kiss. Yours always."

A few days later, on June 23, he wrote:

"I have received your letter, my dear, good Josephine. I am sorry to learn that you have suffered from the journey. But a few days' rest will do you good. I am fairly well. I hunted at Marly yesterday and hurt a finger slightly shooting a boar. Hortense is quite well.

Your big son was slightly unwell, but he is better now. I believe the ladies are going to play *The Barber of Seville.*

"The weather is very fine. I beg you to believe that nothing can be truer than my feelings for my little Josephine. Yours always."

Josephine complained. Her cure was tiring and her husband tried to console her. "Your letter, my dear little wife, told me that you were feeling unwell. Corvisart told me this is a good sign, that the baths will have the desired effect and put you in good condition. But to know you are ill is a keen sorrow for my heart. . . . A thousand kind thoughts. Yours for life."

On July 1 came another letter: "You don't say anything about your health or the effect of the baths. I see you intend to be back in a week. This is a great pleasure for your friend, who is bored at being alone. . . . Please believe I love you and am very impatient to see you again. Everything here is sad without you."

Bonaparte was to some extent acting a part. During his wife's absence he had the pretty singer Louise Rolandeau at Malmaison. Josephine heard of it, broke off her cure and, returning to Malmaison, reproached her daughter.

"You should have prevented her coming here!"

Poor Hortense! Her mother treated her coldly and her husband, who always believed himself persecuted, imagined that the child his wife was expecting was by his brother Napoleon. He had, moreover, convinced himself that he had been made to marry Josephine's daughter merely to hide the result of a love affair between step-father and stepdaughter.

Bonaparte in his turn made a scene, rebuking Josephine for returning and "blaming her for sacrificing her health and the means of perhaps having children to the impulses of ill-considered jealousy."

This immediately brought tears to Josephine's eyes, particularly as in July, 1802, all France was preparing to vote to give Bonaparte the Consulate for life. It was a nightmare for her. Consulate for life practically meant hereditary power. And it seemed that Josephine could have no more children.

At the time of Brumaire Bonaparte seemed to have accepted the situation. "I have no children," he had said one day to Joseph, "and you all say that I cannot have any. In spite of all her good will, I do

not think Josephine will have any more at her age, althou/
wouldn't mind letting others try. So—après moi le déluge!"

Now that the Consulate for life was approaching—some people
were already talking of a monarchy—there could be no more
question of "après moi le déluge." Maternity was an imperious
necessity for Josephine, and a necessity that haunted her. She could
doubtless affirm that she had given her proofs—as witness Hortense
and Eugene—and that the sterility was not hers but her husband's.
Bonaparte did not believe it.

One morning at Malmaison, wishing to prevent her husband from
going hunting, Josephine said:

"How can you think of such a thing? All the animals are pregnant!"

The First Consul had replied, not very kindly, "All right, we'll
have to give it up. Everything here is prolific, except madame!"

12. The Way to the Throne

Now, on the eve of his "reign," the whole clan was excited. The Consulate for life was all very well, but the Bonapartes wanted more. They wanted their brother to have "the right to appoint his successor." There were two solutions: to divorce "the Beauharnais" and marry again or to choose an heir who could be none other than his brother the pale Joseph. He was the eldest—which for Corsicans meant everything.

To combat this scheme Josephine declared to her husband, at Fouché's instigation, "The generals are already saying that they did not fight the Bourbons to put the Bonapartes in their place."

Napoleon was not slow to realize that Joseph was only a mediocrity. How could he impose him on France as a possible successor?

"When you are dead you are dead," he remarked. "Even Louis XIV's will was set aside."

And Bonaparte decided not to predict the future. Josephine breathed again. When the Council of State submitted the text of the two questions to be put before the French people:

1. Shall Napoleon Bonaparte be Consul for Life?
2. Shall he have power to appoint his successor?

Josephine's husband struck out the second question "with a violent gesture."

Then he changed his mind and the second question stood. Probably, as Masson thinks, because Hortense's pregnancy had been announced. If Bonaparte were to adopt Josephine's grandson divorce would be unnecessary, and the wife of the Consul for Life regained hope.

In Paris 60,395 electors voted "yes," there were only 60 opponents. The vote from the royalist department of the Vendée was impatiently awaited. The result was 17,079 "yeses" to 6 "noes." The figures of this victory—"the will of the French people"—were brought to the Tuileries on August 3. Bonaparte was king or emperor in all but the name. His first name—that glamorous name—appeared on the currency and August 15, the new master's birthday, was decreed a national holiday.

The Carib soothsayer's prophecy to Josephine was coming true.

As his first "sovereign" act Bonaparte installed himself in Saint-Cloud in September, 1802, not daring to annex Versailles. And it was at Saint-Cloud, where he spent six million in gold—more than at the Tuileries—that his "reign" began, although a Russian princess, having been received at the new Consular residence, exclaimed, "It's a very great power but it is not a court!"

Of course it could not be like a court except for the boredom. However, it is by following the reports of one of these foreigners eager to know the Consul's household—in this case the letters of J. F. Reichardt, former *Kappelmeister* of Frederick II—that we too shall have the impression of being received by Josephine in the palace in which Louis XIV's brother, the Regent, the Orléans family and finally Marie Antoinette had lived before her. Mme. Bonaparte had installed herself in the Queen's old apartments in the left wing.

On being granted the privilege of a presentation to the First Consul and his wife, one went to Saint-Cloud in the early afternoon. The main courtyard—now the terrace overlooking the Seine—would be crowded with liveried servants and soldiers of the Consular Guard. In the waiting room on the second floor, were four ladies in waiting "in morning dress, elegant but very simple." A palace official would present the new arrivals to the lady in attendance. The day

Reichardt was received this was Mme. de Lauriston. According to him, "She confined herself to slight bows and smiles. Like her companions, she was dressed in white India muslin with a white cashmere wound round her hair." Duroc, the Grand Marshal of the Palace, also received the visitors.

At four o'clock the guests were shown into the audience chamber. The ladies remained standing around the room and the men took their places behind them. Bonaparte, escorted by two officials of "short stature," would come in and begin his tour of the room. "He had reached the third lady when Mme. Bonaparte entered, escorted by two other short officials. She began her tour of the room, and as she made her remarks briefer than her husband's, she had soon caught up with him. She looked older and thinner than I had imagined. She displayed much politeness and consideration, more, perhaps, than the situation required." She was wearing "a white satin morning dress trimmed with broad lace. In her dark-chestnut hair was a kind of diadem with three rows of stones in which were three superb antique cameos."

When the "review" was over there came the filing off. Josephine sat at a corner of the fireplace and the envoys presented those foreigners who were there for the first time. They gave their names and for each one Mme. Bonaparte, bowing her head and half rising, would declare, "Charmed . . . very pleased . . . delighted to see you."

At Saint-Cloud Bonaparte took lunch alone for the most part, when the weather permitted, on the terrace adjoining his study. They dined rather later than in Paris, for at six o'clock—dinnertime at the Tuileries—Josephine and Bonaparte would take a turn round the park in their carriage.

On Sundays the Consul and his wife attended a sung Mass, celebrated by the Archbishop of Versailles, occupying the places where the King and Queen used to sit. Josephine thus had precedence over the other two Consuls, whose position was gradually dwindling. Cambacérès merely gave Mme. Bonaparte his hand to cross the gallery and lead her to her prie-dieu. "There was some piquancy in observing, in that magnificent gallery at Saint-Cloud," wrote Mme. de Rémusat, "the faces of many ex-Conventionals, those modern Brutuses who had so often sworn on the altar of their country that anyone trying to usurp supreme power would perish under their blows. The usurper was there, in their midst, playing his part of master far better than they played theirs as courtiers."

Late in the afternoon of October 10 Josephine, then at Saint-Cloud, was sent for. Hortense was going into confinement at Malmaison. At ten in the evening Mme. Bonaparte became the grandmother of a fine boy!

"Here is our Dauphin!" exclaimed Hortense's ladies.

Josephine's daughter was in raptures. Even Louis appeared happy. Having got it into his mind that his wife was pregnant from his brother's efforts, he had declared that if the child was born before nine months he would never see his wife again. Fortunately, little Napoleon Charles arrived nine months after his parents had stayed at Malmaison. But the respite Louis granted his wife was to be of short duration.

At the end of October, 1802, Josephine was once more on a Consular journey, this time to Rouen. Eugene accompanied his mother and stepfather, the latter traveling on horseback while Josephine followed in a carriage. Passing through Mantes, they left the Evreux road to visit the battlefield of Ivry. Bonaparte ordered the obelisk which had been placed at the spot where Henri IV had rested after the battle to be re-erected. At five o'clock they entered Evreux, where "Mme. Bonaparte, approachable and graciously receptive," "permitted" twenty girls to recite verses and give her a bouquet of flowers, "the simple homage of innocence."

On the façade of the Eure Prefecture were the entwined monograms of M. and Mme. Bonaparte, together with the words: "Faithful in marriage as in victory."

The next day the Consular caravan went through Louviers and arrived at Rouen during the afternoon. On October 31 Bonaparte and Josephine attended a Mass said in the prefecture chapel by Archbishop Cambacérès, brother of the Second Consul. The prelate did not dare hand the paten to the Head of State and his wife. On returning to his rooms Bonaparte exclaimed:

"That man did not pay me the honors given to sovereigns, he did not offer me the paten to kiss. It's not that I care in the least for his paten, but I want him to render to Caesar what is due to Caesar."

And the next day he wrote to the Second Consul: "The Archbishop, who is greatly loved and esteemed here, was kind enough to say Mass for us, but he gave us neither holy water nor a special prayer. We shall have our revenge tomorrow, which is All Saints' Day."

On that November 1 Bonaparte received the public authorities for six hours, standing. Josephine stoically underwent the task with "that amiability and sweetness," said *Le Moniteur,* "which distinguish the person to whom their homage was addressed."

Josephine found time to write to Hortense. "The courier is leaving and I have just time to embrace you, your husband and my grandson with all my heart. We are all well. At Rouen there is general rejoicing, all the inhabitants have been under Bonaparte's windows since he arrived and are always wanting to see him. They can't think of enough praises for him, they're really in a frenzy. I am sending you a song they sing in the streets. . . . Good-by, I'm being asked for my letter. Bonaparte and Eugene embrace you and your mother loves you with all her heart."

After five days' rest they left for Le Havre, and the circuit continued through Dieppe, Gisors and Beauvais. Josephine played her part as sovereign with rare skill. At Dieppe a little girl, Herminie Flouet, brought her a bouquet. Josephine took off one of her bracelets and fastened it on the arm of Herminie who, not in the least shy, immediately held out her other arm. Laughing, Josephine took off another bracelet and herself fastened it on the child's arm.

The example of Rouen, which had given Josephine forty pots of dried preserves and as many bottles of wine, was followed everywhere. Gournay-en-Bray gave her cheeses, a basket of Burgundy and fifty pounds of butter, "an exquisite product of our district."

When the Municipal Council of Beauvais learned that Mme. Bonaparte and the First Consul were to pass through their town on November 13 and 14, 1802, the mayor, M. de La Chaise, delved into the town archives to consult "the reports of what happened during visits by the kings of France, in particular at the arrival of Henri II and Catherine de Médicis in 1555."

A guard of honor, modestly called a company of mounted volunteers, was immediately formed. They were given a gay tricolor uniform of blue coat, white waistcoat and breeches and red plume.

The authorities, the fire brigade, the band, a detachment of the 43rd half-brigade and the guard of honor awaited M. and Mme. Bonaparte at the Pont Saint-Jean, where a triumphal arch of oak branches adorned with ribbons had been erected. The flag Jeanne Hachette had captured from the Burgundians in 1472 was surrounded by girls, each holding a green ribbon tied to the staff. There were also the presents intended for the First Consul and Josephine: a fine, plump sheep weighing 180 pounds, lengths of material of all kinds—vestipoline, espagnolette, sommière, reverbes —and fifty bottles of Burgundy and champagne.

Once the First Consul and his wife had reached the prefecture, temporarily called the Consular Palace, the women guests filed in, but Bonaparte "made a gesture toward the beautiful Creole sitting a little behind him, as though to order them to pay court to his wife."

The dress of white and gold striped gauze with matching turban, which Josephine wore at the ball, was mentioned in the report kept in the archives of the Academic Society of Beauvais. The municipal archives also preserved the menu which was served at midnight. (*Potage au riz, poulardes au riz, pâtés, daubes, saumon, aspic mayonnaise, gâteau de lièvre, turbot en gelée au vin de Champagne, blanc-mange, gâteau à l'anglaise, et desserts.*) Only Josephine and the ladies could sit down. The men supped standing in front of the buffet.

The next morning the Bishop of Amiens said Mass. Two pri-dieu had been placed in front of the altar for M. and Mme. Bonaparte. Before setting off for Saint-Cloud Josephine gave a "private audience" to little Zoé de La Chaise and presented her with a necklace of diamonds—small ones, it is to be presumed—and a medal.

As the First Consul and Josephine reached Saint-Cloud in the evening of November 14, cannons thundered. When, at the beginning of January, the death in Tortuga of Paulette's husband Leclerc was learned, Josephine and her ladies put on Court mourning. On March 12 the Consul and Josephine watched the minting of the first gold pieces bearing his effigy.

All they needed were the titles King and Queen.

On Sunday, March 13, as Bonaparte was playing with Josephine's grandson in his wife's drawing room, it was announced that the diplomatic corps and the people to be presented to him had assembled. Bonaparte charged in, followed by Josephine, and swooped on the English ambassador, Lord Whitworth, saying:

"You want war. We have been fighting for fifteen years. It is already too much. But you want to make war for another fifteen years and you will force me to it!"

The First Consul was only two years off.

Then, turning to the representatives of Russia and Spain, he went on: "The English want war, but although they may be the first to draw the sword I shall be the last to sheathe it. They do not respect treaties."

Lord Whitworth was silent. Once more Bonaparte raised his voice:

"Why all this arming? Against whom are all these measures of precaution taken? I have not a single armed ship of the line in all the ports of France. But if you arm I shall arm too. You may kill France but never intimidate her!"

Everyone present was silent "from astonishment and fear," Hortense relates. "My mother went on talking to the ladies and tried to cover his voice by a few affectionate words to mitigate the bad effect she feared from such a heated argument.

"On returning to his study, the Consul seemed delivered of a great weight. His anger had evaporated. It was my mother and myself who had serious faces."

"Well now," he said, almost laughing, "what's the matter with you, what's happened?"

"You made everyone tremble," Josephine replied. "People will think you ill-tempered. What do you imagine all those ladies will think who don't know you and were so happy to see you? Instead of being good and pleasant to them you go and talk politics. It wasn't the moment for that."

"Did they hear me? It's true, I was wrong. I didn't want to go down today. Talleyrand said things to me that put me in a temper and that great booby of an ambassador had to stick himself under my nose."

At Saint-Cloud, on May 8, 1803, Bonaparte himself wanted to drive the six-horse carriage in which Josephine, Hortense, Caroline and Cambacérès were seated. The carriage ran afoul of a post and was overturned.

"One must render to Caesar the things that are Caesar's," he declared, handing the whip to his coachman, Caesar.

Hortense, who had been thrown twenty paces, suffered most from the accident. Josephine asked her to stay and sleep at Saint-Cloud, but the young woman refused.

"My daughter doesn't love me any more!" cried Josephine, weeping.

"It's quite simple," Bonaparte replied. "Hortense enjoys herself in Paris. We are old and she is bored with us."

"I was in torment," related Hortense, who finally confessed that Louis, still prey to ridiculous jealousy and anxious to leave Napoleon Charles as little as possible with his brother and sister-in-law, had forbidden her to spend the night near the First Consul.

"What!" exclaimed Bonaparte. "Has your husband made such a prohibition? What can be the reason? Has he been taking lessons from the English slander-sheets? Write and tell him he has no power to separate a daughter from her mother. When away from one's husband, where can one find a better support? A wife whose conduct is as pure as yours has the right to speak firmly and not allow such ridiculous obligations to be imposed on her."

Then came another royal, and triumphal, journey. On June 25 Bonaparte and Josephine left for the northern departments of France—now Belgium. At Abbeville trees had been uprooted and set up along the streets to transform them into avenues. Boulogne greeted the First Consul and Josephine with triumphal arches of flowers and leaves. Bonaparte entered the town on horseback while Josephine followed in the carriage. Then the journey in the former "Belgian provinces" really began.

During those forty-eight days Josephine smilingly bore verbose addresses, prolix orations, interminable banquets, everlasting salvos, young girls in white droning endless verses and presenting their perpetual bouquets, prancing guards of honor, illuminations, balls, handing over of keys, bell ringing, songs, hymns, cantatas, Te Deum, anthems, crosses and patens to be kissed in front of churches, sprinklings with holy water, presents of all kinds, from the swans of Amiens to the bay horses of Antwerp, monotonous visits to factories, mills, studios, hospitals, ports, parades, presentations of officials and their wives, soporific performances of allegorical dramas, numberless so-called topical spectacles—all deadly boring.

Although Bonaparte may sometimes have shown weariness, his

wife never gave any outward sign of it. She confined herself to
writing to Hortense: "Since I left Paris my whole time has been
spent receiving compliments. You know me and you can imagine
how much I should prefer a quieter life. Fortunately the company
of my ladies compensates for the bustling life I lead. However, my
mornings, and often my evenings, are spent in receptions. I also
have to go to balls. This would be an agreeable pleasure if I could
share it with you, or at least see you enjoying it. The deprivation my
heart feels most keenly is to be separated from my dear Hortense
and from my grandson, whom I love almost as much as I love his
mamma."

At Ghent the welcome was cool. The inhabitants of the city were
"curious but not enthusiastic."

"These people are pious and under the influence of their priests,"
Bonaparte told his wife. "Tomorrow we must have a long session in
church, win the clergy over by some favor and then we will gain
ground."

This was done and the calculated result obtained.

Coming from Ghent through Saint-Nicolas and Beveren, Bonaparte and Josephine crossed the Scheldt River and entered Antwerp
on July 18. They embarked at the fortress of the Tête de Flandre in
the town barge commanded by Citizen Hoest, captain of the port,
and manned by six rowers in suits of nankeen with blue sashes and
white hats adorned with sky-blue ribbons.

Nothing could be finer than crossing the wide river to arrive in
the largest port in Europe. "The sky was cloudless and the Scheldt
as smooth as glass," reported the *Relation,* a manuscript preserved
in the archives. From every side the cannon thundered, from the
artillery of the citadel, the rampart of Saint-Michel and Fort Saint-
Laurent, to the batteries of the ships in port. All the city bells rang
out wildly, and a military band on the quayside played "appropriate
music."

The authorities, headed by Citizen d'Herbouville, Prefect of the
Deux-Nèthes Department, were waiting on the quay "in the shadow
of a pyramid." It was extremely hot. Bonaparte leaped out of the
barge and "like a flash of lightning was on his Arab steed." There, in
front of the Porte de Bierhoofd, he received the keys to the city and,
according to custom, gave them back, declaring "that they could be
in no better hands than those of the Mayor," M. Werbrouck.

The Consular couple were installed in the prefecture, adorned for the occasion with two Egyptian pyramids "covered with hiero-glyphics and crowned with luminous globes." Illuminations were general—and obligatory—throughout the town.

The next day Josephine stood near Bonaparte while the delega-tions filed past and they drank an old Rhine wine which, "according to ancient usage," had been brought in a cask drawn in a sledge by eight enormous brewer's horses. The drivers wore nankeen and their heads were crowned with vines. Euphoria was general and the President of the Conseil Générale, turning to Josephine, began his speech.

"Madame, occupied as you are with the happiness of Napoleon the Great, you have a sacred right to our good wishes and our gratitude . . ."

Bonaparte had been called Napoleon the Great for the first time. As far as Antwerp was concerned, his reign had already begun. Josephine and Bonaparte had not been married before the altar— their wedding had been only a civil one—but Msgr. de Roquelaure, Archbishop of Mechlin and former Bishop of Senlis in the time of Louis XVI, was unaware of this, or pretended to be. "Madame," he said to Josephine, after numbering her among "the Creator's master-pieces," "madame, having joined yourself to the First Consul by the sacred ties of a holy alliance, you are today surrounded by his fame. This situation is the result of the attractions of your mind, the grace of your character and the charms of your society."

In the evening they went to the Place de Meir, where from the balcony of a house belonging to the mayor's brother, they watched a long display of fireworks.

On the next day, while Bonaparte visited the port and fortifica-tions, officials from the Town Hall, dressed in scarlet uniform with silver braid, brought Josephine a present from the municipality—a painting by Balthazar Ommeganck, an Antwerp painter whom the future Empress was henceforth to patronize. It showed a shepherd and his dog resting at dusk "in the shade of a clump of trees." Near them a few sheep, goats and an ox "completed this group which was the more picturesque in that it was in a way identified with the charming site its painter had chosen near Spa."

At noon on July 21 they left for Brussels. There Bonaparte discovered that the ladies of the city had spent more money on their dresses than his wife had. He reproached Josephine, who burst into tears. Chaptal proved by figures that the First Consul was wrong, but it was undoubtedly the only time in her life that Josephine was reproached with being too economical. Mme. de Rémusat, who was one of the party, was astonished to see that Bonaparte knew by name so many of the soldiers he reviewed and could recall to them their exploits.

"Bonaparte has made a habit of studying the army lists each evening when he goes to bed," Josephine explained. "He falls asleep over the names of the corps and even of some of the individuals in the corps. He keeps them in a corner of his memory, which helps him wonderfully, when occasion arises, to recognize a soldier and give him the pleasure of being singled out by his general."

Perhaps it was after the "frenzy of admiration from the Belgians" —to quote a royalist agent—and on their return to Saint-Cloud, where the final speeches from municipal bodies awaited them, that Josephine, forgetting her fears of royalty, said to her husband, "When are you going to make me Empress of the Gauls?"

Meanwhile the staff received orders that "royalized" the Consulate. On August 25, 1803, Duroc, the Grand Marshal of the Palace, ordered the outriders, their deputies, grooms and coachmen for "the carriages of the First Consul and Mme. Bonaparte" to have their hair powdered as in the old regime. On September 3 one of Louis XVIII's agents in Paris was already speaking in one of his reports "of the reign of Napoleon."

But for the new reign to begin, for the regicides to be able to offer Louis XVI's throne to the First Consul with impunity, a bloody ditch had to be dug between the Bourbons and Bonaparte.

"The monarchical institutions were stalking in the shadow of the Republic," wrote Mme. de Staël. It was not to a king that the Republic was to give itself but to the man who would become "Emperor of the Revolution." Meanwhile Bonaparte did everything by himself, as a contemporary remarked. "Ministers, Councilors of State and Senators hardly dared put forward so much as a recommendation."

Bonaparte, too, had changed. At the end of 1803 he was no longer declaring, as he had to Fouché on January 12 of the same year: "In Paris they think I shall make myself emperor. I shall not do anything of the kind. For three years now I have done great things

under the title of Consul. It should be kept. I do not think a new
name is needed for a new empire."

Events were soon to make him change his mind.

When she went on duty on the morning of February 15, 1804,
Mme. de Rémusat found Bonaparte in his wife's bedroom. Sitting
near the fire, he was holding on his knees little Napoleon, Hortense's
son, then aged seventeen months. He was absent-mindedly playing
with the child, but it was obvious that his thoughts were elsewhere.
Josephine's eyes were very red and she seemed upset. Breaking the
silence, the First Consul looked at Mme. de Rémusat and said:

"Do you know what I have just done?"

Mme. Bonaparte's lady in waiting had not heard the news.

"Well," Bonaparte told her, "I have just given orders for Moreau's
arrest."

That morning at nine General Moreau had been apprehended
and taken to the Temple. Three days earlier, on February 12, a
jailer making his evening rounds in the sinister tower of the Temple
had heard a faint rattle coming from a cell. He had opened the door
and found a body hanging by a cravat from the window bars. The
prisoner was still breathing. He was revived, and advantage was
taken of his comatose condition to question him. His name was
Bouvard de Lozier and he had been arrested that same morning
in the Rue Saint-Sauveur. He was one of those fanatical royalists,
more or less in the pay of England, one of those impenitent
Chouans who had schemed to assassinate Bonaparte. He was
implicated in the conspiracy of Cadoudal, the terrible Georges, who
at that moment was hidden somewhere in Paris and keeping all the
police of the capital overworked. The town seemed to be in a state
of siege, workshops were closed, the streets overrun by patrols, the
walls covered with posters giving the description of Georges and
his accomplices and announcing "that those who conceal brigands
will be considered brigands themselves."

"I live in constant mistrust," Bonaparte confessed to his brother
Joseph. "Every day new plots against my life spring up. The
Bourbons make me their sole target!"

However that might be, Bouvard had confirmed Cadoudal's
presence in Paris and had then reported recent interviews between
Moreau and Pichegru. It appeared that Moreau had thrown in his

lot with the conspirators and wanted Bonaparte's place in order to give it to the Bourbons, or so Bonaparte believed. In reality Moreau had not come to an understanding with Pichegru and had refused to take part in a restoration.

"I cannot put myself at the head of any movement in favor of the Bourbons," he had said. "They behaved so badly that any attempt of that kind would have no success."

Josephine had been unable to hide her tears on hearing the news. As for Mme. de Rémusat, who was a grandniece of Louis XVI's famous minister, she could not hide her stupefaction.

"Ah, you're surprised," Bonaparte went on, trying to justify himself in Josephine's eyes. "It will make a great stir, won't it? People will not hesitate to say I am jealous of Moreau, that it's revenge and such stuff. Me, jealous of Moreau! Good heavens, he owes me most of his fame. It was I who left him a fine army and kept only recruits in Italy. All I wanted was to be on good terms with him. Of course I did not fear him. For one thing, I fear nobody, and Moreau less than most. I've prevented him from compromising himself twenty times. I warned him people would make bad blood between us, he knew it as well as I. But he is weak and conceited. He is ruled by women and the parties brought pressure on him."

He got up, went to his wife and, taking her chin, made her raise her head.

"Everyone hasn't a good wife like mine."

He then noticed that Josephine's tears had started again.

"You're crying, Josephine, why? Are you afraid?"

"No, but I don't like what people will say."

"What would you have? I have no hatred or desire for vengeance. I thought very seriously before arresting Moreau. I could have closed my eyes, given him time to escape, but it would have been said that I did not dare bring him to trial. I have proof to convict him. He is guilty. I am the government. The whole thing must be managed simply."

"He was up nearly all night," Josephine told Mme. de Rémusat, once Bonaparte had left the room, "weighing arguments for and against Moreau's arrest."

Fouché's measures doubled their severity. It might have been the return of the Terror. At the end of the month Pichegru was arrested and, after a lively chase through Paris, Cadoudal was captured in his turn. He was immediately interrogated.

"What did you come to Paris to do?"

"I came to attack the First Consul."

"Had you many people with you?"

"No, because I was not to attack the First Consul until there was a prince in Paris, and he has not yet arrived."

"So the plan was conceived and was to be carried out by agreement with a former French prince?"

"Yes, citizen judge."

Bouvard de Lozier had also confessed that the conspirators were waiting for a prince to arrive before they acted. According to Léridan, a friend of Georges who was arrested with him, this "prince" had already come to Paris on several occasions to give Cadoudal instructions. Greeted with much respect, he was a man of about thirty-five, slender, fair-haired and with an elegant figure. It was the Prince de Polignac, but on that Sunday, March 18, driving to Malmaison with Mme. de Rémusat, Josephine, who appeared very sad, informed her companion that Bonaparte's suspicions had lighted on quite a different person.

"I shall tell you a great secret," she said. "This morning Bonaparte told me that he had sent M. de Caulaincourt to the frontier to seize the Duc d'Enghien. He is to be brought back here." (Josephine made a slight mistake here. Caulaincourt had merely been ordered to hand a letter of explanation and excuse to the Minister of the Elector of Baden.)

"Oh, my God!" cried Mme. de Rémusat. "What will they do with him?"

"I suppose he will be tried."

On learning these events, Mme. de Rémusat nearly fainted—or so she was to claim under the Restoration—and Josephine quickly opened the carriage windows.

"I did what I could," she went on, "to make him promise that the Prince should not perish, but I greatly fear his mind is made up."

"What! Do you think he will have him put to death?"

Josephine remembered that she had been Vicomtesse de Beauharnais and she had not forgotten Penthémont and her friends of the old regime. If her husband executed the Duc d'Enghien, he would make an irreparable breach between the France of yesterday and the France of tomorrow. So Bonaparte, who had been fortunate enough not to have been mixed up in the Revolution, would become the accomplice of the Conventionals. Talleyrand was well aware of this, and urged his master to open the gulf which would definitely separate him from the Bourbons.

Mme. de Rémusat claimed—also under the Restoration, when she had become a household official to Louis XVIII and it was necessary to be exculpated for having served the Usurper—that she had wept bitterly in the carriage taking her to Malmaison. In her "state of emotion" she hastened to put before Josephine "all the baleful consequences of such an event: that stain of royal blood which would satisfy only the Jacobins, the particular interest aroused by that prince above all others, the fair name of Condé, the general terror, the heated anger that would be revived, etc. I touched on all these questions," she added, "only some of which Mme. Bonaparte had envisaged. The idea of murder was what had most struck her. I managed really to frighten her and she promised me to try everything to change this fatal resolve."

Very early in the morning a courier had brought the papers taken from the Duc d'Enghien's house at Ettenheim. Documents proved that the Duke was at the head of a real antirepublican network having ramifications as far afield as Alsace.

Certainly the Duc d'Enghien, in the pay of the English, was betraying the new France, and this was Bonaparte's interpretation.

To this it could be replied that for the Duc d'Enghien this new France did not exist and that M. Bonaparte was only a usurper. His guilt was no less settled in the First Consul's eyes.

Bonaparte had immediately made up his mind. His prisoner was approaching Paris, he would doubtless arrive the next day, March 20, and would be tried without delay. He explained this to Josephine who, keeping her promise to Mme. de Rémusat, begged her husband not to soil his hands with the blood of the Condés: "Women should remain apart from this kind of thing. My policy requires this coup d'état. By it I shall acquire the right to be clement in the future. Impunity will encourage the factions and I shall be obliged to persecute, exile and condemn ceaselessly, to go back on what I did for the émigrés and to put myself in the hands of the Jacobins. The royalists have more than once compromised me in the eyes of the revolutionaries. The execution of the Duc d'Enghien will clear me in the eyes of everyone."

It would seem—in spite of what Napoleon said on St. Helena—that Josephine persisted further.

"The Duc d'Enghien is an instrument of English vengeance," he explained. "After all, he is mixed up in Georges's conspiracy."

"Why did you involve M. de Caulaincourt in this affair, Bonaparte?" she asked. "You thus add to what is odious about it. His parents were formerly attached to the house of Condé."

"I didn't know that," the First Consul replied, "but what does it matter? If Caulaincourt is compromised it won't do much harm, he will serve me all the better. The opposite side will then forgive his being a gentleman."

In the park Josephine recounted this scene to Mme. de Rémusat. Workmen were planting a cypress on the lawn. Josephine watched them, musing.

"Ah, madame!" exclaimed Mme. de Rémusat. "That is the right tree for a day like this!"

Not considering herself beaten, Josephine returned to the attack. This time Bonaparte lost patience.

"Go away, you are only a child, you understand nothing of political necessities!"

"Very well, Bonaparte," she replied. "If you have your prisoner killed you will be guillotined yourself, like my first husband, and it will be in my company this time."

The next morning Josephine greeted Mme. de Rémusat by saying: "It is all in vain. The Duc d'Enghien arrives tonight. He will be taken to Vincennes and tried tonight. Bonaparte has forbidden me to speak to him about it again. He spoke of you," she added. "I confessed that I had told you everything. He has been struck by your sadness. Try to control yourself."

All through that day of March 20 Bonaparte seemed somewhat hesitant, if Josephine is to be believed.

"Pardon for him is in my heart," he is supposed to have told her, "but that is not enough for me. I would like the grandson of the Grand Condé to serve in our armies. I feel strong enough for that."

At dinner that evening he placed little Napoleon on the table and was much amused "at seeing the child touch all the dishes and

upset everything around him." After the meal he played so pleasantly with Josephine's grandson that she looked smilingly at Mme.
de Rémusat as though to say, You see, he is not unkind and we can
be reassured.

Certainly her husband appeared relaxed and thinking of other
things, although the Duc d'Enghien had arrived at Vincennes at five
that afternoon. Later Bonaparte turned to Mme. de Rémusat and
asked her pleasantly:

"Why are you not wearing rouge?"

"I forgot to put it on."

"What! a woman forget her rouge!"

Breaking into laughter, he turned to his wife.

"That would never happen to you, Josephine!"

Then he added, "There are two things which suit women very
well: tears and rouge."

Later, as he was playing chess with Mme. de Rémusat, the noise
of a carriage was heard. General Hulin was announced. The First
Consul rose quickly and joined the commander of the Consular
Grenadiers in the gallery. He appointed him presiding officer of the
military commission which "was to sit immediately at the château of
Vincennes." Everything was to be concluded that night. At Vincennes the tomb was already prepared. That afternoon the governor, the former Jacobin Harel, had given orders for a hole to be dug
in the angle of the Tour de la Reine "for burying garbage." It would
only have to be slightly enlarged.

The next morning when Josephine learned of the travesty of a
trial and of the execution she rushed to Bonaparte's room weeping
"in her morning négligée."

"The Duc d'Enghien is dead," she said, throwing herself into his
arms. "Ah, my dear, what have you done?"

Looking pale, the First Consul is supposed to have replied, "The
wretches acted too quickly."

He seemed to forget that it was he who gave orders "to act
quickly." However, the day before he had also ordered Councilor
Réal to go to Vincennes to interrogate the Duc d'Enghien himself.
As the Councilor had gone to bed early, no one had wanted to
disturb him and the First Consul's order had been placed on his
bedside table. When Réal opened it, in the middle of the night,

everything was over at Vincennes. And the condemned man had asked to see Bonaparte. There is no doubt that if he had been there Réal would have transmitted the Prince's request to his master. It is conceivable that after an interview between the soldier of Rivoli and the soldier of Berstheim blood might not have flowed. But in the absence of the Councilor, Savary was in command. The judges were there only "to render judgment on the spot." They were to obey and they had obeyed. Savary, the executioner, had his sword at their backs. When he arrived at Malmaison, Josephine asked him "in an unsteady voice":

"Well? Has it been done?"

"Yes, madame, he died this morning with, I am forced to admit, much courage. After his death the gendarmes were given permission to take his clothes, his watch and the money he had on him. Not one would touch them."

At the same time Bonaparte was receiving Fontanes, President of the Legislative Body, who had not heard the news. The First Consul wanted to see how he would react on learning not of the execution, which he kept from him at first, but of the trial and condemnation of the Duc d'Enghien.

"I cannot believe it," cried Fontanes, "even when I hear it from you."

"Why not? He was conspiring against the government."

"No matter, that would not be a reason for trying him, for condemning him!"

"Is he above the law, then?"

"No, you must not abuse your strength. You should be magnanimous, set him free. This would tarnish your glory. Do not commit this abuse of power, this act of cruelty. The Jacobins would applaud it."

"There is no longer time, he is dead," said the Consul somberly.

Dinner took place in gloomy silence. Everyone seemed sunk in his own thoughts. Rising from table, Bonaparte—seemingly in answer to this mute reproach—exclaimed violently:

"At least they will see what we are capable of. Henceforth I hope we shall be left alone!"

In the drawing room, where there were other guests who had come from Paris, the atmosphere was terribly oppressive. Josephine, with wet eyes, sitting at the edge of her sofa, worked sadly at her embroidery.

"I am only a woman," she repeated. "I confess it makes me want to weep."

"There are proofs that cannot be denied," exclaimed Bonaparte. "Those people wanted to sow disorder in France and kill the Revolution in my person. I had to defend and avenge it. The Duc d'Enghien was conspiring like anyone else and he had to be treated like anyone else."

After a silence he resumed: "I shed blood, I had to and I shall perhaps shed it again, but without anger and simply because bloodletting is one of the methods of political medicine. I am a statesman, I am the French Revolution, and I shall maintain it."

When Josephine was alone with him she spoke again of her grief and Mme. de Rémusat's tears.

"It is quite simple," he replied. "She is behaving like a woman. None of you understands anything about my affairs, but things will calm down and it will be seen that I have not made a mistake."

Josephine was not sure and when she left Malmaison for Paris on March 24 she was as pale as death. How would the capital greet them now that her husband by shedding blood had opened that breach between the Bourbons and the new France?

That same evening M. and Mme. Bonaparte went to the Opera to take the pulse of the capital. Josephine was not in the same carriage as her husband. As a general rule the First Consul did not wait for his wife's arrival before entering his box. This time he felt that his wife's charm might lighten the atmosphere and tone down the reaction. He waited in the little anteroom of his box until she joined him. Josephine was trembling all over and even he was "very pale." Finally, "with the air of someone marching into fire," he walked forward with his wife. Applause broke out and a smile flowered on Josephine's closed lips.

So, in Chateaubriand's words, the wind had blown and all was over.

Now Bonaparte could take the last step.

"I intended to maintain the Consulate for another two years," he was to tell Mme. de Rémusat, "although with this form of government the words did not match the facts. . . . But this conspiracy was meant to stir up Europe, so Europe and the royalists had to be undeceived. I had to choose between persecution piecemeal or a great coup. My choice could not be in doubt. I imposed silence forever on the royalists and Jacobins."

And the "silence" of the Jacobins would manifest itself as great satisfaction. The Tribune Curée—who called himself "a proved republican"—could say:

"I am delighted. Bonaparte has become part of the Convention!"

In the eyes of the regicides the First Consul had shed the same blood they had. He had become one of them. They could offer him a crown without fearing that he would bring about a restoration of the old monarchy. He would keep it for himself.

They were not to delay long. On March 27, six days after the execution of d'Enghien, the Senate, presided over by Cambacérès, begged the First Consul to render "his work as immortal as his glory."

Mounting the scaffold, Cadoudal was able to declare: "We accomplished more than we planned. We came to give Paris a king and we are giving her an emperor."

The Senate having also raised the question of hereditary power on March 27, Josephine hardly dared breathe as her real reign was now about to begin.

"Bonaparte," she murmured, "do not make yourself a king!"

He shrugged. "You are silly, my poor Josephine. It's your old dowagers of the Faubourg Saint-Germain, your La Rochefoucaulds, who tell you all these tales. You are tiresome."

Of course the new problems were constantly being discussed and no one refrained from talking about them in her presence. One day Josephine exclaimed in front of Fouché and Roederer:

"Bonaparte's real enemies are those who give him ideas about heredity, dynasty, divorce and marriage!"

That throne, whose gold glistened more brightly every day, appalled her. "If I could always be just the wife of the First Consul," she sighed. "That is all I want."

On April 30 Curée—still a "proved republican"—made a speech to the Tribunate. He had been well coached and demanded that the government of the Republic should be entrusted to an emperor and that the empire should be hereditary. There was applause, and on May 4 a delegation from the Tribunate was received by the Senate, whose President declared in complete seriousness:

"In dealing with the Senate you are exercising for the first time that *republican and popular* initiative which the basic laws have given you."

The Senate was willing to have a hereditary empire, but how could this wish be realized when the future sovereign had no heir?

Always fearing to see herself put aside "for sterility," Josephine returned to the scheme her husband had conceived after Hortense's marriage. Why should Bonaparte not immediately adopt his wife's grandson, the First Consul's nephew?

Bonaparte appeared receptive to the idea, but first approached Joseph to ask him to give up his right as older brother.

"I want all or nothing," Joseph replied. "I shall join Sieyès, Moreau himself if necessary, all remaining patriots and lovers of liberty in France, in order to remove myself from such tyranny."

Going beyond this—and yielding to his wife's entreaty—the First Consul asked Louis to entrust his son to him. The future King of Holland bristled.

"Why should I give my son my place in the succession? How have I deserved to be disinherited? What would be my position when this child, become yours, was more highly placed than myself, independent of me, walking immediately after you, looking on me only with uneasiness or perhaps even contempt? No, I shall never consent, and rather than renounce the royalty which is to become part of the heritage you will leave, rather than agree to bow my head before my son, I shall leave France, I shall take little Napoleon and we shall see if you would dare publicly to snatch a child from his father."

Louis went so far as once more to forbid Hortense to see her mother, who had put the "stupid idea" of adoption into her husband's head.

"If you attend to her interests at the expense of mine," he announced to his wife, "I declare that I shall make you repent it. I shall separate you from your son, I shall shut you up in some distant retreat from which no human power can rescue you, and you will pay with unhappiness all your life for your condescension toward your own family. And above all, take care that none of my threats reaches my brother's ears. His power will not save you from my rage."

Hortense's calvary had begun. Louis's "conjugal despotism" soon would know no limits.

"You are not able to love me," he asserted. "You are a woman, consequently a being made up of guile and malice. You are the daughter of a mother with no morals. You are attached to a family I detest—good reason for me to keep watch on all your actions!"

On April 7 Bonaparte declared, "I shall pass a law which will at least make me master of my own family."

The law was voted on May 18, but he had reckoned without the clan.

Where Jerome was concerned there was no problem. He had not asked his brother's permission to marry the American he loved (Elizabeth Patterson, whom Jerome had met in the United States and married in 1803) and so had excluded himself from the system which was being evolved.

There remained Lucien. But Lucien, too, rejected not only the hereditary principle for himself and his children but also the possibility of breaking his union with Mme. Jouberthon, a marriage which Bonaparte had never accepted. The First Consul would have liked to see him marry the Queen of Etruria, now a widow.

"My wife, my son, my daughters and myself are but one," Lucien had replied.

The future Emperor had a violent argument with this most intelligent of his brothers, so violent that when he joined Josephine around midnight he dropped exhausted into a chair, muttering, "That's done it, I have just broken with Lucien and dismissed him from my presence."

Josephine, who still had some leftover kindness for her in-laws, though they hated her more than ever now that Bonaparte was going to make her an empress, tried to defend her brother-in-law.

"You are a good woman to plead for him," her husband told her.

Touched, he rose, took his wife in his arms and, relates an eyewitness, "gently placed her head on his shoulder and went on speaking, his hand resting on that head whose elegance contrasted with the dull, sad face next to it." He told Josephine that Lucien had resisted all his offers. Bonaparte had threatened him and then, changing his tactics, offered his affection. Lucien repeated that he loved his wife, Mme. Jouberthon, and refused to part from her in order to please his brother and become "a French prince."

"But it is hard to find such resistance to matters of such great interest within one's own family," Bonaparte sighed with tears in his eyes. "I must therefore be isolated from the whole world and count only on myself. Well, I shall be self-sufficient and you, Josephine, will console me for everything."

It is certain that the presence of the sterile Josephine was an embarrassment. "It is to be hoped," wrote Fouché coldly a little later, *"that the Empress will die;* that would remove the difficulties. Sooner or later *he* will have to take a wife and have children, for as long as he has no heir there will be the fear that his death will be the signal for dissolution. *His brothers are shockingly incapable and a new party favoring the Bourbons will spring up."*

Since Josephine was alive and adoption impossible, and since his wife had given him no heir, why should the future Emperor not divorce her? The question was brought up again. The clan hated the Creole so bitterly that all its members preferred running the risk of seeing their future throne escape them rather than witness the spectacle of the Widow Beauharnais wearing a crown. But once more Bonaparte held firm. He would not divorce.

In spite of having had many mistresses, he had never been a father. Why make himself ridiculous by divorcing and then not having a child? He was young and the future was his. Why separate from a wife he still loved and whom, in spite of all her extravagance and debts, he reproached with only one thing—her lies, a failing which always irritated him.

"The Empress was pretty and kind," he was to say later to Bertrand, who in his own personal shorthand noted down the conversation, "but untruthful and extravagant to a degree. Her first word was 'no' on the simplest matter because she feared it might be a trap. She would correct herself afterwards."

And then there were her debts.

"She was like that all her life," the Emperor was to say. "Always debts, always hiding them, denying them."

Of course. But does one divorce one's wife because she runs up debts, denies the evidence and constantly lies?

"Yes," Joseph had cried.

Now as he was about to reign as emperor, the clan attacked Bonaparte. In irritation the First Consul confided to Roederer:

"What hypocrites! They say my wife is dishonest and that her children's earnest attentions are put on. . . . My wife is a good woman who does them no harm. She contents herself with diamonds and fine dresses; the trifles of her age. . . . If I had been thrown into prison instead of mounting a throne, she would have shared my misfortune. It is right that she should have a part in my greatness."

It is true—and it had often embarrassed him—that Josephine, with a Creole's naïve and unthinking immorality, often talked shamelessly of her former lovers. Without doubt, she was fickle, light, flirtatious, "even somewhat amorous," as he was to say on St. Helena, and where love was concerned "made a few zigzags." Again, her education often left something to be desired. She seldom, if ever, read anything and holding a pen tired her out. Only the pleasure of adorning herself, ordering a dress, matching a ribbon for her hair could rouse her from indolence.

She was indeed ignorant, but she had nevertheless managed to acquire and retain a certain amount of knowledge which she knew how to use. She was said to have no brains. But she appeared to have enough, or at least to be very clever at making the most of what she had. Her rival, Mme. de Vaudey, said she had "only a quarter of an hour's wit a day." Even this is not so bad. How many women could say as much?

To be convinced that he was right to make his wife an empress, Bonaparte only had to recall with what grace, charm and distinction she received people. One might perhaps reproach her with being almost too welcoming, too easy of approach. But those were the defects of her virtues. And he was pleased, moreover, to find her "usefully captivating."

It was enough also to watch her walk with "a suppleness in her movements, a lightness that gave something aerial to her step without excluding the majesty of a queen." She knew how to assume attitudes full of grace which enchanted him—he was to speak of them with affection fifteen years later on St. Helena.

"She made use of everything art can devise to enhance her charms," he remarked, "but with such mystery that one never was aware of it."

Then there was the point of her beauty. Was Josephine beautiful?

She was more than pretty. Her countenance "was affected by all the impressions of her mind without ever losing that charming gentleness which was its main character." When his wife's "bright and gentle" eyes were turned on him Bonaparte was often touched as in the old days. He loved her "long, silky" chestnut hair, which she dressed so prettily in the morning with a red madras kerchief "which gave her the most attractive Creole air." He loved her skin, whose "transparent satin" amazed him. He loved that body which had lost none of its suppleness, those arms and bosom like those of a girl. He loved the perpetual mobility of her features, which constantly assumed new expressions. Above all he loved that gentle, silvery, caressing voice, whose tones were so enchanting that "one stood still simply for the pleasure of hearing it," that voice which caused him to say to Bourrienne, after Marengo, when the populace were shouting their enthusiasm:

"Do you hear the noise of that continuing acclaim? It is as sweet to me as the voice of Josephine."

Once more Bonaparte refused to separate from his wife, the woman who was to become the Empress.

II. EMPRESS, QUEEN, AND DUCHESS

"Without causing laughter Josephine occupied a throne to which the daughter of the Caesars mounted with no claim to glory."—TALLEYRAND

13. "More Than a Queen"

The prediction of the soothsayer of Martinique to little Rose Tascher de La Pagerie was about to come true.

On Friday, May 18, 1804, while cannon thundered, the Senate led by Cambacérès went to Saint-Cloud to take Bonaparte the decree establishing imperial rank for him.

The President, François de Neufchâteau, congratulated the Emperor on having "brought the vessel of the Republic into port."

"Yes, sire," he repeated, "of the Republic. That word might offend the ears of an ordinary sovereign. Here the word is properly used in the presence of the man who has enabled us to enjoy the institution in the sense in which it can exist among a great people."

On leaving the new Emperor the delegation went to see Josephine.

"Madame," said Cambacérès, "we have just presented to your august husband the decree which gives him the title of emperor and which, by establishing hereditary government in his family, links future peoples with the good fortune of the present generation."

After a silence he went on: "There remains to the Senate a very agreeable duty, which is to offer Your Imperial Majesty the homage of its respect and the expression of the gratitude of the French people. Yes, madame, report proclaims the good you constantly do. It relates how, always accessible to the unfortunate, you make use of your influence with the Head of State only to relieve their distress and for the pleasure of being of service. To this Your Majesty adds that agreeable delicacy which makes gratitude sweeter and the favor more precious.

"This disposition presages that the name of the Empress Josephine will be the sign of consolation and of hope, and as Napoleon's virtues will always serve as example to his successors teaching them the art of governing nations, so the living memory of your goodness will teach their noble spouses that efforts to dry the tears of others are the surest means of reigning over all hearts."

Then, raising his voice, he pronounced: "The Senate congratulates itself on being the first to salute Your Imperial Majesty and he who has the honor to be the spokesman dares to hope that you will deign to number him among your most faithful servants."

Although Josephine had been prepared for the news she was moved. She even felt apprehension and did not leave her apartments all day. Before dinner Duroc, Grand Marshal of the Palace, had told the guests how they were henceforth to address the new dignitaries. The two former Consuls and the sixteen marshals would be called Monseigneur, the Ministers Excellency, the Emperor's brothers, Joseph and Louis Bonaparte, would be Imperial Highnesses and their wives, Julie and Hortense, Princesses. So on several occasions during the meal the new Emperor pointedly referred to "the Princess Louis" and "the Princess Joseph." On hearing these titles two ladies paled visibly: Mmes. Murat and Bacciochi. Napoleon's sisters, in fact were nothing, whereas the Emperor's sister-in-law and "those Beauharnais women" were everything. Elisa confined herself to treating the ladies present with haughtiness, but Caroline, who had less self-control, according to a witness, "drank glass after glass of water to try to compose herself and appear to be occupied, but she was overcome by tears." Napoleon wanted to treat the matter as a joke and began to tease the two women. The next day, after a family dinner, Caroline and Elisa burst out in complaints, tears and reproaches. Mme. Murat dared to exclaim: "Why must I and my sisters be condemned to obscurity and contempt while foreign women are covered with honor and dignities?"

The "foreign women"—the Empress, her daughter Hortense and Julie Clary—said nothing, but the Emperor became angry.

"To listen to you anyone would think I had stolen your inheritance from the late King our father!"

"At the end of the conversation," Josephine told Mme. de Rémusat, "Mme. Murat, beside herself with the excess of her despair and the harshness of the words she had to listen to, fell to the floor in a faint. At this sight Bonaparte's anger disappeared, he grew calm and when his sister came to, he showed an inclination to satisfy her."

On the morning of May 29, in fact, Josephine's two sisters-in-law learned that they would henceforth have the right to be called Imperial Highnesses. In Rome Mme. Letizia read the issue of the *Moniteur* announcing her daughters' victory and hoped to be promoted to the rank of Empress Dowager. Without waiting for that, her friends began to call her Majesty. Napoleon shrugged his shoulders. It was better to treat it as a joke. But after the women came the men. To be sure, MM. Murat, Bacciochi and Borghese were not allowed, at least not for some time, into the imperial drawing room with their wives; yet it was Joseph who began to sulk. He was showered with gold, looked on himself as heir to the Empire—but was not. Ignoring their ill will, Napoleon had reserved to himself the right, if he had no child, to adopt a successor. Joseph's reaction was absurd. Collateral heredity would be justified only if their father, Charles Bonaparte—"Monsieur Père"—had been emperor. It was from this preposterous idea, as Frédéric Masson has shown, that all the follies of Mme. Letizia and her children were to derive.

As for Eugene, he was appointed colonel general, which placed him among the dignitaries, but he remained the most simple of them all and showed no signs of being intoxicated by his new position.

Some people found it difficult to refer to Josephine as "the Empress" and called her "Your Majesty." For General Baron Thiébault, Josephine was, to be sure, enhanced by "precious qualities," embellished with "infinite graces," but to him and to many others she still remained, as he said, "Josephine, the former mistress of Barras, the woman who, for the price of the command of the Army of Italy, became Mme. Bonaparte, the woman who, for a bribe of

500,000 francs, gave the provisioning of the Army of Italy to that dreadful Flachet Company, whose brazen theft caused untold misery and famine to our troops at the siege of Genoa."

But General Thiébault was nonetheless to say of Josephine: "What woman ever united so much seductiveness and dignity! . . . One never approached her without admiration, listened to her without delight or left her without being enchanted with her and her ways."

The new Empress was to use her seductiveness to aid the conspirators who had worked for Louis XVIII and the Comte d'Artois. In June, 1804, Cadoudal's trial ended. Armand de Polignac was to be executed.

One morning Mme. de Rémusat came to Josephine. She had just received a visit from the Duchesse de Polignac, who had begged her "to help her make her way to the feet of the Emperor" to ask for her husband's pardon. Surely only the new Empress could be of help. At first Josephine seemed somewhat afraid. The Emperor was being "so displeased."

"If it were Moreau who had been condemned, I should be more assured of success," she explained to her lady in waiting, "but he is in such a rage that I am afraid he will rebuff us."

While Mme. de Rémusat was trying to persuade Josephine at least to make an attempt, the Emperor came into the room, and the Empress announced "that she had agreed to receive Mme. de Polignac."

At once his voice was raised. Josephine could do as she liked, but as for him he refused to grant an audience to "that woman." He would not see her.

"I cannot grant a pardon," he explained. "You don't see that the royalist party is full of imprudent young men who will renew their efforts again and again if they are not checked by a firm lesson. The Bourbons are credulous, they believe the assurances given them by certain intriguers who deceive them as to the real feeling of the public in France and they will send a throng of victims over to me."

While Napoleon strode up and down the room, Mme. de Rémusat, fortified by Josephine's imploring attitude, began to plead the cause of the unfortunate condemned men.

"What is your interest in these people?" the Emperor interrupted.

"Sire, I do not know them at all and until yesterday morning I had never seen Mme. de Polignac."

"Well, you are pleading the cause of people who came to assassinate me."

"No, sire, I am pleading the cause of an unhappy woman in despair and, I will say, yours also."

The warmth of her plea did not prevent Napoleon from leaving the room in a very bad temper and forbidding the two women "to worry him any more."

He had barely left when Mme. de Polignac's arrival was announced. Josephine went to receive her in a "room outside the apartments," promised to do the impossible to save the Duke and twice made her way into the Imperial study.

The Emperor remained angry. How did she dare ask a pardon for murderers! For the aides-de-camp of the Comte d'Artois who had wanted to assassinate him!

Josephine had to return to Mme. de Rémusat and report her failure. But she was not discouraged and, learning that Talleyrand was now at work with the Emperor, returned to the attack for the third time. This time, aided by Talleyrand, she succeeded in inducing Napoleon to see "this poor woman." The battle was won. Mme. de Polignac threw herself on her knees. The Emperor raised her up and granted Polignac's pardon in these words:

"They are very guilty, madame, those princes who risk the lives of their most faithful servants."

With Josephine's help, other condemned men also obtained their pardons by sending relatives and children to throw themselves at Napoleon's feet.

After having elected an emperor and empress, it was necessary to provide them with a staff worthy of their titles. Josephine found herself surrounded with about a hundred ladies, officers and servants. To her ladies from Consulate days—Mmes. de Rémusat, de Luçay, de Talhouët and Lauriston—Josephine added a maid of honor, a friend of hers related by marriage to the Beauharnais, a royalist, the witty and slightly hunchbacked Mme. de La Rochefoucauld, who bore one of the finest names in France—her salary was to be 40,000 francs. There was also a lady of the wardrobe, Mme. de Lavallette, the niece of Alexandre de Beauharnais and granddaughter of "Aunt Fanny," who, it will be remembered, had married Bonaparte's aide-de-camp. She was "gentle, good, still pretty, in spite of the smallpox," of which she bore the marks. Her salary was 30,000 francs. As Josephine was to be provided with a contingent of twelve ladies in waiting at 12,000 francs a year—later she would have nineteen, twenty-three and finally twenty-nine— there were eight vacancies to be filled when her reign began.

Of her private servants Agathe Rible had followed her mistress to the Tuileries, but in 1804 Josephine no longer had a "favorite." To serve her she had—or would have before the end of 1804—two chief attendants, Mme. de Saint-Hilaire, former lady's maid to Mme. Victoire, who behaved as though she were a duchess, and Mme. Bassan, the wife of a bookseller; four trim, pretty lady's maids— promoted dames d'annonce in the summer of 1805 and called dames rouges on account of their uniforms: they were the Creole Eglé Marchery, Félicité Longroy, Mme. Soustras, widow of an officer, and Mme. Ducrest de Villeneuve, mother of Georgette Ducrest, whom we shall meet later. Finally there was a mistress of the wardrobe, Mme. Mallet, four women of the wardrobe, dressed in black, and five wardrobe girls, in white, who were close witnesses of the Empress's private life. One day in 1805 Mlle. d'Avrillon was taken on and thanks to her *Souvenirs,* we can often be close to Josephine as sovereign.

One woman, La Brisée, looked after Josephine's many dogs. Only the pug—a gift from Charles—was allowed to enter the bedroom. He was acquainted with etiquette and at night, Mlle. d'Avrillon tells us, when the lady's maid on duty shut the Empress's bedroom door he would follow her without hesitation or reluctance. "He would follow us, come into our bedroom, jump on a chair and stay quiet until the morning. Then he would go down to the anteroom and wait, without showing impatience, at the door of his mistress's room, which he would dash into, with a great show of joy, with the first of us who went in."

They found him a mate and when the two pugs died they were succeeded by Alsatians. There was also a hound, which was second in rank. All these dogs "never left the Empress all day, lay down by her on the couch where she made a cashmere cushion for them; they announced visitors as well as the chamberlains and ushers, if not better, and were very aggressive toward anyone who approached their mistress, being particularly fond of the red calves of cardinals."

Not without difficulty a band of braided and gilded chamberlains and officers had been assembled to serve the new sovereign. As a contemporary, Philippe de Ségur, wrote, "with very few exceptions, such as several obscure, poor, ruined noblemen and some others already involved in the fortunes of the Bonapartes, much negotiation and various enticements were needed to persuade a few well-known names to take a place in the new Court."

The Emperor—but not Josephine—was to have his revenge later, when he saw assembled in an antechamber the new chamberlains "engaged" for the occasion of his marriage to Marie Louise. There was a Ségur, a Noailles, a Gontaut, a Chabot, a Béarn, a Turenne, a Contades. The palace marshal then asked Napoleon to be good enough to indicate those who were to begin their service.

"It's all the same to me."

"But, sire . . ."

"Very well," decided the former gentleman-cadet Napoleone Buonaparte, looking over the group as though it were a question of choosing spare horses, "very well, take the fair one and the one with curly hair!"

At the head of her household, with the title of chief equerry, Josephine had managed to get Louis Auguste Jouvenel, Comte de Harville des Ursins, Marquis de Trainel. A friend of Alexandre de Beauharnais, a general and senator, he had entertained Josephine at his home, the Château de Lisy, in February, 1803. He never left Josephine, gave her his hand, stood behind her chair, organized her every move, ordered the escorts, managed the stables, where he ruled over three outriders, four coachmen, eight postilions, twenty grooms and fifty horses (there were twice the number in the next year), and over a dozen carriages of various colors—berlins for travel or for town, calashes or gala carriages, some of which, to the Emperor's fury, had been brought by Josephine from England during the Peace of Amiens.

With the second place, that of first chamberlain, Josephine had been less fortunate. She had obtained only a certain M. Champion "purged of a commoner's condition" a mere century before. He had married Mme. de Rémusat's sister, and this relationship had gained him the second post in the Empress's household. Two other chamberlains, much more noble than he, had obtained only the second and third places: M. de Beaumont, whose nobility went back to the fourteenth century, and the ex-émigré Pierre Raymond Hector d'Aubusson, Marquis de Castelnovel, de Saint-Paul, de Serre and de Melzéard, Comte de la Feuillade, Vicomte d'Aubusson, Baron de la Borne and de la Pérusse.

Deschamps, the private secretary, was an important person. A long-standing friend of Josephine, a former vaudeville writer and spare-time poet, he also sang at the Vaudeville dinners. He was the indispensable intermediary between Josephine and her treasurer Ballouhey, who dealt with expenses for the privy purse and the wardrobe. There were also Bienfaits (Welfare), Secours (Aid) and Pensions, which were managed by the lady in waiting, who, however, always took her orders—always unmethodical and extravagant ones—from the Empress.

In 1804 there were also the Masters of the Horse, Generals de Fouler and de Bonardi de Saint-Sulpice, who were both later to become counts of the Empire. At the door of the apartments stood a porter in green and gold decked with plumes and holding a halberd, which he would thump loudly when his mistress, princes and other dignitaries passed by. Josephine also had in her service four valets, two runners, walking sticks in hand, dressed in green and glistening with gold and plumes, twelve footmen, symphonies in green and scarlet (there would later be twenty-six of them) and finally four household ushers in black, very important people. One was Longroy, father of Félicité the dame d'annonce. Another was the quaint Dumoûtier. One evening he had clumsily caught his foot in the carpet when handing Josephine a cup of tea. He had caught himself, but not the cup, which had broken at the Empress's feet.

"I should do just the same," the Emperor remarked, laughing.

"Of course, sire," retorted the usher, annoyed, "now that Your Majesty has seen how I managed it."

The Empress also had at her disposal some little Negro boys, the two Baguette-Damande brothers, Suaire and Said, and two Mamelukes wearing sword and dagger, nicknamed Marche-à-Terre and Ali.

It was not until July 15 that Josephine showed herself to the Parisians in all her new glory. Accompanied by her sisters-in-law, who pulled wry faces, her ladies in waiting, equerries and chamberlains, she left the Tuileries through the garden—it was the first time anyone had used that way since the fall of the monarchy—and to the sound of cannon her coach with eight horses, and the following carriages with six, entered the Place de la Concorde. The Empress was going in this turnout to witness the taking of the oath by new members of the Legion of Honor.

The procession soon arrived in front of the Invalides, where a fountain had been erected to show off a magnificent trophy, the lion of St. Mark brought from Venice. Josephine and her ladies took their seats on a raised platform opposite the throne. The ceremony went on for three hours as the star had to be presented to nearly 2,000 legionaries. Then they returned to the Tuileries. The Parisians crowded in front of the palace, where a concert was given on the terrace. There were cries of "Long live the Emperor!" and Napoleon, holding Josephine's hand, came to salute the crowd. Finally the Court followed the sovereigns to the end of the long Galerie du Bord de l'Eau, from which they watched the fireworks set off from the far end of the Ile de la Cité.

In July, 1804, Josephine's little world was very excited by their mistress's plan to take the waters at Aix-la-Chapelle, then capital of the Department of La Roer. There could be no question of taking all fourteen ladies to Aix. Four would suffice: Mme. de La Rochefoucauld, Mme. de Luçay, Mme. de Colbert and Mme. de Vaudey. Two lady's-maids would go, also the Chief Equerry, the Comte de'Harville, one master of the Horse, M. de Fouler, and two chamberlains, M. d'Aubusson and André de Beaumont. Also on the journey would be Deschamps, one supervising steward, one regular steward, two ushers, ten footmen, a fleet of chambermaids, and a large delegation of cooks, kitchen servants, coachmen and grooms. In all a train of fifty people.

On July 18 the Emperor left for camp at Boulogne to prepare the invasion of England, and on Monday, July 23, Josephine also set out. She took with her a memorandum of twenty-one manuscript pages dictated by the Emperor to Chaptal, in which every eventuality was foreseen, including the way to reply to speeches and even the amount to be distributed in tips.

"She is a good, easygoing woman," Napoleon had told the Minister. "One must organize her timetable and prescribe her conduct."

The staff for the stables, with berlins, calashes, cabriolets and horses, had gone on before. Josephine traveled by post and each stage required seventy-seven horses driven by twenty-four postilions.

Officers of the gendarmerie rode at the carriage doors and the

subordinate officers went ahead. At Villers-Cotterêts the dragoons came to meet the Empress. The same procedure was followed whenever they passed through small towns, but in prefectural towns such as Soissons, Reims or Liège, regiments paraded, cannons thundered, trumpets blared, drums beat, the authorities, prefects and mayors, addressed their sovereign and little girls in white brought flowers. At each halt the whole staff took their meals with their mistress, as did the colonel of the guard of honor and the officer of gendarmerie, who was instructed to lend an ear to what was said at the Empress's table, obviously for a report to be given to the Emperor.

When Josephine, "preceded by warlike music and to the sound of artillery on the ramparts," made her entry into illuminated Sedan, the main street was hung "with the finest material from the factories" and the crossroads were covered by a dome of blue and white hangings protecting a crown "dazzling with lights."

The next morning Josephine wished to set out again, but the mayor of Sedan had prepared a speech which had to be listened to indulgently. "At last, madame, you are reigning over the hearts of the many inhabitants of the Ardennes as the hero of the century reigns over those of all the French, and if our wishes are granted, he, like our good Henri IV, will associate his dear wife with the honor of the diadem that has been unanimously bestowed on him."

The mayor could rest easy. Like Marie de Médicis, Josephine was to be crowned.

Shouts of "Long live the Empress!" were heard. The order to proceed still could not be given. Eight young ladies in immaculate dresses surrounded their youngest companion, Félicité Petitfils, an orphan. She presented Josephine with a crown of flowers and recited greetings. The Empress had stopped at Sedan the year before when returning from Belgium with Napoleon, so little Félicité, "recalling this memory," recited:

"Last year when we strewed flowers in your path, in our hearts we were awarding you a crown. Encouraged by your kindness, and even happier this day, we come to offer you the emblem of the crown Your Majesty so well deserves."

In exchange for the crown of flowers the Empress gave the orphan a pair of diamond earrings, "a token of her future happiness." Then the procession moved off.

Napoleon may have planned his wife's journey in detail, but beyond Sedan he had mistaken a projected road on the map for an actual road. This soon became obvious, but even in such a case there was no thought of disobeying the master's orders, and the journey across the Ardennes on July 25 was rather like a mountain-climbing expedition. In a driving rain the coaches had to be roped together. Fearing to be overturned, Josephine and her ladies— except Mme. de Vaudey—preferred to get out and splash through the mud. And the night was spent in an indifferent inn at Marche, where most of the travelers had only wooden troughs to sleep in.

The next day the crossing of the Meuse in barges adorned with orange trees and the enthusiastic reception by the people of Liège made them forget the Ardennes misadventure. Finally, on Friday, July 27, Josephine made her entry into Aix-la-Chapelle, still to the sound of cannons and fanfares and between a double line of troops. For Josephine's lodging the fully furnished house of M. Jacoby, Councilor to the Prefecture, had been purchased for 144,000 francs —"one of the finest buildings that adorn the town." In fact it was an incredibly gloomy pile of masonry.

With many sighs the Court camped out until M. Méchain, Prefect of the Roer, resigned himself to giving the Prefecture to Josephine and himself living, somewhat uncomfortably, at the inn. The town was full, invaded, it has been said, by 40,000 strangers attracted by the presence of the new Empress. This was indeed one of the rare events of interest in the old city. Between baths Josephine killed time by chatting with her new lady, pretty Mme. de Vaudey, whom she particularly liked, perhaps because she too had had domestic troubles. This enabled Josephine to complain in her turn and relate all the imperial unfaithfulness to her new favorite.

"I fear," wrote Mme. de Vaudey, quite justly, "that this need to open her heart, to impart all her thoughts and everything that occurred between herself and the Emperor, deprives her of much of Napoleon's confidence. She complains of not having it." But the lady-in-waiting found the Empress likable. But also she wrote: "Josephine is just like a ten-year-old child; she has the same kindness and frivolity; she is easily moved, weeps and is consoled all in an instant. . . . Uneducated, like most Creoles, she has learned nothing, or almost nothing, except through conversation, but as she has spent her life in good company she has acquired very good manners, gracefulness and that manner of speech which, in society, sometimes takes the place of wit. . . . What I find charming about her is that lack of confidence in herself, which is a great merit in her situation. If she discovers intelligence or judgment in any of the people about her, she consults them with very pleasing candor and simplicity."

Josephine saw very few women from the local families, but she received Mme. de Sémonville, wife of the Ambassador to the Hague, Mme. Francheschi, Mme. de Méry, Mme. de Coigny. In the afternoons they would drive to the Borsette spring; they had their silhouettes cut in black paper by Brouch; they gazed at old abbeys or crumbling châteaux; they picnicked, went fox hunting, were taken down into a mine; visited a pin and needle factory.

On August 1 the Empress went to see the mortal remains of Charlemagne. Georges Mauguin recounts that she was presented with a little silver-gilt box called "Noli me tangere." It was wrapped in green silk ribbons held together by a seal bearing an inscription on parchment to the effect that the box had been opened in 1356 and was to be opened again only in exceptional circumstances and by the dean in the presence of the assembled chapter. "On this solemn occasion the box was presented to H.I.M. and the lock, which had resisted the efforts of several canons, opened at once under the Empress's fingers."

One of the Rhenish magistrates wanted to present her with a bone from Charlemagne's arm. Horrified by the gift, Josephine replied "that to sustain her she had the support of an arm as strong as that of Charlemagne." When the Emperor heard this, he was delighted.

Napoleon was the first to admire how admirably Josephine managed her court. In the evenings at Aix, when she did not have tables set out for whist or lotto, she gave a ball to which the German ladies would come wearing the Empress's old dresses, sold to them by her chambermaids. This made her laugh, for she never wore the same dress more than a few times. For distraction there was also the German opera, but it was described as execrable. The famous Picard senior, director of the Théâtre de l'Empératrice—the former and future Odéon—came from Paris to the rescue, but the light comedies he put on were considered just good enough for the servants, and the "little Court" was not amused. As for Picard's *La Femme de quarante-cinq ans,* it was declared "somewhat ill-timed."

Josephine had just turned forty and the forty-five-year-old heroine in the play was presented as a woman who was infirm and over-age where love was concerned.

One evening when the weather was fine Josephine, in spite of M. d'Harville's sighs, proposed to her entourage that they should go on foot to a house where a relief map of Paris was displayed. "When we went out," Mme. de Vaudey reported, "the windows were full of candles and the entire populace were out along our route. We must have been an amusing procession: the gentlemen, with hats under their arms and swords at their sides, offered us an arm and helped us make our way through the crowd, whose ragged clothes formed an odd contrast with our feathers, diamonds and long dresses. Finally we got back to the Prefecture and the Empress then realized she had been somewhat rash. She admitted it frankly."

Napoleon followed his wife's cure from a distance.

"My dear," he wrote on August 3, "I hope soon to learn that the waters are really doing you good. . . . I cover you with kisses." On August 6: "I would very much like to see you. You are always necessary to my happiness." On August 14: "My dear, I have had no news from you for several days. I should like to have been informed of the good effect of the waters and how you spend your time. . . . Let me know by the courier what you intend to do and when you are to finish your baths."

On August 17 he was delighted to have a letter from his wife and a visit from Hortense and her little boy. "I have received your letter," he wrote to his wife. "At the same moment Hortense came into my drawing room with Mr. Napoleon. Louis has let them come here to spend two days to see Boulogne and the sea. She is well. I was very glad to see the dear girl, who is as good, sensible and affectionate as ever. You must go straight to Malmaison. . . . Good-by, my dear, a thousand tender, kind thoughts."

Now that he was emperor, Napoleon sometimes wrote to his wife as "vous"—in jest—as on Monday, August 20, when he announced that he had changed his plans and would join her at Aix-la-Chapelle, the last residence of Charlemagne, where twenty emperors had been crowned. "Madame and dear wife, I shall be at Aix-la-Chapelle in ten days. From there I shall go with you [avec vous] to Cologne, Colbenz, Mainz, Luxembourg . . . You may wait for me, unless you fear you will be tired by such a long journey.

. . . My health is good. I long to see you, to tell you all you are to me and to cover you with kisses. A bachelor's life is a dreary one and there is nothing like a good, beautiful and tender wife."

Four days later, still in good spirits, he warned her: "As I may possibly arrive at night, let lovers beware! I am sorry if this inconveniences them. But one takes one's advantage where one finds it. My health is good. I am working hard. But I am too well-behaved. It's not good for me. So I long to see you and tell you all kinds of nice things."

Napoleon arrived at the Prefecture of Aix-la-Chapelle on September 2, accompanied by Eugene. Josephine was so moved that she wept. In order to make room for the new arrivals all the ladies were obliged to go and sleep at the inn—which was infested with bugs—all, that is, except Mme. de Vaudey, who had become Josephine's favorite. In keeping Mme. de Vaudey near her, "although one cannot state this positively," writes André Gavoty, who has given us a detailed and revealing study of this passing fancy of the Emperor's, "it seems that already, as was to happen with other women, Josephine was hastening her approaching conjugal misfortune by bringing her new friend's attractions too strongly to her husband's notice."

It was, in fact, during the months of September and October that Elisabeth de Vaudey was "noticed" by the Emperor. The lady was desperate on account of serious financial troubles and did everything she could to catch the master's eye. It is not known when she fell into his arms, but in any case it was shortly after Napoleon's arrival at Aix. One evening the Emperor, attracted by Elisabeth's charm, "singled her out" by sending M. de Rémusat to ask her to make a fourth at whist with Josephine, the Duc d'Arenberg and himself. Mme. de Vaudey refused at first.

"There is one problem, she told the chamberlain. "I have never played whist."

Rémusat reported the lady's reply to Napoleon, who answered in his turn, "That doesn't matter."

"It was an order, so I went," Mme. de Vaudey related.

On September 12 Josephine and Elisabeth left for Cologne, where they were to meet the Emperor on the 13th. All the little Court was beginning to suspect Napoleon's interest in Elisabeth. Only Josephine saw nothing. On September 19 Josephine and the woman whom everyone now looked on as the Imperial favorite went aboard the Prince of Nassau's yacht. They sailed up the Rhine toward Mainz, Prefecture of the Mont-Tonnerre Department, but the wind was contrary and in spite of the tugs pulling the little boat, small progress was made. A storm blew up. "Josephine and several of her ladies, who were rather frightened, shut themselves up in a little cabin," wrote Elisabeth de Vaudey. "I wanted to watch a sight new to me. The frequent flashes of lightning revealed behind our yacht the one carrying the other ladies and the Empress's suite. Its large white sails, shaken by a violent wind, stood out against the black clouds covering the sky . . . Gradually the storm died down and we arrived at Bingen at midnight."

Late the following afternoon they reached Mainz, where Napoleon was in a bad temper as his entry into the town had been spoiled by Josephine's delay. They arrived—one by road, the other from the port—and the authorities gathered by the Rhine were not able to address their master. But the streets were strewn with flowers—which was some compensation. There were more receptions. The Rhenish princes had come in force to pay court to the new Emperor. The Court was on exhibition continuously and Josephine and her ladies sighed.

"In the morning we dress at ten for lunch," Elisabeth wrote. "At noon we dress again for the presentations. These often take place at different times and the dress must always suit the kind of people being presented, so that we sometimes change our dress three times in the morning, a fourth time for dinner and a fifth for a ball."

One evening when there was a ball Josephine claimed she was ill, asserted that it would be death for her to go out, and refused to leave her room. The Emperor arrived, treated his wife's fatigue as childishness, "dragged her by one arm out of her bed and forced her to have her hair done and come to the ball." There was another argument between them about Eugene, whom Napoleon thought it unnecessary to present to the German princes.

Nonetheless, Josephine gave her husband all the support she could. We hear of her going alone with her household to visit the Prince of Nassau at the castle of Biberich on the right bank of the Rhine. She reviewed the Prince's troops, presided at luncheon, smiled and adapted herself to the company, proving once more that she was capable of talking and saying nothing and, what is more, doing it gracefully. She was generous and sometimes had reason to regret it. "Yesterday the two Princesses of Hesse-Darmstadt, who were to leave Mainz today, came to dinner," relates Mme. de Vaudey. "In the evening they went to the theatre. As the ladies had no shawls and Josephine was afraid they would be cold, she asked for two to lend them. This morning, when they left, the elder Princess wrote a very witty, pleasant note to the Empress to say that she was keeping the shawls as a souvenir. The note was very well phrased but it did not console Josephine for being deprived of two of what happened to be the finest of her white shawls."

The Emperor and Empress returned to Saint-Cloud by different routes. Napoleon went to Triev and to Luxembourg, while Josephine took a more direct way, for Hortense was shortly to give birth to her second child.

It was a gloomy return. For the Empress had guessed "Bonaparte's" fresh infidelity. She kept Elisabeth at a distance and the latter now traveled in a following carriage. On passing through Nancy on October 4 Josephine was given the same honors as if she were accompanying the Emperor. Amid the trees and arbors a triumphal arch garlanded with flowers had been erected in the Faubourg de la Constitution, formerly the Faubourg de Strasbourg. On the appearance of the procession at six in the evening, music, drums and bells began to sound off. The Empress was addressed, complimented, congratulated, thanked. They wanted to take her to the theatre for the performance of *l'Heureuse Journée ou le passage de S.M. l'Impératrice à Nancy*. Unfortunately, to the great grief of the prefect, who was proud of his idea, Josephine declared she was tired and went to bed.

On October 11, the day before the Emperor's return, a courier arrived from the Hôtel de Saint-Julien, Louis's house in the Rue Cerutti. Hortense was about to give birth. Josephine hurried off and was present at the arrival of another little boy. "When it came time to name my son," Hortense related, "his father wrote 'Louis' on the register, that being the name he wished him to bear. The Emperor crossed it out with his own hand, claiming that all the children in his family should be called Napoleon and that that name should come first."

Mme. de Vaudey had resumed her relationship with the Emperor. Napoleon received the lady in hasty meetings at Saint-Cloud in a little entresol room above his study and his bedroom, which he reached by a side staircase.

One morning, between October 25 and 28, Josephine saw Mme. de Vaudey leave the drawing room for no apparent reason. She guessed that the lady had gone to join her husband and called Mme. de Remusat.

"I am going now to clear up my suspicions," she told her. "Remain in this room with my attendants and if anyone asks where I am say that the Emperor asked for me."

Disturbed, Mme. de Rémusat tried to calm her and dissuade her. Josephine would not listen and went along a little passage. Her absence lasted half an hour. Suddenly she returned to the drawing room by a door opposite that through which she had left. Pale, with "hurried movements," trembling, she seemed very upset and bent over her tapestry to compose herself. Finally, unable to bear it, she summoned Mme. de Rémusat and took her to her room. Sobbing, she told her:

"Everything is lost. What I foresaw is only too true. I went to find the Emperor in his study and he was not there, so I went up by the side staircase to the little room. I found the door shut and through the keyhole I could hear the voices of Bonaparte and Mme. de Vaudey. I knocked loudly and gave my name. You may imagine the agitation I caused them. They were a long time in opening to me and when they did the state they were both in and their disorder did not leave me with the slightest doubt. I know I ought to have controlled myself, but it was not possible, I burst out in reproaches. Mme. de Vaudey began to cry. Bonaparte flew into such a violent rage that I hardly had time to flee to escape his fury. . . . Indeed, I am still trembling," Josephine concluded, "for I do not know to what lengths he might have gone. He is probably coming and there will be a terrible scene."

Mme. de Rémusat was as upset as her mistress.

"Do not make a second mistake," she advised Josephine, "for the Emperor will not forgive you for having taken anyone into your confidence. Let me leave you, madame. You must wait for him. Let him find you alone and try to soften him and repair this great imprudence."

Mme. de Rémusat hastened to return to the drawing room, where

Mme. de Vaudey was. Pale, speaking only in broken phrases, the lady in waiting glanced anxiously at Mme. de Rémusat, wondering if she knew what had happened. Suddenly those present heard a great noise" coming from the Empress's apartments. Mme. de Vaudey rose, ordered her horses and left for Paris. Soon Josephine summoned Mme. de Rémusat. The unhappy woman was in tears. There had been a dreadful scene. Bonaparte, who was furious, had insulted his wife. He had even broken some furniture.

"You must get ready to leave Saint-Cloud," he had told her. "Tired of such jealous surveillance, I have decided to throw off this yoke and from now on listen to the wisdom of the policy which requires me to take a wife capable of giving me children."

"I am irreparably lost," sobbed Josephine.

All the more lost since Napoleon had asked the Pope to come to Paris to crown him and his wife. After some persuasion Pius VII had announced that he was making his preparations for leaving. This news had set off a final effort by the Bonapartes to prevent Josephine's being crowned. It was Joseph who was the spokesman.

"Why crown Josephine since in the end you will have to repudiate her? The interests of France require the Emperor to have direct heirs. Would it not be better for the country and for the Emperor himself to establish the Napoleonic dynasty on the throne by his own descendants rather than by the artificial heredity established by the decree of the Senate of 28 Floréal? The coronation offers the Emperor the opportunity of marrying, as he wishes, a foreign princess or the heiress of one of the great names of France."

The emperor informed Eugene that he had made his decision; he would separate from their mother. While Josephine shed "torrents of tears" and got ready to leave, Eugene declared he would follow her to her retreat.

Hortense preferred to remain outside the conflict.

"I cannot interfere at all," she said to Mme. de Rémusat, "for my husband has positively forbidden me to make any move. . . . Besides, if there is a chance of reconciliation in this affair it comes from the power my mother's sweetness and tears have over Bonaparte. You must leave them to themselves. . . ."

And Napoleon *was* beginning to be shaken by Josephine's sobs. Of course, divorce was of great importance to him. "But," he explained to Josephine, "I have not the courage to take the final resolve and if you show too much distress, if you do it only to obey me, I feel I shall never be strong enough to force you to leave me; but I confess I very much wish you would learn to resign yourself to the requirements of my political needs and that you yourself would spare me all the embarrassments of this painful separation."

Following Mme. de Rémusat's advice, Josephine told the Emperor "that she would await direct orders before descending from the throne on which she had been placed."

The Bonapartes, with the exception of Jerome, rejoiced. This time it was the end of those "Beauharnais" who had been preventing them from sleeping soundly for nearly ten years. The clan shamelessly displayed their joy. Napoleon, disgusted, "wounded by his family's air of triumph," angered at learning that his relatives had dared "to boast of having manipulated him to their ends," confided to Roederer on November 2:

"How can I dismiss this good wife because I am becoming greater? No, it is beyond me. I have a man's heart. I was not borne by a tigress. When she dies I shall marry again and be able to have children, but I do not want to make her unhappy. . . . They are jealous of my wife, of Eugene, of Hortense, of everything about me. . . . I love those children because they are always anxious to please me. . . . I love Hortense, yes, I love her. She and her brother always take my part, even against their mother when she is angry about some girl or such nonsense. If I am making her an empress, it is from justice. Yes, she shall be crowned!"

And that same day he went into Josephine's room to announce the Pope's imminent arrival at Fontainebleau.

"He will crown us both. You must begin making serious preparations for the ceremony."

Mad with joy, Josephine threw herself into his arms.

14. Josephine Crowned

On Sunday, November 25, 1804—Quartidi, 4 Frimaire, Year XIII, day of medlars, for the Revolutionary calendar was still in force—Josephine waited in her apartments at Fontainebleau with beating heart for the arrival of Pope Pius VII, who was coming to Paris to crown the new Emperor and Empress on the following Sunday.

Early that morning she had gone in her carriage to follow the Emperor's hunt. When a courier had announced His Holiness's arrival Josephine had returned to the château while Napoleon pretended to hunt.

"As I am going to my palace at Fontainebleau, which is on the route, I shall thus be able to enjoy His Holiness's company a day earlier" was the message Napoleon had sent the Pope.

Napoleon wanted His Holiness not to think himself superior to the man he was coming to crown. Outside of Notre-Dame the Pope was, Napoleon felt, only a temporal ruler. And to make matters clear, Napoleon did not return to the château to change but awaited his guest at St. Hérem's cross in hunting dress. In order not to seem to be going to meet the Holy Father, the Emperor had had the idea of appearing to interrupt a hunt. The event would thus seem all the more unplanned.

There was a long wait. Finally—it was not half past one—Josephine heard the artillery salvos drowning the sound of bells and soon there rose from the courtyard the rumbling of cannon, then the steps of the escort—an infidel escort, since it was composed of Mamelukes. At the foot of Louis XV's staircase the former Bishop of Autun stood bowing—an apostate and married bishop, Maurice de Talleyrand-Périgord.

The Pope, five cardinals, two Roman princes, four bishops, plus ninety-seven priests, chamberlains, secretaries and servants, installed themselves in the palace. Josephine was getting ready to go to the Holy Father's apartments, but Napoleon asked the Pope to go to the Empress's drawing room "to greet her." With a sigh Pius VII obeyed, left his apartment, and went to bless the *carissima Victoria,* as the Pope persisted in calling her—admittedly a name very suitable for General Bonaparte's wife.

On the second day the Pope dined with Napoleon and Josephine, but refused to attend the concert, a too secular amusement, given afterwards in the Empress's room. On the third day Pius VII accompanied the sovereigns to the shooting range, where there was an extraordinary cannon practice, with leather bullets shot at living human targets. The unfortunate soldiers were probably only slightly bruised, but Josephine found this parody horrible. Pius VII was of her opinion and at their request the Emperor put a stop to this game of living tenpins.

Meanwhile Napoleon appeared very worried. His whole family were still "in a state of frenzy" at the thought that "Mme. de Beauharnais"—as Mme. Mère affected to call her—was to be anointed by the Pope and crowned by her husband. Joseph, speaking for the clan, made a final effort against "that woman."

"The crowning of the Empress is contrary to my interests," he said. "It tends to give the children of Louis and Hortense superior claims to mine; it prejudices the rights of my children in that it makes Louis's children the grandchildren of an empress while mine will be the sons of a bourgeoise."

The Emperor burst out: "To talk to me of his rights and his interests is to wound me in my most sensitive spot. . . . Josephine shall be crowned! She shall be crowned even though it should cost me 200,000 men."

Let us hope—in order to please the historians who support the thesis of a pacifist Napoleon—that anger sometimes induced him to say things he did not mean. Faced with this threatened hecatomb, Joseph gave way and even came to Fontainebeau to make his apology. Napoleon showed his satisfaction.

"I am called on to change the face of the world. At least, I believe so. Remain therefore within a system of hereditary monarchy which promises you so many advantages."

But for all that the Emperor could not sleep. He had "to wage a pitched battle" in order to force his sisters and sisters-in-law to carry the Empress's train in Notre-Dame and to follow her during all the movements of the ceremony. "Mme. Joseph" claimed that "such a task was very painful for a virtuous woman." "For the six days this quarrel has gone on," the Emperor confided in his brother, "I have not had a moment's rest. I cannot sleep and you are the only people with such power over me."

The ladies were so agitated, for they too suffered from insomnia, that it was agreed they should not carry the mantle but "support" it. In exchange they were each given a chamberlain to carry the train of their own dresses. This threatened to cause a certain amount of jostling in Josephine's wake. Fortunately, Joseph, Louis, Cambacé-rès and Lebrun, entrusted with carrying Napoleon's mantle, were not so exigent.

Besides the heavy, traditional mantle, symbol of power—that mantle of "Tyrian purple" 23 yards long adorned with embroidery and lined with Russian ermine and gold bees—Josephine, like the Emperor, had the right to a ring. Hers was adorned with a ruby, emblem of joy, and in Napoleon's shone an emerald, signifying "divine revelation." These rings would be given to them by the Pope, who would accompany the gesture with ritual prayers. The Empress would also put on the crown consisting of eight garlands of laurel and myrtle leaves bearing a little globe surmounted by a cross. She would also wear a tall diadem of gold, diamonds and amethysts—symbols of love and wisdom—which would appear to be part of the crown. Finally, Josephine too would receive the triple unction with the holy oil.

As she was to be thus anointed, Josephine considered herself safe from divorce. It would be impossible to repudiate a woman crowned at one's side—and by the Pope, too. So her conjugal fortune seemed assured forever. One point—not a small one—

obsessed her: she was married only by civil law to the Emperor.
Although for Napoleon the anointing was only a ceremony like the
crowning or the constitutional oath, Josephine considered she was
to receive a sacrament which required confession and communion.

It was not, however, Josephine's Christian feelings which led her
to confess the truth to the Pope, but the conviction that once she
was united to "Bonaparte" in a religious ceremony all danger would
be past. She cleverly waited until Saturday, December 1, the eve of
the coronation, to ask an audience of the Holy Father, who was now
installed in the Pavillon de Flore at the Tuileries. When he received
this information Pius VII nearly fainted. So they had dared to bring
him from Rome to bless a concubine, to give the triple unction with
the chrism reserved for bishops to a couple living in mortal sin! This
time he refused to overlook matters; he would rather leave at once if
the sacrilege was not repaired. He would crown the Emperor alone,
but could not tolerate so much as Josephine's presence in Notre-
Dame.

There could be no question of calling everything off or changing
the arrangements for the ceremony at the last moment. There was
but one solution: to capitulate before Josephine's successful maneu-
ver. At the beginning of the afternoon Napoleon summoned his
uncle, Cardinal Fesch, and informed him of the situation.

"You will celebrate the marriage yourself, but I insist that the
whole affair should be as secret as the confessional. I want no
witnesses."

"If there are no witnesses there is no marriage," Fesch exclaimed.

The Emperor, possibly looking into the future, would not give
way. He would admit no one.

"In that case," sighed the Cardinal, "all I can do is make use of
dispensations."

"Going at once to see the Pope," Mme. Mère's brother related, "I
put to him that I will need very often to ask him for dispensations
and I begged him to grant me all those that were at times
indispensable for carrying out my duties as Grand Almoner."

In this note, which can still be seen in the Archives, the words
"j'aurai besoin" (I will need) were first put in the conditional tense.
It was Fesch who crossed out the *s* with his own hand. Moreover,
the Emperor's uncle seems to have been careful not to explain to
Pius VII that he was asking the head of the Church for an

immediate dispensation to celebrate Napoleon's otherwise illegal marriage on the floor above. One must suppose, however, that His Holiness had guessed the reason for the cardinal's approach. In any case, Pius VII having given his consent—not to the absence of witnesses, of course, but to Fesch's request—the cardinal returned to the Emperor and at four o'clock began the marriage ceremony.

"Sire," he asked Napoleon, "do you declare, acknowledge and swear, before God and in the presence of His holy Church, that you now take to wife and lawful spouse Josephine Rose Tascher de La Pagerie, widow Beauharnais, here present?"

"Yes!" thundered Napoleon.

"Do you promise and swear to be faithful to her in all things, as is a faithful husband's duty to his wife, according to God's command-ment?"

"Yes."

Then it was the turn of "Josephine" Rose Tascher de La Pagerie, widow Beauharnais, who triumphantly agreed to take Napoleon Bonaparte for her husband and lawful spouse.

"*Ego conjungo vos,*" pronounced Fesch.

But Josephine, still worried, asked for a certificate of the cere-mony two days later. After refusing, the cardinal referred the matter to the Emperor, who at first agreed and then, when the thing was done, regretted his gesture—according to Fesch.

Paris was in a fever. People hurried "to one person to get tickets for the day of the ceremony, to another to hire a window to see the procession pass." People went to Foncier's to admire the crowns. The fairy tale was reaching its apotheosis.

With the help of little puppets, dressed in different colored paper and placed on a plan of Notre-Dame, on the Emperor's own table each person was shown what he would have to do at the coronation. Moreover, on the eve of the coronation, in the Salon de Diane, there had been rehearsals with a plan sketched on the floor in chalk.

The next morning, having carefully made herself up, Josephine put on a dress of white satin sprinkled with gold bees, embroidered with silver and shining with diamonds, a dress "edged with fringes" which had cost 10,000 francs—equal to 50,000 present-day francs. She put on white velvet shoes embroidered with gold, costing 650 francs. The imperial mantle was awaiting her at the archbishopric, so she merely wore a "bas de robe" of white velvet costing 7,000 francs. Her gloves were gold embroidered. In her hair was a diadem, different from the one she would wear in church, and valued at 1,032,000 francs—more than five million present-day francs.

With diamonds also in her ears and round her neck and with a jeweled belt at her waist, Josephine, in everyone's opinion, looked fifteen years younger. A high lace collar framed her face and made it even more enchanting—as shown by David's famous painting. When she entered the Emperor's study with her graceful, caressing walk, carrying her head "in a way at once gracious and noble," he smiled, being again under the charm of his "incomparable Josephine."

Napoleon had already put on his white satin breeches embroidered with gold ears of corn, his white silk stockings, his Henri IV style ruff, but by way of a dressing gown he was wearing the jacket of his uniform as colonel of the Chasseurs de la Garde.

When it was nearly time, he donned his purple velvet coat, his little red cloak in the Henri III style adorned with 10,000 francs' worth of laurel leaves and bees embroidered in gold. When he had put on his black felt hat with white plumes and buckled on his sword, whose jasper hilt carried the Regent diamond, Napoleon turned to his wife and ordered: "Let someone look for Raguineau. He must come at once. I want to speak to him."

Raguineau was Josephine's lawyer. Eight years earlier on the eve of his civil marriage Bonaparte had gone with Josephine to see Raguineau and had tactfully stayed in his clerks' office. Standing in a window and "drumming on the panes with his fingers," he had distinctly heard through the door of the office Raguineau "doing all he could to dissuade Mme. de Beauharnais from her projected marriage."

"You are making a great mistake," the lawyer had said. "You will be sorry for it, you are being foolish. You are going to marry a man who has nothing but his cape and sword."

On leaving, Bonaparte had merely said to Josephine, "He spoke like an honest man and I respect him for what he said to you."

The lawyer, astonished at being summoned to the Tuileries on the very morning of the coronation, entered the room. There was Napoleon, in full costume, dazzling.

"Well, M. Raguineau, have I nothing but my cape and sword?"

"The fact is," Josephine was to tell Bourrienne, recounting this scene, "that Bonaparte, who in the days of our intimacy had told me every circumstance of his life he could remember, had never spoken to me of the little rebuff he had received eight years before in Raguineau's office, which he appeared to recollect only on the day of his coronation."

At ten o'clock, while the salvos thundered, Josephine and Napoleon took their seats in the coach upholstered in white velvet and drawn by eight light bays with spotless plumes. Louis and Joseph—silvered and plumed "in the Spanish fashion"—sat facing the Imperial couple. There was a thick bearskin on the floor, but no hotwater bottle, and it was terribly cold.

Clusters of pages in green and gold clung to the front and back of the carriage, which was laden with olive and laurel branches, eagle and palm, coats of arm and crowns, allegorical figures and bees—all dazzlingly gilded. Surrounding this little monument went the aides-de-camp, near the horses, the colonels general of the guard, at the doors, and the equerries, at the back wheels.

In advance of the coach went eight squadrons of cuirassiers, with trumpets and kettledrums, two squadrons of Chasseurs de la Garde, their band sounding loud and clear, companies of Mamelukes, a band, Murat and his staff, the mounted heralds at arms, carriages loaded with high dignitaries, ministers, high-ranking officers and chamberlains.

After the coach came thirteen six-horse carriages for the officers and ladies of the Emperor and Empress, their civilian officers. More grenadiers, gunners, gendarmes, bands. . . .

Such was the glory of Rose Tascher de La Pagerie, Creole from Martinique.

At a quarter to twelve the Imperial coach arrived at the archbishop's palace where the Emperor put on his full costume, while the heavy Imperial mantle was fastened to Josephine and her amethyst diadem put on. The long procession set out on foot for Notre-Dame through a wooden gallery hung with tapestry. After the four ushers—and at a distance of ten paces—came the heralds at arms, the pages, the aides—always at ten paces—the master of ceremonies and the grand master carrying his staff, one behind the other. Then, accompanied by Josephine's chamberlains and equerries, came three marshals dressed in white satin and aflutter with plumes. The first, Sérurier, held the Empress's ring on a cushion; he was flanked by General Gardanne and Colonel Fouler. The second, Moncey, with Colonel Vatier and M. de Beaumont, respectfully carried the basket of purple velvet, twisted and braided with gold and with silver-gilt handles, a basket which was shortly to receive the Empress's mantle. Finally the third, Murat, bore the crown, having d'Harencourt on his left and M. d'Aubusson on his right.

Then came Josephine. The terrible mantle was carried by Hortense, Princess Joseph (Julie Clary), Caroline, Elisa and Pauline. The three last were obviously in a bad temper, lagged behind and, in spite of their agreement with the Emperor, "supported" as little as possible the heavy mantle of thirty square yards. The train of each of them was held by a chamberlain, which made a group of twelve people around that famous Imperial mantle, symbol of "Mme. Bonaparte's" sovereignty. Closing the procession were the maids of honor, the mistress of the wardrobe and the six ladies in waiting.

Then the Emperor's interminable procession began. His mantle was supported by the two Consuls and the two future kings, Louis and Joseph.

At the entrance to Notre-Dame Cardinal Cambacérès presented holy water to Josephine. It was offered to the Emperor by the dyspeptic Cardinal Archbishop de Belloy.

While the orchestra of three hundred musicians attacked the Coronation March, Josephine was accorded a canopy borne by the canons. She was led in procession to her chair in the middle of the choir, near the Emperor's. These were the two "little thrones" with velvet seats. The "great thrones" were at the top of a gigantic platform obstructing the nave, reached by twenty-four steps and built halfway from the center of the church and the high altar. It was at the foot of, and around, this monument that the diplomatic corps and the Ministers were placed. Then, between the throne and the altar, could be seen the members of the Senate and of the Legislative Body, the magistrates and high officers of the Crown. Near the altar, in the front row, were ten archbishops and forty bishops, who had had to robe at police headquarters. In the aisles and transepts were massed the delegations and in the galleries the guests.

Notre-Dame looked strange. Like the façade, the pillars and walls were hidden under a cardboard casing in classical style, which made the basilica look like an antique temple or a Jesuit church. "So much work has been done," an eyewitness sighed, "that God Himself would lose His bearings."

The mistress of the wardrobe and lady of honor took off the heavy mantle and Moncey received it in his basket. Then the honors—crown, ring and mantle in its basket—were placed on the altar, with Napoleon's honors.

The ceremony of anointing followed at once. Josephine and her husband knelt on carpets at the foot of the altar. Having anointed the Emperor, the Pope gave Josephine the holy unction on her head and the palms of her hands. Napoleon had simplified the ceremony. He did not see himself, like the kings of France, lying on his face before the officiant, after having been anointed through holes in his shirt on the chest, the middle of the back and "the folds of the arms." He thought it quite enough for both Josephine and himself to receive the triple unction.

The Mass said by His Holiness terminated at the Gradual. The coronation was to begin.

It had been decided that the Roman Pontifical form would be used, not the ceremony reserved for the King of the Romans crowned Emperor at Rome, but the service *Pro Rege coronando*. It would be enough to substitute *Imperator* for *Rex*. At Napoleon's instigation, a committee formed for the purpose had submitted to the Pope a hash of rites from Rome, Reims, Germany and elsewhere. The Emperor's first care had been to suppress or transform, in the text spoken by the Pope, certain verbs he considered displeasing, such as *eligimus* (whom we have elected) and, for the handing over of the sword *concessum* (yielded), which became *oblatum* (offered).

Having blessed the Imperial regalia—the sword, orb, scepter, hand of justice, collar—the Pope gave a blessing to the two mantles, the two rings, the two crowns.

"Receive this ring which is the sign of the holy faith, the proof of the power and solidity of your empire, by which thanks to its triumphant power, you will conquer your enemies, destroy heresies, hold your subjects united and remain perseveringly attached to the Catholic faith."

Then the Holy Father handed over the mantle to the Empress with these words:

"May the Lord clothe you with His power so that, while you shine externally with the splendor of this garment, you may shine internally by the merits of your virtues in the eyes of God. . . .

There was no question of Napoleon's receiving his crown from the hands of the Pope. It was he who would crown himself and crown the Empress. Had he not raised up the crown of France which he had found fallen to the ground? So, having placed the crown on his own head, he took it off and then came the moment of Josephine's coronation.

The Empress left her chair. She walked forward, knelt before Bonaparte, while the tears she could not repress "rolled onto her clasped hands," wrote Mme. d'Abrantès, those hands "which she raised more to him than to God, at that moment when Napoleon, or rather Bonaparte, was for her her true Providence. There then arose between those two poeple one of those fleeting moments, unique in a whole life, which fill the emptiness of many years."

The Emperor took Josephine's crown, placed it for a second on her head and took it off "with graceful slowness." "But when he was on the point of finally crowning her who was his lucky star, as it was presumed, he was coquettish with her, if I can use such a word," went on Laure d'Abrantès. "He arranged that little crown surmounting the diamond diadem, put it on, took it off, replaced it yet again. It seemed as though he wanted to promise her that the crown would be pleasant and light for her."

What woman in the history of the world has ever received such a present from the man she loved? An empire which was shortly to stretch from Hamburg to Naples, from Brest to Warsaw.

Josephine had risen and slowly, at the Emperor's side, followed by the Pope and the triple procession of princes, cardinals, marshals and high dignitaries, crossed the choir and made her way to the great throne, while the orchestra and choirs rang out.

Not without having been dragged backwards by the weight of their mantles, Napoleon and Josephine managed to reach the top of the structure. This time Josephine's throne was smaller than her husband's and was placed one step lower. The Pope blessed them both in these words:

"May you be established on this Imperial throne and made to

reign with Him in His eternal kingdom by Jesus Christ, King of kings, Lord of lords, who liveth and reigneth with God the Father and the Holy Ghost for ever and ever."

Having embraced the Emperor, he turned to the congregation and intoned: "*Vivat Imperator in aeternum.*"

In reply a shout arose from the assembled crowd: "Long live the Emperor! Long live the Empress!"

Pius VII returned to the altar while the pages and, on Josephine's side, the princesses, maids of honor and ladies in waiting took their places on the steps.

At the reading of the gospel the book was carried in procession for the two sovereigns to kiss. At the offertory the Emperor and Empress and all their suite returned to the altar. For Josephine, Mme. d'Arberg, followed by General Savary, carried the candle with the thirteen symbolic gold pieces, while Mme. de Luçay, escorted by General Lemarois, held the loaf of silver. The loaf of gold was given to Mme. Duchâtel, accompanied by General Cafarelli. For carrying these "honors" the ladies received diamond necklaces worth 20,000 to 30,000 francs.

The sovereigns sat on their "little thrones" while the silver-gilt basin was presented to the Pope. The water flowed from a ewer. Both basin and ewer had been used at the coronation of Louis XVI. The lilies had simply been replaced by Victories, but the L's were still there. After communion they returned to the high thrones.

After Mass the Pope left, not wishing to be present during the civil ceremony or to sanction by his presence the liberty of worship which the Emperor was to mention in the text of that oath he would be unable to keep.

"I swear to maintain the integrity of the territory of the Republic, to respect and cause to be respected the laws of the Concordat and liberty of worship; to respect and cause to be respected equality of rights, political and civil liberty, the irrevocability of the sales of national property, to levy no duty, to impose no tax, except by virtue of the law, to maintain the institution of the Legion of Honor; to govern solely for the interests, happiness and glory of the French people."

Then the herald at arms cried in a loud voice: "The most glorious and most august Napoleon, Emperor of the French, is consecrated and enthroned!"

It was nearly three o'clock. The long ceremony was over. The same procession accompanied the Imperial couple to the archbishopric. A double procession—that of the Emperor and Empress and that of the Pope—returned to the Tuileries by the Rue de la Barrilerie, the Pont-au-Change, the Place du Châtelet, the Rue Saint-Denis and the boulevards. It was night when they entered the Place de la Concorde, where 500 torches, garlands and lanterns made the gold of the coaches shimmer and the diamonds sparkle. Flares were lit on the two palaces, as on all public buildings. Large illuminated stars—symbolic stars 25 yards across placed in the center and on the terraces—lit up the square. The procession entered the great avenue, where it was as light as day, thanks to 62 posts bearing illuminated stars, garlands and lanterns with multicolored glass. The garden, lawns and the château itself were ashine with 38,892 vessels and 15,950 "large-scale" lamps. The illuminators had surpassed themselves "in spite of the harshness of the weather."

At the Tuileries Napoleon thought all the women who had played a part in the ceremony pretty. But it was Josephine dressed as Empress who was most attractive to him. He congratulated her "on the way she wore the diadem" and insisted on her keeping her crown on when she dined alone with him.

All through that glorious day Paris and Notre-Dame had certainly looked on the Empress with the Emperor's eyes. "One would have said," reported Mme. de Chastenay, "that mercy, peace, everything good and gentle, had come from heaven to earth. Josephine was grace personified at that moment. . . . Eyes and hearts were conquered; hers was the triumph on that great day."

Yet, when she was getting into bed with him that evening, Josephine heard her husband murmur, while her fears sprang up again: "To whom shall I leave all this?"

Henceforth, and for five years, this was to be her existence: after a few moments of happiness anguish was always to seize her heart.

For several weeks Paris was all feasts and rejoicing. In the streets, despite the cold, were fireworks, balloon ascensions, traveling shows, balls, tilting at the ring, while the heralds threw the people gold and silver medals commemorating the double coronation.

On December 5 Josephine stoically watched the distribution of the Eagles. The interminable ceremony took place in rain and snow and when, toward the end, the army marched past, splashing through the mud of the Champ-de-Mars, the Empress fled, dripping and barely recognizable.

She smiled charmingly through the boring banquets, the long, solemn audiences her husband gave to all the state departments. On December 16 the city of Paris gave a fete for Josephine. Adhering to the custom of the old regime the Town Hall had been enlarged by a windowed gallery giving a view of the fireworks set off from the Pont-Neuf.

Dressed in silver tulle and gold-embroidered satin, she arrived with Napoleon in the coronation coach. There was a speech at the Pont-Neuf and another on the steps of the Town Hall. Then she was taken to her room, where she found a wonderful silver-gilt toilet set, a present from the city of Paris: mirror, ewer, basin, girandoles, boxes, goblets, bowls, and even a tongue scraper.

Six hundred women were invited to supper and Josephine presided at the Emperor's table.

But then Berthier, the Minister for War, gave a banquet at which Napoleon refused to sit down and Josephine, chatting with her neighbors at the head table, saw that her husband, who had stopped by one of the tables, was leaning over the shoulder of one of the ladies in waiting.

She was charming. Twenty-two years old, dark-haired with a long, pointed nose, according to Hortense, fair with an aquiline nose, according to Mme. de Rémusat, she was allowed by both memorialists to be of medium height, with very pretty teeth and beautiful eyes, dark-blue eyes "with long, silky lids." Josephine's daughter also stated that her complexion, though "without freshness in the morning," was "dazzling at night." In any case, she was attractive, had small feet, a charming smile, danced and sang very pleasantly and with all this greatly pleased Napoleon. Her name was Marie Antoinette Adèle Papin and she had married Charles Duchâtel, then director general of the Registry Office, whose merit in Napoleon's eyes was being thirty years older than his wife.

Napoleon seems really to have been in love with this disinterested young woman who asked nothing for either her family or her friends. He had noticed her for some time, but Josephine first became aware of it only on the evening when the Emperor leaned over the young lady in waiting's shoulder to say:

"You should not eat olives at night, they are not good for you."

Then, addressing Mme. Duchâtel's neighbor: "And you, Mme. Junot, are you not eating olives? You are quite right. And doubly right in not imitating Mme. Duchâtel, who is inimitable."

Eugene had also fallen in love with this young woman and Murat pretended to do so in order to lull the Empress's suspicions. But the Creole's jealousy was always alert and she remembered that for some time now whenever Mme. Duchâtel was on duty the Emperor went down to the ground floor and lingered in her company. Napoleon was indeed very much attracted. If Josephine attended the theatre in a small loge, with Mme. Duchâtel, Napoleon would turn up. "He was less master of himself each day," Mme. de Rémusat related, "and appeared busier. Mme. Duchâtel appeared outwardly cool, but she employed every stratagem of female coquetry. Her dress became increasingly elaborate, her smile more subtle, her glances more studied, and it was soon fairly easy to guess what was happening."

Josephine was quite unaware that even before the coronation Napoleon used to meet Mme. Duchâtel in a little house in the Allée des Veuves. Then one evening at Malmaison, where they had gone in February, Josephine caught her husband proceeding along the tiled, icy corridors to join the fair one. She could no longer be in doubt. Besides, when she had caught her husband walking along "the road to love" she made no bones about listening once more at the door of the Emperor's study. "She was light on her feet," the Emperor was to state. "Moreover, she was always quick enough to nose out any attachment I might have and then she never failed to bring the conversation round to the person she thought it was, and to throw ridicule on her or manage to relate some stories which might put one off her."

This time her stratagem did not work. Mme. Duchâtel seemed firmly established. At once the tears flowed and complaints were made. The Emperor, in fact, had not the slightest intention of installing a "favorite" at court.

"I have no desire for women to rule at my court. They did harm to Henri IV and Louis XIV. My job is much more important than that of those princes and the French have become too serious-minded to forgive their sovereign for having notorious liaisons and maîtresses en titre."

Doubtless Josephine knew this, but she was nonetheless madly jealous and made use of her traditional weapons. "Sometimes," relates Mme. de Rémusat, "she would ask me to go to him and speak firmly to him about the wrong she claimed his new liaison was doing her in the eyes of the world. Sometimes she would get me to spy on Mme. Duchâtel in her own house, where she knew Bonaparte sometimes went in the evening. Her servants were employed to find proofs she sought. Workmen and favorite tradesmen were in her confidence." Napoleon was soon out of patience with this gossip and with his wife's reddened eyes and constant scenes. Josephine thought she had struck a decisive blow by announcing to her husband "that she would end by forbidding Mme. Duchâtel the entry to her apartments."

Exasperated, and not wanting a clash with Josephine, of whom he was sometimes a little afraid, Napoleon summoned Mme. de Rémusat and "let fly about women in general and his own in particular."

"If you do not approve the Empress's inquisition," he told her, "why have you not enough influence over her to stop her? She humiliates both of us by the spying with which she surrounds me. She is providing weapons for her enemies. Since you are in her confidence you must answer to me for her and I shall blame you for all her misconduct."

He also complained to Hortense.

"Your mother's jealousy makes me look ridiculous in the eyes of the world. There is no end to the rubbish talked about me. Do you think I don't know it? It is her fault."

"No, sire," Hortense replied. "There are others whom I blame for it. If they did not try to irritate you instead of calming you, you would be more careful of my mother's feelings. Why do you demand from her more strength than you have yourself? She suffers, she complains. That is natural and if those you think are your friends did not report her complaints to you, or if you knew how to control yourself enough not to reveal your displeasure, I am sure that happiness would return among you. Once more, do not demand of her more strength than you have yourself."

"Your are right," said the Emperor in softened tones. "I see that although in great matters I am great in small ones I am small."

On March 19 the Court went to Malmaison for a few days. From her windows Josephine could see her husband walking in the park with Mme. Duchâtel and young Mme. Savary, who was just twenty. And Josephine wept.

She was sure that Mme. Duchâtel was in the way to becoming maîtresse en titre, and once again the specter of divorce arose before her. She had not even the strength to make vain scenes, but she was extremely sad. If Mme. Duchâtel became pregnant, Napoleon would undoubtedly marry her. Perhaps it was about this time that Josephine spread the idea that her husband was impotent.

"She had told this to Mme. Duchâtel," Napoleon related on St. Helena, "who when *talking* to me one day at Malmaison suddenly burst out laughing.

" 'What is the matter?' I asked.

" 'I was thinking,' she said, 'that the Empress insists that *that* is as clear as crystal, whereas I find that *that* . . .' "

Suddenly one night Josephine thought she was dreaming. "Bonaparte" was alone with her and speaking in the tones of her lover of former days. Yes, he confessed, he had loved Marie Antoinette Duchâtel, but the great passion was no more.

"It is all over now," he added.

Josephine felt the weight that had been on her heart for several months vanish. What was more, the Emperor, having made a few intimate revelations about his love, ended by asking his wife to help him break off the affair.

It may be imagined that she did her best. We know her kindness and Mme. Duchâtel's intelligence and disinterestedness. Matters went off very well and probably more gracefully than in Mme. de Rémusat's account.

Napoleon asked, through Duroc, for the return of the love letters he had sent the young woman. She sent them back without delay, refused the diamond necklace he had offered her but when a return of affection later led him to visit the Allée des Veuves she occasionally agreed to receive her Imperial lover. Josephine was never to know this, however.

15. The Height of Glory

For the moment Josephine was all joy. The Pope had baptized her second grandson at Saint-Cloud on March 24, 1805. Eugene had been appointed a prince of the Empire, Archchancellor of State and Most Serene Highness, and on April 2 she left with the Emperor, who was to be crowned King of Italy at Milan.

Then during a banquet given by the city of Lyons on Holy Thursday, April 11, at the archbishopric, Napoleon apparently met for the first time that exquisite, laughing and ravishing child-woman —or rather bird-woman—Emilie Pellapra, who at the end of 1806 was to give him a daughter, the future Princesse de Chimay, a daughter who would say of her mother: "When you have once known her, no other woman is worth looking at."

We do not know if Napoleon gave the pretty Lyonnaise a "private audience" between April 11 and 16. In any case, Josephine's jealousy was not to be aroused until later.

Now the procession stretched out on the road to the Alps. During the long trip the Empress always assisted her husband and, with all her charm and her smiles, carried off what was already terrible drudgery for them. They had a hard crossing over the Alps and finally came out to the plain and to Turin, where as new sovereigns they were acclaimed.

At Asti the inhabitants had thought that Napoleon and Josephine would be passing through their little town in the middle of the night and had made great preparations to illuminate the houses past which the procession would ride. As the result of a delay the new sovereigns of Italy did not arrive until the next day, April 30, at noon. Not wanting to have gone to so much expense for nothing, the inhabitants lit their lanterns and firepots anyway, a scene which must have looked rather surprising in daylight.

On June 1 the Emperor took his wife to Marengo. By some whim of vanity he had had the clothes he was wearing on the day of the battle brought from Paris. The blue, long-tailed coat was much worn, the embroidery had "turned red," and the hat was all dusty, but it was already a part of history, not to say of legend. While the 25th Division repeated the movements of the battle, Napoleon described to his wife that great day on which Desaix had perished.

Milan, where so many memories awaited Josephine, was decked with flags. The cathedral and principal monuments shone with a thousand lights. There was a grand gala at La Scala, which was lit up as though by daylight.

But once more Josephine's jealousy was aroused. The Emperor seemed attracted by his wife's reader, the fair, delicate and witty Mlle. Lacoste. Josephine had engaged her not for reading—the post was a sinecure—but because this young, dowryless orphan aroused her pity. Napoleon seemed interested in her for other reasons: The Empress therefore demanded that she leave for France and Napoleon gave way. He made only one condition; the reader, who was allowed only into the staff drawing room, wanted to be invited *once* into the Empress's circle. And Josephine had to obey.

On May 26 she was present at her husband's second coronation, this time as sovereign of Italy. Here she was only a spectator, although in the future she would freely be called "Empress and Queen." Napoleon took the iron crown and placed it on his own head, crying, "God gave it to me. Woe to him who touches it!"

And that night in the palace opposite the illuminated cathedral, in the Empress's bedroom, he teased Josephine, pulling her ears, giving her "little pats," tickling her and repeating laughingly, "God gave her to me. Woe to him who touches her!"

She laughed too, trying to defend herself and imploring: "Do stop, Bonaparte!" But he persisted even harder. Mme. Duchâtel, Mme. de Vaudey and the little Lacoste girl were only bad memories then.

While Napoleon watched the guards on maneuvers, presided over the Council of State or received deputations, Josephine made an excursion to Lake Maggiore and Lake Como. Only one mishap— minor, but of importance to Josephine—occurred. Hippolyte's little pug was lost. The whole town of Como was in a flutter. Systematic searches were undertaken, unsuccessfully at first.

After a supper and a night spent in the palace of Isola Bella, in the Borromean Islands, and after ascending the colossal statue of St. Charles, Josephine returned to Milan, where her beloved pug, which had been found at Como, was awaiting her.

There was great news: Eugene had been appointed Viceroy of Italy. At first Napoleon had wanted to create a Kingdom of Lombardy for Joseph or Louis, but the demands of these two, who always took themselves not for Napoleon's brothers but for sons of "Emperor Charles" and "Empress Letiza," had led Josephine's husband to turn to his other family, his relatives by marriage. Napoleon made Eugene Viceroy of Italy, "desiring to give Prince Eugene, our stepson and Chancellor of State of our Empire of France, a striking proof of the trust we have in his sentiments of fidelity to our person."

The Emperor loved his stepson, who was completely submissive to him. This self-effacement, this absence of demands for himself, enchanted the Emperor, who called Eugene his "chevalier sans peur et sans reproche." Moreover, Eugene gave counsel and support to Josephine. She often asked his advice. And when he had a dispute with his wife, Napoleon would often ask Eugene to be the judge. At first Josephine was happy to be the mother of a near-king, but tears came to her eyes when she realized that her dear Eugene would now have to live in Milan, far away from her.

"You are crying, Josephine," said the Emperor. "There's no sense in it. Are you crying because you will be parted from your son? If the absence of your children gives you so much pain, think what I must feel. The attachment you display for them makes me feel very keenly the unhappiness of not having any."

This Imperial blunder, undoubtedly deliberate, increased the new Empress's tears. So he was still thinking about divorce, and the nightmare that had been interrupted by the coronation would begin again.

On June 10 the Emperor and Empress left Milan and stayed two days at Brescia—a place full of memories of love for her. On June 15, before arriving at Peschiera, Josephine traveled again through the district where nine years before she had nearly perished from Austrian bullets. They slept at Verona and spent the next day there. Between Mantua and Bologna they changed horses at Carpi.

When one sees from the municipal archives at Carpi what kind of reception was organized for a mere posting stage one can imagine the size of those given by great towns. Several days earlier the "sound of the bells" of Carpi had been checked, the windows adorned with hangings, as was done for religious processions, and in the principal square was an enormous portrait of Napoleon. The whole route was "strewn with rose petals and wild flowers." The municipal councilors adorned their suits with green and red ribbons with red fringes, and they waited.

Suddenly came the news that "Queen" Josephine would pass through Carpi on June 20, one day before her husband, and might even take luncheon during the halt.

Luckily it was learned that the Imperial cooks would come a few hours in advance to prepare everything.

On the morning of the 20th no cooks appeared. Perhaps the Queen was not going to lunch. In any case, the table was laid and at eight in the morning the municipality proceeded in coaches lent by a few noble, rich families of the town, to the entrance of Carpi. They waited there for two hours before they saw the processions of "H.M. the Empress and Queen" coming from Mantua. At that moment it began to rain, but the beribboned municipal councilors still hurried to Josephine's eight-horse coach and Charles Gabardi, president of the Municipal Council, opened his mouth and began: "Sacred Majesty, we who are the stewards of this town . . ."

With a gesture Josephine interrupted him. Given the weather and her delay, she would relieve the gentlemen from all ceremony. The municipal body resigned themselves to regaining their coaches and following the procession, through puddles where floated rose petals and wild flowers, to the main square. There, as the coaches were halted for changing the horses, Gabardi hurried forward.

"Sacred Majesty, we who are the stewards of this town . . ."

The rain fell more heavily and Josephine interrupted him again.

"Gentlemen, I do not like to see you exposed to this rain. Put your hats on."

Of course, none of the "stewards" covered his head, the rain fell harder and the stoical Gabardi recited his speech, constantly interrupted by the Empress's "Cover your heads, gentlemen."

Soon the shower became a flood. The "Queen" implored:

"Retire, gentlemen, I beg you!"

They had to obey. In any case the horses were changed and the dripping orator had time only to present a soaked petition written by the Capuchin nuns of the town. After a final smile from Josephine the procession moved off under the pouring rain to Bologna.

Gabardi's only consolation was to contemplate the unused luncheon table at the town hall. Perhaps it would be used by the Emperor and King next day. It was not, and on that day the unfortunate Gabardi received the final blow. After hearing "Sacred Majesty, we who are the stewards of this town," Napoleon interrupted him by asking: "Which town?"

At three o'clock Napoleon joined Josephine in Bologna. There were "deafening shouts and vivats" and many of the inhabitants spent the night of June 24 in the square so as not to miss the departure of the King and Queen at four in the morning for Modena and Piacenza.

At Genoa, where Napoleon and Josephine spent six nights in weather that Napoleon found hotter than the Egyptian desert, there were two novelties: the discovery of cockles, which the little Court found an "exquisite dish," and a wonderful evening festival on the sea, where rafts had been turned into floating, flowery islands. The "admiral's galley," in which the Emperor and Empress sat, was manned by a hundred rowers in glittering costumes.

At Genoa Josephine engaged as her new reader pretty Carlotta Gazzani, whose face was of a rare beauty. For the moment she succeeded Mlle. Lacoste in the Empress's suite. In two years' time she was also to succeed Mlle. Lacoste in the Emperor's bed.

The idle life was interrupted on July 6 at ten in the evening by

Napoleon's sudden decision to return to France. The caravan set out for Fontainebleau. After the heat of Genoa the Emperor and Empress, who were inaugurating the new Mont-Cenis road—built in record time—found the pass exceedingly cold. The charming little blue lake was frozen.

Driving at top speed the Emperor and Empress arrived at Fontainebleau, where nothing was ready. Luckily the concierge was General Bonaparte's former cook from Egypt.

"Now then, my man, you must take up your old trade and get us some supper," the Emperor told him.

It was a supper of mutton chops and eggs, which the couple shared, delighted with an escape from the ceremony which was already a burden to them.

On her return Josephine decided to take the waters at Plombière once again. Perhaps the minerals of the Source des Capucins would finally prove effective. When she arrived at Nancy on August 3, 1805, the inevitable triumphal arch awaited her at the foot of Buthegnémont Hill. It was three in the morning when her carriage stopped at Nancy in front of the triumphal arch, where she was subjected to speeches and compliments, in spite of the advanced hour. Josephine, who was dropping with sleep, refused to go on to the Place Napoléon, where a pyramid surmounted by an Imperial eagle perched on a globe had been erected. She went to bed and at twenty past eight in the morning she entered her carriage. This stay of five hours and twenty minutes cost the taxpayers of Nancy 3,397 francs 14 centimes in decorations, ornaments, triumphal arches, firepots, music and "extraordinary services."

From Charmes to Plombières the streets of each town were lined with flowers and adorned with leaves and archways. "A large crowd of citizens," related M. Himbert, prefect of the Vosges, "had gathered from all parts for the pleasure of seeing their sovereign."

It was night when Josephine arrived at Plombières, but the avenue of pines leading to the hotel was illuminated by colored glass and fireworks burst forth when the carriages were seen. A whole troop of cuirassiers and grenadiers was lined up. They had been sent "for her safety," but Josephine wanted to retain only the thirty men of the Imperial Guard. She took up her cure and the expeditions to Mont-Joli or in the Eaugronne valley. She was given a ball, and repaid the invitations by offering a concert and a supper for eighty, given under a vast tent in the courtyard of the Capuchin convent. She also had her full-length portrait painted by a fashionable painter, now forgotten, called Laurent. It cost 6,000 francs—30,000 present-day francs.

She was mainly taking the cure in order to rest after the exhaustion of the past few months and had plenty of time for dreaming and thinking of the future. The future of her son, that is, for at the moment Josephine was principally preoccupied with Eugene.

The vendetta between the Bonapartes and the Beauharnais had received a fresh impulse with Eugene's appointment to the viceroyalty of Italy. Josephine informed Eugene of this, speaking of the "great vexation" displayed by the clan. And she added:

"Murat still plays the courtier. His wife has been ill. That is obvious, for she is greatly changed. She still has that air she calls dignified, which I call stiff, which does not suit her at all. All those people are wrong not to love us. If only they would behave nicely they would not have better friends than us."

The marriage Napoleon was arranging for his stepson was to poison matters still more. He hoped Eugene would marry Princess Augusta of Bavaria, but matters were not yet settled. The engagement of the Elector's daughter to the hereditary Prince of Baden had first to be broken. The Emperor had sent his chamberlain, General de Thiard, to Karlsruhe and there was not too much difficulty made on the Baden side. "No doubt you know that the Prince of Baden's marriage is broken off?" Josephine was able to write happily to her son on August 6, "which gives great hopes for the person you know of. I have seen her portrait. Nothing could be more beautiful."

She loved her son with all her heart. "You must know, my dear son," she wrote to him from Plombières on that same August 6, "that I still sigh at being separated from you and that my eyes are always full of tears every time I think of you or someone mentions you to me." Evidently she did not write to him very often, and Eugene had complained to his sister. "You should not be put out at not receiving letters from mamma," Hortense had replied. "All the time she was in Italy I had only one little one. No one is as lazy as she is. If you knew how she cannot speak of you without weeping you would forgive her indolence."

As she was writing to Eugene Josephine received this letter from her husband, dated Saturday, August 3.

"I have fine armies here, fine flotillas, and everything I want to help me pass the time pleasantly. Only my good Josephine is lacking. But she must not be told that. To have them love us, women must be kept unsure and anxious about the extent and duration of their power. Good-by, madame, a thousand pleasant thoughts."

"The Emperor is always very kind to me," Josephine confided to her son after reading this. "So I do everything that lies within my power to do what pleases him. No more jealousy, my dear Eugene, and what I tell you is quite true. This way he is happier and so am I."

This improved understanding between Napoleon and his wife was partly due to Hortense. She had written to her brother the month before to tell him how much the Court gossip was spoiling the harmony of the Imperial household. "Although I never interfere in anything," she told him, "when I saw the pain all the rumors were giving mamma and the Emperor I thought I ought to speak to General Duroc. I told him that he ought to try to soothe the Emperor, and that it only made him unhappy to be told by people what the Empress was saying to everyone."

Murat, who was standing not far from Duroc and Hortense, was obviously listening. He was told what it was about.

"You are in error," he told Hortense, "as to the people who embitter the Emperor. I only try to calm him down."

Perhaps he did, but the same could not be said for Caroline. On the next day Duroc, or Murat, repeated the conversation to Napoleon and there followed an explanation between Hortense and her stepfather. Napoleon thought her reasoning was sound and both sides made good resolutions. The Empress promised to stop being jealous and the bad counselors promised to be silent. Hortense was able to write to her brother: "Mamma has behaved very well in all this. She is no longer jealous, which is a great thing."

She kept her promise, temporarily, and was indeed no longer jealous, but her laziness was as great as ever. "I do not often hear from you," the Emperor wrote to her on Tuesday, August 13. "You are forgetting your friends, which is bad. I did not know that the

waters of Plombières had the same powers as those of Lethe. It
seems to me that as you are drinking these waters of Plombières
you should be saying, 'Ah, Bonaparte, if I die who will love you?'
That time indeed is a long way off, isn't it? Everything has an
end, beauty, wit, feeling, the sun itself, but what will never end
is the good I desire, the happiness I enjoy and the kindness of
my Josephine."

On Wednesday, August 25, Josephine headed once more for
Paris, after distributing much largess. This time Nancy hoped to be
able to "enjoy" the Empress's presence at some other time than
between three and eight in the morning. A guard of honor had been
raised, newly equipped and was drawn up with the troops from the
garrison, the band and the "beloved children of Victory"—in other
words, retired or half-pay officers. The carriages stopped. Josephine
lowered her window, smiled, replied to two speeches—civil and
military—and then proceeded to the Hôtel de la Paix, now become
the Hôtel Impérial.

She was presented with a *Phytographie encyclopédique,* that is, a
work on the flora of the former province of Lorraine. Then the bells
and drums could be heard. It was time for the illuminations and the
performance of *Le Prisonnier* at the Opera. When Josephine entered
the theater, the curtain was raised. On the stage she saw the
triumphal arch, a replica of the one in the Faubourg de la Constitution.

In the evening of August 30 she was back at Malmaison. She
found the clan's intrigues still going on. "That courtier Murat and
his wife," she told Eugene, "have missed no opportunity, while I
was away, to gain great advantages with the Emperor. They are
quite wrong, because my presence does them no harm at all. They
had strong proof of that last winter." (Murat had in fact been
appointed Prince and Grand Admiral.) "Moreover," Josephine went
on, "they are doing well, since they get everything from the Emperor, who finally appreciates them. Murat has just got himself a
command. They say it is on the Rhine. His wife, who has come from
Boulogne and paid me a visit this morning, struck me as triumphant, having, from what she says, obtained everything she wanted
from the Emperor. Only one thing would frighten me, which would

be their intrigues against my children if we had the misfortune to lose the Emperor."

Josephine added these lines to her letter: "It seems certain that war is declared against Austria. The Emperor has just sent 150,000 men to Alsace. It is said he himself will go there at the end of the month and lodgings have been prepared for our two households."

On his arrival from Boulogne Napoleon confirmed this news. The campaign was about to begin and the Grand Army, then concentrated opposite England, was to leave the shores of the Channel to cross France and enter Germany in "five waves."

One night Napoleon worked until four in the morning with Talleyrand. "Lost in thought and carrying his candlestick," as he recounted the scene later, he was going to bed when he was met by Josephine "looking wild." She threw herself on her husband, asking in a toneless voice, "Was she at least pretty?"

"Since that is what you think, madame," he replied, turning his back on her, "you can sleep in your room and I in my own."

Probably as a result of this scene—and in contradiction to what she had told her son—Josephine's departure for Alsace was not yet fixed. She did everything she could to get permission from her husband to live at Strasbourg during the coming campaign. In the first place, she would thus escape from the clan's hatred and the loathed supervision of Joseph and Louis, and also, where the mail was concerned, she would be only half as far away from the Emperor. Surely, she thought, Napoleon would summon her to him once he had beaten his adversaries, for to her mind victory was certain.

Napoleon gave in. He even agreed to his wife's leaving with him and, according to his custom, traveled night and day. Having left between four and five in the morning of September 24, they reached Strasbourg on September 26 at five in the evening—fifty-eight hours nonstop traveling. Here Josephine lived in the wonderful episcopal palace overlooking the River Ill (the former palace of Cardinal de Rohan, which was rebuilt in the middle of the eighteenth century). With a grant of 60,000 francs, the architect Fontaine had restored the rooms, evicting municipal offices, the archives and even the prisoners, all of which had occupied the building since the town of Strasbourg bought the palace in 1791. The furniture was partly from

Strasbourg, partly from Nancy and Lunéville, and the plate, silver, linen and cooking utensils were sent from Paris. An apartment of fourteen rooms on the second floor over the courtyard (the third floor above the terrace on the river side) had been placed at Josephine's disposal.

Napoleon spent a week with his wife, a week of orations, receptions, speeches and banquets. On October 1 the Emperor crossed the Rhine and Josephine reigned alone for nearly two months, the two months of the "shortest and most brilliant" campaign "ever waged," in the words Napoleon himself used to his wife in a letter to her a fortnight after his departure, the two months of the capitulation of Ulm, the victory of Austerlitz and the entry into Vienna. While Napoleon was increasing his fame and developing his legend, Josephine received visits from German princes, ever more numerous as the French Army advanced into the heart of the Holy Roman Empire. The city was also an obligatory stopping place for everyone summoned to Napoleon, and Josephine gave receptions on one day in honor of the mayors of Paris, on another for a deputation from the Tribunate. Josephine bore with all the speeches, presided over dinners, balls and suppers, went to French and German theatres, organized concerts, summoned from Paris singers or her favorite musician, Spontini, who gave Strasbourg the première of his opera *La Vestale*.

And of course the Empress made innumerable presents, gifts and grants. She bought practically everything offered her and, as the tradesmen well knew, never refused animals, seeds and plants for Malmaison. As often as possible she would take walks outside the town or—she informed Eugene of this novelty—would read while waiting for the couriers.

Only rarely did she remain without news for four or five days. "I am in a good position and I love you," wrote Napoleon on October 2, from Ettlingen. And again, on October 4, before leaving for Stuttgart, where the Elector was to present a performance of *Don Juan* at the Court Theatre:

"I am at Louisbourg (Ludwigsburg). I leave tonight. My whole army is on the march. The weather is superb. My meeting with the Bavarians is accomplished. I am well. . . .

"I am leaving right away to continue my march. You will be without news of me, my dear, for five or six days. Do not be anxious. This is because of the operations about to take place. . . . Good-by, my dear, I love you and embrace you."

On October 10, after crossing the Danube, he was in Augsburg with the former Elector of Trier "who has a very good house." And he continued: "I have been rushing along for eight days. The campaign has opened with some notable successes. I am very well, although it rains nearly every day. Events follow each other very rapidly. . . . Good-by, my dear, I embrace you."

He entered Munich and of October 12 announced: "The enemy is beaten, lost his head . . . In an hour I am leaving for Burgau. I am well, but the weather is dreadful. I have to change my clothes twice a day, it rains so much. I love and embrace you."

At top speed, and under the inexorable rain, he gave the names of towns, villages and rivers a place in history and on October 19, at the abbey of Elchingen, he received Mack, who had come to surrender the Austrian Army. He informed his wife of this on the same day.

"I was more exhausted than I should have been, my dear Josephine. A whole week with my body wet and my feet cold every day did me some harm, but in the course of today, when I did not go out, I have become rested. I have carried out my scheme; I have destroyed the Austrian Army simply by marches; I have made 60,000 prisoners, taken 120 guns and 90 flags and more than 30 generals. I am going to attack the Russians; they are lost. I am pleased with my army. I lost only 1,500, of whom two thirds are only slightly wounded. Good-by, my Josephine, a thousand tender thoughts."

On October 20 the captive Austrian Army of 30,000 men filed past him. "There was never such a catastrophe in all military history," he wrote to her. During the battle around Ulm Napoleon had not written to his wife for some time and Josephine had been upset. "I received your letter through Lemarois. I was sorry to see you were so anxious," he replied. "I have been given details which convince me of your affection for me, but you must have more strength and trust. . . . You must be cheerful, amuse yourself and hope we shall see each other again before the end of the month."

Now he drove on to Vienna and on the evening of November 2 he wrote to Josephine from Haag:

"I am in full march. The weather is cold and the ground covered with a foot of snow. It is very severe. Luckily there is no shortage of wood, here we are still among the forests. I am fairly well. Affairs are going very satisfactorily for me. My enemies must have more worries than I have. I want to have news of you and learn that you are not anxious. Good-by, my dear, I am going to bed."

On November 5 he was at Linz.

"The weather is fine. We are 28 leagues from Vienna. The Russians are not holding out, they are in full retreat. The House of Austria is in great difficulties. All the Court's luggage is being evacuated from Vienna. There will probably be some news in five or six days. I long to see you again. My health is good. I embrace you."

"Events follow each other very rapidly," he had written, and indeed he was already in Vienna, "rather tired," on the evening of November 15. "I have not yet seen the city by day," he went on. "I went through it at night. Tomorrow I receive the notables and authorities. Nearly all my troops are beyond the Danube, pursuing the Russians. Good-by, my Josephine, the moment it is possible I shall send for you. A thousand tender thoughts."

"I shall send for you." These words made Josephine's heart beat. And the next day she received authorization to leave Strasbourg for Munich.

How joyfully she set out on November 28! While the cannon thundered, she started for Kehl, surrounded by her ladies, chamberlains and equerries, a guard of honor escorting her between the double rank of the foot guards. The Grand Duke and Elector of Baden sent his coaches and hussars to meet her.

Her triumphal journey through Baden, Württemberg and Bavaria began, a journey during which electors and electresses, princesses and margraves, following the Emperor's orders, presented their homage to Josephine, "for," as the master wrote proudly to her, "they owe you everything and you owe them nothing, except from civility." There was one special point: "The Electress of Württemberg is the daughter of the King of England, she is a good woman and you must treat her well, but without overdoing it."

After Karlsruhe, Stuttgart welcomed her with pomp and luxury. Banquets, concerts, triumphal arches. At the Opera House they played Paër's *Achilles* and Zingarelli's *Romeo and Juliet*. The Elector, shortly to be the King, of Württemberg was at a loss as to how to associate her with her husband's triumph. It is true that Jerome Bonaparte's future father-in-law was a spectacle in himself. His stomach was so large that his dinner table had to have a deep circle cut in it. He had but one passion, striking clocks, and his apartment "was more like a clockmaker's shop than the bedroom of a reigning prince." To complete the cacophony he had had a chair installed with a built-in organ which began to play when anyone sat down on it. Josephine found it difficult not to laugh.

On December 3 she resumed her journey and at Ulm the procession entered Bavarian territory. Augereau greeted her and announced that there was a great festivity that evening, but since the Empress was "in France" she asked to go to bed. It was doubtless on the day she entered Munich that she received a letter from Austerlitz:

"I have beaten the Russian and Austrian Army commanded by the two Emperors. I am a little tired, I bivouacked in the open for a week and the nights were rather cold. Tonight I am sleeping in Prince Kaunitz's castle, where I shall have two or three hours' sleep. The Russian Army is not only beaten but destroyed. I embrace you."

Two days later, on December 5, he sent her these details:

"I have concluded a truce. The Russians are leaving. The battle of Austerlitz is the finest I have fought: 45 flags, more than 150 guns, the standards of the Russian guard, 20 generals, 30,000 prisoners and more than 20,000 killed—a horrible sight! The Emperor Alexander is in despair and is going away to Russia. Yesterday I saw the Emperor of Germany in my tent. We talked for two hours. We have agreed to make peace quickly. The weather is not yet very bad. Peace has finally been restored to the Continent. Let us hope it soon will be to the whole world. The English will not be able to stand up to us. I shall look forward with much pleasure to the moment that brings me nearer to you. Good-by, my dear, I am fairly well and very anxious to embrace you."

While she was waiting for the Emperor there was such a press of receptions that Josephine, who in this respect snatched at any excuse, did not even have time to write to her husband, who complained on December 10:.

"I have had no news from you for a long time. Do the wonderful

festivities at Baden, Stuttgart and Munich make you forget the poor
soldiers who live covered in mud, rain and blood?"

Four days later, still without news, he wrote these playful lines:

"Great Empress, not one letter from you since you left Strasbourg. You have been through Baden, Stuttgart and Munich without writing us one word. This is neither very kind nor very
affectionate! I am still at Brunn. The Russians have gone; I have a
truce. In a few days I shall see what will happen. Deign, from the
height of your greatness, to pay a little attention to your slaves."

At Munich every day Josephine saw the Electress Caroline, a
charming young woman of thirty, together with her husband, Max
Joseph, whom Napoleon had promised to make King of Bavaria. He
was a simple fellow, not in the least obsessed by his birth. He would
walk alone in the streets of Munich, talking to passers-by and
knowing by name a large number of the inhabitants of his capital.

Josephine was still preoccupied with one thing: her son's marriage to Princess Augusta of Bavaria. For this reason she was
particularly amiable to the Elector and Electress. But Max Joseph
continued to make difficulties. As Napoleon was to recount later, he
would have liked the Emperor to divorce and marry the princess
himself.

"Prince Eugene is only *adopted*," he had told him. "I do not know
what that means. In reality he is merely Vicomte de Beauharnais
and my daughter would only be marrying a French gentleman."

What would the Elector have said if he had known that Eugene
was a vicomte only on his father's authority? That was not all.
Although Augusta's engagement had been broken, the girl still
loved the hereditary Prince of Baden. Little Augusta's governess,
Mme. de Wurmb, had even dared speak to the Emperor about the
princess' love. Napoleon had burst out laughing.

"Really, madame, I think you must be joking. Since when did
princesses marry to satisfy their love? It is politics and state
interests that marry princes. You give me a bad opinion of yourself
and of the education you have given the princess by this display of
ridiculous principles and romantic love."

To cap everything, when the Electress was still Caroline, daughter of the Margrave of Baden, she had nearly married the Duc
d'Enghien. She had in fact been in love with him, but the Margrave,
having become "a mad democrat," in Enghien's own words, had

opposed the union with an émigré and an enemy of Republican France. Caroline, who adored French literature and spent all her evenings reciting poetry, hated Napoleon and did everything she could to prevent Augusta from marrying Eugene. To make them yield required the promise to make the Elector King of Bavaria, which was done on January 1, 1806, and the threat, if they continued obstinate, to give an archduchess, daughter of the Emperor of Austria, to Josephine's son in marriage. Actually, the only one of marriageable age was little Marie Louise, who was nearly fifteen. She was to make her entrance later.

On December 28, the day on which the Emperor left Vienna to join her, Josephine was finally able to announce to her son that his marriage with Augusta was fixed. The Empress thought her future daughter-in-law was charming. "Her appearance is agreeable, she might even be considered beautiful, but I pay much less attention to her external qualities than to those of her mind and heart, since it is on the latter that your happiness depends. You know, my dear, how your mother's heart is concerned with this, but in this respect I think you will have nothing to wish for."

Unfortunately, Josephine's letter and one sent to him by Napoleon two days later reached Eugene only after a note from an inspector of posts written on the 30th and informing him about his marriage. Eugene was vexed at being told in such an offhand way. "Not a word," he wrote, "from the 10,000 people around my mother who could have carried out this task with interest."

On December 31, on arriving at Munich, Napoleon wrote to Eugene again.

"My cousin, I have arranged your marriage with Princess Augusta. She is very pretty. I enclose her portrait on a cup, but she is much better-looking."

Eugene set off at a gallop for Bavaria, with the cup carefully packed in his luggage, and on the morning of January 10 Josephine was waked by the announcement of the arrival of her son, who had immediately gone to present himself to Napoleon. At this news she began to weep: "her son's first visit was not to her." A few minutes later the Emperor came into his wife's room holding Eugene by the hand.

"Here, madame," he said, smiling, "I bring you your great booby of a son."

Josephine wept again, but this time from joy, and begged Eugene to cut his mustaches before being presented to Augusta. He quickly obeyed and with a smooth face made the acquaintance of the fiancée his stepfather had chosen for him. He was pleased by this eighteen-year-old girl whose appearance lacked prettiness, perhaps, but whose contemporaries praised her "nymph's figure" and the freshness of her complexion.

With the speed so much approved by Napoleon, the contract was signed on January 13, Eugene and Augusta were married civilly on the same day, in the great gallery; and at seven the following day the religious ceremony took place in the castle chapel. On January 16 *Castor and Pollux* was given in the Court Theatre. Eugene looked affectionately at his wife. She was certainly much better-looking than on the cup sent by his stepfather. Indeed, love was to come even more quickly than Josephine had hoped.

There was one shadow: Hortense had not been able to come. Louis, who had been prevented from leaving Paris, had not permitted his wife to travel to Munich. "This invitation," she explained to her brother, "has thrown Louis into despair. He would be lost and dishonored if his wife left without him. That I might meet my mother, stepfather and perhaps brother means nothing to him. Being accustomed always to making sacrifices in order at least to have peace, I have given way, but I see I shall still have a lot of trouble about this, much grief if you go away, a scolding from the Emperor for my weakness and from my husband no more happiness than usual. So all I have is the consolation that I am the only one to suffer and that if others cause me sorrow, I at least give pain to no one."

Hortense hoped that the marriage might take place in Paris, after all. When she learned that her brother had been married far from her she was overcome.

"I cannot tell you the grief it gives me. Since I heard of it I have done nothing but weep. What! I am not to be near you at such an important moment! Think of me a little, dear Eugene, for I am the only one to be pitied. Seeing you for a moment would have consoled me for so much grief. I needed this, but I hope you will be happy for both of us. Speak of me to your wife, tell her how much I love her and how sorry I am not to see her. Everyone speaks so well of her that this marriage makes me very happy. But how sorry she will be to leave her family at once. I am sure you will replace them all for her when she knows you, but you will find her regret very natural, for is there anything sadder than separating from one's family? Show her my letter. I want her to know of all my regrets and to love me a little."

Hortense had to be contented with giving a party in Eugene's own house in the Rue de Lille.

Josephine, who had returned to Paris on January 26, 1806, was busy with Augusta's wedding presents, the bill for which came to 200,000 francs. "They were seen by all Paris and thought very beautiful," she wrote to Eugene. Indeed, nothing was too beautiful for her new daughter-in-law.

Napoleon did not share her opinion. He fumed, and in addition, Josephine received a dressing down from her husband because the work he had ordered to be carried out to furnish and modernize Eugene's magnificent house in the Rue de Lille amounted to 1,500,000 francs—and it was not yet finished. Calmelet, that old friend who had become administrator of the Imperial palaces and been entrusted with the work, received a severe reprimand and had to give up his post.

Court life was resumed and Josephine had little leisure. "I have not written to you before, my dear son," she explained to Eugene on February 13, "because since my return I have been leading the most exhausting life, never a moment to myself, going to bed very late and getting up early. The Emperor, who is very strong, bears this active life very well, but my own health suffers from it somewhat."

Eugene's marriage to Augusta had left the Prince of Baden to be disposed of. Napoleon had airily taken his fiancée, so another must be found for him. While the Emperor was still at Karlsruhe he had first thought of his wife's cousin, Stephanie Tascher de La Pagerie.

"It would be just the thing," he declared to Josephine. "Mlle. Tascher is your first cousin. That suits me perfectly. The Grand Duke has been speaking to me, I have just left him. It would be a suitable marriage."

Josephine explained that her cousin was still suffering "from an illness she had brought from Martinique." Napoleon gave way. Since Mlle. Tascher was not available, the Prince of Baden could marry Josephine's former niece, Stephanie de Beaubarnais. She had been abandoned at Penthémont by her father, Claude, and brought up by Mme. Campan. She had romped on the lawns at Malmaison with Hortense during the Consulate. She was very pretty, with blue eyes, a pure complexion, a graceful figure, fair hair and mischievous charm. At the age of seventeen she arrived at the Tuileries. The Emperor found her charming. The little girl, who looked no more than fourteen, divined her power over her "uncle" and abused it. One evening when they were waiting for the Emperor, Stephanie sat down in the presence of Napoleon's sisters. Caroline sent her an order to stand and the master found Stephanie in tears. She related her misfortunes.

"Is that all?" he exclaimed. "All right, then, sit on my knee, you won't trouble anyone."

Undoubtedly the Emperor had been first amused and then disturbed by this child-woman and the Empress's jealousy was aroused. But for the moment Napoleon was occupied with a new flirtation with another of Mme. Campan's former boarders whom Pauline had been happy to introduce to him. Mlle. Dénuelle de La Plaigne was in process of getting a divorce in order to be more completely the Emperor's. She certainly did not love him. She herself related that once, in the Imperial bedroom, while her lover was otherwise occupied she managed to put the clock ahead half an hour without his noticing. "Already!" exclaimed the Emperor, raising his head—and Mlle. Dénuelle found herself at liberty earlier than had been foreseen.

Josephine had reason to be more jealous of Stephanie than of Eléonore Dénuelle. So she decided to speak to the little scatterbrain. She pointed out to her niece "the harm she could do herself if she did not obviously resist Bonaparte's efforts to achieve her seduction." Stephanie promised to behave with more reserve.

However, the Grand Duke Elector of Baden was not satisfied. A "Princess Bonaparte" was one thing, but to unite his son to the niece of the Empress's first husband seemed, not unreasonably, to be a misalliance. Napoleon decided to adopt the girl. She would become "Princess Stephanie Napoleon," live in the Tuileries, take precedence over the Emperor's sisters, be placed near him "in all meetings, parties and at table" and, Napoleon stated, "in the event of Our not being there, she will be placed on the right hand of the Empress." The Grand Duke gave way. Stephanie would be a grand duchess one day. The clan choked with rage. So Mme. Letizia would walk behind the Beauharnais chit! And when Mme. Murat saw "that child" go through the door ahead of her she nearly fainted.

The fiancé arrived in Paris. He was pink and white, and awkward. "Without being exactly ugly," wrote a contemporary, "his face is not very attractive." As may be imagined, Stephanie was not very taken with him, but for the moment she was living in a fairy tale: an Imperial trousseau, a dowry of 15,000 francs, sets of diamonds, nothing was too good for her. The marriage took on considerable proportions. On the evening of April 7 the civil wedding was celebrated in the presence of the whole Court in the Galerie de Diane. The pair were blessed by the Cardinal Legate, and the Grand Chancellor Prince united "His Majesty's daughter" to the Prince of Baden. The next day Josephine, glittering with jewels and giving her hand to the Prince of Baden, walked slowly between two ranks of grenadiers, accompanied by twenty-four pages bearing torches. Although the chamberlains cried, "Come along, ladies, move quickly," Josephine did not hasten her step. It was, Mme. de Rémusat tells us, "one of the points on which she would not yield to her husband's wishes. As she walked extremely gracefully and was unwilling to lose a single one of her advantages, nothing could hurry her and it was behind her that the crush began."

When evening had come, and the banquet was over and the fireworks extinguished, Stephanie refused to let her husband into her bedroom. She wept and grew calmer only when a school friend, Nelly Bourolly, came to spend the night with her. The Prince of Baden was advised to cut his hair, which he wore long in the old fashion. The husband obeyed immediately, but the little wretch burst out laughing and declared her husband was even uglier with his hair "à la Titus." While waiting for his hair to grow again, the husband spent his nights in an armchair—until the day the Emperor lost his temper.

Finally everything was straightened out—at least according to Josephine, who was able to write to Eugene on April 13: "We went to Grignon to visit Marshal Bessières to amuse our newlyweds. They seemed very pleased with each other and I notice the Prince of Baden pays a lot of attention to his wife, looks after her, and I hope this marriage will be happy. We spent the evening playing little

games. The Emperor was good enough to join us and we all arrived
at Saint-Cloud gay and very well."

Two days later there was a ball in the Galerie de Diane. Mme.
de Boigne describes it:

People were placed according to the color of their tickets. Mine put
me in the Galerie de Diane. We did not move around, but the Court
progressed from one room to another. The Empress, the Princesses, their
ladies, their chamberlains, all elaborately dressed, entered behind the
Emperor and took their places on a dais prepared in advance. After
watching a kind of ballet, the Emperor came down off the dais alone and
made a tour of the room, talking exclusively to women. He was wearing
his Imperial costume (which he was soon to give up), white satin jacket
and breeches, white shoes with gold rosettes, a cloak of red velvet embroidered with gold along the seams, the sword flashing with diamonds
outside the cloak. Orders, medals, also of diamonds, and a cap with
feathers all round and turned up with a diamond edging. This costume
may have been a beautiful design but on him, who was short, fat and
awkward in his movements, it was ugly. Perhaps I was prejudiced, but
to me the Emperor looked terrible, he looked like the king of diamonds.

I was standing between two women I did not know. He asked the
first her name and she replied that she was Foacier's daughter.

"Ah!" he said and moved on.

As was his custom he asked me my name too and I told him.

"Do you live at Beauregard?"

"Yes, sire."

"It is a fine place and your husband has done a lot of work on it.
That is a service to his country and I am obliged to him. I am grateful
to everyone who employs workmen. Was he in the English service?"

I found it simpler just to answer yes, but he continued.

"But you are French, completely French, we lay claim to you. You
are not one of those rights one easily renounces."

I bowed.

"How old are you?"

I told him.

"And frank into the bargain! You look much younger."

I bowed again. He began to move away, then returning to me, he
spoke lower, in a confidential tone.

"You have no children, have you? I know it is not your fault, but try
and have some. Believe me, and give it some thought. I am giving you
good advice!"

I was astonished. He looked at me for a moment, smiling quite
graciously, and passed on to my neighbor.

"What is your name?"

"Foacier's daughter."

"Another of Foacier's daughters!" and he continued his walk.

I cannot convey the extreme aristocratic contempt with which this "Another of Foacier's daughters!" dropped from the Imperial lips. . . .

Having made his tour, the Emperor went back to the Empress and the whole gilded troop left without going anywhere near the common people.

Perhaps the Emperor was jealous or perhaps he had already been cured of his penchant for Stephanie. In any case, once the festivities were over Napoleon sent the young couple to Karlsruhe.

Later the Emperor was to busy himself with marrying Stephanie Tascher de La Pagerie to Prince d'Arenberg. She too thought her marriage a disaster. She wept throughout the ceremony, "choked" and had constantly to be handed smelling salts. Pale and exhausted, she was literally dragged to the altar. The elderly and amiable Duc d'Arenberg was distressed. He had said to Josephine, "I think, madame, that in giving my son a charming companion you have given me an Antigone."

"Antigone" refused to go to Brussels and lived in Paris with her husband, seeing him as little as possible. The marriage was never even consummated. The Prince consoled himself by leading a regiment raised at his father's expense and by seeking on the field of battle a counterirritant to his conjugal disappointments.

With two Beauharnais now allied to "real" princely families, Hortense soon to be Queen of Holland and already mother of a little boy of whom it was said he would succeed the Emperor, the shadow of divorce had disappeared. Josephine could be happy.

16. *"What Unhappiness Thrones Bring!"*

Hortense's marriage was going from bad to worse and Josephine found her daughter "so thin that every time I looked at her it brought tears to my eyes." In order not to worry her mother Hortense assured her that it was grief at not having been able to attend her brother's wedding that had brought her to this state. But Josephine was not deceived. Although she appeared to have brought happiness to Eugene, she had to admit having made a terrible mistake in forcing her daughter to marry a pitiful valetudinarian. His stepdaughter's languidness had not escaped the Emperor either.

"Hortense has lost her color," he said to Josephine. "Her husband does not make her happy. We may have to go through a bad time. If she falls in love, it will be intensely, and love can be the cause of great folly."

"She is too reasonable to yield to a caprice," Josephine replied.

"Don't count on it. Look at her walk, listen to her speech. Everything about her indicates feeling, and besides she would not be your daughter otherwise."

Josephine had to agree. Hortense, in fact, was in love. Some time earlier she had fallen in love with a young aide-de-camp of Murat, the son of Mme. de Souza. His name was not Souza, but Comte Charles de Flahaut, from the name of Mme. de Souza's first husband, whose son, however, he was not. M. de Flahaut, thirty-six years older than his wife, had been only an honorary husband to her, having gracefully bowed to the "marriage of the heart" his wife had contracted with a young abbé, who seemed perfectly at home in the Louvre, where the Flahauts lived. Years before, Gouverneur Morris, United States minister in Paris, who was paying the young wife a visit, found her taking a foot bath while "a man of the Church" was undertaking a "pious operation": he was warming the bed of the lady of the house. The young abbé's name was Charles Maurice de Talleyrand-Périgord and was to become one of the cleverest foreign ministers of all time and the father of Charles de Flahaut. M. de Flahaut, a well-bred man of the eighteenth century, courteously accepted this unexpected birth.

The Count having died on the scaffold during the Terror, Mme. de Flahaut became the wife of a Portuguese diplomat, M. de Souza. Her one thought was to see her son well settled. So when she noticed that Hortense looked tenderly at him, she urged her young son to pay court to her. Hortense found Flahaut more and more charming—a word constantly in women's mouths where Talleyrand's natural son was in question—but matters went no further, particularly as Caroline Murat in her turn let her husband's aide-de-camp know that he was very much to her taste. Charles found the Emperor's sister extremely attractive physically and did not have to be begged to give proof of it, while continuing to flirt with Hortense when he met her in society.

This annoyed Caroline, who refused to admit that "a young man of her household," who was in service as much with her as with her husband, could look at another woman. So when his mistress was present Charles avoided being pleasant to Hortense. She understood matters more clearly when one evening, on the Ile de la Jatte near the palace of Neuilly, she came across her sister-in-law and Charles de Flahaut taking a sentimental walk together. After that she tried so obviously to shun him that the young aide-de-camp spoke to his mother. Mme. de Souza went to see Hortense and complain, and during a ball the Princess invited Flahaut to dance. While waltzing—the latest fashion—Flahaut asked her, sighing, why she was angry with him and what he had done.

Hortense's beautiful eyes filled with tears and Charles asked with emotion:

"You had some interest in me, why did you leave me ignorant of it? You would have spared me much grief. . . . Now, although I still love only you, I am tied to another."

Hortense's heart beat faster. Obviously lying, she exclaimed: "No, no, I do not love you. Although I thought so for a moment, it is all over, believe me."

Flahaut hastened to conclude: "Then grant me your friendship. It will console me for all I have lost."

Flahaut had apparently closed the chapter, but Hortense had not. She could not make up her mind to think no more of the charming officer. She could not even succeed in rejoicing at the victories of the French armies. She was to write in her *Memoirs:* "The idea of the dangers threatening a person of whom I thought too often told me how dear he was to me and troubled my joy. If a bulletin arrived I would tremble before reading it, in case in a report of some misfortune I should see his name. One day he was cited for distinguished conduct, another for having received a wound. Fortunately I was alone when I learned this. My lively sorrow would not have convinced people that this interest was inspired only by friendship."

She watched Caroline's reactions and when she found her sister-in-law less anxious than herself she was angry with her. "When I saw her sad and tormented, she became dear to me and I forgave her for the painful moments she often made me endure."

Mme. de Souza was delighted. Her son was protected by the master's sister and sister-in-law. She did not know the Emperor, who disapproved of lapses by the women of the clan and who was irritated by the feats of the young "libertine."

"But he has grace and wit," Josephine had pleaded.

"Wit!" Napoleon exclaimed. "Brrtt! who hasn't that kind? He sings well? Fine gift for a soldier, who by occupation is nearly always hoarse. Ah! he's a handsome lad, that's what affects you women. Well! For my part I don't see anything extraordinary in him."

And Napoleon arranged for the handsome aide-de-camp to be kept away from Paris. At that time, when most of Europe was divided into French departments or vassal states, this was not too difficult.

A new event came to disturb Hortense's life. She was to be made queen. The "appointment" of Louis and Hortense to the throne of Holland hastened matters. Whereas Louis appeared in seventh heaven, Hortense greeted the news sadly. Josephine heard her sigh: "I wish I could be Queen of Holland in Paris."

In tears she begged Napoleon not to "inflict" this throne on her.

"This distinction is flattering to you," Napoleon exclaimed. "You should display feelings worthy of such a high position."

"Ah, sire," cried Hortense, "it is of no use, I shall always have bourgeois feelings, if attachment to one's country, friends and family must be so described."

But Napoleon merely laughed at her. And in a letter to her brother Hortense showed her great grief:

"I cannot think of it without tears coming into my eyes. There are so many people who would be glad to be queen! . . . Why not give them that happiness which will make me so unhappy! I still have hopes, but the Emperor seems set on it and his policy overrules everything. My God, I think I shall die of grief!"

Napoleon's regal gestures did not dazzle Josephine. She was already becoming blasé. Only one thing counted to her: she was already separated from Eugene and now her daughter, too, would live far from her.

"Mamma is not reasonable," wrote Hortense to Eugene, "and I who am the most unhappy, again have to console everyone else."

When Hortense had left for The Hague Josephine needed "a long time to recover," as she wrote to her son. She was "too upset and too unwell" to send news to Eugene. Her grief increased when she heard that a new campaign was being prepared, a double campaign, first against Prussia, then against Russia, which was to take the Emperor to Tilsit the following year, a glorious, bloodstained path passing through Jena, Potsdam, Warsaw, Eylau and Friedland.

On Wednesday, September 24, 1806, at Saint-Cloud, Napoleon received a letter from Berthier announcing that "the Prussians no longer hide their intention" of making war on him. Their armies, tomorrow to be enemies, were approaching the Grand Army's outposts.

With some reluctance the Emperor decided to leave for Mainz the next night without taking Josephine. But the Empress heard of it—it was then nearly four in the morning—and, Constant related, "jumped out of bed, put on the first garment to hand, and ran out of her room in slippers and without stockings. Weeping like a little girl being taken back to school, she crossed the apartments, ran quickly downstairs and threw herself in the Emperor's arms just as he was about to enter his carriage."

He had to take her along. They rode day and night in the Emperor's eight-horse sleeper-carriage. Early in the afternoon of September 26 they arrived at Metz, where a stop of eight hours enabled Josephine's staff to catch up with her in six six-horse coaches, three three-horse carts, two wagons and one carriage. Ladies and officers had driven at breakneck speed from Paris, but were given no chance to rest. That same evening the travelers went on. After driving for another day and night they arrived at Mainz at dawn on Sunday, September 28. They had gone 84¾ stages in three days.

The Imperial couple were installed in the Teutonic Palace, but Napoleon would have to leave soon to join the army. Josephine was in tears, either from emotion or from the fatigue of the journey. She was taken ill with vomiting. The Emperor held his wife in his arms, pressed Talleyrand's hand and—if M. de Rémusat is to be believed —murmured with tears: "It is very painful to leave the two people one loves the most."

He did not leave Mainz until the evening of October 1, 1806. Once more Josephine was in tears. She had received bad news from poor Hortense. "I don't know why you cry," Napoleon wrote to her. "You are wrong to make yourself ill. Hortense is a bit pedantic; she likes giving advice. She wrote to me and I am answering her. She must be happy and gay. Courage and gaiety, that is the recipe." Very convenient! Louis had taken it into his head that his wife was conspiring against him. He had her spied on by his servants and skulked round the palace like a detective. Luckily he had to join the army and Hortense was given permission to go to her mother at Mainz. Little Napoleon went with her. "You would not recognize him," she wrote to Eugene. "If you knew how sweet he is! He is already a man. He never leaves me, keeps me company. I am sad to think that when he is seven I shall have to part with him, for you know that, according to the Emperor's decree, our children have to be brought up at Meudon, but they are left to us until they are seven. I think that when that time comes I shall go to school with them."

Stephanie had also been able to leave Mannheim and now the little Beauharnais clan was together again. As she had her daughter, grandson and niece with her, Josephine was "in grand company," as the Emperor wrote to her. She ought to have been consoled and yet the strange feeling in her heart did not leave her. "Talleyrand has come," wrote the Emperor, "and tells me, my dear, that you do nothing but weep. What do you want, then? You have your daughter, your grandchildren and good news, a great many reasons for being content and happy!"

Everything went "wonderfully" for him, he wrote on October 13. "I have already got fatter since I left, and yet I myself do twenty and twenty-five leagues a day on horseback, in the carriage, every way. I go to bed at eight and get up at midnight. Sometimes it occurs to me that you may not yet have gone to bed." In three weeks he had beaten the Prussians at Jena. "My dear," he announced on October 15, "I carried out fine maneuvers against the Prussians. Yesterday I won a great victory. They were 150,000 men. I made 20,000 prisoners, took 100 guns and flags. I was face to face with the King of Prussia and quite near him. I nearly captured him and the Queen too. I have been in encampments in the field for two days. I am wonderfully well. Good-by, my dear. Keep well and love me."

On the next day: "M. de Talleyrand will have shown you the bulletin, my dear, and you will have seen of my successes. Everything went as I had calculated and no army was more thoroughly beaten and more utterly lost. There only remains to say that I am well and that fatigue, bivouacking, and staying up have made me fatter."

He occupied Potsdam and Berlin and yet she wept. He could not understand it. Josephine's sadness was contagious. "Would you believe that in spite of all that I am sad?" Hortense wrote to her brother. "I see I shall soon have to return to The Hague, which is not gay these days, and although I have had a little peace since being here, this is not very long. But I am not selfish enough to want it to last longer."

Hortense and her mother—together with the young women around them—had only one preoccupation: listening for the horn of the courier bringing news from the army. "It was a race as to who would announce it first," Josephine's daughter tells us. The news, which was excellent, came rapidly, but Josephine's eyes were still clouded with tears. As Frédéric Masson has said, "nothing could be done and during the three months of her stay she had a fear she could not conquer, a sadness she could not explain, an anxiety with no motive, which sprang from those strange, vague presentiments which, at the height Josephine had reached, make one fear, divine and glimpse a fall. What did she read in the cards with which she was familiar and which had already told her so many secrets?" She did in fact seek her future there and had her valet de chambre, Douville, buy her 148 packets each of six packs of cards. She played patience every day and exhausted them all, "the grande, the petite, the moulin à vent and the patience de quinze." One evening the grande patience came out and she had barely put down the last card when the door opened and Cambacérès brought her a letter from the Emperor. Naturally she believed in the cards.

Her heart was moved at seeing how badly Napoleon treated the Queen of Prussia in his victory bulletins. "I received your letter in which you seem annoyed by what I say of the women," he replied to her from Berlin on November 6. "It is true that I hate intriguing women more than anything. I am used to good, gentle, conciliatory women, those are the ones I like. If they have spoiled me, it is not my fault but yours. However, you will see that I have been very kind to one who showed herself to be sensitive and good, Mme. d'Hatzfeld. When I showed her her husband's letter she said to me, sobbing, with great sensibility and simplicity: 'Ah! yes, that's his handwriting!' As she was reading it her tones went to my heart, she distressed me. I said to her, 'Well now, madame, throw that letter in the fire, I shall never be strong enough to punish your husband.' She burned the letter and seemed very happy. Her husband has been very quiet since. Another two hours and he would have been lost. You see how I like good, simple, gentle women, but that is because they are the only ones like you."

With reddened eyes Josephine received the German princes: the Nassaus, the Saxe-Gothas, the Saxe-Weimars, the Hesse-Darmstadts, the Hohenlohes, the Hesse-Rothenburgs. With her mind elsewhere, she was bored at balls, illuminations, visits to gardens, to the opera, to dinners. Yet she carried out all the necessary tasks of her position. She visited the wounded, gave the town of Mainz an indemnity of 8,000 francs for her stay there, then a second sum of

8,000 francs to repay the municipality for building a theatre for her. She spent money, of course, and bought 348,304 francs 94 centimes' worth of jewelry from Nitot père et fils: a diadem, earrings, a bracelet, necklaces and a "garland of hortensias." She ordered a shower of snuffboxes and watches for presentation. Of course she did not forget her daughter-in-law and for the New Year sent her "a bed sheet which is said to be extremely beautiful."

Augusta's first pregnancy went off without difficulty. "I long to hear that my dear daughter has been confined," Josephine wrote to Eugene. "This good news cannot arrive too soon and I expect you to send a courier. Tell him to make haste. I know your fears, but I have none and I am sure everything will go as I hope."

Only the presence of little Napoleon could dispel her grief. Hortense's son was very advanced for his age. On the preceding January 1 he had already written a few lines for his "grandmamma" without having his hand held. His remarks were bandied about. When one day Comtesse d'Arberg said to him while presenting the daughters of Maréchale Lobau and Comtesse Kler: "Monseigneur, I recommend them to your favors," the little man raised his head and replied, "Madame, it is for these ladies to give me their favors."

He loved the Emperor with all his heart and called him "Uncle Bibiche," and he cried one day when a shoemaker was paid in his presence with five-franc pieces.

"I don't want them to give away the picture of my Uncle Bibiche!"

Josephine laughed, but when the child had gone out, relapsed into her sorrow. Only one thing could pull her out of her depression: joining "Uncle Bibiche." He constantly gave her hope that he would soon summon her. "I am distressed to think you are bored at Mainz," he wrote to her on November 16. "If the journey were not too long you could come here, for the enemy is no longer here, he is beyond the Vistula, which is more than 120 leagues away. I wait to hear what you think."

Her thought, of course, was to leave Mainz at once. And Mme. de La Rochefoucauld, who regretted seeing Prussia ill treated, persuaded her to complain and to ask to leave. "I am sorry to see you are sad," he replied, "yet you have reason to be nothing but gay. You should not show so much kindness to people who are unworthy of it. Mme. L . . . [La Rochefoucauld] is a silly woman, so stupid that you ought to know her and not pay any attention to her. Be content, happy in my affection and all you inspire in me. In a few days I shall make up my mind either to summon you here or to send you to Paris. Good-by, my dear. At present you can go to Darmstadt, or Frankfurt, that will distract you." With no feeling of pleasure she went to Frankfurt, to stay with the Prince Primate, who gave receptions, concerts and masked balls for her.

Her gloom continued, and yet she was receiving almost tender letters from Napoleon. "Posnań, December 2, 1806. Today is the anniversary of Austerlitz. I went to a ball in town. It is raining. I am well. I love you and want you. My troops are in Warsaw. It has not been cold yet. All the Polish women are quite French, but there is only one woman for me. Do you know her by chance? I would draw you her portrait, but I would have to flatter the portrait too much for you to recognize yourself in it; yet, to speak truly, my heart would have nothing but good to say of her. These nights are long, all alone."

She dreamed that her husband had met a woman he could love, and she wrote to him about it. He replied: "I have your letter of November 26. I see two things: you tell me I do not read your letters. That is inaccurate. I am vexed with you for your bad opinion. You say this may be the result of some dream in the night and you add that you are not jealous. I noticed a long time ago that angry people always maintain they are not angry; those who are frightened often say they are not frightened. So you are convicted of jealousy. I am delighted! In any case you are wrong. Nothing is further from my thoughts and in the deserts of Poland one thinks little of beautiful women. . . . I gave a ball for the nobility of the province yesterday; quite good-looking women, quite rich, quite badly dressed, although in the Paris fashion."

Once more she insisted. Only one thing could restore her pleasure in life—joining him. "I have your letter of November 27 in which I see your little head is excited," he wrote on December 3. "I remembered the line, 'A woman's desire is a devouring flame.' But you must be calm. I wrote that I was in Poland and that when winter quarters were settled you could come, so you must wait a few days. The greater one is the less one can have a will of one's own. One is dependent on events and circumstances. You can go to Frankfurt or Darmstadt. I hope to send for you in a few days, but not unless circumstances are favorable. The warmth of your letter made me see that you pretty women admit no obstacles. What you want must be. But as for me, I declare I am the most enslaved of men. My master is without pity and that master is the nature of things. Good-by, my dear. Keep well."

Then for a month he kept her in suspense. On December 9: "I see with pleasure that you are gayer and that the Queen of Holland wants to come with you. I long to give the order, but I must wait a few days yet." On December 10: "I love you and want you very much. Good-by, my dear. I shall write to you to come with at least as much pleasure as you will have in coming." On December 12: I long to see things fall out so that I can have you come." For the first time, on December 15, he spoke to her of her possible return to Paris. "I am leaving for Warsaw. I shall be back in about a fortnight. I hope I can send for you then. However, if it were longer I should be glad if you would return to Paris, where you are wanted."

Return to Paris, when for three months she had cherished the illusion that she would join him? Josephine wrote to him begging him to let her leave for Poland. The letter was to arrive in Warsaw at the beginning of January, 1807. Ten days earlier he had not made up his mind. "I should much like to see you," he had written on December 20, "but I hope to be able to send for you in five or six days."

But on December 31, at Pultusk, he had received an important piece of news: Mlle. Dénuelle had given birth to a little boy. The child was asserted to be his, and besides it was astonishingly like him. So he could beget children, and it was Josephine who was sterile.

The idea of the inevitability of divorce must have entered his mind once more. He refused to let himself be softened by his wife and replied to her on January 3: "I received your letter, my dear. Your grief touches me, but one must submit to events. There is too much country to be crossed between Mainz and Warsaw. We must wait until events allow me to go to Berlin before I write to you to come. In the meantime the beaten enemy is retreating, but I have a great many things to settle here. I should prefer you to return to Paris, where you are needed." She wrote again, clumsily insisted, pleaded, putting forward arguments that made him stick to his decision. "My dear, I am touched by everything you say, but what with the cold weather, the very bad roads, which are not safe, I cannot let you expose yourself to so much fatigue and danger. Return to Paris for the winter. Go to the Tuileries. Give receptions and lead the life you are accustomed to leading when I am there. This is my wish. Perhaps I shall not be long in joining you there, but you simply must give up the idea of traveling 300 leagues at this season, across enemy country and in the rear of the army. Believe me, it costs me more than it does you to delay the pleasure of seeing you for a few weeks, but that is what events and the success of my affairs require. Good-by, my dear. Be gay and show firmness of character."

On January 8 he wrote again: "Your sojourn at Mainz is too gloomy. Paris is asking for you, go there, that is what I want. I am more put out than you. I should have liked to spend the long nights of this season with you, but we must bow to circumstances." She wept and told him so. "I am distressed by all you tell me of your grief," he replied. "Why these tears and this sorrow? Have you no more courage? I shall see you soon. Never doubt my feelings and if you want to be still dearer to me, show character and strength of mind."

In her letter she had seemed doubtful about the future. If he had reverses, would he not need her at his side? She wanted also to be the companion of his bad times, if bad times had to come. He protested. "I am humiliated at the thought that my wife is distrustful of my destiny." But he ended affectionately. "Good-by, my dear, I love you, I want to see you and would like to know you are content and happy."

But she could not be happy far from him. This time she was shattered and confessed as much. Then he grew angry, and on January 28 replied to her in displeasure. "I insist you have more strength. I am told you are always crying. For shame, that is very bad! Your letter of January 7 pains me. Be worthy of me and develop a stronger character. Make a proper show in Paris and above all be happy. I am very well and I love you very much, but if you are always weeping I shall think you have no courage or character. I do not like cowards. An empress should have heart."

She had more heart than was needed to make everyone around her happy. What she lacked was a brave heart, and that was what the Emperor meant. She especially lacked courage, as she was constantly thinking of her prophetic dream.

Napoleon's latest letter was dated January 18 and on that day Duroc had finally managed to find the young peasant girl—a ravishing blonde with a dazzling complexion beneath her square bonnet of black fur—who on January 1, 1807, at the last relay before Warsaw, had murmured, blushing:

"Welcome, sire, to our land, our country which waits for you so that it may raise itself."

He himself had been surprised at retaining the memory of that delicate, simple face. The peasant girl who spoke French had astonished and interested him. Her whole person emanated such tenderness. It felt like love at first sight, though he must have imagined himself immune from such flames. However, he had ordered: "Duroc, you must find her for me."

Duroc had found her. She was not a peasant, but the nineteen-year-old wife of the elderly Count Walewski, who was seventy. Her name was Marie. On January 18 Duroc went to invite her to a ball at Prince Poniatowski's. At first she had refused, then—in the hope that he would "restore the motherland"—she had gone to the palace. In the evening she had received a note from Napoleon: "I saw only you, I admired only you, I desire only you. Send a prompt reply to calm the impatient ardor of N."

That same day he had written to Josephine: "Be worthy of me and develop a stronger character."

Meanwhile, at Warsaw, Marie resisted. He pleaded. "You destroy my rest. Oh! give a little joy, a little happiness to a poor heart ready to adore you."

And in order to reach his end and to take to his bed the woman who refused him, Napoleon resorted to shocking stratagems. Blackmail first: "Come! All your desires will be fulfilled. Your country will be dearer to me when you have pity on my poor heart." She had come and he had made a terrible scene, had trampled on his watch, threatening to treat Poland in the same way if she "rejected his heart." Terrified by his "wild look," she had fainted. But then she regained her senses, and was henceforth his.

And on January 23, when Mme. Walewska was his mistress, when she was beginning to love him and he loved her as much as one has time to love with all Europe on his hands, he received a letter from Josephine, naïvely informing him, "I took a husband in order to be with him." "I thought, in my ignorance," he replied in heedless

vainglory, "that the wife was made for the husband, the husband
for his country, his family and glory. Pardon my ignorance; with our
beautiful women one is always learning something."

The letter followed her along the high roads, for on January 15,
1807, Josephine had left Mainz for Paris. She was all the more
depressed since Hortense had left her the night before to return to
The Hague.

On January 26 the Empress was entertained at Strasbourg by the
Prefect Shée. She spent the night of January 28 at Lunéville and
passed through Nancy quite early the next day. After the inevitable
speeches and compliments, she ordered the carriages to go at a foot
pace and stop for a moment before the Hôtel Impérial. There she
accepted the Emperor's portrait presented to her by the wife of the
painter Carbonet and proceeded toward Toul. She spent the night
at the Hôtel d'Oudinot at Bar-le-Duc—where the ubiquitous girls in
white awaited her with their flowers and compliments—and left
next day for Epernay. Finally, to the sound of cannon, she arrived
at the Tuileries on the evening of January 31.

Now that she was back she had to resume her task of making "a
proper show." Josephine obeyed, "grumbling and weeping," as
Napoleon complained in reply to a letter she had sent him before
leaving Germany, a letter "which had distressed him." "She is too
sad," he explained. "That is what comes of not being just a bit
pious. You tell me your happiness is your glory. That is not
generous. You should say, the happiness of others is my glory. It is
not wifely. You should say, the happiness of my husband is my
glory. It is not maternal. You should say, the happiness of my
children is my glory. Now, like nations, your husband, and your
children cannot be happy without a little glory; you should not turn
up your nose at it so much. Josephine, you have an excellent heart
but your reasoning power is weak. You feel things wonderfully, but
you do not reason so well. That's enough quarreling. I want you to
be gay, content with your lot and to obey, not grumbling and
weeping, but with a gay heart and a little happiness."

A few days later she received another note written on the battlefield of Eylau. "There was a great battle yesterday, my dear, and the
victory was mine, but I have lost a lot of men. The enemy's losses,
which are even greater, do not console me. I am writing these few

lines myself, although I am tired, to tell you that I am well and that I love you." On the same day, February 9, at six in the evening he sent her these details: "I am writing a word, my dear, so that you will not be anxious. The enemy has lost the battle, 40 guns, 10 flags, 12,000 prisoners. They suffered horribly. I have lost a lot of men, 1,600 killed, 3,000 to 4,000 wounded.

"Your cousin Tascher is well. I have put him on my staff with the title of aide-de-camp. Corbineau was killed by a shell. I was particularly attached to this officer, who had great merits, and this grieves me. My horse guards covered themselves with glory. D'Allemagne is dangerous wounded. Good-by, my dear. Ever yours."

Josephine had a moment of joy on learning of the birth to Augusta in Milan on March 14 of a little girl, also called Josephine, whose title was to be Princess of Bologna. Eugene sent Josephine some of her granddaughter's hair. "It is a charming present," she wrote to her son, "and I am never tired of looking at it. The color is already the same as her mother's. This is an omen that she will be like her too in face and be as pretty and beautiful as she is."

But for Hortense everything was going from bad to worse. The Hague—where, as the Queen said, she had "neither the pleasures of the town nor those of the country, but only the inconveniences of greatness"—appeared sinister to her. The Dutch, stuck "like posts" before her, had "long faces." They seemed afraid of their sovereigns. And to cap everything, King Louis was becoming more and more of a dreadful tyrant. Hortense wrote of this: "*One*—meaning Louis—has so arranged matters that we are really in a veritable prison. Sometimes I simply cannot help laughing at all the trouble taken about nothing. *One* hides nothing now, because one has become accustomed to the most ridiculous things. Fortunately anyone may judge me, but in a country where I am not known the sight of *one's* behavior may give rise to doubts about me. Although I interfere in nothing, never see so much as a cat, *one* always takes every possible precaution as though quite the reverse was bound to happen. No one can enter or leave after six in the evening. Everyone becomes a spy and it is immediately repeated if anyone coughs or blows his nose."

Josephine was aware of this situation and was oppressed by her grief. Her attendants were not calculated to make her happy either.

The Empress was surrounded by "veritable vipers," in Mme. d'Abrantès' words. Moreover, some of the ladies, royalists at heart such as Mme. de La Rochefoucauld, spread pessimistic rumors. The battle of Eylau had been a terrible massacre. Napoleon had been nearly beaten. His star was on the decline. In Josephine's presence the ladies confined themselves to slight allusions, but they assumed commiserating airs. Naturally Napoleon was not unaware of what was going on. "I hear, my dear, that the unpleasant talk that went on in your drawing room at Mainz has started again. Put a stop to it. I shall be very displeased with you if you do not remedy this. You let yourself be upset by the remarks of people who ought to console you. I advise you to show some character and put all these people in their place."

But she had no heart for it. Some days, as she wrote to the Emperor, Josephine felt she would rather be dead than continue with these perpetual separations and this life too heavy for her weak shoulders. "Your letter distresses me," he replied. "You should not die. You are well and have no reasonable grounds for grief. I think you should go to Saint-Cloud in May, but you must remain in Paris all April. My health is good. Affairs are going well. You must not think of traveling this summer. It is not possible. You cannot be running about to inns and army camps. I want to see you as much as you do and even to live quietly. I know how to do other things besides make war, but duty comes before all. All my life I have sacrificed everything, peace, interest and happiness, to my destiny."

It was easy for him to talk. In fact he was well aware that the clan was still keeping Josephine on tenterhooks and that Mme. Letizia refused to visit her. He wrote to his mother: "Madame, I entirely approve of your going to your country house, but as long as you are in Paris it is fitting that you should dine every Sunday with the Empress, where the family dinner takes place. My family is a political family. When I am absent the Empress is always its head."

He wrote to Josephine that he had "sacrificed everything," but three days later, on April 1, he installed himself for more than two months in the beautiful castle of Finckenstein. Marie had joined him there. Had Josephine guessed that for his "Polish woman" Napoleon had regained the youthful heart of Bonaparte? "As usual, right away," he wrote to her on April 18, "your little Creole head gets excited and upset. Let us talk of it no more." But she continued to talk of it and on May 10 he wrote to her: "I don't understand what you say about ladies who have connections with me. I love only my little Josephine, good, sulky and capricious, who can quarrel as gracefully as she does everything, for she is always pleasant, except when she is jealous. Then she becomes a fiend. But to return to these ladies. If I were to pay attention to any one of them, I assure you I would like them to be pretty rosebuds. Is that the case with the ones you were speaking of?"

He was always afraid that, left to herself, his wife would forget the role he had laid down for her. "I wish you never to dine but with people who have dined with me. The list of your private receptions should be the same and you should never admit to your intimacy at Malmaison ambassadors and foreigners. If you did otherwise you would offend me. Finally, do not let yourself be got round by people I do not know, who would not come to see you if I were there."

Mme. de Chastenay tells us: "The Empress believed in fortune-telling, in all magic, dreams, apparitions almost." On the night of May 5 she was dreaming. Suddenly she saw her little grandson, Napoleon Charles, kneeling before a bronze column, then the apparition "assumed an angel's wings and escaped from sight." Some harm must have come to little Napoleon. And indeed, three days later the terrible news came: the child had just died of croup at The Hague.

On May 10 Josephine set out to meet Hortense. At the château of Laeken outside Brussels the two women mingled their tears. When she arrived Hortense seemed like one dead and Josephine was "seized with grief and terror." The Empress had only a small staff with her and, as the accounts show, took her meals alone with Louis and Hortense. Josephine was crushed. On returning to Saint-Cloud she wrote to her son: "I have greatly suffered, my dear Eugene, and your heart will have felt all my sorrow. You know the state in which my poor Hortense arrived at the château of Laeken. For several days I feared for her, but on returning to Malmaison she wept several times. . . . The tears did her good and I think I can assure you we shall not lose her. Poor Hortense! What a lovable child she has lost. . . . Since the dreadful event I hardly live; I do nothing but suffer and weep. She left on Sunday to visit the spa at Bagnères.

Corvisart sets great store by the effect of traveling and only this hope led me to agree to her leaving. Her health will return but her heart will never be consoled, I can tell that from all that I suffer. The King is very unhappy too. He had at the same time to mourn his son and fear for his wife. Just think, she was paralyzed for six hours."

On the way to Bagnères Hortense wrote to her brother from Orléans: "I no longer feel anything. He is dead, I saw him. God did not wish me to go with him. Yet I should not have left him. Now I cannot die any more for I no longer feel anything and that is why I am well. You do not know all I have lost. He was already a friend to me, no one will ever love me as he did. When I kissed him, an hour before, his eyes were already closed, he said to me 'Good morning, mamma,' he was hardly breathing. If you had seen him choking! I can still hear his breathing! . . ."

The Emperor was more profoundly affected than he told Josephine. "I can imagine all the pain the death of poor Napoleon must cause you," he wrote on May 14. "You can understand the grief I feel." But "Uncle Bibiche" soon recovered. "I wish I were near you so that you would be reasonable and moderate in your sorrow. You have had the good fortune never to lose a child, but it is one of the conditions and sorrows attaching to our human lot. Let me learn that you have been reasonable and are well! Do you wish to increase my grief?" The intensity of Hortense's sorrow surprised him. "Hortense is unreasonable and does not deserve to be loved, since she loved only her children. Try to calm yourself and do not give me pain. For irremediable ills we must find consolations." On June 2 he wrote in astonishment: "Why were you not able to distract her a little? You weep! I hope you will master yourself so that I do not find you all sadness."

Before joining her he had to fight the Russians. He did this at Friedland and informed Josephine on June 15: "My dear, I write just a word, for I am very tired. I have been bivouacking for many days. My children celebrated the anniversary of the battle of Marengo worthily. The battle of Friedland will be as famous and as glorious for my people. The whole Russian Army routed, 80 guns, 30,000 men captured or killed; 25 Russian generals killed, wounded or captured; the Russian guards crushed; it is a worthy counterpart to Marengo, Austerlitz, Jena. The *Bulletin* will tell you the rest. My losses were not great; I maneuvered the enemy successfully.

"Have no anxiety and be happy."

In fact she was, a little. The end of the campaign seemed near. Moreover, sorrow seemed to have drawn her daughter and son-in-law a little closer. Hortense was doubtful about the future and wondered "if it would last," but Louis, as Josephine told Eugene joyfully, paid "the Queen the most affectionate attention. Alas!" she continued, "the lesson has cost them dear, but I hope it will profit them. They will feel that nothing is better than mutual affection and a happiness such as you enjoy." One effect of this lull was the birth, nine months later, of the future Napoleon III. Better still, Louis showed consideration for his mother-in-law and when he went to take the waters he entrusted his second son, little Napoleon Louis, to her. "He is very like his poor brother," she wrote to Eugene. "He has his ways and his voice, but my pleasure in having him near me does not console me for the loss we have suffered."

This loss was more than a grief to her, it was her downfall. All the hopes she had based on the child had crumbled. Thanks to his existence she had had reason to hope she would not be repudiated. Napoleon had considered Hortense's son as his heir. He loved him and the real sorrow he had felt, but had tried to hide, at the child's death enabled Louis to exclaim unpleasantly: "So he was his son!" Hortense's husband was strengthened in his belief by the fact that the Emperor showed no thought of transferring to little Napoleon Louis either the affection he had felt for the elder child or his possible rights of succession. Since December 31 Napoleon had known himself to be the father of a child. Six months after this news, which he had received "with great emotion," his heir presumptive had died, but now there was the possibility that he could provide an heir himself.

This birth and this death, as Louis Madelin has said, were to strike a fatal blow at the Empress's position.

While reading the last letters Napoleon had sent her from Tilsit before returning, Josephine forgot her grief for a while. "The Queen of Prussia is really charming," he wrote on July 8. "She flirts with me a good deal, but do not be jealous, it slides over me like water off a duck's back. Playing the gallant would cost me too dear."

The next day the Emperor left the Tsar and the King of Prussia and on July 10 set out for France. On the 18th he wrote to his wife: "My dear, I arrived at Dresden yesterday afternoon at five, very well, although I was in the carriage for 100 hours without getting out. I am staying with the King of Saxony, with whom I am very much pleased. So I have covered more than half the way to you. One of these fine nights I may well arrive at Saint-Cloud like a jealous lover, I warn you. Good-by, my dear, I shall be very happy to see you again. Ever yours."

At last, on July 27, 1807, haloed with the glory of Tilsit, the Emperor arrived at the château of Saint-Cloud. As she always did on their return, Josephine immediately interrogated Constant eagerly, in a rain of questions.

"Was his journey comfortable? Is he gay or sad? Ill or well?"

She had not seen Napoleon since Mainz, nearly six months before. Without delay—she was expecting this with beating heart—he spoke to her in connection with the death of her grandson "of the necessity in which he might one day find himself of taking a wife who could give him children." She turned pale as he continued:

"If such a thing should happen, Josephine, it would be for you to help me to make such a sacrifice. I would count on your affection for me to spare me all the unpleasantness of this compulsory rupture. You would take the initiative, would you not, and, understanding my position, have the courage to come to the decision yourself to withdraw?"

She undeceived him with her calm reply:

"I shall obey your orders, but I shall never anticipate them."

This was said in the "calm, somewhat dignified tone she knew how to take toward Bonaparte and which was not without its effect," relates Mme. de Rémusat.

Josephine described the scene to her son, who replied:

"I was pleased with your conversation with the Emperor if it really was as you recounted it. You should always speak frankly to His Majesty. To do otherwise would be no longer to love him. If the Emperor continues to harass you about children, tell him that it is not well of him to reproach you with such things. If he believes that his happiness and that of France oblige him to have them, let him have no extraneous consideration. He must treat you well, give you a sufficient settlement and allow you to live with your children in Italy."

Shortly afterward Napoleon had a conversation on the same subject with Hortense. The Queen had come to visit her stepfather, since Louis insisted that little Napoleon Louis return to The Hague. The Emperor sighed.

"His father asks for him; he is not yet seven; I have no right to keep him. He is the only son in the family. If he goes back to Holland he will die like the older one and all France will compel me to divorce. France has no confidence in my brothers, who, moreover, are all ambitious. Eugene does not bear my name and in spite of the trouble I take to ensure the peace of France, there will be complete anarchy after my death. Only a son of mine could settle everything, and if I have not divorced it is only my attachment to your mother that has so far prevented this, for it is the wish of France. This was revealed on the death of your son, who was also thought to be mine. You know the absurdity of such a supposition. Yet you could not have prevented all Europe's thinking that that child was mine! People thought no worse of you on that account," the Emperor went on. "You are generally esteemed, but they believed it."

He paused, then continued: "It was perhaps fortunate that people believed it and for that reason I considered his death a great calamity."

Hortense was terribly shocked by these remarks and the fact that she recounted the conversation in her *Memoirs* seems to prove that it was a dreadful slander. She appears, however, to have said nothing about it to her mother, whose courage revived.

Josephine, indeed, was once more thinking that her husband had again given up any idea of repudiating her. She believed that Napoleon would never dare break the ties—though now very slender ones—binding him to his wife. Perhaps on account of superstition, perhaps because the gentle Creole would take his good fortune and his star with her. Perhaps because, listening for once to his heart, he feared she would make no opposition. Perhaps, too, because he was afraid of public opinion. How would the people like to see *their* sovereign put aside, sent away, exiled by the very man who had crowned her not three years earlier?

She clung to these hopes, but she reckoned without the clan, who worked on the Emperor as soon as they could. His liaison with Marie Walewska spurred on Murat and it was not long before Josephine knew it.

"I have proofs," she wrote to her son, "that while the Emperor was with the army he [Murat] did everything to bring him to a divorce. I was more generous than he, for at the same time I was defending his wife with all my power, but he does not like me and in spite of his protestations toward you, you may rest assured that he has no attachment for you either. . . . Unfortunately the Emperor is too great for anyone to tell him the truth; everyone around him does nothing but flatter all day long. As for me, you know I aspire only to have his heart. If they managed to separate me from him, it is not the rank I should regret. A profound solitude would be what would most please me and, sooner or later, he will realize that all those about him are thinking more of themselves than of him and he will know how he has been deceived. And yet, my dear Eugene, I have no complaints against him and I am glad I can count on his justice and affection."

Jerome was the only exception among the clan. For her husband's youngest brother Josephine was his "dear and beloved little sister." She had charming letters from him, as this one from Breslau at the beginning of the same year: "I am sure you have noticed that I have been telling you for a long time that I love you with all my heart and that I feel more keenly than anyone else the pain of being separated from you. If this is too conceited, blame only your kindness to me and my tender attachment to you. . . . I have procured a few cashmere-style shawls here, made in Moscow. I beg my good little sister to be kind enough to accept them as a proof that I never cease to think of her in all circumstances. Good-by, my good little sister, I embrace you with all my heart."

What a contrast between these affectionate lines and the letters from Caroline, Pauline or Elisa, which are also preserved in the Bibliothèque Thiers! Her sisters-in-law addressed her according to protocol as "Madame" and "Your Majesty," whereas among themselves Josephine was always "the Beauharnais" or, now, "the old woman."

While still at Tilsit the Emperor had proudly announced to Jerome his appointment as head of a kingdom comprising "all the States you will find enumerated herewith." Talleyrand had been charged with inventing a coat of arms for this newly created Kingdom of Westphalia. He had taken a dozen lions, to be found capering in the armorial bearings of the German principalities and duchies, crowned them with an eagle and flanked them with a horse. A queen also was needed, since Napoleon had made his brother divorce Elisabeth Patterson, whom he had married without his consent. Jerome was affianced to Catherine, daughter of the King of Württemberg. She may not have been very pretty, but her curves—later to become generous—her charming mouth and fine hands were not unpleasant to look at. She was dazzled by Jerome's classical face at first glance, and this feeling was to remain with her until she died.

When she arrived, Josephine showered her with attentions and filled up the heavy silences between the two fiancés who had nothing to say to each other.

The marriage—civil on August 22, religious on August 23—was celebrated with unbelievable pomp and ostentation through which Josephine moved with more ease than the young Württemberg girl whose family was allied to all the European courts, but who had arrived from Stuttgart without a shift. Catherine found evenings of backgammon or talk with the Empress's entourage particularly painful. She hoped that everything would be simpler at Rambouillet, where a large part of the court, forty-four people, was to stay September 7 to 17.

Nothing of the kind. It was cold and damp. "François I died here," Catherine wrote to her father, "and it all looks like a prison. Everyone has a tiny bedroom, where in any case we go only to dress and sleep—very little—for we spend the whole time, from eleven to two in the morning, with the Empress. Lunch, needlework, then hunting, for six or seven hours; dinner at top speed, games, music and fine conversation with the Empress. The Princes and Princesses generally dance. As I am the most sensible and the eldest, I remain sitting to watch them and mope, almost dropping with sleep."

Although Josephine kept up her "fine conversation," she detested Rambouillet, but only in a whisper, for her husband found it "charming" and was surprised that anyone could be bored there. He said so a few days later to Talleyrand, when the Court was installed at Fontainebleau from September 21 to November 16.

"I invited a lot of people to Fontainebleau. I wanted them to enjoy themselves. I organized all the amusements; and everyone had long faces and looked worn out and gloomy."

Talleyrand replied, "That is because pleasure cannot be regulated by drums, and here, just as in the army, you always seem to be saying to each of us, 'Now, then, ladies and gentlemen, forward— march!'"

In the midst of the parties the news came to Fontainebleau that Mme. de La Pagerie had died at Trois-Ilets on the preceding June 2. She had been buried on June 10 with all the magnificence the island could muster.

Would the Imperial Court go into mourning for the Emperor's mother-in-law, whom no one knew, apart from Josephine and Stephanie Tascher? In order not to interrupt the festivities at Fontainebleau, it was decided not to mention the event. Josephine kept quiet and hid herself to weep, recounts Mlle. d'Avrillon. But the news could certainly not have further darkened the atmosphere of the palace; it could not have been gloomier.

The walls oozed boredom. Yawns greeted the tedious plays given on Mondays, Wednesdays and Fridays throughout the "grand stay" at Fontainebleau. Out of eighteen shows twelve were tragedies, "those everlasting tragedies," real soporifics which had to be sat through with an air of enjoyment. The Court was dreadfully bored, accord- ing to Mme. de Rémusat. The young women went to sleep with no fear of being wakened by applause, for it was forbidden to applaude in the Emperor's presence. On days when he had been hunting, he sometimes dozed off himself. Josephine woke him only when the final curtain fell and the company separated "sad and discon- tented."

"The Emperor," Mme. de Rémusat reported, "became aware of this feeling. He grew angry, attacked his first chamberlain, blamed the actors and would have liked others to be found." Sometimes he would change the play on the very morning of the performance.

"I wish it," he would say.

"Once the Emperor had uttered this irrevocable 'I wish it,' the words echoed throughout the palace. Duroc and Savary in particu- lar pronounced them in the same tone as he did. M. de Rémusat repeated them to all the actors, who were confused by the efforts of memorizing the unexpected changes. Couriers galloped off in search of the necessary men or materials."

Things brightened up only three times a week, when there was a hunt. Josephine and her ladies wore red velvet dresses embroidered with gold, while Hortense had chosen a blue velvet habit embroidered with silver. The Empress hated following the hunt, her heart recoiled from the carnage. One day at Rambouillet the stag running from the pack took refuge beneath her carriage. Tears streaming from her beautiful eyes, Josephine begged that the animal be spared. When it was, she put a silver collar round its neck so that it would be protected in future.

The Emperor had spared no expense in having Fontainebleau made ready to receive the Court. The rooms had been refurnished, the park renovated and the lake cleaned out by prisoners of war. Swans had been put on it "to prevent the weeds returning" and the celebrated carp, which had been fished up and sold during the Revolution, were to be replaced.

But in spite of its setting the château remained like a slave ship in which everyone "rowed according to the rules" under the Emperor's pitiless eye. However, this did not prevent private thoughts and gossip once the masters had returned to their "quarters."

The Court, being malicious, laughed to see Jerome already neglecting his plump young wife to flirt with pretty Stephanie, who was grieved at now being no more than Princess of Baden, whereas not long before, as Napoleon's adoptive daughter, she had ranked above everyone else.

Of course the Emperor's love affairs were the center of every conversation. It seemed perfectly natural that Napoleon was attracted by the beautiful face of Josephine's reader, the Italian Carlotta Gazzani, who had been biding her time since the Imperial stay in Genoa. She had the finest face in the Court, its pure lines illuminated by black eyes, flashing teeth and a laugh described as "aslant." Needless to say, Josephine wanted to know what was going on and one day, convinced that her husband was receiving Mme. Gazzani, she indulged in her bad habit of trying to enter his study. Constant intercepted her.

"It is impossible, madame, I have definite orders not to disturb His Majesty. The Emperor is working with a minister."

The "minister" was Carlotta. Josephine came back twice and each time Constant prevented her going in. That same evening the Emperor said sternly to his valet:

"The Empress asserts that she has it from you that I was closeted with a lady."

Constant had no difficulty in clearing himself, but it can be seen
that Josephine thought any trick justified to gain her ends.

Nevertheless, on this occasion she did not display extreme jealousy and Mme. Gazzani continued to show respect and devoted
affection to her mistress, while in public the Emperor treated his
"fancy" almost coldly. Josephine was all the more prompt in "deciding to accept with complaisance the amusements which it would
have been impossible for her to oppose very long," since her
husband had confessed that it was nothing but a "liaison in cold
blood." Except for Marie Walewska, Napoleon usually told Josephine about his "affairs," to which he attached not the least importance. Indeed, according to the Empress's maid, "he told her more
than she asked, even mentioned hidden imperfections and, in
connection with another confession, mentioned this or that court
lady who was not involved and had never been made an offer."

Josephine tried to follow the advice of Eugene, who had written
from Monza on September 10: "Don't plague the Emperor and try
to regulate your private expenses. Do not be so kind to everyone
about you, or you will soon be deceived."

Josephine had promised her son to listen to him, but Fouché was
soon to get the poor woman involved in further unhappiness.

One Sunday after Mass, when the Court was still at Fontainebleau, Josephine was standing at a window when she saw Fouché
approaching. He bowed and without any preamble had the effron-
tery to tell her in his sanctimonious voice "that as the public weal
and in particular the consolidation of the present dynasty required
the Emperor to have children, she should make known her wishes to
the Senate so that they would join with her in supporting her
request to her husband for the sacrifice most painful to her heart."

Josephine felt the room going round. Fouché described the scene:
"Her complexion grew red, then pale, her lips swelled and I saw in
her whole person the signs which made me fear a nervous attack or
some other explosion. Stammering, she asked me, 'Have you received orders from the Emperor to make me such a suggestion?' 'I
have received no orders, madame, but I am anticipating future
needs.' Almost with violence she exclaimed, 'On this point I shall
obey only my husband's orders.'"

Fouché, alleging that "he had to confer with one of his colleagues," bowed and withdrew.

The Minister had received no order from Napoleon, but he had spoken to the Emperor and even read him a memorandum. "I pointed out the necessity of dissolving his marriage," he related, "and of forming, as emperor, a new tie, more suitable and pleasant, and of giving an heir to the throne to which Providence had called him. My conclusion was the natural result of the strongest and most solid considerations and arguments which the political requirements and necessities of state could suggest."

"Without giving any positive reaction," Napoleon merely "revealed a glimpse" of his feelings. Undoubtedly, from the political view solely, "the dissolution of his marriage had taken a firm hold on his mind."

"But, on the other hand," he corrected, "I am peculiarly attached, both from habit and from a kind of superstition, to Josephine. The step which would cost me most would be informing her of the divorce."

Fouché, "urged on by an excess of zeal," resolved "to open the breach and summon Josephine to this great sacrifice required by the solidity of the Empire and the happiness of the Emperor."

The Minister cared nothing for the "happiness of the Emperor," but he feared to see Napoleon marry an archduchess, grandniece of Marie Antoinette. Being a supporter of the Russian marriage, he preferred to make the first move and be the artisan of the divorce, so that he would be in a good position to recommend an alliance with the Tsar's sister.

A few days later M. de Rémusat was urgently summoned to Josephine at midnight. He found her "dishevelled, half-undressed and with a disturbed countenance." She had just had a long letter from Fouché. This time the Minister pointed out how fine her self-sacrificing role would be. France would owe its future to her.

"One must not fail to acknowledge, madame, that France's political future is compromised by the lack of an heir for the Emperor. As Minister of Police I am in a position to know public opinion and I know there is anxiety about the succession of such an empire. Consider how much strength His Majesty's throne would have today if it were supported by the existence of a son!"

Fouché ended by asserting that the Emperor was ignorant of his move. "I think, indeed, that it would displease him," the hypocrite said, and he recommended "the greatest secrecy" to the Empress. In a voice broken by sobs Josephine asked Rémusat, "What shall I do?"

"Madame, I strongly advise you to go to the Emperor at once, if he is not in bed, or else first thing tomorrow. Remember you must not give the impression of having consulted anyone. Give him this letter to read, watch him if you can, but in any case show your irritation at this inopportune advice and tell him once more that you will only obey a positive order given by himself."

According to the record left by Mme. Rémusat, Josephine hurried to the Emperor next morning but, according to Hortense, the Empress waited for her husband to be informed. In both versions, however, Napoleon appeared indignant, disowned Fouché and asserted that he had spoken "without orders."

"This is an excess of zeal; and one must not be too much annoyed with him. It is enough that we are determined to reject his advice and that you really believe that I could not live without you."

"I was extremely shocked by Fouché's behavior," Napoleon was to explain on St. Helena. "I would have dismissed him at once for having interfered with what went on in my bed, if that would not have appeared to be repudiating an opinion which it behooved me to favor."

In fact, since the ground had been more or less prepared, Napoleon, as we know from Hortense, asked his wife "what she thought about it." Josephine could only repeat what she had said to him a few weeks earlier.

"I shall never be the first to ask for something which could separate me from you. Our destiny is too extraordinary not to have been determined by Providence and I should be afraid of bringing misfortune on both of us if I separated my life from yours of my own accord."

She had made a good point by arousing the feeling of superstition that lies in the heart of every Corsican. Yet she realized that Fouché had acted to some extent with the Emperor's tacit agreement. As Metternich wrote at the same time: "No minister here dares do what the Emperor has not ordered; above all, none of them would risk repeating the offense." It was significant that Napoleon refused to dismiss his minister. "It was obvious to me," Fouché wrote, "that if he had not already decided on his divorce he would have sacrificed me, instead of confining himself merely to disowning my move."

So the future Duke of Otranto enlarged the breach once more. On Tuesday, November 17, the very day after Napoleon's departure for Italy and Josephine's return to Paris—the Emperor having refused to take her with him—Fouché sent this report to his master:

Paris. In every walk of society people are discussing the causes of His Majesty's leaving Fontainebleau and the motives of his journey to Italy. Everyone explains these causes and motives in his own way. People appeared astonished at not seeing Her Majesty the Empress at the performance of *Trajan* on Tuesday. Some answered that she was unwell, most spoke of the dissolution of her marriage and of the Emperor's alliance with the the the sister of Emperor Alexander. This news has become the talk of all classes in Paris and the truth is that not one of them has not greeted it as a guarantee of imminent peace and of the duration of the state's tranquillity.

On the following Thursday, November 19, Fouché returned to the attack with consummate skill.

Paris. Report. At Court, among the Princes and in all circles, there is talk of the dissolution of the Empress's marriage. At Court there is divided opinion on the subject. The people in the Empress's confidence seem convinced that the Emperor will never make up his mind to this dissolution; they say that the Empress is adored in France, that her popularity is useful to the Emperor and the Empire, that the happiness of each of them is linked to the duration of this union, that the Empress is the Emperor's talisman, that their separation will be the end of his good fortune and other fables of this nature which sound like the tales of fortunetellers. They maintain the Empress in her opinions, dissuade her from any contrary resolution, urge her to appear in public to contradict, by her presence, the rumors that are circulating. The other part of the Court, which looks on the dissolution as something the establishment of the dynasty must necessarily entail, is trying to prepare the Empress for this event, and gives her the advice it thinks suitable for this situation. In the imperial family there is only one opinion: *it is unanimously in favor of the divorce.* In Paris circles there are no two opinions among people attached to the dynasty. They seem quite convinced that only children of the Emperor can assure its duration. Only the egoists and scatterbrains appear indifferent. The malcontents utter hypocritical cries about the fate of the Empress, whom they pity greatly and for whom they have suddenly begun to have feelings the opposite of those they have hitherto displayed.

Nothing had been forgotten. In this same report, among "the most contradictory rumors," the Minister incidentally provided the Emperor with an idea for Josephine's future lot. "Some say . . . that the Empress will be Queen of Naples." On Thursday, December 3, he stated that "the public," interested by the Emperor's journey to Italy, was alleging that he "had gone to prepare the royal retreat for the Empress Josephine."

The next day, Friday, December 4, Fouché again devoted his report to Josephine:

> The moralizing women of the Faubourg Saint-Germain utter loud protests against divorce. Mme. Hamelin spreads abroad the confidences she says she has received from Her Majesty the Empress on this subject. This woman, and several others of her kidney, undertake daily to discuss, provoke and exaggerate the Empress's complaints and griefs. They claim to know perfectly what the Emperor said to the Empress on such and such a day, their conversation before and after the coronation, the differences among the Imperial family, plots being woven against her and the plotters guilty of this, etc. They maintain that the Empress's sterility is not her fault, that the Emperor has never had any children, that the liaisons His Majesty has had with several women have had no results, whereas these women, the moment they were married, became pregnant. . . .

After that Fouché was obligated to put a damper on his campaign. On November 30, extremely irritated by the first two reports, Napoleon sent his minister a stern letter from Venice: "I have already informed you of my opinion as to the folly of the move you made at Fontainebleau with respect to my private affairs. By behaving thus you alienate good opinion and leave the path to which every honest man should keep."

Napoleon's return on January 1, 1808, brought Josephine a little relief. On January 4 they went to see the picture of the coronation David had just finished, that canvas which portrays not the Emperor's coronation but Josephine's. The Empress had indeed been placed at the centre of the composition as the result of a "little intrigue," as Napoleon was to call it, between the painter and Josephine.

"It will make a prettier picture," she had said.

On seeing the picture, Napoleon showed his pleasure and Josephine plucked up courage. She might well have been reassured by the joy he displayed on seeing her painted kneeling so prettily while he prepared to put her crown on her.

But Fouché was on the alert and on January 29 gave the Emperor a further report:

The wife of Isabey, painter, is publishing details on the Empress's private life. She says Her Majesty is constantly in tears, that she has suspicions about the cause of her last indisposition which plunge her into deep grief, that she wants divorce but dares not admit it, that Mlle. Tascher is now the only confidante to whom she opens her heart. Little is said today about the divorce, but people think of it since it is believed certain that the Empress can have no more children.

Murat also worked hard on his brother-in-law. He joined his efforts to those of Fouché and, now, of Talleyrand. The unhappy woman was not unaware of this and wrote to her son on Feburary 10, 1808:

You can easily guess that I have had many causes for grief and I still have. The rumors that were current during the Emperor's absence have not ceased on his return and at this moment have more supporters than ever. It is true that their authors have not been punished; on the contrary, it has been observed that those who tried to belie them have been greeted more coldly. In any case I entrust myself to Providence and to the will of the Emperor. My only defense is my conduct, which I try to make irreproachable. I never go out; I have no pleasure, and I lead a life to which people are surprised I can adjust myself, having been accustomed to being more independent and to seeing a lot of people. I console myself by thinking that I am submitting to the Emperor's wish. I see my stock falling every day while others gain in credit. The favor all goes to Prince Murat and the Princess his wife, to M. de Talleyrand and to Berthier. You know he is to become your first cousin. He is marrying Princess Elisabeth, daughter of the Duchess of Bavaria. The request was made and accepted yesterday.

What unhappiness thrones bring, my dear Eugene! I would sign an abdication on behalf of all my family tomorrow without regret. The Emperor's heart is entirely mine. If I am to lose it I have little regret for the rest. That is my only ambition and the real state of my heart. I know one does not succeed with such frankness and if, like so many others, I could only be cunning I should be much better off, but I prefer to preserve my character. At least I can have my self-respect.

As for you, dear son, remain what you have always been. Continue to render yourself worthy of the Emperor's friendship and let the future bring what it will. I shall never complain of my fate as long as you are happy and I can believe myself certain of your affection.

There was another discussion between the husband and wife that winter. According to the Russian ambassador, Count Tolstoy, Napoleon "in an access of rage" declared to his wife "that she would finally force him to adopt his bastards." According to the diplomat, Josephine seized "promptly" on this solution, but the Emperor's suggestion, uttered in a moment of anger, was not carried further.

On St. Helena Napoleon was to tell Grand Marshal Bertrand one day in January, 1819, that, on the contrary, it was Josephine herself who had suggested that "he have a child by some young lady and pass it off as hers. When she spoke to me of this," the Emperor went on, "I entirely disapproved and had no difficulty in convincing her."

Whatever the case, one thing is certain: Napoleon was constantly thinking of what he considered more and more unavoidable. On April 1, meeting Hortense, who was to give birth that month to the future Napoleon III, he looked at her and sighed: "It hurts me to see you like that. How I should love your mother if she were in the same condition."

17. *"In My Situation . . ."*

On April 2, 1808, Napoleon left Saint-Cloud, followed by thirty-six carriages, on the pretext of inspecting the southern departments. In fact he was soon to proceed to Bayonne, where he was to set up his trap for the Spanish King which would make the first crack in the Imperial edifice. He had not wanted to take Josephine, but as he wished to lure the Spanish royal family to the frontier, he needed a hostess.

"I do not know where I shall put all that crowd," he had written to her, so in order to help him receive "all that crowd" the Empress was summoned to join him at the Château de Marrac at the gates of Bayonne, "a little country house," as he called it, which he bought from its owner, M. Marcqfroy.

Josephine stayed at Bordeaux for a few days, the Emperor having recommended that she "be friendly toward everyone as his pursuits had not allowed him to be so to anyone." Having finished her civilities, she set out for Bayonne. While crossing the moors her carriage was nearly stuck on several occasions, although it was drawn by twelve horses. Finally she arrived at Marrac in the evening of April 27.

Her rooms had been charmingly arranged. Her bedroom was a

355

symphony in violet and yellow silk and the cherrywood bed was surmounted by a crown "with oak leaves and twisted ribbons." Her drawing room of blue satin braided with violet and yellow appeared like "a tent with the curtains looped up." This room was also furnished in cherrywood and the sofas, armchairs and stools were covered with "striped blue Indian silk trimmed with yellow silk with white stars." A bathroom had been installed with a pinewood bath.

Ferdinand, the Prince of the Asturias, had already arrived in Bayonne, having been hailed from Madrid by Savary, the Emperor's head policeman, who had been prodigal with lies and false promises in order to bring him to the feet of his master. "Ferdinand VII" was thus the first to walk into Napoleon's web. He had proclaimed himself King of all Spain, his father having been forced to abdicate in his favor, but Napoleon did not recognize him. Charles IV, the father, for his part, had retracted, claiming that he had abdicated under pressure of events. "Fully relying on the magnanimity and genius of the great Napoleon," he wanted the Emperor to arbitrate the conflict between himself and his son. On this account he had also came to Bayonne, together with his wife and their favorite, Godoy. Two days after Josephine's arrival they made their entry in an ancient coach.

"With her yellow skin the Queen looks like a mummy," the Emperor told his wife. "She has an untrustworthy, ill-tempered appearance and one cannot imagine anything more ridiculous."

As for Charles IV, he was always accompanied by his confessor, whom he summoned by "whistling to him like a dog"; he had a dozen of his watches carried by his valet and when in his coach carried the same number himself, asserting that "it spoiled pocket watches not to be worn."

On seeing his son, the grotesque King rushed at him. "Have you not sufficiently insulted my white hairs? Begone, I do not wish to see you any more."

Then, turning to Napoleon, he sighed. "Your Majesty does not know what it is to have to complain of a son."

One can imagine what kind of atmosphere prevailed during dinner. Even the astonishing behavior of the King of Spain did not cheer those present. He had three jugs of water in front of him, one iced, one hot and one ordinary, and carefully and scrupulously mixed them until he had just what suited him.

That evening he observed that his dear Godoy had been placed at a side table. He did not regain his composure until the "Prince of Peace," as Godoy was called, had been put near him. The King was then able to indulge in his aquatic games and eat with a good appetite.

Louis XIV's descendants were now at Napoleon's mercy.

On April 30 the Emperor wrote to Murat, "I have to clear up the whole affair during these two days." Two days later, in fact, Charles IV addressed his son a letter informing him that his crimes prevented his succeeding to the throne and that "Spain could now be saved only by the Emperor." Godoy was forced to help Napoleon in his task and on May 4 the old King appointed Murat lieutenant general of the kingdom. On the next day Charles IV ceded his kingdom to Bonaparte on the single condition "that the territorial integrity of the kingdom should be respected and no other religion than the Catholic tolerated." In exchange Charles and Marie Louis would receive Compiègne, Chambord and 6,000,000 francs a year.

There remained Ferdinand, who tried to resist and could still legally consider himself King of all Spain. Suddenly there came the news of the bloody Madrid uprising of May 2—the famous *dos de mayo*—harshly suppppressed by Murat. Ferdinand had nothing to do with it, but it gave the Emperor a good excuse. He heard the news when out riding and immediately hurried to Bayonne where, as he told Josephine that evening, having summoned the Prince of the Asturias to meet his father, he accused him of fomenting the rising.

"The blood of my subjects has flowed," old Charles IV shouted, "together with that of the soldiers of my great friend Napoleon. You were concerned in this slaughter."

Like a fury, the Queen also insulted her son, calling him a bastard and demanding that he be taken to the scaffold. Napoleon did not go so far.

"If, between now and midnight, you have not recognized your father as the legitimate King and do not announce this in Madrid, you will be treated by me as a rebel."

Terrified, Ferdinand at last gave way. He was now barely more than a prisoner. When the curtain came down on the drama at Bayonne Joseph, the brother of Emperor Napoleon, could sign "I, the King" and receive these lines of congratulation from his predecessor, Ferdinand: "I beg Your Catholic Majesty to accept the

allegiance I owe him and that of the Spaniards who are with me"—a
nauseating piece of servility.

Napoleon and Josephine stayed at Marrac until July 21 to recover
from this terrible fortnight. Napoleon was now in a very good
humor and played pranks with Josephine like a newlywed. He also
went bathing. "Each one of us," recounts an eyewitness, "was
accompanied by an aquatic lookout, to prevent any English attack.
All the time Napoleon remained in the water a detachment of
mounted guards patrolled the sea, entering it as far as they could
without too much risk." Returning to the beach, Napoleon chased
his wife, pushed her into the sea and took her shoes, which he threw
away. Josephine laughed, was happy, and thought herself back in
the days of the Consulate.

But the lighthearted atmosphere was slightly disturbed by the
glances the Emperor kept giving one of Josephine's readers, Mlle.
Guillebeau, who was quite new to the Court. She read little, but
played the harp very well and, it appears, was "of a rare freshness."
Moreover, as Mlle. d'Avrillon remarked with some envy, the reader
was "burdened with eighteen years." If Napoleon is to be believed,
Josephine had brought Mlle. Guillebeau and Mme. Gazzani with
her purposely. "By giving me a mistress," he was to say, "Josephine
hoped to keep me and so prevent a divorce. Frankly, I was not
pleased with this behavior." So the Emperor was "delighted" when a
letter from Mlle. Guillebeau's mother to her daughter was discovered, from which it was evident that the daughter had been
coached by her mother. "The part she was to play was laid down,
she was advised to be skillful and was also strongly urged without
fail and at any cost to contrive to produce a living result that might
prolong her favor or entail very profitable returns for her."

Josephine had to give orders that the too-complaisant mother
should be summoned at once to take her daughter away. The girl
was entrusted to a lady's maid, who went with her to meet Mme.
Guillebeau. But Mme. Gazzani was still there, prepared to read the
paper to Josephine or to help the Emperor spend a few pleasant
moments.

On leaving Bayonne for Bordeaux and Nantes, the Emperor was
serious and thoughtful. Certainly affairs in Spain were going badly.
He had written to Talleyrand: "This tragedy is in its fifth act, we

shall soon see the denouement." At Bordeaux, when he learned of the French capitulation there—he called it "ignominious," which was excessive—he flew into a terrible rage.

"I have a stain here," he said to Josephine, touching his coat.

He was in an appalling humor—the bright, cheerful days of Marrac were far away—and Josephine's eyes were often red. One evening, when they were still at Bordeaux, she even had an attack of nerves.

Napoleon would have preferred to return quickly to Paris, but he had promised to visit the Vendée.

"It would look as though I was afraid of those people," he said. "I shall go, but I shall accelerate my journey as much as possible."

On Wednesday, August 3, eight carriages left Bordeaux to visit "the western countries." First a kitchen wagon, in which were the cooks, scullions and utensils. Was the Emperor afraid of being poisoned while going through the royalist departments? To the despair of the authorities, who had spared no expense, he wished to eat in Josephine's company from his own kitchen. Next rode a subinspector of posts, an equerry, a page, three cavalry scouts, an outrider, another page, three couriers. Then came seven carriages in which were the colonel quartermaster of the Imperial household, Msgr. de Pradt, the Emperor's almoner, Berthier, Talleyrand, Maret, General Bertrand, Minister Decrès, Duroc, the Grand Marshal of the Palace, Josephine's three ladies, Mmes. de Montmorency, de La Rochefoucauld and Gazzani, and finally the coach. An aide-de-camp and Rustum rode by the doors and an outrider of the Imperial Guard closed the procession.

After a night in the carriages, between Bordeaux and Saintes, a departure from Rochefort at two in the morning and arrival at Niort at seven in the morning, Napoleon and Josephine entered the country of the Giants, as Napoleon had called the Vendéans. All those who had suffered, all who had seen their land ravaged by civil war, all who had seen their families massacred by one camp or the other, all who had fought, whether blues or whites, all wished to acclaim "the pacifier of the Vendée." The former Chouans prepared to shout even more loudly "Long live the Empress!"—Josephine being still considered a royalist.

The Mayor of Fontenay, M. Laval, had been in suspense since

Sunday, August 7, when an officer had come at eight in the evening to announce that the Emperor and Empress would spend the night with him. The officer had tapped the walls, opened the cupboards and even "tapped the barrels in the cellar with a stick."

At nine in the evening, two shouts of "Long live the Emperor! Long live the Empress!" Napoleon and Josephine entered Fontenay beneath a portico bearing "an allegorical group representing the Emperor on an ancient chariot drawn by eight horses and crowned by the spirit of France."

Mme. Laval was in despair. Her Imperial guest refused her sumptuous dinner and ate the modest meal hastily prepared by His Majesty's cook. In order to smooth over this bad impression, Josephine asked one of the daughters of the house to sit down at the piano and, while longing to go to bed, listened with a show of delight as Mlle. Laval sang an aria from *Les Bardes*.

At midnight the Empress and the whole house were wakened by a terrible noise. The Emperor had just received a dispatch from Joseph announcing his intention to abdicate. In a rage Napoleon had broken the large china bowl Mme. Laval had provided for washing his feet.

At three in the morning Josephine was got out of bed and at four they left. Napoleon was in a filthy temper.

The Empress was able to rest for a few hours at the Grande Auberge at Napoléon-Vendée, which they reached in the rain at eleven in the morning. The town, which was being built, was a depressing and deplorable spectacle. It was a muddy building site with a few clay houses rising up here and there. While Josephine was recovering her strength, Napoleon, furious at the condition of the town bearing his name, dug his sword into a mud wall, exclaiming: "I have poured out gold for palaces to be erected and you have built a town of muck."

The Emperor announced that he and the Empress would leave that day. He refused to spend the night in that "caricature of a city." The mayor sighed and excused himself. "We have done little to receive you," he explained, "because we could not do much, but in our hearts are built the altars where burns the purest incense for Your Majesties."

Napoleon and Josephine left at five o'clock. Their journey continued in the rain. They stopped at the house of the lawyer Tortat. Again the Emperor and Empress refused to touch the dinner prepared in their honor. As on the previous evening, they were served by their butler, Leclerc. Josephine accepted only a glass of water and when she had drunk it she immediately had an attack of vomiting. White with anger, Napoleon summoned the subprefect.

"What is this, sir? Do you see this water?"

"Sire," replied the poor man, trembling, "Your Majesty need not have the least anxiety, you are with very honest people."

"But taste it then," Napoleon ordered curtly.

The unfortunate man obeyed, still more nervously, but felt no discomfort. Tortat arrived a few minutes later and found the Emperor standing sulkily with his back to the fire—lit although it was August. Josephine, opposite him, interrupted the lawyer's excuses.

"It's nothing, probably fatigue and the dust of the journey."

Tortat looked at the Empress "with love," as he relates. And he adds: "This excellent Princess was in a very low-cut dress, still very attractive and above all gracious."

Now the dignitaries filed through the room. Josephine questioned her visitors, promised to transmit their requests and intercede with the Emperor. The parish priest, Abbé de Buor, apologized for not having rung the bells.

"Alas, we have not the money to buy any."

"You shall have one, I shall pay for it."

Which is why the bell of Montaigu still bears the joined names "Napoléon-Joséphine."

At one in the morning the travelers left for Nantes, which they reached at three in the morning. Then on August 10, while Napoleon went off at four in the morning to visit Paimbeuf and Saint-Nazaire, Josephine held a reception for a hundred ladies and forty girls from the city. She had a pleasant word for each and in the evening, the Emperor having ridden back from his trip, she went to the Cirque du Chapeau Rouge, where a great ball was held.

Before returning to the relative calm of Saint-Cloud, Josephine and Napoleon, to the accompaniment of flattery, gunfire, speeches, compliments, acclamations and festivities, went through Anjou and Touraine. They spent the night of August 13-14 in their coach,

between Blois and Saint-Cloud, but for all that had to attend a
party given at the Tuileries on the evening of their arrival.

Josephine was unwell, not as a result of the exhausting trip, for in
this respect she was astonishingly resilient, but on account of her
anxieties of the preceding winter. The day Napoleon left for Erfurt
she explained to Eugene: "You know how much distress I had; my
head was affected by it. Last winter I had so much to put up with
that a mass of humors collected and formed a deposit, which luckily
worked outward and gave me terrible pain. In this instance the
Emperor proved his attachment by the anxiety he showed. He
would get up as often as four times a night to come and see me. For
the past six months he has been wonderful to me. So I saw him
leave this morning with regret but with no anxiety for myself. Not
that I have not a few enemies, which I am always surprised at, for I
have never done anyone any harm, but happily they are very few
and several are far from here, for example, Prince Murat. I can
mention him without being unjust. His hatred for me is so strong
that he does not even try to hide it and you would hardly imagine
the things he permits himself to say against me when showing his
desire for a divorce. But I take my revenge on him, as on the others,
by a sovereign contempt and by not trying to harm them, and the
Emperor is too just not to see the difference between their behavior
and mine."

During the few preceding months Napoleon had seemed to be
paying less attention to the everlasting advice of the clan to get rid
of his "old woman." Josephine's "situation," as she wrote to Eugene,
"has greatly changed since Murat's first journey to Spain when the
scales fell from the Emperor's eyes. That family really hates mine,
although I have done them nothing but good. There are some warm
friends here and everything that has happened during the past year
has made me understand many things and many people. I keep
completely quiet about all this and, in my situation, one is often
forced to live with one's enemies, but it is always well to know
them. I meddle in nothing, I ask nothing. . . . As for my debts I
have undertaken new methods of order and economy of which I
have great hopes."

She was sure the Emperor would be pleased. He was still in

Germany and had written to her "as in the old days." I shall soon
be with you. Keep well and let me find you plump and fresh."

Josephine must have smiled with pleasure at reading this and
begun to hope that she would remain empress.

"Is it daylight in the Empress's room?"

In other words, are Her Majesty's shutters open? Such was the
question that was asked through the palace at eight each morning.

Sometimes, with a knowing smile, it was announced that the
Empress had spent the night with the Emperor. This was learned
through Constant, who on going to wake his master between seven
and eight had found Josephine in bed with her husband.

"Are you getting up already?" she had asked. "Stay a bit longer."
He pretended to be surprised. "Aren't you asleep?"

"Then," the valet related, "he would roll her up in the blanket,
patting her cheeks and shoulders, laughing and kissing her."

He would leave her laughing happily in her "Napoleon bonnet" or
"Bavarian fichu." Then she would return to her bedroom.

Her women came in, bringing an infusion or some lemonade,
which she would drink in bed. Soon, after the entrance of her pet
dog, now a black Pomeranian from Vienna, the long business of the
toilette began. The senior women, Mme. de Saint-Hilaire, in service
since August, 1804, and Mme. Bassan were always there but did not
form part of Josephine's "inner circle," any more than the four
dames d'annonce. Their task consisted of announcing to the
Empress the arrival of the Emperor or of a palace official, or
perhaps of a chamberlain with the right of entry into his sovereign's
apartments.

Josephine's only confidants and true "servants" were: the mistress
of the wardrobe, Mme. Mallet, and the four women of the wardrobe: Mme. Charles, former lady's maid to Princess Adélaïde
d'Orléans and then to Hortense, Mlle. Aubert, who dealt with the
linen, Mlle. d'Avrillon, who first worked for Mlle. Tascher, and
finally Mme. Fourneau. There was also the Negress Malvina, who
busied herself with everything and nothing. This little world re-
volved round Josephine at her toilette—a toilette which, after her
daily bath, went on for nearly three hours. As can be seen from the
bills kept at Malmaison, her dressing tables and shelves held pots of

creams and pomades, and crystal bottles containing sweet-smelling Portugal, Naples or Cologne water, orange-flower water, double cassis and elixir of balsam.

Josephine's table also held a great many rouges for her cheeks. Following the demands of fashion, she used an immense quantity— 3,348 francs 10 centimes' worth for the year 1808 being the bills for only two perfumers out of four. In 1809 the Empress's expenses for rouge were even higher, 3,599 francs 72 centimes being paid to Mlle. Martin and Mme. Chaumeton, not to mention the two other suppliers, Gervais-Chardin and the Widow Farjeon.

Napoleon liked this fashion. One evening he pleasantly commanded a lady: "Go and put on some rouge, madame, you look like a corpse."

There was not only rouge, there was white paste as well—a white paste used to efface wrinkles.

A German, Tobias Kving, who called himself a physician-chiropodist, came every two weeks, at a salary of 1,200 francs a year, to look after Josephine's feet. He begged the Empress so insistently to be allowed to carry out his task in an embroidered coat and with a sword at his side that she finally consented.

Then the dressing began. First, the embroidered vest. At the beginning of 1809 she owned 399 of them, not counting those in the laundry. She changed several times a day, for the notebook of her laundrywoman, Mme. Barbin, for the week from March 25 to April 1 showed 18 vests, one "for the bath." She changed handkerchiefs even more frequently according to the *Mémoire de samagestée l'imperatrisse raine*, which mentions 87 handkerchiefs sent to the laundry on January 9 and 117 on the 18th.

Now came the stockings, new stockings naturally, which held up of themselves without garters. There were 158 white or pink pairs piled up in her drawers. Though she changed her vest three times a day, she did not wear knickers. She had only two pairs for riding in, and since the coronation she no longer rode. She had innumerable corsets and petticoats.

Next she had to choose a dress, which often she would wear only once. She would be shown several placed in large baskets. In January, 1809, the count was 676 dresses made of heavy cloth, not to mention others of cambric or muslin. White predominated, but there were also "budding green," purple, orange velvets, blue corded silk, multicolored or embroidered satins, "striped ribbed silks with cashmere style flowers," true cashmeres of every design— 33 of them—dresses of lace and point d'Angleterre, Cossack or Polish jackets, overcoats of dark-green velvet and of white satin edged with sable.

Around Josephine, Mme. de La Rouchefoucauld, M. de Ballouhey, the treasurer in charge of private expenses, and the lady of the wardrobe moved a whole world of milliners, lacemakers, fine laundresses, laundresses for body linen, perfumers, stocking makers, cleaners, shoemakers, dressmakers for corsets or gowns, menders and embroiderers—a whole world proposing new purchases, delivering them without orders, sending bills, dunning, protesting, accepting a discount and dunning once more.

Twice a year Josephine would visit what she called her "tiring room." She would then inspect her "treasures" and divide among her women the many items to be scrapped, some of which had never been worn. In 1809 she discarded 441 of the 676 listed dresses. One day Mlle. d'Avrillon fell heir in this fashion to a completely new bonnet of "black silk lace ornamented with very pretty roses." When Josephine saw her lady's maid wearing this new headdress, she asked her where she had bought it. Mlle. d'Avrillon explained laughingly how it had come into her possession.

"It was made by Mlle. Guérin."

"I think it's charming. Get Mlle. Guérin here, I want her to see it on you so that she can make one for me just like it."

For shoes she had almost too much choice. In 1809 alone she ordered 524 pairs, and she had 265 left over from the year before which she had not worn, and probably never would wear.

Her hair was dressed by Herbault, who entered wearing a sword, or else by the amazing coiffeur-modiste Duplan, who had been the most fashionable hairdresser since the Directory, inventing ravishing coiffures of flowers—roses, jasmine, daisies—or "bears' ears," or curls in ringlets. For the evening he would skillfully weave pearls and diamonds into the hair.

For the mornings Josephine was shown other baskets containing hats and a few of her hundreds of shawls to match the dress she had chosen. She had a passion for shawls. "She made dresses of them," recounts Mme. de Rémusat, "covers for her bed, cushions for her dog. She always wore one all morning which she draped over her shoulders with a grace I have never seen in anyone else. Bonaparte, who thought the shawls covered her too much, would snatch them off and sometimes throw one in the fire, but then she would ask for another one. She bought all that were brought to her and at whatever price. I have seen some of hers that cost eight, ten and twelve thousand francs."

When she was dressed, Corvisart, the Emperor's doctor, would appear. Josephine always thought she had every illness. Apart from a few headaches she was as strong as an ox, which she had to be to stand the Emperor's way of life. Corvisart dealt with his noble patient by gravely ordering pills which were simply made of breadcrumbs.

She also had to choose a pair of white gloves. She ordered them six dozen at a time and in January, 1809, possessed 980 pairs.

Now she was ready. In the antechamber all kinds of tradespeople would be waiting. She had not the strength to send them away without buying something. Sometimes she would acquire a very expensive object "which was of no use to her, simply for the pleasure of buying." But what she bought was always attractive, for, as Mlle. d'Avrillon remarked, "no one had such exquisite taste as she." Of course Josephine was drawn by the English materials and muslins, all the more attractive as their sale was forbidden in France since the establishment of the blockade. She privately shrugged her shoulders on hearing her husband exclaim: "This craze for English muslins is all the more extraordinary since in France we have cambrics which could replace them and which make much prettier dresses. I shall always prefer this material because, when I was young, the first girl I was in love with had a dress of it."

In order to satisfy Napoleon when he asked where certain stuffs came from, she would reply: "This was made in Lyons. . . . This comes from the Saint-Quentin factories."

"Aha!" he would say, rubbing his hands, "this proves the superiority of our products over those of the *others*."

The "others" were the English.

But Josephine sometimes had the goods she wanted sent through Holland. One day—as we know from a report by Fouché—two bales that had been seized and were to be sold by public auction were reclaimed at the last minute "in the Empress's name." Naturally this made an unfortunate impression.

Another time the cases Josephine had ordered, which contained "English percale," had been stopped by the customs and the Emperor had them seized. Seeing that his wife was worried at having no news of her "orders," he said to her:

"Josephine, the greatest grief, of the greatest punishment, a husband can inflict on his wife is to lock up her hats, dresses and silks. I am willing to pardon you this time. I shall have some of the cases that have escaped destruction given back to you, for you must know that it is I who have placed an embargo on what you call your 'orders.'"

He gave them back to her on condition that she would not do it again—and yet he knew her very well!

At eleven o'clock Josephine, who had kept her habits of the Consulate, would lunch generally with seven or eight ladies. Sometimes, when the Emperor was away, a few men would also be invited. Her butler, Richard, served her, assisted by the two chief valets, a Mameluke and the apartment servants. For ten people: soup, four hors-d'oeuvre, two relevés, six entrées, two roasts, six entremets, six desserts. Of course they did not eat of every dish. Usually Josephine, who gave these meals "a quite special charm," would propose to her guests the dishes that were in front of her, for everything was placed on the table at once without any particular order. The dishes were kept hot by plate warmers containing spirits of wine or boiling water. "The Empress," relates one of the valets, "hands us what she has offered her guests and we hand it to the footman attending the person the dish is intended for." Each person had "his" footman, who served, changed the plates and the knives and forks, or brought slices of pâté, which were not placed on the table but on the sideboard. The plates were of silver or silver-gilt. Porcelain plates with a gold design did not appear until the dessert. In the center the monogram J.B. "indicates that these belong to the Empress." "On rising from the table," the valet tells us, "everyone turns round and advances one pace, like noncommissioned officers on parade when the order is given, and they are each offered a blue bowl, which contains another china bowl, all on a tray with a napkin and half a lemon. The china bowl contains water to rinse out the mouth; the blue bowl is used for washing the tips of the fingers."

Then Josephine would play a game of billiards or take up her embroidery. Between two and three o'clock, weather permitting, the

Empress would go for a drive with two or three of her ladies. An outrider preceded the carriage, the equerry on duty galloped at one side and the officer of the Guides at the other. A picket of cavalry followed the page who rode behind the carriage. They would go to the Bois de Boulogne or through Passy to Chaillot, which held some memories for Josephine.

On their return came the grande toilette, at which the Emperor was sometimes present. This was the moment he chose for informing "the household" of his decisions. For he concerned himself with even the smallest details. Josephine had great difficulty stopping Napoleon's orders for economy in laundry. He had decided that henceforth the ladies should be entitled to only one pair of sheets and two towels a month.

While her ladies dressed the Empress, he would amuse himself by patting her shoulders.

"Do stop, do stop, Bonaparte," she would vainly repeat.

"The Empress would force herself to laugh," Mlle. d'Avrillon recounted, "but more than once I have noticed tears in her eyes."

In spite of her facile tears, she was delightfully gay, which was what he most appreciated, particularly in the woman who was now "his partner." She replied sweetly when he gave his opinion on her makeup or on the dress she had chosen. Did he really, as was reported, one day throw his inkwell over a pink and silver dress Josephine was wearing because he did not like it?

She bore his rages with "unalterable gentleness." She always appeared serene and equable. Her "complaisance" could not be equaled, her lady's maid tells us. She was never angry in front of the tyrant the Emperor sometimes was and never yielded to a burst of temper.

"With me she is a woman without claws," said Napoleon.

Josephine remained unmoved when she saw her husband roughly overturn the dining table because, on raising the dish cover, he had found the very crépinettes of pheasant that had been offered to him a month before, and which he had then much enjoyed.

Her serenity and goodness had ended by softening Napoleon's imperious character. She would still intercede with her husband to reverse the order for a servant's dismissal.

"My dear," she would say with her "inimitable grace," "if you would pardon him you would give me pleasure." And he would yield at once.

In theory dinner was served at six, but if he had not come down for Josephine's toilette, Napoleon occasionally kept dinner waiting a long time. One evening he did not leave his study until eleven.

"I think it's rather late," he said to Josephine.

"Past eleven."

"I thought I had had dinner."

She had not dared to let him know and that evening twenty-three chickens had succeeded each other on the spit.

He always found the menu too lavish. He would say to his butler, "You can see you are making me eat too much. I do not like that. It disagrees with me. I want to be served only two dishes."

As he never paid any attention to food, he had no idea of what he was eating. As at his wife's meals, everything was set on the table at once—in the time-honored phrase, à l'ambigu—and he would sometimes start his meal with the sweet.

The cooks tried to arouse the Emperor's interest by giving their pastry the shape of Egyptian, Greek or Roman temples, and Napoleon could be seen devouring an Egyptian pyramid while Josephine picked at the base of the Aventine Hill. He did not pick at his food. He ate so quickly that he sometimes became indisposed. Josephine would then sit by him while the Emperor laid his head on her lap.

"Do you fell better?" she would ask. "Would you like to lie down a little? I shall stay by your bed."

After tea—Napoleon's was given to him with two silver-gilt spoons, one for tasting and one for himself—he would retire, barely saying good night. Josephine pursued her evening by playing backgammon with Beaumont, unless the Emperor sent for her, in which case she would hurry to join him while the guests awaited her return, struggling against sleep.

If those near to her are to be believed, she now had a kind of worship for him, and he was deeply touched by it. Whenever he managed to stop thinking of himself and the Empire—synonymous, incidentally—he was full of attentions for his wife, trying not to forget to come and say good night to her, sending Rustum, even in the middle of the night, to see how she was. Sometimes he would come down himself, which would really wake the Empress.

Some days, if there was gambling, the evening would be somewhat prolonged. Napoleon often won at vingt-et-un, while Josephine preferred la macédoine. She would preside over one table with her ladies while the men made their stakes standing.

Sometimes ceremony weighed heavily even on Josephine's seasoned shoulders—on the evenings when there were Imperial banquets. On the occasion of the grand dinners the silver-gilt ships and caskets were placed on the table, heavy pieces covered with figures, bas-reliefs, bees and stars which can still be seen at Malmaison. These legacies from the old regime had been presented at the time of the coronation by the city of Paris and in theory contained the two sovereigns' knives and forks and napkins, the seasonings, spices and the épreuves—pieces of unicorn's horn or serpent's tongue with which the dishes were "tried" for fear of poisoning. The "sampler," a little cup, also was kept in the ship and was intended for the cupbearer guinea pig who had to "sample" the drinks before the sovereigns. When the Emperor, the Empress and the sovereigns invited to this redoubtable ordeal had sat down, the spectators filed in and watched them eat. Behind each guest were three footmen, one pace apart, Captain Coignet has recounted. "The other footmen communicated with the carvers and passed the plates, without making more than a half turn to take them. When the plate came to the sovereign the first footman presented it and if the sovereign shook his head the plate disappeared and was replaced by another. If the head did not move, the footman placed the plate in front of his master."

Each time a sovereign wiped his mouth the napkin was changed and so by the end of the meal there was "a pile of napkins each used only once" behind them. As the captain remarks, "it may have been imposing, but it was not gay." And Josephine could not wait to regain her apartments.

At midnight she began a careful toilette, carried out with charm and coquetry. Sometimes the Emperor was present and was enraptured. He was to recall on St. Helena the delightful grace with which the Creole went to bed. He would have liked to have her painted in that array, and it may well be supposed that Josephine eschewed curlers and face packs.

To discover how the evenings were spent when the Emperor was away one follows Mme. de Chastenay's reports:

Hardly a week went by, during the winter, without my going to the Tuileries once or twice in the evening. This last winter, in particular,

I was very assiduous. Oddly enough, I usually found myself the only visitor, the whole company being composed of people on duty or in service. I would arrive and have to wait until an usher went to announce me. He came back and opened the door. The Empress was by the fire, playing whist with a lady and two of the men she particularly wished to distinguish. Cardinal Caprara was often her partner. The circle of seated ladies was more or less large. I would go and make my curtsy, then sit down and a lady on duty would politely do the honors. After a few minutes one of the ladies generally suggested gambling, so that the men could sit down. We never played anything, so it did not matter in the least whether one was good at it or not. At eleven it was announced that tea was served. The Empress rose and everyone with her. Then, passing in front of the circle, she would address an obliging word with perfect graciousness to each woman, and often to the men standing behind, all without stiffness or affectation. One replied, chatted almost, and then everyone went to the dining room, where the women took places near a beautiful supper of which the tea was the best thing. Coming back, the numbers varied, for a lot of people slipped away at teatime. The Empress sat down again at her table and played several games of patience by herself. Then the people nearest her would begin to talk and several men would take part. At the far end of the room various people would retire and the Empress herself rose when she thought proper and returned to her apartments. This moment of conversation was what often gave me most pleasure and as far as possible I always placed myself near the patience table after tea. A woman accustomed to the conversation of the most remarkable people, to the private society and the habitual confidence of a man of so many ideas, could not be an ordinary woman.

The Empress's household had been considerably enlarged. In 1805 there were appointed, besides five Italian ladies, Mme. Devaux, whom Josephine had known formerly, the beautiful Mme. de Montalivet, who, it was said, had been loved from afar by Second Lieutenant Bonaparte when in garrison at Valence. Mme. Marescot, another of Josephine's ladies, was married to a former comrade of Captain Bonaparte's at the siege of Toulon. But when General Marescot was implicated in the capitulation of Andujar his wife was obliged to resign. Two ladies from the old regime completed the new appointments: Mme. de Turenne, whose husband was to be faithful to Napoleon up to Waterloo, and Mme. de Bouillé, whose mother-in-law, a Creole from Martinique, was related to Josephine.

In September, 1805, Mme. de Canisy joined the little band of ladies. Dazzlingly beautiful—Mme. d'Abrantès compared her to a

Muse—she had been married at fourteen to an old uncle. She found consolation at Napoleon's Court in the person of Caulaincourt, whom she later married when she was free. In February, 1806, arrived Mme. Maret, a pretty and elegant bourgeoise, whose husband was made Duc de Bassano on August 15, 1809. Finally there were three great ladies: the Marquise de Mortemart, the Duchesse de Montmorency-Matignon, and the picturesque Mme. de Chevreuse, who had carroty hair, the first name of Hermesinde and the Duc de Luynes as father-in-law. She had at first declined her appointment but, being forced to accept, brought outstanding impertinence to the performance of her duties. This "ill-tempered creature," as Fouché called her in one of his reports, made fun of everyone and indulged in all kinds of absurdities. "Among others," Mme. de Boigne related, "I recall that one day when there was a great soirée at the Hôtel de Luynes she set places for M. de Talleyrand's party opposite a bust of Louis XVI set on a table and surrounded with candles and a lot of vases of lilies, forming a kind of altar. She took us to see this arrangement with all the pleasure of a schoolgirl. Although I was almost as definite in my opinions as she was, these tricks struck me as childish and dangerous and I told her so. 'What do you expect! The little wretch (which was what she always called the great Napoleon) victimizes me, so I revenge myself as I can.'"

Napoleon almost flirted with her to "overcome her aversion," but completely in vain. When Hermesinde was chosen as one of the staff of honor to receive the King and Queen of Spain at Fontainebleau, she refused, saying, "It's bad enough to be a slave without having to be a jailer!"

Since the coronation the masculine side of Josephine's household had been increased by the "Most Powerful Lord Comte de Béarn," who in 1805 had solicited a post as chamberlain at 12,000 francs. He was an important addition. Having married Pauline de Tourzel, he was the son-in-law of the last governess of Louis XVI's children, who had accompanied the royal family on the next to the last stages of their agony. Another acquisition was the Prince de Grave who, although he possessed nearly a dozen titles, felt the inexplicable need to add that of imperial count. The Comte de Montesquiou also, a descendant of Clovis and the Dukes of Aquitaine who became the Empress's chamberlain in 1807, was made a baron by

Napoleon's favor. His wife was one day to be the King of Rome's Maman Quiou. The new chamberlains also included M. de Saint-Simon-Courtomer, a certain Du Val, a mounted equerry, M. de Fouler and the ordinary equerries, Colonel de Corbineau, the commander of Berckeim who was from the old Alsatian nobility, and the "handsome equerry" d'Audenarde. To balance the appointments from the members of the aristocracy the post of first equerry held by the Comte d'Harville was given in 1806 to General Ordener, who had kidnaped the Duc d'Enghien and was a Lorrainer whose French was incomprehensible.

Naturally everyone in this little world, from the top to the bottom of the ladder, sought posts and preferments for their cousins or brothers-in-law. "Excessively kind," as Constant was to write, "sympathetic beyond all expression, generous to prodigality," Josephine was incapable of refusing. No one ever knocked at her door in vain. Alms, help, thousands of letters of recommendation ceaselessly left the Tuileries borne by Josephine's valets. She gave to members of the former nobility in particular: 3,600 francs a year to Mme. de Montmorin, 2,500 to Mme. Tascher, nun, 1,800 to Mme. d'Arenberg. Pensions of from 3,600 to 144 francs were received by Mmes. Maille-Brézé, Canillac, d'Agoult, Mmes. Polastron de La Tour, de Luynes, de Fontenelle, Mmes. D'Héricourt de Bligny, de Villars, de Beaujeu, d'Halluin, MM. de Chavigny, Bernard, Calonne, Montalet, etc. She sent help to Mme. de Pardailhan, widow of Mme. de Montespan's grandson, to Mme. de Guerchy, widow of the former ambassador to London, and even a sum to Mme. de Vaudey, her former rival. She bore no malice once the danger was past. It sufficed to have been born in Martinique or in "the islands" to receive assistance. Among the accounts of "the Emperor's good angel," as some called her, can also be found unexpected charities, such as the payment of a pension of 1,200 francs to Mme. Collot d'Herbois.

Gifts to painters, musicians, engravers and sculptors can often be noted. She liked and protected them. And of course there were sudden outbursts of generosity toward those who helped "repair the irreparable ravages of time": 12,000 francs to the hairdresser Duplan, 1,200 francs to her chiropodist, 12,000 to another hairdresser. There were also the sums to assist Mme. Gohier, Mme. de Saint-Ange or Josephine Tallien, her goddaughter.

From September 26, 1804, to December 31, 1809, she distributed in this way 923,803 francs 24 centimes—nearly five million present-day francs. This is a great deal. But are there many women who spend nearly a sixth of their income on charity? In five years Josephine had received from the Treasury, for her clothes, pensions and alms, 5,354,435 francs 44 centimes, more than 25,000,000 present-day francs. "As a result," sighed the Treasurer, "Her Majesty acquired the taste for being even more grand and generous than her means allowed." Undoubtedly if she had opened her purse less often she would not have had a perpetual deficit in her budget. With great injustice, and not very kindly, Napoleon was to say before her death:

"She would give. But would she have deprived herself of anything to give? No! Would she have made a sacrifice to help someone? That is real goodness. She gave, but she dug into someone else's purse."

Her dress allowance had been originally fixed at 360,000 francs a year and she had cleverly brought it up to 600,000 francs. Her heaviest expense was undoubtedly for her dresses—6,000,000 present-day francs in six years. Leroi, whom the Emperor called his wife's "rag merchant," was the principal creditor. For Josephine he was a real master, although this great, effeminate workman was only a hypocrite, a boaster and a rogue. But the Empress wanted to keep her coronation silhouette and Leroi took care to avoid innovations, although he called himself an "inventor," taking himself very seriously. He seemed to die a thousand deaths when he had to serve customers who did not come to him in a carriage. When his daughter was married he asked Josephine for one of the emblazoned court coaches. Unable to refuse anything, she agreed, but when Napoleon heard of the dressmaker's request he exploded:

"What does Leroi take me for? Let him go in a cab if he likes, but I don't intend his shopgirls to be driven around in my carriages!"

Josephine also spent enormous sums on jewelry. She had of course acquired some very beautiful jewels, necklaces or diadems, but she was not a Creole for nothing and, although the wonderful crown jewels were at her disposal, she often bought by the hundreds stones of little value, agates, carnelians, turquoises and even carved cherry stones, simply for the pleasure of looking at them, touching them and then forgetting them in a drawer.

As the accounts at Malmaison show, Josephine regularly ordered numerous rings and jewels of varying value which she took great pleasure in giving away. Toward the first of January each year her room looked like a shop.

At one time she became very fond of turquoises and cameos, as can be seen from a letter she wrote to Pierre Daru, the Crown Intendant, in 1807:

"I am sending you a letter from M. Denon. In the various places he has visited he has reserved a few objects for me, such as cameos and turquoises. The only value of the latter is to make pretty ornaments for women whom their color suits wonderfully. The Empress is no more exempt from coquetry than any other woman, but as the Emperor is her only object she can be forgiven."

She succumbed to every suggested purchase. "What do you expect," she said to Bourrienne one day, "is it my fault? They bring me beautiful things, show them, praise them. I buy them, I am not asked for money, and when payment is asked for I have none. Afterwards it comes to his ears and he gets angry."

She no longer had her profits from military supplies to spend on her whims and could live only by amassing debts, enormous, endless, phenomenal, astronomical debts, faced with which the Emperor exploded. What usually happened was more or less as in 1806. One day that year Napoleon said to Duroc, "those women have tears in their eyes, I am sure there are debts, try and find out what it's all about."

Duroc went down to Josephine. "Madame, the Emperor is convinced you are in debt. He wants to know how much."

Josephine burst into tears and confessed "that she owed 400,000 francs."

"Ah!" exclaimed Duroc. "The Emperor thought it was 800,000."

"No, I swear, but since you must know, it's 600,000 francs."

"You are quite sure it is not more?"

"Quite sure!"

"Well, I shall speak to him."

Returning to the Emperor, honest Duroc told him he had found Josephine bathed in tears. "She is in despair, sire."

"So she's crying! She realizes her crime! Good! But you'll see her debts are enormous. She is capable of owing a million."

"Oh, no, not a million, sire."

"Well how much, then?"

"Supposing it were 800,000 francs?"

"That would be no less scandalous . . . for wretched frills, for letting herself be robbed by a gang of rascals. I must dismiss certain tradesmen and forbid others ever to come to my home."

"But, sire, it is only 600,000 francs."

"Only, you say. You think it nothing. I don't like this game. All right, I'll talk to her."

He spoke to her while she was at table, leaning on the back of her chair.

"So you are in debt, madame?"

In reply Josephine, who knew exactly how to weep and its effect on men, began to sob.

"You owe a million," continued the Emperor.

"No, sire, I swear to you that I owe only 600,000 francs."

"Only, you say, do you think it's a trifle?"

Josephine, well knowing what she was about, sobbed harder. Disarmed, he said gently to her, "Now, then, Josephine, now, then, my little one, don't cry, cheer up."

And he paid. During five years of his reign he was to pay 3,200,000 francs.

The next year Josephine found herself at the edge of a new abyss. She owed nearly three million present-day francs. This time she did not dare speak to her husband. In great anxiety she asked advice of Comte Mollien, the Finance Minister, and Marescalchi, the Italian Foreign Minister in Paris, in whom she had great confidence. The latter was in almost daily communication with Eugene and if anyone could help Josephine it was her son. Marescalchi immediately wrote to Eugene to inform him that his mother owed 600,000 francs, to ask him to help and to tell him that Josephine undertook for her part to pay back 50,000 francs a year. But the creditors really could not wait twelve years. And then there was 6 percent interest on the sum. Perhaps a banker could be found in Milan to lend the Viceroy 600,000 francs.

At first Eugene was horrified and "deeply distressed" at learning his mother's situation, but he pulled himself together, studied the matter, made careful inquiries and replied that no one in Milan could lend such a sum. However, he wrote to Marescalchi, the Empress "is in a difficult situation and must be rescued from it."

And he proposed to advance 50,000 francs a year himself. As a guarantee he offered his word of honor "which will always be worth something in the eyes of honest people," and his possessions in Sologne, Santo Domingo, Martinique, France and Italy. At the end of his long letter Eugene wrote these words which show us his heart: "Nevertheless, I accept with pleasure anything that can honorably cover my mother's deficit and compromise only myself."

On hearing of her son's proposal Josephine was "moved to tears" and her heart overflowed with gratitude. She then confessed the whole truth to Marescalchi. She owed much more and the Minister wrote to the Viceroy: "The Empress's debts are in fact much greater and the total is given as 600,000 francs only on the supposition that there may be a reduction for ready cash." Marescalchi formed a plan: neither Josephine nor Eugene would be named in the transactions with the lenders. He alone would borrow in his own name 150,000 to 200,000 francs, which would enable the creditors to wait. For the rest, the annual payments by Josephine and Eugene would finally wipe out the remaining debt and the interest.

This was done, a least as regards the first payment of 200,000 francs. It would appear that Napoleon settled what remained of the terrifying debt at the time of the divorce.

At the beginning of 1809 the Empress had made good resolutions "of order and economy of which I have great hopes," as she cheerfully asserted. She appointed Mme. Hamelin to manage her budget. Mme. Hamelin—who had 75 dresses given to her for her trouble—decided that the monthly *maximum* for Leroi should be 7,000 francs. She informed him of this and he replied in terms that leave one gasping:

"I beg you, madame, to ask Her Majesty to permit me to present my humble respects and to beg her not to think, as she says, that I find her custom too small to be bothered with it. . . . At the same time I ask you in each letter you are kind enough to send me, to say a word on the health of Her Majesty. This word is the first need of the soul; so pray remember it. . . . You have received the small monthly maximum; I confess that, without your orders, I would not have continued to send things based on the limit Her Majesty imposed. You can see, madame, that it would be difficult to continue at 7,000 francs. We shall always be in arrears and, indeed, that would make great difficulties for me in keeping my books. I should wish then, madame, when I send you the total for the month, that the 7,000 francs should be entered as payment on account, so as not to bring confusion to the paper work."

And Leroi's bill for that year was 143,314 francs 10 centimes.

Now in a panic, Josephine decided to economize at all costs. Not knowing how, she assembled her household to ask advice and in her disarming way she ordered especially for this gathering, a "quite simple" toile gown.

18. The Sentence

During the evening of April 12, 1809, a courier sent by Berthier arrived at the Tuileries. The Austrians had occupied Munich and crossed the Inn River.

"It is war," the Emperor sighed.

Once more he would have to fight in pursuit of the peace that was to evade him until his defeat. And he decided to leave before dawn. At dinner, which was not served until nine, Josephine asked if she could go with him. He agreed; she would stay in Strasbourg.

On April 14 they passed quickly through Nancy, lunching at the Hôtel Impérial, where the guard of honor served them. They soon left and arrived next day in Strasbourg, having traveled 62½ stages in two days. While Josephine went to bed, exhausted, Napoleon crossed the Kehl Bridge.

"Sire, all is lost for us if Your Majesty does not act quickly," the King of Bavaria told him the next day.

"Set your mind at rest, you will shortly be in Munich."

He himself, as he told the King of Württemberg, was going to Vienna.

Josephine's apartments in Strasbourg had been redecorated since her last stay. The waiting room was in blue silk damask with white patterns, the drawing-room furniture was of white and gold wood, the curtains and chair material in "sea-green silk poult." Her bed-room, "in Florentine silk," looked like a purple and gold jewel case. At the corners of the Savonnerie carpet were four swans "bearing a garland of flowers and fruits."

Hardly had she settled in than Josephine heard with sorrow that Eugene had been forced to retreat from the Isonzo to Sacile, where Archduke John beat him on April 16, 1809. Fortunately he took his revenge on May 8 at the Piave and Josephine congratulated him, advising him to write often to Napoleon, "although the Emperor needs no one but himself and his success results from his genius, yet a knowledge of the movements of the army you command may be useful to him and, above all, to you, and in this case as in all others, even of a blunder, you must let him know."

On May 23 Stephanie hastened to Strasbourg followed by the whole Baden family, even the hereditary Grand Duke, who joined Josephine two days later. Catherine, who had been driven from the Westphalian states, took refuge with her sister-in-law and Hortense, too, came to her mother. Hortense was accompanied by her two children, the eldest, whom Napoleon had just named Grand Duke of Berg, and the future Napoleon III, born eighteen days prematurely in the April of the preceding year—a fact which probably disturbed Louis. For her grandchildren Josephine ordered a carriage with four horses and five figures of painted wood, a "large wooden theatre," a box of doll's furniture, and a large box containing a whole army of lead soldiers.

Whenever she was apart from Louis Hortense revived. Napoleon had sent his brother this reprimand: "Your quarrels with the Queen are reaching the public. You control a young woman as one would control a regiment. You have the best and most virtuous wife and you are making her unhappy."

Louis rushed to his wife. "Have you been complaining? Have you slandered me? Now the Emperor is interfering in our marriage."

"I have never said a word!"

"Now, then, admit you have deceived me. I want to know the truth and I will know it. When and with whom? Useless to deny it, or to trick me, I have proofs and I shall show them."

"How can you show me proofs of what does not exist?"

Hortense settled in Baden, where she found the air better than in Strasbourg, but she received a stern letter from Napoleon. The Queen, who had left the territory of the Empire without permission, must return to Strasbourg with her children.

Although she made excursions to Mutzig, to the Orangerie Joséphine or the botanical gardens, the Empress was anxious. She had learned that the Emperor had been wounded at Ratisbon. He tried in vain to reassure her. "The ball that touched me did not wound me," he wrote to her, "it barely grazed the Achilles tendon." On May 9 he wrote to her again: "My dear, I write to you from Saint-Polten. Tomorrow I shall be before Vienna, which will be a month to the day since the Austrians crossed the Inn and violated the peace. . . . My health is good, the weather is superb and the soldiers very cheerful. There is wine here." He was at Schönbrunn on May 10 and the Austrian capital capitulated on the 13th, but Josephine was a prey to dark forebodings.

In fact, the battle of Aspern-Essling on May 21 had not been a victory and on May 22, after Lannes had been mortally wounded, the army had had to withdraw to the island of Lobau. Without Messéna the day would have ended in catastrophe. Josephine was so pessimistic that she could not conceal her anxiety from Metternich, who was passing through Strasbourg as a prisoner to be exchanged with the French ambassador. "I found her keenly preoccupied with the possible results of the event in question," he wrote. "She informed me of what she had learned and I had no further doubt as to the importance of the defeat. The details were so precise and positive that Josephine did not doubt that on my arrival in Vienna I should find negotiations under way. The Empress even considered it possible that I might meet Napoleon on his way back to France."

Did she no longer believe in him? Lannes was dying. The Duchesse de Montebello passed through Strasbourg but refused to stop and it was Josephine who visited her at the inn. Was this the end of the epic? She felt so upset that she decided to take the waters at Plombières. "I thoroughly approve of this journey," Napoleon replied from Schönbrunn, and he ended, "Good-by, my dear, you know my feelings for Josephine, they are unchanging. Ever yours."

Was she deceived? Did she know that on arriving at Schönbrunn Napoleon, more and more in love with Marie Walewska, had summoned his "Polish wife" to join him? Did she know that her rival had left the Rue Chantereine (she lived quite near Josephine's beloved "folly") to be with the Emperor? He had lodged her near Schönbrunn in a small house he had rented for this purpose.

On July 10 Josephine was awakened by one of Napoleon's pages, Ferdinand de Lariboisière. The young man persisted in holding his hat "closely pressed behind him." He had been galloping for three days and the seat was out of his breeches. Staggering with fatigue and sleep—at the relays "he was lifted with his saddle and placed on another horse"—he presented to Josephine a letter from the Emperor announcing the victory of Wagram. "The enemy army is fleeing in disorder and everything is going according to my wishes. . . . A ball touched Bessières in the fleshy part of the thigh, the wound is very slight. Lasalle was killed. My losses are rather heavy, but the victory is decisive and complete. We have more than 100 guns, 12 flags, many prisoners. I am sunburnt. Good-by, my dear, I embrace you."

Full of happiness, Josephine thanked the young page, handing him a ring with a fine diamond, the petit Rosé.

Two days after the victory Napoleon sent Josephine more details from Wolkersdorf. "Everything is going as I wish it, my dear. My enemies are defeated, beaten, utterly routed. They were very numerous and I have crushed them. My health is good today. Yesterday I was a little unwell from an excess of bile as a result of so much fatigue, but it does me a lot of good. Good-by, my dear, I am very well."

On arriving at Plombières Josephine found a deputation from Gérardmer who praised her in dialect, praises of which she can undoubtedly have understood only the word "madame," which occurred twice in eight stanzas.

During this stay at Plombières, which was to be her last, Josephine certainly had as many people to serve her, but she shunned society. She lived retired with Hortense and Stephanie, who had joined her. She spoiled her grandsons and had more toys sent from Strasbourg for them: soldiers of cardboard and painted wood, carriages of all kinds to drag over the floor, and an enormous warship on wheels.

She received visits from Molé and from the elderly, old-fashioned Marquis Stanislas de Boufflers, who tried to make her laugh by telling her risqué stories "from the old times."

As her accounts show, Josephine continued to be very generous. To every page who brought her a letter from the Emperor she gave diamonds worth 1,200 to 4,000 francs. When she stopped at a farm, if only to drink a glass of milk, she made a present. If she found peasants celebrating their golden wedding she gave them a watch and snuffbox. If she met a poor man, a prisoner or a cripple, there was a shower of gold napoleons. For some reason, although it hardly seems like her, she had a store of rosaries which she gave old people. She always had a large reserve of snuffboxes for sub-prefects, postmasters and escort commanders. One day during this last cure she discarded 37 dresses and divided them among her lady's maids.

On August 16 she passed through Nancy on her way back to Paris. The authorities came forward, naturally, and "Her Majesty deigned to greet them and honor with her salutation the crowd that had come to meet her." She invited the commander of the guard of honor to dinner, but appeared worried and did not smile.

When she passed through Saint-Aubin the postmaster's daughter was being married. The marriage contract was brought to Josephine in her carriage and she signed it. At seven in the evening a 21-gun salute marked her arrival in Bar-le-Duc. She dined with Marshal Oudinot, with whom she stayed that night, and left next day for Malmaison.

Napoleon was writing her affectionate letters. "I have your letter from Malmaison. I have been informed that you are plump, fresh and very well. I assure you that Vienna is not an amusing city. I very much wish I was back in Paris."

On August 31 he teased her. "I have had no letter from you for several days. The pleasures of Malmaison, the beautiful hothouses, the beautiful gardens all cause the absent to be forgotten. That is the rule, they say, with all of you. Everyone talks of your good health, but I have no confirmation of this."

Hortense arrived at Malmaison at the beginning of October. As

she wrote later, she found her mother "in despair at the Emperor's
liaison with the young Polish woman." Josephine now knew that
Marie Walewska had joined Napoleon at Schönbrunn. But she did
not yet know the terrible news: one day in September Marie had
told the Emperor she was expecting a child. If all went well it
would be born at the beginning of May, 1810. Napoleon was full of
joy. Now he could really exclaim that it was Josephine who was
sterile. She had made him believe that it was himself. And he had
almost become resigned to it.

Perhaps this was the price he had to pay for his genius, and
perhaps the lack of an heir was the ransom of his fame. Little Léon's
birth to Mlle. Dénuelle had permitted him to hope. But Mlle.
Dénuelle had also, it was asserted, bestowed her favors on Murat,
and sometimes Napoleon was in doubt. Although the gay, flirtatious
Lyonnaise had declared that the girl to whom she had given birth
on November 11, 1806, was also his, Napoleon had been only half
convinced.

This time he was utterly certain and there was no possibility of
doubt. His "Polish wife" could not be suspected. He could father a
child. He could forge the first link in his dynasty. No need now to
make Eugene or one of his nephews his successor. The heir to his
vast empire would be his own son. And that son must come quickly.
He was needed in order to attain the peace that had been evading
him for so many years. As Fouché had said, two years before: "The
English are encouraged in their attacks on the Emperor, as in their
refusal to make peace, by the sole thought that, being without
children and consequently without a successor, on his death the
Emperor will bring down the whole government with him. And his
death was possible at any time."

On October 12, when he was holding a review at Schönbrunn, a
young man approached him to hand him a petition. He had a
strange look and was arrested. His name was Staaps and he was the
son of a pastor of Erfurt. He was searched and found to carry a
knife. Napoleon decided to question him himself.

"What were you going to do with your knife?"

"Kill you."

"Are you mad, young man, or one of the Illuminati?"

"I am not mad. I do not know what Illuminati are."

"You are ill then?"

"I am not ill, my health is good."

"Why did you want to kill me?"

"Because you are the cause of my country's unhappiness."

"Have I done you some harm?"

"The same as to all Germans."

"Who sent you? Who urged you to this crime?"

"No one. It was the inner conviction that by killing you I should render the greatest service to my country and to Europe that placed weapons in my hand."

Napoleon let this "little wretch," as he called him, be shot, a "little wretch" who cared nothing for Plutarch and was not even "a Brutus." Other motives—more serious ones—had impelled him to act. Napoleon had brought kings and emperors to their knees, he had annexed part of Croatia or Carinthia to France, but he had not conquered the people, who carried on the war with knives in their hands.

In these national uprisings the Emperor did not see a presage of the future fall of the God. He thought of only one thing: this abortive attack showed that he was at the mercy of the first madman, both he and his gigantic empire. He had to have an heir, and, therefore, sacrifice Josephine.

As he drove toward France on October 15 he thought only of his divorce and future marriage. Caulaincourt must find out as quickly as possible from St. Petersburg whether Grand Duchess Anna, the Tsar's sister, who was nearly sixteen, would be able to make him a father. For it would be of no use to repudiate a sterile wife in order to marry an adolescent incapable of being a mother.

"Start from the principle that what is needed are children," he had Champagny write to Caulaincourt. As he himself was to exclaim inelegantly, "I am marrying a womb!"

He had no doubts as to the Tsar's agreement to give him this "womb." He had let it be known, just before leaving Vienna, that he agreed "that the words Poland and Polish should disappear not only from all transactions but even from history." This should appease Alexander, who felt ill at the mere word "Polish." Poor Marie, who had given herself to Napoleon only through love of her country and in the hope that Poland would not be erased from the map!

Matters must be settled briskly. He had to have a son, and he had to live, too. If he were to die it could not be his brothers who should succeed him or govern during his heir's possible minority. Joseph now considered himself "His Catholic Majesty." Louis had written without a smile that he now saw "nothing but Holland." Jerome, that comic king, took his role seriously, except on the battlefield, where he paraded like a "satrap," as the Emperor had told him after Wagram.

The clan was so obstinate and so blind in their hatred for "the Beauharnais woman"—that "worthless woman," as Mme. Mère called her—that they had never stopped doing everything to have him repudiate her. They did not realize that if the Emperor were to have a son he would not turn to the "princes" and "princesses" to find a possible successor. Perhaps they too imagined that the sterility was not only on Josephine's side. In the autumn of 1809, as in 1807, 1804, before the coronation or in 1799 on her return from Egypt, the unhappy woman could say, "They will be content only when they have driven me from the throne of France. They are implacable toward me."

While she was awaiting the Emperor's return at Malmaison she was often seen to have tears in her eyes. Sometimes she grew pale or shivered.

"It is very cold," she would murmur, gathering her shawl around her.

It was her heart that was cold. One day, when she could bear it no longer, she took Laure d'Abrantès aside and spoke to her "with sorrow."

"Mme. Junot, you know they all want to destroy me. Tell me what you know about me."

Laure knew nothing, or rather wished to say nothing. Of course everyone was talking about the divorce, "and talking as openly as was possible during the reign of Napoleon of matters concerning his private life."

Josephine almost implored an answer. "Tell me, I beg you, everything you have heard about me. I ask it as a favor."

She continued to speak, to show her heart. In spite of the heat in the greenhouse, her hands were cold and her lips trembled as she resumed, pitifully: "Mme. Junot, remember what I am telling you today, here in this little greenhouse, in this place which is a heaven and will perhaps soon be a hell for me, remember that this separation will kill me."

And, thinking of her terrible sisters-in-law and of Mme. Mère, she concluded, "Well, they will have killed me."

At that moment Junot's daughter, little Josephine, ran up to show the flowers she had been picking. The Empress took her god-daughter in her arms, lifted her up and hugged her so hard, almost frantically, that the little girl was frightened. She looked at her godmother's eyes, saw them misted with tears and flung her arms round her neck.

"I don't want you to cry."

"Ah! if you knew what I suffered every time one of you brought her child to me," Josephine told Laure. "My God! I, who have never felt envious, felt it as a dreadful poison when I saw lovely children. I, being afflicted with sterility, will be shamefully driven from the bed of the man who gave me the crown. And yet, as God is my witness, I love him more than my life, and much more than that throne."

The unhappy woman said this so often that she ended by believing it. Undoubtedly she now loved him, now that it was too late.

She was very happy whenever she received a letter written in his old style. Perhaps he was ashamed of the decision he had reached, or perhaps he wanted to lull her suspicions by pretending to be jealous himself.

On October 21 he wrote announcing his imminent return. "I look forward to seeing you and I await that moment impatiently." He would be in Fontainebleau without doubt on October 26 or 27.

She set out late in the morning of October 26 and learned, on passing through Saint-Cloud, that the Emperor had arrived in Fontainebleau at nine that morning. Her heart beat and she was full of foreboding.

At the same time Napoleon was receiving Cambacérès. "Why has public opinion been alarmed by my absence?" he asked him. "Why have they exaggerated the dangers I have been in? Is it thought that my death would be the signal for a revolution?"

"Sire," replied the Archchancellor, "it is natural that the nation should be anxious about the dangers threatening its sovereign. Although the succession is laid down by Imperial decrees, as long as there is no direct successor the country will never have any confidence about its future."

Cambacérès had no need to be anxious. The Emperor was resolved and had decided on a divorce. It was urgently necessary to establish a hereditary empire. Europe was tamed. Austria, weakened, had become a second-class power and agreed to apply the blockade. At that very moment French mines were blowing up the fortresses of Vienna and the Emperor Francis could see the ruins from his windows. England, which had been defeated at Walcheren, would be beaten. Rome would become a mere French province. "He appeared to be walking in the midst of his glory," Cambacérès was to say.

The Archchancellor immediately put forward some reservations. The French loved "good Josephine" and the repudiation would undoubtedly be unpopular. As the Emperor no doubt intended to marry a princess, this would give rise to more mistrust among the people. Napoleon swept these sentimental objections aside with a gesture. When he was brother-in-law to the Tsar or son-in-law to the Kaisers, the French, who loved glory, would give way. Cambacérès mentioned another obstacle. If the Emperor wished to be able to remarry and to espouse a princess at the altar, his clandestine marriage on the night before the coronation would undoubtedly be put forward as an impediment. Napoleon shrugged his shoulders. It was a forced marriage, celebrated in a hurry, without publication of banns and without witnesses. Cambacérès explained that only the Sovereign Pontiff could break a princely union. The Pope, who was now Napoleon's prisoner, would certainly refuse to be accommodating.

The Emperor was beginning to be annoyed. Since he could not appeal to His Holiness, he would do without him. The diocesan authorities of Paris would be considered competent to have jurisdiction in the matter. It was their business to judge the validity or invalidity of unions contracted before the Church. They would make no more difficulty than for a private individual. They had not done so when, after the Pope's refusal in 1806, they had been asked to dissolve the marriage of Jerome and Elisabeth Patterson.

Cambacérès promised to study the matter. In any case there was no hurry. First there must be the civil divorce and Josephine must be persuaded to make the request herself to withdraw and to sacrifice herself in order to assure the fate of the Empire.

They had just finished their conversation when a carriage stopped in the courtyard. Napoleon hurried out. It was not Josephine but the ladies of her staff.

"And the Empress?" he asked.

"Her Majesty will be here in a quarter of an hour."

"Good," he replied curtly, and retired to his library.

When she arrived at six it was dark night. This time Napoleon did not come to meet her, as was his custom. She was immediately distressed. Leaving her carriage, she proceeded to the ground floor and then to the library, where "His Majesty was working." Napoleon greeted her with the words, "Ah, there you are, madame. That is fortunate, for I was just about to leave for Saint-Cloud."

She wanted to apologize, but she felt the tears rise to her eyes and choke her throat. She was convinced now that he had made up his mind.

It was worse in her own apartments. The communicating door between them and her husband's had been walled up on the Emperor's orders, an order which had been sent from Schönbrunn. However, she hastened to dress and arrange her hair with cornflowers and silver ears of wheat.

"I was not long dressing, was I?" she said, entering the library, where Montalivet and Decrès were now with the Emperor.

He looked at her. She had taken great pains and her blue satin polonaise edged with swansdown suited her wonderfully. But he did not smile; he rose, gave her his hand to go into the dining room and said to the others, "I shall be with you in five minutes."

"But these gentlemen have probably not dined," she remarked, "since they have come from Paris."

"Ah, yes, that's true," he said.

But he had hardly sat down before he left her and went to his study, taking the two hungry Ministers with him.

She questioned Bausset.

"Tell me, if you know, why the private entrance between my apartments and the Emperor's has been closed."

The chamberlain did not know what to reply. Josephine appeared to be resigned, but could not prevent herself saying, "Believe me, there is some mystery behind this."

During the next three weeks—Napoleon and Josephine did not return to Paris until November 16—the Empress began her martyrdom. She forced herself to follow her husband out hunting. With eyes shut she was present at the slaughter of boars in which the Emperor took part with excessive fury, as though trying to escape from himself.

At night she was alone. Alone in her bedroom, now a symphony in violet and white satin, alone in her bed with its columns topped with white plumes. From her windows she could see the lighted windows of Pauline's apartments. The Emperor's sister gave parties to which Josephine was not invited, receptions to which the "little pagan" had asked women who were "very beautiful and very willing." There was even one to whom Napoleon made advances—a plump little fair-haired Italian with blue eyes, Mme. des Mathis. He drove about with her, his sister Pauline acting as chaperon. When he was with Josephine he became unjust, "tormenting" her ceaselessly, according to Hortense, who was a "witness to the continual tears" of the Empress and did not know how to cheer her mother.

The Queen of Holland was very mortified by the Emperor's treatment of his wife. Indeed, she often wished they were separated. "The existence of my family, the future of my children were as nothing to this humiliating attitude. My brother and I were the only people with anything to lose, I would tell myself. He would have to renounce the crown of Italy and my children that of France, to which they were the heirs. This sacrifice was worthy of us and my mother would be happier. Her career was over. At least her life need not be shortened. Her heart would have to detach itself from the one who made her suffer. We would have to forget all the greatness promised us and think only of our mother's peace."

The approaching drama was all the more painful since Jerome and Louis had been summoned and gave the impression of arriving for the kill. The Kings of Bavaria, of Württemberg, and of Saxony and the Grand Duke of Baden also were there to congratulate the conqueror of Austria. Josephine might well feel that they had come to witness the Emperor's "triumph," in which her departure would be the chief attraction.

There was a show every night—*Le Secret du Ménage* and *La Revanche* were given, as well as extracts from Italian operas—but the Emperor no longer left his seat to chat with her. He no longer leaned on the back of his wife's chair. He shunned those reddened eyes. And the Court imitated its master, barely paying the Empress the honors due to her. They seemed to consider her as merely a temporary sovereign.

On November 16 the Court set out for Paris, but Josephine and the Emperor did not travel together. He was on horseback and she, sighing, in her coach.

For two weeks after the return to the Tuileries everyone held his breath. Josephine did not cease weeping and he, who seldom took pity on anyone, was disarmed by those eyes constantly bathed in tears, that sorrowing, imploring look. He still did not dare take the last step.

On November 22 he dictated to Champagny a letter for Caulaincourt, telling him to ask the Tsar officially for the hand of Grand Duchess Anna for the Emperor of the French. On November 27 he wrote to Eugene to leave Milan and hurry back to Paris. Then for three further days he hesitated.

On the evening of Thursday, November 30, dinner was dreadfully silent. Josephine had wept all day and, to hide her red eyes, had put on a large white hat tied under her chin. He stole a glance at her occasionally, but did not speak. He mechanically tapped his glass with his knife. The officers on duty seemed rooted to the ground and did not dare move. The meal was served only for form's sake. All one heard, according to Cambacérès, was "the steady sound of plates being brought and taken away, alternating gloomily with the monotonous voices of the servants."

Suddenly he uttered a deep sigh and asked, "What is the weather like?"

But he did not seem to hear the reply. The semblance of a meal being over, he rose. She followed him with short steps, her handkerchief to her mouth to repress her rising sobs. The chef sent Josephine the Emperor's coffee on a tray carried by a page, but for the first time the Emperor took the cup himself, poured out the coffee, and melted the sugar, looking at the Empress all the time. She saw him, as though in a nightmare, drink, put down the cup and make a gesture to his officers. He wished to be alone with her.

Soon Constant and the chamberlain Bausset heard through the door Josephine's weak voice asking brokenly, "So, it's all over?"

He talked. . . . He was to say himself on St. Helena that he talked a great deal, trying to convince her. "I explained to her that there was no solidity to my dynasty if I did not have a child."

Of course, but he had nephews.

"My nephews cannot replace me; the nation would not understand it. A child born to the purple, on the throne, in the palace of the Tuileries is, for the nation and for the people, something quite different from the son of my brother."

He continued putting forward his point of view, while she tried not to weep.

"The good of the state and the consolidation of my dynasty require me to have children. . . . You have yours, but when I married you you were not capable of having any more. . . . It is not just that you should deprive me of what all men wish."

The tears rose to her eyes. He claimed to suffer more than she did, "since it is I who am giving pain!"

Now she no longer held back her tears.

"No, no, you shall not do it! You would not want to kill me!"

He continued to drug himself with words.

"Do not try to move me. I still love you, but there is no heart in politics, only head. I shall give you five million a year and a principality with Rome as capital."

Josephine sobbed. "No. . . . Please leave me in France. . . . In France. . . . Not far away from you."

He continued implacably: "Divorce is necessary. It will take place because I wish it. Now, there are two ways of doing it: with your consent or without. Choose! I think you have no reasons for hesitating."

In the anteroom Bausset and Constant heard a great cry. The door opened. The Emperor appeared, pale and trembling.

"Bausset, come here!"

The Chamberlain entered the room. Josephine was stretched on the carpet, seemingly hysterical. Then she apparently fainted.

"Bausset, are you strong enough to pick up the Empress and carry her to her rooms by the inner staircase?"

"I think so, sire."

"Good, let's go."

Bausset obeyed, raised Josephine with Napoleon's help and picked her up in his arms. The Emperor took a torch from the table

and opened the door of the drawing room, which led by a dark
corridor to the little staircase leading to Josephine's apartments.
Then he handed the light to the gardien du portefeuille, who always
stood by the little staircase.

"Jacquart, light the steps."

Napoleon wanted to help Bausset by taking Josephine's legs while
the chamberlain held her shoulders. But, being tangled up in his
sword, Bausset held Josephine rather too tightly to his chest and, to
his great astonishment, he heard the incorrigible Creole, who had
not fainted and for whom acting appeared to be second nature,
murmur softly, "You are holding me too tightly."

No doubt she thought a faint necessary to the scene. Once the
Empress had been handed over to her women, the Emperor took
Bausset into his study and strode up and down in great distress. He
uttered disconnected words with difficulty. The chamberlain heard
him exclaim in a disturbed, oppressed voice: "Ah! it's terrible . . .
terrible. The interests of France and my dynasty do violence to my
heart. Divorce is now my harsh duty. I pity her with all my heart. I
thought she had more strength of character. And I was not prepared
for her outburst of suffering."

The Emperor was to recall this dreadful evening when he was on
St. Helena.

"She was in despair and went to bed," he told Grand Marshal
Bertrand, "and partly from real grief, partly from play-acting [he
had not been deceived] behaved as though she were ill and made
scenes for three days. But my decision was based on reason, reasons
of state, and I was not to be moved. Josephine could not say she
had sacrificed her youth to me, as a woman generally can say to her
husband. She was a widow with children. I had married her when
she was a widow. She had not given me children and could not give
me any. Corvisart told me that she had not menstruated since my
marriage and that she had deceived me on that point, that she was a
Creole and consequently had started early, that she had been in
prison, which had had its effect on her, and that I should therefore
make up my mind."

On that same day in 1820 he continued: "All the same, the
Empress had sometimes behaved badly to me. She used to say I
was *no good*, that I was impotent, which always makes a man look

ridiculous. She claimed that therefore the divorce would not lead to anything."

The next day Josephine's levee went off as usual. When the staff entered her bedroom her women found her pale and haggard. They had no suspicions and thought their mistress's doleful appearance was the result of a bad night after an indisposition the day before. When her toilette was finished she sent for Hortense. The young woman came hurrying and Josephine, no longer trying to hold back her tears announced that the die was cast.

"So much the better!" exclaimed Hortense. "We shall all go away and you will be more peaceful."

"But what will become of you, my children?"

"We shall go with you, my brother will think as I do and for the first time in our lives, far from the world with just our family, we shall know happiness."

Josephine grew calmer. With Hortense and Eugene near her the idea of divorce seemed more bearable.

So, probably the same morning, Napoleon found his wife "attractively dressed, as usual."

"I have made up my mind," she said. "I agree to a divorce."

In the evening the Emperor sent for Hortense. She went to his study determined to do anything rather than display the slightest weakness. Napoleon, thinking his stepdaughter was going to beg him to reverse his decision, greeted her curtly.

"You have seen your mother. She has spoken to you. My decision is made. It is irrevocable. All France wishes for the divorce and loudly demands it. I cannot resist its wishes. So nothing will make me change, neither tears nor prayers."

"You are the master and can do what you please, sire," replied Hortense, cold and calm. "No one will cross you. Since your happiness demands it, that is enough. We shall sacrifice ourselves to that end. Do not be surprised by my mother's tears. You should rather be surprised if, after a union lasting fifteen years, she shed none. But she will submit, I am convinced, and we shall all go away, taking with us the memory of your kindness."

"While I was speaking," Hortense said later, "his face and expression changed. I had barely finished when I saw tears flowing freely from his eyes."

"What!" he exclaimed. "Will you all leave me, abandon me? Do you no longer love me? If only my happiness were concerned I would sacrifice it for you, but it is the happiness of France. You should pity me rather for being forced to attain that happiness by giving up my dearest affections."

Now Hortense was weeping too. "Take courage, sire, we shall need it if we are no longer to be your children. We shall have it, I swear to you. By going away we shall know that we are no longer an obstacle to your plans and hopes."

In vain he tried to combat this idea, asserting that Josephine would always be "his best friend" and that he would never cease to regard Eugene as his son. The Queen could only repeat: "Sire, I owe myself to my mother. She will have need of me. We can no longer live near you. This sacrifice has to be made and we shall make it."

On December 5 Hortense left to meet her brother, who had been summoned by Chappe's semaphore, which on the Milan road worked as far as Lyons. The brother and sister met at Nemours. Eugene entered the Queen's carriage.

"Is the event that brings us together good or bad?"

These were his first words.

"Bad."

He immediately guessed everything.

"Is my mother brave?"

"Yes."

"Well, we shall all go away quietly to end our life more pleasantly than we began it, but why have married me to a princess? My poor wife will be the only one to be pitied. She was hoping for crowns for her children. She has been brought up to think highly of them. She thinks I have been summoned to be declared heir to that of France, but she will be brave. She loves me so tenderly and she is so perfect that she must know that one is never made unhappy by doing right."

The Emperor received Eugene on his arrival at the Tuileries; then, after a preliminary conversation, went down with him to Josephine's room, where Hortense was. All four had tears in their eyes. Napoleon agreed, not without sorrow, to the loss of his wife, but wanted to keep those he had always considered his children near him. Like Hortense, Eugene thought this impossible.

"We should be in a false position. My mother might end by being an embarrassment to you. People would allow themselves to attack our family, which they would consider repudiated. The simplest actions would look like concerted plans. Your very enemies would harm us by pretending to be our friends and would arouse unjust suspicions about us in your mind. It is better to leave everything. Show us a place where, far from the Court and its intrigues, we can help our mother bear her misfortune."

The Emperor then found an argument to overcome their resistance.

"Eugene, if I have ever been able to be useful to your life, if I have ever been a father to you, do not abandon me. I need you. Your sister cannot leave me. She owes herself to her children, my own nephews. Your mother does not wish it. With all your exaggerated ideas you would cause her unhappiness. I will say more, you must think of posterity. Remain, if you do not wish it to be said: the Empress was sent away, abandoned, perhaps she deserved it. Is not her role fine enough, if she is still near me and keeps her rank and dignities, to prove that it is a purely political separation which she herself wished, and to give her new claims to the esteem, respect and love of a nation for which she has sacrificed herself?"

Eugene and Hortense agreed to remain, he as Viceroy of Italy, she as Queen of Holland—at least for the moment, for poor Hortense, constantly tortured by her husband, guessed that for her, too, separation was to come, although for quite different reasons. Louis, who had come to Paris on December 1 to witness the carrying out of the sentence on "the Beauharnais woman," had gone to live not in the Rue Cerutti, to Hortense's great joy, but with Mme. Letizia. This enabled the Queen to stay close to her mother.

But Josephine's martyrdom was prolonged until December 15.

Two days after the terrible evening on which her husband had finally plucked up courage to announce his decision, Josephine had to go to a Te Deum in Notre-Dame, one of the last ceremonies she was to attend as a sovereign. But in fact the Empress went to the basilica as a mere spectator.

It was dreadfully cold and Josephine, sitting in the gallery between the Queens of Spain and Westphalia, was trembling all over. It was not only the cold that made her shiver, but the memory of what had happened there five years before. In fact the Te Deum was being sung for the anniversary of the consecration and coronation. Five years earlier, under that same roof, she had received the holy oils from the hands of the Pope, five years earlier Napoleon had crowned her himself, had arranged her little crown, had "put it on and off" with such affection that she had felt the tears falling on her clasped hands, tears of joy, although now she felt she would never weep but from grief.

The next day, when the Hôtel de Ville gave a fete, it was worse. When she arrived, having been commanded to do so by the Emperor, she was greeted by a void. At the foot of the stairs were only Frochot and Junot—the latter in disobedience to his master— and no one else. Mme. Junot and all the ladies, who by custom should have greeted their sovereign, had disappeared. Josephine mechanically climbed the great staircase and when she sat on the throne—doubtless for the last time—her eyes filled with tears.

At last the Emperor arrived. She looked at him, guessing that it was to him she owed her solitude. When she rose to join him for his customary "review," Berthier, who was hurrying after the Emperor, tripped clumsily on the Empress's train and did not even apologize. In everyone's eyes she had already left. Josephine smiled, "as at a blunder," but her eyes were again full of tears and her lips trembled.

During the ball all the sovereigns took their places on the platform, according to court etiquette. The Emperor, the Kings, the Empress and the Queens were in full dress. Josephine sparkled with diamonds. The kings—of Saxony, Westphalia, Württemberg and Naples—hardly dared speak. One could feel that at the slightest word that might have been an allusion to the situation, Josephine, who sat next to the Emperor, would have burst into sobs.

But the fetes continued. Everyone pretended not to know anything. On December 10, a Sunday, the Legislative Body went to the Tuileries. In his speech the Emperor finally made a public announcement of his intentions.

"France," he said, "has need of a moderate, but strong monarchy. I and my family are ready to sacrifice our dearest affections to this."

The bridge was crossed.

On December 11 Berthier gave a party in honor of the foreign

monarchs. When Josephine arrived at the château everyone had
gone out hunting. Only an aide-de-camp waited to give her his arm
as she left her carriage. Seeing that her tears were about to fall, the
officer stammered a few compassionate words. She seized on them.

"Yes, whatever happens, you won't forget me? Whatever happens,
will you?"

She joined the hunt. Her eyes became redder and redder, but
everyone pretended to think it was from the cold. At dinner the
unhappy woman's eyelids were so swollen that Napoleon declared
with affected gaiety, "I intend for all to enjoy themselves. I want no
stiffness or ceremony. We are not at the Tuileries now."

Berthier came forward, smiling. He was determined everyone
should laugh. He had brought the actors from the Variétés Theatre
who were going to perform *Cadet-Roussel maître de déclamation,* a
play by Aude, played by Brunet, which had been running for a
year.

It was dreadful. All the guests were on tenterhooks. The chief
character repeatedly said that he wanted to get a divorce in order
"to have descendants."

"It is sad for a man like myself," he declared, "to have no one to
whom he can transmit the inheritance of his glory. Decidedly, I
shall divorce and marry a young woman by whom I shall have
children."

Increasingly horror-struck, the audience heard his words as he
changed his mind. "I know what my wife is like and I do not know
what the one I shall take will be like."

Berthier was the last to see the appalling blunder he had made in
choosing such a play. He alone, faithful to the Emperor's orders,
was heard to laugh loudly. Suddenly, observing the glares of his
master, he realized and began, as was his habit, to bite his nails
until the blood came.

Josephine "could scarcely contain herself."

"How long have they been performing this play in Paris?" the
Emperor asked Berthier.

"For a year, sire," he stammered.

"Has it been successful?"

"Immensely successful."

"It's annoying. If I had known I should have forbidden it. It

would seem that the censors make it their duty to commit nothing
but blunders."

The Imperial family had been summoned for nine in the evening
of December 14. It was pouring rain in Paris and blowing a gale.

In her bedroom, while her hair was being done, Josephine
glanced from time to time at the paper on which was written the
speech she was to give during the ceremony. But the words swam
before her eyes. She had modified the text, which had been prepared by Cambacérès and Maret, a cold, stiff speech which can still
be read in the National Archives. She refused to declare that she
performed the sacrifice asked of her "with bitterness." She wished to
show that she was "proud" of performing it for "the good of the
country."

The high officers of the Crown and the Princes of the Empire
were already crowding into the throne room, having received the
following invitation: "I have the honor to inform Your Excellency
that the Emperor wishes you to come today, Thursday, December
14, at nine in the evening, to the throne room in the Tuileries
Palace."

H.I.H. Mme. Mère was announced, Their Majesties the King and
Queen of Holland, Their Majesties the King and Queen of Westphalia, Their Majesties the King and Queen of Naples, H.M. the
Queen of Spain, H.I.H. Eugene, Viceroy of Italy, Prince and
Princess Borghese. Only Joseph, the King of Spain, had been unable
to attend. Everyone went into the large study. As they waited for
the condemned woman the Bonapartes rejoiced. As for the Beauharnais, they could hardly repress their tears.

Josephine entered shortly after Napoleon. She crossed the throne
room and entered the study. She was very simply dressed, in a
white gown, a ribbon in her hair, and no jewels. "She was pale but
calm" and leaned on the arm of Queen Hortense, who had gone to
meet her. Eugene was standing near the Emperor, his arms folded,
and trembling so violently that it seemed he might fall at any
moment.

Napoleon rose.

"You are gathered here to listen to the decision which the
Empress and I have been obliged to take. We are divorcing. God

knows how much such a resolve has cost my heart. But there is no sacrifice too great for my courage once I have been shown that it serves the good of France. I should add that, far from ever having had to complain of her, I have, on the contrary, nothing but praise for the affection and tenderness of my beloved wife. She has embellished fifteen years of my life. The memory of them will always be engraved on my heart. . . ."

Josephine began to read the document she had prepared herself.

"With the permission of our noble and dear husband . . . I have to declare that . . ."

But she stumbled over the next words about her sterility, sobs choked her and she held out the paper to Comte Regnault de Saint-Jean-d'Angély. He continued with the reading:

. . . I have to declare that, no longer retaining any hope of having children who would satisfy the needs of his policy and the interests of France, I am glad to give him the greatest proof of attachment and devotion that has ever been given on earth. Everything I have comes from his kindness: it is his hand which crowned me, and from the summit of that throne I have received only tokens of affection and love from the French people. I believe I am acknowledging all these feelings by consenting to the dissolution of a marriage which is now an obstacle to the good of France, which deprives it of the happiness of being one day governed by the descendants of the great man who was so obviously raised up by Providence to efface the evils of a terrible Revolution and re-establish the altar, the throne and the social order. But the dissolution of my marriage will make no change in the feelings of my heart. The Emperor will always find in me his best friend. I know how much this act, required by affairs of state, has wounded his heart, but both of us are proud of the sacrifice we are making for the good of the country."

The Emperor made no gesture. He remained as motionless as a statue, his eyes staring and almost bewildered. After a few empty words from Cambacérès came the signing.

The Emperor signed first, underlining his name with a thick stroke. Josephine wrote her first name just beneath the Imperial line, as though she wished to be protected by it. Letizia simply wrote "Madame," then the pen was handed to Louis. Afterward came Jerome, Murat, Eugene, whose complicated signature looked like a bank manager's, Julie, Hortense, Catherine, Jerome's wife, Pauline and finally Caroline. The signature of Saint-Jean-d'Angély,

who signed at the end after Cambacérès, is almost as long as that of
the Emperor.

It was over.

Napoleon had hardly gone to bed when Josephine entered, her
hair in disorder, her "face completely distorted." She came forward
hesitantly, then stopped, weeping "in a heart-rending way." Constant, who was present, saw her fall on the bed and put her arms
round the Emperor's neck. Great tears fell from his eyes too. He
pressed her in his arms, saying, "Come, come, my good Josephine,
be more reasonable. Now, then, be brave, be brave, I shall always
be your friend."

Choked with sobs, she did not reply. Suddenly Napoleon noticed
that Constant was still there.

"Go away, Constant."

He obeyed. An hour later he saw Josephine leave the room, still in
tears. Like an automaton she walked to her room, where she was to
spend her last night as Empress.

19. The Execution

On Friday, December 15, it was still raining. Two o'clock sounded from the Church of Saint-Roch. It was the time fixed for the departure for Malmaison.

In the courtyard servants were busy with wagons and carriages. The removal had an exotic note, thanks to the presence of the Empress's favorite parrot cackling in its cage and a pair of Alsatian dogs from Strasbourg accompanied by their pups. The Emperor was to hold an inspection and the crowds assembled in the Carrousel could see from a distance the departure and its preparations.

Josephine's last morning was agonizing. She watched her women do the packing. Hortense and Eugene were there.

Since morning Josephine had been wandering round her apartments, which had been redecorated at the beginning of the year and in which the future Empress would doubtless be installed as mistress. At this thought her tears fell faster and it was with sobs that she threw herself into the arms of Napoleon, who had come down with his secretary, Méneval, by the hidden staircase. He kissed her several times "very affectionately."

She fainted—and this time it was not simulated. When she revived, the Emperor had escaped through the ground-floor rooms.

Only Méneval, very embarrassed, as he might well be, remained with her. She asked him if the Emperor had already left for Trianon. Méneval thought so. (In fact he did not leave the Tuileries until two hours later.) Then he was to write to her when he arrived and write to her often. The secretary must speak to him of Josephine. And dear Méneval must say this, advise that. . . . She could not bring herself to leave Méneval, her last link with the Emperor. But she had to go, to pass through that door "beyond which she would be no one," no one but an honorary empress.

Veiled and carrying a handkerchief, accompanied by Hortense and leaning on the arm of Mme. d'Arberg, she crossed the drawing room full of ladies who could not repress their tears, then the hall where were gathered "all the people not kept away by their duties." A "concert of lamentations" was heard, according to Constant, and without a glance behind her Josephine went out into the courtyard, which was still flooded with rain.

It had not stopped raining when her coach arrived at Malmaison. She finally broke the silence she had kept since Paris to observe to Hortense, "If he is happy, I shall not repent."

Her eyes full of tears, she got out of the carriage. Here everything recalled the past, the happy days of the Consulate, those times when she had perhaps begun to be attached to "Bonaparte" and to forget that puppet Charles. All around her were the first signs of flight. The first almoner, one lady of honor and the wardrobe mistress left, and on the next day the Grand Marshal was obliged to call the recalcitrants to order, reminding them that until January 1 their duties to H.M. the Empress Josephine were to be carried out as usual. She had only two visits, from Queen Hortense, accompanied by her ladies, and from the Duchess of Ragusa, Mme. Marmont. The ladies spoke to their sovereign with pitying expressions. Nodding their heads, clutching their handkerchiefs, they seemed to have come to present condolences at a funeral. And Josephine's tears increased.

Augusta, as she had written on December 7 to Josephine, loved her husband "much more than herself," and had a true affection for Josephine. Though she had stayed in Milan, she could imagine the grief of her mother-in-law and her husband. "I think of your sad situation," she wrote to Eugene, "and although I am far away I can

see the joy on the faces of those who have done us too much harm."
When she wrote these lines she still believed that her husband
would have to give up his viceroyalty and, like a heroine of Cor-
neille, she wrote: "When we are removed from the list of the great
we shall be inscribed on that of the happy, will that not be better?
. . . Do not think I feel cast down. No, my Eugene, my courage
equals yours, and I want to prove to you that I am worthy to be
your wife."

Augusta did not imagine that, on the very day after Josephine's
departure for Malmaison, Napoleon had had the cruelty to ask
Eugene to explain to the Senators the reasons for the sénatus-
consulte which was required of them to dissolve the marriage.

At eleven in the morning of December 16, before the members of
the Senate in full costume, before the Kings of Westphalia and
Naples—Murat was still smiling—Eugene mounted the tribune
with beating heart.

You have just heard the draft of the sénatus-consulte which is submitted to your consideration. I feel, in these circumstances, that I should
make clear the feelings which animate my family. My mother and my
family owe everything to the Emperor. He has been a true father to the
Empress's children; in us he has always found the feelings of true children.

Aged forty and in the prime of life, founder of a dynasty, brought to
the throne by a succession of benefits to the people and prodigious feats
of all kinds, it is of the greatest importance for France that he grow old
surrounded by his direct descendants, who would be the guarantee of
that throne from which the country has already received so much good
and which alone should perpetuate his good fortune and glory.

Since it is established that the ties which unite the Emperor to my
mother cannot satisfy this requirement of policy and of the state, I shall
be the first to approve His Majesty's resolution. I join my wish to his, to
that of all France, that sons may be born to him who will be the protectors of our children.

My mother will be happy at the tribute her husband does not cease
to pay her on this great occasion. She will be happy at the testimony of
her own conscience. She will be glad to have fulfilled with courage and
dignity this duty she contracted to the people and to him on the very
day she was crowned at his noble hands. There is nothing left to desire
for her happiness and her glory, once we have noted the touching
regrets and witnessed the struggle, in the heart of a monarch accustomed
to sacrificing everything to the good of France, between his duty toward
the state and the feelings that attached him to his wife.

Everything in His Majesty's life thus bears the seal of his greatness. Great Charlemagne and several of our kings were separated from their wives, but none had so many and such powerful motives, none, in such serious circumstances, had this mark of feeling, I might even say of justice, which characterizes all the Emperor's actions. I rejoice that my post as Archchancellor of State, which gives me the right to sit among you, has enabled me to make plain my feelings. Our family will always be that of the Emperor, at least through attachment, devotion and love."

Then the Senate voted. The marriage was dissolved by 76 votes to 7, with 4 abstentions. The document set forth that "the Empress Josephine will retain the titles and rank of crowned Empress" and that her allowance would be "fixed at an annual income of two million francs from the State Treasury."

Eugene then went to Malmaison to inform his mother. She had been receiving visitors—a whole stream of them. A pale smile lit her face. So she was not forgotten. In fact, Napoleon had spent the day at Trianon asking, "Have you seen the Empress?" So, in order to pay court to the master, they went to see the exile. Seated under Girodet's picture, wearing a vast green hood that shaded her unhappy face, she tried to smile at each person who came to bow before her. But when she recognized a face from Consulate days her heart broke and she made no effort to repress her tears. Of course no member of the clan took the trouble. She was never to see her in-laws again, not even Jerome.

The cold night of December 16 drew on. Suddenly, at Trianon, Napoleon threw down his game of cards and called for a carriage.

"To Malmaison!"

It was a short visit. In spite of the cold they sat on a bench between showers and, although he embraced her on arriving, when he left he merely kissed her hand. On his return, at eight in the evening, he wrote a letter which Josephine was to read before going to bed: "My dear, today I found you weaker than you ought to be. You have shown some courage, you must find still more to sustain yourself. You must not give way to a harmful melancholy and above all you must take care of your health which is so precious to me. If you are attached to me and if you love me you must behave with strength and [make?] yourself happy. You cannot doubt my constant and tender friendship and you would greatly misunderstand my feelings for you if you supposed I could be happy if you are not happy, and content if you are not calm. Good-by, my dear, sleep well, consider that I wish it."

It was easy for him to talk. In spite of the Imperial wish we know from Mme. de Rémusat that Josephine "wept unceasingly and gave one pain to see her." Everything was gloomy and it was pouring rain. At Trianon Napoleon was bored. He was "in a filthy temper" and never stopped thinking of the absent woman. For the only time in his life as sovereign he did nothing for three days. Audiences, council sessions, correspondence—except to her—were suspended. His heart had got the upper hand. On top of everything the rain fell inexorably.

On Sunday, December 17, he supped with Christine de Mathis, the Piedmontese whom his attentive sister Pauline, who was staying at the Petit Trianon, had brought with her. He met her again the next evening, again with Pauline, who was trying to make him start a new chapter. He may have called his feelings for Mme. de Mathis "little friendship," but he took great pleasure in spending his nights with the fair, plump Piedmontese. He merely reproached her with having "no desire."

The Italian's dimpled body did not make him forget the exile and on December 19, before leaving to hunt on the plain of Satory, the Emperor sent Savary for news. It was not very good. Again he wrote to Josephine: "Savary tells me you are always crying. This is not right. I hope you have been able to go out today. I have sent you some game from my hunt. I shall come to see you when you tell me that you are sensible and that your courage has the upper hand. Good-by, my dear. I am sad today. I want to know you are content and to learn that you are recovering your balance. Sleep well."

But she did not close an eye and the next day had "a deplorable morning." Mme. de Rémusat wrote to her husband, who was at Trianon with the Emperor: "She receives visits which renew her grief and then every time something comes from the Emperor she gets into a terrible state." According to the lady in waiting, Napoleon simply had to be made to "moderate his expressions of regret" when he wrote to his ex-wife. Mme. de Rémusat looked after the Empress as well as she could, but Josephine was "gentle, suffering, affectionate, everything that pierces the heart." Undoubtedly "by being affectionate" the Emperor "made her worse," although "with all that," remarked the lady in waiting, "he does not say a word too much."

Taking advantage of a break in the weather, Mme. de Rémusat took the poor woman into the park to "try to tire her body and rest her mind." Josephine was compliant. "I spoke to her, questioned her . . . she yielded to everything, understood my intention and seemed to be grateful to me in the midst of her tears." An hour went by thus, then Mme. de Rémusat heard her murmur:

"Sometimes it seems as though I was dead and had only a kind of vague faculty for feeling that I no longer exist."

Mme. de Rémusat begged her husband to get the master to write to his ex-wife "so as to encourage her" and, above all, "not in the evening," since that gave her "awful and terrible" nights.

Eugene tried, in his turn, to reason with his mother, but quite in vain. And yet, as he had written to Augusta, he thought the Empress "would be happier in her new situation." And, quite sincerely, he had added, "And we as well."

On Friday, December 22, 1809, Cambacérès, seconded by the Minister of Public Worship, both much embarrassed, received four prelates, equally embarrassed at finding themselves there. The four priests were by way of being magistrates, members of the Diocesan Ecclesiastical Court of Paris, a tribunal judging cases of nullity in marriage, whom Napoleon, being one of their subjects, had asked to break his religious ties with Josephine.

Facing the Archchancellor and the Minister of Public Worship were the two Metropolitan and Diocesan ecclesiastical judges, the Bishop appointed by Napoleon to Liège, François Antoine Lejeas, and Canon Pierre Boilesve, and the two Metropolitan and Diocesan Promoters, Abbés Corpet and Henry Rudemare. It is from this last, former curate of Saint-Germain-l'Auxerrois and future vicar of Notre-Dame-des-Blancs-Manteaux, that we know what went on.

Having first given his credentials by declaring himself, by an article of the sénatus-consulte, "authorized to proceed to the proper quarters for carrying out His Majesty's wishes," Cambacérès opened fire in these words:

"The Emperor cannot hope for a child from the Empress Josephine. Yet he cannot, while founding a new dynasty, renounce the

hope of leaving an heir who may assure the peace, glory and
integrity of the Empire he has founded. He intends to remarry and
wishes to marry a Catholic, but prior to that his marriage with the
Empress Josephine must be annulled and my intention is to submit
it to the examination and decision of the Ecclesiastical Court."

Cambacérès' intention had been determined by a simple sentence
written by Metternich to the Austrian ambassador in Paris: "His
Majesty [the Emperor Francis] will never give his consent to a
marriage that does not conform to the precepts of our religion." This
sentence proved that in view of the Tsar's manifest unwillingness to
give his sister to the Emperor in marriage, Napoleon had chosen
"the Austrian marriage."

But only the Pope had authority to dissolve royal unions. When
Louis XII had wished to break his marriage to Jeanne de France—
alleging nonconsummation—he had approached Alexander VI.
Henri IV had acted in the same way in order to repudiate Queen
Marguerite and had turned to Clement VIII. So with one voice the
four prelates exclaimed: "This cause is one of those reserved, if not
de jure at least *de facto,* to the Sovereign Pontiff."

"I am not authorized to have recourse to Rome," replied the
Archchancellor coldly.

"There is no need to send to Rome for the Pope's decision,"
replied Abbé Rudemare. "His Holiness is at Savona."

The abbé was crossing swords with him. Everyone knew, indeed,
that if Pius VII was at Savona and not in Rome it was because
Napoleon had had him abducted by gendarmes and was holding
him prisoner. Undoubtedly there could be no question of asking
him to make a decision. The prisoner would refuse to do his jailer a
service. In diplomatic language Cambacérès merely answered without giving deitals.

"Nor am I instructed to deal with the Pope."

Then, without going further into the matter, he added: "In the
present circumstances that is impossible."

Suddenly Abbé Rudemare had an idea.

"Monseigneur, there is a commission here of cardinals, archbishops
and bishops assembled in connection with Church business."

"They do not form a tribunal," Cambacérès replied once more.
"The Ecclesiastical Court has been set up for dealing with this kind
of case."

"Yes, Prince, between private people, but the high dignity of the persons in question does not permit that Court to consider itself a competent tribunal."

"Why not?" Cambacérès exclaimed. "Is not His Majesty free, if he chooses, to present himself before a tribunal set up for his subjects and composed of his subjects? Who can contest his right?"

"He may do so," admitted Abbé Rudemare, "but this is so contrary to usage that we cannot take it on ourselves to consider ourselves as judges, unless this committee decides we are competent. Disposed as we are to do everything in our power to prove our devotion to His Majesty, we yet cannot refrain from doing all we can to safeguard our responsibility and to put our consciences at rest. In undertaking this affair we present a spectacle to the world, to angels and to men."

"But," replied Cambacérès, "we do not want this affair to become public and to have all the English newspapers getting hold of it. All the documents will be lodged in His Majesty's files and we ask you to keep it a profound secret."

Finally—it had to come—what grounds were the Emperor and Empress putting forward? To enlighten his questioners Cambacérès read the draft request: Napoleon was asking for the annulment of a marriage celebrated in the absence of the parish priest and of any witnesses.

"But does not all Paris know that the religious marriage was celebrated in proper form?" remarked one of the abbés.

Cambacérès then explained that "on Saturday, December 1, 1804, on the eve of the coronation, His Majesty, foreseeing what has now come about, never wished to agree to having his marriage blessed," but that "worn out by the Empress's importunities, he had told Cardinal Fesch to give them the nuptial blessing and that the Cardinal had given it to them in the Empress's bedroom, without witnesses and without the parish preist."

Stupefied, Abbé Rudemare asked to see the certificate of this casual ceremony.

"There is none," relied the Archchancellor.

"Do you have the Emperor's baptismal certificate?"

"I do not."

"But it is a document we are told to procure."

"I cannot procure it, but I have seen it," declared Cambacérès, who had doubtless seen nothing of the kind. And he added: "It seems to me that the word of a prince should be enough for you. We want this affair to be finished quickly and to have the tribunal's decision as soon as possible."

"Monseigneur," replied Abbé Rudemare, "this affair—even if it is decided that the tribunal is competent—must positively be examined and judged like that of any of His Majesty's subjects."

"Do you want to follow the formalities, then?" exclaimed the Archchancellor. "Everything will drag on. I have been a lawyer. Formalities kill a case."

"Sometimes, Monseigneur, but they are very useful in leading to a knowledge of the truth and we cannot evade them without our proceedings being rendered invalid. But there is no doubt that everything will be done with all the respect and deference due to the Imperial Majesty."

In short, the four priests insisted that the question of their competence should be submitted to the "superior knowledge" of a committee to be assembled at the Cardinal's. "Then," writes Abbé Rudemare in his *Narré,* "we separated."

One can imagine the amazement of the four priests as they returned to the archbishopric. The master of Europe wanted to make them believe that he had been constrained and forced to marry Josephine, that he had been "ravished," which were the reasons usually put forward by timid young girls.

Two days later, still without news, the abbé wrote to Cambacérès to explain the scruples of the Ecclesiastical Court, which feared to bring "under its jurisdiction the head of the state." According to him, "the majesty of the throne" seemed "irreconcilable" with the powers of a mere diocesan tribunal. The Cardinals present in Paris would have to be hastily brought together and asked three questions:

1. Was the Diocesan Ecclesiastical Court of Paris competent to pronounce on the validity of Their Majesties' marriage?

2. If it was, would it be justified in judging this case without fulfilling the formalities to which it was subject?

3. Finally, would it not be necessary to go through all the judicial stages?

On January 3, 1810, an archbishop and four bishops met under the presidency of Cardinal Maury, Archbishop of Montefiascone and Corneto, and Cardinal Caselli, Bishop of Parma. Unanimously and with "submission," the prelates declared "that lacking consent, as judicially proved before the competent tribunal, the marriage contracted between His Majesty the Emperor and King and Her Majesty the Empress Josephine was completely null." They then washed their hands of this ticklish affair by adding: "This case falls within the ordinary competence of the Diocesan Ecclesiastical Court."

The Court was forced to be content with these decisions "which said nothing," Rudemare sighed, "of the form of procedure to be followed." They first heard Cardinal Fesch, who related how he had clandestinely blessed Josephine and Napoleon, having first asked the Pope to allow him to "make use of dispensations." Not without embarrassment he revealed that on December 4, two days after the clandestine ceremony, Josephine had asked him for "a certificate of the administration of this nuptial blessing." After twenty-two days of wavering he had finally agreed to this demand and given the Empress the desired document:

"But," Fesch added cautiously to the investigators, "I was extremely surprised when, having told the Emperor what I had done, I was sternly reproached by him and he revealed that everything he had done had been merely with the aim of calming the Empress and yielding to circumstances. He declared that once he had founded an empire he could not renounce having direct descendants."

The investigators then turned to Berthier, Prince de Neuchâtel—"a goose I made into an eagle," Napoleon was to say—who, like a good courtier anxious to please his master, brought an accusation against the Emperor of having *knowingly* deceived Josephine and the Church by *deliberately* rendering Uncle Fesch's blessing invalid.

"We declare on our soul and conscience and under oath," he wrote, "that to our knowledge . . . at the time of the coronation Their Majesties received the nuptial blessing without this ceremony's being accompanied by the prescribed solemnities in the presence of the necessary witnesses; that this unusual procedure was followed simply by the express wish of the Emperor, who did not wish the said nuptial blessing to be registered; that we have several times been in a position to hear His Majesty say that he had not wished to bind himself and that he considered himself in no way tied by an act which did not have the prescribed marks or ceremonies."

Duroc could not refuse to make a similar declaration on behalf of his dear emperor. The former priest Talleyrand, fourth and last witness, knew better than Berthier and Duroc the worth of a declaration in this matter. However, he did not hesitate to say "that on several occasions His Majesty the Emperor said in our presence that the blessing he had let himself be given a few days before the coronation could not be an obstacle to what he foresaw he would have to do one day in the interests of the crown; that in consequence he did not consider himself otherwise bound by a ceremony which had not been preceded or accompanied by any of the substantial conditions of marriage laid down by canon law, such as the presence of his own parish priest and of the necessary witnesses." The former Bishop of Autun was quite aware that the presence of the parish priest, and even of witnesses, was unnecessary since Fesch had obtained from the supreme head of the Church all the dispensations "indispensable for fulfilling his duties as Grand Almoner."

By this time it was January 6. At noon on the 7th, a Sunday, a commissaire brought Abbé Rudemare a letter from Sieur Guieu, Mme. Mère's chief secretary and "with authority from H.S.H. the Prince Archchancellor." He warned the Promoter that his conclusions were expected the next day, January 8, at eleven, "threatening me," Abbé Rudemare related, "with His Majesty's anger if the judgment was not given on that day at the time mentioned."

The poor man worked all night, and was ready, but it was not until the Tuesday that the Court met. If the *Narré* is to be believed, Guieu "embroidered for half an hour or more on the Emperor's nonconsent, saying that he had never had any intention of making a contract . . ."

His conclusions—it could not be otherwise—declared:

1. That the marriage between Their Majesties must be regarded as null and invalidly contracted and null *quoad foedus* (as a contract) lacking the presence of his own priest and of the witnesses required by the Council of Trent and the rules . . .

In explanation of this opinion Rudemare launched out on some unfortunate hair-splitting. According to him, Cardinal Fesch "having asked only for the dispensations which were sometimes necessary for him to fulfill his duties as Grand Almoner, and *not having particularised or especially named the extraordinary and vicarial functions he was to exercise with regard to His Majesty,* was unable to receive and had not received either the dispensation as regards witnesses or the power to take the place of the parish priest."

So, according to the Promoter, Pius VII had not known what dispensation the Cardinal had been talking about, although he had just heard Josephine's admission. This was taking His Holiness for a fool. Moreover, if one was to believe Abbé Rudemare, so entangled in this unsatisfactory case, the Pope had been deceived, and deliberately deceived, by Cardinal Fesch.

It was now the turn of the Diocesan Official, Canon Pierre Boilesve. After underlining "the difficulty of resorting to the visible head of the Church, whose *de facto* province it has always been to hear and determine such extraordinary cases," the canon finally gave his judgment. According to him, Napoleon and Josephine were free from any contract, might marry again and might not "haunt and frequent each other without incurring canonical sanctions."

The Metropolitan Promoter, Abbé Corpet, then spoke. For his part he refused, "from respect for His Imperial and Royal Majesty," to consider the nonconsent of the husband and based his argument only on the absence of witnesses and parish priest, which were decisive causes of nullity.

Abbé Lejeas gave the final judgment, that of the Metropolitan Official. This was the most servile one. The appointed Bishop of Liège—he had not yet gone to his see and was never to be consecrated—found a new argument, perhaps indicated by Cambacérès and of a subtlety worthy of a Jesuit. According to him, "the civil contract of Their Majesties having been solemnly dissolved by the sénatus-consulte of December 16 last, and this dissolution having been dictated by motives of the highest importance which are necessarily invariable, it becomes henceforth impossible in this particular case to base the rehabilitation of the religious tie on a preceding civil contract which can no longer exist." Apart from this, no witnesses, no parish priest: no marriage. And he paid "homage to the faith and virtues" of Cardinal Fesch in these words:

"His eagerness to comply with the desires of Her Majesty the Empress, the hope, perhaps, of one day completing and perfecting his work, and finally that unexpected request from the Empress, must have overwhelmed him and prevented the reflections he would have made given a few moments more."

In short he attempted to prove that Pius VII had been deceived by Fesch and that Napoleon had deceived everyone—including Josephine. So, with little self-satisfaction, they had completed their work.

On opening *Le Moniteur* of January 14 Josephine could read that "the Diocesan tribunal of the Ecclesiastical Court of Paris" had "declared, by a judgment of 9th instant, the nullity, as regards the spiritual tie, of the marriage of His Majesty the Emperor Napoleon and Her Majesty the Empress Josephine" and that "the Metropolitan Ecclesiastical Court had "confirmed this judgment on the 12th of this month."

Meanwhile the Emperor's letters to Josephine had become less affectionate—perhaps on M. de Rémusat's advice. On December 23 he had merely announced, "I hope to see you tomorrow and find you cheerful and well-balanced." He did go to Malmaison as a visitor, taking care not to leave the drawing room or meet Josephine in her private apartments, as he had formerly done. The next day, being Christmas, Josephine went to Trianon with Hortense and the Emperor made them stay to dinner. As formerly, she presided at the meal opposite him. Nothing seemed changed. The officials and pages on duty remained standing during dinner, which was served with the customary speed, but in profound silence, and Josephine did not swallow one mouthful. "The Emperor," Hortense reported, "wiped his eyes two or three times without saying anything and we left immediately after dinner."

Napoleon returned to the Tuileries, but couriers, usually pages, constantly galloped between Malmaison and the Tuileries. Napoleon would question them on their return and if he heard that "the page this morning" had seen her cry, he would scold her. She must put a better face on it. To amuse her he got the sovereigns of Württemberg and Bavaria, then in Paris, to go to Malmaison, and Josephine again had the illusion of being the Empress.

At his levee the Emperor would often say, "Have you been to see the Empress Josephine?"

The courtiers would bow, embarrassed, not knowing what to

reply, and trying to give an affirmative or a negative flavor to the bow.

"Gentlemen, this won't do," Napoleon would then say. "You must visit the Empress Josephine."

Immediately "the road to Malmaison was covered with carriages. Mme. de Chastenay was one of the first to visit Malmaison:

The Empress was not in the drawing room to begin with and it was full. Finally the poor woman appeared. As usual she went to the first person in the circle, who was Mme. Clément de Ris. Josephine, holding back her tears, hesitated and could only stammer.

"Your Majesty seems to me to have got much fatter," said Mme. Clément de Ris.

At this unsuitable word a smile appeared on the afflicted woman's lips.

"I would not have thought so," she replied.

And she arrived in front of me already moved. I raised my eyes to hers. The tears with which they were reddened quickly affected me and I was at once in tears myself. Poor Josephine thanked me for showing such affectionate interest in her. She told me I was kind and added that she greatly needed to keep all her courage.

The conversation soon took on that general aspect and lively turn which that distinguished woman had the art of giving it. After a few moments we went into a gallery which she herself had had built in very fine proportions. It was adorned with the best-chosen pictures of the most famous painters. A barely completed picture was on the stand at the end of the gallery. It was the portrait of the Empress herself by Prud'hon. It was younger than she and perhaps somewhat embellished. "It was the work of a friend rather than of a painter," she said, with much grace.

Mme. de Metternich also went to Malmaison. Josephine had asked her to come. Hortense and Eugene received the ambassadress, who could not believe her ears when she heard the Queen of Holland confide, as she took her aside:

"You know we are all Austrians at heart, but you will never guess that my brother has had the courage to advise the Emperor to ask for your Archduchess in marriage."

At that moment Josephine entered the room and Mme. de Metternich, more and more astonished, heard her declare:

"I have a scheme which occupies me entirely and which alone, if it succeeds, will give me hope that the sacrifice I have just made is not completely wasted. It is that the Emperor should marry your archduchess. I spoke to him about it yesterday and he told me that his choice was not yet made, but I think that it would be if he were sure of being accepted in your country."

"I should consider this marriage a great happiness," the ambassadress replied prudently.

But, thinking of the fate of Marie Antoinette, she could not help adding, "Perhaps an Austrian archduchess would find it painful to settle in France."

"We must try to manage that," Josephine said again. Then she gave a hint of a threat. "Your emperor must be made to see that his ruin and that of his country is certain if he does not consent and it is perhaps the only means of preventing the Emperor from breaking with the Holy See."

Meanwhile, according to Hortense, the Emperor's letters "became more infrequent" and Josephine "was always waiting. My mother had a little study from which she could see the high road. Each time she was told of a hunt in the forest of Saint-Germain, she would stay at the window until she had seen the Emperor's carriage pass and return. I began to fear that this sacrifice was costing her more than I had at first believed."

When he came to see her his visits were always the same. The moment she heard the sound of carriages in the alley Josephine went out to greet the Emperor at the threshold of the "cage." They did not embrace. If it was fine she took Napoleon's arm, or his hand, and they went and sat down in the park, while the officers accompanying the Emperor stayed with her ladies.

Perhaps a little more gold might soften her sorrow. So on January 6, the day after a visit during which, as he wrote to her, he had been under her spell, the Emperor once more applied himself to the vexing financial problem, Josephine's eternal abyss of debt. After working with Josephine's treasurer and deciding to pay the heavy arrears, he gave orders for the normal payment for 1810 to be made and granted a supplement of 400,000 francs, not only "for the extraordinary expenses of Malmaison," so that Josephine could "have what she wanted planted," but also to pay for the recently bought set of rubies, "which is to be valued by the Intendance" as he wanted no "thefts by jewelers." He added 5,000 to 6,000 francs which were "in the safe at Malmaison." "You can take them to buy your silver and linen." Finally he ordered a porcelain dinner service for her. "They will take your orders so that it may be very beautiful."

As she was now her own mistress, Josephine saw Rousselin again, the former secretary to General Hoche and Bernadotte and now, as a note from Fouché to the Emperor shows, connected with the police. "These tête-à-tête are not considered decorous," he concluded. As to why she saw him, the Minister explained: "M. Rousselin has the merit in the Empress's eyes of having given her, after the death of General Hoche, the letters she had written to that general, but in the eyes of many people M. Rousselin is an intriguer who keeps bad company, who at one time caused talk about the Prince de Ponte-Corvo [Bernadotte] and today causes talk about the Empress."

On several occasions Rousselin sent in his name at Malmaison and sometimes spent two hours with Josephine. They recalled the past, and there is no trace in Fouché's notes of any protest from Napoleon on this subject. She also saw Mme. Tallien, now Princesse de Caraman-Chimay. The two former queens of the Directory embraced each other and Josephine once more gave free rein to her tears. It was now a ritual. She wept at every visit and recounted "her misfortunes." She also wept when she received the page bringing her the Emperor's letters and once more Napoleon scolded her.

At dawn on January 17 the Emperor asked M. d'Audenarde to go himself to find out how Josephine was. On the equerry's return he wrote a few illegible lines: "He tells me you have no courage since being at Malmaison. Yet that place is full of our feelings which cannot and should not change, at least on my side. I much want to see you, but I must be sure that you are strong and not weak. I am a little weak too and that makes me terribly unhappy."

In Savona the Pope was deeply distressed on reading *Le Moniteur* and learning that an incompetent tribunal had dissolved the union of Napoleon and Josephine.

"The Church's principles have been overthrown," he sighed, "and disorder has triumphed."

On January 21, the seventeenth anniversary of Louis XVI's execution, the Emperor summoned the members of the Council to have their opinion as to "the most favorable alliance for French interests." Conforming to Napoleon's wishes (and Josephine's), the majority declared for Marie Louise of Austria, the niece of Marie Antoinette and Louis XVI.

The "Pope in bondage" was, as we know from his "jailer," "sunk in grief" at learning that Napoleon, who in his eyes was still married, was about to lead the Austrian Archduchess to the altar. Fourteen cardinals yielded, but thirteen other princes of the Church, unexpected partisans of Josephine, decided to protest "canonically" and refused to attend the Emperor's religious marriage. They were nicknamed "black cardinals," for Napoleon compelled them to doff their cardinals' cassock for the cassock of a simple priest. They were put under house arrest and "abandoned to the charity of the faithful."

At Malmaison tears were still flowing. Josephine thought only one thing could calm her, a return to Paris. On December 16 the Emperor had given her the Elysée Palace "to enjoy during her lifetime. The King of Saxony had left it and admittedly the Murats had moved in, as the palace had belonged to them before the divorce, but they had no right to remain there. Moreover, on January 30 Napoleon had remarked on this subject: "I should be glad to know you were in the Elysée and very happy to see you more often, for you know how much I love you." But Josephine was not sure. From all sides she was told that her presence in Paris would embarrass the Tuileries, which was true, and place the high officials in a delicate position just at the time when the talk was all of the new marriage. The Emperor soothed her. "I told Eugene that you preferred to listen to the gossips of a great city than to what I told you; that people mustn't be allowed to tell you cock-and-bull stories that upset you. I have had your possessions moved to the Elysée. You must come to Paris at once. But be calm and contented and trust me entirely."

This letter was dated on the evening of Saturday, February 3. The next day a further letter brought joy back to Malmaison. Josephine was authorized to return. She settled in the Elysée Palace the same week in which this news appeared in *Le Moniteur:* "There is to be a marriage between His Majesty Emperor Napoleon, King of Italy, Protector of the Confederation of the Rhine, Mediator of the Swiss Confederation, and Her Imperial and Royal Highness the Archduchess Marie Louise, daughter of His Majesty the Emperor Francis, King of Bohemia and of Hungary." The Emperor had summoned the Austrian Ambassador on February 7 to inform him of his decision, for with a man like Napoleon there was no question of "asking for the Austrian's hand" and awaiting a reply.

While Berthier prepared to go to Vienna to marry Marie Louise as proxy, Josephine, still plaintive, waited for all the many items of news that showed her reign was over. Ball succeeded ball, the Emperor was seized with a passion for dancing, going to the theatre and hunting, and, feeling young again, thought only of the plump Archduchess he was to take to his bed. He repeated as ungallantly as ever: "I am marrying a womb!"

On January 30, 1810, he had already abolished the prerogatives of his brothers and their descendants in favor of his own direct heirs. He was building the empire of his son, the son he was sure he would have, and on February 17 he divided up the Papal States into the departments of the Tiber and Trasimeno, over which the future King of Rome would rule.

Meanwhile all Paris, including the fashionable tradesmen, was preparing for the coming important event. The ladies of the Court and the high dignitaries can hardly be blamed for thinking of the "New" Empress when they visited the "Old" one. Josephine herself even had Marie Louise's future chamberlains to dinner. And, if a note by Fouché is to be believed, "they declared they would protect her interests with the future Empress." What humiliation!

Napoleon came to the Elysée and left as soon as he had arrived, for he cared less and less for those eyes reddened by tears. Though on February 20, as he was going to hunt with Bessières at Grignon, he thoughtlessly suggested that his ex-wife go with him. But Josephine, with her usual tact, thought this escapade would not be proper or worthy of them, since at that date Marie Louise must have known of her destiny for at least four or five days. "There may be something in your remarks," he replied. "Perhaps it might not do for us to be under the same roof during the first year."

Life became more painful and visits much rarer. The news that Josephine's apartments had been destroyed by fire hardly provoked any emotion. Paris was talking of nothing but the wedding presents, the new Empress's dowry, fixed at four millions, the amazing

trousseau being sent to the Archduchess, part of which was to go to
Braunau, where the remise was to take place, copied from the
ceremony of Marie Antoinette's marriage. Josephine did not even
dare leave her residence for fear of provoking among the passers-by
a sympathy she could not bear. The newspapers continued to pity
her and seemed to enjoy mingling news about both empresses. The
Emperor was angry. "I told you," he wrote to Fouché, "to see that
the newspapers did not talk about the Empress Josephine. But they
do nothing else. Today again *Le Publiciste* is full of her."

Le Publiciste of March 9 had announced Josephine's departure
for Malmaison. The day before, Marie Louise had hung the miniature of her future husband round her neck and the next day, March
10, Napoleon wrote to the Archduchess, "I am counting the moments. The days seem long to me and this will continue until the
day when I have the happiness of receiving you."

Her arrival was expected on March 28 at Compiègne and it
seemed impossible that Josephine should be so near Paris on that
day. She would have to be got away.

It was on February 7 that Napoleon first thought of the Château
de Navarre, near Evreux. The castle owed its name to Jeanne de
France, Comtesse d'Evreux and Queen of Navarre, to whom it had
belonged. She had built a castle there, which was later demolished
to make way, at the end of the seventeenth century, for a hideous
square building erected by the second Comte d'Evreux. Napoleon
had never set foot inside it—which was his excuse for lodging his
dear Creole, whose good taste was proverbial, in the château
considered the ugliest in France.

The estate, more or less legally confiscated from the Bouillon
family, had been state property for a year. On February 15 Navarre
was put up for sale and purchased by the Intendant du Domaine
Privé. On March 11 the Emperor signed letters patent raising the
domaine of Navarre to a duchy, as under the old regime, in favor of
his ex-wife, "wishing to give the Empress Josephine a fresh testimony of his affection." Now Josephine was a duchess.

On March 12 he wrote to her: "My dear, I hope you will have
been pleased at what I did about Navarre. You will have seen in it a
fresh proof of my wish to be pleasant to you. Take possession of
Navarre. You could go there on March 27 and spend April there."

On March 19 the feast of St. Joseph was celebrated simply at

Malmaison. The Emperor and the Court left Paris on Tuesday, March 20, for Compiègne, where Marie Louise was awaited. Napoleon was feverishly excited and full of impatience. To please his nineteen-year-old wife he took dancing lessons with Josephine's daughter. On March 24 he wrote to Marie Louise: "How I wish I were happy enough to see you and tell you all my feelings of affection. The telegraph informed me yesterday that you had a cold. I beg you to take care of yourself. I went hunting this morning; I am sending you the first four pheasants I killed as a token of the dues owing to the sovereign of my most secret thoughts. Why can I not be in the page's place and take my oath as your liegeman, on my knees, with my hands between yours? In any event, accept it in spirit. In spirit, too, I cover your beautiful hands with kisses."

On March 20 Josephine welcomed to the Elysée her gentle daughter-in-law, whom Eugene had fetched from Italy to attend the wedding. Tuesday, March 27, came and went and Josephine did not set out. That evening Napoleon had gone to meet his new wife and, brushing aside the program laid down, had taken her to Compiègne. It was not a marriage but an abduction. That evening, without waiting for the religious ceremony, she became his wife and the next day he said with greedy satisfaction to one of his aides-de-camp: "My dear fellow, you should marry a German. They are the best women in the world, gentle, kind, simple and as fresh as roses."

It was not until that day, Wednesday, March 28, as night was falling—a night which Napoleon was again to spend with Marie Lousie—that Josephine decided to leave. Now that another woman had taken her place with the Emperor she was really no one. Henceforth when people said "the Empress" they would mean Marie Louise. Even Mme. de Rémusat, whose husband was at Compiègne, sometimes called Josephine "the other one."

She must have wept when leaving for Navarre, and yet she was calmer. At her request the Emperor had appointed three chamberlains to follow her to her new retreat: MM. de Turpin, de Viel-Castel and Louis de Montholon. Turpin had recently become Josephine's lover and consoler.

The Comte de Turpin-Crissé had the attractively medieval Christian name of Lancelot. The son of the Marquis de Crissé, he was charming and a talented sketcher and watercolorist. Above all, he was twenty-seven and very attractive. André Gavoty describes him when he first met Josephine. "Chestnut locks curling over his forehead and temples, large, laughing eyes with well-marked eyebrows, a straight nose, a wide, clean-shaven mouth, a long, oval face with a rounded, dimpled chin gave this face a pleasing and sympathetic expression. He had . . . the open countenance of a landed gentleman who would not hang back from a roast partridge."

He did not hang back from Josephine either. He had been recommended by Hortense and the ex-Empress had bought from him three pictures he had painted during a stay in Italy. She was twenty years older than he and she was quickly attracted to this young man who looked at her admiringly. Love is the one sure elixir of youth and in May, when her cousin Maurice Tascher saw her at Navarre, between the young and pretty Stephanie d'Arenberg and Stephanie of Baden, he exclaimed, "One would take her for the elder sister of the Graces!"

The portrait drawn by Bausset dates from this year. "It was impossible," he wrote, "to have more grace of manner and bearing. Her eyes and her looks were enchanting, her smile full of charm, all her features and her voice were extremely gentle. Her figure was noble, supple and perfect. The purest taste and most skilled elegance presided at her toilette and made her appear much younger than she actually was."

Much younger, indeed. A few days after the divorce Josephine had even been offered marriage by Frederick Louis of Mecklenburg-Schwerin, whose duchy was part of the Confederation of the Rhine. He was fifteen years younger, but he had loved the Empress since 1807. Josephine had even consented, in that year, to go secretly with him to the Vaudeville Theatre. The Emperor had called her to order and, according to Mme. de Rémusat, had lectured his wife, "not wishing to be the target of any jest." Talleyrand, to whom the Emperor had given a free hand in the matter, had advised the young Duke to go and look after his duchy. But learning that Josephine was now free, he had come forward again, and had been refused. The ex-Empress could not think of exchanging her widow's dowry, as André Gavoty so accurately calls it, for Mecklenburg-Schwerin.

And then there was sweet Lancelot, the chamberlain of her heart, who in himself was enough to console her. She needed no one else.

20. La Marmite

On learning that the divorced Empress was coming to live outside Evreux, M. Roland de Chambaudoin, Prefect of the Eure Department, was very excited. "Let us outdo each other in zeal," he declared, "to express our gratitude for such a precious boon." He was no less feverish in his reception of the youth of Evreux who came "in a spontaneous impulse" to propose the creation of a guard of honor. The scheme was agreed to and, among other preparations, five coaches were hired for the twelve young ladies who would go to meet Josephine. Then flowers were ordered to be presented to her—these expenses amounted to 84 francs 47 centimes.

Meanwhile M. de Chambaudoin was wondering how far his attentions to the ex-Empress should go. On March 17, 1810, he consulted the Minister of the Interior about this, explaining with satisfaction, "I am trying to imbue my conduct with all the aplomb of a civil servant and a man of forty-three."

He and his aplomb were dashed at receiving a letter from the Minister of the Interior, who had learned of the creation of a guard of honor and "was not able to conceal" how "irregular in form" this decision appeared to him. He ended his letter with a fatal blow for the prefect: "I hope therefore that this will be the last time I have to note such an error." M. de Chambaudoin was unaware that his minister had written this rebuke after leaving the Emperor's study.

Napoleon had even conveyed to the prefect an order to make sure that the department's newspaper made no mention of Josephine's arrival.

Chambaudoin was all the more contrite since he had had Josephine's letter announcing her arrival widely advertised and the news published in the *Journal d'Evreux et de l'Eure*. But what had been ordered could not be countermanded. The great day—Thursday, March 29, mid-Lent, 1810—arrived. And the "joyous entry" of "Mme. la Duchesse de Navarre" took place in accordance with the prefect's dreams.

The moment the carriages appeared the band burst out with "Where can one be happier than in the bosom of one's family?" The National Guard drew up in line and the inhabitants, who had turned out in a body, shouted, "Long live the Empress Josephine!" The mounted guard of honor of thirty-three men and officers lined the road. Their jackets were puce, enlivened with an orange collar, their waistcoats white and their breeches royal blue—not to mention three-cornered hats with white plumes and immaculate sashes around their waists. Leaning out of the window of the Opale, Josephine accepted the bouquet ordered by M. de Chambaudoin and abstractedly listened to the prefect's protestations of devotion as he expressed "all his joy and all that of his department in receiving into its bosom the model of goodness, virtue and grace."

Then the carriage proceeded, surrounded by the guard of honor. Behind came other carriages and numerous wagons holding 673 dresses, a huge collection of riding habits, corsets, shawls, chemises, and 198 pairs of silk stockings, 685 pairs of shoes, 980 pairs of gloves and 87 hats.

There were also the horses, for Josephine brought a whole stable with her.

The relay was at Pacy, where the inevitable white-clad girls presented flowers. On their arrival at Evreux the bands played, the cannon thundered, the bells of Notre Dame cathedral and Saint-Taurin rang out and Josephine, hearing a second speech, might have thought herself back in the good old days. The procession moved at a snail's pace through the town, while the Empress, as the prefect wrote in his report, "greeted everyone on her way in the most gracious manner."

When, two miles out on the road to Conches, Josephine saw her new residence standing on marshy ground cut by ponds, lakes and canals, she thought it was a nightmare: an equilateral cube, itself standing on a pedestal of stairs and lawns and topped with a crown of chimneys, and in its center a dome perched on a rotunda with six windows and cut off on top to make a platform. This had been intended for a statue of Turenne, uncle to the second Comte d'Evreux. Fortunately the pedestal remained empty, but it gave the château an unfinished look, and the whole structure resembled a cooking pot and the inhabitants of Evreux had nicknamed it "La Marmite."

Josephine's coach drew up. On the terrace "two little young ladies" disguised as shepherdesses presented flowers and two be-ribboned lambs, and then sang.

Josephine mounted one of the four stone staircases located on each façade of La Marmite. These led to four lobbies which all ended in the same marble-paved drawing room, which rose the entire height of the building, receiving light only through the windows in the dome. One corner of the house was reserved for Josephine, another contained two reception rooms, one of which was used as a chapel on Sundays. On the second floor the apartments, dripping with water, dilapidated, practically unfurnished, with rotten woodwork, smoky chimneys and drafty windows, were squeezed around the strange drawing room with its lofty ceiling where a veritable gale blew. A smaller château was not far away, but it was in even worse state than La Marmite.

That evening, as she slipped between the damp sheets of her bed, Josephine thought of her "joyous entry" and sighed: "Didn't you think, Mlle. d'Abrillon, that they seemed to be offering their con-dolences to me?"

Meanwhile M. de Chambaudoin was writing his report. He was not unaware that Mme. Gazzani, who accompanied the Empress, had been the Emperor's mistress and so, being a thorough toady, he felt it necessary to add to his letter: "One cannot but have a very favorable opinion of a lady whose features are so regular and whose beauty is so perfect."

Thinking thus to have "softened" his master, the prefect took it

upon himself next day to change the name of the Rue du Départe-
ment to the Rue de l'Impératrice, and the Rue Saint-Taurin became
the Rue Joséphine, which it remains to this day.

Grumbling and envying those who had been chosen to serve "the
new one," the suite shook down as best it could. Josephine had
retained a court befitting a queen. She had a large palace staff and a
whole army of servants. Several members of the Court had found
excellent excuses for not going to Navarre. The desertion most
wounding to Josephine was that of Maréchale Ney, Hortense's
companion. When her husband wrote that he would separate from
her if she did not send in her resignation as lady in waiting, she
went to Malmaison and was cruel enough to show this letter from
"the bravest of the brave" to the ex-Empress. Josephine advised
her to yield, and not long afterward Mme. Ney, then Duchesse
d'Elchingen, became lady in waiting to Empress Marie Louise.

The head of the household, Mme. d'Arberg, had remained faithful. She always guided her mistress cleverly but firmly and through
her presence was to prevent many mistakes by the exile.

Another important personage, the gentle Comte André de Beaumont, a former chamberlain who had been with Josephine since she
became Empress, did not desert either, but he had just been elected
a deputy and might have to go away. But he could not do enough to
try to please the exile and displayed a gallantry worthy of the old
regime. In his zeal, which the members of the "little Court" considered excessive, he even sometimes did the work of the valets de
chambre.

Mmes. de Colbert, de Canclaux, Octave de Ségur, d'Aguesseau,
d'Audenarde and de Viel-Castel—the two last being "honorary
ladies"—had come or were coming to Navarre, but Mme. de
Turenne and Mme. Walsh made various excuses for not joining the
Empress in her Norman château. As for Mme. de Rémusat, her
health did not allow her to resume her post until somewhat later.

Deschamps, her principal secretary, had also kept his post. Being
the Emperor's private secretary as well, he had been obliged to give
up this position in order to stay with the Empress. But Josephine
paid him the salary he had lost by preferring her to her ex-husband.

Only one of the three chamberlains, Montholon, had chosen to
stay in Paris. But Turpin de Crissé was there, which was what

mattered to Josephine. The Comte de Viel-Castel, with whom Josephine was said to have had a romance in 1791, also was present.

Mme. Gazzani, whose husband was receiver general of the Eure Department, had decided to stay. There were a few changes among the wardrobe and tiring women, with whom Josephine was quite intimate. The Empress had lost her hairdresser, Duplan, and felt this particularly keenly, for even long before she became Mme. Bonaparte Duplan had done Josephine's hair and he also cut the Emperor's. Napoleon, thinking that only Duplan could do the new Empress's hair properly, sent for him.

"What do you earn from the Empress Josephine?" he asked.

"Twelve thousand francs, sire."

"I appoint you hairdresser to the Empress Marie Louise, I will pay you the same, but you must not dress the hair of anyone else."

"Sire, Her Majesty the Empress Josephine allowed me to dress other people's hair and that brought me in as much again."

"Well," Napoleon concluded, "I shall give you 24,000 francs, but on condition that you do not dress the hair of anyone but the Empress Marie Louise."

When she heard of this "bad turn," as she considered it, Josephine was "wounded to the quick" and tears filled her eyes. "It made a profound impression on her," related Mlle. d'Avrillon, "because she saw in it the prelude to other sacrifices that might later be required of her."

Over this little world reigned the new intendant general, Pierlot. He was full of his own importance and the little Court led him a hard life. He wanted to economize, but started badly by doing away with the coffee served to the lady's maids after meals. His decision gave rise to a storm which died down only when Josephine restored the coffee.

The Court settled in, or rather camped out, as best it could. As Josephine wrote to Hortense, Navarre might one day become "a very beautiful place," but at the moment "everything needs repairing." How could she stay there? "The people I have brought with me have only a tiny bedroom each, of which the door and window do not shut."

"If the Emperor asks for news of me," she also wrote to Hortense, "tell him my only occupation is thinking of him." She was thinking less of him than of Paris and Saint-Cloud, where there was a constant succession of wedding celebrations. Everyone who saw the Emperor was struck by his "air of triumph." His face "beamed with happiness and joy." On April 3, when Josephine wrote to her daughter that "the life I lead is a country life," Napoleon, with Marie Louise at his side seated on Josephine's throne, received the whole Court and the public authorities.

Josephine's only diversion was the arrival of tradesmen from Paris. She could still wear a new dress every day. Her greatest activity, aided by the "pleasant, gay and very learned" bishop, was to give alms, found scholarships at the seminary and place girls in convents. But the evenings were gloomy. Fortunately she still had her beloved Lancelot, "gentle, agreeable and good company," said Laure d'Abrantès, who was generally very severe on her contemporaries. But Josephine wanted to be alone, or almost alone, with him. Her dream was to take the waters with a suite of a few close friends. Meanwhile she had to put up with the damp, inconvenient Marmite. She had to swallow affronts, such as her armorial bearings sent to her by the Conseil du Sceau. It did include a golden eagle and silver stars, but also showed the martlets and pales of the Taschers and Beauharnais. It was undoubtedly a ducal coat of arms. It was quartered, whereas the Imperial family could display a "whole coat."

Why did Hortense not join her mother? Once Napoleon's divorce was pronounced Louis arrived in Paris, all excitement. Since his brother had repudiated the "Beauharnais woman," perhaps he, too, could get rid of his wife. He had written, "Sire, I beg Your Majesty to approve my separation from the Queen my wife. I propose to give her the house she inhabits and 500,000 francs from my civil list. I ask from your justice that I may keep my eldest son with me and that the Queen may keep the youngest."

A series of divorces in the Bonaparte family would certainly risk raising a smile, so the Emperor had first ordered a family council, which was summoned in due form by Cambacérès. Then, to bring his arrogant brother down a peg, he had sent him a gracious note in which he reproached Holland for violating the Franco-Dutch Treaty and resuming relations with England. "I shall not hide from you," Napoleon had added, "that my intention is to unite Holland to France, thus freeing myself from the perpetual insults leveled at me

by the ringleaders of your cabinet. In fact the mouths of the Rhine
and the Meuse ought to belong to me. It is a fundamental principle
in France that the valley route of the Rhine is our frontier. . . . I
have enough grievances against Holland to justify declaring war.
However, I intend to make no difficulties about any arrangement
which will give me the Rhine frontier."

Thus forewarned, Louis, terrified at the thought that his brother
was about to take his states from him, changed his tone and agreed
to resume a sort of common life with Hortense. Josephine's daughter, who had been delighted at the thought of being rid of her
husband, was shattered by the decision.

"Madame, I have long been wishing to speak to you," Louis said
to her. "The Emperor has refused to consent to a separation which
we both desired. You cannot therefore be free and independent of
your husband."

"What happiness do you expect from our reunion?"

"I know that it is not possible, it is not what I ask, but you are
Queen of Holland. It is there that you should live and I shall not
suffer you to be anywhere else."

"What is your reason for wanting me there?" Hortense replied. "If
you fear my being at the Emperor's Court, I do not care to stay
there. My mother is now in retreat. I shall go and live with her. I
can do nothing for your happiness. Let me finish my life in peace.
Think no more of me. Consider me as one dead."

"That is quite different. Look at the Emperor of Austria; he
remarried at once."

Without having had the courage to go to Navarre, Hortense set
out on April 6, as though "preparing for death," on the road to
Amsterdam, where Louis, in his desire for a reconciliation, had had
all the doors from his apartments to the Queen's walled up.

Before going to Belgium with Napoleon and Marie Louise,
Eugene went to see his mother. Navarre immediately assumed a
less gloomy appearance. The Viceroy organized expeditions between showers—the park was so wet that Josephine wore a kind of
sabot for these walks.

In the evening there were charades and games. For the first time
the Marmite echoed with laughter. The "action" charades, it appears, were extremely comical, especially when the great tragedian
Talma came to help.

Eugene did not stay long. His wife, who was unwell, was expecting him in Paris, but he took a letter from his mother to the Emperor. Josephine wanted to return to Malmaison and, needless to say, asked for a few hundred thousand francs to render Navarre more inhabitable. Napoleon, being in the middle of his honeymoon, had no time to reply and gave Eugene a verbal answer for his mother. Vexed, Josephine sent her former husband a letter in which for the first time she assumed a tone of ceremony far from her usual custom.

> Navarre, April 19, 1810.
> Sire, I have received from my son the assurance that Your Majesty consents to my returning to Malmaison and is good enough to grant me the advances I requested to make the château of Navarre inhabitable.
> This double favor, sire, has to a great extent dissipated the anxieties and even fears which Your Majesty's long silence had aroused in me. I feared I was entirely banished from your memory. I see that I am not. I am today therefore less unhappy, and even as happy as it is henceforth possible for me to be.
> I shall go to Malmaison at the end of the month, since Your Majesty sees no objection, but I must tell you, sire, that I should not so soon have profited by the freedom Your Majesty gives me in this respect if the house at Navarre did not require, both on account of my health and that of the people in my household, urgent repairs. My plan is to remain but a short time at Malmaison. Perhaps I shall shortly leave it to take the waters. But while I am at Malmaison Your Majesty may be sure that I shall live as if I were a thousand leagues from Paris. I have made a great sacrifice, sire, and I feel its extent more each day. But be this sacrifice what it may, on my side it shall be total. Your Majesty will not be troubled in your happiness by any expression of my regrets.
> I shall always wish that Your Majesty may be happy. Perhaps I shall also wish to see you again, but Your Majesty may be certain that I shall always respect your new position. I shall respect it in silence; trusting in the feelings you formerly had for me, I shall not ask for any fresh proof, I shall expect everything from your justice and your heart.
> I merely ask one favor which is that you should yourself condescend to find a means sometimes to convince both myself and those about me that I still have a small place in your memory and a great place in your esteem and friendship. Whatever this means may be, it will soften my sorrow without, it seems to me, compromising what is of the greatest importance to me, Your Majesty's happiness.

Josephine was undoubtedly always capable of surprises. This time she had won. He replied:

My dear, I have received your letter of 19 April. It is written in a very bad style. People like me never change. I do not know what Eugene said to you. I did not write because you did not and I wanted to do everything that pleased you. I see with pleasure that you are going to Malmaison and that you are contented. I shall always be glad to have news of you and give you mine. I say no more until you have compared your letter with mine and after that I leave you to judge who is the better friend, you or I. Good-by, my dear, keep well and be just to yourself and to me.

Eugene brought this letter and Josephine immediately took up her pen:

A thousand, thousand tender thanks for not having forgotten me. My son has just brought me your letter. [In this letter Josephine returns to calling Napoleon *tu.*] How eagerly I read it, and yet it took me some time, for there was not a word that did not make me weep, but the tears were very sweet! My heart has returned to me intact, as it will always be. There are sentiments which are part of my very life and will end only with it. I should be in despair if my letter of the 19th displeased you. I do not recall all its expressions, but I know what painful feelings dictated it, grief at having no news from you.

I wrote to you on leaving for Malmaison and since then I wanted many times to write to you, but I guessed the reasons for your silence and I feared to importune you with a letter. Yours was balm to me. Be happy! Be as happy as you deserve! My whole heart says this to you. You have given me my share of happiness and a token keenly felt. Nothing can be of so much value to me as a token of your remembrance.

Good-by, my dear, I thank you as much as I shall always love you.

All this may seem a little exaggerated, but she knew "Bonaparte" and knew how to manage him. She would have done anything to get permission to leave Navarre. She also needed money. Navarre must be made inhabitable. She also wanted the Emperor to see to the marriage of her two Tascher cousins. Eugene was instructed to convey these wishes to the master. He was also to speak of her plans for the future.

"Eugene tells me you want to take the waters," wrote Napoleon from Brussels, where he had gone with Marie Louise. "Don't restrict yourself in any way. Pay no attention to the Paris gossips; they are a lot of idlers and far from understanding the true state of affairs. My feelings for you have not changed and I am anxious to learn that you are happy and contented."

Napoleon agreed to arrange for the elder Tascher—Louis, who had written to Josephine from Martinique in December, 1806—to

marry the Princesse de la Leyen, niece of the Prince Primate. As for
the younger, Henri, he was a "little wretch" who had failed in his
duty. "He had left the French Army in Madrid" without informing
Napoleon, following "an impulse of love" and forgetting all his
obligations to the Emperor. He could do what he liked and marry
whom he would, it made no difference to him. The Emperor
"greatly" approved Josephine's plans "for all the expenses at Navarre," but he would give nothing beyond what had been arranged.
He merely authorized advances of 600,000 francs, on the one hand,
and 100,000 to be used at Malmaison.

On May 15 Josephine finally returned to Malmaison. The park
was full of flowers, the beds were carpets of double hyacinths and
precious tulips. The purple-flowered magnolia had not suffered too
much from the winter. Her greatest pleasure was in revisiting her
greenhouses and aviaries, where one parrot repeated "Bonaparte!
Bonaparte!" all day and another is said to have spoken Spanish very
well and danced to the sound of the guitar.

The ex-Empress might well be proud of her work. From the days
of the Consulate she had continually embellished it. "It is an
enchanted place," declared Mme. de Rémusat. In 1806 Josephine
had taken on the famous Berthault, architect and gardener, whom
some people compared to Louis XIV's architect, Le Nôtre. He had
enlivened, refreshed and "given breath" to the park by constructing
cascades, waterfalls and lakes. The rivers embraced islands full of
flowers. Near the Temple of Love the prospect of water and lawns
was studded with enormous clumps of rhododendrons. On the
canal, according to an eyewitness who visited Malmaison in 1810,
"float pretty boats and black swans with red beaks and many other
water birds." In front of the château was a multitude "of pages,
chamberlains, valets in gold braid, and Basques"—the ex-Empress's
green and gold footmen—who fluttered around the barouches "with
an immense parasol in the center." The horses and postilions, it
appears, were "charming."

The previous year Josephine had managed to get 800 exotic
plants from Booz, the director of the Schönbrunn gardens. One
wonders if Marie Louise knew this.

She might also have felt proud as she passed through the galleries, antechambers and reception rooms of her house. Malmaison

had become a real museum. It took no fewer than seventy-nine sittings, each of more than two months, to inventory everything she had accumulated there.

She liked to admire and show off her stones or cases of minerals, her collections of antiques or precious vases and particularly her paintings. She possessed 110 Old Masters, including pictures by Albano, Correggio, Raphael, Leonardo da Vinci, Veronese, Dürer, Rembrandt, Teniers, van Dyck, Holbein, Ruysdael, Murillo.

The Emperor and Marie Louise were in Belgium, so visitors, principally from the Faubourg Saint-Germain, came in crowds to Malmaison. There were rarely fewer than twelve guests to lunch and twice the number to dinner. Moreover, meals were no longer served at the double. There was time to taste and savor the iced cakes invented by the Italian chef Ruccesi. In the evening four butlers, wine waiters, and a footman for each guest, performed as at the Tuileries. After dinner the guests would listen to a concert while the famous Garat sang. Josephine showed her close friends the letter Napoleon had written her: "I very much want to see you. I expect to be at Saint-Cloud on the 30th of the month. My health is very good. I should like to know that you are content and well. Let me know the name under which you wish to travel. Never doubt the truth of my feelings for you; they will last as long as I do. It would be unjust of you to doubt them."

The Emperor did not come to see her until June 13. "I had a day of happiness yesterday," Josephine told Hortense. "His presence made me happy although it brought a renewal of all my sorrows . . . one would wish to experience such emotions often. All the time he was with me I was brave enough to hold back the tears I felt were about to flow, but after he left I felt very miserable. He was good and kind to me, as always, and I hope that he read in my heart all the affection and devotion which fills me."

The Emperor had embraced Josephine's grandson, the younger son of Louis and Hortense, whom she had with her. They spoke in particular of Hortense. The three months she had spent in the Dutch mausoleum had been dreadful for Josephine's daughter. "This isolation in a foreign country filled me with terror," she was to relate. "Death, which formerly had had a pleasing aspect and which I had longed for, now appeared terrifying. 'What am I doing here?'

I asked myself. 'What? Must I perish far from my country without one friendly hand to soften my last moments, without being able to take a fond farewell of all those I love? Why did they let me go and why did I decide to do so?' I cherished but one idea—to leave that country and resume my freedom." Louis never spoke to her except to say good morning in the morning and good night before retiring to his apartments. So on June 1 Hortense left Amsterdam forever and took refuge in Plombières. This time Napoleon finally realized that Louis was a tyrant and agreed to the husband and wife's living apart in the future. Within three weeks he was to learn, with rage, of Louis's abdication and flight to Austria.

"Should I have expected such an insult from the man to whom I have been a father?" Napoleon exclaimed. "I brought him up on my slender pay as artillery lieutenant, I shared my bread and my mattress with him. Where has he gone?"

He had gone to Graz, where he decided to put his kingdom under the protection of the Tsar. Napoleon paid no attention. Eight days later he annexed the Kingdom of Holland to France and divided it up into French departments. As a result, Hortense—that unfortunate girl, as the Emperor called her—gained her freedom and two million in revenues, plus the Grand Duchy of Berg for her elder son. She learned this good news while at Plombières. She also had a letter from her mother, asking her to join her at Aix-les-Bains. Mme. de Souza was to be there and, most important, her son Flahaut.

"I had just passed the first stage," she wrote, "when I saw afar off two horsemen galloping rapidly along. When one's mind is full of a single object, we think we see it everywhere. I exclaimed, 'I was right!' on seeing one of them. My heart beat strongly, but I hid my emotion and showed only surprise when M. de Flahaut and M. de Pourtalès, my mother's equerry, drew near the carriage."

Josephine, who had been at Aix for more than a month, had rented a quiet house for her daughter "with a four-sided roof of brown tiles." On the terrace were pots of flowers.

The ex-Empress was traveling under the name of "Comtesse d'Arberg." She had with her only her dear Lancelot, Mme. d'Audenarde and the last-named's lover, the equerry Pourtalès. Josephine passed through Lyons incognito, refusing to receive the colonel of gendarmes and the mayor's assistant, and, with her two women and her dog Askim, settled into the Chevaley house at Aix which was called "the palace" because she was living there. A nearby cottage had been rented where Turpin and Pourtalès could live while awaiting the arrival of Mme. de Rémusat, who was to resume her duties on June 29.

Josephine was happy. No more uniforms, visits or etiquette. As Frédéric Masson says, she was "a bather who took her usual companions with her . . . not a sovereign." In the morning there were showers, baths and rest, then lunch in "the palace." In the afternoon, a drive in the carriage with the Imperial livery. Back at four, sometimes at five. At six the little Court dined, then had another outing. "At nine," Mme. de Rémusat told her husband, "we play, we sing a little afterward and at eleven we go to bed. As you see, we lead a very regular little life."

Eugene and Augusta were in Geneva. So, under a tropical heat, Josephine made a brief excursion to Lake Leman, but Turpin did not go with her. Her son and daughter-in-law might have said something about his presence.

On her return she resumed her spa routine. Crowds gathered as the ex-Empress passed. "The pretty carriage, the fine horses, the liveries and our dresses all make a great impression," Mme. de Rémusat wrote to her husband, "and amid all that the gentle and always benevolent face of my mistress. People come from Chambéry, Geneva, Turin and Grenoble just to see her. Everyone shows great interest in her. What pleases me is that no one appears to assume that she is estranged from the Emperor, for she is given many petitions for him." With "remarkable kindness" she promised to help. But would she? The ex-Empress's tact was greatly admired by Mme. de Rémusat. The "Duchesse de Navarre" had quickly learned the art of making "quite simple a situation which at first seems embarrassing." In fact she had no vanity, did not "try to attract attention" and spoke "of the Emperor as she should and when she should."

On July 26 the little band—the "colony," as Mme. de Rémusat called it—spent a happy day at the Abbey of Hautecombe. Lancelot made a charming sketch of the Empress wearing a "hooded cape trimmed with ostrich feathers" and looking through a telescope.

Then, "with an affectionate hand," he portrayed her sitting under an umbrella near the famous intermittent spring. On their return a real tempest broke. The wind blew violently through the garlands, sails and ornaments intended to give their boat a festive air. Turpin and Pourtalès behaved with courage, holding the Empress's hands and "prepared to save her." Flahaut began singing ballads. Mme. de Rémusat sang too, but only to herself and, she tells us, "I recommended my soul to God above this accompaniment." By hard rowing the sailors managed to reach port, where a crowd had gathered. "For an inhabitant of the oceanic islands dying in a lake would have been a sad fate," wrote the Emperor.

When Hortense arrived in Aix Josephine found her "pale, thin, very depressed, always prone to weep without knowing why." Hortense herself gives us the reasons for her "spleen." The mere sight of handsome Colonel de Flahaut produced "an impression increasingly difficult to hide and too strong for my weak health. It was the first time I had seen him constantly since beginning to love him. My eyes were ceaselessly filled with tears." He himself did not weep and his heart beat quite steadily. "I ended by loving her," he was to admit, "for I had so many proofs of her devotion." During this August of 1810—"the happiest time of my life," as she called it—Hortense gazed at Charles with admiration.

There was a rumor at Aix, reported by Mme. de Rémusat, that Marie Louise was pregnant. Josephine immediately wrote to her ex-husband for news. "The Empress is in fact four months pregnant," he replied. "She is very well and greatly attached to me."

During a short trip to Geneva—"she hurried through the night to get there"—Turpin remained at Aix "in solitude" with Mme. de Rémusat. But a few days later Josephine, leaving her daughter to her love affair, decided to go touring. She went to the Hôtel d'Angleterre, or Hôtel Dejean, among the vines at Sécheron on the shores of Lake Geneva. Voltaire had stayed there. Byron, Goethe, Chateaubriand and Musset were to come. "We went there," recounted young Georgette Ducrest, "convinced that everything would be turned upside down by the presence of such important people and sure that the ordinary visitors would have been sent away to make room for this court. What was our surprise, on arriving, to find everything apparently as calm as before the arrival of the Empress, who traveled with the simplicity of a rich private person.

"Mme. d'Audenarde, who had been a lady in waiting since the divorce, showed us into a very small room with no antechamber. That was where Her Majesty slept. She was in negligee, but looking much better than when she was on the throne. She had grown plumper, without her figure's losing its perfection. Her complexion was less brown and the charm of her pleasant and noble manners made her the most attractive of women."

The Genevans gave an entertainment on the lake for Josephine. Decorated, beflagged and beribboned boats full of musicians escorted the little vessel drawn by two swans in which the Duchesse de Navarre was seated. In the evening the ex-Empress was saluted by a display of fireworks. But Josephine preferred making trips with her favorite chamberlain and a few close friends as chaperons. They visited Ferney and supped and spent the night at the Auberge de l'Union at Bex. After visiting the Castle of Chillon and the church at Vevey—which provided more sketches of her by Turpin—they spent the night at the Lion d'Or in Lausanne. After a short stop at Sécheron they set off again for the valley of the Arve and "Chamouny." Mlle. d'Avrillon, who chronicled the excursion, relates: "We got out every time we met anything of interest on the road. M. de Turpin made quick sketches. He drew Her Majesty and the ladies with her several times. He portrayed them in different groups each time he saw them sitting down for a few moments' rest, which was often necessary. Our second journey ended at Chamouny, where we slept at the Priory. At that time it was a rather bad inn."

The ascent of Le Montenvers, starting from Chamonix, was made on horseback by Josephine and on mules by her suite. Eighty people, including guides and porters, accompanied them. They reached the Mer de Glace in sedan chairs. Josephine walked over a large part of the glacier, but everyone's teeth were chattering for, although summer was barely over, it was very cold. Turpin sketched the Duchess huddled in her wraps and protecting her complexion with a sunshade. Josephine declared that the walk was wonderful but on her return to Chamonix threw herself fully clothed on the bed, exhausted.

The next day they went for a picnic at Servoz, an open-air lunch recorded by Turpin, and finally returned to Geneva on September 20.

Hortense had left Aix and Flahaut and come to join her mother. Josephine gave her a letter, which she was to hand to the Emperor.

The Queen, who has come to spend two days with me, is leaving me tomorrow to return to Paris. She hopes soon to have the happiness of seeing you. Permit me to recommend her to your friendship, which is our only hope. She will give you this letter, which I write with a disturbed heart, for every moment makes me feel more keenly the embarrassment of my situation. As I approach the time I had set for the end of my journey I become more uncertain what I should do. Bonaparte, you promised not to abandon me. Here is a circumstance in which I need your advice. I have only you in all the world. You are my sole friend. Speak frankly to me. May I return to Paris or should I stay here? Of course I would rather be nearer you, especially if I had a hope of seeing you. But if this hope is not promised me, what shall I do all this coming winter? Whereas, by prolonging my absence for another seven or eight months I hope that circumstances will become more favorable for me, since the Empress will have acquired fresh rights to your love.

I am asking the Queen to talk to you about my affairs and to enter into all the details which I cannot write. She will tell you how dear you are to me and that there is no sacrifice which would weigh on me if your peace is in question.

If you advise me to stay I shall rent or buy a little country house on the shores of the lake. I only want to know if there is any objection to its being near Lausanne or Vevey if I find a situation that suits me better. I may perhaps return next summer to take the waters at Aix, which do me good. This will be another year of absence, but a year I shall be able to bear from the hope of seeing you after that and from the thought that my conduct is approved by you.

So do decide what I must do and if you cannot write to me get the Queen to let me know what you intend.

Ah! I beg you, do not refuse to guide me! Advise your poor Josephine! It will be a proof of friendship and you will console her for all her sacrifices.

At this point she received a letter from Mme. de Rémusat, written at Napoleon's request:

You remember that you sometimes regretted as I did that, at the moment of his marriage, the Emperor did not press for a meeting between the two people who, he flattered himself, would meet easily because he joined them in his affections [Josephine and Marie Louise]. You have since told me that he hoped that a pregnancy, by reassuring the Empress as to her rights, would give him the means to fulfill this wish of his heart. But, madame, if my observations have not deceived me, the time has not yet come for such a meeting. . . . What would you do here, madame, amid the joy caused by this pregnancy, at the time of the birth of a child so impatiently awaited, among the sounds of the feasts which will follow this event? What would the Emperor do, who would be bound to pay every consideration required by this young mother's condition and would still be disturbed by the memories of the feelings he retains for you? He would suffer, although your delicacy would not exact anything, but you would suffer too. You would not hear without pain the cries of so much rejoicing, being perhaps yourself forgotten by a whole nation or become the object of the compassion of some who would pity you, perhaps from a party spirit. Gradually your situation would become so painful that only a complete disappearance would restore everything.

Tears came to Josephine's eyes as she wondered whether Napoleon would permit her to stay in Paris or demand that she go to Milan. While waiting for his reply she resumed traveling. Accompanied by Mlles. de Mackau and d'Avrillon, and of course by Turpin, Josephine left Sécheron and spent the night at Morges. The next day, following the road which winds round the foot of the Jura, she passed near Orbe, stopped at the château of Montchoisi, where she met an old acquaintance, Mme. du Plessis d'Aumale.

Josephine was now expected at Neuchâtel for a week. She had wanted to have a boat "decked with flags and with a dais." The prefect of Nidau placed his own launch at her disposal, which gave her "much enjoyment, in spite of its shortcomings."

Josephine installed herself in Louis de Pourtalès's house in the Faubourg de l'Hôpital. Her room, newly papered in red and gold, looked over the lake. Her first impression was all the more attractive since musicians gave her an aubade.

The next day Josephine, with a white plume in her hat, went to La Chaux-de-Fonds. Here she refused the dinner prepared in the hotel, which had the somewhat too royalist name of the Fleur de Lys, and contented herself with potluck at the Auberge de la Balance. From there she went to Locle and then to Le Crêt-Vaillant where musicians had been got together for an aubade, but the concert was execrable "because they are not accustomed to playing together." The next day Josephine visited the Saut du Doubs in the rain. More musicians, who this time seemed fortunately to know each other better, were stationed in boats and "a delicious music" accompanied the trip.

She spent a fortnight as a guest of the Berne government in the Gasthof zum Falken. It was an old inn, well known since the fifteenth century, which faced the Rue du Marché.

On Monday, October 7, in "a juive of lilac levantine silk with cap of the same" and a long, heavy gold chain round her neck, she had lunch at the famous Enge restaurant built on a plateau from which there was a beautiful view. She and the seventeen people with her were served, after the soup and hors-d'oeuvres, with hare pâté, trout au bleu, young turkey, chicken with tarragon, ham, salad, creams, compotes and pastries, all washed down with Malaga, Bordeaux and the delightful Neuchâtel wine. It must be assumed that she did not taste of everything. Nevertheless, it cost the Berne treasury 288 francs for the head table and 1,143 francs for the other guests, not to mention 45 francs "breakage."

While digesting they watched an "Alpine entertainment": brass band, solo on the Alpine horn, procession of flocks to the sound of their bells, and mountain wrestling. Finally Josephine left the restaurant. "We had our fill of looking at her," wrote an eyewitness. "She has a nice face, beautiful features rather past their prime." She found the Bernese women's costume so charming that she ordered one to take to Malmaison. She also paid 314 francs for a charabanc in which she decided to visit the Oberland. On October 15 she was the guest of M. de Mülinen at Thoune—"a pleasant diversion for her sad, desolate heart," wrote Turpin. Then to Interlaken, where the Jungfrau gave her dear chamberlain another chance to use his pencils. On October 17 she was back in Berne and on the 18th she left. That evening Josephine arrived at the Auberge de la Couronne at Soleure, where she spent the night. In the afternoon she had watched a "dancing assembly" of ladies and girls wearing various Swiss costumes.

"I have not enjoyed myself so much for a long time," she declared on leaving.

It was in Berne that the ex-Empress received the Emperor's reply.

"Go and see your son this winter," he wrote, "return to Aix next year or spend the spring at Navarre. I should advise you to go to Navarre straightaway if I did not fear you would be bored there.

My opinion was that this winter you could properly be only at Milan or Navarre. After that I approve anything you do, for I do not want to interfere with you at all. Good-by, my dear. The Empress is four months pregnant.

"I am appointing Mme. de Montesquiou governess to the Children of France. Be content and do not get excited. Never doubt my feelings."

Josephine quickly made up her mind. Since the Emperor made no mention of Paris she would settle down at Navarre.

"I find many objections to going to Italy, particularly to spending the winter there," she wrote to Hortense. "If it were for a journey of one or two months I would gladly go to see my son, but staying there longer is impossible. Besides, my health, which had become stronger, has become very bad during the past two weeks. My doctor advises rest and at Navarre I shall have plenty of time to look after myself. . . . I would like to have another line from you before fixing my departure for Navarre, so that I know if the Emperor approves my spending the winter there. Write to me frankly about this. I confess that if I had to leave France for more than a month I should die of grief. At least I shall have the pleasure of seeing you sometimes at Navarre, my dear Hortense, and this is such a great happiness for me that I must prefer the place which brings me nearest to my dear daughter. Good-by, I embrace you with all my heart. Kiss my grandsons for me."

In a postscript she added what was for her the most important point. "If I went to Italy I am sure that several people who are attached to me would resign." Would Turpin have been one of those? He loved his mother so much that perhaps he would not want to be separated from her for several months.

The next day Josephine went to Lausanne, where she saw the Tsar's sister-in-law, that "pretty brunette" Grand Duchess Constantine, nee Coburg. In Lausanne she refused to receive Mme. de Staël, at that time exiled by the Emperor's orders.

"In the next book she published," declared Josephine, not without reason, "she would not fail to recount our conversation and God knows how many things she would make me say which had never entered my head."

She was right to shun Mme. de Staël even if she probably did not know that Mme. de Staël had once said to Bonaparte, when he was

still living in the Rue Chantereine, "Josephine is a fool not worthy to
be your wife. I am the only woman who would suit you."

On her way back to Geneva she stopped at Morges at the Château de Vufflens, where she admired the Alpine plants growing
among the rocks. Mme. Eynard-Chatelain entertained her next day
at Rolle. "She is so thoughtful," she wrote, "that one forgets the
Empress and thinks only of the woman who wishes to please
everyone, and it is impossible not to like her. For the rest, her
clothes would have pleased you less than her personality. Imagine a
dress of sky-blue levantine silk, fastened at the neck and not
showing a trace of linen . . . a blue hat with blue feathers and a
yellow cashmere shawl embroidered with many-colored bouquets.
. . . She has had a charming face and still looks well."

Mme. Eynard-Chatelain's son, young Alfred, offered Josephine
flowers. "When she asked Alfred his age," related Mme. Eynard,
"and he replied in a clear voice, 'I am five, madame,' I was terrified
he was going to add, from politeness, 'And you?'"

Before leaving Switzerland Josephine bought a house for 145,000
francs, the Pregny-la-Tour estate at Le Petit Sacconex, "a large main
house, three dependent buildings and other small adjoining buildings, three courtyards, three terrace gardens, an orchard with a tree-
lined avenue to the east, a little wood, a field of sainfoin, a cherry
orchard, vines and a large meadow. Also, on the edge of the lake, a
little port surrounded by walls and a little building intended for the
sport of fishing." She was to make use of this purchase only once,
but she had such pleasure in buying, particularly useless objects.

Of course Josephine cheated about the orders from Napoleon,
who did not want to have his ex-wife at the gates of Paris. She
stopped for a few days at Malmaison, which was visited by all those
who wanted to find fault with the regime. It was a kind of fashion,
even when not actually signifying opposition to the Tuileries. People
found pretexts for visiting "the old one" if they were not on good
terms with "the new one." They pretended to pity the divorced
woman, they entered her house as entering a sacristy condole with
a family in mourning. So the Emperor had made Marie Louise godmother to Josephine's last grandchild! What a lack of tact! If we
can believe Bourrienne, who had for a long time been in disgrace,
Josephine greeted the Emperor's former secretary by holding out
her hand sadly.

"Well, my friend?"

Then, according to him, she launched into a long complaint.

"I have had my fill of misfortune. He has left me, abandoned me. He gave me the empty title of empress only to make my shame more noticeable. Ah! how well we judged him. I never had any illusions about my fate, and what would he not sacrifice to his ambition? . . . He did everything with a cruelty you could never imagine. . . . You cannot imagine, my friend, everything he has made me endure. . . . I cannot think how I have not succumbed. Can you conceive what a torture it has been for me to see descriptions of rejoicing everywhere? And when he first came to see me after his wedding, what an interview! . . . How cruelly he speaks to me about the child he is to have. . . . It would be better to be exiled a thousand leagues from here, and yet a few friends have remained faithful to me and that is now my sole consolation whenever I am able to have one at all."

She saw her tradespeople, chose her dresses, bought shawls, stockings and hats, heard their complaints about "the other one," who let her mistress of the wardrobe choose dresses for her.

Napoleon, who was at Fontainebleau, was astonished that Josephine should delay in leaving Malmaison. He sent Cambacérès to hasten her departure. In a rainy November Navarre should be delightfully green. Finally she consented to set out.

This time the prefect had taken precautions and had offhandedly asked the Minister if he should bother to greet "Josephine," as he dared call her, at Chauffour. Should he take the trouble to call out the guard of honor? He begged that "a few lines" should be written on what his behavior should be "toward Josephine." The Minister was even more offhand than the prefect, for on M. de Chambaudoin's own letter he scribbled these three cutting words, "Nothing to reply."

"Having no reply," wrote the unfortunate prefect, "I merely had the road lit by members from the gendarmerie." But he did order illuminations and the loudest possible shouts of "Long live Josephine!" He himself went to the château, where, he wrote, "I was very well received."

Before leaving Malmaison Josephine had written to her son to explain her reasons for choosing to live at Navarre. "I should have preferred Milan. You know how much I wanted to spend some months with you, but you cannot imagine all the rumors there were about this. People said I had been ordered to Italy and would never return to France. Even the people of my household became uneasy. All feared a journey which would have no limit. So I was obliged to give up what would have pleased me most and not to leave France, at least this year."

In the same letter, dated November 19, she wrote: "It seems that the Empress Marie Louise has not spoken about me and has no desire to see me. We are completely in agreement about this and I should only have agreed to see her to please the Emperor. It appears, too, that she has more than an antipathy for me and I cannot see the reason for it, for all she knows of me is the great sacrifice I made for her. Like herself, I desire the Emperor's happiness and this feeling should bring her closer to me. But none of this will affect my conduct. I have laid down the line I must follow and I shall not depart from it. This is to live in retreat far from everything, but with dignity and without asking for anything but peace. My occupations will be the arts and botany. In the summer I shall take the waters."

Finally she stated: "I shall spend this winter at Navarre, where I am going this week. I needed those few days I spent in Malmaison to rest after my journey to Switzerland. I saw very few people there. Those who, in former days, appeared very attached to me have not all given proof of remembering me. I forgive them heartily. I recall only those who have not forgotten me and I do not think of the others. I hope I shall be able to find happiness around me and in the affection of my children, for I am sure that my dear Eugene will always love me as I love him."

21. Duchesse de Navarre

"Tranquility is such a precious gift."—JOSEPHINE

On the morning of December 4, 1810, young Georgette Ducrest de Villeneuve, niece of Mme. de Montesson and Mme. de Genlis, was full of excitement. One of Josephine's coaches was to call for the girl in Paris and take her with her mother to Navarre, where they had been invited to stay for a few months. When the carriage with the Imperial arms, drawn by six horses, followed by a groom and with footmen on the box, stopped in front of the Ducrests' modest house Georgette was dazzled. She usually traveled, as she tells us, in "heavy, dirty stagecoaches." As the relays had been arranged in advance, the speed with which they covered the 68 miles to Navarre delighted the travelers. They did an average of 11 miles an hour, an almost Imperial pace.

The château was all lit up when the coach entered the great avenue. A "troop of footmen"—there were now about a hundred servants—hastened to unload trunks and boxes. Mlle. d'Avrillon who, as "lady of the wardrobe," was part of Josephine's "personal staff," led the travelers to their room. The owner's absence had enabled the architect Berthault to carry out much work and the Marmite had become inhabitable. The château was now well heated by a hot-air stove and forests of wood were burned in the fire places. Forty-two steres (cubic meters) of wood and fifteen tons of coal were consumed each day.

Mme. Ducrest and her daughter were calmed by Mlle. d'Avrillon. Of course, the Empress would not see them until next day. They could rest. "I breathed again," writes Georgette, "at the thought that I had a whole night to prepare myself for being presented. I had not been scared at Malmaison when I made my visit, because the room was so full of people that it was like any other gathering I had been to and I was not noticed in the crowd, but I told myself that, far from Paris, some distraction was needed and that someone as awkward as I might be would prove a very amusing one for the courtiers whom I imagined to be all mocking and impertinent."

But suddenly there was a knock at the door and Mme. d'Aude-narde appeared. Her Majesty wished to see her two guests at once. Immediately there was panic and the bustle of dressing. Fortunately no choice had to be made. In order to spare expense for her household and her guests Josephine had decided that all the ladies should wear "dark green" dresses of any material. At the moment this uniform seemed heavy and ugly to Georgette. "Mme. d'Aude-narde, with great kindness, tried to dissipate what she called my terror, and assured me that people were as indulgent in the drawing room at Navarre as anywhere else."

Trembling, Mlle. Ducrest went downstairs and entered an ante-room where thirty footmen waited—to Georgette it seemed more like two hundred. Then came a reception room with four valets de chambre in embroidered coats and wearing swords and then another reception room where the usher on duty waited to announce Josephine's guests. The poor girl, fearing "to appear haughty," made curtsy after curtsy, even to the valets, and finally entered the card room, where Josephine was passing the evening at her usual game of backgammon with a "respectable old man," M. Bourlier, Bishop of Evreux.

Three more curtsies and then Mme. Ducrest and her daughter stood before the ex-Empress. Josephine was smiling—that smile which had always won hearts.

Mme. d'Arberg stood near the ex-Empress. She was still running the household and trying, but in vain, to dam the tide of tradesmen who still came as frequently from Paris and who, with such a good customer as Josephine, were not put off by two days' journey and bad lodgings at Evreux. Georgette noticed with pleasure that besides the Empress's usual ladies there was a group of young girls in the room. There was Mlle. de Mackau, who hoped to become a baroness and was to be appointed a lady in waiting after Christmas, the two Mlles. de Castellane and Stephanie d'Arenberg, who still obstinately refused to live with her husband, for whom she felt the same insurmountable aversion as after her terrible wedding night. Her nervous attacks which "were terrifying," her sensitivity "which was killing her," did not prevent Napoleon from threatening her: "I shall have you taken to Brussels between two gendarmes."

"As you wish, sire," she had replied. "At least, if I am seen to arrive like that people will know I am not coming of my own accord."

Meanwhile she was happy with her Imperial cousin. They talked about their beloved Martinique, which they would never see again, and Stephanie let herself be flirted with by M. Chaumont de Guitry, who was to be appointed equerry on December 26. *He* seemed to be able to manage the Princess' nerves quite well.

This little world, which also included Turpin-Crissé and Pourtalès, formed the habit of meeting in Georgette's apartment in the evening. At the beginning of her stay, indeed, the girl did not dare eat during meals for fear of committing some blunder. When Mme. d'Arberg informed Josephine, the latter, touched and amused, ordered a chicken and some Malaga to be sent up every evening to Mlle. Ducrest, who shared it with her new friends. Gradually she risked eating in public and soon considered she knew as much as her neighbors—which did not put an end to the tradition of the midnight feasts.

"Luncheon, at ten in the morning, and dinner, at six," Georgette tells us, "were composed of only one course, except for dessert, which was the second. The soups, hors-d'oeuvres, entrées, roasts and entremets were all served at once." Behind Josephine's chair, as at the Tuileries, were a butler, two valets, a Basque courier and a footman. Pineapples and bananas came from the Malmaison hothouses.

After luncheon, while Josephine worked at her embroidery and others sketched, one of the chamberlains, generally Viel-Castel, read the latest novel aloud. At two they would pile into three four-horse carriages and drive to the forest of Evreux. Josephine had tried to shake off Imperial etiquette by refusing the ceremonial outriders, but the Emperor had decided that as his first wife had been "anointed Empress and Queen," this quality was "indelible" and therefore she could not get a breath of fresh air without being accompanied by a uniformed equerry prancing at the right door, an officer at the left and fourteen horsemen of the 8th Cuirassiers, provided by the Evreux garrison, following.

When the weather was unfavorable they would take a stroll along the canals in the park. Josephine went every day to the greenhouses, where the horticulturist Bonpland was acclimatizing duplicates from Malmaison. During one of these walks a camellia, one of those Josephine had introduced into France, was given to Georgette Ducrest, which, as may be imagined, provoked much jealousy.

If it was raining, the reading went on until four, after which there was time off until dinner. It was then that Josephine would chat with some intimate friend. The subjects of conversation were always the same: the divorce, life in the old days, and above all, "is he still thinking of her?" Josephine spoke of the Emperor "with moderation and tact." As Mme. de Rémusat said, the deserted woman tried "with the best will in the world" to "replace her memories by her hobbies."

"The life I lead," she wrote to Eugene, "is that of a country lady. I never have much company. I now have seven or eight ladies with me and a man or two, no more, when an equerry is here, which makes the château appear rather like a convent. . . . I was unwell for the first few days after my arrival, perhaps on account of the damp. I was given an emetic, which broke the fever, and I should be very well now were it not for a slight weakness in my eyes. However, they are still good enough for me to see my grandson, if he were here." Her daughter-in-law, Augusta, had just given birth to a boy.

Josephine listened indulgently to the gossip of her little court. She was amused at learning that M. de Pourtalès, already the lover of Mme. Gazzani, was trying at the same time to carry on an intrigue, more sentimental and "honorable," with Louise de Castellane. She patronized other love affairs, which also ended in marriage. M. la Briffe was to marry Mlle. de Colbert and Mlle. de Mackau had fallen in love with a visiting general, M. Wattier, by the grace of the Emperor Comte de Saint-Alphonse. Following the example of the mistress of the house—her feelings for Lancelot were a secret only to newcomers—there was a certain laxity in the château. The position of this Empress *in partibus* was a false one and consequently the efforts to make Navarre an Imperial residence like Fontainebleau or Compiègne partook of make-believe. It was life in a country house rather than a palace, which incidentally, was much pleasanter for everyone. Equerries and chamberlains wore their uniforms as little as possible and if a young lady's maid had charm and wit why should she not go with "the gentlemen and young ladies" on a sleigh ride? In fact this was how it happened that Mlle. d'Avrillon was thrown out of a sleigh on January 9 and broke her left leg in two places. Turpin was present when the bone was set and described the operation to Josephine in detail. The ex-Empress bought a mechanical bed so that the invalid's sheets could be changed without hurting her too much.

And life went on, from incident to incident. "I have already told you about life at Navarre," Josephine wrote to Eugene on January 20. "It is still the same and I am becoming used to it. Tranquillity is very pleasant! Ambition is the only thing that can make one dissatisfied with it, and, thank God, I do not suffer from this. I only wish I was better placed for seeing you; then I would lack little. Hortense came a few days ago. She is going back to Paris tomorrow. She is so thin and changed that it gives me almost as much pain as pleasure to see her. I wish I could give her my health, which is very good at present. It began to freeze again yesterday, which will increase our walks and decrease the readings in the drawing room."

The composer Spontini came to Navarre to present his *La Vestale*, which he had dedicated to Josephine. The ladies and officers of the household who possessed, or thought they did, passable voices had studied the choruses of *La Vestale* and *Fernand Cortès*. The composer's presence made the actors nervous and inhibited their style, but Spontini declared nevertheless that everyone "sang wonderfully."

Josephine announced that there would be a jewel lottery on the first of the year. "Everyone impatiently waited for what fate, *helped by Her Majesty*, would bring them. M. de Barral, the Archbishop of Tours, an intelligent but rather absent-minded man, did not notice the way in which the lots were drawn. The first was for him. It was a superb ruby ring surrounded by diamonds. He was enchanted and declared with amusing good faith that it could not have hap-

pened better, since he could wear it, and that he would have been
very much embarrassed to get a necklace or a pair of earrings,
which he would have had to have changed. He perceived that the
Empress was helping chance only when two or three palace ladies
got exactly the same things and the chamberlains identical pins."
Mme. Gazzani received a bracelet "of large colored stones mounted
in diamonds." Instead of being touched at seeing that the Empress
bore her no grudge, she pouted at not receiving a cross of brilliants
like those given to the palace ladies.

When Hortense visited her mother court etiquette was re-
established, and in imitation of the ex-Queen of Holland's household, Josephine's little court brought out their silk dresses and
uniforms.

Eugene was always glad to relax at Navarre. "It is bad enough to
be forced to undergo all the gloomy consequences of power when
I am in Milan," he said. "At least let me be allowed to amuse myself
a little here. *The task of being a king is very hard when one has not
been brought up to it.*"

He forbade the ushers to announce him, so that the court ladies
would not have to rise every time he entered his mother's drawing
room. "I have seen him choose to go through the garden in the
pouring rain," wrote Georgette Ducrest, "in order to enter by the
gallery without the announcement he disliked."

On March 18 a long line of carriages arrived from Evreux. These
contained "all the great ones of the town," who were coming twenty-
four hours in advance to wish the Duchess of Navarre a happy
celebration on St. Joseph's day. Girls in white carrying flowers
brought a bust of Josephine and grouped themselves around it to
recite their congratulations. In the evening it was the turn of the
members of the little Court, who disguised themselves as Norman
peasants and chanted verses.

The gift which probably pleased Josephine most was the pack of
cards painted by Turpin-Crissé showing the faces of the chief
people at court. Josephine was the Queen of Hearts and Lancelot
the knave of Diamonds. Already a comte and the son of a marquis,
Lancelot had just been made an imperial baron by Napoleon.

Shortly afterward Turpin gave his mistress further pleasure by
presenting her with the collection of his sketches from Switzerland
and Savoy bound in red leather and imprinted with a gold J. There

Josephine found Hautecombe and its fountain, the Mer de Glace, the old castle of Aix, and she slipped between the pages a little bouquet of dried flowers, those Turpin had given her on a mountain walk. (The album can still be seen at Malmaison.) She was so happy that she asked Turpin to paint a picture from one of the sketches. He agreed. "This magnificent landscape was brought to the Empress, who was delighted," Georgette tells us. "Having displayed it for the admiration of everyone who came, she approached the artist and drew him into a window.

"'This is for you,' she said, putting into his hand bank notes for the agreed price, and a diamond worth 900 francs. 'This is for your good mother. But if I have not guessed her tastes rightly, tell her that I shall not be annoyed if she changes this poor token of my friendship for whatever suits her. She will at least see my desire to prove to her all the pleasures her son's work has given me.'"

The mayor had invited Josephine to dinner on March 20, for the feast of St. Joseph, but Josephine refused and sent her maison d'honneur in her stead. She was alone with Mme. d'Arberg when she heard the sound of guns and bells far off. She thought it might be more celebrations of her feast day. A few minutes later she was enlightened by the arrival of the Evreux director of posts, who came in his ceremonial uniform. He had just received a courier from Lavallette who announced the birth to Marie Louise and Napoleon of a son, the King of Rome. He watched Josephine's reactions. At first he noticed a slight contraction of the face, but she soon controlled herself. This birth undoubtedly gave even more importance to the woman who had succeeded her and the ex-Empress would undoubtedly fall further into the background, but the arrival of an heir to the great Empire proved, as she often said, "that her sacrifice had not been in vain." And she forced herself to smile as she replied:

"The Emperor can have no doubt of my lively interest in an event that fills him with joy. He knows that I am inseparable from his destiny and that I shall always be happy at his happiness."

Next morning Josephine received some consolation from the arrival of Prince Eugene, who had been sent by the Emperor to give her details of the birth. She immediately wrote to Napoleon to congratulate him and on March 22 the page Leblond de Saint-

Hilaire, staggering with fatigue and announced by the usher as "coming from the Emperor," brought her the happy father's reply. "My dear, I received your letter. I thank you. My son is plump and healthy. I hope he will do well. He has my chest, my mouth and my eyes. I trust he will fulfill his destiny. I am still very pleased with Eugene. He has never given me any anxiety." As thanks for his swift journey the young page received from Josephine a diamond pin worth 25,000 present-day francs.

Eugene managed to make his mother laugh by describing the antics of Caroline and Pauline, who pretended to feel faint with emotion and happiness.

Josephine's son left Navarre before the grand ball his mother gave to celebrate the birth of the little King. "Everyone shouted and rushed around," related Georgette, who watched the preparations with amusement. ". . . We tried on our dresses and the gentlemen their grand uniforms. Some no longer knew how to wear them; some never had known. M. Pierlot amused us greatly by his embarrassment at wearing the velvet jacket embroidered with silver, and the plumed hat stuck on his head like the classic nightcap. . . . The enormous bow of his white satin scarf fell right in the middle of his chest; his sword caught on all our dresses; in fact he was the most comical figure I have ever seen."

When the time came for the ball, Josephine, followed by her household, made her entry covered with diamonds, as at the Tuileries. She held a "review" of the guests and sat down in a chair, which this time somewhat resembled a throne.

Georgette's account continued:

> Her Majesty offered to lend me a set of jewels to wear on the great day, but I thought I should not dare move if I were wearing anything valuable that did not belong to me, so I refused and decided, although regretfully, to wear only my modest pearl necklace. which at least would not keep me from dancing. Mlles. de Mackau and de Castellane, who had accepted the Empress's offer, would have preferred to be in my shoes in the course of the evening.
>
> After each dance they asked if anything was missing from their rich jewels and it could be seen that they hardly dared to move, they were so afraid of losing something.

A false floor had been laid over the tiles of the great drawing room. The work must have been hastily done, or else the dancers were more numerous than had been expected, for M. de Clermont-Tonnerre, who admittedly was very fat, broke through the boards and a carpenter had to be summoned in the middle of the ball to get him out. But the supper, up to the standards of the Tuileries, made everyone forget the incident.

The old financial problems continued to arise, naturally, and Josephine went on piling up debts. Money flowed on an Imperial scale. M. de Monaco refused to travel otherwise than in a six-horse carriage preceded by an outrider and a courier. One morning her chief butler told Josephine that it was impossible to have fewer than twenty-two tables for the servants, who were served separately.

"There is a hierarchy among the lower classes much more marked than in Her Majesty's drawing room."

Josephine went to find Mme. d'Arberg, who was unwell, and so held a conference at her bedside.

"Can you imagine anything like the waste I have to put up with? The cooks won't eat with the kitchen maids and the scullions, or the floor polishers with the furnace attendants. As the dames d'annonce do not dine with me, your women refuse to dine with theirs. The etiquette belowstairs is ruining me. Mme. d'Arberg, you simply must set this to rights."

Mme. d'Arberg tried to reduce the number of tables but could not bring it below sixteen, still a large number considering, as Georgette Ducrest reveals, that "the footmen and stable staff were not fed."

The Emperor sent Mollien to try to stem the tide. The total of debts was found to be 1,159,494 francs 65 centimes. Part of the deficit could be met by selling wood from Navarre and Malmaison, for as Napoleon told Mollien: "She can no longer count on me to pay her debts. I have no right to add to what I already do for her. The future of her family must not rest on me. I am mortal, more so than anyone."

Mollien explained that Josephine had promised, weeping, to do everything not to exceed three million in 1812.

"But you should not have made her cry," exclaimed the Emperor, sincerely distressed.

And he immediately wrote to her: "I was angry with you about your debts. I don't want you to have any. On the contrary, I hope you will save a million each year for your granddaughters' marriages. However, never doubt my friendship for you and don't upset yourself about it."

To the end both he and she remained in character.

In April Napoleon permitted his ex-wife to return to Malmaison. She went back to Navarre again for just a few weeks during the summer of 1811, but after that, from September on, she remained at Malmaison for the autumn, winter and the spring of 1812 and returned to her Norman home only at the coming of the dark hours.

Josephine was happy to be back in her beloved Malmaison. Her bedroom had been redecorated. She was delighted, and with reason, by her new bed designed by Jacob Desmalter. Surmounted by an oval canopy, it was supported by four cornucopias and the headboard was flanked by two wooden swans. The décor and chairs were purple, the windows and bed draped in muslin and all was embroidered with gold.

The silver-gilt toilet set given by the city of Paris at the coronation was placed between the two windows. Josephine had forbidden the slightest change in "the most beautiful bedroom one could see," that of the Emperor, in which the Roman bed placed on a platform covered with tiger skins was "of an antique shape, simple and irreproachable." She would sometimes go into this room, where a "spacious tent" took the place of curtains, to revive her memories. In the Emperor's study his pen was placed at the inkstand. Everything remained "as before." The globe still bore "the marks of some impatient movements."

"My relics," she would say, herself brushing the dust off familiar objects that recalled the past.

Was there not some affection in this? Was she not cultivating a grief which was beginning to die down?

At Malmaison there was a life of perpetual receptions. To be received one applied to the dame d'honneur, who fixed a day, and the visit always ended with an invitation to luncheon or dinner in the near future. It was no longer the easygoing life of Navarre, and Josephine was the only one not to regret this. By nine in the morning the ladies of the household and those who were staying in the château, such as Georgette Ducrest and her mother, had to be in full dress and the men were ordered to wear uniform or embroidered jacket to receive the guests. The latter had to be dressed in the same way and to assemble well before the time fixed for luncheon. After the meal, which lasted three quarters of an hour, came a game of billiards won, naturally, by the most important guests. Soon the crowd of afternoon visitors arrived.

Georgette Ducrest said:

When the weather permitted we would visit the greenhouses. Every day we went by the same path, talked of the same things, the conversation turning on botany, on Her Majesty's liking for this interesting science, on her prodigious memory, which enabled her to name all the plants. In fact, one uttered the same sentences, at the same time, almost every day, which made these walks boring and tedious. On setting foot in this pretty avenue, which I thought charming on the first day, I would be attacked by such violent yawns that I could hardly overcome them to reply and keep up a conversation which was wearying in its monotony. After examining even the stamens of the rarest flower we would go and admire the black swans (infinitely less beautiful than the white, but the latter had the misfortune of being more common). . . . One listened once again to the chamberlain on duty describing the difficulty of naturalizing them. He would solemnly assert that they could be acclimatized only at Malmaison. . . .

The people who came in the morning were dismissed at the arrival of Her Majesty's carriages, which indicated that she was going out. . . . She rarely detained the ladies to drive out with her. As at Navarre, she would indicate those of her household who were to follow her. We entered other carriages, crossed the park and for two hours traveled round the Bois de Butard. We never went in any other direction. We would come back to dress more elaborately for dinner, to which twelve or fifteen people were always invited.

As they ate, it was customary to assert that one had never drunk better milk or eaten better butter than that of Malmaison. The dairy products came from a herd of cows imported from Switzerland and tended by a young Bernese couple, who wore the dress of their canton. Moreover, the wife of the janitor at Malmaison, who was of English origin, excelled at making Cheshire cheese and mouphines, or muffins, of which Josephine was very fond. She asked her son to send her some "good cheeses" from Italy.

Georgette continued.

At midnight Her Majesty would retire, and we would go up to our rooms. The next day we began all over again and, unless something out of the way happened, each day was like the next. Nothing could be gloomier than this *hybrid* life, if I can so call it. We were not solemn enough for a court and much too stiff for an agreeable gathering. Everyone watched everyone else and no intimacy was possible. . . . Instead of the interesting readings and pleasant conversation of Navarre we had always to put up with the boring commonplaces employed in society, from which one retained only a keen regret at having spent one's time saying or hearing them.

Indeed, what could they talk about? Not of the Emperor, nor of "the other one," nor of the Court at the Tuileries, nor of the war. They spoke little of the Parisian theatres, to which Josephine did not go. There remained only marriages and births. Josephine adored arranging marriages. The Duchesse de Navarre had become simply a private person.

With the winds of marriage blowing through the staff, Josephine always opened her purse, spending 400,000 francs. She also made presents of rare plants—bulbs, shrubs and plants—which often arrived at their destination dead or rotten. No matter, they could be replaced. Purple magnolias, Amaryllis Josephiniae or oleanders left the Malmaison greenhouses every day at Josephine's expense.

It never even occurred to her that she could economize other than in words.

"What a pretty dress your Majesty is wearing today," exclaimed M. de Pourtalès. "That cashmere would make very attractive waistcoats."

She immediately asked for a pair of scissors and laughingly cut up her skirt, distributing pieces to the men around her. During their walks many of the women guests received the shawl Josephine was wearing. "It suits you so well. Keep it in memory of me."

In a letter to Eugene she listed what she had done for the Taschers, the La Pageries, the du Verger de Sanois.

"I am sorry to see you have been incorrectly informed about my Tascher cousins. M. Niepce, who deals with their affairs, asked me to guarantee 60,000 francs for Louis at the time of his marriage, which I did. . . . As for Henry Tascher, I did not know he needed money, as the King of Spain gave him a million when he got married. I bought a set of diamonds for his wife for 30,000 francs. Last January I paid Leroy's dress bill of 32,000 francs for him." And so it went.

Josephine liked giving so as to see happy people around her. She noticed that for traveling to Paris Turpin had only a shabby cabriolet drawn by a horse unworthy of her dear Lancelot. So one morning, when the chamberlain asked a servant to bring out his modest conveyance, what arrived was an elegant tilbury with a thoroughbred horse. It was a present from Josephine, who had also had the Turpin-Crissé arms painted on the door.

Josephine was staying at Navarre for a few weeks when, at the end of August, she received this letter from the Emperor. "Put your affairs in some kind of order. Do not spend more than 1,500,000 francs and lay as much by every year. That will make a reserve of 15 million in ten years for your grandchildren. It would be nice to be able to give them something and be of use to them, instead of which I am told that you are in debt, and that is very bad. Attend to your affairs and don't give to everyone who wants something. If you wish to please me, let me learn that you have amassed a great treasure. Consider what a bad opinion I should have of you if I knew that with an income of three million you were in debt."

Josephine tried to defend herself and wrote to Eugene: "The Emperor speaks very kindly to me about my debts. It would seem that they have been grossly exaggerated to him, but I am confident he will soon hear no more of them. I am setting my house in order and I do not permit myself any new expense." Except, of course, for her dresses. Leroy still ruled Josephine and supplied her with goods costing 10,000 or 15,000 francs a month.

At Malmaison it was still unusual to see Josephine wear the same dress twice; it was almost a matter of etiquette, though fashion had scarcely changed since the day Bonaparte saw the Creole for the first time. Dresses had merely stopped being transparent and were now cut from heavier materials.

Josephine sometimes liked to moralize. One day she had all her jewels spread out on a large table to show to the girls of the little Court. Interrupting their cries of admiration, she explained "kindly":

"It is to dissuade you from developing a mania for jewels that I have had mine brought out. Having seen such beautiful ones you will not wish for mediocre ones, particularly when you think that I have been so unhappy although I possessed such rarities. When I began on my astonishing destiny I took pleasure in these trifles, many of which were given to me in Italy. Gradually I became very tired of them and I wear them now only when I am forced to do so by my new rank in society. Besides many events might deprive one of these superb but useless things; have I not come into possession of Marie Antoinette's jewels? Is it certain that I will keep them? Believe me, young ladies, you should not envy this luxury which does not bring happiness."

Yet she would have been made exceedingly unhappy if she had been restricted to ordering in a month what Leroy delivered in one week.

She felt she was being moderate. "You may be sure," she wrote to Eugene, "that I have suffered much from this deprivation, but I am beginning to enjoy its fruits, for as a result of the care I have taken my debts will all be paid off at the end of this month and I am glad of it, less for my own peace of mind than in the hope of doing what may please the Emperor. I could have made the task difficult by spreading it out over next year, but the Emperor's intentions would not have been so well carried out and the thought that he will be pleased with me gives me the courage to bear sacrifices."

However, she decided to enlarge Malmaison and, in order to find the necessary money, asked the architect Fontaine to suggest that the Emperor should buy the Elysée Palace. Napoleon was delighted. It seemed to him almost indecent to have his ex-wife possibly living less than half a mile from the Tuileries now that Marie Louise was with him. But he had no intention of loosening his purse strings further. He suggested an exchange of the Elysée, which on December 16, 1809, had cost the Treasury 852,317 francs 78 centimes, for the magnificent château of Laeken outside Brussels, which Bonaparte had bought when still First Consul. The former palace of Schönnenberg and of Prince Charles of Lorraine had been restored a few years before and in 1811 the apartments had been redecorated when Marie Louise passed through. Moreover, there were the famous greenhouses, equal to those at Malmaison.

Josephine accepted the exchange, although this did not bring her the necessary sums for transforming Malmaison. She was never to go to Laeken; the ladies and gentlemen of her household uttered such cries—courtiers' cries, worse than a real scene. To expel Josephine, exile her 37 stages from Paris, would be a real act of tyranny.

In short, Malmaison stayed as it was.

Before knowing Marie Louise Napoleon had thought, somewhat naïvely, that his two wives might meet. He gave up this scheme on noticing, not without satisfaction, that the Archduchess was as jealous as the ex-Vicomtesse. At the mere name of Josephine uttered in her presence she had the vapors, and yet she had imagined that the "preceding Empress was eighty." One day, on leaving Saint-Cloud by the swing bridge, the Emperor suggested, as they came to the turning for Malmaison, that they might visit the house, Josephine being then at Navarre.

"The garden is pretty."

In reply the "new one" burst into tears. He calmed her.

"I was only suggesting an outing. If you don't want to go, that's the end of it, but you must not cry on that account."

The exiled Empress, however, wanted to meet the Archduchess. Napoleon dissuaded her.

"You are wrong. Today she believes you are old and does not think of you. If she saw you with all your charms you might make her anxious and she would ask me to send you away. I should have to do it. You are all right as you are. Keep quiet!"

Josephine, flattered, did not persist. Yet one day when Napoleon came to see her without telling "the other one" she asked his permission to see the little King. The Emperor was evasive, then explained to Mme. de Montesquiou, the King of Rome's governess: "It would hurt the Empress so much that I cannot make up my mind to authorize such an undertaking."

"Leave it to me, sire," she replied. "Just give your approval afterwards."

"I agree, but mind you do not get into trouble."

The governess then let Josephine know, by the King of Rome's first equerry, Baron de Canisy, that she was taking the child to the Park of Bagatelle on the next Sunday.

So that our secret should not be guessed I had agreed with M. de Canisy that on entering the carriage I should say that I left him the choice of our outing. Shortly afterward I called him back to say that if the child needed to stop we would go to Bagatelle. In due course we arrived there. On entering the courtyard M. de Canisy announced with an air of astonishment that the Empress Josephine was there. I replied: "We have gone too far to turn back. It would be improper."

She was in the little room at the back. She had us come in at once. She knelt before the child, sank into tears and kissed his hand, saying, "My dear child, you will one day know the extent of the sacrifice I have made for you. I rely on your governess to make you understand it."

After spending an hour with the child and me she wanted to see those at present in the young King's service. She was amiable as always, so much so to the nurse that as we returned to the carriage this woman said: "My goodness, how pleasant this one is! She has said more to me in a quarter of an hour than 'the other one' has in six months."

22. "Poor Josephine!"

In May, 1812, the Empire was at its height, but only the façade of the edifice remained intact, hiding the cracks. The "beginning of the end" was not far distant. Pending the time when the house of cards should collapse, the Napoleonic glory was emitting its final rays. At Dresden, before the departure for Russia, there was a crowd of kings, princes and more or less sovereign dukes around the two Imperial couples of France and Austria. And when they went to table Napoleon kept on his hat. Everyone else had his hat in his hand, even the Emperor Francis—he was giving his arm to his daughter Marie Louise.

Eugene, who had passed through Paris on his way to assume command of the IV Corps of the Grand Army, had finally persuaded his mother to go to Milan. She had often promised him to do so and Augusta was again pregnant. Since the child's father would be far away, the grandmother could replace him. Josephine agreed without enthusiasm. She was so comfortable at Malmaison, whereas in the Viceroy's palace in Milan there would be all the drawbacks of a court—and a foreign court at that. She made one condition, that she might travel under another name, and Eugene informed his wife:

"She will arrive incognito. Then she will receive all the people

461

presented at court, on one day the authorities and on the next the ladies and their husbands. After that the authorities will be admitted to her presence just as you receive them on ordinary Sundays. So the Senate are not to come in a body, nor the Council of State, nor the Tribunal, but you will present them, as they are presented to you on Sundays and they will be mentioned by name to the Empress. In this way speeches will be avoided. So now you understand: all the people presented must be told to come at a certain time and first the Ministers and the President will be shown in and then ten or twelve people at a time."

After twelve days' hard traveling Josephine, under the name of Mme. d'Arberg, arrived in Milan in the evening of July 27, 1812, and was housed in the Villa Bonaparte in the apartments usually inhabited by Eugene. She found her daughter-in-law "wonderful," as she wrote to her son, and her grandchildren "adorable." "There are none prettier or more amiable." Auguste Napoleon, the future Duke of Leuchtenberg, who was to marry Maria II, Queen of Portugal, was a "Hercules of a child." The elder granddaughter, Josephine, the ex-Empress's godchild—in 1823 she married Oscar I, who reigned over Sweden and Norway—was "a beauty," and the "lively and intelligent" face of the younger, Eugénie, who was later ruling Princess of Hohenzollern-Hechingen, was her grandmother's joy.

On July 31, not without some difficulty, Augusta gave birth to Amélie, "the kitten," as Eugene called her, who was one day to become Empress of Brazil and who, at the moment, "gives great hopes for her face and strength." "I am more and more enchanted with your children," added Josephine in her letter to Eugene. "Your son is very strong, very gay and very gentle. We now get on very well. Yesterday, after writing you my evening letter, I gave it to him to give the equerry and I told him it was for papa. He kissed the letter and took it to the equerry."

In spite of her joy at getting to know her grandchildren, Josephine did not linger in Milan. Court life did not amuse her. Augusta was undoubtedly "charming, beautiful and fresh," but Milan is very hot in August. So after a month, while little Josephine wept on hearing her grandmother's carriage leave, the ex-Empress set off again, crossed the Alps and arrived in Aix-les-Bains. She received letters from Augusta and was touched to learn that Eugene's son

prayed every evening for his parents and "for the other mamma."
"That is charming," Josephine replied. "I can no longer embrace him
or his sisters, but I often think of them."

She found Aix very melancholy that year and missed Plombières.
She took baths and douches every morning at the thermal establishment. These were no longer to cure her sterility but to treat her
imaginary ailments. She met the two Clary sisters there, Queen Julie
"good and kind as usual," and Princess Désirée "looking very well."
Then the ex-Empress spent three weeks at Pregny on Lake Geneva,
the house she had bought the year before. The house was full of
flowers but "very hastily furnished." They were "camping out" and
it was a good excuse for taking liberties with etiquette. Josephine
allowed people to sit down in her presence and they played blind-
man's buff and hot cockles in the park, as at Malmaison in the old
days. Crowds came from Geneva and everyone found the hostess
"full of charming urbanity and consideration." No constraint about
her," they added, admiring her simplicity. Naturally she kept her
visitors to dinner. "This dinner," a sympathetic Genevan tells us,
"is at six thirty. At seven thirty we return to the drawing-room and
talk for an hour, after which she sits down to whist and plays for fun.
There are two tables. The rest of the company play children's games
or even tig, forfeits and so on. At half past ten she wishes the
company good night and retires. There is no awkwardness or
stiffness in these gatherings. One is merely obliged to pay great
attention to one's dress. One tries to please and be well bred, in
short, it is good society."

On October 4 she went to the Prefecture of Geneva, then capital
of the Mont-Blanc Department, to a reception celebrating Napoleon's victory over the Russian armies. A few days later the Emperor
was to begin his terrible retreat.

On October 21 she left the shores of Lake Geneva. One of the
Genevans gave an ungallant sigh of relief. "The Empress is leaving
and, although she had made herself liked, most people are pleased.
The kind of life we have been leading since she came here does not
suit our habits."

On October 23 Josephine was driving peacefully toward Paris. At
the same time Malet and his unwitting accomplices were trying to
overthrow the Empire. Once back in Malmaison she wrote to her

son: "My journey would have been happy if I had not learned, on arriving at Melun, of the trouble Paris had been experiencing the previous morning. . . . One consolation is that Paris took no part in it. The consternation was general, but it did not last long. After a few hours everything became as calm as before. If there could have been the slightest danger to the King of Rome and the Empress I do not know what I should have done, but I am sure I should have followed my first impulse: I should have gone with my daughter to join them."

Josephine did not understand the gravity of the situation or, rather, drew no conclusion from it. It was the knell of the regime.

Admittedly this comic-opera conspiracy had had little chance of success, but for all that it had shaken the enormous, hybrid and perpetually hungry Empire. Above all, Malet had proved that the hereditary Empire was only a point of view. No one that morning, among the prefects, functionaries and officers to whom the Emperor's death had been announced, had thought of the King of Rome, still less of shouting: "The Emperor is dead, long live the Emperor!" Had Josephine's sacrifice been in vain? She realized even less what was going on since the Russian catastrophe had not yet begun. She had not really understood the reasons for the burning of Moscow. She merely knew that the Emperor and the Grand Army had arrived in the Russian capital and this news had surprised her no more than Napoleon's entry into Vienna, Cairo or Madrid.

Josephine concluded only one thing from the Malet affair, that the Emperor's life might be in danger. "Take care of his safety," she recommended Eugene, "for the rogues are capable of everything. Tell the Emperor from me that he is wrong to go and live in palaces without knowing whether they are mined."

And suddenly into that life at Malmaison made up of trifles, daily routine and banalities, abruptly, between two visits to the swans or the greenhouses, between two strolls in the garden, burst the news of the Russian catastrophe, the dreadful drama of the most horrible retreat in history. At Malmaison they watched for the couriers. "Every day brought fateful details which caused a shudder," wrote Mlle. d'Avrillon. "We were the more frightened since twenty years of uninterrupted success had taught us to think setbacks impossible."

Josephine trembled for the Emperor, but even more for Eugene.

When she finally received a letter, which was two or three weeks old, she breathed again. "I have passed from the most acute anxiety to great happiness. My son is alive!"

On December 19 she learned that on the previous evening the Emperor, unrecognizable, unshaven, wrapped in a pelisse, had re-entered Paris alone with Caulaincourt, after a 14-day journey. He was soon to come to see her at Malmaison, but we do not know what they said to each other.

Murat, to whom Napoleon had left the command of the remnants of the Grand Army, forgot his heroism, turned into a whimperer and deserted—under the pretext of incipient jaundice—and Josephine learned with distress that the onerous inheritance had fallen to her son. His diligent mind, his professional conscience, his honesty, the "good student" side of his character, his courage and intelligence enabled Eugene to carry out the operations successfully and to receive the Emperor's approval.

"We all made blunders," Napoleon was to say later. "Eugene alone made none."

Josephine had become much more maternal than formerly, or rather grandmotherly. Her greatest pleasure was to have children at Malmaison. She even invited and spoiled little Alexandre and his mother, Marie Walewska—an ironical sight. When Queen Hortense went for her cure at Aix-les-Bains in June and July, 1813, Josephine was happy to have her grandsons Napoleon and Louis with her. The latter was nicknamed "Oui-Oui."

When the two boys had studied hard during the week Josephine had them to lunch and dine with her on the Sunday. She got two mechanical toys from Paris—two gold hens that laid silver eggs. She gave one to each of her grandsons and told her daughter, "I gave them on your behalf, as coming from Aix."

More than fifty years later Oui-Oui, then the Emperor Napoleon III, was to remember with affection the days spent at Malmaison:

I can still see the Empress Josephine in her ground-floor drawing room, covering me with caresses and already developing my self-esteem by making the most of my clever remarks. For my grandmother literally spoiled me, whereas from my earliest childhood my mother was careful to curb my faults and develop my good qualities. I remember that as soon as we arrived at Malmaison my brother and I were free to do what we liked. The Empress, who was passionately fond of her plants and greenhouses, allowed us to cut the sugar canes to suck them and she always told us to ask for everything we wanted. One day, on the eve of some feast, when she said the same thing, my brother, who was three years older than I and consequently more sentimental, asked for a watch with our mother's portrait. But when the Empress said to me, "Louis, ask for whatever would give you most pleasure," I asked to walk through the mud with the little common children on the street. This should not be thought a ridiculous request, for as long as I was in France, where I stayed until I was seven, one of my greatest griefs was always going to town in a carriage with four or six horses.

The two grandsons were still at Malmaison when Josephine heard that Adèle de Broc, Hortense's inseparable friend, had been drowned before her eyes in the Grésy cascade. Josephine immediately wrote to her daughter, "I am so anxious that I am sending my chamberlain, M. de Turpin, to you so that I can get firsthand news of your health. . . . I should not delay in coming myself if my presence and care could be of use to you."

Lancelot went and returned and was able to calm Josephine. Hortense was intensely grieved, but had decided to prolong her stay at the spa, and Josephine could keep her grandsons with her a little longer.

"Their health remains wonderful. They have never been more hearty and well. Little Oui-Oui is always kind and pleasant to me. Two days ago, when he saw Mme. de Tascher leave to join her husband at the spa, he said to Mme. de Boucheporn, 'She must love her husband very much if she is leaving grandmamma.' Don't you think that's charming? That same day he went for a walk in the Bois du Butard. The moment he reached the great avenue he threw his hat in the air, crying, 'Oh, how I love nature!' Few days go by without one or the other amusing me by his lovable ways. They enliven everything about me, so you may imagine how happy you have made me by leaving them with me."

Things were not going well for Napoleon, but who would have imagined that the end was so near? So Josephine busied herself with enlarging her estate. Pierre Schommer, who was the curator of Josephine's estate for many years, has told us of her last acquisitions. She enriched Malmaison "with the lake of Saint-Cucuffa, which fed her waterfalls. She extended in the direction of the Côte d'Or of Rueil, she made sure of the hills of Buzenval and brought about the harmonious unity of Malmaison by adding the twenty acres of Bois-Préau."

The great Empire was crumbling. It was the beginning of the battle of France. Bernadotte went over to the coalition and the Allies would have liked Eugene to do the same, thus following the example of his father-in-law, the King of Bavaria, who on November 22, 1813, sent the Prince of Thurn and Taxis to him to persuade him to change camps. His family would be "assured of a favorable destiny in Italy." He was even offered kingship "of a country to be agreed on." Eugene immediately wrote to the Emperor: "I need little reflection before assuring the King of Bavaria that his son-in-law was too honest to commit such a cowardly action, that to my last breath I should hold to the oath I had taken, which I repeated, to serve you faithfully; that the fate of my family is and would always be in your hands and that, finally, if misfortune ever fell on us I thought so highly of the King of Bavaria that I was convinced in advance that he would rather see his son-in-law a private person, but an honest man, than a king and a traitor."

It is a pleasure to read these lines written during the last months of the Empire when the rush of betrayals had already started.

Augusta's attitude compels admiration. She was born a Wittelsbach and so that Josephine might be as proud of her son as she herself was of her husband, sent her mother-in-law all the relevant documents, adding: "Nothing good, noble and great coming from our excellent Eugene can astonish us, but for all that I have, since yesterday, been even happier and prouder to be the wife of such a man and, so that you may share my joy, I hasten to send you a copy of a letter he wrote me after refusing a crown that was offered him if he would agree to be an ingrate, a coward, in fact to betray the Emperor as the King of Naples has."

Yet Augusta was once more pregnant and Eugene thought he might ask the Austrian Marshal de Bellegarde permission for his wife to stay in Milan or Monza for her lying-in. The Marshal said he would refer to Vienna. At that time, apart from exceptional cases, it took twelve days to send a letter from Paris to Milan and receive the reply. This lapse of time gave rise to a series of misunderstandings. Napoleon appears not to have been informed of the exact tenor of Eugene's request. Worse, he seems to have gathered only one thing—that Eugene, formerly his adopted son, "was in touch with the enemy." So he wrote to Josephine to prepare her for the Viceroy's possible treason. The ex-Empress immediately wrote to her son: "Do not lose a moment, my dear Eugene, whatever the difficulties, redouble your efforts to carry out the order the Emperor has given you. He has just written to me about it. He intends you to betake yourself to the Alps, leaving only the Italian troops in Mantua and the Italian strongholds." Her letter ended with these words: "France above all, France needs all her children. Come, then, my dear son, hasten. Your zeal will never have better served the Emperor. I can assure you that every moment is precious. I know that your wife was preparing to leave Milan. Tell me if I can be of use to her. Good-by, my dear Eugene, I have time only to embrace you and tell you to come quickly."

A few days later the Emperor, learning the truth from Eugene's aide-de-camp Tascher, was completely reassured. He merely wrote to the Viceroy from Nangis on February 18, the day of the battle of Montereau: "My son, the Vicereine must go immediately to Paris for her lying-in, my intention being that she should not, in any circumstances, remain in country occupied by the enemy." Then Napoleon left Nangis to fight at Montereau, uttering a sentence which was to make the fortune of print sellers: "Go on, my friends, fear nothing. The bullet to kill me has not yet been made." He had all Europe against him, he was writing to Eugene between two battles, and the tone of his letter can be forgiven.

But Eugene was wounded at receiving his stepfather's orders through his mother. It was the first time such a thing had happened. Following Eugene's reply to the Prince of Thurn and Taxis, Napoleon had contented himself with saying: "I recognize Austria's policy. That is the way she makes so many traitors.'

Eugene therefore wrote to his mother: "Your letter took me aback. I did not think that after all this time I had to give the Emperor proofs of my fidelity and devotion. I can see only one thing in all this, which is that I have enemies and that they are jealous of the honorable way, if I may say so, in which I have extricated myself from a very difficult situation."

And on February 27 he sent a letter by the same courier to the Emperor, expressing surprise that his stepfather should imagine that he "needed to be urged" to "draw nearer" to France. The treachery of Murat, who had just gone over to the enemy, enabled him to end by affirming that he considered he deserved neither the Emperor's reproaches nor his lack of confidence.

When he finally received Napoleon's letter of February 19, ordering "his son" to get Augusta to leave at once for Paris for her lying-in, Eugene was deeply "hurt and afflicted by the form of this order," and he told his stepfather so. But Augusta did not complain. She rebelled. She was the daughter of a king, a real king, and she gave herself the luxury of writing the Emperor such a letter as he was not accustomed to receive:

I did not expect [she wrote], after all the proofs Eugene is constantly giving you of his attachment, that you should require him to risk the health and even the life of his wife and children, the only blessing and consolation he has in the world. . . . We do not practice intrigues and we have no other guide than honor and virtue. It is sad to have to say that, in recompense, we have had only grief and mortification heaped on us, which we have nevertheless borne in silence and with patience. . . . What have I done to deserve such a curt order to leave? When I married I did not think matters would come to this pass. The King my father, who loves me tenderly, suggested, when matters were going so badly, that he should take me in so that I might be confined in peace. But I refused, fearing that this step would reflect badly on Eugene's conduct, although his actions spoke for him, and I intended to go to France. Since then I have been ill and the doctors have told me that I would be taking a great risk if I made such a long journey at present, as I am already in the eighth month of pregnancy.

Augusta did not want to go to Paris or to Malmaison with Josephine. She would stay with Eugene, who was still in Italy. "I shall leave Milan if the enemy should come," she added, "but my duty and my heart make it a law for me not to leave my husband, and since you require me to risk my health I at least wish to have the consolation of ending my days in the arms of the man who has all my affection and is all my happiness."

Eugene, dazzled by his wife's "beautiful soul" and "fine character," made two copies of Augusta's letter and sent them to his mother and sister. Josephine's daughter-in-law was undoubtedly often ill-treated by Napoleon. Being the wife of the Emperor's adopted son, she should have had precedence over the other princesses of the family. Yet she, a Wittelsbach, always had to give way.

When she married, Napoleon had promised the couple the Italian succession and now he spoke only of the Grand Duchy of Frankfort. Admittedly a few days later, on March 15, at the Congress of Châtillon, Caulaincourt received orders to tell the Allies that the Emperor was resigning the crown of Italy in favor of Prince Eugene Napoleon.

Less than two weeks later the Austrians, Russians, Prussians and Swedes would be in Paris. Yet the Emperor felt ashamed. On March 12 he wrote to Augusta from Soissons to apologize and explain his attitude. "I thought that with your temperament you might have a difficult delivery in a country which is a theatre of war and amid enemies and that the best thing for your safety was to come to Paris. Admit your injustice and I rely on your heart to punish you."

He could not help being ironical to Eugene. "It is unfortunate for the age in which we live that your reply to the King of Bavaria should have won you the esteem of all Europe. For my part I did not congratulate you because you only did your duty and that is simple. However, you already have your reward, even in the opinion of the enemy, whose comtempt for your neighbor is unbounded." His neighbor, of course, was the unfortunate Murat.

But already this whole affair had lost its importance. France was conquered. Louis XVIII was packing his trunks, the future Charles X was following the Allied armies, at a distance, and in Marie Louise's court, as in Josephine's, people conspired while making bandages for the wounded. Abstentions, even betrayals, had begun. The Viel-Castels, the Rémusats, the Pourtalès, the Montalivaults, even the Turpins, thought only of the return of the lilies, and for some days several of them had been making their contribution behind Josephine's back.

On Tuesday, March 29, it was raining. From the Tuileries Marie Louis, the King of Rome, the ministers, the treasurer and the coronation coaches set off for the Loire. At Malmaison Josephine entered her carriage to flee to Navarre. Only sixteen Guards remained at the château. To stay longer, when the Cossacks were at Bondy, would be madness. The ex-Empress could not even ask Napoleon's advice. He was somewhere behind the enemy armies. So in deep distress she left Malmaison in tears, wondering when and how she would return to her beloved château.

Everything had crumbled in a few weeks. She did not know what would become of her or how she would live, as she had nothing but debts. Hortense had brought her 24,000 francs, the Duchesse d'Arenberg 25,000 and Henri Tascher 7,500. Josephine had diamonds and pearls sewn into the hem of her "wadded skirt." Fearing that there would be no relays, the fugitive took her own horses and carriages with her and it was impossible to do more than 31 miles a day.

In the evening of March 30 the ex-Empress finally reached Navarre, just as Paris had surrendered and Napoleon, at Juvisy, was exclaiming: "If I had arrived sooner all would have been saved!"

Josephine did not learn the news until the next day from a courier sent by Hortense. The ex-Queen of Holland also arrived at Navarre with her two sons. She had refused to obey either Marie Louise, as Regent, or Louis, both of whom had ordered her to join the Court at Blois.

During the week of April 2 to 9 a succession of news came to Navarre. "Our hearts are broken by all that is happening," she wrote to a friend, "and above all by the ingratitude of the French. The newspapers are full of the most horrible insults. If you have not read them, do not take the trouble, they would make you sick."

In succession Josephine heard of the Allies' refusal to treat with the vanquished leader, the creation of a provisional government, Napoleon's first abdication, reserving the rights of Napoleon II, the granting of the governorship of the Island of Elba to the former master of 132 French departments, the second abdication, renouncing the crowns of France and Italy for himself and his heirs and finally the expected arrival in Paris of the Comte d'Artois.

On April 9 Josephine wrote to Eugene: "What a week I have gone through, my dear Eugene! How I suffered from the way they treated the Emperor! What insults in the newspapers, what ingratitude on the part of those he had most honored! But there is no more hope. *Everything is over; he is abdicating. As for you, you are free and released from every vow of fidelity. Anything more you do for his cause will be useless. Act for your family. . . .* I live in terrible fear and anxiety." By April 9 she had undoubtedly seen the issue of *Le Moniteur* of April 6, which published the letters of adherence to Louis XVIII by Napoleon's generals. To prolong the French Army's resistance in Italy would have been a folly which Eugene might have committed.

The Treaty of Paris was signed on April 11. Article VII settled

Josephine's future. "The annual revenue of the Empress Josephine will be reduced to a million in land or treasury scrip. She will continue to enjoy all her personal property and real estate and can dispose of it according to French law."

With no more service d'honneur and no more pensions to pay, Josephine could still lead a princely life on five million present-day francs. Queen Hortense and her children received an income of 400,000 francs, while "a suitable establishment outside France will be given to Prince Eugene, Viceroy of Italy."

There was no reason for Josephine to stay in Navarre, particularly as she had heard from Mlle. Cochelet that the Russians were very well disposed toward her. The Tsar wished to set the Beauharnais against the Bonapartes and it was said that Eugene was being talked of as a candidate for the throne of Italy. This last was somewhat exaggerated, but certainly the Russians and Austrians wished Josephine and her children nothing but good. Alexander was anxious to know Hortense, "for he serves her interests as though they were his." Prince Metternich, for his part, recalled "the kind actions" of Hortense and her mother to his wife and children and asked after the health of the "ladies at Navarre." Even Prince Leopold, Marie Louise's uncle, was "perfect" to Josephine and her daughter. "All he wants is to be useful to both of them." And Caulaincourt, speaking for the Emperor, advised a return to Malmaison. So on Wednesday, April 13, the day after the Comte d'Artois's entry into Paris, Josephine went back to her beloved home. The previous night Napoleon had tried to poison himself at Fontainebleau and that same morning Marie Louise arrived at Rambouillet, where her father was to join her. Everything was over.

If Josephine had stayed forty-eight hours longer at Navarre she would have returned to Malmaison with a guard of honor wearing white cockades—the gracious suggestion of the Duc de Berry, who was crossing Normandy at the same time.

The *Journal des Débats* of April 16 announced: "The mother of Prince Eugene has returned to Malmaison." If the new government did not know what to call the ex-Empress, this was not the case with Emperor Alexander, who on the same day, preceded by Prince Tchernicheff, visited Josephine and gave her all her titles. He appeared charmed by her "gentleness" and her "lack of control." At this point Hortense joined her mother and Alexander in the park.

Alexander, who apparently found Hortense very attractive, was all smiles and politeness, but the ex-Queen of Holland remained cold and dignified when the Tsar, caressing her children, declared, "What would you like me to do for them? Let me look after their interests."

Without enthusiasm she replied, "I thank Your Majesty, and I appreciate his interest in me, but I wish nothing for my children."

When Alexander had gone, Josephine scolded her daughter for her "air of coldness."

"It would have been out of place," Hortense replied, "to show attention to a man who has just declared himself the Emperor's personal enemy and who, moreover, has destroyed my children's life and that of the family whose name I bear."

Josephine undoubtedly had no such scruples and "maneuvered," as Paul Fleuriot de Langle has said, in an attempt to "pull her chestnuts out of the fire." Of course she was thoughtless, she always had been, and one cannot help feeling uncomfortable at the sight of her throwing herself on the necks of the conquerors, but it is equally certain that Josephine was looking at things more as a sovereign than as a Frenchwoman. She was adopting the tone customary with crowned heads when the wars were over. When she reigned she had seen kings and queens, emperors or empresses conquered by Napoleon come to dine with him and address him as "my good brother." Napoleon had married the daughter of the man he had twice forced to leave his capital. The Tsar himself, who had been beaten by Napoleon, had embraced him at Tilsit. Alexander, of course, had helped to dethrone the Emperor. But Josephine had been repudiated by Napoleon four years before and was no longer his wife.

On that same Saturday, April 16, Napoleon, who was to be at Fontainebleau for four more days, wrote to Josephine. It was the last letter he would send her and he addressed her as *vous*—perhaps in case the courier was captured by the enemy. *Vous*, as in his first letter on October 28, 1795, nineteen and a half years before.

I wrote to you on the 8th of this month and perhaps you did not receive my letter, we were still fighting and it is possible that it was intercepted. Now communications must be re-established. I have made up my mind, I do not doubt that this note will reach you. I shall never repeat what I used to say to you. Then I complained of my position, now I am glad of it. My head and mind are free of an enormous weight.

My fall has been great, but at least it is useful, from what they say. In my retreat I shall replace the sword by the pen. The history of my reign will be an interesting one. I was seen only in profile, but I shall show the whole of myself. What things shall I make known! How many men have been wrongly judged! . . . I loaded thousands of wretches with gifts. What have they done for me in these last days?

They have all betrayed me, yes, all. I except that good Eugene, so worthy of you and me. May he be happy under a king able to appreciate the impulses of nature and honor!

Good-by, my dear Josephine. Be resigned, as I am, and never lose the memory of the man who has never forgotten you and never will forget you.

Napoleon

P.S. I hope to have news from you on the island of Elba. I am not very well.

Many royalists came to Malmaison, either prompted by curiosity or remembering what "good Josephine" had done for the émigrés. Visitors from former days came in crowds. One day, seeing a regular frequenter of the house wearing a white ribbon, she could not help saying with a smile, "Should you not have left that with the hall porter?"

On the day Louis XVIII entered Paris General de Lawoestine came to lunch at Malmaison and drew such a picture of the gouty King and his joyous entry "in the nineteenth year of his reign" that Josephine and her little court could not help laughing. Since Alexander had promised to return, Josephine summoned Leroi and in the second fortnight of April ordered white embroidered muslin dresses costing 6,209 francs 75 centimes. The Tsar did, in fact, come, but more on account of Hortense. He had been snubbed by her and wanted to win her over. He hardly spoke to Josephine, but paid a great deal of attention to the ex-Queen, caressing her children and holding them on his knees. Hortense could not help sighing, "Their only support is an enemy."

"I cast off my original reserve and become more unrestrained," she admitted. A few days later the Tsar wished to visit Saint-Leu. Hortense invited him together with Tchernicheff. Josephine did the honors, but Alexander had eyes only for her daughter and during luncheon, at which he sat next to her, he confided to her:

"You do not know that today there is a solemn service in Paris in honor of King Louis XVI and Queen Marie Antoinette. All the foreign rulers are to be there and I was remarking to Tchernicheff as we came here what a peculiar position I am in. It was in antagonism to your family that I came to Paris full of enmity and it is solely them I have pleasure in visiting. I am doing you harm; I do good to others and it is among you that I find affection. Moreover, I ought to be in Paris today with the other sovereigns and here I am at Saint-Leu!"

After the meal, while Josephine, who was tired, remained in the house, the Tsar walked alone in the park with the Queen. They confided in each other. She spoke "of the cruelest griefs" of her life. She confessed that since the death of her eldest son she lived in perpetual expectation of misfortune.

"But you have friends," he told her. "You are unjust toward Providence."

No doubt Alexander wished to be that Providence. He also made confidences which led Hortense to inquire why he had deserted the Tsarina.

"I cannot go into all the details with you," he replied. "Please do not speak of it any more. My wife has no better friend than myself, but we will never be reunited."

Their friendship certainly never went as far as some scandal-mongers have asserted. Yet the Tsar's feelings for Hortense had useful results. The King granted her the title of Duchesse de Saint-Leu. As a result of this some thought that Louis XVIII, King of France and Navarre, would confirm the ex-Empress's title of Duchesse de Navarre, which would have had some piquancy. Moreover, he received Prince Eugene "extremely well," as Josephine's son was to tell Augusta, and this is certain, Louis XVIII "spoke to him of the good his mother had done in France." The King even sent the Duc de Polignac to Malmaison "to thank the Empress Josephine on his behalf for the zeal she had displayed in trying to save the life of the Duc d'Enghien." The Duc de Polignac "took advantage of this visit" to express his personal gratitude to Josephine. He would never forget that if he was still alive he owed it to her who in 1804 had managed to have his wife granted an audience.

Eugene was in hopes of receiving a throne, but even with the Tsar's help it was not an easy matter.

"From all I have learned," he wrote to his wife on the day he arrived, "we must not expect to be too well treated. Everyone wants

a share of the cake. Each one makes enormous claims and it is true
to say that the most sacred family ties count for nothing in politics.
They wanted to give us Genoa, so that they would not have to give
us anything on the Rhine. If Frankfurt, Mainz, etc. are mentioned,
this one claims it. If Berg or Cologne, then that one. In short, I do
not know what little corner they will take to ensure a home for us,
since everything encroaches on someone's claims or interests."

Eugene, as we know, ended as Duke of Leuchtenberg, a Bavarian
principality carved out of his father-in-law's possessions.

Mme. de Rémusat conceived an extraordinary idea. She thought
Josephine ought "to give some mark of deference to the family
summoned to reign over France." A somewhat ridiculous letter was
drafted in which the ex-wife of "the Usurper" was made to write
"that she no longer knew what she was or what she had been" and
begged the King "to determine her existence." Josephine felt the
impropriety of such a step and asked advice of Alexander, who
apparently replied: "A letter like that would disgrace you. Get rid of
all intriguers and go-betweens. I am sure the King requires nothing
like that from you. No one has any thought of making you leave
France or of disturbing your peace. If necessary, I shall be your
guarantor."

The Tsar's friendship for her brought the conquerors to Malmaison. Grand Duke Constantine, the King of Prussia, the German
princes, were all seen there, including Frederick of Mecklenberg-
Schwerin, who was still in love with Josephine. Having given up in
despair, he had married Caroline of Saxe-Meiningen and was now
the father of a little girl of three months.

They formed a motley crowd—there was a mixture of uniforms
from many battlefields—and were more at ease at Malmaison than
at the Tuileries. It was "at Napoleon's wife's house," as Frédéric
Masson says, that they met and fraternized.

However, according to Mme. Cochelet, the ex-Empress was
assailed by gloomy thoughts.

"I cannot conquer my sadness," she said one day. "I do all I can
to hide it from my children, but that makes me suffer the more. I
am beginning to lose heart. . . . Do you know what will happen
when the Tsar leaves? None of the promises to him will be fulfilled
and I shall see my children unhappy and I cannot bear the thought,
it hurts me terribly. I am already grieved by the fate of Napoleon,

who has fallen from so much greatness and is banished to an island far from France, which has abandoned him. Must I also see my children wanderers without any fortune? I feel that this thought is killing me."

On May 14 at Saint-Leu, where she had gone to receive the Tsar, Josephine felt a sudden chill while taking a drive in a carriage. She returned to the château, drank an infusion of orange flowers, and then lay down for a little before going to the dining room, where, however, she ate no dinner. She had a good night and thought she was cured as she returned to Malmaison.

During the next few days she did not put off any of her visitors, and received among others Mme. de Staël. After the latter's departure, Josephine's cheeks were red and she appeared agitated and upset.

"I have just had a painful interview," she told Mme. de Saint-Aulaire and the Duchess of Reggio. "Would you believe that among the questions Mme. de Staël was pleased to put to me she asked if I still loved the Emperor? She seemed to be trying to analyze my state of mind in the face of this great misfortune. . . . Would I, who never ceased to love the Emperor throughout his good fortune, cool toward him today?"

On May 23 she felt worse, but still received Grand Duke Constantine, the King of Prussia and his whole family. With them she made the classic excursion through the park and took them to see the greenhouses and the menageries. Eugene, who had spent the day at Malmaison, told his sister that evening that he had left their mother "tireder and more unwell." Josephine had appeared very affected at learning from a newspaper that the body of little Napoleon, Hortense's first child, was to be exhumed from Notre-Dame and buried in a parish cemetery.

Hortense came to Malmaison and found her mother low-spirited and still entirely taken up with the article she had read the day before.

"They dare interfere with graves," she moaned. "It is just like the Revolution."

Josephine began to have difficulty in speaking, but she had no fever, her pulse was normal and her doctor, who had diagnosed a simple cold, reassured the Queen.

"Your Majesty is wrong to be worried."

The next day, May 24, her cough became dry, but the mistress of Malmaison wanted to make the effort to receive the Grand Dukes Nicholas and Michael. She overestimated her strength and Hortense did the honors in her stead.

On May 25 she had a fever, but Dr. Horeau was still not worried. "The doctor says it is only a cold in the head," Eugene wrote to his wife, "but I do not think she is at all well." His mother's body, in fact, was covered by an "eruption" which, however, disappeared the same evening. Hope revived, but she had a bad night and Hortense insisted that a vesicant should be applied to the patient's throat.

On the morning of Thursday, May 26, the young woman, "astonished" at the inefficacy of the remedy, wanted another doctor to be called in. Josephine was against it. "It would vex my doctor."

On Friday, May 27, the Tsar's chief surgeon, the Scotsman Sir James Wylie, came to Malmaison to announce a visit from his employer on the next day. Josephine immediately began seeing to the preparations for the dinner, but on leaving her room the doctor could not conceal his anxiety. That "labored" breathing, increasingly dry cough and "vacillating" pulse caused him to say to Hortense, "I think Her Majesty is very ill, she should be covered with vesicants."

Horeau finally became worried and declared that the patient's head was "affected as though she were in a state of intoxication." "Seized with fright," Hortense summoned the best doctors in Paris. Drs. Bourdois de La Motte, Lamoureux and Lassarre arrived at Malmaison on May 28. They diagnosed a purulent sore throat and prescribed strong remedies, but the disease had made terrible progress. At this point Alexander arrived at Malmaison. Eugene, who was also unwell, received him and it was agreed to conceal his presence from the patient. "The Tsar canceled his engagement," she was told, whereas he spent all Saturday at the château in Eugene's room.

"I am sure," sighed Josephine, "that he is embarrassed at having nothing new to tell us about Eugene's future and has qualms about coming."

In the evening Hortense took Josephine's two grandchildren in to see her.

"The air is not good here," Josephine told her. "It might harm them."

She had a very bad night. Her breathing became more and more wheezing and her fever rose. Hortense had gone to get some rest and the lady's maid who was watching over the ex-Empress heard her mutter, "Bonaparte . . . the island of Elba . . . the King of Rome."

These were Josephine's last words, or at least the last that could be understood. The next morning, May 29, Whitsunday, she held out her arms to Hortense and Eugene, but her malady choked her and the words she tried to utter were unintelligible. Her face was distorted.

Abbé Bertrand, her grandsons' tutor, administered extreme unction to the dying woman. Hortense fainted, and was carried from the room. When she regained her senses, Eugene was there. He took his sister in his arms and burst into tears.

"All is over."

Josephine was fifty-one—the same age as Napoleon would be when he died.

It was noon. At the same hour Napoleon was leaving the church of Porto-Ferrajo on Elba where he had attended High Mass. In the evening he went to a ball given in the town hall for the feast of the patron saint of the little town which was now his capital.

"Poor Josephine. She is happy now!" he sighed, when he learned of her death from a letter by Caulaincourt to Mme. Bertrand. Neither Hortense nor Eugene had thought of informing him. And for two days the banished man refused to leave his house.

She lay between the curtains of white taffeta and gold-embroidered muslin that draped her bed, dressed in a pink satin wrap and with one of her pretty morning caps on her head. She seemed to smile.

Béclard, head of the Anatomical Department of the Faculty, the apothecary Cadet-Gassicourt and Dr. Horeau carried out the autopsy. They found the whole of the trachea in a bad state. The membrane was purple in color and tore at a touch. The lungs, which adhered to the pleura, and the bronchi were seriously attacked. All the other organs appeared "perfectly healthy." Josephine had died of pneumonia and a "gangrenous sore throat."

The registrar of Rueil was perturbed. How was he to frame the death certificate? Finally he wrote these astonishing words announc-

ing the death of "the Empress Josephine, Wife of Napoleon Bonaparte, Commander in Chief of the Army of Italy."

On May 30 the Duke of Mecklenburg-Schwerin wrote to Mlle.
Cochelet: "Mademoiselle, my grief is too strong to be described.
You know my feelings too well not to realize what I suffer. My first
thought, after the subject of our tears, is for our excellent Queen. I
am sure this fatal blow will crush her. I dare not write to her, but I
ask you as a favor to speak to Her Majesty of me and of my most
lively and sincere interest. After her own family I do not think there
exists a being more devotedly attached to the Empress than myself.
So it is with all my soul that I weep for her loss."

This was not a mere form of words, as was seen at the funeral on
Thursday, June 2. "He shed tears," an eyewitness related, "prayed at
the foot of the catafalque and put the edge of the pall to his lips."

According to court etiquette Hortense and Eugene were not
allowed to be present at the removal of the body or the burial.

Josephine was leaving Malmaison. Her heart and organs, placed
in a silver-gilt box, were carried by a valet in a long mourning cloak
who walked before the coffin. Everyone wanted to follow the
procession from the château to the church on foot, and the mourning coaches were empty. In front—a last attention from the Tsar—
marched a detachment of the Imperial Russian Guards, whose
muffled drums beat continuously. The National Guard of Rueil
lined the route. The dead woman's two grandsons—Hortense's
children, one ten and the other five—were the chief mourners.
General Sacken represented the Tsar. Then came the Duke of
Mecklenburg, the Grand Duke of Baden, and those Beauharnais
and Taschers who were in Paris. Then a crowd of marshals, generals
and French and Allied officers.

The church at Rueil, where Josephine was to be buried—her
remains are still there—was draped under the funeral hangings
which showed no coats of arms, monogram or crown. Nothing
would have been satisfactory—not the arms of the French Empire,
nor of the Beauharnais, nor of Navarre, nor even a simple "J." For
all that, the funeral cost Eugene 15,703 francs 75 centimes. The
clergy of Notre-Dame, some of whom had taken part in the coronation, officiated. The choir of the Madeleine sang. The Archbishop of
Tours, Msgr. de Barral, former chief almoner to the Imeprial Court,
handled a difficult situation and won Louis XVIII's approval with
his funeral oration:

"How many unfortunates, whose fidelity to the illustrious race of the Bourbons condemned them to live far from their country, owe it to her persistent and touching intercession that they were returned to their families and to the land that gave them birth! How many have seen opened through her efforts the prison doors which rashness and, often, unjust charges had closed upon them! How many were snatched from the sword of the law at the moment it was about to attack them!"

By next day the hawkers in Paris were shouting the titles of the latest pamphlets: "The life and death of the late Empress Josephine, first wife of Napoleon Bonaparte"; "The Will of the Empress Josephine, discovered this morning in her château of Malmaison"; "Interesting and Unpublished Anecdotes from the life of the Empress Josephine." Thousands of copies were sold of the ballad of "Prince Eugene at his mother's tomb," and of a print showing Josephine's son meditating by a column bearing an urn with the letter "J" on it.

The Royal House seems to have been willing to continue paying the pension for "M. de Buonaparte's" first wife. A memorandum in the National Archives shows that the supplement of 83,333 francs 33 centimes was paid on June 6, when Josephine's body had been in its temporary resting place in Rueil cemetery for four days. Her remains were to wait eleven years before being placed in the church beneath the monument which can still be seen there and which was ordered by Hortense and Eugene. The sculptor Cartellier showed her with clasped hands. In prayer? She prayed so little! The attitude rather recalls the morning when she knelt in Notre-Dame before the Emperor, who was about to place the Imperial crown on her head.

In 1815 on the evening of Tuesday, March 21, the day after his arrival in Paris from Elba, the Emperor went to Malmaison. He had that morning told Hortense he was coming.

"If I arrive at night," he had said, "I shall be able to indulge in my feelings with no fear of interference from anyone."

The moment he got out of his carriage he said to the ex-Queen: "I wish to see the Empress Josephine's bedroom. No, Hortense my dear, stay here. I shall go alone, it would upset you too much." And he went up to the second floor.

Malmaison saw him again eleven days after Waterloo. He had abdicated once more and had asked Hortense to give him hospitality. The park was a mass of flowers.

"Poor Josephine," he murmured as he left the carriage which had brought him from the Elysée Palace, "I always seem to see her leaving the path to pick one of the roses she loved so much!"

And he repeated, "Poor Josephine!" Hortense could not repress her tears.

"In any case, she would have been very unhappy now," he resumed. "There was only one thing we quarreled about—her debts, and I scolded her enough about them."

The next day Hortense heard him sigh: "How beautiful Malmaison is! How happy I should be to be able to stay here!"

But the provisional government had just refused his offer to resume command of the army under the name of "General Bonaparte."

"Is he making fun of us?" Fouché had exclaimed.

Now it was all over. "Nothing remains to me except to leave." He slowly moved away from Josephine's daughter and went up to the second floor by the little side stairs linking his study to his bedroom. There he took off his uniform, laid down his sword, put on a brown coat and, carrying a round hat, went to Josephine's apartments.

On his return to the Tuileries, exactly a hundred days earlier, he had questioned Dr. Horeau.

"You did not leave the Empress throughout her illness?"

"No, sire."

"What, in your opinion, was the cause of that illness?"

"Anxiety . . . grief . . ."

"Do you think so? What caused the grief?"

"The things that were happening, sire. Your Majesty's situation." Above all, what was happening, and what would happen to her. He also asked, "Ah! Did she speak of me?"

"Often, very often."

"Good woman! Good Josephine! She really loved me, that woman, did she not?"

"Oh, yes, sire. One day she said that if she were Empress of the French she would have crossed Paris in an eight-horse carriage, with all her household in full livery, to join you at Fontainebleau and never leave you."

"She would have done it, sir. She was capable of doing it."

Before starting off on the way to his last exile he opened the door of the circular bedroom, the bedroom draped in purple, gold-embroidered beaver cloth. Memories swept over him.

His sacrifice in parting from her had brought him no happiness. The legend was right. It seemed that in repudiating his partner he had lost his star, the star which shone when he was at her side, the star which, after darting a few rays at the beginning of 1812, died, by a disturbing coincidence, when Josephine was no more than an exile. As one of his veterans had said when things began to go badly, "He should not have left 'the old one.' She brought us luck, and him too."

The divorce and its sequel—the marriage with an archduchess and the birth of the King of Rome—had marked the culminating point of his more than human destiny. Tragically soon after that came the beginning of the end.

On June 26, 1813, he had said to Metternich, "I was very stupid to marry an archduchess. I committed an unpardonable blunder." By divorcing his partner he seemed to have parted also from good fortune.

He stood musing before the bed watched over by the two swans with folded wings.

"She was so graceful as she went to bed and as she dressed. I should have liked an Albani to see her then and draw her. . . . She was a woman in every sense of the word, changeable, lively and with the best heart. . . . She was the woman I most loved."

His eyes were full of tears as he left the room. Then he entered his carriage and started on the road to St. Helena.

There, on the evening of April 26, 1821, a few days before he died, Napoleon was to express the wish that if the Bourbons refused to place his remains at Saint-Denis, he might be buried near Josephine.

Sources

After the publication, between 1896 and 1900, of four large works on Josephine by Frédéric Masson it might have been thought that, although the great historian had maliciously concealed his sources, everything about Napoleon's wife had been said.

But it was not so. Since then many documents have been brought to light. First of all Frédéric Masson himself published letters from Josephine to her son, a collection soon complemented by *Les Beauharnais et l'Empereur* by Jean Hanoteau, a work which also contains the Empress's correspondence with Queen Hortense and letters written by the latter to Prince Eugene.

More recently that amazing research worker Louis Hastier was able to publish four letters from Josephine to Hippolyte Charles, and thanks to him we now know about *Le Grand Amour de Joséphine*, which is, in fact, the title of M. Hastier's book. Recently, too, André Gavoty, whose work I admire deeply, has provided revelations on every page of his *Les Amoureux de l'Impératrice Joséphine* and of the two first volumes of *Drames inconnus de la Cour de Napoléon*.

There was also the publication of the *Cahiers* of Grand Marshal Bertrand, which were so patiently and cleverly deciphered by M. Paul Fleuriot de Langle and which provide often unexpected echoes of Josephine from St. Helena. Finally there is the *Police secrète du Premier Empire*, Fouché's daily reports to the Emperor published by Ernest d'Hauterive and continued by Jean Grassion.

We should also mention the valuable collection of 265 letters from Napoleon to Josephine, the unexpurgated publication of which we owe to M. Jean Savant. It includes several hitherto unpublished letters by the Emperor. Some have been reproduced with Napoleon's own peculiar spelling and abbreviations. I thought it better not to follow this example, for this method was employed with only a few of the letters. It seemed preferable to me to standardize them, thus making the texts more readable.

I undoubtedly owe the most valuable part of my book to the work of my predecessors, but I must thank those who enabled me to bring it to a successful conclusion. First, Mme. R. Mardinier, who gave such skilled and devoted assistance to my researches in various archives. Then Pierre Schommer, who kindly placed at my disposal documents preserved at Malmaison or copied by himself. I must also thank M. Bernard Mahieu, librarian at the *Archives Nationales,* who is kindness personified, Mlle. Michaud, librarian at the *Bibliothèque Thiers,* and my excellent colleague Paul Fleuriot de Langle, librarian at the *Bibliothèque Marmottan.* I am also greatly obliged to Mme. Gagnerot, to M. Ritter von Jantsch, who carried out research for me in Austria, to M. Victor-Charles-Massance, a descendant of Captain Charles, who brought me a letter proving that Hippolyte Charles remained on the best terms with Queen Hortense.

Finally—and above all—I am deeply grateful to Dr. Rose-Rosette, Mayor of Trois-Ilets, and Mme. Rose-Rosette, the present owners of La Pagerie, and also to M. and Mme. Jean-Charles, who with typical Martinique kindness guided my steps through Josephine's native island and answered my many questions.

I found unpublished or forgotten documents in the following archives: *Archives Nationales:* Fia. 559 (passage through Moulins in 1797, journey to Antwerp in 1803, journey to Aix-la-Chapelle, passage through Rethel and Sedan in 1804, journeys to Plombières, passages through Nancy and Epinal, etc.); F7 459 (her arrest in 1794, removal of seals in 1795); AF IV 1220, 02 41, 02 25 (coronation and anointing); 02 1214, 02 24, 02 47, 02 48 (her household); 02 560 (Fontainebleau); 02 33, 02 77, 02 560, 02 18 (travels); 02 767, AF IV 83 (Strasbourg); 02 17, 02 652, 02 639 (Marrac); 02 46, 02 47, 02 30, 02 41 (Mainz); 02 1238, 02 16 (Laeken); 02 124 (stables, horses 1810); 02 16 (Duroc's orders); AF IV 1224, 02 33 (aid and charities); AF IV 1507, AF IV 1508 F7 3720, F7 3721 (police reports about her in 1810); AF IV 1220 (divorce); AA 41 (marriage of Mlle. de Castellane); 03 2717 (dowry, household of Louis XVIII); and many researches into the 02 series.

Malmaison Archives: Two letters from Josephine written in 1799; photocopy of the 1809 inventory; salaries, bills, invoices, various notes, etc. Inventory of the furniture of Malmaison "in conformity with the act of sale of 2 Floréal, Year VII." (Copy made by M. Pierre Schommer.)

Bibliothéque Thiers (Fonds Masson): *Fonds* 29 (Tascher de La Pagerie archives). Particularly touching letter from King Jerome and others, far less so, from Napoleon's sisters—Caroline, Pauline, Elisa—to Josephine. Letter from Louis Tascher to Josephine, etc.

Bibliothéque Thiers (Fonds Masson): *Fonds* 29 (Tascher de La her mother-in-law Josephine (Rosebery collection).

Private archives: Alexandre de Beauharnais's will. La Pagerie Archives (property of Dr. Rose-Rosette).

Bibliography

Abrantès (Laure Junot, duchesse d'). *Mémoires sur Napoléon, sa cour et sa famille.*
———. *Les Salons de Paris.*
Alanic (Mathilde). *Le mariage de Hoche.*
Almeras (Henri d'). *La Vie parisienne sous la Révolution et le Directoire.*
———. *La Vie parisienne sous le Consulat et l'Empire.*
Arjuzon (Caroline d'). *Hortense de Beauharnais.*
———. *Joséphine contre Beauharnais.*
Arnault. *Souvenirs d'un sexagénaire.*
Aubenas (J. A.). *Histoire de l'impératrice Joséphine* (2 vol.).
Aubry (Octave). *Bonaparte et Joséphine.*
———. *Vie privée de Napoléon.*
Aulard. *Paris sous l'Empire.*
Avannes (Dr). *Esquisses sur Navarre.*
Avrillon (Mlle d'). *Mémoires.*
———. *En habillant Joséphine.*
Baguenier. *Joséphine à la Malmaison.*
Baguenier-Désormeaux. *Pages d'Histoire.*
Bainville (Jacques). *Napoléon.*
Barault-Roullon. *L'Impératrice Joséphine et la famille de Beauharnais.*
Barrante. *Souvenirs.*
Barras. *Mémoires.*
Bartel (Paul). *La Jeunesse inédite de Napoléon.*
Bausset. *Mémoires.* (3 vol.).
Beauharnais. (voir *Hortense* et *Eugène*).
Belliard. *Mémoires.*
Bernardy (Françoise de). *Charles de Flahaut.*
Bertaut (Jules). *L'Impératrice Joséphine.*
———. *La Reine Hortense.*

489

————. *Napoléon ignoré.*

————. *Napoléon aux Tuileries.*

————. *Les Parisiens sous la Révolution.*

————. *Madame Tallien.*

Bertrand (Grand Maréchal). *Cahiers de Sainte-Hélène* (3 vol.), publié par P. Fleuriot de Langle.

Bessand-Messenet. *La France après la Terreur.*

Beugnot (Comte). *Mémoires.*

Bochsa (Mme). (voir Georgette Ducrest).

Boigne (Mme de). *Mémoires* (2 premiers vol.).

Bonaparte (Lucien). *Mémoires écrits par lui-même.*

Bord (Gustave). *L'Hôtel de la rue Chantereine.*

Bouchot (H.). *La Toilette à la cour de Napoléon.*

Bouillé (Louis-Amour de). *Souvenirs* (2 vol.).

Bourgeat (Jacques). *Lettres à Joséphine.* (recueillies et commentées par).

Bourguignon. *Les Adieux de Malmaison.*

Bourrienne (de). *Mémoires* (4 vol.).

Brochet (Régis). *Napoléon et Joséphine en Vendée.*

Bude (Eugène de). *Les Bonapartes en Suisse.*

Cabanès (Dr). *Légendes et curiosités de l'Histoire.*

————. *Une mort d'impératrice.*

Campan (Mme). *Journal privé.*

Caro (A.). *Le Général Santerre.*

Castelnau (J.). *Mme Tallien.*

Caulaincourt. *Mémoires.*

Chaptal. *Mémoires.*

Chastenay (Mme de). *Mémoires.*

Chastenet (Jacques). *Manuel Godoy.*

Chaumont (de). *Le Prince Eugène et l'impératrice Joséphine.*

Chuquet (A.). *Episodes et portraits.*

Clary-et-Aldringen (comte de). *Trois Mois à Paris en* 1810.

Chochelet (Mlle). *Mémoires, sur la reine Hortense.*

Coignet (capitaine). *Cahiers.*

Coittant. *Mémoires sur les Prisons.*

Cole (Hubert). *Joséphine.*

Collignon. *Joséphine à Navarre.*

————. *Napoléon dans l'Eure.*

Constant. *Mémoires.*

Constant (Charles de). *Correspondance* (Bibl. de Genève).

Costa de Beauregard. *Mémoires.*

Coston (Baron de). *Les Premières Années de Napoléon Bonaparte.*

Dean Paul (Sir John). *Journal du voyage à Paris au mois d'août* 1802.

Decaux (Alain). *Laetitia, mère de l'Empereur.*

Delandine. *Passage à Lyon de LL. MM. I et R en 1805.*

Desgenettes. *Souvenirs.*

Dielsbach (Fr. de). *Mémoires.*

Driault (Edouard). *L'Impératrice Joséphine.*

———. *Napoléon le Grand.*

Dubor (Georges de). *Joséphine Bonaparte.*

Ducrest (Georgette). *Mémoires sur l'Impératrice Joséphine* (3 vol.).

Dupont. *Pauline Fourès.*

Durand (Vve du général). *Anecdotes sur la famille de Napoléon Bonaparte.*

Eliott (Mrs). *Mémoires.*

Eugène (Prince). *Correspondance.*

———. *Mémoires.*

Fabry. *Mémoire de la campagne de* 1796.

Fain (Baron). *Mémoires.*

Fleischmann (Hector). *Joséphine infidèle.*

———. *Une maîtresse de Napoléon (Mlle George).*

Fleury de Chaboulon. *Mémoires.*

Fouché. *Mémoires.*

Fouques (Victor). *Napoléon et Joséphine à Châlons-sur-Marne.*

Fuye (Maurice de la) et E. Guéret. *Rouget de Lisle inconnu.*

Ganière (Dr Paul). *Corvisart.*

Garros (L.). *Itinéraire de Napoléon Bonaparte.*

———. *Napoléon, cet inconnu.*

Gavoty (André). *Les Amoureux de l'impératrice Joséphine.*

———. *La Grassini.*

———. *Les Drames inconnus de la cour de Napoléon* (1804).

———. *Les Drames inconnus de la cour de Napoléon* (1805–1806).

Gaxotte (Pierre). *La Révolution française.*

Gay (Sophie). *Joséphine à Aix-la-Chapelle.*

George (Mlle). *Mémoires.*

Girod de l'Ain. *Désirée Clary.*

Giuliani (Albert). *Les Amours lyonnaises de Napoléon.*

Gohier. *Mémoires.*

Goncourt (E. et J. de). *Histoire de la Société française pendant la Révolution et le Directoire* (2 vol.).

Gourgaud (Général). *Journal* (2 vol.).

Gravereaux. *La Malmaison. Les roses de l'Impératrice.*

Grégoire (Louis). *Le Divorce de Napoléon et de l'impératrice Joséphine.*

Hanoteau (Jean). *Le Ménage Beauharnais.*

————. *Les Beauharnais et l'Empereur.*

Hastier (Louis). *Le Grand Amour de Joséphine.*

Hauterive (Ernest d'). *La Police secrète du Premier Empire* (4 vol.). (le quatrième volume a été publié par M. Jean Grassion).

Herrissay (Jacques). *Joséphine à Navarre.*

Holzhausen (P.). *Bonaparte et la société parisienne.*

Hortense (la reine). *Mémoires.* Préface et notes de Jean Hanoteau. (3 vol.).

Houssaye (Arsène). *Notre-Dame de Thermidor.*

Houville (Gérard d'). *La Vie amoureuse de l'impératrice Joséphine.*

Imbert de Saint-Armand. *La Citoyenne Bonaparte.*

————. *La Femme du Premier Consul.*

————. *La Jeunesse de l'Impératrice Joséphine.*

————. *La Cour de l'Impératrice Joséphine.*

————. *Les Dernières Années de l'impératrice Joséphine.*

————. *Portraits de femmes françaises.*

Iung (Th). *Lucien Bonaparte et ses Mémoires* (3 vol.).

Jacquin (et Duesberg). *Rueil, le château de Richelieu et la Malmaison.*

Janssens (Jacques). *Joséphine de Beauharnais et son temps.*

————. *L'Impératrice Joséphine.*

Kielmannssegge (Comtesse de). *Mémoires sur Napoléon Ier.*

Kunstler (Charles). *La Vie privée de l'impératrice Joséphine.*

Lachouque (Ct Henry). *Bonaparte et la cour consulaire.*

Lamarque (général). *Souvenirs, Mémoires et Lettres.*

Larevellière-Lépeaux. *Mémoires.*

Lariboisière (général). *Souvenirs.*

Larroumet (Gustave). *Petits Portraits. La vraie Joséphine.*

Las Cases. *Mémorial* (ed. Marcel Dunan).

La Tour du Pin (marquise de). *Journal.*

Lavallette (comte de). *Mémoires et Souvenirs* (2 vol.).

Lenormand (Mlle). *Mémoires historiques.*

Lenotre (G.). *Vieilles Maisons, Vieux Papiers* (Ire et VIe séries).

————. *La Maison des Carmes.*

————. *Les Tuileries.*

————. *Napoléon (Croquis de l'épopée).*

————. *En suivant l'Empereur. (Autres croquis de l'épopée).*

————. *Le Château de Rambouillet.*

Lescure (M. de). *Le Château de Malmaison.*

————. *L'Amour sous la Terreur.*

Levy (Arthur). *Napoléon intime.*

————. *Les Dissentiments de la famille impériale.*

Lezai-Marnésia (Mme). *Souvenirs.*

Lhospice (Michel). *Divorce et dynastie.*
Lorédan. *Mme de Lavallette.*
Lucas-Dubreton. *Mme de Lavallette.*
Macdonald (maréchal). *Mémoires.*
Madelin (Louis). *Histoire du Consulat et de l'Empire.* (8 premiers volumes).
———. *Fouché.*
Marco de Saint-Hilaire. *Le Petits Appartements des Tuileries* (2 vol.).
———. *Mémoires d'un page* (1).
Marmont (maréchal, duc de Raguse). *Mémoires* (9 vol.).
Masson (Frédéric). *Joséphine de Beauharnais.*
———. *Madame Bonaparte.*
———. *Joséphine impératrice et reine.*
———. *Joséphine répudiée.*
———. *Napoléon et sa famille* (13 vol.).
———. *Le Sacre et le couronnement.*
———. *Napoléon et les femmes.*
———. *Napoléon chez lui.*
———. *Huit conférences sur Napoléon* (part: *Malmaison et Joséphine*).
———. *Jadis et Aujourd'hui* (II série. *La Mort de Joséphine*).
Mathiez. *Le Directoire.*
Masuyer (Valérie). *Mémoires.*
Maugras (G.), et de Croze-Lemercier. *Delphine de Custine.*
Mauguin (Georges). *L'Impératrice Joséphine.*
Maynard (Paul). *L'Impératrice Joséphine.*
Maze-Sensier (Alph.). *Les Fournisseurs de Napoléon et des deux impératrices.*
Melchoir-Bonnet (Bernardine). *Napoléon et le Pape.*
———. *Savary, duc de Rovigo.*
Meneval (Baron de). *Mémoires.*
Mercier. *Tableau de Paris.*
Metternich (Pce de). *Mémoires.*
Miot de Melito (comte). *Mémoires.*
Montgaillard (Cte de). *Souvenirs.*
Montier *Robert Lindet.*
Nabonne (Bernard). *La Reine Hortense.*
Napoléon. *Correspondance générale* (32 vol.).
Nézeloff (Pierre). *L'Impératrice Joséphine.*
Normand (Suzanne). *Telle fut Joséphine.*
Ollivier (Albert). *Le 18 Brumaire.*
Ouvrard. *Mémoires.*
Papillard (François). *Cambacérès.*

Pasquier (Chancelier). *Mémoires.*
Pellapra (Emilie de). *Mémoires.* Publiés par Mme la princesse Bibesco.
Pfister. *Les Passages de Napoléon et de Joséphine dans la Meurthe.*
Pichevin (R.). *L'Impératrice Joséphine.*
Pillon (Edmond). *Aspect et figures de femmes.*
Planat de la Faye. *Le Prince Eugéne en 1814.*
Potocka (comtesse). *Mémoires.*
Pourtalès. *Correspondance* (archives de Neuchâtel).
Reboux (Paul). *Comment fut aimée l'impératrice Joséphine.*
Redhead Yorke. *Paris et la France sous le Consulat.*
Reichardt (J. F.). *Un hiver à Paris sous le Consulat.*
Reinhardt. *L'Impératrice Joséphine.*
Rémusat (Mme de). *Mémoires.* (3 vol.).
————. *Lettres à son mari* (2 vol.).
Renouard. *Histoire de la Martinique.*
Reval (G.). *Les Grandes Amoureuses romantiques.*
Rochard (C.). *Dans les coulisses de l'Histoire.*
Robert (Henri). *Les Grands Procès de l'Histoire* (7e série).
Robert (S.). *Les Séjours de l'impératrice Joséphine en Suisse.*
Robiquet (Jean). *La Vie quotidienne au temps de la Révolution.*
Roederer. *Mémoires* (4 vol.).
Roncière. *Mémoires* (4 vol.).
Roncière (Sainte Croix de la). *Joséphine, impératrice des Français, reine
    d'Italie.*
Rousselin (A.). *Vie de Lazare Hoche.*
Roustam. *Mémoires.*
Rovigo. *Mémoires.*
Savant (Jean). *Napoléon et Joséphine* (Edition intégrale des lettres de
    Napoléon à Joséphine).
————. *Tel fut Barras.*
————. *Napoléon raconté par les témoins de sa vie.*
Savine (A.). *Le Jours de la Malmaison.*
Schuermans. *Itinéraire générale de Napoléon.*
Ségur (Ph. de). *Mémoires.*
Simiot (Bernard). *De quoi vivait Bonaparte.*
Sorel (Albert). *Le Couvent des Carmes sous la Terreur.*
————. *Histoire de la Martinique.*
Stendhal. *Vie de Napoléon.*
Talleyrand. *Mémoires.*
Tercier (général). *Mémoires politiques et militaires.*
Terrasse (Claude). *Napoléon à Fontainebleau.*
Thibaudeau. *Mémoires.*
Thiébault (général, baron). *Mémoires* (3 vol.).

Thiry (Jean). *Le Coup d'Etat de Brumaire.*

Tortat. *Mémoires.*

Turquan (Joseph). *L'Impératrice Joséphine.*

———. *La Générale Bonaparte.*

———. *Stéphanie de Beauharnais et la duchesse de Chevreuse, dame du palais.*

———. *Napoléon amoureux.*

———. *La Citoyenne Tallien.*

———. *Une fille adoptive de Napoléon: Stéphanie de Beaucharnais.*

Villat (Louis). *La Révolution et l'Empire* (2 vol.).

Vandal. *L'Avènement de Bonaparte* (2 vol.).

Villenzo. *Journal d'un Milanais.*

Vivent (Jacques). *Barras.*

Welschinger (Henri). *Le Divorce de Napoléon.*

———. *La Censure sous le Premier Empire.*

Relation du passage et du séjour de LL. MM. I. et. R. à Troyes.

Passage à Lyon de LL. MM. en 1805.

Le Moniteur; Le Constitutionnel; Le Publiciste; Le Journal des Débats; Le Journal d'Evreux et de l'Eure, etc.

Catalogue Charavay: (No 29864) "*Requeste introductive pour la Dame Marie-Rose Tascher de La Pagerie contre le sieur Alexandre, François Marie, vicomte de Beauharnais, son mary.*"

Catalogue de la vente Brouwet.

PERIODICALS

"*La Revue des Etudes Napoléoniennes*":

La Malmaison avant Joséphine. Louis Bigeard. (X-XI. 33).

Joséphine de Beauharnais à Croissy. Louis Bigeard. (III et IV. 36).

Le Contrat de mariage du citoyen Bonaparte et de la citoyenne de Beauharnais. Burgraeve (IV. 36).

Un soir de ventôse an IV à l'hôtel de Mondragon. Henry Clouzot. (VII. 35).

La Malmaison de Joséphine. Edouard Driault. (III. 33).

Les Dernières Années de l'impératrice Joséphine. Edouard Driault.

Fête lyonnaise du Premier Empire. François Dutacq. (I. 35).

Le Premier Consul dans les Flandres. Théo Fleischmann. (IV. 23).

Napoléon et Joséphine à Carpi. Alphonso Morselli. (VIII. 30).

La Malmaison et Navarre. Journal de Piout. (II. 23).

Le Passage à Beauvais du Premier Consul et de Joséphine. Vinot Préfon-
taine. (XII. 35).

Dettes de l'impératrice Joséphine. Cte. Philippo Visconti. (II. 35).

Voyage en Normandie (tome XLI. p. 265).

"Bulletin de l'Institut Napoléon":

Visite de Malmaison. F. Boyer (I. 49).

La Mort de l'impératrice Joséphine. Paul Fleuriot de Langle. (VII. 64).

Quelques révélations sur les biens de Joséphine. Serge Grandjean (VII.
64).

Joséphine, les camées, les turquoises et les fleurs. Suzanne d'Huart. (VII.
64).

L'Impératrice Joséphine et le retour du gothique sous l'Empire. Guy et
Denise Ledoux-Lebard. (VII. 64).

Joséphine, amateur de jardins à la Malmaison. Pierre Schommer. (VII.
64).

Autour du mariage de Napoléon et de Joséphine. Madeleine Tartary (X.
49).

CONFERENCES AND MISCELLANEOUS

Le seul véritable amour de Napoléon: l'impératrice Joséphine. René
Arnaud. *Les Annales* (I. 1935).

L'Impératrice Joséphine, dernière souveraine couronnée. Alain Decaux.
Miroir de l'Histoire (VI. 1953).

Bonaparte et les siens vus par une étrangère. Mme Divoff. *Revue Uni-
verselle* (15-X-1929).

Une soeur inconnue de la reine Hortense. André Gavoty. *Revue des
Deux-Mondes* (Ier-XII. 1952).

Il y cent cinquante ans mourait l'impératrice Joséphine. Conférence du
Dr. Guy Godlewski, publiée par *les Annales* (III. 1964).

Les Collections de l'impératrice Joséphine à Malmaison et leur dispersion.
Serge Grandjean. *La Revue des Arts* (Nos IV et V 1959).

Douze ans de ma vie. Hamelin. *Revue de Paris.* (Ier-XI-1926).

Une éminence grise de Barras: Bottot. Louis Hastier. *Revue des Deux
Mondes* (Ier-VIII. 1952).

L'Impératrice Joséphine, bienfaitrice de l'horticulture et de l'agriculture.
Conférence par Paul Maynard.

Récit de Mme de Montesquiou (publié à la suite des *Souvenirs* du comte
Anatole de Montesquiou).

Index